Generations

Generations

Age, Ancestry, and Memory
in the English Reformations

The Ford Lectures 2018

ALEXANDRA WALSHAM

OXFORD
UNIVERSITY PRESS

OXFORD
UNIVERSITY PRESS

Great Clarendon Street, Oxford, OX2 6DP,
United Kingdom

Oxford University Press is a department of the University of Oxford.
It furthers the University's objective of excellence in research, scholarship,
and education by publishing worldwide. Oxford is a registered trade mark of
Oxford University Press in the UK and in certain other countries

© Alexandra Walsham 2023

The moral rights of the author have been asserted

First Edition published in 2023

Impression: 1

Published in the United States of America by Oxford University Press
198 Madison Avenue, New York, NY 10016, United States of America

British Library Cataloguing in Publication Data
Data available

Library of Congress Control Number: 2022946084

ISBN 978-0-19-885403-6

DOI: 10.1093/oso/9780198854036.001.0001

Printed and bound by
CPI Group (UK) Ltd, Croydon, CR0 4YY

Links to third party websites are provided by Oxford in good faith and
for information only. Oxford disclaims any responsibility for the materials
contained in any third party website referenced in this work.

For my PhD students, past, present, and future

Preface and Acknowledgements

It feels as if this book has been a generation in the making. In the period since its first inception, I have accumulated many debts and I am glad to have the opportunity to acknowledge them here.

I begin by warmly thanking the electors to the Ford Lectureship in British History at the University of Oxford, who invited me to deliver the lectures in the Hilary Term 2018. The honour of being selected to carry on this distinguished tradition is accompanied by a particularly daunting sense of responsibility. I was filled with trepidation as I mounted the marble steps to the cavernous South Schools each Friday afternoon, but I found a warm, loyal, and receptive audience. I am grateful to Steve Gunn for being such a gracious host, and to all those who kept coming and saved me from the embarrassment of being moved to a smaller room. Among them were Susan Brigden, Susan Doran, the late John Elliot, Felicity Heal, Clive Holmes, Paulina Kewes, Lyndal Roper, Steve Smith, Andrew Spicer, and Keith Thomas. The members of Oxford's early modern British history seminar made the lectures the subject of a thought-provoking discussion, from which they have benefited in the process of the revisions that have expanded them into this book. I also thank the Warden and Fellows of All Souls College who welcomed me into their midst during that time as a Visiting Fellow and provided a quiet and leafy retreat in Iffley.

A second debt is to the Leverhulme Trust, which awarded me a Major Research Fellowship between 2015 and 2018. The luxury of space and time this afforded enabled me to transform a slippery and ephemeral idea into something more concrete. The Trust's generosity has been matched only by its patience and forbearance in awaiting the fruits of these endeavours. This project has also been shaped by the AHRC collaborative grant on 'Remembering the Reformation' of which I was co-investigator with Brian Cummings between 2016 and 2018. I owe much to Brian and to the other members of the team—Ceri Law, Karis Riley, Bronwyn Wallace and Tom Taylor—for inspiring insights, lively conversations, and plenty of laughter. The research we undertook together in Lambeth, Cambridge, and York, the events we organized, and the publications we co-edited have fed into and cross-fertilized my work on generations in decisive ways.

Thirdly, I wish to express my appreciation to the staff of all the libraries and archives I have visited in the course of this project. Archivists in the county record offices scattered around the country in which so many family papers are deposited have been unfailingly helpful. Closer to home, my many debts to colleagues in the Rare Books and Manuscripts Rooms in the Cambridge University Library over three decades are hard to repay. I was privileged to hold the Mary Robertson Visiting Fellowship at the Henry E. Huntington Library in May 2018, and I thank Steve Hindle, its Director of Research, for making this possible. I am also extremely grateful to the Folger Shakespeare Library for inviting me to deliver a semester-long Spring Seminar on 'The Reformation of the Generations' between February and April 2016, the participants in which played a key part in the conceptualization of this project in its early stages. My stay in Washington enabled me to immerse myself in the Folger's manuscript collections. It was also greatly enlivened by those whose time there coincided with mine, especially Claire Bowditch, Emma Depledge, Paul Dover, Christopher Highley, and Elaine Hobby.

Versions of the chapters that comprise this book have been heard by audiences in Britain, Ireland, France, Germany, the Netherlands, Australia, South Africa, Canada, and the USA, and their comments and questions have helped to refine it. Several long-suffering friends have read it in whole or part, and I thank them for their help and encouragement, especially when my confidence in it was wavering: Brian Cummings, David Hall, Paulina Kewes, Harriet Lyon, and Peter Marshall. Brian and Peter were particularly astute about how to revise the Introduction. The anonymous readers for Oxford University Press offered constructive criticism and helpful advice which I have tried my best to implement. At Oxford University Press, Stephanie Ireland and Cathryn Steele have been very supportive and understanding editors, while Donald Watt and Thomas Deva have provided expert assistance on the production side.

The beginnings of this project lie in Exeter, but most of the research and writing which has led to this book has been undertaken since my arrival in Cambridge in October 2010. Here I have benefited from being part of a large and vibrant community of scholars. My fellow early modernists, including Melissa Calaresu, Paul Cavill, Gabriel Glickman, Arnold Hunt, Clare Jackson, Mary Laven, John Morrill, Kate Peters, Helen Pfeifer, Ulinka Rublack, Richard Serjeantson, and David Smith have been stimulating companions. Sachiko Kusukawa has been the very best of friends during the most difficult times. The final phases of preparation have been prolonged by two factors: my responsibilities as Chair of the Faculty of History and the concurrent complications created by the pandemic. The latter has presented many challenges, though two weeks of hotel quarantine in Sydney provided an oasis of concentrated time in which to focus on revising the chapters. I want to thank the academic and administrative colleagues with whom I have worked most closely during this period—Chris Briggs, Lucy Delap, Liz Haresnape, and Liz Partridge. Much of the work on this book took place while I was a fellow of Trinity College, and I owe all my friends there much gratitude. More recently, Julie Barrau, Peter Burke, Liesbeth van Houts, David Maxwell, and Emma MacKinnon have made Emmanuel a consoling place of asylum. In West

Wratting, I have the kindest of neighbours. Although separated by distance, my parents and sister have always been there when I have needed them most. The dedication, however, salutes the next generation: my PhD students, past, present, and future, from whom I learn so much. I am full of admiration for their achievements and full of gratitude for their continuing support and affection.

West Wratting, 29 December 2021

Contents

List of Abbreviations and Conventions

AAW	Archives of the Archdiocese of Westminster, London
AHR	*American Historical Review*
BCH	*British Catholic History*
BL	British Library, London
Bodl.	Bodleian Library, Oxford
BM	British Museum, London
CL	Congregational Library, London
CRO	Cheshire Record Office, Chester
CRS	Catholic Record Society
CS	Camden Society
CSP Dom	*Calendar of State Papers, Domestic Series, of the Reigns of Edward VI, Mary, Elizabeth and James I, 1547–1625*, ed. R. Lemon and M. A. E. Green, 12 vols (1856–72); *Calendar of State Papers, Domestic Series, of the Reign of Charles I, 1625–1649*, ed. J. Bruce et al., 23 vols (1858–97); *Calendar of State Papers Domestic Series [of the Commonwealth] 1649–1660*, ed. M. A. E. Green, 13 vols (1875–86).
CUL	Cambridge University Library
DCRO	Durham County Record Office, Durham
Devon HC	Devon Heritage Centre, Exeter
Dorset HC	Dorset History Centre, Dorchester
DRO	Derbyshire Record Office, Matlock
DWL	Dr Williams's Library, London
EHR	*English Historical Review*
FHL	Friends' House Library, London
Fitz.	Fitzwilliam Museum, Cambridge
FSL	Folger Shakespeare Library, Washington DC
GA	Gloucestershire Archives, Gloucester
HEHL	Henry E. Huntington Library, San Marino, CA
HJ	*Historical Journal*
HLQ	*Huntington Library Quarterly*
HMC	Historical Manuscripts Commission
JBS	*Journal of British Studies*
JEH	*Journal of Ecclesiastical History*
JRH	*Journal of Religious History*
LLRRO	Leicester, Leicestershire, and Rutland Record Office, Wigston Magna
LPL	Lambeth Palace Library, London
LRO	Liverpool Record Office, Liverpool
NLS	National Library of Scotland, Edinburgh
NLW	National Library of Wales, Aberystwyth

NPG	National Portrait Gallery, London
NRO	Norfolk Record Office, Norwich
NS	New Series
NYCRO	North Yorkshire County Record Office, Northallerton
ODNB	*Oxford Dictionary of National Biography*
OED	*Oxford English Dictionary*
OS	Old Series; Original Series
P&P	*Past and Present*
PS	Parker Society
RH	*Recusant History*
RQ	*Renaissance Quarterly*
SA	Shropshire Archives, Shrewsbury
SCH	Studies in Church History
SCJ	*Sixteenth Century Journal*
Somerset HC	Somerset Heritage Centre, Taunton
SP	State Papers
SRO	Staffordshire Record Office, Stafford
STC	A. W. Pollard and G. R. Redgrave, *A Short-Title Catalogue of Books Printed in England, Scotland, and Ireland and of English Books Printed Abroad 1475–1640*, 2nd edn, rev. and enlarged by W. A. Jackson, F. S. Ferguson, and K. F. Pantzer, 3 vols. (1976–91)
Surrey HC	Surrey History Centre, Woking
TNA	The National Archives, Kew
TRHS	*Transactions of the Royal Historical Society*
V&A	Victoria and Albert Museum, London
WAAS	Worcestershire Archive and Archaeology Service, Worcester
Wing	D. Wing, *Short-Title Catalogue of Books Printed in England, Scotland, Ireland, Wales and British America and of English Books Printed in Other Countries 1641–1700*, 2nd edn, rev. and enlarged by the Index Committee of the Modern Language Association of America, 3 vols (New York, 1972–88)
YML	York Minster Library, York

Original spelling, punctuation, and capitalization are retained in all quotations, with occasional exceptions in the interests of clarity. The use of i and j, u and v, however, has been modernized. In citations from manuscript sources, standard abbreviations and contractions have been silently expanded. Greek letters have been transliterated. For the sake of consistency, signature numbers are cited in Arabic numerals throughout. Dates are given in Old Style, except that the year is reckoned to begin on 1 January. The place of publication is London, unless otherwise stated. All biblical citations are from the Authorized Version of 1611, except where indicated.

List of Illustrations

Introduction

In October 1641, the godly London artisan Nehemiah Wallington knew that he was witnessing history in the making. He watched in wonder as the churches of the city were purged of 'supersticious' images left over from the days of 'popery' and introduced during the Laudian era. In his own parish, St Leonard's Eastcheap, an 'Idoll in the wall' was removed, ancient funeral brasses and a candlestick were defaced, and medieval stained-glass windows were shattered. Determined to keep a record of these momentous events for posterity, he gathered up some fragments of the broken lights 'to keep for a remembrance to show to the generation to come what God hath done for us, to give us such a Reformation that our forefathers never saw the like'. Preserved in one of the many voluminous notebooks he wrote during his life, summarized in another, and bequeathed to his children as a legacy, Wallington's words and actions highlight the interconnections between age, ancestry, and memory in the context of the successive stages of unsettling religious change which England experienced during the sixteenth and seventeenth centuries. They emphasize the role of the family as a critical forum in which both historical consciousness and confessional identities were forged. They underline the intense and powerful link that people felt with their dead ancestors and their living and unborn descendants. And they illuminate how senses of the past converged with hopes for the future in the two hundred years following the Henrician break with Rome in 1534.[1]

This compelling vignette draws into focus the key themes of *Generations*. A revised and expanded version of the Ford Lectures in British History 2018, the book examines a cluster of closely interrelated questions. How did the young, middle-aged, and old respond to the theological, liturgical, and cultural upheavals that comprised the English Reformations? What part did ties of blood and bonds of kinship and fellowship play in facilitating and complicating ecclesiastical change and spiritual conversion? In what ways did the languages of age and ancestry help to conceptualize religious transformations between 1500 and 1700? To what extent did the Reformation itself 'age' as it made the transition from an illicit protest movement to a mature, institutionalized Church? Did those

---

[1] BL, Additional MS 21, 935 (Nehemiah Wallington, 'A Bundel of Marcys', fo. 148r); summarized in FSL, MS V. a. 436 (Nehemiah Wallington, notebook 1654, p. 86). The relevant section of the BL manuscript is transcribed and printed in David Booy (ed.), *The Notebooks of Nehemiah Wallington, 1618–1654* (Aldershot, 2007), p. 131.

who witnessed, embraced, and resisted its different phases come to consider themselves members of a distinct generation? How did memory of these developments mutate with the passage of time? When and why did contemporaries begin to think of their own era as a decisive juncture in Christian history?

This study adopts the rich and resonant concept of generation as its analytical framework. 'Generation' is a fertile term with multiple meanings in modern usage. It describes the act and the fact of bringing something into existence, in particular a living organism, whether an animal, plant, or human being. A synonym for the reproduction, procreation, and propagation of species, by extension it is sometimes deployed to denote the development of ideas and the effect of technological inventions such as wind and electrical turbines. Simultaneously, it is widely used as a collective noun to refer to a set of people born and living in the same era, a group of coevals who are often assumed to hold similar cultural attitudes. It is also a conventional shorthand for the average number of years that it takes for children to grow up, become adults, and have offspring of their own—generally between twenty-five and thirty. In this respect, it is an emblem of the unending loop that is the life cycle. In turn, the word is frequently invoked as a unit of chronology and periodization.[2] Generation is thus a concept that focuses our attention on three important themes, as well as the triangular relationship between them: the mystery of engendering living creatures; the idea of a social cohort or virtual community sharing a common location in time; and the mental structures by which we measure and comprehend the unfolding of history itself.

Generation is a revealing new lens through which to inspect England's Reformations. Foreshadowed by episcopal initiatives and dissident tendencies that were already present in the late medieval Church, these impulses not merely spanned the reigns of Henry VIII and his late Tudor heirs, Edward VI, Mary, and Elizabeth, but continued to provoke both heated political and ecclesiastical debate and local friction under their Stuart successors. The repeated attempts to recast and subvert the Church of England that marked the period between c.1530 and 1700 reflected its contested genesis. They also fomented fresh discontents that further fragmented it and threatened to destabilize English society. The revolutionary events of the 1640s and 1650s, during which civil war broke out, an anointed king was tried and executed, and monarchy replaced by the radical constitutional experiment of the English republic, were themselves a function of its unresolved tensions. They were driven by a series of dynamic but ultimately abortive efforts to correct and perfect what many regarded as an unfinished reformation. Convinced that it had not yet properly begun, others looked forward to its imminent dawn and the advent of Christ's reign on earth. The destructive verbal and physical violence unleashed by these decades was formative and scarring

---

[2] *OED*, s.v. 'generation'.

for the generation that experienced it. The troubles this precipitated rumbled on after the restoration of Charles II in 1660, stimulating new efforts to recapture the original essence of the Tudor religious settlements and to revive the thwarted priorities of the puritan era. The later Stuart period entailed an attempt to come to terms with this double legacy, a dangerous cocktail that fuelled more inter- and intraconfessional conflict and catalysed the coup that led to the ejection of James II and the accession of William and Mary. The fires it ignited were not extinguished by the legislation of 1688–9 and continued to break out long after 1700, leaving a lasting mark on English culture. Its afterlives still trouble us today.

Reformation was never a single event or a coherent entity, not least because parties and groups competed to define the meaning of religious developments that were steadily receding from living memory. Intrinsically plural and unstable, it was a shimmering mirage whose shape and significance depended on the perspective of those who observed and remembered its constituent elements. *Generations* seeks to enrich our understanding of the passions that this movement produced both in its initial unruly stages and in the subsequent spasms of strife and antagonism to which it gave rise, as well as the more gradual process by which its ideals and contradictions became permanently embedded in everyday life.

This book also endeavours to make several broader methodological interventions. It lays down a series of challenges to scholars working on other societies and periods. It reopens an older debate about the utility of the idea of the generation in historical inquiry and applies it to an era in which discussions of it have hitherto been conspicuous by their relative absence. An attempt to detect and document a particularly elusive phenomenon, it offers a foundation upon which subsequent studies might build and from which new insights may spring. A further aspiration is to foster greater awareness of how the archive of the English Reformations came into being. This book approaches the generations as windows and gateways to the early modern past it tries to recover. It places the very processes by which our knowledge of this era has been formed under scrutiny. The concept of generation invites us to contemplate the connections between memory and history, as well as the legacies—personal and scholarly, intimate and intellectual—that human beings perennially feel compelled to bequeath to posterity. As Friedrich Nietzsche wrote in his *Untimely Meditations*, we 'cannot learn to forget but cling relentlessly to the past', which repeatedly returns 'as a ghost' to disturb the peace of later moments.[3]

---

[3] Friedrich Nietzsche, 'On the Uses and Disadvantages of History for Life', in *Untimely Meditations*, ed. David Breazeale, trans. R. J. Hollingdale (Cambridge, 1997), p. 61.

Reformations and Generations

Reformation historiography has often been an exercise in genealogy, a search for precursors. The first Protestant historians were apologists for a faith that appeared to its opponents to have no pedigree. Their principal task was thus to establish the ancestry of this 'new religion': to recover the hidden brotherhood of believers who had kept the light of the Gospel alive and who gave legitimacy to the reformers' claim that they were merely renewing apostolic Christianity in its pristine purity. The factions and sects into which the Reformation splintered in the sixteenth and seventeenth centuries likewise had an intrinsic propensity to tell a linear and teleological story of triumph over persecution and adversity, of stoical survival against the odds, and of splendid isolation from corrupting influences that threatened their separate identity and ideological integrity. Protestant nonconformists, radical sectarians, and Catholics wrote vertical histories of their descent as dissenters. Afflicted by a form of tunnel vision, they fostered an illusion of continuity with a heroic past that telescoped time, exaggerated the exclusivity of these movements, and occluded evidence of lateral and horizontal connections with rival groups.[4] Ironically, in the case of the official Church of England the dominant paradigm is of more recent provenance. It is a side effect of the Victorian reinvention of the Reformation and the myth it created to buttress the evolving priorities of nineteenth-century Anglicanism.[5]

Traditional denominational perspectives have waned within the academy over the last few decades, though the possibility of moving beyond confessional paradigms and the validity of writing religious history from a position of neutrality both remain live issues.[6] Against this backdrop, the origins, impact, and repercussions of the English Reformation continue to be the subject of stimulating debate. Controversies have raged about whether it sprang up spontaneously from below or was imposed upon the populace by the Tudor state; whether it was fast or slow; whether it was enthusiastically welcomed or fiercely resented; whether it was a dismal failure or a resounding success; and whether it created a society comprised of convinced Protestants or just a nominally Protestant nation. Christopher Haigh spoke memorably of its 'premature birth', 'difficult labour', and the 'sickly child'

---

[4] Patrick Collinson, 'Towards a Broader History of the Early Dissenting Tradition', in C. Robert Cole and Michael E. Moody (eds), *The Dissenting Tradition: Essays for Leland H. Carlson* (Athens, OH, 1975), pp. 3–38; repr. in Patrick Collinson, *Godly People: Essays on English Protestantism and Puritanism* (1983), pp. 527–62. See also the similar remarks of Christopher Hill, 'History and Denominational History', *The Baptist Quarterly*, 22 (1967), 65–71.

[5] Diarmaid MacCulloch, 'The Myth of the English Reformation', *JBS*, 30 (1991), 1–19; Peter Nockles and Vivienne Westbrook (eds), *Reinventing the Reformation in the Nineteenth Century: A Cultural History*, special issue of the *Bulletin of the John Rylands Library*, 90 (2014).

[6] See Brad Gregory, 'The Other Confessional History: On Secular Bias in the Study of Religion', *History and Theory*, 45 (2006), 132–49; *idem*, 'Historians' Metaphysical Beliefs and the Writing of Confessional Histories', *Fides et Historia*, 43 (2011), 9–17; Andrea Sterk and Nina Caputo (eds), *Faithful Narratives: Historians, Religion, and the Challenge of Objectivity* (New York, 2014).

which it brought forth. Its advance was impeded by a tide of conservative resistance and foot-dragging at parish level and its eventual entrenchment was a consequence of the slow attrition of those who clung tenaciously to the 'old religion'.[7] Patrick Collinson explored the protracted *Birthpangs of Protestant England* and probed the 'painful complications' of later stages of its life cycle with characteristic subtlety, including a mood change 'from iconoclasm to iconophobia' around 1580.[8] The underlying theme of Eamon Duffy's arresting evocation of 'traditional religion' in *The Stripping of the Altars*, meanwhile, is lament for its untimely demise. He concluded his book by remarking that by the middle of Elizabeth's reign, Protestantism had settled into its status of the new orthodoxy: 'a generation was growing up which had known nothing else, which believed the Pope to be Antichrist, the Mass a mummery, which did not look back to the Catholic past as their own, but another country, another world'.[9] For John Bossy, the 'death' of the medieval church was the precondition for the emergence of what he called 'the English Catholic community'. The internal conflicts by which it was blighted were the 'posthumous convulsions' of that process, while its history to 1603 was 'a progression from inertia to inertia in three generations'.[10]

These arguments have prevailed to the extent that the English Reformation is now widely regarded as a prolonged and incremental process that extended over many decades and, indeed, centuries. John Spurr has deployed the term 'post-Reformation' to refer to the period 1603–1714: even as this phrase recognizes the continuing repercussions of the seismic upheavals of the Tudor era and the ongoing struggle to interpret them, it also implies that the phenomenon in question was, in some sense, over.[11] Peter Marshall's more recent, magisterial study of *Heretics and Believers* brings its story to a close in the 1590s.[12] However, the end point of reform in England has been stretched well beyond this terminus by other

---

[7] Christopher Haigh, 'The English Reformation: A Premature Birth, A Difficult Labour and a Sickly Child', *HJ*, 33 (1990), 449–59; and see *idem, English Reformations: Religion, Politics and Society under the Tudors* (Oxford, 1993). The first part of Haigh's title alludes to Anne Hudson, *The Premature Reformation: Wycliffite Texts and Lollard History* (Oxford, 1988).

[8] Patrick Collinson, *The Birthpangs of Protestant England: Religious and Cultural Change in the Sixteenth and Seventeenth Centuries* (New York, 1988). Ch. 4 is a revised version of his Stenton Lecture, *From Iconoclasm to Iconophobia: The Cultural Impact of England's Second Reformation* (Reading, 1986).

[9] Eamon Duffy, *The Stripping of the Altars: Traditional Religion in England 1400–1580* (New Haven, CT, 1992; 2nd edn, 2005), p. 593.

[10] John Bossy, *The English Catholic Community 1570–1850* (1975), p. 11; *idem*, 'The Character of Elizabethan Catholicism', *P&P*, 21 (1962), 39–59, at 57.

[11] John Spurr, *The Post-Reformation 1603–1714* (Harlow, 2006), pp. 1–2. See also his 'The English "Post-Reformation"', *Journal of Modern History*, 74 (2002), 101–19. The phrase was also deployed by John Bossy in the title of *Peace in the Post-Reformation* (Cambridge, 1998).

[12] Peter Marshall, *Heretics and Believers: A History of the English Reformation* (New Haven, CT, 2017). See his '(Re)defining the English Reformation', *JBS*, 48 (2009), 564–86, esp. 567–8, 576–7.

scholars. Via the notion of a 'long Reformation', its parameters have been expanded to encompass the years up to 1800.[13]

These trends partly take their cue partly from the scholarship on Continental Europe. Anglophone historians have, nevertheless, been slow to apply the notion of a 'second reformation', familiar from the German literature, to the British Isles. This signals a shift of gear as Lutheranism lost ground to the conception of reform most closely associated with John Calvin, the Frenchman born a full generation after the former Wittenberg monk in 1509. It is also indicative of the tensions that emerged as Protestantism moved into its implementation phase, as doctrinal boundaries hardened, and as an ethic of moral discipline became a defining feature of the 'late Reformation'.[14] Although Alec Ryrie has charted the 'strange death of Lutheran England' in the late 1540s and 1550s, as Zwinglian and Calvinist theology began to eclipse that of Martin Luther, a generational model of ecclesiastical development has not been widely adopted.[15] However, Anthony Milton's important new account of the reshaping of the Church of England between 1625 and 1662 in the crucible of the Civil Wars, Interregnum, and the Restoration has changed this definitively for the mid-seventeenth century. The multiple varieties of reformation—Laudian, episcopalian, Presbyterian, Congregationalist, and Cromwellian—that he investigates were competing strategies for tackling the confusing inheritance of the 'unresolved' reformation of the sixteenth century and shifting it in new directions. 'England's second Reformation' was not a strange hiatus or anomaly, but the climax of a century-long battle over the identity of the established Church, its history, and its formularies. The 1662 settlement did not mark a return to the pre-war status quo. Complicated and coloured by the schemes of the previous two decades, it inaugurated a fresh bout of contestation about the religious past that played itself out in subsequent decades.[16]

[13] Nicholas Tyacke (ed.), *England's Long Reformation 1500–1800* (1998); Lucy Bates, 'The Limits of Possibility in England's Long Reformation', *HJ*, 53 (2010), 1049–70. See also John McCallum (ed.), *Scotland's Long Reformation: New Perspectives on Scottish Religion, c.1500–c.1660* (Leiden, 2016); David Loewenstein and Alison Shell (eds), 'Early Modern Literature and England's Long Reformation', special issue of *Reformation*, 24, no. 2 (2019); Peter G. Wallace, *The Long European Reformation: Religion, Political Conflict, and the Search for Conformity, 1350–1750*, 3rd edn (2019).

[14] For some of the relevant scholarship, see Heinz Schilling (ed.), *Die Reformierte Konfessionalisierung in Deutschland: Das Problem der "Zweiten Reformation"* (Gütersloh, 1986); Bodo Nischan, *Prince, People and Confession: The Second Reformation in Brandenburg* (Philadelphia, PA, 1994); Harm Klueting, 'Problems of the Term and Concept "Second Reformation": Memories of a 1980s Debate', in John M. Headley, Hans J. Hillerbrand, and Anthony J. Papalas (eds), *Confessionalization in Europe, 1555–1700: Essays in Honor and Memory of Bodo Nischan* (Aldershot, 2004), pp. 37–49. See also Amy Nelson Burnett, 'Generational Conflict in the Late Reformation: The Basel Paroxysm', *Journal of Interdisciplinary History*, 32 (2001), 217–42.

[15] Alec Ryrie, 'The Strange Death of Lutheran England', *JEH*, 53 (2002), 64–92. For a refinement, see David Scott Gehring, 'From the Strange Death to the Odd Afterlife of Lutheran England', *HJ*, 57 (2014), 825–44.

[16] Anthony Milton, *England's Second Reformation: The Battle for the Church of England 1625–1662* (Cambridge, 2021). A. G. Dickens anticipated Milton in applying this phrase to the mid-seventeenth century in *The English Reformation* (1964), p. 336.

Robert Ingram's analysis of the aftermath of the revolution of 1688, *Reformation without End*, meanwhile, finds that such conflicts remained at the centre of public political debate in the era of the Enlightenment: the fundamental questions about truth and Christian history that had preoccupied people in the sixteenth century continued to promote discord as well as release creative energies.[17] For Jeremy Gregory too, reformation is a process that lacks both 'a straightforward beginning' and a finite stopping point, and which rippled over into the nineteenth century.[18] At the other end of the chronological spectrum, there has been fresh interest in its late medieval antecedents, in the currents of critique and renewal that were in motion within Christianity before the break with Rome. Investigations of the roots of evangelicalism within orthodoxy as well as heresy and the 'family resemblances' and interdependencies between different strands of vernacular religion are beginning to nuance long-standing assumptions about its genesis and lineage.[19]

Despite the striking metaphors invoked by historians and the prevailing scholarly consensus that religious change took place over a lengthy period, comparatively little attention has been paid to the relationship between the life cycle and England's Reformations. By contrast with the categories of class, nation, and gender, age has been a neglected dimension of our understanding of this religious movement until rather recently. Susan Brigden's inspiring work on the role of youth in its early, disruptive phases is now being complemented by studies of childhood within the Catholic and nonconformist traditions,[20] while David Cressy's wide-ranging survey of rites of passage is undergoing refinement in the light of new research on the multiple ways in which contemporaries perceived and interpreted the path from birth to death and from infancy to adulthood.[21] Alec Ryrie's

[17] Robert G. Ingram, *Reformation without End: Religion, Politics and the Past in Post-Revolutionary England* (Manchester, 2018).
[18] Jeremy Gregory, 'The Making of a Protestant Nation: "Success" and "Failure" in England's Long Reformation', in Tyacke (ed.), *England's Long Reformation*, pp. 307–33, at 313, 316. See also Nockles and Westbrook (eds), *Reinventing the Reformation*.
[19] Among others, see Shannon McSheffrey, 'Heresy, Orthodoxy and Vernacular Religion, 1480–1525', *P&P*, 186 (2005), 47–80; Robert Lutton, *Lollardy and Orthodox Religion in Pre-Reformation England: Reconstructing Piety* (Woodbridge, 2006); Robert Lutton and Elizabeth Salter (eds), *Pieties in Transition: Religious Practices and Experiences, c.1400–1640* (Aldershot, 2007); J. Patrick Hornbeck, *What is a Lollard? Dissent and Belief in Late Medieval England* (Oxford, 2010), esp. 'Introduction: Family Resemblances', pp. 1–24; Fiona Somerset, *Feeling like Saints: Lollard Writings after Wyclif* (Ithaca, NY, 2014); Peter Marshall, 'Catholic Puritanism in Pre-Reformation England', *British Catholic History*, 32 (2015), 431–50; *idem*, *Heretics and Believers*, part I.
[20] Susan Brigden, 'Youth and the English Reformation', *P&P*, 95 (1982), 37–67; Lucy Underwood, *Childhood, Youth and Religious Dissent in Post-Reformation England* (Basingstoke, 2014); Tali Berner and Lucy Underwood (eds), *Childhood, Youth and Religious Minorities in Early Modern Europe* (Basingstoke, 2019).
[21] David Cressy, *Birth, Marriage and Death: Ritual, Religion, and the Life-Cycle in in Tudor and Stuart England* (Oxford, 1997); Alexandra Bamji, 'The Catholic Life Cycle', in Alexandra Bamji, Geert H. Janssen, and Mary Laven (eds), *The Ashgate Research Companion to the Counter-Reformation* (Farnham, 2013), pp. 183–201; Caroline Bowden, Emily Vine, and Tessa Whitehouse (eds), *Religion and the Lifecycle in England, 1500–1800* (Manchester, 2021). See also my 'The Reformation of the

Being Protestant traces the stages of spiritual growth that people traversed during their lives, sometimes in tandem and sometimes in tension with key biological turning points.[22] Norman Jones's investigation of the 'cultural adaptation' of English society comes closest to the present project in charting the manner in which Protestantism was gradually assimilated by individuals and institutions, though the Reformation he describes is a 'moderately short' one accomplished over three generations. By the early seventeenth century people were living in a 'reconstructed culture' and inhabiting a different 'mental world'.[23]

If interest in how the ecclesiastical and theological revolutions of the sixteenth and seventeenth centuries affected different generations is increasing, historians have been less inclined to ask questions about how these developments were affected by the passage of the generations. Nor have they exploited the notion of the generation as a social cohort as a tool for exploring its course and consequences or its conscious identification as a seminal early modern event. This book makes a novel and emphatic case for doing so.

It has often been assumed that as a form of imagined community the generation is a symptom and by-product of modernity, and, in particular, of the accelerating tempo of change that is held to be one of its principal effects. Pierre Nora linked its advent to the French Revolution and saw it as 'the daughter of democracy' and of the principle of equality.[24] An early template was laid by Auguste Comte in the 1840s, who regarded generational succession as a driving force for progress, but it was the thought-provoking interventions of François Mentré, José Ortega y Gasset, and Karl Mannheim in the 1920s and 1930s that really made the case for the generation as a key dynamic of historical development. It was in the work of these pioneering theorists that the idea that a group of coevals might share a common outlook gained traction, partly in reaction to the Marxist preoccupation with class. For Mannheim, 'mere chronological contemporaneity' was insufficient to create generational consciousness: as a form of identity derived from one's position in time, it had to coincide with participation in a 'common destiny' associated with living through moments of profound dislocation, rapid transition, and cultural rupture.[25]

Generations: Youth, Age and Religious Change in England, *c.*1500–1700', *TRHS*, 6th ser., 21 (2011), 93–121.

[22] Alec Ryrie, *Being Protestant in Reformation Britain* (Oxford, 2013), part V ('The Protestant Life').

[23] Norman Jones, 'Living the Reformations: Generational Experience and Political Perception in Early Modern England', *HLQ*, 60 (1999), 273–88; idem, *The English Reformation: Religion and Cultural Adaptation* (Oxford, 2002), esp. 6, 196–8.

[24] Pierre Nora, *Realms of Memory: Rethinking the French Past*, 3 vols, trans. Arthur Goldhammer (New York, 1996–8), vol. i, *Conflicts and Divisions*, pp. 502–3, 508, and ch. 3.

[25] Auguste Comte, *Cours de philosophie positive*, 5 vols (Paris, 1830–42), vol. iv, pp. 635–41; François Mentré, *Les Générations sociales* (Paris, 1920); Jose Ortega y Gasset, *El tema de nuestro tiempo* (Madrid, 1923), trans. by Mildred Adams as *Man and Crisis* (New York, 1962), pp. 30–84; Karl Mannheim, 'Das Problem der Generationen', *Kölner Vierteljahreshefte für Soziologie*, 7 (1928), trans. as 'The Problem of Generations', in *Essays on the Sociology of Knowledge: Collected Works*,

Part of a broader programme to develop a sociology of knowledge, Mannheim's concept of generations has worked its way into the lexicon of the social sciences. As a sociological problem, it has offered a route to understanding age-related conflicts and the temporal disorientations connected with crisis and catastrophe. Avoiding the unhelpful dualism of self and society, in the words of Philip Abrams, it foregrounds 'the mutual phasing of two different calendars: the calendar of the life cycle of the individual and the calendar of historical experience'.[26] While there are dangers in assuming the existence of a bridge between the biological rhythm of individual lives and the chronology of external events, it is necessary to remain alert to the possibility of interconnections between the two.[27] Some sociologists have suggested restricting the term to refer to kinship descent, but the majority have followed an earlier preference for largely cutting it loose from its 'genea-logical anchor' and approaching it as a type of cohort.[28] They have approached the generation as 'a form of dwelling in time and space' and as 'a vehicle for thought and action', as a mode of subjective perception and a cognitive structure that provided people with specific ways of understanding and acting upon their experiences in a world that seemed to be in turmoil. Situated in the present, but oriented towards the past and future, it is a discourse in which myth and mission are closely intertwined.[29]

Most historians who have utilized generation as a heuristic device have like-wise defined the generation as a social and cultural rather than a biological phe-nomenon. A significant flurry of studies was inspired by the generational tensions manifested in the student revolts of 1968, together with an outburst of theorizing. The clash of the generations and the role that the discontinuities between them played in the transmission of ideology and political experience became fashion-able themes. The concerns of the present provoked a rediscovery of the cleavages between old and young and the coalescence of age and social cohorts into self-conscious entities in the past.[30] In an article published in 1974, David Herlihy

ed. Paul Keeskemeti, vol. v, (1952), pp. 276–320, esp. 207, 306, 320. Important later interventions include Julián Marías, *El método histórico de las generaciones* (Madrid, 1961), trans. by Harold C. Raley as *Generations: A Historical Method* (Tuscaloosa, AL, 1970). For an analytical overview, see Hans Jaeger, 'Generations in History: Reflections on a Controversial Concept', *History and Theory*, 24 (1985), 273–92. This is a translation of an article originally published in *Geschichte und Gesellschaft*, 3 (1977).

[26] Philip Abrams, *Historical Sociology* (Shepton Mallet, 1982), ch. 8 ('The Historical Sociology of Individuals: Identity and the Problem of Generations'), p. 240. See also Ron Eyerman and Bryan S. Turner, 'Outline of a Theory of Generations', *European Journal of Social Theory*, 1 (1998), 91–106; June Edmunds and Brian S. Turner, *Generations, Culture and Society* (Buckingham, 2002).

[27] Jaeger, 'Generations in History', 275.

[28] For concerns about its polysemous usage, see Norman B. Ryder, 'The Cohort as a Concept in the Study of Social Change', *American Sociological Review*, 30 (1965), 843–61; Matilda White Riley, 'On the Significance of Age in Sociology', *American Sociological Review*, 52 (1987), 1–14; David I. Kertzer, 'Generation as a Sociological Problem', *American Review of Sociology*, 9 (1983), 125–49, at 128.

[29] Judith Burnett, *Generations: The Time Machine in Theory and Practice* (Farnham, 2010), p. 125; Karen R. Foster, *Generation, Discourse and Social Change* (New York, 2013), ch. 1, esp. p. 23.

[30] Lewis S. Feuer, *The Conflict of Generations: The Character and Significance of Student Movements* (New York, 1969); Herbert Butterfield, *The Discontinuities between the Generations in History: Their*

urged medievalists to consider the significance of generational balances and relationships in the study of medieval history, but his call to arms fell largely on deaf ears, at least within the Anglo-American academy.[31] Indeed, Herbert Butterfield doubted the importance of age-related conflicts before 1900.[32] By contrast, German scholars of the Middle Ages and early modern era have been more active in pursuing these promising lines of inquiry.[33]

Nevertheless, the chief laboratory for investigations of the generation as a historical phenomenon remains the nineteenth and twentieth centuries. In particular, Robert Wohl's *The Generation of 1914* (1980), Alan Spitzer's *The French Generation of 1820* (1987), Mary Fulbrook's *Dissonant Lives: Generations and Violence through the German Dictatorships* (2011), and Roy Foster's *Vivid Faces: The Revolutionary Generation in Ireland 1890–1923* (2014) have sensitively reconstructed the mentality of groups of people born around the same time and traced how traumatic events foster senses of purpose and solidarity.[34] The situations in

---

Effect on the Transmission of Political Experience (Cambridge, 1971); Alan B. Spitzer, 'The Historical Problem of Generations', *AHR*, 78 (1973), 1353–85; Anthony Esler, (ed.), *The Youth Revolution: The Conflict of Generations in Modern History* (Lexington, MA, 1974); *idem, Bombs, Beards and Barricades: 150 Years of Youth in Revolt* (New York, 1971); Annie Kriegel and Elisabeth Hirsch, 'Generational Difference: The History of an Idea', *Daedalus*, 107 (1978), 23–38.

[31] David Herlihy, 'The Generation in Medieval History', *Viator*, 5 (1974), 347–64. One exception to the comparative neglect of the premodern manifestations of this phenomenon is Anthony Esler, *The Aspiring Mind of the Elizabethan Younger Generation* (Durham, NC, 1966).

[32] Butterfield, *Discontinuities*, p. 21.

[33] See Sabine von Heusinger and Annette Kehnel (eds), *Generations in the Cloister: Youth and Age in Medieval Religious Life/Generationen im Kloster: Jugend und Alter in der mittelalterlichen vita religiosa* (Zurich, 2008); Dina de Rentiis and Ulrike Siewert (eds), *Generationen und gender in mittelalterlicher und frühneuzeitlicher Literatur* (Bamberg, 2009); Finn-Einer Eliassen and Katalin Szende (eds), *Generations in Towns: Succession and Success in Pre-Industrial Urban Societies* (Newcastle, 2009); Christian Kuhn, *Generation als Grundbegriff einer historischen Geschichtskultur: Die Nürnberger Tucher im langen 16. Jarhundert* (Göttingen, 2010); Mark Häberlein, Christian Kuhn, and Lina Hörl (eds), *Generationen in spätmittelalterlichen und frühneuzeitlichen Städten (ca. 1250–1750)* (Constance, 2011). Stimulated partly by the Göttingen graduate programme in Generationengeschichte, the concept has been extensively deployed and theorized in German scholarship, though the emphasis remains on the modern era. See Ulrike Jureit and Michael Wildt (eds), *Generationen: Zur Relevanz eines wissenschaftlichen Grundbegriffs* (Hamburg, 2005); Sigrid Weigel, Ohad Parnes, Ulrike Vedder, and Stefan Willer (eds), *Generation: Zur Genealogie des Konzepts—Konzepte von Genealogie* (Munich, 2005); Ulrike Jureit, *Generationenforschung* (Göttingen, 2006); Ohad Parnes, Ulrike Vedder, and Stefan Willer, *Das Konzept der Generation: Eine Wissenschafts und Kulturgeschichte* (Frankfurt am Main, 2008); Björn Bohennkamp, Till Manning, and Eva-Maria Silies (eds), *Generation als Erzählung: Neue Perspektiven auf ein kulturelles Deutungsmuster* (Göttingen, 2009); Harald Kündemund and Marc Szydlik (eds), *Generationen: Multidisziplinäre Perspektiven* (Wiesbaden, 2009); Hartmut Berghoff, Uffa Jensen, Christina Lubinski, and Bernd Weisbrod (eds), *History by Generations: Generational Dynamics in Modern History* (Göttingen, 2013).

[34] Robert Wohl, *The Generation of 1914* (Cambridge, MA, 1980); Alan B. Spitzer, *The French Generation of 1820* (Princeton, NJ, 1987); Mary Fulbrook, *Dissonant Lives: Generations and Violence through the German Dictatorships* (Oxford, 2011); Roy Foster, *Vivid Faces: The Revolutionary Generation in Ireland 1890–1923* (Harmondsworth, 2014). Other contributions include D. L. Shaw, *The Generation of 1898 in Spain* (New York, 1975); Marvin Rintala, *The Constitution of Silence: Essays on Generational Themes* (Westport, CT, 1979); Mark Roseman (ed.), *Generations in Conflict: Youth Revolt and Generation Formation in Germany, 1770–1968* (Cambridge, 1995); Stephen Lovell (ed.), *Generations in Twentieth-Century Europe* (Basingstoke, 2007).

which individuals find themselves leave a 'decisive imprint' on their outlook and create a 'transient unity'. Whether identified by themselves or by external observers, the generations these scholars reconstruct are less 'an army of contemporaries making its way across the territory of time' than 'a magnetic field at the center of which lies an experience or series of experiences'.[35] The associated insight that generations are frequently recognized with the benefit of hindsight has been a vital stimulus for my own investigation. According to Robert Wohl, generations are 'not born; they are made'; to quote Roy Foster, they are 'made not only by conscious processes of identification and rejection in the lives of the protagonists, but also retrospectively'.[36] In short, they are often artefacts of memory. They are constituted by traditions of remembering and forgetting the past which operate in dialogue with dreams and visions of the present and future. As Pierre Nora comments, they often revolve less around the recollection of events that their members have experienced than those they have not: 'a painful, never-ending fantasy that holds them together far more than what stands in front and divides them'.[37]

The idea of writing 'history by generations' is currently undergoing a revival. The recent *American Historical Review* conversation on this topic is a sign of the times.[38] Fresh interest in generational dynamics is perhaps not surprising in a context in which tensions between the generations seem to be again on the rise and in which people are once more acutely conscious of temporal rupture. Climate change and the coronavirus pandemic, the campaign to address historic racial injustice, and dramatic political disjunctures such as Brexit and the Russian invasion of Ukraine are all cultivating renewed awareness of how the generations contribute to the making of history.[39]

Generations takes inspiration from this body of literature, but it also insists that we must be attentive to the plural and fluid meanings of the word 'generation' in the late medieval and early modern era. In the sixteenth and seventeenth centuries, as now, it was sometimes used to describe a set of individuals of the same age or a group of people who coexisted in a particular epoch. It was also invoked to measure the lifespan, the interval between birth and death, the 'time that a man dwelleth in the worlde'. A figure of duration and an index of chronological progression, as the Canterbury minister Thomas Wilson delineated in his *Christian dictionarie* of 1612, it also denoted 'a history or narration of things which happen unto any persons'. The term was predominantly employed, however, to define a body of genealogical descendants: a succession, pedigree, or 'race' of persons

---

[35] Spitzer, *French Generation*, pp. 14, 32; Wohl, *Generation of 1914*, p. 210.

[36] Wohl, *Generation of 1914*, p. 5; Foster, *Vivid Faces*, p. 7.

[37] Nora, *Realms of Memory*, i. pp. 498–531, quotation at p. 525. See also Fulbrook, *Dissonant Voices*, p. 18.

[38] 'AHR Conversation: Each Generation Writes Its Own History of Generations', *AHR*, 123 (2018), 1505–46. With the exception of myself, all the contributors are modernists.

[39] On the resurgence of 'generationalism' in recent social and political discourse, see Jonathan White, 'Thinking Generations', *The British Journal of Sociology*, 64 (2013), 216–47.

sharing a common ancestry. In turn, this was integrally linked to the use of generation to identify 'the first beginning of a thing' and its coming into being. It pinpointed the moment of origin of a living creature.[40] The gradual displacement of the word 'generation' by 'reproduction' reflects changing understandings of conception and procreation in European culture. The intellectual developments that lay behind this are typically associated with Charles Darwin's theory of the biological evolution of species, but they were also a function of subtle, longer-term shifts in philosophical and scientific thinking.[41]

Contemporary senses of the word had their roots in Scripture, especially the Old Testament. Part of the social universe of the English Bible, they reflected the manner in which its early modern translators rendered a variety of cognate nouns in Hebrew and Greek for vernacular readers.[42] The book of *Genesis* is itself a genealogy which tells the story of the Creation of Adam and Eve and the posterity they engendered. Divinity itself was understood in generational terms: the Christian God is both a Father and a Son, begotten by a mysterious union between the Holy Spirit and the Virgin Mary. The miraculous conception of Jesus is a prelude to his redemptive death on the cross at Calvary, which made him the saviour of the world. Suffusing the medieval liturgy and its Protestant successor, the Book of Common Prayer, the language of generations reflects the conviction that the people of God are, by extension, his spiritual family and children. In the words of 1 Peter 2:9, they are 'a chosen generation' who have been 'called...out of darkness into the marvellous light'. Elected as partakers of the holy promises he made to Abraham and his seed forever, they will be preserved from age to age by his merciful providence. Poised between hope and assurance, gratitude for blessings past, and anticipation of the felicity that awaited the Lord's 'inheritance' in heaven, such statements gave expression to a sense of inclusion and shared identity. Elsewhere, 'generation' is deployed in a prophetic and denunciatory mode to demarcate those who resist Christ's gospel, stand in opposition to the truth, and persecute the faithful. Evil and adulterous, ungrateful and hypocritical, these are generations of 'serpents' and 'vipers' against whom God and subsequent ages will rise in judgement. Here 'generation' is part of a vocabulary of discrimination that identifies a hostile other and attributes collective culpability to it.[43] Such passages

---

[40] *OED*, s.v. 'generation'; Thomas Wilson, *A Christian dictionarie* (1612; STC 25786), pp. 188–9, 221, 223. See also R[obert] F. H[errey], *Two right profitable and fruitfull concordances, or large and ample alphabetical tables* ([1580?]; STC 13228b), s.v. 'generation'; Andrew Willet, *Hexapla in Genesin, that is, A sixfold commentarie upon Genesis* (1632; STC 25684), pp. 64, 148–9.

[41] See Nick Hopwood, 'The Keywords "Generation" and "Reproduction"', in Rebecca Flemming, Nick Hopwood, and Lauren Kassell (eds), *Reproduction: Antiquity to the Present Day* (Cambridge, 2018), pp. 287–304. Raymond Williams traces the shifting inflections of the word in *Keywords: A Vocabulary of Culture and Society* (1976), pp. 140–2.

[42] See Naomi Tadmor, *The Social Universe of the English Bible: Scripture, Society and Culture in Early Modern England* (Cambridge, 2010).

[43] See Matthew 12:39, 41 and 23:33; Mark 8:12; Luke 11:29, 32.

encapsulate the multivocality of the word 'generation' in early modern England. Like its linguistic cousins and close synonyms, it floated across several discursive domains—theology, law, history, and natural philosophy—and was employed figuratively as well as literally.[44]

In the sixteenth and seventeenth centuries, then, the genealogical, social, and historical dimensions of this concept were tightly intertwined. Keeping its mutability in mind and all its connotations in play, this book explores how the English Reformations shaped the horizontal and synchronic relationships that early modern people formed with their kith and kin, as well as the vertical and diachronic ones that tied them to their forebears and heirs.[45] It examines the overlapping entities that were families of blood and families of faith and considers how these developed over the course of a religious movement that began as a project of evangelical conversion but evolved into a birthright passed down from mother and father to daughter and son. The same patterns can be detected in those who rebelled against and broke away from it in later generations. The recurrent theological and cultural upheavals of the era were repeated attempts to effect the *regeneration* of both institutions and souls. They not merely transformed the generations that participated in and witnessed them; in significant respects, they also reconfigured the relationship between the realms of the living and the dead and the nexus between memory, history, and time. Accordingly, this book contends that in the context of early modern England, generations were born as well as made.

Approaching and Locating the Generations

Generations resists the temptation to divide individuals into groups based on age or self-identification in favour of acknowledging the fruitful ambiguities and porous boundaries that surrounded this conceptual category in the period. It eschews a prosopographical approach because this carries the risk of assuming that the outlook of the selected cohort is representative, homogeneous, and predetermined by their birth date, life stage, or historical experiences. Conscious of the similar dangers associated with reconstructing the collective mentality of 'a vast sea of anonymous coevals',[46] it pays close attention to the idiosyncratic biographies of individual men, women, and children. The picture it paints is an intricate mosaic of the stories these people told about themselves, others, and the times in which they lived. It is one that acknowledges their agency in shaping the very events by which generational awareness itself was created.

---

[44] See *OED*, s.vv. 'age', 'youth', 'heritage', 'inheritance', 'posterity', 'patrimony', and 'legacy'.
[45] Following the lead of Burnett, *Generations*, p. 24, and see ch. 1.
[46] Spitzer, *French Generation*, p. 11.

At the same time, this book foregrounds the family as a key domain in which the generation as both an idea and an experience was forged. It recognizes it as a critical forum in which questions of age, ancestry, identity, and memory coalesced. *Generations* is not, however, simply a new history of the early modern family.[47] Nor is it family history writ large. As conventionally practised, this too is a genealogical enterprise suffused by filial loyalty and pride. Conservative and sometimes sentimental in character, it tends to prioritize the steady succession of the generations at the expense of the transformations taking place around them. If the visibility of generations as social cohorts is often a function of revolutionary developments, the study of generations as kinship structures frequently privileges continuity. As I show in the chapters that follow, the family was not only a source of stability and an instrument of perpetuity; it was also a locus of conflict and a framework in which change occurred. It stretched backwards and forwards in time and outward in space to encompass a wider penumbra of relatives and friends beyond the household. In the context of high rates of infant, child, and maternal mortality and of the vulnerability of people of all ages to premature death, the links in the generational chain were extremely fragile. Repeatedly broken and reconstituted by remarriage, families were hybrid structures within which the blood ties binding adults and children were variegated. Moreover, some, including the unmarried, widows and widowers, and monks and nuns, remained on their peripheries, though still integrated into wider networks of kinship.

The church, congregation and sect is the third form of community which *Generations* places under the spotlight. It investigates the full range of groups into which Christianity dissolved in the wake of the schism from the Church of Rome initiated by Henry VIII and under the pressure of subsequent events, especially the Civil Wars and the Interregnum. Despite the reigning ideal of religious uniformity, which was seen as a recipe for political order and social harmony, the ironic effect of England's successive and serial reformations was to foster pluralism, entrench diversity, and create the conditions for confessional coexistence. Membership of the multiple, overlapping communities of faith that this process engendered was both voluntary and involuntary. It was the product of royal fiat and personal conversion, choice and birth. The boundaries of orthodoxy were constantly being redefined, and people could easily find themselves on the wrong side of the law.

This study encompasses adherents of the established Church of England, a capacious institution that proved capable of accommodating competing tendencies. Its inclusive ecclesiology, in combination with the principle of outward conformity, enabled it to incorporate people who harboured significant scruples and reservations, including church papists and puritans. The emergence of a new style

---

[47] For this historiography, see Chapter 2.

of churchmanship (sometimes described as 'avant-garde conformity') in the 1590s, the advance of anti-Calvinist or Arminian ideas, and the rise of Laudianism in the 1630s provide evidence of the changes of ecclesiastical and theological mood that occurred as it rethought its relationship with Rome and with Reformed churches abroad. However, this book also extends to those who separated out into dissenting congregations and joined radical sects. It investigates Roman Catholics who took the path of recusancy and supported the cause of Counter-Reformation, alongside those Protestants whose disillusionment with the Church of England led them, whether reluctantly or enthusiastically, into nonconformity: Presbyterians, Baptists, and Congregationalists. After two decades of wrangling, many of these puritans were ejected and marginalized from it in 1662. Others who feature in these pages include Familists, Quakers, Muggletonians, and Fifth Monarchists. If some of these mystical families of love, societies of friends, and apocalyptic brotherhoods declined and disappeared, others adapted themselves to survive the challenges of a changing environment and thrived. The book additionally incorporates the later Lollards, whom the reformers heralded as their spiritual forebears. It traces the life cycles of these churches, congregations, and sects and how they evolved over time. It observes affinities and parallels between these groups and their histories, but it also tries to do justice to the doctrinal and temperamental differences that distinguished and divided them.

This book may be described as a social history of a cluster of potent ideas and their practical ramifications in culture and behaviour. In some recent work, an unfortunate dichotomy has emerged between polemic and piety: between the study of ecclesiastical politics and the study of devotional identities and styles. *Generations* resists this divorce, as well as the associated apartheid between private faith and public doctrinal division. Early modern spirituality was inflected by religious controversy and vice versa. Confessional antagonism was not detached from practical divinity; quotidian routines carried the potential to ease frictions but also to provoke confrontation and violence.[48]

I also seek to explore the mutually constitutive relationship between theology and lived religion. Historical anthropology has had the less than salutary effect of exiling doctrine from the reconstruction of past praxis. *Generations* reinforces calls for theological ideas to be reintegrated into the analysis of religious culture and sensibility. It shows how beliefs about salvation and sin, predestination and damnation, divine will and human nature shaped modes of conduct and daily life, and it teases out the tensions between soteriological anxiety and family and community dynamics. Less a static canon than a pulsing tissue, theology was in

---

[48] See John Coffey, 'Foreword', in Elizabeth Clarke and Robert W. Daniel (eds), *People and Piety: Protestant Devotional Identities in Early Modern England* (Manchester, 2020), pp. xvii–xviii, discussing Peter Lake's criticism of Alec Ryrie's *Being Protestant* and the latter's response. See also the thoughtful remarks of Jessica Martin, 'Early Modern English Piety', in Anthony Milton (ed.), *The Oxford History of Anglicanism*, i: *Reformation and Identity c.1520–1662* (Oxford, 2017), pp. 395–411, esp. 410.

constant evolution. It was a script that was repeatedly rewritten in the light of experience.[49] In short, this book advocates a social and cultural history of religion with the theology put back.[50]

It is as hard to pin down a generation as it is to catch a cloud in a butterfly net.[51] Rooted in extensive archival and bibliographical research, this book draws upon a wide range of sources. It attends to the rhetorics and representations of age and ancestry alongside textual, visual, and material traces of the affective ties that bound the generations together. It mines biblical commentaries and works of systematic theology, as well as the pastoral treatises in which preachers and ministers explicated key precepts for lay readers. It exploits the polemical diatribes that contemporaries launched against their opponents and the controversies about ecclesiastical history and dynastic politics which they prosecuted in print. Extensive use is made of sermons, broadsides, catechisms, and liturgies. These too were manifestations of the twin impulses to persuade and educate, inspire and indoctrinate, which underpinned the competing Protestant, Catholic, and radical Reformations.

Medical and midwifery treatises provide insight into early modern ideas about sexual generation and heredity that both inflected and informed discussions of the life cycle of faith. Forms of life-writing also loom large: sixteenth- and seventeenth-century diaries, memoirs, journals, obituaries, and biographies yield a rich seam of evidence of how religious change was experienced and internalized by individuals. They also attest to the powerful impulses that led their writers and compilers to preserve this on paper for the edification of their relatives, friends, disciples, and descendants. Setting aside the anachronistic paradigm of autobiography, this book firmly situates such texts in the corporate and communal contexts from which they arose. It places them on a continuum with chronicles, registers, and histories and treats them as a mode of commemorating past generations and as an instrument for communicating with future ones. Many of the manuscript sources I discuss have been discovered among family papers bequeathed to national libraries and deposited in local record offices—an untapped treasury that deserves fuller investigation. Indeed, the very existence and survival of these genealogical residues is key to the arguments about the significance of the generational transmission of memory that this study develops.

---

[49] In this it reinforces the work of Brian Cummings, *The Literary Culture of the Reformation: Grammar and Grace* (Oxford, 2002); Leif Dixon, *Practical Predestinarians in England, c.1590–1640* (Farnham, 2014), esp. p. 24; Jonathan Willis, *The Reformation of the Decalogue: Religious Identity and the Ten Commandments in England, c.1485–1625* (Cambridge, 2017), esp. pp. 10–11, 353; David D. Hall, *The Puritans: A Transatlantic History* (Princeton, NJ, 2019), esp. pp. 11–12.

[50] To redeploy a phase used by Patrick Collinson in another context: *De Republica Anglorum, or History with the Politics Put Back* (Cambridge, 1990).

[51] A metaphor borrowed from Peter Burke, *Varieties of Cultural History* (Cambridge, 1997), p. 1: 'How can anyone write a history of something which lacks a fixed identity? It is rather like trying to catch a cloud in a butterfly net.'

The same is true of the array of objects that appear as illustrations—from paint-ings, portraits, and pedigrees to domestic utensils and furniture, personal posses-sions, and sacred relics. Handed down as legacies and heirlooms, these artefacts are tangible residues of the processes I place under the microscope. Their jour-neys and itineraries through time are as revealing as those of the men, women, and children to whom they belonged and by whom they were inherited.

These sources have been chosen because they illuminate how senses of reli-gious subjectivity and confessional identity became entangled with conceptions of people's place in the age hierarchy and their family's lineage. They permit us to gain intimate glimpses of the ways in which individual lives were shaped by polit-ical and ecclesiastical events that often seemed outside the control of those whom they most affected, but which they nevertheless helped in vital ways to advance, subvert, and shape. It is a premise of this project that record-keeping and storytell-ing are key mechanisms for facilitating contact and conveying information between, across, and within generations. Reflection and narration are critical ingredients in the creation of senses of solidarity and generational consciousness.[52]

Alert to the complex intersections between generation, rank, and gender, *Generations* attempts to probe the lives of contemporaries from across the social and age spectrum, even as it acknowledges that the voices of the young and the poor are more difficult to recover than those of literate adults from the middle and upper rungs of the hierarchy. The picture it presents is skewed towards people who were both educated and pious, but it does its best to incorporate members of society who have left little in the way of written testimony and made no discern-ible mark on the historical record. Finally, while the geographical focus of ana-lysis is England, the book calibrates its findings in relation to historiographies that extend beyond these islands. It keeps other parts of Britain and the Atlantic world on its horizon. While the religious settlements that comprised the English Reformations were idiosyncratic, the patterns of generational conflict and con-solidation it produced have pertinence for other contexts and cultures. The Erastian reforms of the Tudors were repeatedly contested by alternative visions that pitted the establishment against its critics and encouraged resistance. As the wheels of fortune and time turned, erstwhile protesters became the guardians of tradition. 'The complicated dance of acceptance and reaction' each generation had with its predecessor finds echoes in other parts of Europe which were con-vulsed by religious upheaval and turmoil, especially the Low Countries, France, and the Holy Roman Empire.[53]

This book conducts its investigations over the long chronological period between *c*.1500 and 1700 precisely because it conceptualizes the Reformation as a

---

[52] See June Edmunds and Bryan S. Turner (eds), *Generational Consciousness, Narrative and Politics* (Lanham, MD, 2002), 'Conclusion', esp. p. 181.
[53] Jones, *English Reformation*, p. 10.

multistranded and protracted process that spanned several generations. Each of its thematically organized chapters traverses the whole period and intertwines discussion of the genealogical, social, and historical dimensions of its subject, though the precise ratio differs. Perhaps the aptest metaphor for describing it is the kaleidoscope. With every twist of the cylinder, the pieces of coloured glass and mirror are rearranged and a new image emerges into view.

Chapter 1, 'Youth and Age', explores the part played by people of all ages in the making of England's long Reformation. It tests suggestions that the successive phases of ecclesiastical and cultural upheaval entailed forms of youthful rebellion and assesses the intergenerational tensions between children and parents, adolescents and elders, to which these revolutionary events were perceived to give rise. Defining age as a stage of spiritual growth as well as a biological phase, it also probes the paradoxes of a society that distrusted novelty and revered antiquity even as it praised childish innocence and sometimes denigrated the senility of the very elderly. It engages critically with scholarship on religious childhood alongside the idea that the authority of the aged was steadily eroded in the course of the sixteenth and seventeenth centuries.

Chapter 2, 'Kith and Kin', investigates how the Reformations affected patterns of religious practice within the family, a broad umbrella term that encompassed both kith and kin. It considers the revival of domestic religion and its role as both a bulwark and challenge to the status quo, together with the concurrent development of households both divided by faith and united by fervour and zeal. It then turns to assess the surrogate familial and sibling relationships that members of the rival churches and congregations engendered by the English Reformations developed with their fellow believers, contesting claims that the early modern period saw a weakening of ties of spiritual kinship. It stresses instead the resilience of formal and informal forms of religious fraternity against the backdrop of ecclesiological fragmentation.

The themes of Chapter 3, 'Blood and Trees', are ancestry and genealogy. Where previous studies have focused primarily on the social dimensions of early modern England's genealogical fever, here I argue that the biblical and secular dimensions of this enterprise cannot be neatly separated and that they had wider purchase and reach than has yet been recognized. I examine the interconnections between contemporary assumptions about sex and original sin, pregnancy and childbirth, race and heredity, and show how these evolved in relation to competing teachings about salvation, especially the doctrine of predestination. A further topic of discussion is the lively deployment of genealogy as a polemical device to trace the lineage of particular churches and sects back to Christ and to depict their confessional enemies as the spawn of Satan and the Antichrist.

Chapter 4, 'Generations and Seed', demonstrates that religious change fostered a strong sense of belonging to a special cohort of godly people bound by common experience and defined in contradistinction to the false and 'froward' generations that opposed and tormented them. It explores how the Reformation helped to forge forms of generational awareness closely connected with the workings of memory but also with missionary zeal to transform the future and to usher in a glorious new phase of history. These developments are assessed in conjunction with the pressing questions that devout men and women from all denominations faced about the spiritual fate of their dead ancestors and the emotional dilemmas surrounding the problem of whether or not they could save their own children. Attentive to evolving attitudes towards nature and nurture, I trace the growing importance that religious communities attached to the family as a means of transmitting religion to the next generation and the powerful resonance of the Old Testament promise to the seed of Abraham.

Chapter 5, 'History and Time', turns to the relationship between the religious turbulence of the era, the arts of history, and the sciences of time. It examines the emergence of official and alternative histories of reformation and considers how some contemporaries came to view this as a past event rather than an ongoing process. It argues that the end product of these developments was not a single unitary vision, but rather multiple conflicting ones that corresponded with the several frames of temporal reference, analogical and linear, liturgical and historical, that coexisted in this culture. Fraught with ambiguity about when (and if) the Reformation had started and ended, such accounts catalysed controversies that have left a lasting imprint on our understanding of the early modern period. These public memories became entangled with family history and genealogy in ways that expand our understanding of how the past was circulated and interpreted and how the passage of time was experienced.

Chapter 6, 'Memory and Archive', is a study of the transmutations of memory that occurred during the two centuries between Henry VIII's break with Rome and the revolution of 1688–9 that brought William and Mary to the throne. It investigates shifting attitudes towards commemoration and memorialization before exploring the ways in which contemporaries selectively remembered and creatively edited their own lives in accordance with the ever changing environment in which they found themselves. In the process it sheds fresh light on how perceptions of the English Reformations evolved as the generations that directly witnessed the religious events of the sixteenth and seventeenth centuries gave way to those whose knowledge of them was second-hand, as well as to the curious mixture of resentment and nostalgia that accompanied these transitions. Focusing as much on the form as the content of the texts and objects that men, women, and children left as legacies, it highlights the agency that biological and spiritual families exercised in creating and curating the archives, libraries, and museums upon which we rely. Thereby, they became both the mediators and the curators of our knowledge of the religious past.

Having described the architecture of this volume, the last remaining task is to draw out some of its salient arguments. How does this book contribute to the histories of the Reformations and of the generations? First, it adds texture and nuance to the lazy commonplace that England underwent a long Reformation. It refines this monolithic model, which has become coterminous with the early modern period as a whole, by focusing attention on the moving parts of the generations. It shows that competing perceptions of its starting point, speed, and duration coexisted with each other. These also depended upon the perspective of observers and actors, which shifted over the course of their own life cycles. The Tudor Reformations were neither fast nor slow, but both at the same time. Viewed from the vantage point of the present or with the benefit of hindsight, they looked different. As they retreated into the distance, contemporaries confused their initial with their subsequent stages in ways that further complicated their legacies. Understood as a phenomenon that proceeded in phases, reformation itself was conceived generationally.

A second historiographical problem that this book attempts to address is the question of how change arises out of continuity. Continuities born of compromise at many levels—political, ecclesiastical, civic, and domestic—have been seen as key to easing the passage to the Protestant era and mitigating the impact of the mid-seventeenth-century religious revolution. The bonds of family and blood and the cycle of the generations must be part of the explanation for why many people complied with developments they resented, as well as why others turned away from settled orthodoxies and embraced exotic new ideologies. They not only deepen our understanding of both the spiritual epiphanies contemporaries experienced and the pragmatic calculations they were obliged to make in response to unforeseen events; they also show how these were interlinked.[54]

Thinking in generational terms helps to recapture the inner dynamics and kinetics of a movement that began as a war between rival confessions but later became a series of internecine struggles within the same churches and sects. These often revolved around squabbles about how to preserve their purity and rekindle their primitive zeal. Generations served as a coil and a spring: they absorbed shocks and bounced back. But they may also be compared to a spiral that swirls in unexpected rather than predictable directions. Highlighting the vicissitudes, accidents, and contingencies that mould history, they help us to evade the seductive appeal of teleological stories of origin.[55]

---

[54] Cf. the distinction that underpins Ethan H. Shagan, *Popular Politics and the English Reformation* (Cambridge, 2003), quotation at p. 309.

[55] Nietzsche and Foucault described this methodology as 'genealogy' and contrasted it with traditional 'history'. Friedrich Nietzsche, 'On the Genealogy of Morality', in *Beyond Good and Evil/On the Genealogy of Morality*, trans. Adrian del Caro (Stanford, CA, 2014); Michel Foucault, 'Nietzsche, Genealogy, History', in *Language, Counter-Memory, Practice: Selected Essays and Interviews*, ed. Donald F. Bouchard, trans. Donald F. Bouchard and Sherry Simon (Ithaca, NY, 1980 edn), pp. 139–64.

Thirdly, this book argues that the English Reformations and the generations exercised influence on each other in both directions. It demonstrates the ways in which the Reformations transformed the generations: by severing the link between the living and the dead and by reconfiguring relations between children and parents, young and old, kith and kin. Simultaneously it points to their role in creating them: in fostering fertility, procreation, and family formation; in forging senses of collective identity rooted in shared aspirations and experiences of suffering; and in empowering people to believe that they could shape the future. In reverse, it suggests that the generations crafted and fashioned the Reformations: they did so through deliberate and concerted action, but also by recording their experiences in writing and print, by preserving the memory of the ancient and recent past, and by constructing poignant personal archives to pass on to posterity. The mixture of selective remembering and strategic forgetting this entailed has left a decisive mark on the historiography of religion in the early modern period. To study the generations is to delve into its genealogy. It is to investigate how the competing narratives that still colour it came into being.

1

Youth and Age

'[A]ll that were before Christ were in the infancye and childhood of the worlde', declared William Tyndale in the prologue to his translation of the book of Leviticus published in Antwerp in 1530. The ceremonies of the Old Testament, he wrote, were 'unto them as an A.B.C. to lerne to spell and read, and as a nurce to fede them with milke and pappe'. Under the Law, people were like 'babes and children', who saw 'but thorowe a cloude' and lacked the capacity to comprehend the truth fully. It was not 'untyll the full age were come' that God would 'delyver them from their shadowes and cloudelight and the hethen out of their dead slepe of starcke blinde ignorancy'. With the coming of Christ and the advent of the Gospel, religion had reached adulthood and maturity.[1]

At the time Tyndale was writing, the long-standing tendency to map the historical growth of Christianity onto the human life cycle was acquiring a novel inflection. Evangelical Protestants readily appropriated it as an analogy for the Reformation itself. In 1550, William Salesbury, who later translated the New Testament into Welsh, thanked God for his clemency in delivering him from bondage to the 'blynde popyshe heresy':

> as I was thus tangeled, and abhominablye deceyved, and trayned, and brought up in tender age, in the Popes holilyke Religion before Christes second byrthe here in Englande, even so were the Jewes before hys fyrste byrthe in Judea wonderously deceyved, and shamefully seduced and that by the fayned newe Doctryne that their Popes...hadde brought into their churche.[2]

Salesbury thought of his own time as the dawn of a new era and compared his personal liberation from darkness to the nation's deliverance from Roman Catholicism. Just as Judaism had been superseded by Christianity, so had he and his country grown in faith and progressed to a high stage of spiritual development in the heady middle decades of the sixteenth century.

---

[1] 'A Prologe in to the thirde boke of Moses called Leviticus', in [*The Pentateuch*], trans. William Tyndale ([Antwerp, 1530]; STC 2350), sig. A1v–2r. Tyndale alluded to 1 Corinthians 13:11–12. The rendering in the King James Version is 'When I was a child, I spake as a child, I understood as a child, I thought as a child: but when I became a man, I put away childish things. For now we see through a glass, darkly; but then face to face: now I know in part; but then shall I know even as also I am known.'
[2] William Salesbury, *The baterie of the popes botereulx, commonly called the high altare* (1550; STC 21613), sigs F1v–2r.

The statements by Tyndale and Salesbury quoted above reflect the pervasive cultural influence of the Ages of Man in early modern England. Deployed by classical writers such as Pythagoras and Aristotle and by biblical exegetes from Augustine to Isidore of Seville, this was a moral, theological, and didactic trope of considerable conceptual resonance. Comprising between three and twelve stages, it correlated an individual's journey from cradle to grave with the historical progression of the world from Creation to Doomsday. Sometimes conflated with the cycle of the four seasons of the year or with the six architectural orders, it was a powerful paradigm for describing how both the body and soul and the earth and its inhabitants evolved over time.[3] It was also a ubiquitous iconographical theme. From wall paintings and stained-glass windows in churches to tapestries and murals in manor houses, the topos of the Seven Ages of Man migrated into the realm of prints and engravings and remained a favourite pictorial and literary motif (Fig. 1.1). Often visualized as a stepped pedestal or staircase, it presented human life as a process of ascent from infancy to the prime of life and then of downward descent to 'decrepit' old age and death. Reflecting the typological mindset that marked early modernity, it established a compelling parallel between *aetatis mundi* and *aetatis hominis*.[4]

The conventional polarity between Youth and Age into which this scheme was compressed enjoyed similar allegorical utility (Fig. 1.2). These polyvalent terms likewise alluded to phases in the human life cycle, spiritual growth, and history itself simultaneously. 'Age' could refer both to a distinct period of time within an individual's life and to the whole 'race or course' from birth to death.[5] This was a pairing fraught with ambivalence: if youth was synonymous with innocence and receptivity to divine influences, it was also associated with ignorance, idleness, insubordination, and sin. Children both symbolized the hope of new life and

[3] See, e.g., the series of Dutch prints entitled *Theatrum vitae humanae* (Antwerp, 1577), in which old age corresponds with 'ruina'. For devotional and didactic deployments, see Nathaniel Crouch, *The vanity of the life of man* (1688; Wing C7355); John Bunyan, *Meditations on the several ages of mans life: representing the vanity of it, from the cradle to his grave* (1700).

[4] See Samuel C. Chew, *The Pilgrimage of Life* (New Haven, CT, 1962), pp. 144–74; J. A. Burrow, *The Ages of Man: A Study in Medieval Writing and Thought* (Oxford, 1986); Elizabeth Sears, *The Ages of Man: Medieval Interpretations of the Life Cycle* (Princeton, NJ, 1986); Mary Dove, *The Perfect Age of Man's Life* (Cambridge, 1986); Michael E. Goodich, *From Birth to Old Age: The Human Life Cycle in Medieval Thought, 1250–1350* (Lanham, MD, 1989). On the life cycle, see also Deborah Youngs, *The Life Cycle in Western Europe, c.1300–c.1500* (Manchester, 2006); Philippa Maddern and Stephanie Tarbin, 'Life Cycle', in Sandra Cavallo and Silvia Evangelisti (eds), *A Cultural History of Childhood and Family in the Early Modern Age* (Oxford, 2010), pp. 113–33. For some prints and illustrations of the ages of man, see [*The Ages of Man*] (Thomas Jenner, c.1630); Johannes Comenius, *Orbis sensualium pictus*, trans. Charles Hoole (1672; Wing C5584), pp. 76–7; *The life of man demonstrated in their several ages* (John Overton, late 17th century); *As in a map here man may well perceive, how tyme creeps on til death his life bereave* (late 17th century); Malcolm Jones, *The Print in Early Modern England: An Historical Oversight* (New Haven, CT, 2010), pp. 27–34. The literary *locus classicus* is William Shakespeare, *As You Like It*, II.vii.

[5] OED, s.vv. 'youth' and 'age'. Levinus Lemnius, *The touchstone of complexions generallye appliable, expedient and profitable for all such, as be desirous & carefull of their bodylye health*, trans. Thomas Newton (1576; STC 15456), fos. 29r–v.

Fig. 1.1 *The ages of man* (London, c.1630).

carried the taint of inherited depravity. Age had an equally double-edged quality. On the one hand, it was proverbially linked with gravity and wisdom; on the other, with stubbornness and senility. Esteem for the elderly as bearers of tradition and emblems of authority coexisted with irreverence and disrespect. Youth and age were opposites, but they were also analogues: the aged returned full circle to a second childhood. In juxtaposition they served as a 'myrrour meete for all mankynde' of the transience and vanity of life, the frailty of the flesh, and the

Fig. 1.2 *An allegory of youth and old age* (oil, English school, late 16th century).
Source: ART Collection/Alamy Stock Photo.

inevitability that all would eventually perish. In short, they functioned as a memento mori. Contemporary perceptions of the young and the old were filtered through the sieve of these contradictory but durable stereotypes, which in turn shaped lived experience.[6]

---

[6] On childhood and youth, see Steven R. Smith, 'Religion and the Conception of Youth in Seventeenth-Century England', *History of Childhood Quarterly*, 2 (1975), 493–516; Keith Thomas, 'Children in Early Modern England', in Gillian Avery and Julia Briggs (eds), *Children and their Books: A Celebration of the World of Iona and Peter Opie* (Oxford, 1989), pp. 45–77; Shulamith Shahar, *Childhood in the Middle Ages* (New York, 1990); Paul Griffiths, *Youth and Authority: Formative Experiences in England 1560–1640* (Oxford, 1996); Ilana Krausman Ben-Amos, *Adolescence and Youth in Early Modern England* (New Haven, CT, 1994); P. J. Goldberg and Felicity Riddy (eds), *Youth in the Middle Ages* (York, 2004); Anna French (ed.), *Early Modern Childhood: An Introduction* (Abingdon, 2020). On old age, see Hallett Smith, 'Bare Ruined Choirs: Shakespearean Variations on the Theme of Old

Refracted through the dominant theories of Galenic and Hippocratic medicine, ageing was understood as a physiological process of sensory impairment
and bodily decay. Natural philosophers and doctors identified the shifts in complexion, humour, moisture, and temperature that accompanied its stages. Often
these were elaborated in relation to the zodiac and astrological calendar.[7] This
was a society, moreover, in which there were settled conventions about when
childhood ended (typically 14) and when old age began (usually 60), but it was
also one in which the boundaries between these categories were porous and slippery, as well as further complicated by gender and social rank.[8] The interfaces
between the intermediary stages of adolescence and adulthood were no less difficult to discern and dependent upon marital, economic, and legal status. Although
an impulse to measure age numerically was growing, chronological precision was
in many ways less significant than function. Far from a transparent, universal
fact, age was a culturally negotiated category.[9] It was a sliding scale calibrated in
accordance with physical vitality, sexual knowledge, academic learning, vocational qualification, financial independence, and civic and political responsibility.
Ecclesiastical rites of passage such as baptism, confirmation, and marriage served
as additional markers of life stage. These were overlaid by subjective assessments
of grades of spiritual attainment. Religious maturity was not regarded as the
exclusive preserve of the elderly: the Bible provided ample evidence that iniquity
was often ingrained in those advanced in years, while the exemplary piety of tender babes sometimes put to shame those who stood above them in the age hierarchy. Part of a common Christian heritage, these cultural constructions were the
prism through which people perceived demographic realities.

Age', HLQ, 39 (1976), 233–49; Georges Minois, History of Old Age: From Antiquity to the Renaissance,
trans. Sarah Hanbury Tension (Chicago, 1989); J. T. Rosenthal, Old Age in Late Medieval England
(Philadelphia, PA, 1996); Shulamith Shahar, Growing Old in the Middle Ages, trans. Yael Lotan (1997);
Paul Johnson and Pat Thane (eds), Old Age from Antiquity to Post-Modernity (1998); Erin J. Campbell,
Growing Old in Early Modern Europe: Cultural Representations (Aldershot, 2006); Nina Taunton,
Fictions of Old Age in Early Modern Literature and Culture (New York, 2007); Albrecht Classen (ed.),
Old Age in the Middle Ages and the Renaissance: Interdisciplinary Approaches to a Neglected Topic
(Berlin, 2007); Keith Thomas, 'Age and Authority in Early Modern England', Proceedings of the British
Academy, 62 (1976), 205–48; Steven R. Smith, 'Growing Old in Early Stuart England', Albion, 8 (1976),
125–41; Pat Thane, Old Age in English History: Past Experiences, Present Issues (Oxford, 2000), chs.
2–4; Susannah R. Ottaway, L. A. Botelho, and Katharine Kittredge (eds), Power and Poverty: Old Age
in the Pre-industrial Past (Westport, CT, 2002); Pat Thane (ed.), The Long History of Old Age (2005),
chs. 3–4; Susannah R. Ottaway, The Decline of Life: Old Age in Eighteenth-Century England
(Cambridge, 2004).

[7] See Lemnius, Touchstone; Henry Cuffe, The differences of the ages of mans life: together with the
original causes, progresse, and end thereof (1607; STC 6103).

[8] For some of these complications, see Alexandra Shepard, Meanings of Manhood in Early Modern
England (Oxford, 2003), esp. chs 1–2; Lynn A. Botelho, Old Age and the English Poor Law, 1500–1700
(Woodbridge, 2004); Alexandra Shepard, Accounting for Oneself: Worth, Status, and the Social Order
in Early Modern England (Oxford, 2015).

[9] Thane, Old Age, p. 5. See also Corinne T. Field and Nicholas L. Syrett, 'Chronological Age: A
Useful Category of Historical Analysis' and Pat Thane, 'Old Age in European Cultures: A Significant
Presence from Antiquity to the Present', both in AHR, 125 (2020), 371–84 and 385–95, respectively.

YOUTH AND AGE   27

Early modern England had an age profile very different from our own: just 8% of the population was over 69, while some 40–50% of the population was under 21. These statistics, however, obscure the very high rates of infant and child mortality in this society. One in three or four children died before the age of 15 and many of these did not live beyond their first birthday. If individuals survived into adulthood, they had a reasonable chance of living to a ripe old age, although significant numbers of women expired during childbirth. Life expectancy was around 60, so people appeared older at a younger age than they do now.[10]

Skewed towards youth, this was, at the same time, a gerontocratic society, in which patriarchal deference to elders was both prescribed and expected. Monarchs, parents, masters, and ministers were figures to whom their subjects, children, servants, and parishioners owed the same respect due to the Almighty himself. Long portrayed as the white-haired and bearded ancient of days, God the Father's status as an emblem of eternity was accentuated rather than attenuated by the English Reformations. The reformers may have repudiated anthropomorphic depictions of the deity in favour of the abstract symbol of the Hebrew tetragrammaton, but such images evidently lingered on in the imagination for many generations.[11]

This chapter investigates how the categories and concepts of youth and age were implicated in England's long Reformation and traces shifting perceptions of intergenerational relations as the movement progressed from infancy to maturity. It asks whether, and in what ways, age mattered in the context of Reformation and how, in turn, the Reformations themselves might be said to have aged. It explores the role that people at different life stages were thought to have played in advancing and resisting its tumultuous first phases and in its implementation and institutionalization as the orthodox faith. It also probes some of the paradoxes of a religious experiment that at once craved the imprimatur of age and encouraged its adherents to experience a new or second birth. It suggests that these rhetorics tell us as much, if not more, about contemporary preoccupations and modes of subjectivity as they do about the social and emotional dynamics of religious change. They illuminate how people from all points on the religious spectrum comprehended the unsettling developments that were occurring around them. In particular, many believed that the successive stages of England's contested Reformation had been accompanied by discord and strife between the old and the young.

[10] See E. A. Wrigley and R. S. Schofield, *The Population History of England 1541–1871* (Cambridge, 1989 edn), p. 528, and see pp. 215–19, 443–50; Roger Schofield and E. A. Wrigley, 'Infant and Child Mortality in England in the Late Tudor and Early Stuart Period', in Charles Webster (ed.), *Health, Medicine and Mortality in the Sixteenth Century* (Cambridge, 1979), pp. 61–95.
[11] Thomas Rogers reproved such depictions in *The English creede consenting with the true, auncient, catholique, and apostolique Church in al points, and articles of religion* (1587; STC 21227), p. 18.

This chapter is less interested in assessing the truth of this claim than in examining why events were framed in these conflictual terms and in asking what this might mean.[12] It proceeds from the assumption that formative experiences and social behaviours both condition and are conditioned by the scripts and repertoires available in any given culture. It focuses attention on the evolving relationship between ideas of human development and spiritual progress and traces how the religious impulses it investigates reconciled the tensions between charisma and discipline. In sum, this chapter approaches age, like generation, as both a biological phenomenon and a social construct.

Youth and Age

As Susan Brigden demonstrated in a seminal essay, during the earliest phases of the Reformation, its enemies and critics castigated it as a disorderly outbreak of youthful enthusiasm. They blamed it on 'lewd laddys' and 'beardless boys' who were captivated by evangelical ideas and who used them as an excuse to cock a snook at their elders.[13] In the 1520s, Thomas More was incensed by young scholars like John Frith who presumed to dispute with more experienced doctors of theology, advancing their arguments 'so sagely' as if these senior scholars were 'but very babys'.[14] The lay Catholic polemicist Miles Huggarde similarly berated the insolence of 'yonglinges', whose 'merye conceipts' and 'novelties' had infected the populace with poison, corrupted their consciences, and turned them against the Church of Rome.[15] 'Young' and 'old', 'man' and 'boy', were 'key terms in a vocabulary of insult'. As Paul Griffiths has commented, 'they helped to cast aspersions and trim reputations in a society in which age was one principle of order'.[16]

It became a commonplace to suggest that the natural appetite of youths for liberty drew them to Lutheranism. Writing in 1546, the Dominican prior William Peryn feared that heresy had 'crepte secretly in to the hartes of many of the yonger and carnall sorte' via the 'evell & pestiferous bokes' flooding in from Continental Europe. His own preaching and publishing were designed to combat 'the encresse of that mischeuous lady (amonge the unstable & vulgare people)'.[17] In a sermon preached at Paul's Cross in 1546, John Feckenham inveighed against the 'bringing up of the youth of England in heresies', exclaiming to the 'venerable senators and

[12] I draw inspiration here from Ilena Isayev, 'Unruly Youth? The Myth of Generational Conflict in Late Republican Rome', *Historia*, 56 (2007), 1–13.

[13] Susan Brigden, 'Youth and the English Reformation', *P&P*, 95 (1982), 37–67.

[14] Thomas More, *The co[n]futacyon of Tyndales answere made by syr Thomas More knyght lorde chau[n]cellour of Englonde* (1532; STC 18079), sig. Ee1v.

[15] Miles Huggarde, *The displaying of the protestantes* (1555; STC 13558), fo. 7r.

[16] Griffiths, *Youth and Authority*, pp. 101–2.

[17] William Peryn, *Thre godlye and notable sermons, of the sacrament of the aulter* (1546; STC 19785.5), sig. *2v.

ancient fathers' present: 'What a world shall it be when they shall have the rule, for if they have the swing it will be treason shortly to worship God' himself. Protestantism, in his view, provided a licence for dissolute living and a mandate for rebellion.[18] According to the Marian dean of Norwich, John Christopherson, too many adolescents made a 'mery mockery of their parents', railing against their fathers as 'old doting foole[s]' who fasted on Fridays and disdaining their mothers for 'mumbling' over their rosary beads. They condemned their 'superstitious folye' and vowed never to walk in 'the papisticall pathes' of their progenitors.[19] Huggarde painted an equally evocative picture of the young people of the capital who refused to attend church on holy days and flocked in clusters, 'either skorninge the passers by or, with their testaments utter[ing] some wyse stuffe of theyr owne devise'.[20] Such enormities were seen as a direct consequence of promiscuous bible-reading and rabble-rousing preaching. Infiltrating schools and universities and perverting servants and apprentices, heresy threatened to turn the world upside down and to foment anarchy.

The fruits that came of this 'newe fanglet' doctrine included the dissolution of household discipline: children were disobedient to their parents, and servants could no longer be trusted by their masters and mistresses. The only solution to this pernicious state of affairs, declared one early Elizabethan Catholic, was to 'retourne backe againe to the steppes of good fathers afore us'.[21] In a sermon preached to the citizens of London on St Andrew's Day 1557, Cardinal Reginald Pole had offered a similar diagnosis and proposed a comparable cure. The roots of disobedience to the true Church lay in the disorderly behaviour of the young, and it was incumbent upon their elders to restrain them: 'Do you thinke the youthe ys to be borne withal yn suche matters of religion, when they do so muche contrarye to the example of theyr fathers touching religion?' If they failed to set a proper example, 'there ys small hope of remedye'.[22]

In presenting Protestantism as a revolutionary movement with alluring appeal to young people, conservative clerics and commentators anticipated an idea that has firmly entrenched itself in modern sociology and psychology. The hypothesis that the young have a particular propensity to reject the status quo and rebel against the established conventions upheld by their elders was much debated in the scholarship on generational conflict fostered by the student uprisings in Europe and America in 1968. Correspondingly, it has often been assumed that

[18] *Letters and Papers, Foreign and Domestic, of Henry VIII*, xxi (2) *September 1546–January 1547*, ed. James Gairdner and R. H. Brodie (1910), no. 710, pp. 370–1.

[19] John Christopherson, *An exhortation to all menne to take hede and beware of rebellion* (1554; STC 5207), sig. C2r–v.

[20] Huggarde, *Displaying*, fos 85v–87v.

[21] James Pilkington, *The burnynge of Paules church in London in the yeare of oure Lord 1561* (1563; STC 19931), sigs A5v–6r.

[22] John Strype, *Ecclesiastical Memorials Relating Chiefly to Religion*, vol. iii, part 2 (Oxford, 1822), pp. 497–8.

the old are instinctively resistant to change.[23] The resulting model of friction and confrontation finds one of its taproots in the early modern period. It is indebted not merely to the medieval literature of the ages of man but also to the popular convention in Renaissance poetics that pitted the old against the young in generational debate and battle.[24] Contemporaries viewed the turbulence of their own era through the same lens.

Children and adolescents were certainly perceived to be prominent in incidents of carnivalesque inversion directed at the Catholic Church and its clergy during Protestantism's initial phase as an illicit protest movement. In London and other locations, they were said to have hurled nasty words and made rude gestures towards priests, dressed dead cats up in Mass vestments, and cast their caps contemptuously against the holy sacrament of the Eucharist. They composed satirical ballads and jests, disrupted sermons, and engaged in other high-spirited juvenile pranks that undermined the dignity of bishops and monks, including throwing a pudding at Edmund Bonner.[25] Their words and actions gave expression to an undercurrent of anticlericalism that alarmed the ecclesiastical hierarchy. The festive rituals by which they ridiculed the clergy and liturgy were reminiscent of seasonal pastimes such as Christmas and May games. Building on a tradition of sanctioned youthful misrule, they also found precedents in the traditional moral economy that permitted apprentices to sack brothels on Shrove Tuesday and the informal punishment of adulterers by forms of rough music.[26] Spurred to action by evangelical preaching denouncing the material culture of Catholic idolatry, young people appear to have eagerly participated in illicit image-breaking, revelling in the opportunity to destroy religious objects that were also symbols of authority. They thought of themselves as warriors and dragonslayers. Smashing statues and decapitating standing crosses in the name of godly reformation was fun: sport and solemnity were not enemies but twins.[27]

[23] This paradigm has more often been applied to the modern era than earlier periods. See, e.g., Philip Abrams, 'Rites de Passage: The Conflict of Generations in Industrial Society', *Journal of Contemporary History*, 5 (1970), 175–90; L. M. Singhvi (ed.), *Youth Unrest: Conflict of Generations* (New Delhi, 1972); Lewis S. Feuer, *The Conflict of Generations: The Character and Significance of Student Movements* (New York, 1979); Anthony Esler, *Bombs, Beards and Barricades: 150 Years of Youth in Revolt* (New York, 1971); idem (ed.), *The Youth Revolution: The Conflict of Generations in Modern Society* (Lexington, MA, 1974); Alan B. Spitzer, 'The Historical Problem of Generations', *AHR*, 78 (1973), 1353–85; idem, *The French Generation of 1820* (Princeton, NJ, 1987). A significant earlier contribution is Louis Mazoyer, 'Catégories d'âge et groupes sociaux: Les Jeunes Générations françaises de 1830', *Annales*, 10 (1938), 385–423. Freud himself wrote that 'the progress of society in general rests upon the opposition between the generations': 'Family Romances', in *The Penguin Freud Reader*, ed. Adam Phillips (2006), p. 422.

[24] See Steven Marx, *Youth against Age: Generational Strife in Renaissance Poetry* (New York, 1985).

[25] Brigden, 'Youth and the English Reformation'.

[26] Natalie Zemon Davis, 'The Reasons of Misrule', in her *Society and Culture in Early Modern France* (Stanford, CA, 1975), pp. 97–123; S. R. Smith, 'The London Apprentices as Seventeenth-Century Adolescents', *P&P*, 61 (1973), 149–61; Martin Ingram, 'Ridings, Rough Music, and the "Reform of Popular Culture" in Early Modern England', *P&P*, 105 (1984), 79–113.

[27] See Margaret Aston, 'Iconoclasm in England: Official and Clandestine', in Clifford Davidson and Ann Eljenholm Nichols (eds), *Iconoclasm vs. Art and Drama* (Kalamazoo, MI, 1989), pp. 47–91.

The hostile observers through whose eyes we see these episodes instinctively interpreted them as evidence of youthful insubordination and intergenerational tension. Sometimes, however, such incidents were condoned or stage-managed by adults. When the famous moving Rood of Boxley was exposed as an ingenious fraud by Hugh Latimer in 1538, the mechanical crucifix was thrown down to the boys in the crowd to break into pieces.[28] At the time of the dissolution of the monasteries, redundant images were deliberately given to children to play with. Preaching in Bristol later that decade, the conservative cleric Roger Edgeworth painted an evocative picture of how such popish 'trumperies' were turned into toys and made the subject of 'childish' games that instructed the young in the tenets of the new faith. 'What haste thou there?,' the father asks his daughter; 'I have here myne ydoll,' she replies, before both fall into fits of corrosive laughter.[29] This studied process of desacralization continued into Edward's reign, when parents and parish officials in Lincolnshire handed over confiscated pyxes and other liturgical equipment to their toddlers and infants.[30] Sacred things were, thereby, literally reduced to playthings. Such strategies for disenchantment replicated the vocabulary deployed to discredit holy objects and miracle tales: polemicists regularly denounced them as vain trifles and foolish baubles.[31] As Joe Moshenska has shown, the ambiguity of these actions allowed children's play to assume a disturbing and powerful life of its own, beyond the control of their elders. They not only educated the child about the triviality of these items; they also encapsulated 'in miniature the decisive historical transformation under way in the Reformation, in which centuries of childish error will be swept away and replaced with newly pristine truth'.[32]

Orchestrated acts of adolescent rebellion could spill over into spontaneous misbehaviour. The irreverent tippling, piping, dancing, hopping, and singing in which local adolescents engaged in the disused chapel of St Anne's holy well at Buxton in Derbyshire during Edward's reign was said to have been 'suffered' by an evangelical layman called Roger Cottrell to undermine the reputed sanctity of this traditional site of Catholic pilgrimage. But the 'affray' that they subsequently made against 'honest, sage, and discrete persons' who demanded that they 'desist from their foolish youthful fashions' forthwith and 'hear God's service' caused

---

[28] Charles Wriothesley, *A Chronicle of England during the Reigns of the Tudors, from* AD *1485 to 1559*, 2 vols., ed. William Douglas Hamilton, CS (1877), i. 74–6.

[29] Roger Edgeworth, *Sermons very Fruitfull, Godly and Learned*, ed. Janet Wilson (Cambridge, 1993), p. 143.

[30] *English Church Furniture, Ornaments and Decorations, at the Period of the Reformation: as Exhibited in a List of the Goods Destroyed in Certain Lincolnshire Churches*, AD *1566*, ed. Edward Peacock (1866), 55, 108.

[31] See, e.g., William Turner, *A new dialogue wherin is contyened the examination of the messe of that kynde of priesthood, whych is ordained to saye messe* ([1548]; STC 24363), sig. B8r; Henri Estienne, *The stage of popish toyes: conteining both tragicall and comicall partes* (1581; STC 10552).

[32] Joe Moshenska, *Iconoclasm as Child's Play* (Stanford, CA, 2019), at pp. 128–9.

consternation and led to a legal case in the Court of Chancery in Mary's reign.[33] Harnessing youthful high spirits carried risks. Light-hearted jesting and horse-play could all too easily exceed acceptable bounds. It is unclear how far the mock battles between two factions of schoolboys at Bodmin in 1548—'the one whereof, they called the olde religion; the other the new'—were directed and sanctioned by their teachers. These too ended in violence, when a calf was shot by a candlestick which one of them had converted into a makeshift gun. Thereafter, these contests were sharply repressed.[34] Children's games absorbed and mimicked the religious conflicts and passions of the surrounding adult world.

The instabilities that such episodes engendered sometimes tested the limits of official tolerance in a febrile political environment. The 18-year-old maiden Elizabeth Croft who pretended to be a white 'byrde that spake in the wall' in Aldersgate Street in London in 1554 and uttered seditious words against the king and queen, as well as the sacraments of the Mass and confession, was made to confess publicly that she had been coached in her role as the Holy Spirit by 'divers lewd' and 'mischevous persons' who had given her a whistle. The promotion and preaching of heresy by young girls was especially offensive to the authorities, because it subverted the age and gender hierarchies simultaneously. Youthful masculine unruliness might be excused as a stage on the path to adulthood, but it could not be condoned in pubescent women. Presenting the pronouncements of this 'poore wenche' as the product of her seduction by evil heretics and making her openly renounce their 'noughty opinions' at Paul's Cross was regarded as the best mechanism for restoring civil and ecclesiastical order.[35]

For their part, Protestants were willing to countenance temporary reversals of the social structure because they believed they were living through extraordinary times. Scripture taught that 'out of the mouths of babes and sucklings' the Lord proclaimed truth.[36] It predisposed them to think that, in moments of crisis, God employed children and youths as the instruments of his will to instruct their parents and to facilitate the conversion of older people. Usurping the place of mothers, fathers, ministers, and masters was not presumption but piety: it was one of the emergency measures to which the Lord resorted when normal ones failed.[37] It also reflected the conviction that those of tender years were themselves

<hr />

[33] TNA, C 1/1322, fo. 57r. See also Ethan H. Shagan, *Popular Politics and the English Reformation* (Cambridge, 2003), p. 267.

[34] Richard Carew, *The survey of Cornwall* (1602; STC 4615), fos 124v–125r. See A. G. Dickens, 'The Battle of Finsbury Field and Its Wider Context', in James Kirk (ed.), *Humanism and Reform: The Church in Europe, England, and Scotland, 1400–1643* (Oxford, 1991), pp. 271–87.

[35] Wriothesley, *Chronicle*, ed. Hamilton, ii. 117–18; Huggarde, *Displaying*, fos 119v–120r; John Stow, *The chronicles of England from Brute unto this present yeare of Christ. 1580* (1580, STC 23333), p. 1092.

[36] Psalms 8:2.

[37] On child prophets, see Anna French, *Children of Wrath: Possession, Prophecy and the Young in Early Modern England* (Farnham, 2015), ch. 5.

a constituent part of the priesthood of all believers. As the German reformer Johannes Oecolampadius said in a sermon addressed to 'yong men, and maydens' and translated into English in 1548, 'Children be as much consecrated to god, as though they were anointed preestes, or shaven into any order of relygyon.'[38] Their theological knowledge could be upheld as a humiliating example to their elders. In the diocese of Gloucester, an Edwardian curate praised a little girl for reciting the catechism and shamed an adult man by challenging him to declare the Ten Commandments, Lord's Prayer, and the Articles of the Faith as accurately as she could.[39]

Such stories reinvigorated the medieval hagiographical theme of the *puer senex*, the old child who transcends his stage in the biological life cycle and displays prescient wisdom.[40] In mid-Tudor England, this contributed to the creation of a potent myth about Edward VI, whose identity as a latter-day Josiah, the youthful Hebrew king famous for destroying idols, was already present in embryo during his lifetime. Writing in 1548, John Champneys prayed for his preservation, so that, 'lyke as the godly kyng Josias being yong of age in the begynynge of his time' had destroyed the priests and prophets of Baal, extinguished false gods, and restored the true worship of God, so might he too work to reinstate 'the true lebertle of ye gosple of christe' within his dominions and realms.[41] In retrospect, after Edward's premature death, these exhortations to imitate the godly Old Testament ruler settled into a pious legend about the actual achievements of the boy king. Hopes and dreams congealed into facts of history. Indeed, his early demise cemented his reputation for precocious zeal. This found expression in John Foxe's *Actes and monuments*, which praised him as 'a prince although but tender in yeres, yet for his sage and mature rypenes in witte' the equal of many of greater longevity.[42]

Feeding the impression that the Tudor Reformation had been led by brave young people, Foxe likewise shone a spotlight on the Protestant martyrs in their late teens and early twenties who bravely faced the fires at Smithfield and other sites of execution, ready to die in defence of the Gospel.[43] John Frith was described, even by his opponents, as 'young in yeares, olde in knowledge'.[44] Reprimanded as a 'naughty boye' by the official whom he upstaged by displaying

---

[38] Joannes Oecolampadius, *A sarmon…to yong men, and maydens*, trans. John Foxe (1548, STC 18787), sig. B4r–v.
[39] F. D. Price, 'Gloucester Diocese under Bishop Hooper 1551–3', *Transactions of the Bristol and Gloucestershire Archaeological Society*, 60 (1938), 51–151, at 145.
[40] Shulamith Shahar, *Childhood in the Middle Ages* (1990), pp. 15–16.
[41] John Champneys, *The harvest is at hand, wherin the tares shall be bound, and cast into the fyre and brent* ([1548]; STC 4956), sig. A7r–v.
[42] John Foxe, *Actes and monuments* (1583; STC 11225), p. 1294.
[43] See also Sarah Covington, '"Spared not from Tribulation": Children in Early Modern Martyrologies', *Archiv für Reformationsgeschichte*, 97 (2006), 165–82.
[44] Foxe, *Actes and monuments* (1583 edn), p. 2126.

a profound understanding of Scripture, the 19-year-old apprentice William Hunter faced his death courageously, refusing the promise of pardon if he recanted, taking up a faggot and embracing it in his arms as the flames consumed him. Hunter's parents urged him to stand fast and 'to continue to the ende in that good way which God had begon'. They were proud 'to beare such a childe, which could finde in his heart to loose his life for Christes names sake'. But in other cases the victims defied their mothers and fathers as well as magistrates and priests.[45] Convinced he had been 'borne & brought up in ignoraunce vntill nowe of late yeares', Thomas Tomkins boldly declared that his 'parents, kinsfolkes, frendes, and acquaintaunce', as well has his godparents, 'did erre, and were deceiued' in believing in the real presence in the Eucharist. For this impertinence, he was committed to Newgate and went to the stake, sealing his faith in the fire in con-firmation of weaker Christians.[46] Protestant narratives fitted these heroic and articulate youths into well-established typologies of holy sacrifice, but they also strove to distance them from the child saints canonized by the Catholic Church. John Bale juxtaposed Anne Askew and her 'constant brethren' with the alleged victims of Jewish ritual murder, including Hugh of Lincoln and William of Norwich, declaring that their martyrdoms were 'but babyish in comparison with these, the verity having by them no small furtherance'.[47]

Foxe's martyrs were celebrated and commended not merely for their refusal to bow to the wishes of their parents and masters, but also for their temerity in reproving their backwardness in religion. In a document that Foxe accidentally omitted from his voluminous book, William Maldon recalled how he had been whipped by his father with a great rod for reading and quoting Scripture and for denouncing reverence to the crucifix as 'plain idolatry'. William's insolence in tell-ing his father that he needed no other 'scholmaster but God' drove his parent into a furious rage. The fact that his son bore his punishment without shedding a tear only riled him further. Fetching a halter, he had placed it round his neck and threatened to strangle him. William wept for the 'griefe of the lake of knowledge' in him.[48] Looking back on their childhood and adolescence from middle and old age, people remembered their early lives in alignment with the empowering sto-ries of suffering that became integral to Protestant identity in later generations. The common thread in these accounts is the child's lament for the spiritual benightedness of his progenitors.

The Bible persuaded children that they had a moral and filial duty to assume the role of tutor to their unenlightened elders. In the early 1530s, the law student Robert Plumpton felt compelled to instruct his 'moste deare mother' and to warn

---

[45] Ibid., pp. 1535–8.   [46] Ibid., p. 1535.
[47] *Select Works of John Bale, D.D., Bishop of Ossory*, ed. Henry Christmas, PS (Cambridge, 1849), p. 192.
[48] John Gough Nichols (ed.), *Narratives of the Days of the Reformation, Chiefly from the Manuscripts of John Foxe the Martyrologist*, CS, ser. 1, vol. 77 (1859), pp. 348–51.

her that unlesse she took 'heede to the teaching of the Gospell', she would never enjoy 'favour with God'. Sending her a copy of Tyndale's New Testament, he urged her to read it and see the 'marvelous things hyd in it'.[49] This kind of role reversal was evidently not uncommon in the mid-Tudor period. Conservatives like John Christopherson commented disapprovingly on the many boys who were sent away to school and exposed to the influence of 'some lewd Lutherane' who presumed to send epistles to their parents exhorting them to 'leave their papistry and blind ignoraunce'.[50] The young felt impelled to impart the truth to their blood relatives, even when this contravened the accepted structures of honour and deference and fractured relationships.

Writing in the mid-Elizabethan period, the Lincolnshire clergyman Francis Trigge insisted that although the world now marvelled at the familial dissensions that had accompanied the early Reformation, they had been foretold in the New Testament. In Luke 12:52–3 Christ had warned his disciples that he did not come to bring peace to the earth, but rather division:

> For from henceforth there shall be five in one house divided, three against two, and two against three. The father shall be divided against the son, and the son against the father; the mother against the daughter, and the daughter against the mother; the mother in law against her daughter in law, and the daughter in law against her mother in law.[51]

Intergenerational conflict was not an indictment of the Gospel, but rather a hallmark of its authenticity and truth, duly prophesied in Scripture. It was an eschatological sign that God was at work in the world.

The edifying memoirs of Protestant divines who had forsaken their friends and relatives to follow Christ collected by Samuel Clarke in the mid-seventeenth century exemplified these assumptions. Laurence Chaderton, first master of Emmanuel College, Cambridge, preferred 'an heavenly before an earthly Inheritance' as the price of adhering to the true religion. Converted by his Saffron Walden schoolmaster and shaped by his experiences at Christ's College in the mid-1570s, Arthur Hildersham refused to go to Rome to train for the Catholic priesthood and was 'cast off' by his father.[52] Late sixteenth- and seventeenth-century Protestants readily acknowledged that the onset of the Reformation in the reigns of Henry VIII and Edward VI had been accompanied by hurly-burlies

---

[49] *Plumpton Correspondence: A Series of Letters, Chiefly Domestick, Written in the Reigns of Edward IV, Richard III, Henry VII, and Henry VIII*, ed. Thomas Stapleton, CS, 5th ser., 8 (1896), pp. 233–4.

[50] Christopherson, *Exhortation*, sig. C2r.

[51] Francis Trigge, *An apologie or defence of our dayes, against the vaine murmurings & complaints of manie* (1589; STC 24276), pp. 15–16.

[52] Samuel Clarke, *A general martyrologie...whereunto is added the lives of thirty two English divines* (1677; Wing C4515), pp. 145 and 114–15, respectively.

Fig. 1.3 Hugh Latimer (*c.*1485–1555), chaplain to Anne Boleyn, bishop of Worcester (1535–9), and Protestant martyr (oil, English school, 16th century).

Source: Reproduced by kind permission of the Master and Fellows of Clare College, University of Cambridge.

within families and between the generations. They remembered their own lives and those of their parents in accordance with biblical passages that provided a blueprint for Christian behaviour.

These images of exemplary evangelical youth found their counterparts at the other end of the age spectrum in the guise of elderly confessors, the vigour of whose faith belied the infirmities attendant upon their advanced years. Commemorative portraits depicted Hugh Latimer with a pair of spectacles hanging from his neck to aid his failing eyesight (Fig. 1.3). But according to the account of his death incorporated in Foxe's *Actes and monuments* he had been physically rejuvenated in the midst of his martyrdom. He went to the stake 'a withered or crooked sely old man' dressed in a threadbare gown in 1555, but the prospect of bearing witness to the Protestant faith made him stand 'bolt upright, as comely a father as one might lightly behold'.[53] Rawlins White, burnt at Cardiff, was likewise transformed at the prospect of meeting his Maker: 'where as before he was wont

---

[53] Foxe, *Actes and monuments* (1570 edn), p. 1937.

to go stowping, or rather crooked, through the infirmitie of age, having a sad countenaunce and a very feeble complexion', he too assumed the stature and demeanour of a man in his prime, while his white hair and beard afforded 'a shew and countenance to his whole person that he seemed to be altogether angelicall'.[54]

The perception that these martyrs regained their youthfulness as they faced death was the obverse of the idea that children were closest to God. This too attests to the resilience of ancient rhetorical tropes associated with youth and old age. The capaciousness of the latter category in early modern England is highlighted by the case of the Suffolk weaver John Dale, who was set in the stocks in a cage for the 'words he spake in ferventnes of spirit against the superstitious religion of Rome'. After disparaging a Catholic priest and his curate as 'miserable & blind guides' and members of an 'indurate hard harted, peruerse, & crooked generation', he was thrown into a dungeon, where he later died aged 46. He and his 70-year-old fellow prisoner, Richard Yeoman, were both described as 'old men'.[55]

Protestantism clearly won support from people from all stages of the life cycle. By the late sixteenth century, however, the dominant view was that the elderly had, on the whole, resisted the Reformation. Stubborn persistence in popery had become synonymous with the habitual conservatism of those in their dotage. It was widely supposed that those advanced in years regretted the demise of the medieval Church and persisted in following the 'old beaten ways' of their predecessors.[56] Their misguided yearning for the past irked many ministers. In a dialogue between 'Civis' and 'Puer' (City and Child) devised by John FitJohn in 1577, the latter is made to state 'I have harde my Father and mother say, I would the olde learning were up agayne.'[57] Writing in 1617, John Favour complained:

Are not these words...in the mouthes of all the old superstitious people of this land?...When we prayed to our Lady, and offred tapers on Candlemasse day...then we had plentie of all things, and were well, we felt no evill. But since we have left the religion of our fathers...we have scarsnesse of all things.

He feared that the young imbibed these mistakes from their elders. The local people of Christchurch in Hampshire even attributed the decline of salmon in their river to the cessation of the Mass, saying that they were 'wont to come up when they heard the sacring Bell ring'. 'The pretence is still, that the former way was the *Old way*, and that *Old way* was the best way.'[58] Early modern preachers thus anticipated the sociological insight that nostalgia is an inherently generational concept in which age hankers after the time of its youth. Thriving on the

---

[54] Ibid., pp. 1728–9.   [55] Foxe, *Actes and monuments* (1583 edn), pp. 2045–6.

[56] See Trigge, *Apologie*, pp. 14 and 16.

[57] John FitJohn, *A diamonde most precious, worthy to be marked instructing all maysters and servauntes* (1577; STC 10929), sig. C1v.

[58] John Favour, *Antiquitie triumphing over noveltie* (1619; STC 10716), p. 8.

subjective apprehension of temporal transition, it finds in the life cycle 'fertile terrain for its flowering'.[59]

The idea that the elderly were unreceptive to cultural change was also a perennial theme of ballad literature. *Times alteration: or the old mans rehearsall, what brave dayes he knew* (1629) makes no reference to the ecclesiastical upheavals of the era, but it too sums up this piece of proverbial wisdom. Its narrator grumbles that the good hospitality, friendship, and plenty that prevailed in 'times of yore' have decayed and been replaced by bribery, extortion, corruption, and greed.[60] Such complaints frequently fused with longing for the pre-Reformation world. 'Traditions' and 'old wives' tales' became a shorthand and byword for continuing adherence to Catholic error and for the dross of 'superstitious' rubbish that had suffocated the truth. Old nursemaids and dames were constantly blamed for passing on idle fables and foolish tales to the children under their care. This was a rhetoric to which Protestantism added a confessional edge. Edwin Sandys was among those who complained of the 'dotages of silly women', and stories of miracles and relics were regularly equated with the legends of Robin Hood and dismissed as evidence of popish imposture and credulity.[61] Stubborn persistence in old fashioned rituals was a further element of this evolving stereotype. Thomas Wilson evoked the image of an 'old grandamme' in the 'dotynge world, when stockes were saintes, and dumme walles spake', 'devoutly kneling upon her knees before the ymage of our Ladye'. For him, it was indicative of blind ignorance.[62] The woodcuts of toothless, wrinkled old women with crutches that adorned pamphlets about witchcraft also helped to cement gendered stereotypes of age that increasingly acquired a religious dimension, sharpened by the belief that the 'weaker sex' was peculiarly vulnerable to seduction by Satan. Elderly women were denigrated in cheap print more often than men, whose trademark beards gave them an aura of authority and gravity.[63]

Regardless of sex, the religious illiteracy of the elderly became notorious. Quizzed about his knowledge of Christ by the preacher John Shaw in the 1640s, a Cumbrian man aged about 60 is said to have replied: 'Oh sir...I think I heard of that man you spake of, once in a play at Kendall, called Corpus Christi play, where there was a man on a tree, and blood ran down.' He professed he was 'a good

---

[59] See Fred Davis, *Yearning for Yesterday: A Sociology of Nostalgia* (New York, 1979), pp. 52–3 and ch. 3.

[60] Martin Parker, *Times alteration: or, The old mans rehearsall, what brave dayes he knew a great while agone, when his old cap was new* (1629; STC 19271). See also Chapter 6 below.

[61] Edwin Sandys, *Sermons made by the most reverende Father in God...Archbishop of Yorke, primate of England and metropolitan* (1585; STC 21713), p. 11. See Adam Fox, *Oral and Literate Culture in England 1500–1700* (Oxford, 2000), pp. 174–8.

[62] Thomas Wilson, *The arte of rhetorique* (1553; STC 25799), fo. 77v.

[63] See L. A. Botelho, 'Images of Old Age in Early Modern Cheap Print: Women, Witches and the Poisonous Female Body', in Susannah R. Ottaway, L. A. Botelho, and Katharine Kittredge (eds), *Power and Poverty: Old Age in the Pre-Industrial Past* (Westport, CT, 2002), pp. 167–86; Alison Rowlands, 'Witchcraft and Old Women in Early Modern Germany', *P&P*, 173 (2001), 50–89.

churchman' who constantly attended Common Prayer; 'yet he could not remember that ever he heard of Salvation by Jesus Christ, but in that play'.[64] Although the story was told primarily to highlight the consequences of clerical neglect in the 'dark corners of the land' and the quasi-paganism of the rural peasantry, it underlines the point that the old were perceived to be the principal impediments to the building of a truly Protestant nation.

In a society in which age was less a numerical than a relative concept, it remains difficult to judge whether or not the first half century of the Reformation was marked by the tensions and biases embedded in contemporary discourses. The flashpoints of generational strife upon which surviving records alight may reveal more about the inherited anxieties regarding youth and age that this process exacerbated than about the actual roles played by the young and old. Their voices are muffled, and we see their experiences largely through the distorting prism of other observers or refracted through the faulty medium of their own memories.

Antiquity and Novelty

Visual and verbal representations that privilege Protestantism as a religion of young people sit uneasily with the fact that from the outset the proponents of Reformation were eager to claim the mantle of age. In a culture that regarded novelty with suspicion as a sign of illegitimacy, the biggest handicap that faced the infant Protestant movement was its lack of antiquity. Its earliest defenders and polemicists invested much energy in responding to the accusing question fired at them by their Catholic enemies: 'Where was your Church before Luther?' In common with Protestant propagandists and historians across the Continent, the strategy they adopted was to assert that Protestantism was not in fact a 'new religion' but rather the Old Faith, a reincarnation of the primitive purity of Christianity in its earliest apostolic phase. 'Reformation' entailed the rehabilitation of an institution that had been corrupted and tarnished over time and in which the guiding light of truth had become dim and dark. It entailed the rebirth of a religion that had degenerated as the centuries following the redeeming sacrifice of Christ had passed. Like the Renaissance, it was a movement that claimed to turn back the clock to an earlier stage in the life cycle of Christian civilization. And one of its most striking by-products was the identification of the intervening centuries as a degenerate stage: the invention of the very concept of the Middle Ages.[65]

---

[64] 'The Life of Master John Shaw', ed. Charles Jackson, in *Yorkshire Diaries and Autobiographies in the Seventeenth and Eighteenth Centuries*, Surtees Society, 65 (Durham, 1877), pp. 138–9.

[65] See Jennifer Summit and David Wallace (eds), 'Medieval/Renaissance: After Periodisation', special issue of *Journal of Medieval and Early Modern Studies*, 37 (2007). See esp. Margareta de Grazia, 'The Modern Divide: From Either Side', pp. 453–67.

These were central themes in the disputations in which evangelicals engaged with the bishops and officials who interrogated them from the 1520s and 1530s onwards. In a heated exchange that took place during his examination and trial in 1555, the Marian martyr John Philpot was challenged 'how olde your religion is', to which he boldly replied, 'It is older then yours, by a thousande years and moe'.[66] This was the stimulus for many of the controversial works that poured from the presses in the sixteenth century. Miles Coverdale's translation of Heinrich Bullinger's *The old faith* (1547) provided an 'evident probacion...that the Christian fayth (which is the right, true, old and undoubted fayth) hath endured sens the beginnyng of the worlde'.[67]

Christopher Rosdell's *Godlie and short discourse* on this subject, published in 1589, also set out to demonstrate that 'the Reformation at this day in England is not a bringing in of a newe Religion, but a reducing againe of the olde and auncient fayth'. Its aim was to show that it was the Romanists rather than the reformers who had hidden a collection of invented traditions 'under the visard of antiquitie', together with 'a huge heape of hypocrisie, and a store basket of all Apostacie'. It traced the first planting of the truth by Joseph of Arimathea in the first century A D and its renewal by King Lucius, before setting out how, under the influence of subsequent bishops of Rome, it had declined into corruption and how far they had 'fallen from their first foundation' on key doctrinal issues. In his dedicatory epistle to the countess of Hertford, Rosdell compared the Gospel to 'a true and natural mother that hath beene long absent from hir house and familie', who on returning home was unknown by her own offspring: 'even so, the ancient and Apostolicall religion hath beene so long absent, and lacking to her Christian children, than nowe at her returne shee is almost a straunger to all, and in deed knowen but to a few'.[68] Turning the tables on his opponents in the same way, Josias Nicholls's *Abrahams faith* (1602) insisted that it was not Protestantism but popery that was 'a false, bastard, new, upstart, hereticall and variable superstitious devise of man'. He too sought to unveil Catholicism as a religion that promoted a 'new broacht and monstrous heresie' under the cloak of the faith planted by Christ and his disciples Peter and Paul.[69] The Jacobean anti-Catholic polemicist Robert Abbot launched further attacks designed to 'dismask' Catholicism of 'that

---

[66] Foxe, *Actes and monuments* (1583 edn), p. 1821.

[67] Heinrich Bulllinger, *The olde fayth an evident probacion out of the holy scripture, that the christen fayth (whiche is the right, true, old and undoubted fayth) hath endured sens the beginnyng of the worlde*, trans. Miles Coverdale (1547; STC 4071).

[68] Christopher Rosdell, *A godlie and short discourse shewing not onely what time the inhabitants of this land first receyved the Christian faith: but also what maner of doctrine was planted in the same* (1589; STC 21320), sigs A2r–v, A3v.

[69] Josias Nicholls, *Abrahams faith: that is, the olde religion* (1602; STC 18538), title page, sigs A3r, B2v.

antiquity which they pretend for it'.[70] This was a fake patina, a counterfeit antiquity forged to deceive the unwary laity.

Exiled Catholic controversialists responded robustly, denouncing the 'new gospel' as a product of the seditious preaching of the Wittenberg monk 'of late begonne'. Thomas Harding declared it 'a newe church of late yeres set up by Sathan' in 1565, 'a Babylonish tower' built on the foundations of the ancient heresies that it had successfully resurrected.[71] The same arguments were echoed by John Rastell in a tract that declared that the uninterrupted persistence of his own faith was clear evidence of its verity, adding that its theology was further authenticated by the 'godly and grave heads' who upheld it. By contrast, it was impossible for the churches of England and Geneva to prove an unbroken chain of succession extending back to the apostles.[72] After 1600, Matthew Kellison, professor at Rheims and later president of Douai College, and Richard Broughton, a leading figure in the early Stuart mission, took up the cudgels, renewing the attack on the Church of England as a patchwork of 'gross absurdities' and 'novelties'.[73] In turn, Matthew Sutcliffe intervened to counteract Kellison's 'scurrilous' intervention 'in disgrace of the true religion'.[74] Philip Woodward set about refuting the various treatises on this topic written by the intemperate convert Thomas Bell, intent upon 'discovering' the 'divers contradictions' in the works of this 'newe ragmaster of rascall'.[75] This rather unedifying circus went on for the rest of the century. The bitter confessional battles that divided early modern England were in considerable part a politics of age.

The same rich paradoxes were explored in contemporary plays. In an anonymous interlude entitled *New custom*, first published in 1573, Perverse Doctrine, 'an old Popish priest' and his elder colleague Ignorance join forces with the character of Hypocrisy ('an old woman'), to dispute with 'New Custom', a minister and preacher 'not past twenty years old', who personifies Protestantism. The resulting

[70] Robert Abbot, *A defence of the Reformed Catholicke of M. W. Perkins…Wherin…their religion is dismasked of that antiquity which they pretend for it…* (1606; STC 48.5); idem, *The true ancient Roman Catholike. Being an apology or counterproofe against Doctor Bishops Reproofe of the defence of the Reformed Catholike* (1611; STC 54).

[71] Thomas Harding, *A confutation of a booke intituled an apologie of the Church of England* (Antwerp, 1565; STC 12762), fos 15v, 42r–v, 133v.

[72] John Rastell, *A replie against an answer (falslie intitled) in defence of the truth* (Antwerp, 1565; STC 20728).

[73] Matthew Kellison, *A survey of the new religion detecting manie grosse absurdities which it implieth* (Douai, 1603; STC 14912); Richard Broughton, *The conviction of noveltie, and defense of antiquitie. Or demonstrative arguments of the falsitie of the newe religion of England* ([Douai, 1632]; STC 1056). See also Edward Maihew, *A treatise of the groundes of the old and newe religion* ([English secret press, 1608]; STC 17197.5).

[74] Matthew Sutcliffe, *The examination and confutation of a certaine scurrilous treatise entituled, The survey of the newe religion* (1606; STC 23464).

[75] Philip Woodward, *Bels trial examine. that is a refutation of his late treatise, intituled The triall of the newe religion* (Rouen [Douai], 1608; STC 25972.2); Thomas Bell, *The tryall of the new religion contayning a plaine demonstration, that the late faith and doctrine of the Church of Rome, is indeede the new religion* (1608; STC 1832); idem, *The Catholique triumph* (1610; STC 1815).

exchanges replay the themes of intergenerational tension and dissension explored in the preceding pages. Perverse Doctrine is incredulous at the 'Young men' who think themselves 'to be meddlers in Divinity' and the boys who carry the Bible about with them conspicuously and quote from it liberally. These are matters, he says, that should be left to those 'of riper age'. Denounced as a 'pestilent knave' and 'miscreant villain' who has 'revoked diverse old heresies out of hell', New Custom replies that popery is merely a confection of the 'inventions of men' that had crept in 'through coveteousness, and superstition' over the centuries. He denies that he is an upstart heretic and declares his real name to be Primitive Constitution, insisting that 'a thousand, and a half, ... [is] surely my age'. Later in the play Perverse Doctrine ventriloquizes the wistful regret of the elderly for the passing of the era before the Reformation:

> since these Genevan doctors came so fast into this land,
> Since that time it was never merry with England.
> First came New Custom, and he gave the onsay,
> And sithens things have gone worse every day.

The interlude concludes with Perverse Doctrine seeing the error of his former ways and repenting of his 'forepassed demeanour'. Light of the Gospel, Edification, Assurance, and God's Felicity provide comfort and hope that he too can find salvation through faith alone. In the end, the young minister around whom this didactic dialogue revolves triumphs over his elderly Catholic rivals. In the process, the play vindicates Protestantism's claim to be the true old religion rather than a false new one.[76]

Reformed writers revelled in these inherited riddles. Taking inspiration from 1 Corinthians 13, Protestants frequently presented their faith as one whose adherents had 'put away childish things' and attained the deeper knowledge of those who had reached the years of discretion and reason. The anonymous author of *A caveat for the Christians agaynst the arch-papists* (1548) confidently declared that 'We be past chyldehod, away than wyth childish phantasies. For the houre commeth and now is, when the true worshippers worship the father in spirite, and in truth.'[77] In a sermon first published in 1576, the puritan preacher Edward Dering similarly contrasted the maturity of Protestant belief with the infantile state in which papistry kept its besotted followers. Disparaging the signs and wonders by which the Catholic laity were fed in 'milkepannes and greasie dishes', he said that his own religion had no need of such things. These may have been important aids 'when doctrine was more obscure' and 'when we were unbeleeving', but the Lord

---

[76] *A new enterlude no lesse wittie: then pleasant, entituled new custome deuised of late* (1573; STC 6150). I am grateful to Andrew Hope for drawing this play to my attention.

[77] *A caveat for the Christians agaynst the arch-papist* ([1548]; STC 5195), sig. B7r.

had now removed them as redundant swaddling bands and walking frames. Miracles had ceased and in the current age it was by reading the Bible that men and women were taught the true religion.[78] Richard Sheldon's *Survey of the miracles of the church of Rome* (1606) likewise dismissed such external spectacles as 'poore and childish conceits', beguiling for 'simple people' but superfluous for those who were fully enlightened by the candle of the Gospel.[79] Protestantism, in short, was envisaged as a form of Christian adulthood.

Traditional rites and ceremonies were accordingly described as 'childish'. Thomas Becon used the same adjective to castigate the ignorance of parish priests, saying that it 'wold make your hert to blede for to consider that such blind curates should have the charg of Christes congregation'.[80] The Elizabethan preacher John Stockwood urged his congregation to abandon the practices of their forefathers and 'let our olde auncient customes vaile their bonnet to the worde of the Lorde', reproving those who clung to the 'old heathenish religion and Idolatrie' sanctioned by the 'prescription of time'.[81]

Yet if Protestantism repeatedly claimed that it had come of age, as we shall see later, it also often described its disciples as people who had put off the 'old man' and turned into 'new' ones, exchanging the rigidities of the law for the rejuvenating nectar of the reformed faith. This Pauline theme permeated Protestant discourse and was commonly utilized as a shorthand for the project of reformation itself. The cultural matrix surrounding the concepts of antiquity and novelty, old and new, childhood and age was both fertile and contradictory.

In a further twist, as Warren Wooden has shown, sixteenth-century Catholics often exploited the topos of childhood as a device for recalling heretics to the bosom of the Mother Church.[82] Marian bishops and priests treated Protestants as children who needed to be weaned back from error and schism. 'Beinge but as babyes, and God's suckynge chyldren', declared Leonard Pollard, prebendary of Worcester, in 1556, people could best avoid the 'cruell daunger of that mischievous beaste the devyll' by remaining 'within the house of our father which is the Catholike Church'. Adult Christians should endeavour to emulate the 'chyldyshe simplicitie' and 'loving obedience' of the young by humbly deferring to the clerical hierarchy who had cure of their souls.[83] The papal legate Cardinal Pole

---

[78] Edward Dering, *XXVII lectures or readings, upon part of the epistle written to the Hebrues* (first publ. 1576), repr. in *Maister Derings workes* (1590; STC 6676), pp. 116–17.

[79] Richard Sheldon, *A survey of the miracles of the church of Rome* (1606; STC 22399), p. 49.

[80] e.g. *Newes from Rome concerning the blasphemous sacrifice of the papisticall masse with divers other treatises very godlye & profitable*, trans. Randall Hurlestone (Canterbury, [1550?]; STC 14006), sig. B3r; Thomas Becon, *The jewel of joye* ([1550?]; STC 1733), sig. C8v.

[81] John Stockwood, *A sermon preached at Paules crosse on Barthelmew day, being the 24. Of August. 1578* (1578; STC 23284), pp. 55–6.

[82] Warren W. Wooden, 'The Topos of Childhood in Marian England', *Journal of Medieval and Renaissance Studies*, 12 (1982), 179–94.

[83] Leonard Pollard, *Fyve homilies of late, made by a ryght good a. vertuous clerke* (1556; STC 20091), sigs E2r–3v.

adopted the same tone in his homilies addressing a laity that had been tossed and turned by two decades of religious change. He urged the English to become *parvuli*, 'lyttle babes', 'without the whiche Scripture is not onelie unprofitable but it is noisome and perniciouse'. They should abandon the heresies with which they had flirted and return to the maternal fold of Rome. The metaphor of 'childship' was a vital tactic in persuading the populace that without proper guidance the Bible could prove pernicious. Pole warned of the dangers of presuming to 'be your owne masters, whiche were as much to make yoursellfes father and mother to your self'.[84] A riposte to the priesthood of all believers, this was a model in which Catholicism took the role of the loving parent and diligent tutor, wielding the rod of discipline as well as the carrot of compassion in an effort to reclaim its delinquent children.

The text of the New Testament to which leading figures in Mary's short-lived Counter-Reformation naturally turned was Matthew 18:3: 'Except you will be convertyd, and make lyke unto lytill children, you shall not entre in to the kingdom of heaven.'[85] It is telling that this text was explicated in what was possibly the last Boy Bishop sermon delivered in England, written by Richard Ramsay, almoner of Gloucester Cathedral. The 'foolish' festivities of the season of Childermass, including the annual ceremony on Holy Innocents Eve in which youth symbolically supplanted their clerical elders for a day, were a casualty of a Henrician proclamation of 1541. Their revival after 1553 was a vehicle for reminding people that unless they renounced heresy, they were on a fast track to hell. The sermon declared that it was 'a childysh poynt for any Christian man to waver in his faith...[and to] be caried from the doctrine of his awncient relligion in to a new fanglyd doctrine', lamenting 'how many witless childer and childysh people' in the realm had been 'caried hyder and thyder, from one opinion to another, as childer ar caried with an apple, or wyth a puffe of wynd, as thei that have strength to resist nothing, which is reproveable in men that should have constanncie and discrecion'.[86] In short, succumbing to the temptations of Protestantism was shameful in people who had reached adulthood. Although English Catholics were never again in a position to deploy this rhetoric from the position of institutional dominance that lent it weight and credibility, they nevertheless continued to regard heresy as a symptom of childish imbecility.

[84] Rome, MS Vat. Lat. 5968, quoted in J. W. Blench, *Preaching in England in the Late Fifteenth and Sixteenth Centuries: A Study of English Sermons 1450–c.1600* (New York, 1964), pp. 50–1.

[85] For patristic and medieval exegesis of this passage, see Tim Gorringe, 'Parvulus: The Idea of the Little Child in Medieval Preaching and Commentary', in Sabine von Heusinger and Annette Kehnel (eds), *Generations in the Cloister: Youth and Age in Medieval Religious Life* (Zurich, 2008), pp. 65–73.

[86] 'Two Sermons Preached by the Boy Bishop', ed. John Gough Nichols, *The Camden Miscellany*, 7 (1875), p. 21.

Maturity and Middle Age

After Elizabeth's accession in 1558, Protestantism was restored to its position as the established religion. Its transformation over the course of the queen's long reign from an illegitimate protest movement into the official orthodoxy relied on the cooperation of the clergy who served its parishes and the hundreds of unpaid office holders who comprised what Patrick Collinson famously dubbed the 'monarchical republic' of Tudor England.[87] This prolonged transitional phase was both steadied and complicated by continuities in personnel: by the many priests who retained their posts by conforming with the ecclesiastical alterations ordered by the state and by the churchwardens, constables, and magistrates whose responsibility it was to see that the law was implemented. Some such vicars of Bray catered for the conservative tastes of their congregations with improvisations that mimicked the Mass. Others, including William Sheppard, the former Augustinian monk of Leeds Priory in Kent who served as a dedicated pastor of the Essex parish of Heydon between 1541 and 1586, eased the process of liturgical change through the very familiarity of their presence during these tumultuous decades. Sheppard never underwent a formal conversion. But he gradually discarded his older beliefs about purgatory and his habit of devotion to the Holy Name of Jesus and absorbed some of the values of the Church he served. He came to respect the 'decent Rits' commanded by the Queen's Injunctions and sought to deter the fairs and Sunday sports that kept 'a gret company of people of the younger sort' from hearing sermons.[88] These were men of middle age, whose longevity operated as a soft pedal and brake and whose replacement by university-trained ministers emphatically committed to the Protestant faith took several generations. The local officials charged with enforcing the statutes and injunctions were adults in the same stage of life. They were the appointed delegates of monarchs who regarded themselves as nursing 'fathers' and 'mothers' to their people.

Tudor and Stuart England was essentially ruled by men in their 40s and 50s.[89] Stretching from 35 to 50, 'flourishing and middle age' was understood as a distinct phase of the life cycle. According to Henry Cuffe, this was when a man came to 'the highest degree of perfection in the temper of his body, & continueth in that flourishing livelinesse, without any notorious decay'.[90] 'Middle age' carried few of the negative connotations it does today: rather, it represented the 'prime' and

---

[87] Patrick Collinson, 'The Monarchical Republic of Queen Elizabeth I', *Bulletin of the John Rylands Library*, 69 (1987), 394–424. See also John F. McDiarmid (ed.), *The Monarchical Republic of Early Modern England: Essays in Response to Patrick Collinson* (Aldershot, 2007).

[88] On Sheppard, see Mark Byford, 'The Price of Protestantism: Assessing the Impact of Religious Change on Elizabethan Essex: The cases of Heydon and Colchester, 1558–1594' (DPhil thesis, University of Oxford, 1989), p. 42.

[89] Keith Thomas, 'Age and Authority in Early Modern England', *Proceedings of the British Academy*, 62 (1976), 205–48, at 211.

[90] Cuffe, *Differences of the ages*, p. 119.

'perfect age of man's life', the apex of human existence. It was the age at which Adam was created *ex nihilo* and in which Christ's salvific ministry had reached its height. Linked with exuberance, strength, 'ripeness', and maturity, it was closely related to *gravitas* and located between *juventus* and *senectus* by late classical and early medieval writers.[91] It succeeded the estate of manhood.

Like the categories of youth and age, manhood was culturally conditioned and linked with social status. It was demarcated by the acquisition of rights and responsibilities: to marry, to inherit, and to bequeath. For men, it entailed a transition from being dependent to having dependants: the setting up of a separate household and becoming a husband and master, carer, and provider. Crucially, fatherhood proved their masculinity and placed them in 'a genealogical chain'.[92] However, as Alex Shepard has demonstrated, patriarchy was riddled with contradictions in theory and practice.[93] While women were generally thought to reach their physical peak earlier, maternity was equally critical as a marker of life stage. Adults were individuals who exercised authority over others. The extent of their autonomy and self-government was contingent upon their own place within the social and gender hierarchies in a variety of ways: widowhood, for instance, could bring financial independence as well as acute vulnerability. Like gender, adulthood was a relational category.[94]

Historians puzzled by the comparative absence of concerted resistance to the Tudor Reformations should perhaps pay more attention to the factor of age.[95] In seeking an explanation for the so-called 'compliance conundrum', we might investigate the ways in which married couples with young children and dependent elderly relatives were obliged to make choices that subordinated their own beliefs and instincts to the imperative of maintaining family stability. Outward conformity must have been a tempting option for people weighed down by parental and household duties. The life cycle of poverty that exposed such men and women to economic destitution was paralleled by a religious one.[96] For many the safety and welfare of their spouses and offspring must have been paramount. Overt dissidence was a reckless course of action that might place this in jeopardy.

---

[91] Mary Dove, *The Perfect Age of Man's Life* (Cambridge, 1986), esp. chs 1, 4.

[92] Ruth Mazo Karras, *From Boys to Men: Formations of Masculinity in Late Medieval Europe* (Philadelphia, PA, 2003), p. 16.

[93] On adulthood, see Youngs, *Life Cycle*, ch. 6. On manhood and its variations, see Shepard, *Meanings of Manhood*, chs 1, 3.

[94] Newcastle University hosted an online workshop devoted to 'Adulthood as a Category of Historical Analysis' on 7 September 2021 (https://www.ncl.ac.uk/hca/events/item/adulthood/, accessed 10 June 2022).

[95] Christopher Marsh, *Popular Religion in Sixteenth-Century England: Holding Their Peace* (Basingstoke, 1998), pp. 197–219.

[96] See Tim Wales, 'Poverty, Poor Relief and the Life-Cycle: Some Evidence from Seventeenth-Century Norfolk', in Richard M. Smith (ed.), *Land, Kinship and Life-Cycle* (Cambridge, 1984), pp. 351–404; Susannah R. Ottway and Samantha Williams, 'Reconstructing the Lifecycle Experience of Poverty in the Time of the Old Poor Law', *Archives*, 23 (1998), 19–29.

Circumstances likewise militated against pursuing the path of exile. Recollecting how his parents had steadily conformed themselves to the Church of England, the Welsh Benedictine Augustine Baker underlined the dilemmas felt by his father when the reign of Queen Mary came to an end:

> he was in his mind and affection so much troubled or offended thereat, that if he had not then bin in the state of a married man and a father (as he was) of children living, he would (as I have very credibly understood) upon such change made by Queen Elizabeth, for Catholick religions sake have forsaken the kingdom, and gone overseas and lived there, in some Catholick condition. But his conjugal estate, and the care he ought to have of his children, dashed such inclination and desire of his; so that he remained in such condition.[97]

Baker's regret at his parent's steady descent into a state of religious neutrality was tinged with understanding that his life stage had played a key part in shaping his course of action. The obligations of married adulthood were far more constraining than those of singledom. Against the backdrop of the succession of bewildering reversals that marked the mid-sixteenth century, it was these men and women especially who were compelled to forge 'new consciences to navigate the unprecedented circumstances in which they found themselves' and to become, in Ethan Shagan's words, 'de facto collaborators with the regime's spiritual programme'.[98]

Ironically, the comparative invisibility of adults in the historical record is a function of the fact that they wrote it. It is through the eyes of individuals such as the long-serving vicar of the Devon village of Morebath Christopher Trychay that we see the slow and incremental progress of a Reformation that perhaps the majority reluctantly embraced only after the event. The churchwardens' accounts in which for fifty-four years between 1520 and 1574 Trychay registered his community's response to these developments are texts that are tinted by the eccentricities of his own advancing age. They allow us to track his begrudging reconciliation with a religious experiment that was gradually settling into a permanent state of affairs.[99] Many of those who returned *omnia bene* ('all is well') in response to episcopal visitation articles and other bureaucratic questionnaires were middle-aged men with their hands full, too busy to document the minor misdemeanours that impeded religious reform with due diligence. The 'unacknowledged republic' of office holders upon which the early modern state depended for the implementation of its policies was a network of householders

---

[97] *Memorials of Father Augustine Baker and Other Documents Relating to the English Benedictines*, ed. J. McCann and H. Connolly, CRS 33 (1933), p. 19.

[98] Shagan, *Popular Politics*, pp. 309 and 287, respectively.

[99] Eamon Duffy, *The Voices of Morebath: Reformation and Rebellion in an English Village* (New Haven, CT, 2001). See Chapter 6, below, p. 453.

juggling multiple, competing responsibilities. Both state formation and the progress of reformation were shaped by this matrix.[100]

Meanwhile, for those who had converted to Protestantism, the problem became how to capture the charisma and bottle the zeal that had compelled them to embrace the Gospel and impart it to the next generation. To be born after 1558 was to be born into, rather than born again, in the Protestant faith. The key task that the Church and state now faced was one of education and indoctrination, of ensuring that as children grew up, they also advanced in spiritual maturity. The traditional mechanisms for marking stages in the religious life cycle were liturgical: baptism and confirmation. The reformers upheld baptism as a sacrament, but their theology transformed it from a carrier of salvific grace into a symbol of the infant's admission as a 'lively member' of the Church on earth. Stripping it of the 'superstitious' rites that had surrounded it in the pre-Reformation world— from the use of salt and spittle to the adjuration to 'accursed Satan' to depart— they remodelled it as a sign of the God-given faith by which believers were justified. Invoking the language of regeneration, cleansing, and remission, the liturgy for baptism in the Book of Common Prayer continued to speak of it as 'mistical washinge away of synne'. Its formulae implored God to grant that 'the olde Adam maye be so buried, that the newe man may be raysed up in them' and spoke of children as being 'grafted' and 'adopted' into Christ's flock.[101] As we shall see in Chapter 4, it tacitly nurtured the idea that baptized children were thereby made into 'partakers of his everlasting kingdome' and 'heyres of everlasting salvacion'. It consoled and reassured anxious parents by implying that their precious offspring numbered among the elect.[102]

Christening thus retained a key place in Protestant life. A social ritual as well as a sacred one, marked by the giving of gifts such as baptismal spoons, it incorporated children into the Christian community, starting them on their spiritual journey towards sanctification. The second stage in this process was confirmation.[103] Children were anointed with chrism and blessed by the bishop to mark their transition into full membership of the church. After the Reformation, this ceased to have the status of a sacrament and was downgraded to a mere ceremony of

---

[100] Mark Goldie, 'The Unacknowledged Republic: Officeholding in Early Modern England', in Tim Harris (ed.), *The Politics of the Excluded, c.1500–1850* (Basingstoke, 2001), pp. 153–94.

[101] Brian Cummings (ed.), *The Book of Common Prayer: The Texts of 1549, 1559, and 1662* (Oxford, 2011), pp. 141–6.

[102] See Chapter 4 below. On baptism, see David Cressy, *Birth, Marriage, and Death: Ritual, Religion, and the Life-Cycle in Tudor and Stuart England* (Oxford, 1997), ch. 5; Will Coster, *Baptism and Spiritual Kinship in Early Modern England* (Aldershot, 2002), ch. 2; Karen L. Spierling, *Infant Baptism in Reformation Geneva: The Shaping of a Community, 1536–1564* (Aldershot, 2005). Anna French provides a nuanced discussion in 'Infancy', in *eadem* (ed.), *Early Modern Childhood*, pp. 74–93.

[103] S. L. Ollard, 'Confirmation in the Anglican Communion, 1500–1800', in *Confirmation or the Laying on of Hands*, i: *Historical and Doctrinal* (1926), pp. 60–245; S. J. Wright, 'Confirmation, Catechism and Communion: The Role of the Young in the Post-Reformation Church', in *idem* (ed.), *Parish, Church and People: Local Studies in Lay Religion 1350–1750* (1988), pp. 203–27.

initiation. Some radical Protestants demanded that this 'dumb' and 'frivolous' ceremony, which was superfluous to the mystery of salvation, be abandoned altogether. John Hooper, bishop of Worcester and Gloucester during Edward's reign, conspicuously refused to carry it out.[104] Following a partial hiatus in confirmation in the middle years of the sixteenth century, however, a resurgence of the rite occurred in the later Elizabethan period. In the Jacobean era some dioceses were overwhelmed by the number of candidates who presented themselves: Tobie Matthew, for instance, confirmed more than a thousand at Ripon in Yorkshire in 1607.[105] These too were occasions attended by celebration and festivity. Confirmation evidently remained an important communal ritual in the later seventeenth and eighteenth centuries. Its significance as a popular rite of passage and as an agent for fostering in young people a sense of belonging to the Protestant Church of England has perhaps been underestimated. Its traditional title, 'bishopping' and its enthusiastic revival by Laudian divines in the 1630s should not occlude its compatibility with the priorities of those on the Church's more evangelical wing, for whom it represented a crucial opportunity to entrench the high standards of spiritual understanding idealized by Calvin and his disciples and to police access to the Eucharist.[106]

According to the Prayer Book, confirmation should only take place when boys and girls came 'to the yeres of discrecion', could consent 'with their owne mouth' to the promises made on their behalf by their godparents at their christening, and were capable of reciting 'in theyr mother tong, the articles of the faith, the lordes prayer, and the tenne commaundementes'. It was 'most mete to be ministred, when children come to that age, that partly by the frayltie of theyr owne fleshe, partly by the assautes of the world and the devil, they begin to be in daungier to fall into sinne'. It was to serve as a shield against temptation. The medieval Catholic Church had confirmed children at a young age, typically between 5 and 10 and sometimes even in infancy, but Protestantism delayed it to a later stage, following the precedent of the primitive Church, which had ordained the sacrament to 'them that were of perfecte age', properly instructed in the truth of Christ's religion, and able to articulate their understanding of it in their own words.[107] Admission to Holy Communion thus became dependent on the attainment of an

---

[104] Diarmaid MacCulloch and Pat Hughes, 'A Bailiff's List and Chronicle from Worcester', *Antiquaries Journal*, 75 (1995), 235–53, at 247.

[105] See Kenneth Fincham, *Prelate as Pastor: The Episcopate of James I* (Oxford, 1990), pp. 123–9; Rosamund Oates, *Moderate Radical: Tobie Matthew and the English Reformation* (Oxford, 2018), p. 201.

[106] For its seventeenth- and eighteenth-century history, see James F. Turrell, '"Until Such Time as He Be Confirmed": The Laudians and Confirmation in the Seventeenth-Century Church of England', *The Seventeenth Century*, 20 (2005), 204–22; Phillip Tovey, *Anglican Confirmation 1662–1820* (Farnham, 2014). For a fuller development of the argument outlined in this paragraph, see my 'Coming of Age in Faith: The Rite of Confirmation after the English Reformation', in Frances Knight, Charlotte Methuen, and Andrew Spicer (eds), *Rites of Passage*, SCH 59 (Cambridge, forthcoming).

[107] Cummings (ed.), *Book of Common Prayer*, p. 58.

appropriate level of religious knowledge. It became more closely aligned with puberty and adolescence than with the earlier phases of childhood. As Keith Thomas once commented, the official age of religious adulthood was raised by the Reformation.[108] The unworthy parishioners whom puritan ministers deliberately excluded from the holy feast on the grounds of spiritual ignorance were effectively being reclassified as children.

Confirmation was closely linked with catechizing. Perceived as a vital device for restoring corrupt Christendom and for weaning the populace from popery, this had been a linchpin of the early Reformation in England, as in Luther's Germany, from the beginning.[109] Catechesis had its origins in the apostolic era, when it was associated with the conversion of adult neophytes from a state of unbelief. A prelude rather than sequel to baptism, it was designed to prepare them for the spiritual rebirth that would initiate them fully into the Christian community.[110] The same aspiration underpinned the revival of catechizing in the sixteenth century, but it also became a vital tool of confessionalization, helping to forge a populace that was more self-conscious of the doctrines that delineated the boundaries between competing faiths and churches and of the responsibilities of good citizenship and godly obedience to one's superiors.

The first Protestant catechism to be published in English was a translation of a Latin and German work by the Strassburg reformer Wolfgang Capito prepared by the exiled former friar William Roye in 1527. An exposition of the Creed and the Lord's Prayer, it was a vehicle for instructing the young in the reformed theology of justification by faith, predestination, and the sacraments. Filled with sharply anticlerical and anti-popish recriminations against the 'belly bestes' of monks, Roye's version had a racy vernacular character. He ingeniously reversed the roles of the original interlocutors, turning this into a dialogue between a 'Christen father and his stobborne Sonne', whose questions emanate from curiosity about the new Protestant creed. Just two copies of the first edition of this subversive book survive.[111] Its reissue in 1550 coincided with a flurry of similar publications

---

[108] Thomas, 'Age and Authority', p. 224.

[109] Gerald Strauss, *Luther's House of Learning: Indoctrination of the Young in the German Reformation* (Baltimore, MD, 1978). For England, see Philippa Tudor, 'Religious Instruction for Children and Adolescents in the Early English Reformation', *JEH*, 35 (1984), 391–413. The most extensive study of the catechism in England is Ian Green, *The Christian's ABC: Catechisms and Catechizing in England, c.1530–1740* (Oxford, 1996). See also idem '"For Children in Yeeres and Children in Understanding": The Emergence of the English Catechism under Elizabeth and the Early Stuarts', *JEH*, 37 (1986), 397–425.

[110] See Green, *Christian's ABC*, 14.

[111] Wolfgang Capito, *A lytle treatous or dialoge very necessary for all christen men to learne and to knowe*, trans. William Roye ([Strassburg, 1527]; STC 24223.3). For a modern edition, see William Roye, *A Brefe Dialoge bitwene a Christen Father and his Stobborne Sonne: The First Protestant Catechism Published in English*, ed. Douglas H. Parker and Bruce Krajewski (Toronto, 1999). See Anthea Hume, 'William Roye's "Brefe Dialoge" (1527): An English Version of a Strassburg Catechism', *Harvard Theological Review*, 60 (1967), 307–21.

that appeared after the accession of Edward VI to supplement the short catechism incorporated in the Book of Common Prayer.

Printed in 1547, another catechism opens with the child responding to the question 'What art thou' by describing him- or herself as 'a creature of God', 'the sonne of Adam', and 'as touching my newe and seconde byrth...a chrystian'. It goes on to underline the evils of idolatry and image-making emphatically.[112] Edmund Allen's *Christian introduccion for youth* (1548) also took the form of a conversation between a Maister' and a 'Scholar' who was made to 'answere as he hath before been taught'.[113] The following year, the former Carmelite friar John Bale prepared a similar *Dialogue* in the guise of a dinner table conversation between his two young sons John and Paul, in which the elder instructs the younger, contrasting the Gospel with the 'leven of Pharisees' and the empty 'tradicions of men' and insisting that God 'never distributeth his gyftes to ye measure of age' and often gave the benefits of his grace to children, who were reserved to his 'secrete workynge'.[114] John and Anne Hooper took inordinate pride in the academic achievements of their little daughter Rachel, reporting to her godfather Heinrich Bullinger in Zurich that she understood English, French, German, and Latin 'very tolerably' in February 1550 and that she had learnt the Decalogue, Paternoster, Apostles' Creed, and several Psalms by heart in under three months, only two years after her first teeth appeared.[115] In the preface to the bulky catechism Thomas Becon prepared for his 5-year-old son, he similarly boasted that his offspring were drilled in the precepts of the Protestant faith from their very cradles.[116] Devices for indoctrination, such catechisms envisaged a situation in which Protestantism was aligned with the structures of parental and political authority.

Most of these texts were written for use in domestic settings. Adapted from the Nuremberg catechism and dedicated to the young king, Thomas Cranmer's *Catechismus* (1548) claimed that the Reformation would have met with less opposition had it not been for 'greate negligence of theducation of the youth' of the realm. Catechizing was conceived as an instrument for feeding those of 'tender age' with the 'swete milke' and 'pappe of goddes holy worde', as well as training them in how to behave towards magistrates, ministers, mothers, and fathers. Tellingly, Cranmer also had a secondary audience in mind: people of 'the older sorte', who, though zealous for the truth, had been 'brought up in

---

[112] Cummings (ed.), *Book of Common Prayer*, pp. 59–62; *A fruteful and a very Christen instruction for children* (1547; STC 14106), sig. A6r, B2v–3r.

[113] Edmund Allen, *A christian introduccion for youth conteinyng the principles of our fayth & religion* (1548; STC 359), sig. A2r.

[114] John Bale, *A dialoge or communycacyon to be had at table betwene two children* (1549; STC 1290), sigs A2v, A4r–v.

[115] *Original Letters Relative to the English Reformation*, ed. H. Robinson, PS (Cambridge, 1846), i. 74–5, 107.

[116] Thomas Becon, *The workes of T. Becon* (1564; STC 1710), fo. cclxxxvii v.

ygnorance' and might benefit 'by hearing of their children, [and] learne in theyr age, that which passed theym in their youth'. This catechism was designed to do double duty, benefiting both parents who had been unlucky enough to grow up before Protestantism became the official faith of the land and their more fortunate children.[117]

An official programme of Protestant catechizing in homes and schools was revived after 1558, facilitated by the revised Prayer Book and the influential version prepared and published by Alexander Nowell, dean of St Paul's in 1570.[118] By the 1580s, however, the reformers' heady optimism about the salutary effects of this ambitious educational programme had begun to wane. The surge of catechetical works that appeared from the middle decades of Elizabeth's reign balanced the neo-Augustinian pessimism about human nature that was a hallmark of Calvinism with the conviction that children could be nurtured in their nascent faith and enabled to reach a deeper understanding of it through diligent instruction from their earliest years.[119] Although 'utterly destitute of all pietie' and corrupted by inherited concupiscence, they were, nevertheless, pliable. As William Gouge put it, just as clay and wax 'while they are soft receive any impression' and 'twigs while they are tender are bowed any way', so too could sons and daughters be moulded by their parents.[120] A similar tension lay at the heart of the wider project to build the new Jerusalem through education: Protestant theology taught that salvation was a free gift from the deity, but it also clung to the view that learning could indeed incline one to godliness and awaken in the elect a desire for salvation.[121]

The proliferation of catechisms also reflects a developing sense of disillusionment about the receptiveness of the young to a Reformation that was now in its second generation rather than the first flush of youth. As Ian Green has suggested, this converged with concern about the resistance that other contemporaries still exhibited to the Protestant message.[122] The dedicatory epistles and titles of such books reflect a determination to bring both 'children in yeeres and children in understanding' properly up to speed.[123] The 'novices in the schoole of Christ' to

---

[117] Thomas Cranmer, *Catechismus. That is to say a shorte instruction into Christian religion for the synguler commoditie and profyte of children and yong people* (1548; STC 5994), sigs (?)iiir, (?)ivr, (?)vir; sigs M3v–6r.

[118] For the Book of Common Prayer catechism, see Cummings (ed.), *The Book of Common Prayer*, pp. 59–62, 151–4, 426–30; Alexander Nowell, *A catechisme, or first instruction and learning of Christian religion. Translated out of Latine into Englishe* (1570; STC 18708).

[119] See Barbara Pitkin, '"The Heritage of the Lord": Children in the Theology of John Calvin', in Marcia J. Bunge (ed.), *The Child in Christian Thought* (Grand Rapids, MI, 2002), pp. 160–93.

[120] William Gouge, *Of domesticall duties* (1622; STC 12119), pp. 537, 544.

[121] For a subtle exploration, see John Morgan, *Godly Learning: Puritan Attitudes towards Reason, Learning and Education, 1560–1640* (Cambridge, 1986).

[122] Green, '"For Children in Yeeres and Children in Understanding"'.

[123] John Stalham, *A catechisme for children in yeeres and children in understanding* (1644; Wing S5183).

which they are directed were the elderly as well as infants, 'simple' and 'ignorant people' who had fallen through the cracks in what puritans regarded as an imperfect ecclesiastical system.[124] Invoking St Paul's Epistle to the Hebrews 5:13–14, William Crashaw's 'countrey catechism' of 1617 declared that 'every one that useth Milke, is unskilfull in the Word of Righteousnesse, for he is a Babe' and that 'strong meate' was only suitable for those 'that are of full age' in their faith.[125] The Nottinghamshire preacher Richard Barnard agreed that within the Church of England there were two sorts of 'Babes', 'babes in yeeres, and Babes in knowledge, though auntient for yeeres'.[126] Exploiting the ambiguous boundary between age as a marker of biological stage and age as an index of spiritual development, the explicit objective of some of these texts was the religious rehabilitation of backward adults. Parish ministers remained convinced that a lamentable number of people still required spoon-feeding in elementary Christian teaching. Simon Ford, rector of Old Swinford in Worcestershire, was still harping on this Pauline theme three-quarters of a century later: published in 1684, his catechism was designed for 'the more adult Children, and other Elderly Persons that need it'.[127] The passage of time did not diminish the clergy's conviction that in spiritual terms much of the populace had yet to pass infancy.

The urgency attached to catechizing in churches, schools, and homes was a product of anxiety that the Almighty would surely punish a society that displayed so little gratitude for the blessings it had received. The preface to James Leech's *Plaine and profitable catechisme*, published in Cambridge in 1605, lamented the 'miserable times wherein we live', in which the number of 'wicked atheists, superstitious papists, prophane worldlings, carnall gospellers, vaine and idle professors' was daily increasing. Like many of the preachers who thundered from the pulpit of Paul's Cross in the Elizabethan and Jacobean period, he surmised that the Lord had a controversy with England, as with Israel of old, and that many thousands had 'not yet learned the very beginnings of the doctrines of Christ'.[128]

---

[124] D. V., *An enlargement of a former catechisme which contained in briefe the grounds and principles of Christian religion that shewed what we ought to beleeve* (1641: Wing V2), title page.

[125] William Crashaw, *Milke for babes. Or, a north-countrie catechisme* (1618; STC 6020), sig. A1v. See also Nicholas Byfield, *The rule of faith: or, An exposition of the Apostles Creed so handled as it affordeth both milke for babes, and strong meat for such as are at full age* (1620; STC 4233.3); William Dickinson, *Milke for babes. The English catechisme, set downe in the Common-Prayer Booke, breifly explaned for the private use of the younger and more unlearned sort of his parishioners of Apleton, in the county of Berks* (1628; STC 6822); Hugh Peters, *Milk for babes, and meat for men, or, Principles necessary, to bee known and learned, of such as would know Christ here, or be known of him hereafter* ([Amsterdam?], 1630; STC 19798.5); John Cotton, *Milk for babes...chiefly, for the spirituall nourishment of Boston babes in either England: but may be of like use for any children* (1646; Wing C6443).

[126] Richard Barnard, *Two twinnes: or two parts of one portion of Scripture* (1613; STC 1964), pp. 9–10.

[127] Simon Ford, *A plain and profitable exposition of, and enlargement upon, the church-catechism* (1684; Wing F1493), title page.

[128] James Leech, *A plaine and profitable catechisme, with certain prayers adjoined, meete for parents and housholders to teach their children and servants* (Cambridge, 1605; STC 15363.3), sigs A2r–3v.

Godly Protestants remained petrified that the true faith would not survive unless radical political and pastoral remedies were applied to reform the Church further. Against the backdrop of assassination plots and succession crises, the fragility of the 1558 settlement constantly preyed on their minds. Many feared that the Reformation was indeed a sickly child that might not survive.

Concern that, like Israel before her, sinful England might finally be cast off by God reached a new peak of intensity in the 1640s. Parliamentary fast sermons revitalized the theme that the Lord, like a long-suffering husband, would soon lose patience and sever his connection with a nation that was guilty of 'spirituall whoredome'. This second marriage would end in the same way as the first: in anger, recrimination, and judgement. Mingling parental and marital metaphors, the clergy warned England's 'backsliding children' to repent lest the Almighty carry out his threat to undo the knot between him and his people.[129] In 1640, Stephen Marshall used the anniversary of Elizabeth's accession on 17 November to indict 'the extreame daring, bold audaciousnesse' of the current 'generation of men' and to beseech it to abandon the superstition and idolatry in which it persisted. 'This day eighty two yeares agone, the Lord set up the Gospell among us, and tooke us to be a nation in Covenant with him', but his tolerance was wearing thin, and it was a wonder that he had not already 'wholly forsaken us long agone'.[130] After 'four score yeers' of being irradiated by the 'cleer beams' of Protestant doctrine, William Price declared the following year, the continuing propensity of the English nation to relapse to idolatry would surely cause him to sue his unfaithful spouse 'by a Bill of divorce'.[131]

Echoed in dozens of sermons, such claims mimicked the lachrymose tone of the prophetic books of the Old Testament. They reflect the widespread perception that as Protestantism aged, the spontaneous enthusiasm assumed to have marked its earliest phases had faded into indifference and apathy. Now it was necessary to adopt alternative strategies to shake people out of their sinful complacency. Such statements attest to an emerging strain of nostalgia for the early days of the Reformation, when the true mettle of believers had been tried and tested in the crucible of persecution. Like all nostalgias this one was the product of a potent mixture of selective forgetting and misremembering. It was symptomatic of the fact that the religion of Protestants had moved into middle age.

---

[129] See Thomas Case, *Spirituall whoredome discovered in a sermon preach'd before the Honourable House of Commons assembled in Parliament* (1647; Wing C843), p. 33; James Nalton, *Delay of reformation provoking Gods further indignation* (1646; Wing N122), p. 3; John Strickland, *Mercy rejoicing against judgement* (1645; Wing S5973), p. 14.

[130] Stephen Marshall, *A sermon preached before the honourable house of commons* (1641; Wing M776), pp. 33–5, 30.

[131] William Price, *Mans delinquencie attended by divine justice intermixt with mercy* (1646; Wing P3401), p. 39.

The Progress of Patriarchy

A further index of the accompanying shift of priorities in the later sixteenth and seventeenth centuries is the surge of didactic literature designed to inculcate piety appropriate to different stages in life. It is telling that many such tracts were directly addressed to Youth and Age. Others took the form of staged conversations between them, in which the latter tutors the former on his spiritual journey through life. Predicated on the ambivalent stereotypes already discussed, if these underlined the capacity of people at both ends of the age spectrum to attain a special relationship with God, they also stressed their propensity to be seduced by the Devil and to fall into dissolution and vice. Childish innocence was twinned with iniquity, and seniority was frequently accompanied by incorrigibility and clogged with self-inflicted misery.

In two sermons preached in Dover and published in 1621, John Reading declared that too many young people deceived themselves that there was plenty of time to repent before it was too late: 'This is the reason why we have so many youthfull old men, Children of age'. The best course of action was to 'bee an happie old man in thy youth, as some are unhappy young in their age'. It was not 'gray haires and wrincles' that begot 'the Crowne of glorie'; a holy life spent in devotion to God was 'the onely way to an honorable and comfortable old age'.[132] The Sussex divine John Maynard's *Memento for young and old* (1669) took up the same conventional theme, encouraging his readers to 'regard not those who scoff in their carnal folly at the uniting of these two together, Youth and Holiness, as at an unequal match'. He also reproved those who gave over the spring of their age to fornication, drunkenness, and vanity, warning that these shameful practices would come back to haunt them in later years.[133] The Congregationalist minister Thomas Brooks's bestselling *Apples of gold for young men and women*, first published in 1657 and in its seventeenth edition by 1693, similarly described 'the happiness of being Good betimes, and the honour of being an Old Disciple'. Youth, 'the Primrose of your daies', was the fittest time for cultivating godliness and serving the Lord in preparation for the 'Winter of old age'. In turn, it was 'no honour for an old man to bee in coats, nor for an old man to bee a babe in grace. An A.B.C. old man is a sad and shameful sight'. 'What [could be] more ridiculous', he asked, 'than (*puer centum annorum*) a childe of an hundred years old?'[134] The ubiquity of this trope in homiletic discourse is indicative of a pastoral problem

---

[132] John Reading, *The old mans staffe, two sermons, shewing the onely way to a comfortable old age* (1621; STC 20792), pp. 5, 7, 21.

[133] John Maynard, *A memento to young and old* (1669; Wing M1451), p. 81. See also Thomas Doolittle, *The young man's instructer, and the old man's remembrancer* (1673; Wing D1906).

[134] Thomas Brooks, *Apples of gold for young men and women, and a crown of glory for old men and women* (1657; Wing B4922A), title page, sig. a1v, pp. 28, 56.

that Protestant soteriology not only failed to solve but may even have served to reinforce.

Others played on the paradoxes at the heart of early modern English culture by admonishing both those starting their journey to faith and those who already had 'one Foot in their Graves'. Their aim was to reclaim what they regarded as a 'degenerate Age' and to ensure that the next generation was better instructed than the present one. Preaching at Guildhall Chapel in the late 1690s, John Strype insisted that 'the Future Good of the Universe depends upon the Sobriety of Youth' and urged the 'Aged Persons' in his congregation to match the maturity of their years with contrition and spiritual wisdom.[135] It behoved those who had 'gone thro' the various Stages & States of Life' to prepare themselves for death by devout prayer and meditation, knowing that those who began and ended well would receive the crown of life.[136]

The authors of many of the 'monitors' and 'remembrancers' that emanated from English presses in the sixteenth and seventeenth centuries dwelt on the providential judgements that befell those who failed to heed these oft-repeated lessons: the slow descent from a misspent youth into the squalor of habitual sin and a woeful death. Dedicated to the adolescent males of the parish, Robert Abbot's *Young-mans warning-peece* (1636) told the story of the Kentish apothecary William Rogers, who, despite his religious upbringing, 'kicked against the pricks'. He began to delight in vain company and fell into an inveterate wickedness that manifested itself in failure to attend church and exposed him to the intense and painful sickness from which he died, bitterly lamenting his earlier failure to mend the error of his ways.[137] Replicated in ballads sung to the tune 'Fortune my Foe' or 'Aim not too high', this proved to be a very popular formula.[138] Its alter ego was the story of *The young-mans victory over the power of the devil*, a broadside about a virtuous 15-year old student from the parish of St Giles in London who had steadfastly resisted the temptations of Satan. This was often printed with a cartoon that illustrated two types of life cycle, contrasting the pious pilgrim's progress from the schoolroom to heaven with the rake's progress from learning to gambling, evil company and greed, and, henceforth pursued by a horned demon, to hell (Fig. 1.4). Such texts were regarded as 'Necessary to be set up in all Houses' for the edification of children and adolescent servants.[139]

---

[135] John Strype, *Lessons moral and Christian, for youth and old age in two sermons preach'd at Guildhall Chappel, London* (1699; Wing S6022), p. 67, sigs A2r–3r, p. 2.

[136] NYCRO, PR/KN 23/1/7 (Commonplace book, 18th century), 'To an aged person'.

[137] Robert Abbot, *The young-mans warning-peece: or A sermon preached at the burial of William Rogers, apothecary* (1636; STC 60.3), p. 13.

[138] *Young-mans repentance, or, the sorrowful sinners lamentation* ([1686]; Wing Y124).

[139] *The young-mans victory over the power of the devil. Or, strange and wonderful news from the city of London* ([1693]; Wing Y126A). See also *The young-mans conquest over the powers of darkness* (1684; Wing Y115).

Fig. 1.4 *The young-mans conquest over the powers of darkness* (London, 1684).

John Bunyan's *Life and death of Mr Badman* is another manifestation of the Restoration vogue for allegorical biographies of sinners.[140]

The themes of inexpensive ephemera and of the practical divinity produced by godly Protestant divines converged in other ways too, not least in underscoring the respect that the young owed to their elders. Songs about the divine punishments meted out to ungrateful and hard-hearted children who failed to care for their aged parents, ignored their cries for aid, and allowed them to sink into poverty numbered among the era's ballad bestsellers.[141] They correspond to the cautionary tales collected in anthologies such as Thomas Beard's *Theatre of Gods judgements* about the unhappy fates that had befallen disobedient sons and daughters throughout the ages.[142] Stories of obstinate and ungodly offspring subjected to the wrath of the Almighty demonstrated the duty of keeping the fifth commandment to 'Honour thy father and thy mother'. As Jonathan Willis has commented, this injunction expanded to encompass a whole range of superiors, becoming 'a divinely instituted charter for the maintenance of secular authority and temporal hierarchy'. 'The idealised model of childhood deference' it enshrined 'formed the prototype for all other subordinate relationships', a pattern that people were expected to emulate at every stage of their lives.[143] It also correlated with the reverence people owed to God himself, in whose shoes his earthly counterparts and deputies stood. Beard recounted the story—'worthy to be remembered of all'—of 12-year-old Denis Benfield, who was struck dead on her way home from school the day after calling the Lord 'an old doting foole'. Her corpse, half-blackened, was buried in Hackney the same night. Her terrible correction by the hand of the Almighty for blasphemous impertinence underscored the gravity of her double offence against the deity and the elderly rolled into one.[144] Disrespect for the old, who carried upon them 'a print of Gods eternitie', was, by extension, a derogation of his own majesty.[145]

The reassertions of the correct order of patriarchal relations these stories embody were characteristic of a society in which Protestantism was becoming an agent of moral discipline and a trusted ally of establishment values. The youthful defiance of authority to which adults had turned a blind eye in the earlier phases

[140] John Bunyan, *The life and death of Mr Badman, presented to the world in a familiar dialogue between Mr Wiseman, and Mr Attentive* (1680; Wing B5550).

[141] *The ungrateful son: or, An example of God's justice upon the abuseful disobedience of a false-hearted and cruel son to his aged father* ([1688–92]; Wing U65). See Alice Tobriner, 'Old Age in Tudor-Stuart Broadside Ballads', *Folklore*, 102 (1991), 149–74.

[142] Thomas Beard, *The theatre of Gods judgements: or, a collection of histories out of sacred, ecclesiasticall, and prophane authours concerning the admirable judgements of God upon the transgressours of his commandements* (1631; first publ. 1597; STC 1661), pp. 214–26.

[143] Jonathan Willis, *The Reformation of the Decalogue: Religious Identity and the Ten Commandments in England, c.1485–1625* (Cambridge, 2017), pp. 89–104, at 89, 98.

[144] Ibid., p. 184.

[145] John Dod, *The bright star which leadeth wise men to our Lord Jesus Christ, or, a familiar and learned exposition on the ten commandements* (1603; STC 6967.5), p. 33.

of the Reformation now became the target of tighter regulation by those worried that bad behaviour and ill manners were threatening to alienate England from God. The rising tide of business in the church courts and the raft of local decrees and by-laws issued by city fathers and secular officials were driven, at least in part, by anxiety about an epidemic of adolescent misconduct and juvenile delinquency that was thought to be undermining the very foundations of the social order itself.[146] *Guides to godliness* directed towards apprentices were animated by the conviction that previous generations 'were never so leaudly and wickedly given, never so vaine and so licentious, never so full of scoffing and derision, never so insolent and contemptuous of God and good men, as they be in these dayes'.[147]

Alongside restraint of boisterous games and disorderly misrule, concern about the apparently irrepressible promiscuity of the young was acute. A total of 61% of cases of sexual crime brought before the London court of Bridewell in the years 1574–6 and 1597–1610 involved illicit liaisons between individuals in service within the same household. This was one of the ways in which the authorities sought to control 'the unfolding of the life-cycle' and prevent the indentured from taking 'a short cut to adulthood'.[148] In Earls Colne in Essex most of those accused of incontinency before the local ecclesiastical tribunal were also in their early twenties.[149] The age profile of offenders, many of whom were seasonal workers passing through the village, bears out the contemporary commonplace that too many accounted fornication 'no sin at all, but rather a pastime, a dalliance and but a touch of youth'.[150] The visibility of delinquent youth in the records of the Elizabethan and early Stuart Reformation of manners is an index of the perennial concern that the moral values of young people were seriously out of kilter with those of their elders. It reflects renewed apprehension of a generation gap and of generational disjuncture.

This also found expression in the literature of social complaint. The dicing, dancing, drinking, plays, and other idle pastimes against which Elizabethan 'anatomisers' of abuses such as Philip Stubbes railed were the leisure activities in which young men and women spent their spare time and for which they forsook Sunday services. They played a critical part in the economy of courtship that clerical and

---

[146] Martin Ingram, *Church Courts, Sex and Marriage in England, 1570–1640* (Cambridge, 1987), pp. 264–74; Griffiths, *Youth and Authority*, chs 5–7.

[147] B. P., *The young-mans guide to godlinesse. Or the prentises practise on earth, that hopes for a freedome in heaven* (1619; STC 19057.5), fo. 43v.

[148] Griffiths, *Youth and Authority*, pp. 281, 94. On apprenticeship as an agent of maturation and coming of age, see Steven R. Smith, 'The London Apprentices as Seventeenth-Century Adolescents', *P&P*, 61 (1973), 149–61; Ilana Ben-Amos, 'Service and the Coming of Age of Young Men in Seventeenth-Century England', *Continuity and Change*, 3 (1988), 41–64.

[149] Robert von Friedeburg, 'Reformation of Manners and the Social Composition of Offenders in an East Anglian Cloth Village: Earls Colne, Essex, 1531–1642', *JBS*, 29 (1990), 347–85, at 369–73.

[150] The 'Homily against Whoredom and Uncleanness', in *Certaine sermons or homilies appointed to be read in churches* (1687 edn; Wing C4091I), p. 119.

lay moral crusaders sought to restrain.[151] It is telling that so many of these treatises take the form of dialogues between figures at different stages in the life cycle. Christopher Fetherston's *Dialogue against light, lewde, and lascivious dauncing* (1582) is a conversation between Minister and Juvenis, who defends his attendance at taverns rather than church, protesting 'Tushe tushe, wee will have our swindg while we be yong, age wil come soone ynough, and it will make us forsake all these sportes: and then will wee be sober and vertuous.'[152] The interlocutors in John Northbrooke's 1577 treatise on this topic were Youth and Age. The intergenerational tensions it embodies are resolved in the final pages, when the former thanks the latter for the 'fatherly instructions' that have led him to see the error of his evil ways.[153] A verse dialogue composed by the serving man James Yates in 1582 also begins with a 'lustie' Youth boldly insisting that 'grisseled Age' has 'no force to banish my delite'. It ends with the former feeling the effects of the 'stroake' of time and meekly admitting that his earlier 'vauntes were all in vaine.'[154]

The satisfying conclusions to these didactic fictions clash with the chorus of popular complaints about the officious interventions of 'busy controllers'. Puritans who refused to indulge the harmless frivolities of youth and to 'allow some fleshly liberty' and 'latitude' to them, were looked upon as spoilsports and killjoys.[155] The godly's concerted assault upon the traditional culture of 'Merry England' provoked deep resentment in a context in which the ecclesiastical calendar had been pruned of many days of licensed festive mischief. The abolition of Christmas festivities as pagan remnants in 1644 seemed a further direct blow against the culture of youth and the notion of holy play.[156] If puritanism was 'one half of a stressful relationship', a key fault line along which it was fractured was age.[157]

The sharper moral rigorism that was a feature of English Protestantism from the 1580s may be seen as a barometer of changing priorities. Patrick Collinson's influential but contested claim that the Reformation underwent 'a cultural about-face' in the mid-Elizabethan period, moving from an iconoclastic to an iconophobic phase, is itself a theory of generational change. It charts a shift in mood from mirth to sobriety as early evangelical exuberance in the use of the popular media of song, drama, and satirical cartoons gave way to growing distrust of these

---

[151] Philip Stubbes, *The anatomie of abuses* (1583; STC 23376).

[152] Christopher Fetherston, *A dialogue agaynst light, lewde, and lascivious dauncing* (1577; STC 10835), sig. B8v. For an earlier articulation of this theme, see R. Wever, *An enterlude called lusty Juventus* ([1550?]; STC 25148).

[153] John Northbrooke, *Spiritus est vicarius Christi in terra. A treatise wherein dicing, dauncing, vaine playes or enterluds with other idle pastimes [et]c. commonly used on the Sabboth day, are reproued* (1577; STC 18670), p. 72.

[154] James Yates, *The castell of courtesie.... Also a dialogue betweene age and youth* (1582; STC 26079), sigs C1r–3r.

[155] Maynard, *Memento*, p. 78.

[156] Ronald Hutton, *The Rise and Fall of Merry England: The Ritual Year 1400–1700* (Oxford, 1994).

[157] Patrick Collinson, *The Birthpangs of Protestant England: Religious and Cultural Change in the Sixteenth and Seventeenth Centuries* (New York, 1988), p. 143.

deceptive vehicles for teaching the truth. Mature Protestantism, Collinson contended, ceased to be a religion of protest at ease with the streets, inns, and alehouses and became intractably hostile to these milieux. A 'more fastidious and inhibited generation' distanced itself from accustomed rituals of 'good fellowship' and 'company keeping'.[158] Although the harder edges of this thesis have been refined by more recent scholarship, there remains considerable value in the suggestion that the temperament of the Reformation altered as it entrenched itself at the heart of the ecclesiastical and political establishment.

Zealous Protestants who believed that they had a duty to be their brothers' keepers also regarded themselves as guardians of the souls of their social inferiors, and of their children when they were absent or neglected to instruct them adequately. This justified an unprecedented level of intrusion into the lives of destitute families, as Patricia Crawford showed in her important work on early modern London. The rhetoric of acting *in loco parentis* served to disempower natural parents. State and charitable institutions such as foundling hospitals and nurseries took their place as surrogates better able to breed up the offspring of the poor in religion and good citizenship. The education that these children received was designed to preserve their bodies and souls and counteract the 'wicked and debauched Principles' they had 'sucked in' with their mothers' milk.[159] Private benefactors who bequeathed money to teach boys and girls the Bible and catechism assumed the same responsibility after their deaths.[160] The prevalent ideal of public and civic fatherhood underpinned the paternalistic reform programmes energetically pursued in cities and provincial towns in this period. These too were underpinned by an inclusive language of parenthood that conceptualized social discipline as a tool of spiritual improvement.[161]

Similar attitudes infused the government of schools and universities. Academic authorities were willing to tolerate the bravado and camaraderie of carnivalesque misrule lubricated by alcohol and sex as rites of passage into manhood that did not inherently threaten the patriarchal order. Young bachelors claimed 'libertie from time to time in their Christmas merriments and sports to punish misdemeanours and faults' committed by college servants and inferior officers. But when masculine misdemeanours and student high jinks spilled over into insubordination, contravening the gravity and civility expected of scholars, their

---

[158] Collinson, *Birthpangs*, ch. 4, citations at pp. 111, 107–8. This thesis is also developed in *idem, From Iconoclasm to Iconophobia: The Cultural Impact of the Second English Reformation* (Reading, 1986).

[159] Patricia Crawford, *Parents of Poor Children in England, 1580–1800* (Oxford, 2010), ch. 5. The quotations are taken from *An account of the general nursery, or colleg of infants* (1686; Wing A294), pp. 11–12.

[160] See, e.g., SA, P257/Q/1/1 (will of Joseph Jones, 1729).

[161] Paul Slack, *From Reformation to Improvement: Public Welfare in Early Modern England* (Oxford, 1998), esp. ch. 2.

perpetrators could find themselves hauled up before college deans or the proctors and bedels who serviced the vice chancellor's court.[162]

Younger children came under close scrutiny too: irreverent behaviour by boys and girls that disrupted liturgical services became the subject of episcopal scrutiny. In 1634, the authorities at Salisbury Cathedral sought to redress 'ye ordinarie trudginge up and downe of youths, and clamours of children to ye great disturbance of ye preachers in their sermon'.[163] It proved difficult to invest the ceremony of confirmation with due decorum: the crush of young candidates who came to receive the bishop's blessing, pushed forward by overeager parents, often made these rather carnivalesque occasions. Joseph Hall of Exeter recalled the 'tumultuous affectation' that surrounded the rite when he administered it in his diocese, and later in life, Richard Baxter remembered receiving it as a schoolboy alongside classmates who went to 'as a May-game'.[164] Laudians determined to preserve the beauty of holiness justified the policy of railing off altars by explaining that the Lord's table needed to be preserved from 'profane abuses', including boys rioting, leaning, stepping, leaping, sitting, standing and casting their hats upon it. Matthew Wren, bishop of Ely, was horrified to report that servants had been seen to hold infants and toddlers over it 'till they defiled it'.[165] But concerns about youthful mischief cut across the divisions that were appearing within the Church of England. In May 1644, the churchwardens of St Mary's in Chester, took steps for the 'Reformacion' of the disorders committed by boys and girls, vowing that the sworn men of the parish would sit in the choir and body of the church to suppress the same and take down the names of the offenders. If their fathers and masters did not duly discipline them, they themselves would be prosecuted under the law.[166] Children and infants were expected to sit in serried ranks without fidgeting, and to be seen and not heard.

The hiatus of the Civil Wars aside, the progressive institutionalization of the Church of England was accompanied by a reinvigoration of patriarchy. Youth's inferiority to age was reasserted in mainstream Protestant discourse and the duty of the population to honour and respect monarchs, magistrates, and ministers as they did their fathers and mothers was firmly underscored. Senior clerics refused to brook resistance to their authority by younger men: John Whitgift reproved a puritan minister from Kent who presumed to correct him as a 'beardless boy, yesterday bird, new out of shell' with undisguised contempt.[167]

[162] Shepard, *Meanings of Manhood*, ch. 4, at p. 99. See also Keith Thomas, *Rule and Misrule in the Schools of Early Modern England* (Reading, 1976).

[163] Cited in Wright, 'Confirmation, Catechism and Communion', p. 208.

[164] Joseph Hall, *Cheirothesia: or, a confirmation of the apostolicall confirmation of children: setting forth the divine ground, end, and use of that too much neglected institution* (1651), pp. 16–17, 82; *Reliquiae Baxterianae: or, Mr Richard Baxters narrative of the most memorable passages of his life and times*, ed. Matthew Sylvester (1696), p. 250.

[165] *Parentalia: or, memoirs of the family of the Wrens*, ed. Stephen Wren (1750), pp. 76–7.

[166] CRO, P20/13/1 (Churchwardens' accounts of St Mary's, Chester, 1536–1684), 9 May 1644.

[167] Cited in Patrick Collinson, *The Elizabethan Puritan Movement* (1967), p. 254.

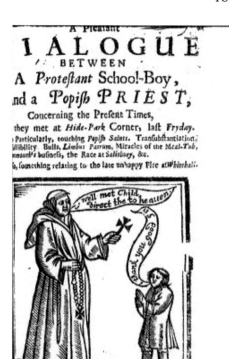

Fig. 1.5 *A pleasant [d]ialogue between a protestant school-boy, and a popish priest concerning the present times* (London, 1698), title page.
Source: © British Library Board, 1078.k.20 (1). All Rights Reserved/Bridgeman Images.

As in every society, young people remained unruly and ill-disciplined. They regularly pushed back against the dictates of their parents and elders, but they often did so in ways that reflected the domestication of the Tudor Reformations. The outbreaks of adolescent disorder and violence against Catholics and nonconformists in the capital that coincided with the Popish Plot and exclusion crisis in the late 1670s and 1680s were an outlet for confessional prejudices that were ingrained in young people from birth. Apprentices and scholars burnt effigies of Whig and Tory figures and symbols, engaged in mock violence, and presented petitions to the king.[168] When older tropes about role reversal were brought out of mothballs, they often served to reinforce rather than subvert the status quo. Published in 1698, *A pleasant [d]ialogue between a protestant school-boy, and a popish priest* (Fig. 1.5) is a spirited exchange in which the child outwits his adult Catholic interlocutor. His quick-witted responses on the topics of saints, transubstantiation, papal infallibility, purgatory, and miracles parrot the opinions of the

---

[168] See Tim Harris, *London Crowds in the Reign of Charles II: Propaganda and Politics from the Restoration until the Exclusion Crisis* (Cambridge, 1987), pp. 166–9, 174–80, 186–8, 212–13.

boy's father, who calls the Pope the Whore of Babylon and regales his son with tales of popish cruelty and treason. His opponent is always on the back foot, unable to refute the teachings of the 'damned Hereticks' who have ruined this impudent little 'saucie villain'.[169] Upbeat and ebullient, cheap print of this kind demonstrates that anti-Catholic pastime was emerging as a critical device for the socialization of the young. It was one the instruments that helped to create both a Protestant nation and successive generations of self-conscious Protestants.

Ageing in Faith: Rebirth and Regeneration

By the second half of the seventeenth century, Protestantism had become a geron-tocracy. Celebratory biographies of old people as models of pious longevity pro-liferated. The virtues of elderly 'saints' cast the vices of the inveterate sinners who were their peers into sharp relief. The death of the 'very aged and religious matron' Frances Walbank inspired a sermon on Psalm 16:31 ('The hoary head is a crowne of Glory') and an exhortation to its hearers to walk in the ways of righteousness and 'shine as lights in the midst of a crooked generation'. 'Living monuments of Honour', the elderly were 'God's deputies and vice-roys here in the world'.[170] The gentlewoman Anne Mickle-thwait was a veritable Dorcas, whose advanced years rendered her 'disciple-ship the more Honourable' and whose conversation was 'a dayly sermon to the young women about her'.[171] Mrs Martha Hasselborn, who expired on 13 March 1695 in her ninety-fifth year, faced her end with 'admirable Calmness and Resignation, and long continued Faith and Hope...dropping into the Grave like Fruit from the Tree, when "tis fully Ripe"' and serenely uttering the words 'I waited patiently for the Lord.' Like Sarah in the Bible, who had reached 127, she was 'a long example of Piety, to the very last step of Humane Life'.[172]

The yardstick against whom godly old men were compared was Abraham, who had died aged 175, some way short of the biblical record holder, Methuselah, who had reached 969 (Fig. 1.6). John Dethick, father of a former Lord Mayor of London, was 'the picture of a good old man'. He was more than 90 when he died, 'an age that did as kindly ripen him for the Grave as that of Abraham'. Like the latter, Dethick grew in faith as he grew in years.[173] John La Motte, son of Walloon refugees

---

[169] *A pleasant [d]ialogue between a protestant school-boy, and a popish priest concerning the present times* (1698; Wing P2541A).

[170] Thomas Hodges, *The hoary head crowned. A sermon preached at Brackley at the funerall of Frances Walbank. A very aged and religious matron* (1652; Wing H2320), pp. 31, 9, 10.

[171] Josiah Hunter, *Dorcas revived the second time: or a sermon preached at the funeral of Mrs Anne Mickle-thwait* (1660; Wing H3765B), p. 33.

[172] Timothy Rogers, *The happiness of a quiet mind both in youth and old age...in a discourse occa-sioned by the death of Mrs Martha Hasselborn, who died March 13th, 1695/6 in the 95th year of her age* (1696; Wing R1851), pp. 4–5, 104.

[173] William Knapp, *Abraham's image in one of his sonnes: or the picture of a good old man* (1658; Wing K667), p. 33.

Fig. 1.6 Methuselah: the longest living patriarch, aged 969. Miscellany of Thomas Trevelyon (1608).

Source: Folger Shakespeare Library, Washington DC, MS V.b.232 (1), fo. 47r. Folger Digital Image Collection.

and alderman of the city of London, was another who was said to have shared the wisdom, judgement, and understanding of the Hebrew patriarch, the grace within him contrasting with the wrinkles and creases outside.[174] While most of those memorialized were of middling and upper-class status, humble parishioners could also be the subject of eulogies. The London artisan Nehemiah Wallington carefully copied into one of his notebooks a 'worthy speech' about 'Old Father Staminate', a true disciple from whose poor cottage emanated fervent and faithful prayers that belied his lack of 'book learning'. 'So Lively did he beare the Image of God in him', commented Wallington, 'that me thought in him Christ Jesus walked alive upon the earth'.[175] The long lives enjoyed by such men enhanced the temptation to present them as mirror images of their biblical archetypes, air-brushing out their personal foibles and failings. Affectionate memory and com-passion for grieving relatives aided this process of editing.

The same is true of Samuel Clarke's mid-seventeenth-century *Lives* of eminent divines. Derived from the funeral sermons delivered by colleagues and friends, these too transformed those whom they commemorated into paragons of godly devotion and Aristotelian moderation. 'Magazeens of religious patterns', they conceived of their subjects as living commentaries on Protestant doctrine. Accordingly, they must be situated on a continuum with prescriptive literature. Shaped by a 'selective but intense amnesia', they were also part of a polemical attempt to defend the benign inclusiveness of the puritan tradition in the face of renewed persecution.[176]

The 'holy gravity' of dedicated ministers such as John Carter, a 'cedar tree' who preached well into his eighties, was encapsulated visually in the engraved por-traits that prefaced their posthumously published works and Clarke's encomiastic *Lives*. William Gouge was said to have resembled Moses 'towards his latter end in his visage' and was his 'exact Effiges' in spirit. Thomas Gataker went prematurely grey, 'which made him to be thought elder than he was, because he had long appeared ancient in the eyes of the world'.[177] John More, 'the Apostle of Norwich', carefully cultivated his persona as a prophet by growing the longest beard of his generation.[178] Such texts offer insight into the cultural values that they simultan-eously helped to disseminate and which in turn served as a template for contem-porary conduct.

---

[174] Fulk Bellers, *Abrahams interment, or, The good old-mans buriall in a good old age* (1656; B1826). See also Chapter 5 below.

[175] FSL, MS V. a. 436 (Notebook of Nehemiah Wallington, 1654), pp. 182–5.

[176] See Patrick Collinson, ' "A Magazeen of Religious Patterns": An Erasmian Topic Transposed in English Protestantism', in idem, *Godly People: Essays on English Protestantism and Puritanism* (1983), pp. 499–525; Peter Lake, 'Reading Clarke's *Lives* in Political and Polemical Context', in Kevin Sharpe and Steven N. Zwicker (eds), *Written Lives: Biography and Textuality, Identity and Representation in Early Modern England* (Oxford, 2008), pp. 293–318, at 311.

[177] Samuel Clarke, *The lives of thirty-two English divines famous in their generations for learning and piety, and most of them sufferers in the cause of Christ* (1677; Wing C4539), pp. 138–9, 234, 242, 260.

[178] J. M. Blatchley, 'More, John', in *ODNB*; Henry Holland, *Herōologia Anglica hoc est clarissimorum et doctissimorum* ([1620]; STC 13582), 209.

The longevity of such individuals was conventionally regarded as a sign of divine blessing. Those who exceeded their allotted span of years were heralded as providential wonders. One broadside described how 80-year-old Mr John Macklin had not only regained his eyesight, hearing, speech, and strength but also grown 'fine young tender hair' on his hitherto bald head. This walking miracle was still to be found living in Northumberland in 1657, aged 116.[179] The status of the aged as figures on the threshold of death accorded their utterances an aura of divine authority. Scripture endorsed the idea that the old were sometimes selected as the conduits of divine messages via prophecies and dreams.[180] Stories about centenarian visionaries and seers who foresaw the future and preached repentance perpetuated a long tradition of reverence for the words of ancient men and women. The prophecies of two old men from Toulouse who claimed to 'be above a thousand years old' were summarized in a Restoration ballad and 155-year-old Margaret Hough of Cheshire was acclaimed as a new Mother Shipton in another published in 1657. Her grumbles about the Commonwealth government and the 'whims whams, and trims trams, new plays and old Games abroad now adaies', as well as her sound prediction of an imminent 'great alteration', acquired prophetic significance during this turbulent time.[181] Strange news of this kind derived its credibility from the widespread assumption that those nearing the end of their lives could be privileged with special insight.

This was replicated at the other end of the age spectrum. Children too were believed to be particularly capable of functioning as vessels of spiritual messages. The Bible teaching that it was 'out of the mouths of babes and sucklings' that the truth would be proclaimed coloured perceptions of young people who made pious pronouncements. The willingness of adults to recognize them as genuine prophets was contingent and limited. William Withers, the son of a Suffolk husbandman, fell into a coma on Christmas Eve 1580 and awoke ten days later to denounce pride and immorality with the vehemence of 'a second Daniel' and 'a learned Divine'. Local ministers and worthies were impressed by this 11-year-old boy who gave eloquent expression to their own moral and ecclesiastical priorities.[182] In general, though, English Protestantism became less

---

[179] *The old mans life renewed by heavenly providence. or, A strange (yet true) relation of one Mr. Macklian [sic], a man of an hundred & sixteen years old* (1657; Wing O206aA). See also William Turner, *A compleat history of the most remarkable providences both of judgment and mercy* (1697; Wing T3345), part II, ch. 32.

[180] Joel 2:28; Acts 2:17.

[181] *The worlds wonder. Giving an account of two old men, lately known and seen in the city of Tholouze in France, who declare themselves to be above a thousand years old a piece* ([1675–80]; Wing W3593). This is summarized in BL, Sloane MS 947, fo. 86r. *A new prophesie: or some strange speeches declared by an old woman living now in Cheshire* ([1657]; Wing N723).

[182] John Phillips, *The wonderfull worke of God shewed upon a chylde whose name is William Withers, being in the towne of Walsam, within the countie of Suffolke* (1581; STC 19877), sigs A8r, B1r–2v. See also Alexandra Walsham, '"Out of the Mouths of Babes and Sucklings": Prophecy, Puritanism and Childhood in Elizabethan Suffolk', in Diana Wood (ed.), *The Church and Childhood*, SCH 31 (Oxford, 1994), pp. 285–99.

open-minded in this area over time. Where early evangelicals were receptive to the possibility that God might deploy children and adolescents to help plant the Gospel, their successors were more inclined to suspect that their premonitions were 'an illusion of Satan'. Just as prophecy had ceased when the apostolic church came of age, so did a Church of England that was settling into permanency begin to turn against juvenile seers who threatened the hegemony of the professional clergy. Along with that of other 'babling and talkative', 'unruly and disordered' people, William Perkins saw their appearance as a sign of the last days of the world.[183] Clerical scepticism about child prodigies was sometimes tempered by a sense that desperate measures were necessary to reclaim sinners resistant to the preaching of ordained ministers and to combat unbelief and atheism. Ecstatic utterances that overturned conventional hierarchies and contradicted official orthodoxies were more liable to be attributed to diabolical delusion.

The vulnerability of the young to satanic assault and temptation was a cultural commonplace, the alter ego of their status as potential divine agents. Diagnoses of demonic possession gave expression to the hermeneutic struggle to decipher the root cause of adolescent malaise and misbehaviour that overturned the natural subservience of sons and daughters to their parents and of laypeople to ordained ministers.[184] As Anna French has argued, they were also a function of contemporary fears and anxieties about the spiritual status of children in the wake of a Reformation that had reduced the soteriological efficacy of the sacrament of baptism.[185] The rash of cases of this kind that occurred in pious Protestant households in the later sixteenth and seventeenth centuries may be seen as somatic signs of the intergenerational conflicts that could arise in intensely religious domestic environments: from the aspiring Derbyshire boy preacher Thomas Darling and Mary Glover, the daughter of a godly London shopkeeper, to the devout but troubled Fairfax children of Fewston in Yorkshire whose tribulations were narrated in a manuscript tract written by their father in the early 1620s.[186] Marked by a mixture of edifying speeches and irreverent outbursts, such episodes provide evidence of religious energies and passions that refused to be neatly channelled in the directions encouraged by adults. The tensions between youth and age that had divided families along confessional lines were now being played out inside them.

[183] William Perkins, *A fruitfull dialogue concerning the end of the world*, in *Workes* (1631; STC 19653b.5), p. 468.
[184] David Harley, 'Explaining Salem: Calvinist Psychology and the Diagnosis of Possession', *AHR*, 101 (1996), 307–30.
[185] Anna French, *Children of Wrath: Possession, Prophecy and the Young in Early Modern England* (Farnham, 2015), pp. 7, 63–4, 78, and chs 3–4.
[186] J. A. Sharpe, 'Disruption in the Well-Ordered Household: Age, Authority and Possessed Young People', in Paul Griffiths, Adam Fox, and Steve Hindle (eds), *The Experience of Authority in Early Modern England* (Basingstoke, 1996), pp. 187–212. For the Fairfax possessions, see *Daemonologia: A Discourse on Witchcraft as it was Acted in the Family of Mr Edward Fairfax, of Fuyston in the County of York, in the Year 1621*, ed. William Grainge (Harrogate, 1882).

On their sickbeds and in the midst of serious illnesses, the young entered a liminal zone in which they commanded the attention and secured the respect of their elders, at least temporarily.[187] The spiritual prowess of those who died before attaining adulthood became legendary. The young Warwickshire gentlewoman Cicely Pickering was a 'vertuous daughter' who 'excelled all others of her sexe and age' and whose knowledge 'oustript' that of people of 'farre longer standing in the Schoole of Christianity'. The dying words of this 12-year-old, a 'matchlesse patterne' of patience in suffering, were so compelling that the preacher of her funeral sermon, John Bryan, thought that she spoke through the Holy Ghost.[188] 'Even from his bairnlie age', William Michel, the son of a Scottish pastor, who died in 1634 aged 24, before he could fulfil his own vocation to become a minister, 'had the wit of a Man, the knowledge of a Scholler, & the carriage of a Christian'.[189] Nathaniel Mather, brother of the more famous Cotton, was only 19 at his death in 1688, but displayed the understanding of one of 90, albeit without the grey hairs that usually attended that venerable age. His tombstone is inscribed with the epitaph 'an aged person' (Fig. 1.7).[190] It embodied the biblical topos that one could be 'young in years, but old in grace', live 'much in a little time' and die 'an hundred years old'.[191] By the later seventeenth century, the exemplary 'early piety' of those who died prematurely had generated a genre of moralistic literature directed towards children themselves, including the popular anthology compiled by James Janeway. Among those he described was the pious 6-year-old boy who preferred praying over playing and read the Scriptures with 'great Reverence, Tenderness and groans...till tears and sobs were ready to hinder him'.[192]

The central feature of the affective and experimental variety of Protestant piety that these texts commemorated was the process of 'regeneration'. Derived from Ephesians 4:22–4, the Pauline idea of casting off 'the old man, which is corrupt according to the deceitful lusts' and taking on the new one 'created in righteousness and true holiness' had been a rallying crying from the earliest days of the Gospel.[193] Over time the associated notion of becoming a new creature in Christ

---

[187] See Hannah Newton, *The Sick Child in Early Modern England, 1580–1720* (Oxford, 2012).

[188] John Bryan, *The vertuous daughter. A sermon preached at Saint Maries in Warwick, at the funeral of the most vertuous and truly religious yong gentlewoman, Mistris Cicely Puckering* (1640; first publ. 1636; STC 3956), sig. A2v, pp. 10–11, 18.

[189] Robert Baron, *Epitaphs upon the untymelie death of that hopefull, learned, and religious youth, Mr William Michel* (Aberdeen, 1634; STC 17857), sig. E2r.

[190] Cotton Mather, *Early piety, exemplified in the life and death of Mr. Nathanael Mather, who...changed earth for heaven, Oct. 17. 1688* (1689; Wing M1096), p. 60.

[191] Hodges, *Hoary head crowned*, p. 15, alluding to 2 Chronicles 34:3 and Isaiah 65:20.

[192] James Janeway, *A token for children being an exact account of the conversion, holy and exemplary lives and joyful deaths of several young children* (1676; Wing J478), pp. 19–26. See also William Bidbanck, *A present for children. Being a brief, but faithful account of many remarkable and excellent things utter'd by three young children, to the wonder of all that heard them* (1685; Wing B2864aA).

[193] See William Tyndale, *A path way i[n]to the holy scripture* ([1536?]; STC 24462), sig. E6r; John Bradford, 'A comparison betweene the old man and the new', in *Godly meditations upon the ten commaundmentes...whereunto is joined...a comparison between the old man and the now [sic]* ([1567];

Fig. 1.7 Tombstone of Nathaniel Mather, 1688, Charter Street Burial Ground, Salem, MA.

Source: Photograph by Joseph R. Modugno.

(2 Corinthians 5:17) seems to have acquired more rather than less importance in the Protestant mind. Some divines equated the 'second birth' of which Scripture spoke with baptism, the 'laver' of regeneration. This tendency was particularly pronounced within the circles of avant-garde conformists, Laudians, and their later seventeenth-century heirs: indicative of the high status they accorded the sacraments, Lancelot Andrewes, John Buckeridge, Edmund Reeve, and Jeremy Taylor all deployed it in these terms.[194]

STC 3493.5), fos 91r–66r [vere 96r]; Thomas Becon, *The demaundes of holy scripture, with answeres to the same* (1577; STC 1718), sigs C2v–3r, F8v–G1r.

[194] Lancelot Andrewes, *XCVI sermons* (1629; STC 606), p. 675; John Buckeridge, *A sermon preached before his majestie at Whitehall, March 22, 1617* (1618; STC 4005), p. 40; Edmund Reeve, *The communion booke catechisme expounded* (1635; STC 20830), pp. 10, 62–3; Jeremy Taylor, *A discourse of baptisme, its institution and efficacy upon all believers* (1652; Wing T315), p. 40.

YOUTH AND AGE 71

For others, however, regeneration was a process that occurred later in life. It was an intensely emotional experience for which people hoped and strove in their search for reassurance that they were among those predestined to salvation. To be regenerated was to be awakened from sin, effectually called, and made a member of the elect. According to Thomas Wilson's *Christian dictionarie* (1612) this 'worke or act of Gods wonderfull power' involved 'our incorporation and ingrafting into Christ by Faith, whereby wee have our spirituall being of Children in the Kingdome of grace, as by Carnall generation we have Naturall Being in the Kingdome of this world'. 'Begotten anew by the Immortall seede of the word', people underwent a 'reformation'.[195] Preachers such as Samuel Hieron described how those whom he had predestined to salvation became the 'adopted' offspring of God, it being his 'good pleasure to admit them into his family' and to make them heirs of eternal happiness. When the regenerate were said to be 'borne of God', he stressed, this was 'a borrowed speech, spiritually to be understood of a new relation, but not of any naturall descent'.[196] In a Christmas sermon of 1602, Robert Abbot similarly spoke of the 'second nativity' of those renewed by the interposition of the Holy Spirit.[197] Based on a series of lectures delivered in Banbury, William Whately's treatise of regeneration entitled *The new birth* of 1618 expounded this theme at greater length. Like the Lancashire puritan Isaac Ambrose's *Prima*, first published in 1650, it went through several editions.[198]

A hallmark of the puritan conversion narratives that emerged in the seventeenth century, the many accounts of regeneration that have come down to us involved processes of self-fashioning and reinvention that were ineluctably coloured by retrospection.[199] The very act of recording was sometimes a stimulus to evangelical rebirth. Looking back to their childhood and youth, diarists and religious autobiographers assimilated their own lives to the tropes about personal metamorphosis set in motion by St Augustine, whose adolescent dalliances with sin and pilfering of fruit from orchards were frequently evoked. In the case of Nehemiah Wallington, conversion was not the result of a single moment of

---

[195] Thomas Wilson, *A Christian dictionarie* (1612; STC 25786), pp. 394–5 and 51.

[196] Samuel Hieron, *The trial of adoption*, in *All the sermons of Samuel Hieron* (1614; STC 13378), pp. 314, 349. See also Stephen Denison, *The new creature. A sermon preached at Pauls Crosse, January 17. 1619* (1619; STC 6607), pp. 73–4.

[197] Robert Abbot, *The exaltation of the kingdome and priesthood of Christ* (1601; STC 51), p. 45.

[198] William Whately, *The new birth: or a treatise of regeneration delivered in certain sermons* (1618; STC 25308); Isaac Ambrose, *Prima the first things... or the doctrine of regeneration, the new birth, the very beginning of a godly life* (1650; Wing A2964). Other texts on this theme include John Andrewes, *The converted mans new birth describing the direct way to go to heaven* (1629; STC 595); Richard Bartlet, *The new birth: in which is brought forth the new creature* (1654; Wing B984); Edward Tharpe, *The new birth, or birth from above presented in foure sermons* (1654; Wing T838).

[199] Patricia Caldwell, *The Puritan Conversion Narrative: The Beginnings of American Expression* (Cambridge, 1983); D. Bruce Hindmarsh, *The Evangelical Conversion Narrative: Spiritual Autobiography in Early Modern England* (Oxford, 2005); Kathleen Lynch, *Protestant Autobiography in the Seventeenth-Century Anglophone World* (Oxford, 2012); Abigail Shinn, *Conversion Narratives in Early Modern England: Tales of Turning* (2018). See also Alec Ryrie, *Being Protestant in Reformation Britain* (Oxford, 2013), pp. 436–41.

revelation but of a prolonged period of struggle for assurance. It entailed repeated rueful recollection of his youthful iniquity and repeated vows to resist temptation (including his addiction to writing itself). Despite being brought up in godliness 'from a childe like yong Timothi', he had lived in a 'vile and sinfull condition', being 'a very forward and disobedient crying childe', given to petty theft and other juvenile misdemeanours. The purchase of a Geneva bible spurred him towards spiritual renewal, but his progress in faith was interrupted by bouts of suicidal despair and moral backsliding.[200] Known only by the initials A.O., another believer lay 'in a sad agony, wrastling with temptations, perplexed between hope and feare' for months until they found comfort by reading a book called *The new birth*.[201] In turn the 'experiences' of these individuals were published to encourage and console 'the new born in Christ, that tho' they are not as it were beyond the Month, or mature enough to go alone', yet they 'were not Still-born' and could indeed call themselves children of the Lord.[202]

Although conversion was often a complex process extending over many years, memory and convention sometimes had the effect of telescoping it into a discrete event. For Samuel Rogers, it was a consequence of hearing a particular sermon that touched his heart around the age of 13 and persuaded him to abandon the hypocrisy of his former life. He too experienced recurrent crises of doubt that were resolved by penitential renewal, one of which he described as 'a second conversion'.[203] The Welsh Presbyterian Christopher Love set aside the 'former pleasures and sinfull pastimes' of his youth and became a 'new borne babe' in his mid-teens through the preaching of William Erbury, whom he ever after revered as 'a father towards a Child'.[204] Philip Henry remembered that 'The Lord was graciously pleased to bring me home effectually' by means of his schoolmaster Richard Burley in 1647.[205] By contrast, Richard Rothwell only received 'the spirit of adoption' and experienced 'the sensible work of grace upon his soul' well into his ministry, after being reproved by a grave colleague for sabbath-breaking. It was the afflicting hand of God in taking away her firstborn baby that brought the gentlewoman Jane Ratcliffe to the knowledge that she was his own adopted daughter. The pangs of this 'New Birth' were as bitter and painful as labour itself.[206] An anonymous narrative among the papers of the Fortescue family of Devon describes 'the signe of new Creature begun in me' alongside the mental

---

[200] David Booy (ed.), *The Notebooks of Nehemiah Wallington, 1618–1654: A Selection* (Aldershot, 2007), pp. 31, 265, 266–9.

[201] Vavasour Powel, *Spirituall experiences, of sundry beleevers* (1653; Wing P3095), pp. 87–93, at p. 90. The text in question is probably one of those listed in n. 189 above.

[202] *A collection of experience of the work of grace* (1700; Wing D1827A), p. 39.

[203] *The Diary of Samuel Rogers, 1634–1638*, ed. Kenneth Shipps and Tom Webster, Church of England Record Society (Woodbridge, 2004), p. 3.

[204] BL, Sloane MS 3945, fos 80r–81v.

[205] CRO, DMD/O/1 (Letters and papers of the Henry Family, including extracts from the diary of Philip Henry, *c*.1670s), unfoliated booklet transcribed in 1878.

[206] Clarke, *The lives of thirty-two English divines*, pp. 68, 377.

troubles by which the writer was afflicted after the birth of 'little Gatty' and a subsequent infant. She thanked God that he had raised her up and enabled her 'to see the fruite of my wombe againe with life' and prayed that he might 'give me a heart to Improve it'.[207] In these examples, the corporeal experience of pregnancy and parturition served not merely as a metaphor but also as a catalyst for the spiritual regeneration of the soul.[208]

These motifs of metamorphosis had surfaced in sixteenth-century accounts, such as the history of Thomas Bilney, the Cambridge divine who recorded how he had chanced upon a passage in Erasmus's Latin translation of the New Testament. '[T]hrough God's instruction and inward working', this had exhilarated him, bringing 'a marvellous comfort and quietnesse, in so much, that my brused bones leapt for joy'.[209] Peter Marshall has excavated other evidence of their presence in the early years of the Reformation, prior to the re-emergence of full-blooded conversion narratives in the seventeenth century.[210] Judith Pollmann sees the temporary hiatus in this tradition as a side effect of its determination to dissociate itself from novelty and its preference for stressing the recovery of old truths. She suggests that the model of second birth at the heart of this genre was predicated on assumptions about rupture that were at odds with the reformers' insistence on the unbroken continuity of their religion.[211] While this may underplay Protestantism's capacity to contain and resolve creative tensions, the increased visibility of the conversionary dynamic in reformed piety certainly coincided with its progression from a dissident faith to an established Church. It reflects the eagerness of those whose membership of this institution was involuntary to regain the empowering zeal of the active convert. It also indexes a further species of reformed nostalgia: the desire of serious Protestants to experience the heart-stopping feeling of liberation they projected back onto those who had personally witnessed the early flowering of the Gospel.[212]

Regeneration was a life course event that, looking back from the vantage point of middle age, many located in the time of their youth. Indeed, some even redated their birthdays to the moment when they came to a true understanding of their justification by faith and election through grace. As early as 1536, a Dominican

---

[207] Devon HC, 1262M/O/FZ/2 (Fortescue family papers, volume of thoughts on religious matters, 1664–78), fos 1r, 3r, 4v–5r, 9r.

[208] On this theme, see Victoria Brownlee, 'Literal and Spiritual Births: Mary as Mother in Seventeenth-Century Women's Writing', *RQ*, 68 (2015), 1297–1326; Abigail Shinn, 'Gender and Reproduction in the *Spirituall experiences*', in Simon Ditchfield and Helen Smith (eds), *Conversions: Gender and Religious Change in Early Modern Europe* (Manchester, 2017), pp. 81–101, esp. 88.

[209] Foxe, *Actes and Monuments* (1583 edn), p. 1005.

[210] Peter Marshall, 'Evangelical Conversion in the Reign of Henry VIII', in *idem* and Alec Ryrie (eds), *The Beginnings of English Protestantism* (Cambridge, 2002), pp. 14–37.

[211] Judith Pollmann, 'A Different Road to God: The Protestant Experience of Conversion in the Sixteenth Century', in Peter van der Veer (ed.), *Conversion and Modernities: The Globalization of Christianity* (New York, 1996), pp. 47–64.

[212] See Ryrie, *Being Protestant*, pp. 422–7.

friar who was a follower of Hugh Latimer was known as 'Two-Year-Old'.[213] This quirky practice gathered momentum as Protestantism entrenched itself. Preaching in London in September 1624, Samson Price urged: 'Let us consider how long it is since wee were borne, and, number our years, not from the time of our old birth, but *New birth*.'[214] The godly adopted this custom with alacrity. Ignatius Jurdain, mayor of Exeter, died in 1640 not in the seventy-ninth year of his life, but the sixty-fifth, 'For so long he reckoned since the time of his effectuall Calling'.[215] Lady Elizabeth Langham of Cottesbrook in Northamptonshire, who expired four years later, was said to have esteemed her 'second birth' better than her first, glorying less in her noble blood and earthly pedigree than in having been reborn in Christ.[216] A commemorative sermon occasioned by the demise of the 'most Religious young Lady' Mary Hampson, the only daughter of a Buckinghamshire baronet, in 1677 likewise stressed that her natural descent was less to be celebrated than the fact that via 'the Sacrament of Regeneration' she had 'past into Gods Family, and in Truth did become his Child' in her tender years.[217]

Although conversion was often recalled as an adolescent experience that took place in one's teens, in reality it was no respecter of age. Its unpredictable occurrence destabilized, even as it re-energized a Church that had now moved from infancy and childhood into its adult stages. Protestant mothers and fathers worried as much about facilitating the second birth of their offspring as their first, which, it was said, entailed 'lesser toil'. Until this occurred, declared Joseph Waite's *Parents primer* (1681), every child was in essence 'a dead child' still stained by original sin, notwithstanding their baptism. The sooner their conversion occurred, the closer the relationship between their biological and spiritual age. The longer it was delayed, the greater the misalignment between these two sliding scales. 'An old man converted a little before his death' would accordingly have 'this Epitaph on his Tomb [*Here lies a very Old Man of 3 years old*]'.[218]

Conversion was a vital, if turbulent juncture in the Christian life course, a key stage in what contemporaries frequently described as a 'race'. But it was by no means the end of their journey in faith. The elect passed through a series of stages

[213] 'Two-year-old' is cited in Marshall, 'Evangelical Conversion', p. 32.

[214] Samson Price, *The two twins of birth and death* (1624; STC 20334), p. 22.

[215] Clarke, *Lives of thirty-two English divines*, p. 407.

[216] Simon Ford, *Hesychia Christianou, or A Christian's acquiescence in all the products of divine providence* (1665; Wing F1485), p. 169. Similarly William Fawcit's 'second-birth [did] qualifie him more then his first birth, whereby hee became the very Top and Honour of all his kindred': Edmund Layfield, *The soules solace* (1632; STC 15334), p. 118.

[217] *A commemoration sermon...Occasioned by the death of a most religious young Lady Mary Hampson* (1678; Wing C5545A), p. 19.

[218] See *The fathers legacy: or counsels to his children in three parts* (1678; Wing F555), p. 166; Joseph Waite, *The parents primer and the mothers looking glasse* (1681; Wing W222), pp. 128–9. Augustine's mother Monica was said to have been 'more troubled at the second birth of her sonne, then at the first': Samuel Burrowes, *Good instructions for all youngmen and maides* (1642; Wing B6135), p. 9. See also Chapter 4 below.

on their way to glorification in heaven, including justification and sanctification.[219] Some envisaged this as a process resembling botanical growth. An engraved 'emblem' tracing the path from conception to resurrection at the Last Judgement published around 1639 takes the form of 'The tree of man's life'.[220] For others it was generational in another sense. Reinvigorating an ancient paradigm rooted in Neoplatonism and Christianized by Augustine and Aquinas, spiritualists described the several ages of the soul that followed its rebirth. The system of spiritual perfection developed by the Dutch mystic David Joris depicted progression to eternal life in diagrams that took the form of concentric circles divided by grades, times, and days. This left its mark on the thinking of Hendrik Niclaes, the founder of the Family of Love, which took root in England in the 1550s. Through baptism and regeneration believers became 'godded with God' and transformed into new creatures. They advanced towards religious maturity in a manner akin to their movement through the human life cycle. H. N. spoke of those who had 'growen-upp obedientlie in the Service of the Love; from the Youngnes of their Understandinge, till unto the Old-aige of the Man Christ' and made it clear that those who did not join the Family were damned.[221] His own spiritual precocity was exemplary: aged 8, he had reputedly disputed with his father's confessor so learnedly that his opponent could not decide whether this was 'childishnesse' or godly wisdom.[222]

Within mainstream Protestantism the allegory of the ages of man was equally resonant. No one elaborated it more assiduously than the ejected Congregationalist minister Ralph Venning. His posthumously published *Christ's school* (1675) identified four classes of regenerate believers: babes, little children, young men, and fathers. These categories denoted not stages of human life but degrees of spiritual attainment. 'Of all Saints', he wrote, 'the Babe-Saint hath the least grace and the most corruption.' All had an obligation to set aside 'Babish-carnality' and to strive 'to grow up to be Fathers in Israel and gray-hair'd in righteousness'. Yet even 'a Father saint', Venning declared elsewhere, 'is but a child'. He modestly described himself as a young man at best. His text highlights the widespread perception that numerical age and level of maturity in faith often diverged.[223] The processes of

[219] See William Perkins, *A golden chaine* (1600; STC 19646), chs 36–8, 48.
[220] *The tree of man's life, or an emblem declareing the like* ([1639–50]). BM, 1847,0723.10.
[221] H[endrik] N[iclaes], *Exhortatio. I. The first exhortation of H.N. to his children, and to the famelye of loue. by him newlye perused, and more distinctlye declared* ([Cologne], 1574; STC 18557.5), p. 43.
[222] For the medieval heritage, see Dove, *Perfect Age*, ch. 6. David Joris, *T'Wonder boeck* ([Vianen, 1584]; first publ. 1542). I am grateful to Gary Waite for drawing this text to my attention. H. N., *Exhortatio I* ([Cologne, 1574]; STC 18557), fo. 43r; Tobias, *Mirabilia opera dei: certaine wonderful works of God which hapned to H. N. even from his youth* (1650; STC 24095), pp. 10–13. I owe this reference to Emily Robson.
[223] Ralph Venning, *Christ's school consisting of four classes of Christians: I. Babes, II. Little children, III. Young men, IV. Fathers* (1675; Wing V201), pp. 66, 235, 379; idem, *Canaans flowings. Or a second part of milk & honey* ([1654]; Wing V199), p. 47. For a fuller discussion, see my 'Second Birth and the Spiritual Lifecycle in Early Modern England', in Caroline Bowden, Emily Vine, and Tessa Whitehouse (eds), *Religion and the Lifecycle in Early Modern England* (Manchester, 2021), pp. 17–39.

regeneration and rebirth that featured so prominently in Protestant piety in the seventeenth century were both intensely emotional and unpredictable. Sometimes they converged with confessional boundary-crossing. Celebrated as converts by one side and denounced as apostates on the other, individuals who abandoned one Church for another were themselves in search of a kind of second birth. They were people yearning to reach a higher state of grace and to grow in Christ. The pungent apologetic that accompanied such shifts of allegiance occludes the internal evangelical upheavals and 'turnings' that brought about decisions to defect from an institution within which they no longer believed they could find eternal salvation.[224] James Wadsworth's *English Spanish pilgrime* (1629) presented his return to 'the bosome of his true mother the Church of England' as a rebellion against the adopted faith of his father, a graduate of Emmanuel College who had been 'perverted' to popery in 1604 and sent his son to be educated in St Omer, from whence he returned to Madrid to serve in the army of Philip III. James's conversion coincided with him reaching the age of 18, attaining his 'yeeres of discretion' and reading Scripture and religious controversy.[225] Challenging the unity of families and providing ammunition for competing clerical hierarchies, such episodes shed further light upon the complex interconnections between the spiritual life cycle and its biological counterpart.

Rejecting and Perfecting Reformation

Roman Catholicism provides another laboratory in which this relationship can be explored. Approaching the English Catholic community from the perspective of the generations revitalizes old debates about the role of continuity and tradition, conversion and mission, in its making. Whether we accord more importance to the recusant Marian clergy who helped arrest the death of the medieval Church or the Tridentine priests who assisted in forging what John Bossy prefers to call a sect, we confront the paradoxical fact that by the 1570s and 1580s the revival of the Old Religion was spearheaded by a movement of youth. The exodus of academic exiles to the Low Countries and Italy in the 1550s and 1560s was followed by a second wave of younger men eager to enter the seminaries, committed to returning to England to reclaim their misguided countrymen from heresy, and inflamed by the desire to become martyrs of the Counter-Reformation. By the

---

[224] Michael Questier, *Conversion, Politics and Religion in England, 1580–1625* (Cambridge, 1996), esp. ch. 3.

[225] James Wadsworth, *The English Spanish pilgrime* (1629; STC 24926), p. 77. See Abigail Shinn, 'Father Figures: Paternal Politics in the Conversion Narratives of Thomas Gage and James Wadsworth', in Hannah Crawforth and Sarah Lewis (eds), *Family Politics in Early Modern Literature* (Basingstoke, 2013), pp. 211–28.

late sixteenth century, remarks Susan Brigden, it was Catholicism rather than Protestantism that 'had the appeal of exotic and forbidden fruit'.[226]

As Lucy Underwood's careful study of the *Responsa scholarum* of the English Colleges at Rome and Valladolid has shown, most of those who entered seminaries in the Elizabethan era were adolescents. Mediated by the scribes who recorded their replies to extensive questionnaires about their lives prior to arrival, these documents afford glimpses of youths who severed ties with their families in order to join the Catholic Church. Between 1598 and 1619, nearly 62% of those admitted in Rome said that they were converts, two-thirds of whom professed that this had occurred before the age of 21, with a significant proportion being under 14. Frequently the flight of these youths from 'schism' or Protestantism appears to have been accompanied by conflict with their fathers and mothers, though these narratives, like those about early evangelicals, bear the imprint of inherited stereotypes of intergenerational rebellion. They also allowed young men to criticize church-papist parents who preferred a life of lax conformity to 'perfect union' with the true Church, or, worse still, languished in the 'darkness of heresy' and required urgent spiritual help. They sanctioned disrespect for misguided heretical elders and gave licence to subversions of the age hierarchy. They correlated becoming Catholic with advancing into adulthood. Recusancy and formal reconciliation with the Church of Rome through absolution were envisaged as rites of religious passage, regardless of the age at which they occurred.[227] Henry Chaderton, who entered the English College aged 46 or 47 in 1559, determined to become a Jesuit, described his long journey out of Protestantism, which included a period of study at Douai, where 'though bearded and 26, he began rudiments with schoolboys aged 7 to 12'.[228]

Histories and memoirs of the foundation of the English seminaries cemented the impression that it was 'an influx of young men from England flying from heresy' who had spearheaded this movement. Robert Persons insisted that the students who petitioned for the transformation of the English hostel in Rome into a Jesuit college were possessed less by 'a youthful spirit of sedition and tumult' than by commendable zeal for the future of the Catholic faith in England. The ejection of the warden, Dr Morrice Clennock, a man 'much advanced in years', was presented as a victory for a younger and more ardent generation. Age was an

---

[226] Brigden, 'Youth and the English Reformation', 67.

[227] Lucy Underwood, 'Youth, Religious Identity and Autobiography at the English Colleges in Rome and Valladolid, 1592–1685', *HJ*, 55 (2012), 349–74. See also *eadem*, 'Catholics', in French (ed.), *Early Modern Childhood*, pp. 149–50; *eadem*, *Childhood, Youth and Religious Dissent in Post-Reformation England* (Basingstoke, 2014), chs 1–2; *eadem*, 'Persuading the Queen's Majesty's Subjects from their Allegiance: Treason, Reconciliation and Confessional Identity', *Historical Research*, 89 (2016), 246–67.

[228] *The Responsa Scholarum of the English College, Rome, Part One: 1598–1621*, ed. Anthony Kenny, CRS 54 (1962), p. 55.

exacerbating element in the 'domestical difficulties' of the English mission.[229] A hostile perspective on this early modern student revolt was provided by Anthony Munday's racy exposé of his 'Romayne lyfe' published in 1582 after he had rejoined the Protestant fold.[230]

Scurrilous anti-Catholic tracts that uncovered the practice of seducing innocent young girls to enter foreign nunneries without parental consent responded to another dimension of the traffic of young converts across the Channel.[231] The obituaries of religious women preserved by their convents provide further evidence of how childish dissidence was both memorialized and sanctified. Although most of those who entered as novices were the daughters of 'vertuous Catholics', some did so against the will of their parents. In 1663, Catherine Holland defied her Protestant father and converted in order to enter an Augustinian cloister in Bruges and escape 'the Slavery of Marriage'. Begging his pardon, she refused his offer of liberty of conscience if she returned home, after which he ceased writing to the daughter who 'had forsaken him, and strayed from his Obedience'. Following her mother's death, she became 'a Stranger to all the rest of my Kindred'.[232] The dates on which such women were professed and took their final vows became their birthdays as well as their wedding anniversaries. Often coinciding with the adoption of a religious vocation, the conversion of the soul was conceived as a second nativity in the Catholic no less than in the Protestant world.[233] Their inner spiritual journeys were mapped onto the life cycle. The fifty panels that comprise the 'Painted Life' of Mary Ward, who founded the controversial Congregation of Jesus or Institute of the Blessed Virgin Mary, trace her path from infancy to death. Commissioned and produced after her death in 1645, they tell the story of a precociously devout child whose first uttered word was 'Jesus' and who grew up to become the foundress of an order of unenclosed missionary nuns (Fig. 1.8).

Back in England, those who had chosen obedience to God over obedience to their earthly elders became the stuff of hagiographical legend. The corporal chastisements of Alice Harrison, who was converted by reading Catholic books and cut adrift by her parents, were described as 'persecutions'.[234] A *vita* of John Maxey,

---

[229]   Robert Persons, 'A Storie of Domesticall Difficulties', in *Miscellanea II*, CRS 2 (1906), pp. 96–9.

[230]   Anthony Munday, *The English Romayne lyfe* (1582; STC 18272).

[231]   Thomas Robinson, *The anatomy of the English nunnery at Lisbon in Portugall* (1622; STC 21123), pp. 8–9; John Gee, *The foot out of the snare* (1624; STC 11704), pp. 66–70; *idem*, *New shreds of the old snare* (1624; STC 11706), pp. 113–20.

[232]   Catherine Holland, 'How I Came to Change my Religion', transcribed and edited from a manuscript in the English Convent of Nazareth in Bruges as an appendix to Victoria Van Hyning, *Convent Autobiography: Early Modern English Nuns in Exile* (Oxford, 2020), pp. 267–341, quotations at pp. 314–17.

[233]   See, e.g., BL Add. MS 5813, fos 32r–33r; Leon de Vennes, *The second nativity of Jesus, the accomplishment of the first (viz) the conversion of the soul* (Antwerp, 1686: Wing P526A).

[234]   John Kirk, *Biographies of English Catholics in the Eighteenth Century*, ed. John Hungerford Pollen and Edwin Burton (1909), pp. 111–12, 262–3.

Fig. 1.8 The birth of Mary Ward, first panel of the *The Painted Life of Mary Ward* (oil, Germany, 17th century).

Source: Geistliches Zentrum Maria Ward, Augsburg. © Congregatio Jesu MEP. Photograph: Tanner/ Nesselwang.

who entered the English College at Valladolid in 1602, told how his own father had betrayed him to the authorities when he returned to England as a missionary in 1616 and wished that his body be buried in the prison rubbish heap.[235] Robert Persons transcribed the inspiring letter that the Cornish youth and Douai student John Typpett penned from his cell in Newgate Prison in response to his father's threat to disown him after he was sentenced to be whipped and branded in 1578. Undaunted, Typpett told how the sacrifice of the martyrs had kindled 'the love of the Catholic faith in the hearts of us boys and children, as the excessive desire of worldly goods has the power of stifling it in the hearts of you old folk'. If he was indeed cast off, he wrote, 'then God alone shall be my Father, whose holy Providence will not fail me', unlike his earthly one 'which must soon return to dust'.[236] Others endured 'a kind of martyrdom' at the hands of the 'hot heretics' who were their schoolmasters: George Jerningham and his brother, who bore their punishments with patience, were commemorated in the Chronicle of

---

[235] Edwin Henson (ed.), *Registers of the English College at Valladolid 1589–1862*, CRS 30 (193), p. 72n.
[236] Persons, 'A Storie of Domesticall Difficulties', in *Miscellanea II*, pp. 80–2.

St Monica's of Louvain in the midst of a mini-biography of their religious sister Christina.[237]

Recounted in the Jesuit Annual Letters and absorbed into the community's arsenal of exemplary narratives, these and other episodes idealized adolescent insubordination. They reflect the inversions of the age hierarchy that were celebrated during the first phase of the Catholic response to the Tudor Reformations.[238] Some young people who aspired to sainthood have largely disappeared from the historical record. The visions of 14-year-old Elizabeth Orton from Flintshire in support of recusancy, purgatory and the Mass in the spring of 1581 were heralded as divine revelations in a manuscript tract that circulated clandestinely among local Catholics. Her ecstasies also inspired several of her classmates to refuse to attend Protestant services. Compelled to confess that she had been coached to fabricate these by the 'vile runnagate papist' who was her village schoolmaster in front of a congregation at Chester Cathedral, this holy maid of Wales became the subject of a mocking pamphlet by the soldier-poet Barnaby Rich which sealed her reputation as a false prophetess. Her public humiliation as a fraud has overshadowed her significance as a symbol of the Elizabethan Counter-Reformation's status as an episode of youthful rebellion.[239] Theologically predisposed to identify signs of spiritual grace in children, Catholics pinned their hopes and dreams of overthrowing the Protestant regime on young people.

The tropes of role reversal embodied in such stories find extended expression in Robert Southwell's famous epistle to his elderly father exhorting him to forsake the world and embrace the true faith, first published in 1597. The humble opening from a 'dutifull sonne' acknowledges the respect he owes to his natural progenitor but explains why he must now 'open a vent to my zealous affection, which I have so long smothered and suppressed in silence'. Though a father has preeminence over the body of his offspring, in the sphere of the soul both are 'of equall proximity' to God. Despite the diversity in 'the degrees of our carnall consanguinity', devotion to Christ trumps earthly hierarchies. Hence Southwell's audacity in tutoring his parent, a task in which he claims the warrant of Scripture, which repeatedly demonstrates that God does not 'measure his endowments by number of yeeres'. 'Hoary senses are often couched under greene lockes and some are riper in the springe, then others in the Autumne of their age.' Presenting

---

[237] *The Chronicle of the English Augustinian Canonesses Regular of the Lateran, at St Monica's in Louvain*, ed. Adam Hamilton, 2 vols (Edinburgh, 1906), ii. 40–1.

[238] See Alison Shell, '"Furor Juvenilis": Post-Reformation English Catholicism and Exemplary Youthful Behaviour', in Ethan H. Shagan (ed.), *Catholics and the 'Protestant Nation': Religious Politics and Identity in Early Modern England* (Manchester, 2005), pp. 185–206; Lucy Underwood, 'Recusancy and the Rising Generation', *BCH*, 31 (2013), 511–33.

[239] Barnaby Rich, *The true report of a late practise enterprized by a papist, with a yong maiden in Wales* (1582; STC 21004); NLW, Great Sessions (Flintshire Gaol Files), 4/970/5/19 (Certificate of recusants, April 1581). For a full account of this episode, see my 'The Holy Maid of Wales: Visions, Imposture, and Catholicism in Elizabethan Britain', *EHR*, 132 (2017), 250–85.

himself as a physician supplying 'medicinable receites against your ghostlye mala-
dyes', he reminds his father that he is now 'in the waining' of his years and on his
'finall voyage...not far of from the stint and period of your course'. He earnestly
implores him to set aside the 'cravant [craven] cowardice of flesh and bloud' and
repent before it is too late. The letter ends with a crescendo of rhetorical questions
that enshrine the uncompromising assertion that its recipient cannot hope to find
salvation in his current state. It evokes a vision of the 'weeping & gnashing of
teeth' in hell, to which he will descend unless he takes steps to return to 'the folde
of Gods flocke'. This is a text in which the supreme imperative of ensuring spiritual regeneration supplants the structures of deference associated with biological
generation.[240]

The tone of N. N's 1623 *Epistle* of a young gentleman imprisoned for his religion sent to his Protestant father explaining his motives for conversion was less
domineering, but it too described its subject's religious transformation as involving the exchange of a natural parent for the tender one he has in heaven. His
father apparently carried the original letter about with him, showed it in public
places, and made it 'his common Table-discourse' in taverns and inns, though
whether in pride or in contempt is unclear.[241] The other side of the story is provided by a didactic dialogue entitled *A mothers teares over hir seduced sonne*
(1627), in which the latter ('now at Doway') is implored to forsake the harlot who
has seduced him, come out of Babylon and Sodom, and return to his ageing and
affectionate parents, who are 'as full of griefs as yeares'. As well as providing
instruction to her own prodigal child, this anonymous text speaks to a second
reader, who is likewise in need of instruction as 'a child in yeares or understanding'. For all its familiar formulae, it too illuminates the heartache of a family
severed by a son's overpowering conviction that his mother's demands are 'unjust'
and 'unnaturall'.[242]

These published works find parallels in manuscript, including the poignant
private letter that the Nottinghamshire gentleman Robert Markham wrote to his
mother and father following 'his departure beyond the seas' in August 1592.
Begging pardon for his decision to embrace the Catholic faith, he beseeched them

---

[240] Robert Southwell, *An epistle of a religious priest unto his father: exhorting him to the perfect for-
saking of the world* ([1597?]; STC 22968.5), pp. 1, 4–5, 11, 9, 15, 23, 29, 26, 46. This was appended to *A
short rule of good life*. A later edition was printed at St Omer in 1622 (STC 22970). See Hannah
Crawforth's insightful discussion in '"A father to the soul and a son to the body": Gender and
Generation in Robert Southwell's *Epistle to his father*', in Simon Ditchfield and Helen Smith (eds),
Conversions: Gender and Religious Change in Early Modern Europe (Manchester, 2017), pp. 61–80.
The text also deliberately inverts the genre of the father's legacy or advice to his son, on which,
see Chapter 6 below.

[241] N. N., *An epistle of a Catholicke young gentleman, (being for his religion imprisoned.) To his
father a Protestant who commaunded him to set downe in writing, what were the motives that induced
him to become a Catholicke* (Douai, 1623; STC 18330), sig. A2r–v.

[242] *A mothers teares over hir seduced sonne: or, a dissuasive from idolatry* (1627; STC 24903.5),
sigs A6r, B3v, pp. 1. On the genre of mother's legacies, see Chapter 6 below.

to read the few lines he penned with so many tears that he could hardly see to write and with such 'ynward greef' that he could not 'endure to read them' again. He knew that his 'hasty jorney' would greatly pain them and that his reconciliation with Rome would 'hazard the stayning of our house and name with treason' but hoped that they would forgive him when they knew how tormented in conscience and 'distract of sences' he had been. He closed desiring their daily blessing and wishing them every prosperity. Freighted with emotion, Markham's letter exasperated his father, who sent it on to Lord Burghley as evidence of 'hys lewde and undutyfull practyce', evidently hoping this would be sufficient to prevent him from being tainted by association with his son's disloyalty. Robert's intention to pursue a military career raised the terrifying spectre of treason: his father implored him to pledge never to fight for Spain against the queen, and his elder brother urged him to turn his militant tendencies against the Ottoman Turks instead.[243]

This pattern of fracture was repeated in subsequent decades. The conversion of the young Tobie Matthew to Catholicism in Florence in 1607 caused a considerable stir in the Church of England and was a source of extreme embarrassment to his father, who had only recently been elevated to the archbishopric of York. Tobie's stubborn persistence tried and tested his parents, though their attempts to persuade him to return to the Protestant faith in which he had been born and baptized were usually done rather 'by sighes and short wishes' than by 'long discourses' and fierce strictures. His mother, who was 'wont to be as busie with scripture, as if it had been some glove upon her fingars ends', frequently told him that she prayed for his soul. His own reciprocal intercessions for hers went unheeded in turn. As he recalled in 1640, she 'went out of the world, more like an ignorant childe of foure yeares old, then like a talking Scripturist of almost forescore'. In short, he was ashamed of her.[244] Tobie's autobiography attests to the gulf of mutual incomprehension that had opened up between the generations.

Augustine Baker's memorials of his childhood in the 1560s are suffused by the same sense of embarrassment and disjuncture. In them, he lamented the lukewarm religion of his parents, who had been reduced by the simple passage of time to mere 'neutrals in religion, viz. neither indeed true Catholicks, for perfect knowledge, belief and practice, nor yet meer Protestants or otherwise heretickes in their belief, though schismaticall, by their externall accommodation of themselves to the schismaticall service of the English Church', and who consequently stood in grave risk of damnation. In the wake of his own successful conversion from 'profane atheism', he spoke of them condescendingly but affectionately as if

---

[243] BL, Lansdowne MS 72, fos 121r, 122r; *Markham Memorials*, ed. Clements Markham, 2 vols (1913), i. 103–7.

[244] FSL, MS V.a.269 ('A true historicall Relation of the Conversion of Tobie Matthew to the holie Catholick Fayth; with the antecedents and consequents therof'), quotations at pp. 219–20, 223–5.

they were children.[245] Infantilized by heresy, they fulfilled the stereotype of elderly impiety that found a mirror image on the other side of the confessional divide.

However, the tensions between parents and children reflected in the foregoing examples should not be overstated. While Catholic martyrologies are littered with edifying stories of interfamilial conflict, their compilers also made polemical mileage out of cases where young and old were in close ideological alignment. The mother of the Somerset layman John Bodye, executed at Andover in 1583, celebrated his heroic sacrifice by making 'a great Feaste to her neighbors, as her sonnes marriage day'.[246] When the Staffordshire-born priest William Hartley was hanged, drawn, and quartered on 5 October 1588, his mother was one of the witnesses, 'rejoicing exceedingly that she had brought forth a son to glorify God by such a death'.[247] The contradictory images that coexist in the pages of hagiography make it a deceptive hall of mirrors as a source for gauging the intergenerational dynamics of the English Counter-Reformation.

Like Protestantism, Catholicism accorded great importance to education. Among the indulgences Pope Gregory XIII granted at the request of William Allen in 1576 was the promise that those that 'teachethe yong folkes & other ignorant p[er]sons to forsake suche principles as they have learnyd of heretyckes & shall instructe them [in] ye catholicke faythe shall gaine an hundred years of pardone'.[248] Schoolmasters and parents were both expected to play their part in preventing the haemorrhage of children from the old faith. Catechizing was as vital an arm of the struggle to reverse the Reformation as it was to plant it. Initially written for the benefit of the 'young Schollers' he taught in exile in Louvain, Laurence Vaux's little catechism of 1568 was intended for the instruction of 'children and ignorant people' in England.[249] Other manuals followed, including translations from famous Jesuit catechisms written by Peter Canisius and Robert Bellarmine. Like their Protestant counterparts, these too sought to supply 'holsome milke' for 'infants and sucking babes' and 'strong meate' for those more advanced in their faith.[250] Raising the next generation went hand in hand with re-educating adults who had lapsed into heresy and schism and transforming

---

[245] *Memorials of Augustine Baker*, ed. McCann, p. 16.   [246] AAW/HIS/A/4/22, p. 118.

[247] Richard Challoner, *Memoirs of Missionary Priests*, ed. John Hungerford Pollen (1924), p. 150.

[248] Aelred Watkin, 'Sixteenth-Century Indulgences for English Catholics', *Downside Review*, NS 38 (1939), 46–54, at 48.

[249] Laurence Vaux, *A catechisme, or a Christian doctrine necessarie for chyldren and the ignorant people* ([Louvain, 1568]; STC 24625.5), 'The Author to the Reader' (sigs A3r–[4]v).

[250] *Certayne necessarie principles of religion, which may be entituled, a catechisme conteyning all the partes of the Christian and Catholique faith* (Douai [London], [1579–80?]; STC 4568.5), sigs ¶3r–7v. Peter Canisius, *A summe of Christian doctrine*, trans. Henry Garnet ([1592–6]; STC 4571.5); Robert Bellarmine, *A shorte catechisme...Illustrated with the Images*, trans. Richard Gibbons (Augsburg, 1614; STC 1843); *An ample declaration of the Christian doctrine*, trans. Richard Hadock (Douai, [1604]; STC 1836); Jacobus Ledisma, *The Christian doctrine in manner of a dialogue betweene the master and the disciple* (1597; STC 15353).

individuals of all ages into confessionally self-conscious adherents of a Church under the cross.[251]

The young Catholics who thrust themselves into the limelight must not been allowed to eclipse those in the middle and later phases of life. It is also important to acknowledge the substantial number of older lay Catholics who appear in official records. Visitation data from Yorkshire in 1615 reveals that more than 60% of adults returned as recusants were in their forties and 40% over the age of 50. While it is tempting to attribute the high proportion of the elderly here to survivalism, several of those presented appear to have been recent converts, a tribute to the vitality of the mission on the north York moors. Yet the visibility of the old in this and other Catholic communities may itself be an optical illusion, a product of the possibility that as people aged and relinquished their social and domestic responsibilities, they withdrew into recusancy. Like Protestant conformity, Catholic dissent may partly be an artefact of life cycle stage.[252]

By the mid-seventeenth century, it is clear that converts made up a much smaller proportion of those admitted to seminaries, colleges, and convents, most of whom were the children of families who had taken in the faith with their mothers' milk. Missionary priests who evaded arrest became revered figures within the de facto parishes they served over many years. William Barrow, alias Harcourt, entered the Society of Jesus in 1632 at the age of 23, but he was not sent back to England until 1646, where he laboured for three and a half decades before being caught up in the storm surrounding the Popish Plot. At the time of his apprehension in London in 1679, aged 70, he was 'venerable for his grey hairs...having been reserved till this time to meet with that death which he had every day prayed for for twenty years'.[253] The normal order of patriarchal relations was gradually restored at the same time as the community became increasingly tight-knit and endogamous. Resistance to Protestantism less frequently required young men and women to repudiate their parents, and vice versa. Catholicism regained its status as a hereditary faith. The Counter-Reformation had itself come of age.

It is probably no coincidence that this period witnessed a concomitant shift in the character of Catholic catechisms and their transformation into instruments for the inculcation of household religion. In Thomas Vincent's *Childes catechism* (1678) the father quizzes his child. After 1700, many others were prepared for gentlemen's children and the rural poor over whom they had paternal direction,

---

[251] See Underwood, *Childhood, Youth and Religious Dissent*, ch. 3; Alexandra Walsham, 'Wholesome Milk and Strong Meat: Peter Canisius's Catechisms and the Conversion of Protestant Britain', *BCH*, 32 (2015), 293–314. For the broader European project, see Karen E. Carter, *Creating Catholics: Catechism and Primary Education in Early Modern France* (Notre Dame, IN, 2011), esp. chs 1–3.
[252] Bill Sheils, 'Household, Age and Gender among Jacobean Yorkshire Recusants', in Marie B. Rowlands (ed.), *Catholics of Parish and Town 1558–1778* (1999), pp. 144–6.
[253] Challoner, *Memoirs of Missionary Priests*, p. 526.

whose illiteracy prompted the creation of pictorial 'eye catechisms'.[254] Such texts seem symptomatic of the fact that eighteenth-century Catholicism had largely reconciled itself to its minority status and begun to concentrate on retaining its existing adherents rather than recruiting new ones. Pious myths about intergenerational conflict continued to sustain the community, but its instinct for missionary outreach had partly been displaced by the task of consolidation.

The cycle of generational change I have described may also help to explain the developments within the later Elizabethan and early Stuart Church of England that cumulatively altered its theological, liturgical, and ecclesiological priorities. The challenges to Calvinist predestinarianism that began to emerge in the 1590s, the concurrent and subsequent reorientation of attitudes towards the Church of Rome and England's reformed sister churches, and the reassertion of ceremonies, sacraments, and the 'beauty of holiness' that became a hallmark of Laudianism in the 1630s can fruitfully be illuminated through this prism. The 'avant-garde conformity' that foreshadowed more decisive changes in the direction of the wind was a measure of the distance travelled from the early days of the Reformation and the emergence of a body of clergy who did not remember them first-hand and interpreted their significance differently.[255] Figures like Lancelot Andrewes and Samuel Harsnett, who were born in 1550s and 1560s and grew to manhood in the fourth quarter of the sixteenth century, developed a perspective on their Church's history that nurtured a rival understanding of the apostolic purity its first founders had endeavoured to recover. In turn, they were overtaken by a generation of even younger divines convinced that the Edwardian and Elizabethan Reformation had been betrayed and distorted by a Calvinist faction, among whom John Cosin and Peter Heylyn figure prominently.

The terms in which the Laudian bishop Matthew Wren defended himself against the charges laid against him in the early years of the Long Parliament are telling in this regard. Reducing liturgical practice to what had been previously established ought not to be reputed a 'scandalous Innovation' but rather a judicious 'Renovation' of what had subsequently lapsed into disuse. His own policies imitated those of that 'grave divine' Lancelot Andrewes, who 'had conversed with most of these holy Fathers, which lived in the Church at the beginning of the

---

[254] [Thomas Vincent], *The childes catechism wherein the father questions his child* (Paris, 1678; Wing C3875). See also J. D. Crichton, 'Challoner and the "Penny Catechism"', *RH*, 15 (1981), 425–32; Geoffrey Scott, 'The Poor Man's Catechism', *RH*, 27 (2005), 373–82.

[255] Peter Lake, 'Lancelot Andrewes, John Buckeridge, and Avant-Garde Conformity at the Court of James I', in Linda Levy Peck (ed.), *The Mental World of the Jacobean Court* (Cambridge, 1991), pp. 113–33; Peter McCullough, '"Avant-Garde Conformity" in the 1590s', in Anthony Milton (ed.), *The Oxford History of Anglicanism*, i: *Reformation and Identity, c.1520–1662* (Oxford, 2017), pp. 380–94; Kenneth Fincham and Nicholas Tyacke, *Altars Restored: The Changing Face of English Religious Worship 1547–c.1700* (Oxford, 2007). See also Nicholas Tyacke, *Anti-Calvinists: The Rise of English Arminianism, c.1590–1640* (Oxford, 1987); Anthony Milton, *Catholic and Reformed: The Roman and Protestant Churches in English Protestant Thought 1600–1640* (Cambridge, 1995); idem, *England's Second Reformation: The Battle for the Church of England 1625–1662* (Cambridge, 2021), ch. 1.

Reformation under Queen Elizabeth'. Andrewes, who had been Wren's mentor from his own youth, was his link to the generation that had instituted this 'first Reformation'. 'In as much as New and Old are Terms of Relation, and are said but respectively to former or later Things', his own actions were no more to be sanctioned than those of the first Protestant reformers, whom the papists had similarly condemned as 'novatores' for restoring what had been practised in 'primitive times'. He swiftly turned the allegation of introducing illegal novelties back upon his puritan opponents. It was they who were guilty of perverting the essence of the sixteenth-century settlement. 'Let the old Usages carry it,' he concluded.[256]

Peter Lake's powerful new account of the process by which these trends gained momentum and came to dominate the upper echelons of the ecclesiastical hierarchy during the personal rule of Charles I is partly couched in terms of the dynamic interactions between 'old lags' and 'young Turks'. This was an alliance of individuals of different generations—veterans of the last decade of Elizabeth's reign and clever younger men 'in a hurry' and 'on the make' who saw the opportunity to acquire influence by riding the wave of ideological change that was transforming the Caroline Church. The crucible for the Laudian revolution was, not surprisingly, the universities. Once again cocky students and ambitious early-career ministers in Oxford and Cambridge took pride in publicly deriding and undercutting senior academics, including Regius Professors of Divinity, whose views seemed misguided. These constellations formed alongside others between true believers and fellow travellers and produced a movement that understood itself as an attempt to restore the Church's true catholicity and to reincarnate the original vision of the Reformation.[257] The opposition it faced helped provoke the Civil Wars, but some of those at its forefront weathered the Interregnum to be reinstated and advanced to livings and sees after 1660s and to become elder statesmen of Restoration Anglicanism. By the 1670s and 1680s, the novelty of the style of worship and churchmanship that had precipitated conflict was settling into orthodoxy, at least within some reaches of the Church of England, though it continued to exhibit the capacity to absorb divergent agendas, including forms of Calvinist conformity.[258]

Similar generational patterns can be discerned within the dissenting Protestant tradition, especially the radical sects that flowered in the vacuum created by the collapse of religious regulation and censorship after 1642. These too were movements that seem to have attracted youthful converts. Carried away by the promise

[256] *Parentalia*, ed. Wren, pp. 81, 91, 99. For the same strategy, see Peter Heylyn, *The parable of the tares expounded & applied* (1659; Wing H1729), pp. 324–5.
[257] Peter Lake, *On Laudianism: Piety, Polemic and Politics during the Personal Rule of Charles I* (Cambridge, forthcoming), esp. Part 5, chs 4–5. I am grateful to Professor Lake for permission to cite this in advance of publication.
[258] See esp. Kenneth Fincham and Nicholas Tyacke, *Altars Restored: The Changing Face of English Religious Worship, 1547–c.1700* (Oxford, 2007); Stephen Hampton, *Anti-Arminians: The Anglican Reformed Tradition from Charles II to George I* (Oxford, 2008).

of the dawning millennium and Christ's impending return to reign on earth, young men and women were prominent in the ranks of those who became tub preachers, engaged in unruly revolt against the ecclesiastical establishment, destroyed surplices, prayer books, and Laudian innovations such as altar rails, and generally embraced the opportunity for sexual and moral antinomianism. Or so it seemed to Royalist journalists such as John Taylor, who derided the adolescent basketmakers, hay-weighers, buttonmakers, and chimney sweeps who joined 'peevish Sects' and became 'holy brothers of the separation'.[259] 'In these later times of Reformation', lamented William Harvey in *The sectaries downefall* (1655), 'every beardless Boy, and broken Shop-keeper, will step into a Pullpit, and there (Parrat-like) prate what they know not themselves, and indeed, how should they doe otherwise, when they speake that which God never put in their mouthes'.[260] Intraclerical squabbles in puritan London were also expressed in generational terms: in 1648 John Goodwin lambasted his rival William Jenkyn as a 'yongling Elder, or, Novice-Presbyter', reducing his errors to 'one, or both, of those two unhappy Predicaments of Youth, Ignorance & Arrogance'. In turn, Jenkyn dismissed him as a 'Blinde Guide' or 'Doting Doctor'.[261] Benjamin Keach's anti-paedobaptist tract *War with the devil* (1684) likewise took the form of a dialogue between an old apostate and a young professor.[262]

The topsy-turvy world of the 1640s and 1650s was thus one in which the young were perceived to be disobeying their elders. In his memoirs, Edward Hyde, earl of Clarendon, bemoaned the effects of these anarchic decades:

> parents had no manner of authority over their children, nor children any obedience or submission to their parents…every one did that which was good in his own eyes. This unnatural antipathy had its first rise from the beginning of the rebellion, when the fathers and sons engaged themselves in the contrary parties, the one choosing to serve the king, and the other the parliament.

But it was also, in his eyes, a product of the 'several sects in religion, which discountenanced all forms of reverence and respect, as relics and marks of superstition'.[263] Intoxicated with dangerous ideas that threatened the patriarchal hierarchy and social order, in revolutionary England youth once more seemed to be out of control. Christopher Hill himself suggested that sectarianism might be

---

[259] John Taylor, *A swarme of sectaries, and schismatiques* (1642; Wing T514), pp. 3, 8.

[260] William Harvey, *The sectaries downefall* (1655; Wing H1093A), p. 20.

[261] John Goodwin, *Neophytopresbyteros, or the yongling elder, or, novice presbyter* (1648; Wing G1183), title page; William Jenkyn, *The blinde guide, or the doting doctor* (1648; Wing J645).

[262] Benjamin Keach, *War with the devil: or, the young mans conflict with the powers of darkness* (1678; Wing K104A).

[263] Edward Hyde, *The Life of Edward, Earl of Clarendon, Lord High Chancellor of England…in which is included A Continuation of his History of the Grand Rebellion Written by Himself*, 3 vols (Oxford, 1827), vol. i, pp. 358–9.

seen as a form of contest between the generations and against patriarchal authority in the home.[264]

This was a time when the idea that children might be commissioned to speak prophetically in place of their elders flourished anew. Struck blind and dumb, 16-year-old Sarah Wight's prodigious ability to recite Scripture during her mystical trances made her a celebrity among the godly of Civil War London. The authenticity of her ecstatic experiences was attested by her Congregationalist and later Particular Baptist minister, Henry Jessey, who also wrote *A looking-glass for children*.[265] A decade later the sobering pronouncements made by the 'wise virgin' Martha Hatfield following a convulsive illness became no less famous (Fig. 1.9). They were recounted by her uncle, James Fisher, vicar of Sheffield but

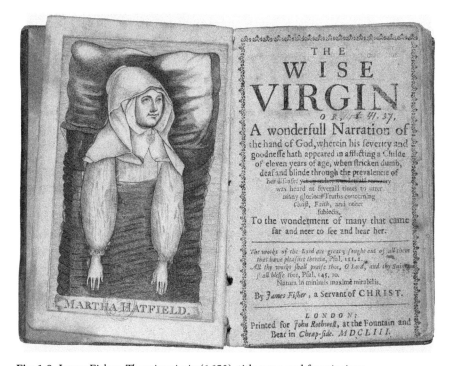

Fig. 1.9 James Fisher, *The wise virgin* (1653), title page and frontispiece.
Source: Cambridge University Library, 8. 41. 37. Reproduced by kind permission of the Syndics.

---

[264] Christopher Hill, *The World Turned Upside Down: Radical Ideas during the English Revolution* (Harmondsworth, 1975), p. 189.
[265] Henry Jessey, *The exceeding riches of grace advanced by the spirit of grace, in an empty creature (viz) Mrs. Sarah Wight* (1658; Wing J692); *idem, A looking-glass for children. Being a narrative of God's gracious dealings with some little children*, ed. H. P. (1673; Wing P29).

also pastor of a gathered congregation in the city, in a tract that co-opted the utterances of this 'poor weak unlikely instrument' to combat the threat to his ministry presented by the Quakers.[266] The revelations of Arise Evans regarding the imminent Apocalypse initially met with a more hostile reception: his neighbours thought he ought to be kept at home by force, because he was 'in the flower of his age, and his bloud boileth in his Veins, and his great strength hath brought him to his Frenzy'.[267] Medical theories about the distinctive humoral make-up of adolescents, combined with long-standing views about the moral ambiguity of youth, continued to shape perceptions of extraordinary behaviour. Tumultuous events provided a temporary sanction for what might otherwise have been dismissed as childish tantrums and diabolical delirium.

They also inspired further episodes of defiance against patriarchy. Agnes Beaumont was 20 when she came under the spell of the charismatic Baptist John Bunyan and joined his congregation at Gamlingay in 1672. When her widowed father heard of this, he locked her out of the house for two days and ordered her to break with Bunyan's church. She agonized before deciding that there was no way to reconcile her conscience with obedience to him, for 'He that forsaketh not father and mother and all that he hath, is not worthy of me.' The clashes that ensued led to the rumours that she had contrived his sudden death and was engaged in an illicit affair with the preacher.[268] But this too was an account coloured by hindsight. It conformed with the model of intergenerational tension embedded in the Bible and reanimated by the turbulent decades of the early Reformation.

Others filtered their experiences through another set of commonplaces we have already encountered, contrasting their religious lives prior to conversion with the state of enlightenment to which they had progressed thereafter. Alluding to St Paul's Epistle to the Corinthians, the Ranter Laurence Clarkson [Claxton] recorded his transformation in terms resonant of the journey from childhood to adulthood, contrasting the routinized puritanism of his youth with the overpowering sense of divine presence that later overtook him: 'My God was a grave, ancient, holy, old man, as I supposed, sat in Heaven in a chair of gold, but as for

[266] James Fisher, The wise virgin. Or, a wonderfull narration of the hand of God, wherein his severity and goodness hath appeared in afflicting a Childe of eleven years of age (1653; Wing F1004). See also Nigel Smith, 'A Child Prophet: Martha Hatfield as the Wise Virgin', in Gillian Avery and Julia Briggs (eds), Children and Their Books (Oxford, 1989), pp. 79–93.
[267] Arise Evans, An echo to the voice of heaven (1652; Wing E3457), p. 32.
[268] Agnes Beaumont, The Narrative of the Persecutions of Agnes Beaumont, ed. Vera J. Camden (East Lansing, MI, 1992), p. 58. On Beaumont, see Bernard Capp, 'The Travails of Agnes Beaumont', in Bronach Kane and Fiona Williamson (eds), Women's Agency and the Law, 1300–1700 (2013), pp. 111–24. Capp offers a wider exploration of this theme in 'Conversion, Conscience, and Family Conflict in Early Modern England', in Tali Berner and Lucy Underwood (eds), Childhood, Youth and Religious Minorities in Early Modern Europe (Basingstoke, 2019), pp. 319–40.

his nature I knew no more than a childe.' His own growth in faith coincided with
a deeper understanding of the Lord less as a distant and domineering father than
as a loving patron and intimate friend closer to his own age.[269]

The Society of Friends provides a particularly revealing illustration of the foregoing themes. Early Quakers revelled in a carnivalesque overturning of the age
and social hierarchies. If their use of the familiar 'thee' and 'thou' and refusal to
doff their hats as a mark of respect to their elders and superiors were disruptive,
impolite, and troubling, the daring forms of protest in which they engaged,
including 'going naked for a sign', were seen as immature in the extreme. This too
was a movement that seemingly spread like wildfire, led by young men such as
James Parnell, who boldly pitted themselves against the authority of ordained
clergymen and compared their encounters to the contest between the little 'strip-
ling' David and the 'proud boaster' Goliath described in the Bible. These were the
terms in which he characterized his dispute with Thomas Drayton, 'an ancient
Country Minister' from Huntingdon, quoting the proverb of Solomon that 'a
poor and wise Child, is better than an old foolish King' and impertinently declaring that even 'a Babe may comprehend thee, and tell thee of thy foly, and when
thy thinkest of thy beard or age (as thou sayest) confusion of face may cover
thee.'[270] Quakers were unapologetic about the household division they fomented,
recalling how Christ had come 'to set at Variance, Father against Son, and son
against Father'. They urged their followers to shun older relatives who tried to
coerce them into abandoning their flirtation with the sect as if they were the very
'Instruments of Satan'.[271] Like early evangelicals and Catholics, they recollected
with pride the sometimes violent intergenerational conflicts that their conversion
created. The autobiography of Thomas Ellwood incorporates an extended account
of his bitter tussles with his father after he began to attend Quaker meetings,
which extended to buffets around the head and 'whirrets on the ear'.[272] When
Richard Davies joined the sect in 1657 and left off the 'dry, dead and formal
Praying' practised by his parents, his father took a staff, beat him violently, and
'against natural Affection...chained him out of Doors in a cold frosty Night'.
Published posthumously by his son for the edification of later Friends, his
testimony resonated with the ingrained commonplace that the early years of

[269] Laurence Clarkson [Claxton], *The lost sheep found, or, The prodigal returned to his fathers house* (1660; Wing C4580), p. 6.
[270] James Parnell, *Goliahs head cut off with his own sword* (1655; Wing P531), title page, pp. 2, 12; Thomas Drayton, *An answer according to the truth, that trembles not, nor quakes, nor quayleth* (1655; Wing D2147), 1.
[271] James Parnell, *A collection of the several writings given forth from the spirit of the Lord* (1675; Wing P528), 67–8. See also Adrian Davies, *The Quakers in English Society, 1655–1725* (Oxford, 2000), pp. 195–201.
[272] Henry Morley (ed.), *The History of Thomas Ellwood Written by Himself* (1885), pp. 53–6, 59, 62.

Quakerism were marked by friction between youth and age and the experience of being hated and forsaken by one's own close relations.[273]

These were struggles that caused anguish to both parties, torn as they were between emotional attachment and ideological commitment. Mothers and fathers concerned about the spiritual fate of their offspring clashed with children convinced that they owed a higher allegiance to God. Disowned by their natural progenitors, some converts sought out surrogate parents and 'tender nurses' and affectionately remembered their role in nurturing their faith in the time of their 'Religious Childhood'.[274] The author of one relation, known only by his or her initials, J. G., recounted how it had pleased the Lord 'to call me from amongst my relations, to bear testimony unto his name' at the tender age of 11. Readers were exhorted to remember that Christ required one to yield 'whatsoever is dear or neer unto him', fathers and mothers, sisters and brothers, and cleave unto him.[275] When Edward Burrough's parents died within ten days of each other, he ignored the call to return home to attend their funerals, reasoning that the departure of 'the old man and old woman, my father and mother according to the flesh' was a lesser priority than publishing the truth.[276]

Unsurprisingly, such cases loomed large in the Quaker imagination. Yet not all of those attracted to the faith did so against the wishes of their elders. Elizabeth Stirredge of Thornbury in Gloucestershire acknowledged the 'honest parents' who had brought her up as a god-fearing child and remembered that her father had 'prophesied the Friends many years before they came', predicting correctly that he would not live to see their appearance.[277] Affection may well have played tricks with Elizabeth's memory, but it is clear that sometimes parents and children joined the sect together or in quick succession. The story told by the accounts of 'convincement' that the early Friends wrote and published so prolifically is not always one involving a war between the generations. It is often one of family concord in the face of oppression. When Alice Hayes became an 'Experimental Witness' of the dealings of the Lord, her father-in-law cursed and threatened her fiercely, but not long afterwards God brought him to a sense of his error

---

[273] *An account of the convincement, exercises, services and travels, of that ancient servant of the Lord, Richard Davies* (1765), p. 39. See also John Crook, 'Truth's Progress', in *The design of Christianity* (1701), p. 264; FHL, MS VOL 62/5, item 27 (Margaret Ellis, 'Concerning my Experience of the Dealings of the Lord with me from my Youth').

[274] Thomas Ellwood, *The history of the life of Thomas Ellwood* (1714), p. 100. See also Naomi Pullin, ' "Children of the Light": Childhood, Youth, and Dissent in Early Quakerism', in Berner and Underwood (eds), *Childhood, Youth and Religious Minorities*, pp. 99–126, esp. 101–6.

[275] J. G., *A faithfull testimony for the Lord wherein is proclaimed the mighty day of his power* (1663; Wing G670), title page and pp. 5–6.

[276] Cited in Vann, *Social Development*, p. 174.

[277] *Strength in weakness manifest: in the life, various trials, and Christian testimony of Elizabeth Stirredge* (1711), extracted in David Booy (ed.), *Autobiographical Writings by Early Quaker Women* (Aldershot, 2004), p. 120.

and in due course her husband too was convinced that she suffered for the truth.[278] The intoxicating rhetoric of conflict adopted by early Friends belies a more complex reality: Richard Vann's study of Buckinghamshire and Norfolk suggests many converts to the sect were adult heads of household aged around 30.[279] Youthful Quakerism turns out to be partly a mirage.

In due course, the Society of Friends grew out of the unruly enthusiasm that had marked its early years. The transformation of the Quakers into a sober and respectable people was a gradual process, but also a strategy for deflecting persecution and securing the sympathy of their conforming neighbours. It entailed forgetting some of the excesses of the sect's initial stages, downplaying its claims to supernatural agency and approbation, and reasserting the importance of filial obedience.[280] It also involved a concerted campaign on the part of the leaders of the movement to instruct the young. George Fox had written a catechism for children as early as 1657, but the emphasis on education grew in subsequent decades and many similar primers poured from the Quaker presses. Spiritual formation was no longer left to the Holy Spirit alone; it required diligent human intervention to prepare the way for the Light to penetrate the soul. Vehicles of intraconfessional polemic, such texts indoctrinated children in the faith they had inherited from their parents rather than adopted in defiance of them, cultivating hostility to priests and 'teachers' as 'blind guides' and 'old Creatures', and condemning churches as 'steeple-houses'. William Smith's *New primmer* of 1668 was constructed 'by way of question and answer, as from a child's enquiry after the truth, to be informed by the father', though like earlier catechisms it anticipated readers of all ages.[281] By the 1680s, the duty of deference to parents and schoolmasters was firmly entrenched. A text commemorating the Dutch Quaker John Matern, who had served as a tutor to the children of a Middlesex family for the space of six years, incorporated a series of touching testimonials from his erstwhile pupils,

[278] *A legacy, or widow's mite'; left by Alice Hayes, to her children and others* (1723), pp. 47–9. See also Pullin, 'Children of Light', pp. 106–7.

[279] Richard T. Vann, *The Social Development of English Quakerism 1655–1755* (Cambridge, MA, 1969), p. 84. For the emphasis on defiance of parents in the first generation, see pp. 174–6. See also *idem*, 'Nurture and Conversion in the Early Quaker Family', *Journal of Marriage and Family*, 31 (1969), 639–43.

[280] For the transformation of Quakerism, see Barry Reay, *The Quakers and the English Revolution* (1985), ch. 6; Rosemary Moore, *The Light in Their Consciences: The Early Quakers in Britain 1646–1666* (University Park, PA, 2000), ch. 17.

[281] George Fox, *A catechisme for children* (1657; Wing F1756); George Fox and Ellis Hookes, *A primmer and catechism for children* (1670; Wing F1883B); William Smith, *A new primmer wherein is demonstrated the new and living way* (1662; S4321). See Walter Joseph Homan, *Children and Quakerism: A Study of the Place of Children in the Theory and Practice of the Society of Friends, Commonly Called Quakers* (Berkeley, CA, 1939), ch. 2; Jerry W. Frost, 'As the Twig is Bent: Quaker Ideas of Childhood', *Quaker History*, 60 (1971), 67–87; and Alexandra Walsham, 'Nature and Nurture in the Early Quaker Movement: Creating the Next Generation of Friends', in Morwenna Ludlow, Charlotte Methuen, and Andrew Spicer (eds), *Churches and Education*, SCH 55 (2019), pp. 161–76.

the precocious elegance of which its editor attributed to the 'Lords work'.[282] The quarterly and yearly meetings of the Friends also devoted growing attention to education in the first half of the eighteenth century, stressing how vital this was for steering the young onto 'the path of purity'.[283]

Membership of the society was in the process of becoming a birthright, but this did not lessen the emphasis on the need for regeneration. The contrast between 'spiritual and carnal birth' had been prominent in Quaker thinking from the beginning, but the importance attached to 'convincement' increased in its second and subsequent generations. Fox and his successors likewise described a life cycle of faith that began in childhood and ended in old age.[284] Convincement involved casting off a mere historical faith for living knowledge of the truth. It too entailed becoming a 'new begotten babe'. Since Quakers repudiated the doctrine of pre-destination, this was less a process of acquiring assurance of one's elect status than of actively embracing the indwelling Light.[285] The impassioned preachers who brought people to a true apprehension of the Gospel were understood as genera-tive fathers of their little flocks of followers.[286] Over time, however, the experience of convincement seems to have shifted: elation and confidence gave way to strug-gle and doubt. Many later Friends strove in vain for the feeling of spiritual rebirth that had overtaken the sect's first enthusiastic converts.[287]

A further side effect of Quakerism's advance to maturity and middle age was renewed reverence for the aged. By the late seventeenth and early eighteenth cen-turies, stories of the divinely ravished but disorderly adolescents who had spear-headed the evangelical initiatives of the 1650s and 1660s had to compete with tales of ancient Fathers and Mothers of Israel. Celebrations of exemplary 'early piety' coexisted with accounts of Friends who had reached an impressive age.[288] The last dying words and final departure of a 78-year-old Cornishwoman from St Austell, Loveday Hambly, who had endured various stints in jail for her refusal

[282] *The testimony of that dear and faithful man, John Matern... With several testimonies of sensible children who had been under his tuition*, ed. A. P. (1680; Wing P683), sig. A2v, pp. 20–31.
[283] *Extracts from the Minutes and Advices of the Yearly Meeting of Friends held in London, from its First Institution* (1783), pp. 77–9.
[284] George Fox, *The state of the birth temporal and spiritual* (1683; Wing F1921); Robert Barclay, *An apology for the true Christian divinity* (1678; Wing B720), p. 37. See also William Rogers, *The Christian-Quaker, distinguished from the apostate and innovator, in five parts* (1680; Wing R1858), part I, p. 26: 'In the Church of Christ, there are Babes, Young Men, and Fathers; there are the Weak, and the Strong.'
[285] FHL, MS VOL 62/5, p. 7 (Richard Moore to Charles Lloyd, 6th of the 3rd month, 1662). On convincement, see Vann, *Social Development*, ch. 1; Hilary Hinds, *George Fox and Early Quaker Culture* (Manchester, 2011), ch. 1.
[286] See Su Fang Ng, *Literature and the Politics of Family in Seventeenth-Century England* (Cambridge, 2007), pp. 201–3.
[287] Nikki Coffey Tousley, 'The Experience of Regeneration and Erosion of Certainty in the Theology of Second-Generation Quakers: No Place for Doubt?', *Quaker Studies*, 13 (2008), 6–88.
[288] John Whiting, *Early piety exemplified in the life and death of Mary Whiting a faithful handmaid of the Lord, who departed this life in the 22th year of her age* (1681; Wing W2019).

to pay tithes, were recorded and set forth, together with 'farther Testimonies concerning her life and conversation'.[289] Samuel Watson was lauded for his ongoing 'labour in the work of the truth' when 'Gray Hairs Cover'd his Head' and 'Weakness of Body, and Old Age came upon him'. He was remembered as a 'nursing father' to fellow members of the sect.[290] Now it was men and women who had maintained their faith over several decades of trials and tribulations who were upheld as Quaker heroes. John Story, who had suffered persecution and imprisonment in Salisbury jail, was 'but young as to number of years, between fourty and fifty, but he fulfilled a great time, if Wisdom be Gray-hair, and undefiled Life, old Age'. He himself spoke 'much in Commendation of many Antient Brethren which are Deceased, whom the Lord raised up to Preach and Publish the Everlasting Gospel in the beginning'.[291] Portraits of demure Quaker children may be paired with the pictorial memorials of elderly Friends that adorned the walls of their meeting houses.[292]

Once again traditional patriarchal values reasserted themselves in a context of the sect's institutionalization. As in the case of the mainstream Reformation, later attempts to recapture its original zeal focused renewed attention on the young and denigrated apathetic old believers as children and infants in understanding who hindered the reinvigoration of the fervent faith that had animated its earliest disciples. This was one prime reason why tales of family discord and generational conflict continued to be cherished and entered into collective myth and memory.

This chapter has examined the complicated relationship between the human life cycle, stages of individual spiritual growth, and the evolution of the multiple religious impulses that comprised England's long and troubled Reformations. It has explored how contemporary perceptions of youth and age, childhood and adulthood, were coloured by ancient topoi and shaped in accordance with biblical prototypes and precepts, as well as by processes of selective remembering and sentimental retrospection. We rarely have direct access to the experience of young and old people in this society: more often than not their actions and voices are refracted through the lenses of those in middle age, whose own role in mediating change was critical. The resulting images of godly and ungodly children and of devout and incorrigible elders are both projections of prevailing preoccupations and carefully studied acts of religious self-fashioning.

---

[289] A relation of the last words and departure of that antient and honourable woman Loveday Hambly of Trigangeeves, in the parish of Austell in the county of Cornwal ([1683]; Wing H472).

[290] A short account of the convincement, gospel-labours, sufferings and service of that ancient and faithful servant and minister of the Lord Jesus Christ, Samuel Watson (1712), pp. v, viii.

[291] John Wilkinson, The memory of that servant of God, John Story, revived (1683; Wing W2241), pp. 8, 26.

[292] A portrait of Sarah Walker (1756–1839) once displayed in the Gildersome meeting house is now in the Leeds University Special Collections.

Nevertheless, the recurrent metaphors of youthful enthusiasm and sober maturity, innocence and wisdom, irresponsibility and senility, that I have traced illuminate some important dimensions of the Reformation of the generations. Their prevalence reflects the perception that contemporaries were living through a profound historical moment. The frequency with which the ecclesiastical upheavals of the sixteenth and seventeenth centuries were recalled in this way attests to a widespread sense that these events had eschatological significance. They marked a key stage in the spiritual growth of the nation and of the world as a whole, a temporal juncture almost as decisive as the birth of Christ itself. Looking back with the benefit of hindsight, they observed patterns that were familiar from the Bible. They wistfully recalled the glory days in which the Gospel had vanquished popery through the agency of children and 'yonglings', even as they reasserted the duty of deference to the patriarchal order. The pious legend of Edward VI as the godly young Josiah is one of the enduring legacies of this strain of nostalgia. His credentials rose as disillusionment with Elizabeth's commitment to perfecting her Reformation set in: by the 1590s, she fitted the mould of a grumpy old woman. In turn, the reputation of the Virgin queen mellowed as discontent with her Stuart successors accelerated.

As we have seen, these tropes of generational conflict had a life cycle of their own. In a social universe permeated by Scripture, people expected religious revolution to be accompanied by the overturning of parental authority and by episodes of juvenile and adolescent rebellion. Indeed, they needed it to conform to the pattern of generational disorder to prove its divine source of inspiration and endorse its authenticity. This depended, in turn, on proving its longevity. Such assumptions fused with early modern society's allergy to novelty and respect for antiquity to complicate the onset of Protestantism and to provide ammunition for its Catholic opponents. Wrapping itself in the mantle of age, the Tudor Reformation disguised its recent origins by claiming to embody apostolic purity. Subsequent attempts to reform and renew it likewise deployed the language of regeneration and rebirth. One consequence was to reinforce the tendency to perceive age less as a series of chronological milestones than as a relative, sliding scale and to use it as a gauge for measuring personal religious progress and the inner travels of the soul.

It has been argued that the authority of the aged was steadily eroded in the course of the sixteenth and seventeenth centuries and that English society moved in the direction of age discrimination as its demographical profile tipped towards youth.[293] The evidence assembled here, however, paints a different picture. It suggests that while gerontocratic attitudes were eclipsed in the first stages of revivalist movements fuelled by evangelical zeal, their potential for resurgence should not be underestimated. The ageism implicit in the Reformations coexisted with

---

[293] Thomas, 'Age and Authority', esp. p. 248. See also Minois, *History of Old Age*, ch. 9.

an ingrained respect for the authority of age that paradoxically became most clearly apparent when it was contested. The family remained the bedrock of the state and the nursery of the Church. In the end, all the religious movements I have placed under the microscope sought to reinforce the conventional age hierarchy and to ensure that households of people related by blood were also households bound together by faith. It is to these themes, and to the links between spiritual and biological kinship, that Chapter 2 turns.

2
Kith and Kin

The Holy Family is one of the most recognizable symbols of Christianity, an iconographical motif that has engendered a vast array of ecclesiastical art over the centuries. Yet while the image of the Madonna and child has a very ancient lineage, depictions of Mary and Jesus alongside Joseph predominantly date from the late medieval period. This is not, of course, a normal family: it is an extremely unusual one. The impression of intimacy conveyed by some fifteenth-century paintings occludes the complexity of this family unit and the extraordinary circumstances that created it. Christ is not the son of the couple represented, but the product of a supernatural union between a young Virgin and the Holy Spirit. Joseph is merely a guardian and step-parent standing in for Jesus's real but absent Father in heaven. Long portrayed as elderly, increasingly he was recast in the guise of a younger man, capable of taking on the responsibilities unexpectedly thrust upon him. The demure, maternal figure of Mary, meanwhile, was a far cry from the powerful empress and queen depicted in earlier images or the indulgent Mother of Mercy sheltering sinners under her protecting cloak and intervening to persuade Christ to save unworthy thieves and murderers who inhabited the popular imagination for much of the Middle Ages.[1]

This Trinity is also a rival to and replacement for another one: the maternal trinity of Mary, Jesus, and his grandmother Anne. Fed by such texts as the Golden Legend, the late medieval cult of Christ's wide 'kindred' also expanded organically to include Anne's husband Joachim, Mary's cousins Elizabeth and John the Baptist, and other relatives linked by marriage or blood, including several apostles (Fig. 2.1).[2] Gradually, this large, multigenerational, and rather incestuous holy family was superseded by a smaller one.

---

[1] For shifting perceptions of the Virgin, see Miri Rubin, *Mother of God: A History of the Virgin Mary* (New Haven, CT, 2009). On Joseph, see David Herlihy, *Medieval Households* (Cambridge, MA, 1985), pp. 127–30. See also John Bossy, *Christianity in the West 1400–1700* (Oxford, 1985), pp. 95, 124–5.

[2] See, e.g., Lucas Cranach, *The Holy Family and Kindred* ([Germany], 1509–10). BM, 1852,0612.32. A painted version is Cranach's 1509 triptych, for which, see Bolo Brinkmann (ed.), *Cranach* (2007), pp. 19–20. On the late medieval iconography of holy kinship, which was popular in family chapels, see Pamela Sheingorn, 'Appropriating the Holy Kinship: Gender and Family History', in Kathleen Ashley and Pamela Sheingorn (eds), *Interpreting Cultural Symbols: St Anne in Late Medieval Society* (Athens, GA, 1990), pp. 169–98; Mellie Naydenova-Slade, 'Late Medieval Holy Kinship Images and Family Commemoration: The Evidence from Thornhill, West Yorkshire and Latton, Essex', in Caroline M. Barron and Clive Burgess (eds), *Memory and Commemoration in Medieval England: Proceedings of the 2008 Harlaxton Symposium* (Donington, 2010), pp. 218–33.

Fig. 2.1 Lucas Cranach the Elder, *The Holy Family and Kindred* (woodcut, Germany, 1509–10).

Source: © The Trustees of the British Museum, 1852,0612.32. Artokoloro/Alamy Stock Photo.

The advent of Protestantism coincided with a corresponding reconceptualization of the deity as a stern and forbidding patriarch: a wrathful Old Testament Jehovah intolerant of those who contravened his commandments and prone to punish his wayward children, whose all-seeing eye searched out their faults and offences and whose omniscience stretched to their innermost secrets. Calvinists banished the genial old gentleman who had stared out of stained-glass windows. They transformed God into a mysterious and inscrutable figure whose actions were often unfathomable and whom it was presumptuous for mere mortals to question. At the same time they downgraded Mary, confining Christ's mother to the margins of Protestant piety and ensuring that she no longer grabbed so much of the limelight in a manner that smacked of idolatry. Baroque Catholicism responded by reactivating her cult and turning her into a mascot of the resurgent and militant Church of Rome, albeit one who now behaved more deferentially to the redeemer of mankind and who understood her subordinate place in the social hierarchy.[3]

---

[3] See Diarmaid MacCulloch, 'Mary and Sixteenth-Century Protestants', in Robert Swanson (ed.), *The Church and Mary*, SCH 39 (Oxford, 2004), pp. 191–217; Bridget Heal, *The Cult of the Virgin Mary in Early Modern Germany: Protestant and Catholic Piety, 1500–1648* (Cambridge, 2007).

How far these developments were symptomatic of wider shifts in human society and household structure remains a matter of dispute. Some historians have seen them as indicative of religious changes that greatly reinforced the age and gender hierarchies. They have read them as evidence of the masculinization of religion, of the closing off of avenues for the expression of independent forms of female spiritual agency, and of the inscription of women within the home as subordinates to their husbands.[4] In turn it has been tempting to correlate the renewed emphasis on divine paternity and patriarchy that was one of the by-products of Reformation with the contemporary reconfiguration of family dynamics that stressed the duty of children and servants to obey the dictates of their male elders and masters. The observation made by the Jacobean puritan minister Richard Sibbes that 'the word *Father* is an epitome of the whole Gospel' has regularly been quoted as an emblem of how contemporaries understood and sought to reorder relationships in the temporal realm.[5] However we choose to interpret these developments, they are important and intriguing ones, related in intricate ways to the religious upheavals that shaped the early modern era.

This was a context in which Christianity conventionally described itself using the languages of family and kinship. In Ephesians 3:15, St Paul had written of the 'whole family' of Christ's followers in heaven and earth and in Galatians 6:10 he equated the congregation of the elect with the 'household of faith'. Articulated repeatedly throughout the middle Ages, these compelling metaphors were also pervasive in early modern England. It remained common and comforting for those who lived in hope of salvation to call themselves the 'children of God'. The religious conflicts of the sixteenth and seventeenth centuries served to entrench these tendencies further. Yet they also multiplied and complicated the connections between the biological families into which people were born and the eternal, spiritual families of which they also yearned to be members.

This complex web of relationships is the subject of the second chapter of this book. In entitling it 'Kith and Kin', I deploy a pair of Old English terms that were then, as now, used both as antonyms and synonyms.[6] Like the words 'family' and 'friends', they were utilized loosely and interchangeably to delineate a variety of social networks that spilled out beyond the perimeter of the domestic household and crossed the porous and ambiguous boundaries between public and private in this society.[7] 'Kin' was frequently applied not merely to blood relations but

---

[4] See especially Lyndal Roper, *The Holy Household: Women and Morals in Reformation Augsburg* (Oxford, 1989); Merry Wiesner, 'Nuns, Wives and Mothers: Women and the Reformation in Germany', in Sherrin Marshall (ed.), *Women in Reformation and Counter-Reformation Europe* (Bloomington, IN, 1989), pp. 8–28.

[5] Richard Sibbes, *Works*, 7 vols, ed. A. B. Grosart (Edinburgh, 1853), vol. v, p. 25.

[6] OED, s.vv. 'kith' and 'kin'.

[7] See the important work of Naomi Tadmor: 'The Concept of the Household-Family in Eighteenth-Century England', *P&P*, 151 (1996), 111–40; *eadem, Family and Friends in Eighteenth-Century*

also to individuals and groups linked by other forms of affinity. And if 'kith' was usually employed to denominate a body of acquaintances and friends, it was sometimes loosely (and confusingly) used to encompass people to whom one was allied through ancestry or by custom and law. The value of this dyad for my current inquiry lies in its capacity to highlight all three dimensions of the generational relationships I seek to investigate simultaneously: to illuminate the dual status of generation as a genealogical phenomenon as well as a social and historical cohort. It draws attention to the links that individuals had with their living relatives, peers, and friends at the same time as the bonds that tied them with their dead ancestors and future descendants. The latter connections are tackled in subsequent chapters; the former comprise the subject of this one. It explores how England's Reformations affected perceptions and patterns of religious practice within the overlapping and intersecting entities, literal and figurative, that contemporaries described as their Christian kindred.

In doing so, this chapter attempts to steer the historiography of the early modern family in fresh directions. It moves beyond older debates about household structure, sentiment, and the self that have preoccupied previous scholars to ask different questions about domestic relations against the backdrop of repeated cycles of ecclesiastical and cultural upheaval.[8] The family is examined as a paradigm and ally of the political order alongside the ways in which, paradoxically, it challenged established structures of order. If it was understood as a key instrument for inculcating uniformity and orthodoxy, it also served as a device for fostering religious diversity. The nuclear unit of the parents and their offspring occupies a central place in this discussion, but it also attends to the ties created by remarriage and adoption, including those between full and half-siblings and between stepmothers, fathers, and children.[9]

England: Household, Kinship, and Patronage (Cambridge, 2001). See also Erica Longfellow, 'Public, Private, and the Household in Early Seventeenth-Century England', *JBS*, 45 (2006), 313–34. For the emergence of the modern division of public and private, see Michael McKeon, *The Secret History of Domesticity: Public, Private, and the Division of Knowledge* (Baltimore, MD, 2006).

[8] On household structure, see Peter Laslett and Richard Wall (eds), *Household and Family in Past Time* (Cambridge, 1972), esp. pp. 125–203; Robert Wheaton, 'Family and Kinship in Western Europe: The Problem of the Joint Family Household', *Journal of Interdisciplinary History*, 5 (1975), 601–28. On the 'surge of sentiment' within the early modern and Protestantism as the midwife of the modern family, see Philippe Ariès, *Centuries of Childhood: A Social History of Family Life*, trans. Robert Baldick (New York, 1962); Stephen Ozment, *When Fathers Ruled: Family Life in Reformation Europe* (Cambridge, MA, 1983), esp. chs 1–2. This chapter builds on the foundations of the rich social history of the family inaugurated by Lawrence Stone's *The Family, Sex and Marriage in England, 1500–1800* (1977). Key contributions include Ralph A. Houlbrooke, *The English Family 1450–1700* (Harlow, 1984); Rosemary O'Day, *The Family and Family Relationships, 1500–1900: England, France and the United States of America* (New York, 1994); Anthony Fletcher, *Gender, Sex and Subordination in England, 1500–1800* (New Haven, CT, 1995); Will Coster, *Family and Kinship in England 1450–1800* (Harlow, 2001); Helen Berry and Elizabeth Foyster (eds), *The Family in Early Modern England* (Cambridge, 2007). See also n. 32 below.

[9] See Stephen Collins, 'British Stepfamily Relationships, 1500–1800', *Journal of Family History*, 16 (1991), 331–44; Lyndan Warner, 'Stepfamilies in Early Modern Europe: Paths of Historical Enquiry', *History Compass*, 14 (2016), 480–92; *eadem* (ed.), *Stepfamilies in Europe, 1400–1800* (New York, 2018);

A further aim is to engage critically with lingering assumptions about the declining significance of kinship ties, both natural and artificial. These are partly a function of teleological narratives about the birth of the modern family which presuppose that the extraneous branches possessed by its predecessors were steadily pruned away. But they have another source too: John Bossy's insistence that the 'translation' of Christianity in the West involved the erosion of bonds of communal solidarity at the expense of individual ones. In his view, the weakening of forms and structures of spiritual fraternity was one of the principal consequences of the religious reform movements of the sixteenth and seventeenth centuries.[10] This chapter suggests, on the contrary, that they were in many ways reinvigorated by England's interlocking Protestant and Catholic Reformations. If biological families were central to these intertwined projects of religious renewal, so were religious ones. It argues that in evaluating their effects and implications we must recognize the vitality of both familial and quasi-familial relationships, of kith as well as kin.[11] Attention must be paid to the religious sisters, brothers, friends, and cousins that the Reformations engendered as well as the premium that, in various different ways, they placed on maternity and paternity. One striking side effect of the confessional conflicts of the era was to foster the reciprocal processes by which families related by blood, marriage, and obligation became families bound together by a shared commitment to particular versions of the Christian faith, and vice versa.

Little Commonwealths and Wicked Conventicles

Aristotle's treatise on *Politics*, written around 350 BC, was a key source for the pervasive early modern idea that the family was the basic building block of human society.[12] In his famous *De republica Anglorum* of 1583, Sir Thomas Smith gave expression to the precept that the domestic household was a model for and

eadem, 'Family, Kin and Friendship', in Amanda L. Capern (ed.), *The Routledge History of Women in Early Modern Europe* (Abingdon, 2019), pp. 53–76. On siblings, see Naomi J. Miller and Naomi Yavneh (eds), *Sibling Relations and Gender in the Early Modern World: Sisters, Brothers and Others* (Aldershot, 2006); Amy Harris, *Siblinghood and Social Relations in Georgian England* (Manchester, 2012); Bernard Capp, *The Ties that Bind: Siblings, Family, and Society in Early Modern England* (Oxford, 2018).

[10] See John Bossy, 'Blood and Baptism: Kinship, Community and Christianity in Western Europe from the Fourteenth to the Seventeenth Centuries', in Derek Baker (ed.), *Sanctity and Secularity: The Church and the World*, SCH 10 (Oxford, 1973), pp. 129–43; *idem*, *Christianity in the West*, esp. pp. 95, 124–5.

[11] On the continuing importance of kin, see David Cressy, 'Kinship and Kin Interaction in Early Modern England', *P&P*, 93 (1986), 38–69; Coster, *Family and Kinship*, ch. 5; Naomi Tadmor, 'Early Modern English Kinship in the Long Run: Reflections on Continuity and Change', *Continuity and Change*, 25 (2010), 15–48.

[12] Aristotle, *Politics*, ed. Steven Everson (Cambridge, 1988), bk 1, §2 (pp. 2–3).

microcosm of the state and commonwealth.[13] Its status as a breeding ground for good citizenship was widely reiterated by other political thinkers. Sir Robert Filmer's *Patriarcha*, probably completed by 1642 but only published posthumously in l680, likewise argued that the government of the family by the father was the true origin and template for all legitimate rule and a pattern for divine-right monarchy. Presenting kings as the nursing fathers of their subjects, *Patriarcha* traced the beginnings of this regime to Adam and his successors as described in the book of Genesis.[14] Such commonplaces were closely linked with the belief that the family was a seminary for the propagation of true religion. Behind these assumptions lay the conviction that disorder, deviance, and delinquency within the household undermined the very foundations of the established civil and ecclesiastical order.

It is against this backdrop that official anxiety about the family and household as key sites for religious dissent in the early stages of the English Reformation must be assessed.[15] In the eyes of the authorities, these were the principal domains in which heresy sheltered and lurked, and from which it spread. Coloured by ancient stereotypes deployed against the Cathars and Waldensians, attempts to nip the pest of fifteenth-century Lollardy in the bud repeatedly targeted the schools and 'conventicles' held in private houses. Gatherings such as those hosted by Hawisia Moone of Norfolk brought together family members, neighbours, and friends: in 1430, she admitted that she had been 'right hoomly and prive' with many local heretics.[16] The perception that the natural nest of heresy was the family home has undoubtedly skewed the historical record, contributing to the mistaken impression that women were more prominent in this underground movement than men. As Shannon McSheffrey has commented, 'the familial nature of the sect paradoxically both favoured and restricted their involvement'; it ran along, rather against the grain of patriarchy.[17]

Lollardy drew considerable strength from ties of dependency and kin. These were cemented by the perceived tendency of its adherents to 'contract matrimonie only with them selves, and not with other Christians'.[18] The snapshots provided by fifteenth- and early sixteenth-century interrogations and trials for heresy reveal how frequently families seemed to have shared a common commitment to

---

[13] Thomas Smith, *De republica Anglorum. The maner of governement or policie of the realme of England* (1583; STC 22858), pp. 12–13.

[14] Robert Filmer, *Patriarcha, or, The natural power of kings* (1680; Wing F922).

[15] Aspects of the argument articulated in the first half of this chapter are anticipated in my 'Holy Families: The Spiritualization of the Early Modern Household Revisited', in John Doran, Charlotte Methuen, and Alexandra Walsham (eds), *Religion and the Household*, SCH 50 (Woodbridge, 2014), pp. 122–60.

[16] *Heresy Trials in the Diocese of Norwich, 1428–31*, ed. Norman Tanner, CS, 4th ser., 20 (1977), p. 140.

[17] Shannon McSheffrey, *Gender and Heresy: Men and Women in Lollard Communities 1420–1530* (Philadelphia, PA, 1995), p. 20 and ch. 4 on the family.

[18] John Foxe, *Actes and monuments* (1583; STC 11225), p. 822.

heterodoxy. In the Oxfordshire villages of Burford and Ginge, three generations of the Colins family were identified as Lollards; in Tenderden and the surrounding area in Kent, Agnes Grevill was one of the leaders of a local conventicle that included her husband, their two sons, a daughter, and a trusted servant.[19] So determined were the authorities to prevent children from being seduced by their parents that when William Tylsworth was burnt as a heretic at Amersham around 1506, his only daughter was compelled to set fire to her father. The same penance was imposed upon the offspring of John Scrivener when he was executed in 1522.[20]

Similar preoccupations shaped the Henrician campaigns against underground congregations of evangelicals, the Edwardian drives against Freewillers and Anabaptists, and the efforts of the Marian Church to uproot domestic cells of dissident Protestants. They too conflated clandestine assemblies of people who met to expound Scripture and read godly books with dangerous sects which they feared might prove the fountainhead of mass rebellion.[21] More than a few of those burnt at the stake in the 1550s had been apprehended at such privy assemblies. In the Essex village of Great Bentley the underground conventicle centred on William Mount and his wife Alice. The hand of his stepdaughter Rose Allin was gratuitously burnt with a candle 'til the very sinowes crackte asunder' when she dared to answer back to a magistrate who exhorted her to counsel her parents to be 'better catholicke people', saying 'Sir, they have a better instructour then I.'[22] This was a case of family solidarity that can only have cemented the view that heresy found a natural haven in the household and enhanced the ambivalence and suspicion that surrounded it.

For their part, early Protestants celebrated these connections, seeing the family as a crucible for the renewal of the ideals of apostolic Christianity steadily corrupted by the papacy and priesthood in the course of the Middle Ages. Their sense of affinity with the house churches to whom St Paul had addressed his epistles found expression in the language of kinship which suffuses the letters that evangelical ministers wrote to their followers. Nicholas Ridley described his as 'the very household and family of God' on the eve of his death in Oxford in 1555, and John Bradford addressed his congregation as 'his good brethren and sisters'.[23] Often the spiritual families that these individuals nurtured incorporated blood relatives.

[19] Anne Hudson, *The Premature Reformation: Wycliffite Texts and Lollard History* (Oxford, 1988), pp. 135–6.

[20] Cited in McSheffrey, *Gender and* Heresy, p. 97. The role of Tylsworth's daughter in igniting the fire that burnt him was invoked in John Shaw's *Mistris Shawe's tomb-stone or, the saints remains* (1658; Wing S3029), p. 95.

[21] See J. W. Martin, 'Tudor Popular Religion: The Rise of the Conventicle', in *Religious Radicals in Tudor England* (London and Ronceverte, 1989), pp. 13–39; Patrick Collinson, 'Night Schools, Conventicles and Churches: Continuities and Discontinuities in Early Protestant Ecclesiology', in Peter Marshall and Alec Ryrie (eds), *The Beginnings of English Protestantism* (Cambridge, 2002), pp. 209–35.

[22] Foxe, *Actes and monuments*, pp. 2006–7.   [23] Ibid., pp. 1777, 1631, respectively.

John Foxe's *Actes and monuments* includes many stories of martyrs determined to ensure that their spouses and children remain steadfast in the faith after their deaths, men like Thomas Haukes, who entrusted his son to the guardianship of a fellow evangelical and asked that he be 'brought up in the feare of the Lord...and always be pricked forward with fatherly instructions to folow my footsteps'. Laurence Saunders's tender care for his wife and baby boy on the eve of his death was presented as a model of the religious solicitude that should be displayed by husbands and parents, as well as a vindication of the Protestant practice of clerical marriage.[24] John Rogers likewise implored his evangelical friends to take care of the soul of his widow and 'the little soules' of his ten surviving children.[25]

The images of the godly family and responsible patriarch incorporated in the 'Book of martyrs' sit somewhat uneasily alongside incidents in which people obey the biblical imperative to forsake one's family in order to bear witness to the faith of Christ. They are in tension with episodes that embody the claim that God requires his disciples to set aside ties of affection and abandon relatives and acquaintances in order to obey their divine Father. 'Let not the remembraunce of your children keep you from God' was John Careless's final admonition to his wife Margaret. 'The Lord himselfe will be a father and a mother, better then ever you or I could have bene, unto them. He himselfe wil do all thinges necessary for them: yea, as much as rock the Cradle, if need be.'[26] In a letter written to a devout matron by the name of Mistress Wilkinson urging her to flee to a place where she could serve the Lord, Thomas Cranmer said that carrying the burden of an unquiet conscience was far worse than the loss of the family one would leave behind. Wherever one found Him truly honoured, 'there we can lack neither frend nor kin'. John Hooper used the same argument to prove that true faith could not be 'kepte secrete in the heart' and to reprove Nicodemite 'mass gospellers', saying that true confession was surrounded by many dangers but that those who were pulled back by 'the love of wyfe, children, brother, Syster, kin, [and] frends' would incur the wrath of Christ and his Father in heaven. Bradford similarly exhorted 'the unfayned professours of the gospell' throughout the realm to remember Abraham, who 'was counted a fole to leave his own country and frends, kyth & kinne, because of Gods worde: but dearly beloved, we know it proved otherwise'. It is not surprising that these edifying letters, which echoed the tenets of the Pauline epistles, became revered as monuments of the martyrs and were collected and published by Miles Coverdale.[27]

Evangelical Protestantism navigated the tension between upholding the family as a locus of religious fervour and seeing it as a potential impediment to following

---

[24] Ibid., p. 1669. See also D. Andrew Penny, 'Family Matters and Foxe's *Acts and Monuments*', *HJ*, 39 (1996), 599–618, esp. 604–7.

[25] Foxe, *Actes and monuments*, p. 1497. [26] Ibid., p. 1922.

[27] Miles Coverdale (ed.), *Certain most godly, fruitful, and comfortable letters of such true saintes and holy martyrs of God* (1564; STC 5886), pp. 23, 158, 433.

Christ. Ultimately, the duty of resisting the temptations of familial affection overrode one's obligations to dependants and relatives. This could also justify reversals of the normal order of gender relations and legitimize defiance of a model of patriarchal authority in which women were understood as the underlings of men. In a context in which theories of political resistance and disobedience to an ungodly husband developed in parallel, it could validate a rearrangement of power within the marital union. When a sanctified spouse found herself in conflict with an unbelieving partner, she might have legitimate grounds for separation from him, though this was often glossed by the advice that patient resignation was usually the best course of action. As Susan Wabuda has commented, 'if this was a revolt, it was of the most stealthy, humble and self-limiting kind'.[28] Nevertheless, wives like Anne Askew who rebelled for the sake of the gospel sometimes garnered praise rather than condemnation. In 1556 Careless himself implicitly sanctioned this when he counselled a woman induced to attend Mass by her husband to beware that her greatest 'foes' lay within her own home. The same phrase was echoed in a supplication of Suffolk and Norfolk householders to Queen Mary's commissioners, which declared:

> let no man beleue his frend, or put confidence in his brother. Keepe the doore of thy mouth from her that lyeth in thy bosome: for the sonne shall put his father to dishonour, and the daughter shal rise agaynst her mother, the daughter in law agaynst the mother in the law: and a mans foes shalbe even they of his owne houshold.[29]

As we saw in Chapter 1, young people who revolted against the directives of their backward and benighted parents were also frequently upheld as shining heroes in the first phases of the Reformation. Such family troubles were symptomatic of a climate in which the temporary overturning of conventional domestic hierarchies was not merely expected but even welcomed as a telltale sign of divine intervention to restore the Christian religion to its primitive purity. Once again, the Bible supplied a mandate for role reversal, albeit one that was constrained by circumstance and hedged about with caveats and qualifications.

Domestic Duties and Spiritual Seminaries

Enthusiasm for such domestic inversions visibly declined after Protestantism settled into the shoes of the official faith. Its institutionalization was accompanied by

[28] Susan Wabuda, 'Sanctified by the Believing Spouse: Women, Men and the Marital Yoke in the Early Reformation', in Marshall and Ryrie (eds), *Beginnings of English Protestantism*, pp. 111–28.
[29] Foxe, *Actes and monuments*, pp. 1932 and 1904, respectively.

renewed stress on the duty that women and children owed to the paterfamilias and on the role of the family as a bastion of orthodoxy. These tendencies strengthened as the generation of converts gave way to a generation of people who became members of the reformed Church simply by virtue of being born after 1558. The secular and ecclesiastical authorities eagerly co-opted heads of households into a programme designed to create Protestants, less through blinding revelation than diligent education. Edicts and injunctions were issued that required parents and masters to ensure that their children, apprentices, and servants attended church services and sermons and were catechized in the tenets of the faith by their parish ministers. Some local authorities even levied fines on defaulters.[30]

A multitude of works offering guidance about family governance and describing how to foster domestic piety that poured from Tudor and early Stuart presses served as the engine of what Christopher Hill described as 'the spiritualization of the Protestant household'.[31] This voluminous body of prescriptive literature was not a novel product of the Reformation: it had important late medieval and humanist precedents. Among the fifteenth-century muniments of the Throckmorton family of Coughton in Warwickshire is a little manuscript text (evidently once rolled up and carried around in a purse) containing brief instructions for a devout layman. Print facilitated the dissemination of similar guidance, for which there was a growing appetite. The Bridgettine monk Richard Whitford's bestselling *Werke for householders* was first published in 1530, and a similar 'glasse', describing itself as 'verye godly and fruitfull' appeared in 1542.[32]

[30] See, e.g., *Elizabethan Episcopal Administration*, ed. W. P. M. Kennedy, 3 vols. (1924), vol. ii, pp. 93–4, 119, 127–8; vol. iii, pp. 346–7; Richard L. Greaves, *Society and Religion in Elizabethan England* (Minneapolis, MN, 1981), pp. 293–4.

[31] Christopher Hill, 'The Spiritualization of the Household', in *Society and Puritanism in Pre-Revolutionary England* (1964), pp. 443–81. Older studies include C. L. Powell, *English Domestic Relations, 1487–1653* (New York, 1917); Edmund S. Morgan, *The Puritan Family: Religion and Domestic Relations in Seventeenth-Century New England* (New York, 1944); L. L. Schücking, *The Puritan Family: A Social Study from Literary Sources* (1929; 1969). For more recent contributions, see Patrick Collinson, 'The Protestant Family', in *The Birthpangs of Protestant England: Religious and Cultural Change in the Sixteenth and Seventeenth Centuries* (New York, 1988); Anthony Fletcher, 'The Protestant Idea of Marriage in Early Modern England', in Anthony Fletcher and Peter Roberts (eds), *Religion, Culture and Society in Early Modern Britain: Essays in Honour of Patrick Collinson* (Cambridge, 1994), pp. 161–81; idem, 'Prescription and Practice: Protestantism and the Upbringing of Children, 1560–1700', in Diana Wood (ed.), *The Church and Childhood*, SCH 31 (Oxford, 1994), pp. 325–46.

[32] On the Coughton Court roll, see 'W. A. Pantin, 'Instructions for a Devout and Literate Layman', in J. J. G. Alexander and M. T. Gibson (eds), *Medieval Learning and Literature: Essays Presented to Richard William Hunt* (Oxford, 1976), pp. 398–422. Richard Whitford, *A werke for housholders or for them ye have the gydynge or governaunce of any company* (1530; STC 25422); *A glasse for housholders wherin thei may se, bothe howe to rule thiem selfes [and] ordre their housholde verye godly and fruytfull* (1542; STC 11917). On Whitford, see Lucy Wooding, 'Richard Whitford's *Werke for Housholders*: Humanism, Monasticism and Tudor Household Piety', in John Doran, Charlotte Methuen, and Alexandra Walsham (eds), *Religion and the Household*, SCH 50 (Woodbridge, 2014), pp. 161–73. See also Margo Todd, 'Humanists, Puritans and the Spiritualised Household', *Church History*, 49 (1980), 18–34; Kathleen M. Davies, 'Continuity and Change in Literary Advice on Marriage', in R. B. Outhwaite (ed.), *Marriage and Society: Studies in the Social History of Marriage* (1981), pp. 58–80.

Demand for vernacular books that described how fathers and masters should order their families, teach them the Paternoster, Ave Maria and Creed, and inculcate moral and spiritual rectitude was rising in an environment in which the religious laity were eager to find ways of mimicking monastic discipline and spirituality in their own homes and in which classical ideas about the household as the 'beehive' of civic society were circulating anew.

Nevertheless, Protestantism gave a fillip to these impulses, not least by abolishing monasticism and elevating married life as the mode of human living of which God most approved onto a pedestal. It accorded respectability to male householders and surrounded female celibacy and singlehood with a degree of suspicion.[33] It revived the exemplary figures of Priscilla and Aquila, Nymphas and Philemon described in St Paul's letters to the early Christians as a model for early modern householders and underlined the duty of those who occupied the office of 'private bishops' to make their own families miniature churches. Henry Reginald's translation of the German minister Christopher Hegendorff's *Domestycal or housholde sermons* made these Lutheran precepts available to English readers in 1548, concluding with a prayer that beseeched God to grant that man and wife might be conjoined in faith, as in flesh, and 'so bringe up the frutes of our bodyes, our children, with all our servauntes and famylye in thy feare and love'.[34] A year later Anthony Scoloker produced a translation of a Dutch text entitled *The ordenary for all faythfull Christia[n]s*. This book incorporated a series of biblically inspired injunctions regarding the reciprocal duties of parents and children, masters and servants, and husbands and wives. It was bound with a collection of prayers suitable for daily use and illustrated with woodcuts. In one of them, a father holds a scourge signifying his commitment to the strict godly correction that was deemed necessary to control 'untamed' offspring, while the mother instructs her daughters in practical skills in the background (Fig. 2.2). The book disseminated the ideals of evangelical family life and the imperative of bringing up children in 'the nurtour and informacion of the Lord' in both visual and textual form.[35]

This genre of literature became a staple of the religious publishing industry in the later sixteenth and seventeenth centuries. Godly Protestant writers such as Richard Greenham, John Dod and Robert Cleaver, William Perkins, Josias

---

[33] See Alexandra Shepard, *Meanings of Manhood in Early Modern England* (Oxford, 2003), esp. pp. 87, 213; Amy M. Froide, *Never Married: Singlewoman in Early Modern England* (Oxford, 2005), pp. 157, 219; Christine Peters, 'Singlewomen in Early Modern England: Attitudes and Expectations', *Continuity and Change*, 12 (1997), 325–45.

[34] Christopher Hegendorff, *Domestycal or householde sermons, for a godly householder, to his children and family*, trans. Henry Reginald (1548; STC 13021), esp. sigs A2r–4r, E7r–8r.

[35] Cornelius van der Heyden, *A [bryefe] summe [of the whole] Byble a Christyan instruc[tion for] all parsons yonge and [old] to the whych [is] anne[xed] the ordenary for all degrees*, trans. Anthony Scoloker ([1549?]; STC 3017), sigs. J7r–K1r. The text was printed separately in two other editions: STC 5199.7 and 5200.

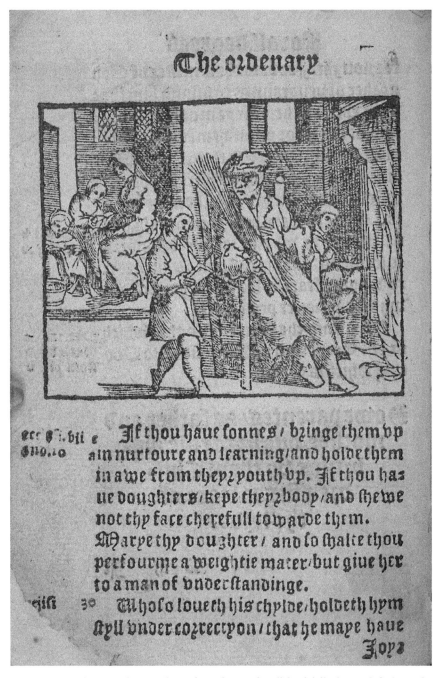

Fig. 2.2 Cornelius van der Heyden, *The ordenary for all faythfull Christia[n]s,* bound with A *[bryefe] summe [of the whole] Byble*, trans. Anthony Scoloker (1549?), sig. B3v.

Source: © British Library Board, 1121.d.37. All Rights Reserved/Bridgeman Images.

Nicholls, and William Gouge who produced popular treatises of *Domesticall duties* and *Christian oeconomie* saw the creation of godly households as a 'seed-plot' for the Reformation that the Lord had begun but not yet perfected in England. Often invoking metaphors of agriculture and husbandry, they saw it as a vital mechanism for establishing a truly reformed commonwealth, 'bringing foorth an holy generation', and ensuring that the candle of the Gospel was not taken away from the nation again. Accordingly, they underlined the risk that through careless attention to this duty the 'whole countrie may fall into Idolatry and destruction'.[36] It was a source of disorder that would eat away at its core. Unless people 'give Religion some roume at home', said Thomas Watts, England would never become a truly godly realm. Sixty years of experience had taught the elderly author of *The office of Christian parents* (1616) that 'loose, negligent, and disorderly government' of households had been 'the bane both of Church and commonwealth'.[37]

Comparing patriarchs to preachers and pastors, watchmen and prophets, such books underscored the weighty obligations that fathers had to nurture the souls as well as the bodies of those under their charge. They declared that negligence in this area was tantamount to spiritual murder. Robert Cawdrey evoked the image of children and servants 'spewing and foming on their faces, continuall curses in hell' upon these 'cut throats of their salvation'.[38] John Downame's *Guide to godly-nesse* said that the blood of those who perished would lie upon the heads of those who neglected their office as God's 'Vice-gerents and Deputies'.[39] The rod of correction that the Lord had placed in the hands of heads of households was to be exercised in imitation of the compassionate chastisement by which He tried and trained the elect; it was an integral part of their duty of care. Such texts delineated a model of reformed masculinity in which male heads of household carried

---

[36] Richard Greenham, *A godly exhortation, and fruitfull admonition to vertuous parents and modest matrons* (1584; STC 11503.3); John Parker, *A true patterne of pietie, meete for all Christian household-ers to looke upon, for the better education of their families* (1592; STC 19217); R[ichard] C[awdrey], *A godlie forme of householde government*, ed. John Dod and Robert Cleaver (1612 edn; first publ. 1598; STC 5386); Joseph Hall, *Salomons divine arts of, 1. Ethicks, 2. Politickes, 3. Oeconomicks* (1609; STC 12712); William Perkins, *Christian oeconomie: or, a short survey of the right manner of erecting and ordering a family, according to the Scriptures* (1609; STC 19677); William Gouge, *Of domesticall duties* (1622; STC 12119); Thomas Carter, *Carters Christian commonwealth; or domesticall dutyes deciphered* (1627; STC 4698); William Jones, *A briefe exhortation to all men to set their houses in order* (1631; STC 14741). Quotation from Josias Nichols, *An order of household instruction* (1596; STC 18539.5), sigs B2r, B4r. An excellent overview of this literature is provided by John Morgan, *Godly Learning: Puritan Attitudes towards Reason, Learning and Education 1550–1640* (Cambridge, 1986), ch. 8.

[37] Thomas Watts, *The entrie to Christianitie, or, an admonition to housholders* (1589; STC 25128), sig. A5v, echoing Greenham, *Godly exhortation*, sigs A7v–8r; *The office of Christian parents* (Cambridge, 1616; STC 5180), sig. A3r.

[38] [Robert Cawdrey}, *A godlie forme of householde government: for the ordering of private families* (1610; STC 5385.5), sig. A4v. See also Gouge, *Domesticall duties*, p. 537.

[39] John Downame, *A guide to godlynesse or a treatise of a Christian life* (1629; STC 7144), pp. 329, 341, and see pp. 144–51, 328–40. See also Thomas Gouge, *A word to sinners, and a word to saints* (1670; Wing G1379A), p. 226.

quasi-ministerial responsibilities.[40] As Lewis Bayly's bestselling *The practice of pietie* declared, 'that which the Preacher is in the Pulpit, the same the Householder is in the house'.[41] Taking up the text of Joshua 24:15 ('but as for me and my house, we will serve the Lord'), they laid down a blueprint for domestic devotion involving family prayer, Bible-reading, psalm-singing, catechizing, and Sabbath observance that was designed to transform the households in which it was practised into 'a kind of paradise upon earth'.[42]

Wives played a critical part in the building of these 'spirituall temples' too. The role played by the Protestant theology of the household in strengthening patriarchy and constraining women's room for manoeuvre should not be overstated.[43] Many writers cited the story of young Timothy, nourished in the Christian religion by the formidable combination of his mother Eunice and his grandmother Lois. Like 'the fruitfull vine' that grew up the wall of a house, women had a responsibility to supply their children and servants with the 'golden apples' of pious instruction.[44] Their role was to 'poure good liquour' into the vessels of their offspring, 'the savour whereof shall sticke in them', and to 'sowe in their mindes the seede of religion and godlinesse'.[45] They were to nurse up their infants in a double respect: by the milk that flowed from their breasts and by the knowledge of God that they dispensed through teaching.[46] It was widely noted that the 'love of the mother exceeds that of the father in fervency' and that, though weaker in judgement, women were stronger in passions had more influence over their children, especially in their 'pliable and tender years'.[47] According to Barthélemy Batt's *Christian mans closet* (1581), maternal discipline was 'wonderful effectuall' in the sphere of early childhood education.[48] One of the defining features of patriarchal Protestantism, the task of instructing the young in the faith of Christ, was incumbent upon their spouses too. A catechism translated from French by

[40] See Karen E. Spierling, 'Father, Son, and Pious Christian: Concepts of Masculinity in Reformation Geneva', in Scott H. Hendrix and Susan C. Karant-Nunn (eds), *Masculinity in the Reformation Era* (Kirksville, MO, 2008), pp. 95–119; Janay Nugent, 'Reformed Masculinity: Ministers, Fathers and Male Heads of Households, 1560–1660', in Lynn Abrams and Elizabeth L. Ewan (eds), *Nine Centuries of Man: Manhood and Masculinities in Scottish History* (Edinburgh, 2017), pp. 39–57. See also Karen Harvey, *The Little Republic: Masculinity and Domestic Authority in Eighteenth-Century Britain* (Oxford, 2012).

[41] Lewis Bayly, *The practice of pietie directing a Christian how to walke that he may please God* (1616; STC 1606.5), p. 343.

[42] Perkins, *Christian oeconomie*, p. 670.

[43] See nn. 4 and 32. Christine Peters offers a more subtle interpretation of how gender roles were reshaped in the context of the Reformation in *Patterns of Piety: Women, Gender and Religion in Late Medieval and Reformation England* (Cambridge, 2003).

[44] Nicholls, *Order*, sigs B2v, B6r–v. See also Gouge, *Domesticall duties*, pp. 546–7.

[45] Cawdrey, *Godlie forme*, p. 59.

[46] See John Dod and Robert Cleaver, *A plaine and familiar exposition of the ten commandments* (1612; STC 6959), pp. 196–201; Gouge, *Domesticall duties*, pp. 430, 482.

[47] Bodl., MS Jones 14, item 3 (George Hakewill, 'The Wedding Robe, or a treatise touching the unlawfulness of Protestants marriages with Papists divided into three parts'), fo. 313v.

[48] Barthélemy Batt, *The Christian mans closet: wherein is contained a large discourse of the godly training up of children*, trans. William Lowth (1581; STC 1591), fo. 54v.

the 'godlie Matrone' Dorcas Martin took the form of a dialogue between a mother and child.[49] While women were envisaged as subordinate helpmeets to their husbands in this culture, the gendered dimensions of marriage and parenthood should not eclipse the extent to which rearing the young in devotion was understood as a mutual responsibility and a collaborative endeavour. In Gouge's words, it was 'a joynt duty belonging to both'. Many such texts addressed mothers and fathers as a conjugal unit.[50] The moral authority accorded by motherhood must be recognized at all levels of society: as Alex Shepard has shown, among the labouring majority, women shouldered many of the burdens of caring for and training children.[51]

Nor can we afford to ignore the role played by step-parents in nurturing spiritual development. Conduct books anticipated the need for advice in this sphere and encouraged new partners to love, tender, and cherish the orphaned infants who came under their care 'as their own father and mother did'.[52] The seriousness with which contemporaries assumed the responsibilities that came with remarriage and the attachments that could build within blended families is occluded by the stories about cruel stepmothers that circulated in this culture. Such stereotypes were the alter ego of contemporary ideals, which they cast into sharp relief. So too does the moral outrage that surrounded the 'unnaturall grandmother' Elizabeth Hazard, the London fruitseller who drowned her 2-year-old grandchild in a tub of water in July 1659, 'without any fear or remorse of conscience' and at the instigation of the Devil. This 'infernal Hag' was the very opposite of the conscientious elderly relatives concerned for the welfare of their grandchildren's souls who populated the outer rings of the Protestant household.[53] And as Bernard Capp has recently shown, siblings too frequently played a part in tutoring younger

---

[49] 'An instruction for Christians, conteining a fruitful and godlie exercise', trans. Dorcas Martin, in *The monument of matrones conteining seven severall lampes of viriginitie*. ed. Thomas Bentley (1582; STC 1892), pp. 221–44. See also Robert Abbot, *Milk for babes; or, a mothers catechism for her children* (1646; Wing A69aA); Paula McQuade, *Catechisms and Women's Writing in Seventeenth-Century England* (Cambridge, 2017).

[50] e.g. Carter, *Carters Christian commonwealth*, pp. 97–165; Gouge, *Domesticall duties*, p. 547. On motherhood, se Patricia Crawford, 'The Construction and Experience of Maternity in Seventeenth-Century England', in Valerie Fildes (ed.), *Women as Mothers in Pre-Industrial England: Essays in Memory of Dorothy McLaren* (1990), pp. 3–38. Margaret J. M. Ezell contests the repressive nature of domestic patriarchy in *The Patriarch's Wife: Literary Evidence and the History of the Family* (Chapel Hill, NC, 1987), chs 1–2. See also Peters, *Patterns of Piety*, ch. 13; Alexandra Walsham, 'The Mother's Legacy: Women, Religion, and Generational Transmission in Post-Reformation England', in Susan C. Karant-Nunn and Ute Lotz-Heumann (eds), *The Cultural History of the Reformations: Theories and Applications* (Wolfenbüttel, 2021), pp. 227–47.

[51] Alexandra Shepard, 'Provision, Household Management and the Moral Authority of Wives and Mothers in Early Modern England', in Michael J. Braddick and Phil Withington (eds), *Popular Culture and Political Agency in Early Modern England: Essays in Honour of John Walter* (Woodbridge, 2017), pp. 73–89, esp. p. 85.

[52] Cawdrey, *Godlie forme*, p. 239.

[53] *The unnatural grand mother, or a true relation of a most barbarous murther* (1659; Wing U86), pp. 6–7.

children, castigating their wayward behaviour and exhorting them to piety and godly life. Taking to heart the sobering lesson of squabbling Cain and Abel enshrined in Genesis 4:9, they were expected, quite literally, to be their brothers' keepers.[54]

Sons, daughters, and servants owed 'awful respect' and 'filiall or child-like feare' to their parents, employers, and elders, who, as Cawdrey commented, 'beare the image of God'.[55] They were to accept instruction humbly and bear correction patiently, knowing that this sprang from 'their deare and natural love towards thee…even from thy birth'.[56] To disobey and resist with 'rough words' and 'froward countenance', declared John Dod and Robert Cleaver, was a vicarious form of rebellion against the Lord himself.[57] It was a contravention of the Fifth Commandment to 'Honour thy father and thy mother'.[58]

Such texts underscored the blessings God that bestowed on godly households and the punishments that befell those that became 'dennes of Theeves', 'sinckes of sinne', and 'habitations of divills'.[59] Families who failed to serve the Lord were no better than 'companies of prophane and gracelesse Atheists' who drew down divine vengeance upon their heads.[60] The preservation of Noah and his relatives in the Ark was contrasted with the terrible fate that had overtaken wicked Achan and his household. Family worship was seen as a singular means of deflecting divine judgement. The story of the devout Swiss family whose home was the only building in a village of ninety houses to survive a devastating earthquake in 1584 was commonly cited as a remarkable providence. The fact that its head and master, with his wife and children, were 'at that very time upon their bended Knees praying and seeking of God' was accorded particular significance.[61]

The dysfunctional families evoked in popular pamphlets and plays about domestic crime were inversions of the pious ones delineated in this prescriptive literature. The case of Enoch ap Evan, who mercilessly killed his mother and younger brother and bedfellow John following a heated household dispute about the legitimacy of kneeling to receive Communion in 1633, was deployed as a

---

[54] Capp, *Ties that Bind*, chs 6–7.   [55] Cawdrey, *Godlie forme*, p. 342.
[56] Carter, *Carters Christian commonwealth*, pp. 177–8.
[57] Dod and Cleaver, *Plaine and familiar exposition*, pp. 183–95.
[58] See also Gervase Babington, *A very fruitful exposition of the commandments by way of questions and answers for greater plainnesse* (1596; STC 1098), pp. 88–98. On the Fifth Commandment as a model for deference to social superiors more broadly, see Jonathan Willis, *The Reformation of the Decalogue: Religious Identity and the Ten Commandments in England, c.1485–1625* (Cambridge, 2017), pp. 89–112.
[59] Matthew Griffith, *Bethel, or a forme for families* (1633; STC 12368), p. 395; Wats, *Entrie*, sig. B1r; Richard Bernard, *Josuahs godly resolution in conference with Caleb, touching household government for well ordering with a familie* (1612; STC 1953), sig. A3r.
[60] Perkins, *Christian Oeconomie*, p. 670.
[61] Samuel Slater, *An earnest call to family-religion: or, a discourse concerning family-worship being the substance of eighteen sermons* (1694; Wing S3961), p. 71.

warning of the evils of separatism, as well as a rerun of Cain's assassination of Abel.[62] Sensational stories about sons who murdered their parents and siblings reveal the dark underside of Protestant domestic religion.

Nevertheless, the imperative of building a Christian household was broadly shared. It was an issue upon which there was considerable consensus within the late Elizabethan and early Stuart Church and which ameliorated the latent tensions that brimmed over into civil war in the 1640s. The author of *Bethel, or, a forme for families*, a 500-page manual published in 1633 was Matthew Griffith, a lecturer at St Dunstan in the West and a defender of clerical privileges who sympathized with the Laudian programme and had his livings sequestered in 1643. He too lamented the 'Supine neglect, if not wilful contempt of Family-duties' and declared that it was not surprising that profanity reigned in English society when 'we will not begin reformation at home'. Warning that all household members 'must feare God and the King, and must not meddle with those that be seditious', he too saw the pious patriarchal household in which kith and kin gathered to serve the Almighty as a bulwark of the civil and ecclesiastical order.[63] E. Nisbet's *Foode for families* (1623) was a 'wholesome' conversation between a father and son on the subject of rendering due allegiance unto Caesar.[64] The Royalist clergyman Richard Allestree's influential *Whole duty of man*, first published in 1659 laid similar stress on the correlations between the duties owed to magistrates, ministers, and parents: honour, reverence, obedience, and prayer.[65] These were precepts endorsed by those who sought to sweep out the popish dross that persisted within the Church of England. They likewise revered it as a cradle of true Christian obedience, albeit one that was periodically rocked by dilemmas of conscience.

From whichever wing of the Church of England the authors of these tracts emanated, the key message they conveyed was that unless households conformed themselves with the pattern laid down in Scripture, Protestantism itself was in serious danger of foundering. Conformity to the ordinances of public worship was insufficient; this had to be complemented by zealous daily prayer at home. Families who set aside service to God and did the 'devil's business', declared Philip Goodwin in his *Religio domestica rediviva* (1655), laid themselves open to external calamities. Like a house without locks or bolts, they were unprotected from Satan's

---

[62] Peter Studley, *The looking-glasse of schisme…a briefe and true narrative of the execrable murders, done by Enoch ap Evan, a downe-right separatist, on the bodies of his mother and brother* (1634; STC 23403). See also Frances Dolan, *Dangerous Familiars: Representations of Domestic Crime in England, 1500–1700* (Ithaca, NY, 1994); Lucy Munro, 'Family Politics and Age in Early Modern England', in Hannah Crawforth and Sarah Lewis (eds), *Family Politics in Early Modern Literature* (2017), pp. 229–46.

[63] Griffith, *Bethel*, pp. 2, 429–30. On Griffith, see *ODNB*.

[64] E. Nisbet, *Foode for families: or, an wholesome houshold-discourse: in which all estates and sorts of people whatsoever are taught, their duties towards God, their alegeance to their king, and their brotherly love and charitie one to another* ([1623]; STC 11126.5).

[65] [Richard Allestree], *The whole duty of man laid down in a plain way for the use of the meanest reader* (1659; Wing A1159), part XIV (pp. 278–305).

machinations.[66] The London pastor Robert Abbott envisaged the Christian family as a residence erected, finished, and furnished by the Lord: without the sure foundations that followed from employing God as 'the Surveyor, Framer, Joyner', and 'sole workman', the result would be 'an old ruinous building of sinne'.[67] Daniel Cawdrey's *Family reformation promoted* of 1656 was animated by the same convictions, as well as by the fact that bulky books like Gouge's *Domesticall duties* were too expensive for the purses of the poorer sort, who required shorter and lest costly summaries.[68] The reader of a copy of Gouge's tract now in the Andover-Harvard Theological Library certainly seems to have found it somewhat tedious: he wrote 'And so forth and so forth and so forth...' in the margins.[69] By contrast, when the wife of Nehemiah Wallington gave birth to his first daughter in 1622, he immediately went out and bought an edition of his own, newly conscious of his responsibilities as a householder with two servants, having 'the charge of so many Souls': 'for I was resolved with Joshua that I and my house will sarve the Lord'. A few years later he extracted from it a list of thirty-one articles, to which all were required to subscribe. These included the payment of a farthing to the poor box for lying in bed after 6 a.m. on Sunday and other fines for delinquency in Bible-reading and sermon repetition and for uttering profanities.[70] One surviving example constructed from mahogany and painted with the words from Matthew 5:34, 'Swear not at all', affords insight into the material equipment for moral admonition that filled the devout Protestant home.[71]

The lessons laid out in such manuals were even more pithily encapsulated in engraved broadsides like *The good hows-holder* (1607). This encouraged patriarchs to build the foundations of their families on rock rather than sand and to rule them with 'a warie head and charie hand' (Fig. 2.3).[72] Taking the form of a triptych combining biblical verses about the two Protestant sacraments of baptism and Communion with the table of the Ten Commandments, Thomas Jenner's *The Christians jewell* advertised itself as 'fit to adorne the hearte and decke the house of every Protestant'. Reproducing the iconography of the reredos in the London church of St Mary Overy, mounted on the wall, it quite literally helped to transform a private residence into a domestic temple.[73] In middle- and

---

[66] Philip Goodwin, *Religio domestica rediviva, or, Family-religion revived* (1655; Wing G1218), pp. 68, 26.

[67] Robert Abbott, *A Christian family builded by God, directing all governours of families how to act* (1653; Wing A68), pp. 3–4.

[68] Daniel Cawdrey, *Family reformation promoted. In a sermon on Joshua, chap. 24. Ver. 15* (1656; Wing C1627), sig. A3v–4r.

[69] See https://hdslibrary.tumblr.com/post/139486595399/domestical-duties-blah-blah-blah-though-the-book, accessed 28 May 2022.

[70] FSL, V. a. 436 (Nehemiah Wallington, notebook 1654), pp. 13–14.

[71] Edward Town and Angela McShane (eds), *Marking Time: Objects, People and their Lives, 1500–1800* (New Haven, CT, 2019), p. 273. This item is dated 1762.

[72] *The good hows-holder* (1607; STC 13851).

[73] *The Christians jewell [fit] to adorne the hearte and decke the house of every Protestant* ([1624]; STC 23499).

The good | Howf-hol-der.

The good Howf-holder, that his Howfe may hold,
Firft builds it on the Rock, not on the Sand,
Then, with a warie head and charie hand
Prouides (in tyme) for Hunger and for Cold:
Not daintie Fare and Furniture of Gold,
But handfom-holfom (as with Health dooth ftand),
Not for the Rich that can as much command
But the poor Stranger, th'Orfan & the Old.

And (thea) to thefe fo ftand fill open wide,   For, Thrifts right Pud of Magnificence:
Hee nether wings with Wrongs, nor rocks his Rents: As Protean Parfions of new Prodigalitie
But fhuns the charge of wanton Wafte & Pride: Haue quafht t'em-out ill aocient Hofpitalitie.

PRINTED AT LON-
DON, IN THE
BLACKE
FRIERS
1607.

Fig. 2.3 Gyles Godet, *The good hows-holder* (London, 1607).
Source: © The Trustees of the British Museum E, 6.38.

upper-class houses this was reinforced by the schemes of interior decoration analysed by Tara Hamling—by chimney breasts, firebacks, plaster ceilings, wall panels, furniture, and tapestries bearing biblical motifs derived from single sheet prints and emblematic title pages. Together with portable objects such as cushions and crockery, they reminded the members of the spiritualized families in which they were used that nothing could escape the surveillance of the Almighty.

The actions of all—from eating and drinking to waking and sleeping—were under his constant scrutiny.[74] A revealing early description is provided by the Henrician evangelical Thomas Becon's *Christmas bankette* (1542), a didactic dialogue between Philemon and the guests he has invited to partake in a feast consisting of several courses of divine instruction. The doors, windows, tables, chairs, stools, cups, and dishes of this fictional household are all objects that speak, rehearsing key lessons from the holy Scriptures that helped to turn it into a nursery of piety and, indeed, 'a nother heaven'. One of the visitors commends his host by wishing that 'all Bysshoppes & Curates would waite & attent upon theyr parysshes wyth no lesse dilygence than you do on your flock'. This home was a model for ecclesiastical governance.[75]

Sanctifying the settings in which families heard God's word and lived their everyday lives, such inscriptions further blurred the boundaries between the house and the church. Downgrading the importance of formal rites of consecration, Calvin and his disciples defined these as any place where two or three of the faithful gathered for prayer.[76] The commercial success of psalters and compilations of godly prayers is indicative of their capacity to unite Protestants of various stripes. In an image inserted in a 1563 music book in which the Psalms are conveniently arranged for singing in four parts, the father sits at an authoritative distance from his wife and children and is in command of the scene.[77] Group portraits of the godly families who inhabited such houses are comparatively rare. The prolific Dutch and Swiss genre of paintings depicting pious households seated around a table and saying grace before a meal had few counterparts in England.[78] The portrait of William Brooke, 10th Baron Cobham, and his wife, sister, and children dated 1567, now at Longleat House, is perhaps its closest cousin (see Fig. 6.13).[79] In the painting that James Pilkington, bishop of Durham,

[74] Tara Hamling, *Decorating the 'Godly' Household: Religious Art in Post-Reformation Britain* (New Haven, CT, 2010); *eadem* and Catherine Richardson, *A Day at Home in Early Modern England: Material Culture and Domestic Life, 1500–1700* (New Haven, CT, 2017). On 'speaking crockery', see also Juliet Fleming, *Graffiti and the Writing Arts of Early Modern England* (2001), pp. 145–58, at p. 151; and Andrew Morrall, 'Inscriptional Wisdom and the Domestic Arts in Early Modern Northern Europe', in Natalia Filatkina, Birgit Ulrike Münch, and Ane Kleine-Engel (eds), *Formelhaftigkeit in Text und Bild*(Wiesbaden, 2012), pp. 121–38.
[75] Theodore Basille [Thomas Becon], *A Christmas bankette garnyshed with many pleasaunt and deynty disshes* ([1542]; STC 1713), sigs A6r–B6v.
[76] John Calvin, *Institutes of the Christian Religion*, trans. Henry Beveridge, 2 vols (Grand Rapids, MI, 1989 edn), vol. ii, p. 180.
[77] Thomas Sternhold, *Tenor of the whole psalms in foure partes* (1563; STC 2431). On household prayer, see Alec Ryrie, *Being Protestant in Reformation Britain* (Oxford, 2013), ch. 14. One example is Edward Dering, *Godly private praiers, for housholders to meditate upon, and to saye in their families* ([1578]; STC 6688).
[78] Wayne Franits, 'The Family Saying Grace: A Theme in Dutch Art of the Seventeenth Century', *Simiolus: Netherlands Quarterly for the History of Art*, 16 (1986), 36–49; Andrew Morrall, 'The Family at Table: Protestant Identity, Self-Representation and the Limits of the Visual in Seventeenth-Century Zurich', *Art History*, 40 (2017), 336–57.
[79] Susan E. James and Katlijne Van Der Stighelen, 'New Discoveries concerning the Portrait of the Family of William Brooke, 10th Lord Cobham, at Longleat House', *Dutch Crossing: Journal of Low Countries Studies*, 23 (1999), 66–101. See Chapters 3 and 6 below and Fig. 6.13.

Fig. 2.4 Commemorative painting of the Pilkington family commissioned by James Pilkington, bishop of Durham (oil, original painted 1566; reproduced 1835).

Source: Parish church of Rivington, Lancashire.

commissioned as a memorial to his father, who built the church in Rivington, Lancashire, in 1566, his parents Richard and Alice kneel on either side of a table, with their seven sons and five daughters behind them in serried ranks, their hands raised in gestures of prayer. James appears among them in clerical dress but also preaches from a pulpit in the right-hand pillar. The setting is an ecclesiastical one, but the inscriptions include exhortations that pithily summarize the precepts of Protestant family religion: 'Fathers teach your children nurture and learning of the Lord' and 'Children obey your parents in the Lord' (Fig. 2.4).[80]

Exemplary regimes of household piety were more often captured in writing. The father of Dutch pietism, Willem Teelinck, spent nine months as a visitor in the home of a godly Banbury citizen in 1604 and described its routines in the preface to his own *Huysboeck* (1639).[81] William Hinde's 1641 *Faithfull remonstrance of the holy life and happy death* of the Cheshire puritan John Bruen praised his earnest performance as a family patriarch and described how he made his

---

[80] The original was badly damaged in a fire in 1834. A replica based on a careful copy painted by a descendant hangs in the church of the Holy Trinity, Rivington, Lancashire. Another, a simplified version, is at Bishop Auckland Castle. The latter is reproduced in Ryrie, *Being Protestant*, p. 367.

[81] See Hamling and Richardson, *Day at Home*, pp. 129–30.

home into 'a little Bethel' and 'a common nursery for the Churches of God'. The 'wholesome admonitions' and 'mild rebukes' by which he brought his wife to 'a higher pitch and degree of knowledge and of grace' and the 'rod of correction' he applied to the corruptions of his children and servants made him a puritan governor par excellence, albeit almost a cardboard cut-out that bears an uncanny resemblance to those described in the prescriptive texts on which he evidently relied.[82] The devout Margaret Corbet, who died in 1656 and was one of the few women to feature in Samuel Clarke's *Lives* of Christians eminent in their generations, was likewise a model of maternal piety whose endeavours to instruct her 'hopefull little ones in the holy Scriptures' were compared to those of Eunice and Lois in relation to Timothy.[83] Thomas Cawton, sometime minister of St Bartholomew's behind the Royal Exchange and latterly preacher to the English congregation of Rotterdam in Holland, was recalled as 'a true Pater familias'.[84] Art and life, Scripture and social reality are hard to distinguish in accounts that were carefully moulded to highlight the intrinsic moderation of puritanism and to present family religion as a conservative and stabilizing force in English society.

The case of Little Gidding reminds us that these ideals also took root in reaches of the Church of England that have retrospectively (and misleadingly) been seen as the embryo of Anglicanism. The informal spiritual community established by Nicholas Ferrar and his extended family (his mother, siblings John and Susanna and their children) followed a strict routine in accordance with the Prayer Book.[85] The divines eulogized in Thomas Fuller's rival collection of 'moderne divines', *Abel redevivus* (1651) less frequently appear as paragons of family religion, though John Jewel was said to have conducted prayers with his family at 5 a.m. and to have called his servants to account each evening at 9 p.m. The unmarried Lancelot Andrewes was also 'exempllary' in the public devotions he conducted for his household in his 'decently and reverently adorned' chapel at Ely, but his biographer laid more emphasis on the 'private and secret' ones in which he spent many hours each day and over which he spilt 'abundant teares'.[86] Domestic piety is conspicuous by its comparative absence from the memoirs of his successor in

---

[82] William Hinde, *A faithfull remonstrance of the holy life and happy death, of John Bruen of Bruen-Stapleford in the County of Chester* (1641; Wing H2063), pp. 49, 51, 53, 65.

[83] Samuel Clarke, *The lives of thirty-two English divines, famous in their generation for learning and piety, and most of them sufferers in the cause of Christ* (1677; Wing C4539), p. 414, alluding to 2 Tim. 1:5. See also Jacqueline Eales, 'Samuel Clarke and the "Lives" of Godly Women in Seventeenth-Century England', in Sheils and Wood (eds), *Women in the Church*, pp. 365–76.

[84] Thomas Cawton, *The life and death of that holy and reverend man of God Mr Thomas Cawton* (1662; Wing C1653), pp. 60–1.

[85] Joyce Ransome, ' "Voluntary Anglicanism": The Contribution of Little Gidding', *The Seventeenth Century*, 24/1 (2009), 52–73; *eadem*, *Web of friendship: Nicholas Ferrar and Little Gidding* (Cambridge, 2011).

[86] Thomas Fuller, *Abel redevivus, or the dead yet speaking. The lives and deaths of the moderne divines* (1651; Wing F2400), pp. 309–10 and sig. [*3r–v]. The life of Andrewes is interpolated between pp. 440–1 of the main text.

this diocese, Matthew Wren, despite the fact that he was happily married and had twelve children, six of whom survived to adulthood.[87] These subtle differences of emphasis alert us to diverging priorities that will re-emerge in the next section.

It is striking that so many of the Protestant households described by contemporary writers were clerical ones. This was a comparatively recent species of family, a product of Protestantism's firm repudiation of a celibate priesthood. Whereas the medieval clergy were figures detached from the biological chain by virtue of vows of chastity, their reformed counterparts participated in it via the act of reproduction. For all the apocalyptic anti-Catholic bile that the former Carmelite friar John Bale directed against the illicit sexual liaisons of the English 'votaries' and despite the Church of England's vigorous promotion of marriage as the true vocation of the reformed ministry, hostility to married clergy and especially married bishops was slow to dissipate. In 1562, there were many who still 'kycke[d] agaysnt the lawful maryage of the faythful ministers of the church' according to John Veron.[88] It was not merely outspoken Catholics who denounced Protestant bishops and clergy as 'hormasters' and knaves and their wives as harlots and concubines.[89] The suits of defamation and slander that continued to be brought before the ecclesiastical courts long after the Elizabethan settlement suggest that some still regarded ecclesiastical families as an unseemly aberration. The sentiments of Hugh Holland of King's Sutton in Northamptonshire, who was cited in 1610 for saying that 'the world was never merry since priests were married', were echoed in other presentments. Allegations that the offspring of Protestant ministers were illegitimate 'brats' also rumbled on for more than a century.[90] The Cambridge vice chancellor's court books record an injury case of 1604 about a certain Thomas Bradbury who had allegedly called Theophilus Field 'a scurvy fellowe and a foole' and sent him an offensive letter enclosing a poisonous plaster and containing the words 'if he be a minister's son he is a bastard'.[91] Similar charges were made against the bailiffs of Great Yarmouth in Norfolk in 1640 for their several misdemeanours and abuses against the town's two vicars, Edward Barker and Matthew Brookes, which included spreading defamatory

---

[87] *Parentalia: or, memoirs of the family of the Wrens*, ed. Stephen Wren (1750), pp. 1–134.

[88] John Bale, *The actes of the Englysh votaries* (Antwerp, 1546; STC 1270); John Veron, *A strong defence of the maryage of pryestes* (1562; STC 24687), sig. A2r. On clerical marriage, see Eric Carlson, 'Clerical Marriage and the English Reformation', *JBS*, 31 (1992), 1–31; Helen L. Parish, *Clerical Marriage and the English Reformation: Precedent, Policy and Practice* (Aldershot, 2000); *eadem*, '"It Was Never Good World Sence Minister Must Have Wyves": Clerical Celibacy, Clerical Marriage, and Anticlericalism in Reformation England', *JRH*, 36 (2012), 52–69.

[89] See, e.g., Devon HC, 3799M/3/O/8/2 (Report of speeches of Browne, a merchant, 1596).

[90] Christopher Haigh, *The Plain Man's Pathways to Heaven: Kinds of Christianity in Post-Reformation England* (Oxford, 2007), pp. 204–5. For the earlier tradition of concern about clerical unchastity, see Martin Ingram, *Carnal Knowledge: Regulating Sex in England, 1470–1600* (Cambridge, 2017), ch. 8.

[91] CUL, VCCt.III 11 (Vice Chancellor's Court records, 1577–1605), no. 30.

libels and calling the children of the former 'Preists bastards'.[92] Evidently not everyone revered dedicated pastors like Herbert Palmer, whose painful labours and impressive vigilance reputedly transformed his household into 'a garden without weeds'.[93]

Nevertheless, antagonism towards married ministers and their wives was abating. At the parish level, antagonism and ambivalence were gradually giving way to accommodation.[94] By the seventeenth century, this novel brand of Protestant family had become an accepted feature of the post-Reformation landscape.[95] So too had the associated phenomenon of the clerical dynasty. The renowned Shropshire puritan Thomas Gataker followed the example set by his father (who had been chaplain to the earl of Leicester and later pastor of St Edmund's Lombard Street) and took holy orders, while the sober carriage and grave deportment of John Carter, minister of Belstead in Suffolk and author of one of the classics of the household governance genre, had not only made his family into 'a little church' but inspired his own son to enter the ministry.[96] Three of James Pilkington's brothers were also clergymen, all educated at St John's College, Cambridge; one joined him in exile during Mary's reign. His own sons, Joshua and Isaac, died young, but were probably also intended for ordination. A descendant of his daughter Ruth married Dr Thomas Fuller, author of the *Worthies* and *Abel redevivus*.[97] Philip and Matthew Henry were members of a Presbyterian family whose diligent attention to such duties turned their houses into seminaries as well as sanctuaries, in which devout students cohabited with sons who themselves subsequently trained for the ministry. Relatives edited Philip's memoirs to strengthen the impression that he was a 'perfect pattern of Primitive Christianity' in this, as in other respects. His wife Katherine was similarly celebrated as 'a very Discreet Manager of her Family Affairs' and an exemplar of Christian 'oeconomy'.[98]

---

[92] London, Parliamentary Archives, HL/PO/JO/10/1/60, fo. 103. I am grateful to Danny Buck for this reference.

[93] Clarke, *Lives of thirty-two divines*, p. 190.

[94] Anne Thompson, *Parish Clergy Wives in Elizabethan England* (Leiden, 2019), esp. ch. 6.

[95] An important contribution is Michelle Wolfe, 'The Tribe of Levi: Gender, Family and Vocation in English Clerical Households, circa 1590–1714' (PhD thesis, Ohio State University, 2004). See also Tom Webster, *Godly Clergy in Early Stuart England: The Caroline Puritan Movement, c.1620-1643* (Cambridge, 1997), ch. 1; R. Emmet McLaughlin, 'The Making of the Protestant Pastor' and Susan C. Karant-Nunn, 'The Emergence of the Pastoral Family in the German Reformation', both in C. Scott Dixon and Luise Schorn-Schütte (eds), *The Protestant Clergy of Early Modern Europe* (Basingstoke, 2003), pp. 60–78, 79–99.

[96] Clarke, *Lives of thirty-two English divines*, pp. 248–9 and 135, respectively.

[97] Leonard, John, and Lawrence: see John Pilkington, *History of the Pilkington Family of Lancashire and its Branches, from 1066 to 1600*, 3rd edn (Liverpool, 1912), pp. 104–15.

[98] Matthew Henry, *An account of the life and death of Philip Henry, minister of the gospel* (1698; Wing B1100A), ch. 4 and preface, sig. A4r. For the couple's exemplary credentials in the realm of family religion, see W. Tong (ed.), *An account of the life and death of the late Reverend Mr Matthew Henry, Minister of the Gospel at Hackney, who died June 22nd, 1714, in the 52d year of his age* (1716), pp. 124 and 10. On the editorial strategies, see Patricia Crawford, 'Katharine and Philip Henry and Their

It would be wrong to regard these complimentary accounts as mere panegyrics. Such individuals internalized the biblical exemplars of family religion: in 1672 Mary Blackmore, wife of the ejected preacher of St Peter's Cornhill, William Blackmore, wrote to 9 nine-year-old son Chewning, who was away at school, urging him not to neglect to read the Scriptures daily, 'that thou mayst, as young Timothy did, know them from a child & therby become wise unto salvation & fit to be servisable to God in your generacion'. He too became a dissenting minister in Worcester.[99] In other instances, denominational differences emerged over time. Nonconformist fathers produced episcopalian offspring and vice versa. Isaac Archer, vicar of Chippenham in Cambridgeshire, was the son of the puritan divine William, who disapproved of his ordination as deacon and priest within the Restoration Church of England but still sent him the gift of his sermons in manuscript.[100] The filial ties that bound the generations often proved more resilient than particular ecclesiastical allegiances.

Some dynasties gained a reputation for championing godly domesticity in print. Daniel Cawdrey's *Family reformation promoted* was a piece of filial mimicry, a sequel to Robert Cawdrey's *Godlie forme of householde government*. His son complained that the original author of this classic had been concealed by its subsequent editors, Dod and Cleaver, who had claimed the credit for it by putting their own name on the front cover rather than that of their 'deceased brother', who was its 'first Father'.[101] In puritan New England, multiple members of the Mather family entered the ministry, leaving a legacy that stretched across several generations. The most famous of these was Increase, but his three siblings (Samuel, Nathaniel, and Eleazar) were also clerics. In turn his own son Cotton, who was named after his maternal grandfather John Cotton, another eminent divine who had emigrated to Massachusetts in 1633, took holy orders.[102] Within such families, religious vocation seemed to run in the blood.

Family Religion

The mass ejection of dissenting Protestants on Black Bartholomew Day 1662 had the effect of reinvesting 'family religion' with a subversive edge and revealing its

---

Children: A Case Study in Family Ideology', in *eadem, Blood, Bodies and Families in Early Modern England* (Harlow, 2004), pp. 175–208.

[99] DWL, MS 12.40 (Original Letters and Papers of the Blackmore family), item 6.

[100] CUL, Additional MS 8499, transcribed in *Two East Anglian Diaries, 1641–1729: Isaac Archer and William Coe*, ed. Matthew Storey (Woodbridge, 1994), pp. 93–4. See Hannah Yip, 'The Familial Afterlives of Parochial Sermons in Early Modern England', *Reformation*, 27 (2022), 125–40. I am grateful to Dr Yip for permission to cite this prior to publication.

[101] Cawdrey, *Family reformation promoted*, sig. A2v–3r.

[102] Robert Middlekauff, *The Mathers: Three Generations of Puritan Intellectuals, 1596–1728* (New York, 1971).

capacity to function as a Trojan Horse. It reignited concerns about the porous boundary between the household and the 'seditious' conventicle that had never entirely evaporated. Illicit gatherings to recite sermons and read the Bible that took place in the covert arena of the home had been a source of ongoing anxiety to the Elizabethan authorities, who saw them as a rival to the public liturgy of the Book of Common Prayer. Together with private fasts, they remained something of a thorn in the side of the Church in the Jacobean era. They were forms of puritan voluntarism that perennially troubled the religious establishment, serving as a supplement to parish worship that could easily become an alternative to it. Archbishop John Whitgift admitted that there were occasions when, upon some 'urgent cause', it was appropriate for the word to be preached and the sacraments administered in domestic contexts but insisted that this did not open 'any window to secret and schismatical conventicles' of the kind defended by the Presbyterian leader Thomas Cartwright.[103] Anti-puritan propaganda and satire such as Richard Bancroft's *Survay of the pretended holy discipline* (1593) saw household piety as a sinister threat to the ecclesiastical and political status quo, comparing consistories erected in private homes to 'a Parish not of many but of one familie'.[104] The anonymous author of *The house-holders helpe* of 1615, a dialogue between a gracious gentleman and his eldest son, may well have been a deprived minister. He directly confronted the charge that domestic conferences led by lay heads of households placed them in competition with the clergy and trespassed on their office as preachers and teachers, defending their roots in Christian antiquity. Sermon repetition was an approved method of 'whetting our spiritual dullnesse', notwithstanding the fact that puritans were 'much derided, scorned, and mocked for it'. He also overtly advocated domestic catechizing where public instruction was lacking.[105] Other puritans strenuously upheld the legality of 'the joining together of Christians of sondry familyes', insisting that this had 'gods allowance and approbation' 'even in these tymes and in such a church as ours is'.[106] Scholarly opinion has been similarly divided on how far such gatherings were corrosive of parochial identities. Christopher Hill's insistence that they opened a door to centrifugal forms of sectarianism contrasts with Patrick Collinson's conviction that they did more to enrich than to undermine mainstream Protestantism from within.[107]

---

[103] John Ayre (ed.), *The Works of John Whitgift, D.D.*, 3 vols (Cambridge, 1851–3), vol. i, p. 211.

[104] Richard Bancroft, *A survay of the pretended holy discipline* (1593; STC 1352), p. 98.

[105] R. R., *The house-holders helpe, for domesticall discipline* (1615; STC 20568), pp. 26–8 and 20–1.

[106] BL, Additional MS 4275 (Ralph Thoresby, collection of letters of conformist and nonconformist divines), fo. 281r.

[107] Hill, 'Spiritualization'; Patrick Collinson, 'The English Conventicle', in W. J. Sheils and Diana Wood (eds), *Voluntary Religion*, SCH 23 (Oxford, 1986), pp. 223–59; *idem*, *The Religion of Protestants: The Church in English Society 1559–1625* (Oxford, 1982), ch. 6. Cf. the different emphasis of *idem*, 'The Godly: Aspects of Popular Protestantism', in *idem*, *Godly People: Essays on English Protestantism and Puritanism* (1983), 1–17. In a note on p. 18 Collinson indicates his shifting opinion on puritanism's capacity to serve as 'a solvent of parochial religion and as congregationalist in potential'.

The writers of many works on household governance were at pains to stress that withdrawal from public church services into the realm of the private household was not permissible: only at the Last Judgement would the Lord sift the wheat from the chaff and divide the sheep from the goats. Until then, in the home as in the church, the regenerate and unregenerate would intermingle. Thomas Paget's *Demonstration of family-duties* (1643) was written in exile in Amsterdam, where he had fled after being driven from his position at Blackley in Lancashire because of his nonconformity and where he ministered to the English church alongside his elder brother John. His book defended the practice of inviting friends and neighbours to join blood relations in religious exercises at home on special occasions. But Paget also stressed that 'consociation, or joyning together in Church-fellowship' was 'more eminent, and more worthy than worship in families'. He sharply reproved those who 'under a pretence of better profiting themselves in reading of good books at home, and private devotions, doe neglect to converse with God and his people in the publick ordinances'.[108] While households should be little congregations of the saints, there was no justification for divorcing them from the wider body of the faithful that comprised the national Church.

Contemporary concerns that such practices challenged the inclusive ecclesiology of the Church of England and fostered the formation of tiny gathered churches cannot, however, be completely dismissed. Some books about 'family Reformation' recommended barring 'wicked companions' and incorrigible sinners from the homes of the godly in the interests of preserving their purity as domestic congregations of the elect. In calling upon householders to exercise 'a Church-like Discipline' and denounce 'a lesser Excommunication of refractorie offenders', they arguably paved the way for a kind of domestic independency.[109] Both before and during the English Revolution household religion did sometimes function as a bridge to separatism and as a crucible for congregationalism. Lubricated by covenant theology, it fostered a sense of exclusivity that could encourage the expulsion of the unregenerate from the miniature church that was the family household.[110] It provided a platform on which some drifted out of the disintegrating Church of England into experiments in sectarianism. What had initially seemed the key to consummating the imperfect sixteenth-century Reformation became a route to the creation of individual kingdoms of spiritual kith and kin that fragmented it as a single, coherent vision.

During the 1640s and 1650s, it was the beleaguered supporters of episcopacy and the superseded liturgy who became a dissident underground religion.

[108] Thomas Paget, *A demonstration of family-duties* (1643; Wing P168aA), pp. 82–6, 105–10.
[109] Cawdrey, *Family reformation promoted*, pp. 57 and 25–6, respectively.
[110] Helen Hajzck, 'Household Divinity and Covenant Theology in Lincolnshire, c.1595–c.1640', *Lincolnshire History and Archaeology*, 17 (1982), 45–9.

Some public worship continued in defiance of the status quo, but others were compelled to practice their faith clandestinely. In these conditions, insisted a minister in 1657, 'tis fit the Church should come to private houses'. As John Evelyn recorded in his diary, performed by a sequestered minister, Prayer Book services and rites—from baptism and churching to Christmas and the Eucharist— took place in the discreet setting of the home. He heard sermons in his library and other rooms. While lamenting that the Church of England had been 'reduced to a Chamber & Conventicle', in July 1656 he reported 'a great meeting of zealous Christians, who were generaly much more devout & religious, than in our greatest prosperity'.[111] This situation also served as a fillip to the development of a distinct strand of domestic spirituality that built on the collections of private prayers prepared by the Calvinist conformist Daniel Featley and the Laudian John Cosin in the 1620s. Featley did not 'confine Devotion to her chamber' but gave her 'the Liberty of her house', appending a catechism entitled *The summe of saving knowledge* to his *Ancilla pietatis*.[112] Jeremy Taylor, who became chaplain to the earl and countess of Carberry in Herefordshire during these decades, was inspired to compose his rules and exercises of holy living and dying, and in enforced exile the Royalist Edward Hyde similarly devoted himself to preparing prayers and meditations on the Psalms for the benefit of his children.[113] An index of decreasing ambivalence about devotional solitude, the portrait of the soon-to-be executed king's pious contemplations in the *Eikon Basilike* provided a model for the followers of a tradition that had now become a repressed minority.[114] Temporarily, until the tables were turned again in 1660, it was on the receiving end of ongoing suspicion about secret activities that took place within the seclusion of the household.

The Restoration settlement had the effect of pushing many Presbyterians into the wilderness of schism against their own inclination and will. It compelled puritan dissent once again to retreat into the domestic realm, and it turned the meetings that ministers ejected from the public pulpit held in private homes into forms of criminal dissidence. The Conventicle Acts of 1664 and 1670 illustrate the

[111] Edward Hyde, *Christ and his church* (1658; Wing H3862), sig. A2r; *The Diary of John Evelyn*, ed. E. S. de Beer, 6 vols (Oxford, 1955), vol. iii, p. 181, and see pp. 75, 76, 78–9, 89, 90, 92, 144–5, 147, 188, 190, 195. See Judith Maltby, 'Suffering and Surviving: The Civil Wars, the Commonwealth and the Formation of "Anglicanism", 1642–60', in Christopher Durston and Judith Maltby (eds), *Religion in Revolutionary England* (Manchester, 2006), pp. 158–80, esp. 166–7.

[112] Daniel Featley, *Ancilla pietatis: or, the hand-maid to private devotion* (1626; STC 10726). *The summe of saving knowledge* was bound with this: sig. A2v. John Cosin, *A collection of private devotions* (1627; STC 5816).

[113] Jeremy Taylor, *The rule and exercises of holy living* (1650; Wing T371A) and *The rule and exercise of holy dying* (1651; Wing T361B); Edward Hyde, 'Contemplations and Reflections upon the Psalms of David', in *A collection of several tracts* (1727), pp. 369–770. See Ian Green, 'Varieties of Domestic Devotion', in Alec Ryrie and Jessica Martin (eds), *Private and Domestic Devotion in Early Modern Britain* (Farnham, 2012), pp. 21–44, at pp. 17–18, 30.

[114] *Eikon basilike. The pourtraicture of his sacred majestie in his solitudes and sufferings* (1649; Wing E270). See Erica Longfellow, '"My Now Solitary Prayer": *Eikon Basilike* and Changing Attitudes towards Religious Solitude', in Ryrie and Martin (eds), *Private and Domestic Devotion*, pp. 65–83.

difficulty that officials had in distinguishing between illicit gatherings and more innocent forms of 'family religion': they defined the conventicle as an assembly of more than five people 'over and besides those of the same household' or of a similar number 'where there is no family inhabiting'.[115] The conventicle's status as an unlawful event, in short, rested on the presence of non-resident kith as well as natural kin: on the admission of friends into the elastic institution that was the early modern family.

In this context the practice of domestic piety once again stirred anxiety and skirted the edges of the law. Nonconformists such as Thomas Jolly looked back to the precedents set by the apostles in early Christian times, who had visited their disciples house by house, to justify the ingenious ways in which they evaded the legislation, in his case by dividing his congregation into groups of four and repeating his sermons from a makeshift pulpit.[116] Dissenting ministers and laypeople exploited legal loopholes in the fundamental ambiguity about whether the family was a public or private space and an entity beyond the jurisdiction of the state. As a consequence, tracts reiterating conventional and uncontroversial wisdom about godly household government now carried an undercurrent of defiance against the establishment. The Baptist John Bunyan's *Christian behaviour* (1663) described its author on the title page as 'a Prisoner of Hope'. Amidst chapters full of familiar advice, it also addressed the question of how a wife was to conduct herself in relation to an unbelieving husband. He answered that the latter's 'salvation or damnation lyeth much in thy deportment or behaviour before him' and that the woman should 'bare with patience his unruly and unconverted behaviour'. Even if he was 'a sot' or 'a fool', he was her lord and master. Bunyan's book provided no sanction for subverting patriarchal authority.[117]

The circumstances of persecution in which dissenting Protestants found themselves highlighted the inherent inconsistencies within this ideology, which had always acknowledged that there were situations in which wives, children, and servants might be justified in resisting the dictates of male patriarchs, namely when they required them to act in defiance of divine law. These concessions were carefully calibrated, but it was nevertheless acknowledged that there were limits to the subjection that subordinates owed to their superiors. In the end, their higher duty to their Father in heaven had to prevail. There was a sin in yielding to wicked parents, especially those who forbade them from 'the doing of any necessary duty commanded of God'.[118] The 'veritable charter of authoritarianism'

---

[115] 16 Car. II, c. 4 (1664); 22 Car. II, c.1 (1670).

[116] Henry Fishwick (ed.), *The Note Book of the Rev. Thomas Jolly* AD *1671–1693*, Chetham Society, MS 33 (Manchester, 1895), pp. xxi, 63.

[117] John Bunyan, *Christian behaviour, or, The fruits of true Christianity shewing the ground from whence they flow, in their godlike order in the duty of relations, as husbands, wives, parents, children, masters, servants, &c: with a word of direction to all backsliders* (1663, Wing B5493), pp. 69–74.

[118] See Gouge, *Domesticall duties*, pp. 325–9, 467–9; Carter, *Carters Christian commonwealth*, pp. 198–200.

that appeared to be inherent in the Fifth Commandment was not without its vulnerabilities.[119] There was also space for legitimate opposition to a profane spouse. The prophetess Anne Wentworth, who apostatized from the Baptists in the 1670s, excused her disobedience to her 'earthly husband' by saying that she owed deference to God as her divine householder and 'heavenly Bridegroom'. In the process, she reinforced accepted assumptions about the gender hierarchy, even as she exposed the forms of domestic resistance theory that had been inherent in patriarchy from the beginning.[120] The household itself was a sort of monarchical republic within which allegiances were as precarious and contingent as its own relationship with the formal ecclesiastical and civil order.[121]

This is not to say that 'family religion' became the exclusive property of those on English Protestantism's left wing in the latter half of the seventeenth century, any more that it had been before the Civil Wars. On the contrary, as the belated appearance of Filmer's *Patriarcha* in print in 1680 reveals, it remained a critical ally of royal authority.[122] In a variation on a standard theme, Robert Sanderson, consecrated bishop of Lincoln in 1660, had called the paterfamilias 'a kind of petty Monarch'.[123] A 1685 broadside containing 'household observations, fit to be observed by wife, children, and servants' also explicitly draws a parallel between deference to fathers and husbands and deference to kings. The associated image is a picture of the royal court rather than a private home and the plaque above the central doorway is inscribed 'A Family well govern'd, is like a Kingdom well Rul'd'. Other sentences underline the role of hereditary rulers as loving fathers and the correlation between servants and subjects.[124]

Adorned with title pages invoking the model of Joshua and his family at prayer, guides to 'domestical duties' and household religion such as *The godly mans delight* (1679) continued to be produced by authors from all points on the ecclesiastical spectrum (Fig. 2.5).[125] As Andrew Cambers and Michelle Wolfe have emphasized, 'family religion' was an element of evangelical piety that

---

[119]   Willis, *Reformation of the Decalogue*, p. 104.

[120]   Warren Johnston, 'Prophecy, Patriarchy, and Violence in the Early Modern Household: The Revelations of Anne Wentworth', *Journal of Family History*, 34 (2009), 344–68, esp. 353–5. See also Diane Willen, 'Godly Women in Early Modern England: Puritanism and Gender', *JEH*, 43 (1992), 561–80.

[121]   The allusion is to Patrick Collinson, 'The Monarchical Republic of Elizabeth I', repr. in his *Elizabethan Essays* (1994), pp. 31–57. On the subordination of the claims of the natural family to the divine authority of God the Father, see Jonathan Sircy, 'Becoming Spiritual: Authority and Legitimacy in the Early Modern English Family', *Renaissance Papers* (2009), 55–65.

[122]   On Filmer, see Gordon J. Schochet, *Patriarchalism in Political Thought: The Authoritarian Family and Political Speculation and Attitudes especially in Seventeenth-Century England* (Oxford, 1975), chs 7–8.

[123]   Robert Sanderson, *Fourteen sermons heretofore preached IIII. Ad clerum, III. Ad magistratum, VII. Ad populum* (1657; Wing S605), p. 291.

[124]   *The husband's instructions to his family, or household observations* (1685; Wing H3809B).

[125]   T.W., *The godly mans delight or A family guide to pietie* (1679; Wing W121).

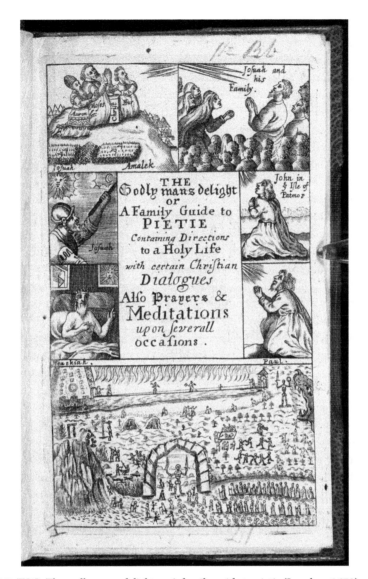

Fig. 2.5 T.W., *The godly mans delight or A family guide to pietie* (London, 1679), title page.
Source: © British Library Board, 843.f.27. All Rights Reserved/Bridgeman Images.

cemented the ecumenical connections and breached the artificial divide between moderate nonconformists and conforming members of the Church of England sympathetic to godly ideals. It was a form of religious sociability that facilitated the inclusion of visitors in the devotions of the nuclear family and its live-in relatives and other dependants. It fostered forms of cooperation and fraternity that cut across the polarities between Dissent and Anglicanism that still distort modern historiography.[126] A commitment to encouraging it united clerics of different temperaments. John Tillotson, future archbishop of Canterbury, preached on this subject at St Lawrence Jury in July 1684, lamenting the 'mischievous and fatal consequences' of its neglect 'in this loose and degenerate Age'.[127] His concerns were shared by the Presbyterian Richard Baxter, whose *Poor man's family book* (1674) and *Catechizing of families* (1683) were designed to disseminate the same message to those of humbler rank, as well as to serve as a makeshift when 'the ministry is defective' and a corrective to 'publick failings'.[128] Oliver Heywood thought that there was 'no better Remedy than Domestick Piety' for the general 'inundation of profaneness' that had overtaken late seventeenth-century England and no more effective mechanism for preserving 'the power of Godliness'.[129] The deprived London divine Samuel Slater, whose *Earnest call to family-religion* (1694) compared households whose members omitted daily prayer together to heathen ones filled with 'barren Soil', and commanded patriarchs to purge the orchards and vineyards of which they had charge of noisome weeds. He urged them to admit none as servants, apprentices, or visitors 'but those who will keep you company while walking with God'. '[L]et Birds of a Feather get together', he remarked; 'what have Birds of Paradise to do with Vultures and Owls?' In turn, he exhorted servants to avoid families who were negligent in their religious exercises, citing the example of Lot fleeing the iniquitous city of Sodom before its destruction. Lodgers should not flinch from admonishing their masters to pull up their socks as spiritual fathers, though this should be done in a polite and friendly manner. If such warnings were ignored, at least one had the satisfaction of a clear conscience.[130]

Creating devout Christian households continued to be seen as key to the elusive goal of rebuilding the unity of a nation that was riven with religious conflicts and frictions. Many saw internal divisions within them as both a cause and an effect of civil dissension. Indeed, this was one argument deployed against the granting of religious liberty. Daniel Cawdrey said that licensing pluralism would cause endless rifts in families and undermine the authority of heads of

---

[126] Andrew Cambers and Michelle Wolfe, 'Reading, Family Religion, and Evangelical Identity in Late Stuart England', *HJ*, 47 (2004), 875–96.

[127] John Tillotson, *Six sermons…II. Family religion* (1694; Wing T1268), pp. 83, 50.

[128] Richard Baxter, *The poor man's family book* (1674; Wing B1352); idem, *The catechizing of families a teacher of housholders how to teach their housholds* (1683; Wing B1205), sig. A6v. Baxter reflected on this in *Reliquiae Baxterianae, or, Mr. Richard Baxters narrative of the most memorable passages of his life and times faithfully publish'd from his own original manuscript by Matthew Sylvester* (1696; Wing B1370), p. 191. Part 2 of his *A Christian directory* was entitled *Christian oeconomicks: or the family directory* (1677). A broadside summarizing these books is *Mr. Baxters rules & directions for family duties shewing how every one ought to behave himself in a Christian behaviour, suitable to that relation in which God hath placed him* (1681; Wing B1379). See also William Payne, *Family religion: or, the duty of taking care of religion in families, and the means of doing it* (1691; Wing P903).

[129] Oliver Heywood, *A family altar erected to the honour of the eternal God* (1693; Wing H1765), sig. A2r, p. 82.

[130] Slater, *Earnest call*, pp. 310–11.

households: this would 'serve to discover the iniquity of that so much cal'd for cursed Toleration'.[131] In this sense the legislation of 1689 sanctioning coexistence was a mixed blessing. If it allowed dissenting minorities to practise their religion, it simultaneously had the potential to erode the pillars of patriarchal authority. The domestic *cuius regio, eius religio* exercised by the paterfamilias was threatened by the form of parliamentary indulgence that accompanied the Glorious Revolution, even as it legalized private household meetings that had previously been tarred with the brush of sedition and treason.[132] At least in the eyes of some, toleration jeopardized the neat convergence between the biological family and the spiritual family of God that zealous Protestants saw as the objective of household reformation.

The restatements of this ideal that appeared in print in subsequent decades must be seen as a reassertion of its value in shifting circumstances. They bore witness to ecumenical initiatives designed to build bridges between conformity and dissent.[133] They reflected the perception that family religion was a powerful weapon against the infidelity and unbelief that seemed to be pervading English society, a suitable remedy for what Thomas Bray, the founder of the SPCK, called 'the general Apostasy from Christianity'.[134] Yet texts like Matthew Henry's *Church in the house* (1704) also attest to the ongoing perception that the household was a critical site for salvation. The home took on new importance as a spiritual haven in the wake of the 1688 Revolution. It was a nursery in which to nurture 'a seed to serve the Lord, which shall be accounted to him for a Generation'. Diligent performance of these duties, said Henry, was the best way of ensuring that piety was passed down from parents to children and made into a family 'Heir-Loom', and thereby of securing the prosperity of the English nation and the Protestant faith.[135]

Seedbeds of Subversion?

One variety of household religion that remained untouched by the provisions of the Act of Toleration of 1689 was Roman Catholicism. Catholics were not

[131] Cawdrey, *Family reformation promoted*, pp. 28–30.
[132] As the nonconformist John Rastrick commented in a memoir recounting the momentous developments of 1688: HEHL, MS HM 6131, fo. 55v, printed in Andrew Cambers (ed.), *The Life of John Rastrick, 1650–1727*, Camden 5th ser., 36 (2010), p. 128. For the household as a site of domestic *cuius regio, euis religio*, see Morgan, *Godly Learning*, p. 143.
[133] See, e.g., David Jones, *A sermon of the absolute necessity of family-duties, preached to the united parishes of St Mary Woolnoth, & St Mary Woolchurch Haw in Lombard Street* (1692; Wing), p. 28.
[134] Thomas Bray, *An appendix to the discourse upon the doctrine of the baptismal convenant: being a method of family-religion* (1699; J936), sig. A3v.
[135] Matthew Henry, *A church in the house. A sermon concerning family-religion* (1704), p. 43. For a similar statement, see Slater, *Earnest call*, p. 80. See also William J. Sheils, 'The Act of Toleration, Household Worship and Voicing Dissent: Oliver Heywood's *A Family Altar* (1693)', in Elizabeth Clarke and Robert W. Daniel (eds), *People and Piety: Protestant Devotional Identities in Early Modern England* (Manchester, 2020), pp. 79–94.

beneficiaries of the decision to permit Dissenters to meet for worship in public buildings. Celebration of the Mass and administration of the other sacraments remained illegal activities that found a natural place of refuge in the private houses of the recusant aristocracy and gentry. This pattern had established itself in the Elizabethan period in response to the penal legislation that punished Catholics who withdrew from their parish churches and relied on secret services said by itinerant missionaries and by the resident chaplains they employed to provide them with spiritual sustenance for their souls and to perform liturgical rites of passage. By the late seventeenth century, some Protestants were willing to turn a blind eye to what went on behind the closed doors of the seigneurial households around which the community clustered in the countryside, at least in times of relative peace and freedom from political crisis. The ambassadorial residences, with their associated chapels, that formed a key focus for Catholic life in the capital were zones into which the jurisdiction of the Stuart state technically did not reach and to which adherents of Rome came to exercise their consciences more freely. Although vulnerable to symbolic displays of popular violence, they relied on a version of what Benjamin Kaplan has called 'fictions of privacy', though the overt performance of 'popery' in London also raises questions about the applicability of that model to England.[136]

The home was a vital forum in which the Old Religion found asylum. The manors of Catholic gentlemen and aristocrats served as hubs for missionary priests who often combined their role as private chaplains with the task of serving a wider penumbra of faithful people in their vicinity. The strategy of perching as 'sparrows on the rooftop' in the attics of wealthy recusants and of residing 'in private houses after the old example of the Apostles in their day' bore fruit in reconciliations and conversions that built a new community. This community extended outward from the circles of close kin who lived therein towards the wider body of kith who came within their orbit.[137] These domestic cells developed a strong sense of identification with the early Christian congregations and of their own

<hr/>

[136] Benjamin J. Kaplan, 'Fictions of Privacy: House Chapels and the Spatial Accommodation of Religious Dissent in Early Modern Europe', AHR, 107 (2002), 1031–64, at 1062. See also idem, 'Diplomacy and Domestic Devotion: Embassy Chapels and the Toleration of Religious Dissent in Early Modern Europe', Journal of Early Modern History, 6 (2002), 241–61. Emily Vine explores the anxiety that surrounded minority homes and the distrust of privacy in '"Those Enemies of Christ, if They are Suffered to Live Among us": Locating Religious Minority Homes and Private Space in Early Modern London', London Journal, 43 (2018), 197–214. Mark Allen is currently engaged in a Cambridge PhD on ambassadorial and royal chapels in early seventeenth-century London which considers these themes.

[137] For differing perspectives on the significance of this strategy, see John Bossy, The English Catholic Community (1975); Christopher Haigh, 'From Monopoly to Minority: Catholicism in Early Modern England', TRHS, 5th ser., 31 (1981),129–47 and idem, 'The Continuity of Catholicism in the English Reformation', in idem (ed.), The English Reformation Revised (Cambridge, 1987), pp. 176–208; T. M. McCoog, '"Sparrows on a Rooftop": "How we Live where we Live" in Elizabethan England', in T. M. Lucas (ed.), Spirit, Style, Story: Essays Honoring John W. Padberg, S.J. (Chicago, 2002), pp. 237–64, at p. 355.

autonomy. It is telling that when Lord Vaux of Harrowden was presented with his entire family and retinue of servants for refusing to attend Protestant services in May 1581, he claimed 'his house to be a parish by itself', a kind of peculiar or proprietary church.[138] Lower- and middling-sort Catholics relied on having access to the chapels of the rural gentry, the upper rooms of townhouses, and the barns owned by wealthy farmers in which Mass was said and the sacraments dispensed. Their ability to participate in the attenuated liturgical life of their proscribed religion depended on the connections and friendships they forged with like-minded neighbours—on a sense of affinity with fellow members of the little family of God who had resisted the Reformation and clung faithfully to the Mother Church.[139]

Described in the memoirs of Jesuit priests and in the hagiographical accounts of devout laypeople written by their clerical confessors, the intensity of these Catholic regimes of piety bears comparison with those in the godly Protestant households already described. Locally known as 'Little Rome', Battle Abbey in Sussex was a centre of exemplary recusant devotion, where Lady Magdalene Montague kept three priests and elaborately decorated the private chapel to which large numbers of visitors resorted alongside those resident in her own house. Her daily round of prayer, meditation, recitation of the rosary, and penance was a mirror image of the cycle of humiliation, thanksgiving, and searching self-scrutiny practised by puritan families.[140] In the north, the home of Dorothy Lawson at St Anthony's near Newcastle upon Tyne was another beacon of Catholic religiosity served by the Jesuits Henry Morse and Richard Holtby. According to her chaplain and biographer William Palmes, she kept her household carefully and behaved 'like a Martha', reading the lives of the saints and other pious books to her maids, catechizing lapsed Catholics, distributing charity to the widows and poor, and assisting women in childbirth with relics for the soul and cordials for the body.[141] At Osgodby in Yorkshire in the 1620s, the Babthorpe family diligently assembled each evening at 9 o'clock for the litanies and every Sunday and saint's day for sermons and spiritual lessons, regularly confessing and receiving the Eucharist.[142] Devout Catholic women regarded the diligent performance

---

[138] Godfrey Anstruther, *Vaux of Harrowden: A Recusant Family* (Newport, 1953), p. 113.

[139] Bill Sheils, 'Household, Age and Gender among Jacobean Yorkshire Recusants', in Marie B. Rowlands (ed.), *Catholics of Parish and Town 1558–1778*, CRS Monograph Series 5 (1999), pp. 131–52, at pp. 137–8.

[140] *An Elizabethan Recusant House Comprising the Life of Lady Magdalen Viscountess Montague (1538–1608)*, ed. A. C. Southern (1954). On Battle, see Michael Questier, *Catholicism and Community in Early Modern England: Politics, Aristocratic Patronage and Religion, c.1550–1640* (Cambridge, 2006), ch. 7.

[141] William Palmes, *Life of Mrs Dorothy Lawson, of St Anthony's, near Newcastle-upon-Tyne, in Northumberland*, ed. G. Bourchier Richardson (Newcastle upon Tyne, 1851).

[142] 'Father Pollard's Recollections of the Yorkshire Mission', in John Morris (ed.), *Troubles of our Catholic Forefathers Related by Themselves*, 3rd ser. (1877), p. 468.

of menial chores as part of their vocation: the 'holy housework' in which they engaged was a form of mortification akin to the sanctified manual labour carried out by the religious.[143]

The attachment that many members of these households, and especially matrons, displayed to the cult of the Blessed Virgin of Loreto surely owed much to the fact that it centred on a holy house that had provided a harbour of security for the Mother of Christ. The miraculous flight of the Holy House from Palestine to safety in Italy was a metaphor for their own condition of inner exile and their desire to find a mental and physical place of refuge and retreat. Post-Reformation Catholics built on an older tradition of devotion that had inspired the erection of replica chapels by churchmen and laymen alike, including the London ironmonger John Andrew, who constructed one of timber a quarter of a mile from his house in the early years of the sixteenth century in honour of this 'blessid lady'.[144] In Elizabethan Northamptonshire, Elizabeth Vaux dedicated her entire home to Our Lady of Loreto, creating a heart of gold as a pledge of her vow, which she intended to send to the Holy House itself as a token of her devotion.[145] A miracle of portable Catholicism, this cult had special resonance for a community displaced by its official disestablishment from the church into the household.[146]

Filtered through the lens of the admiring clergy who described them, these Catholic families were hothouses in which the spirit of the Counter-Reformation blossomed. The forms of holy domesticity they professed were inspired not just by spiritual literature translated from other European vernaculars, but also by devotional texts specifically composed for the circumstances in which English Catholics found themselves—for a community that could only give overt expression to its religious convictions within the confines of the home.[147] Although Catholicism's close alliance with the family was in part a marriage of convenience, it was also a continuation of older trends. It must be situated in a line of succession that extends back to the devout Christian humanist households of Lady Margaret Beaufort and Sir Thomas More, to the orthodox domestic piety that drove the lucrative late medieval market for primers and inspired the building of

---

[143] See Frances E. Dolan, 'Reading, Work, and Catholic Women's Biographies', *English Literary Renaissance*, 3 (2003), 328–57, at 338–45.

[144] TNA, PROB 11/19/377 (Will of John Andrewe otherwise called Geilis of All Hallows Gracechurch, London, 15 March 1520). I am grateful to Jason Scott-Warren for this reference.

[145] John Gerard, *The Autobiography of an Elizabethan*, trans. and ed. Philip Caraman (1951), p. 163. On Loreto, see Orazio Torsellino, *The history of our B. Lady of Loreto*, trans. T[homas] Price (St Omer, 1608; STC 24141); Louis Richeome, *The pilgrime of Loreto. Performing his vow made to the glorious Virgin Mary mother of God* (Paris, 1629; STC 21023); J[ohn] S[weetnam], *The paradise of delights. Or the B. Virgins garden of Loreto* ([St Omer, 1620]; STC 23531).

[146] See Karin Veléz, *The Miraculous Flying House of Loreto: Spreading Catholicism in the Early Modern World* (Princeton, NJ, 2019).

[147] Robert Southwell, *A short rule of good life. To direct the devout Christian in a regular and orderly course* ([1596–7]; STC 22969), chs 8–9.

private chapels, and to the quasi-familial late medieval mystical movement known as the Brethren of the Common Life.[148]

Recent scholarship by Abigail Brundin, Deborah Howard, and Mary Laven on Renaissance Italy has revealed the extraordinary vibrancy of domestic piety in what became one of the heartlands of Catholic renewal. Evoking an image of the sacred home as a porous and permeable zone, a space filled with material aids to intercession and meditation, and a place of empowerment for the laity, they speak of a 'quiet campaign' to tame and reclaim it as a site of devotion.[149] At the same time the household was 'a fragile entity' within which heterodox ideas and illicit practices bordering on 'superstition' could flourish.[150] Such work refines and qualifies Marc Forster's contention that, tainted by association with secrecy and heresy, religious practices centred on the family and household were a marginal feature of Baroque Catholicism before the eighteenth century.[151]

The Counter-Reformation generated its own literature of household government and its own theories of Christian upbringing. These, in turn, were underpinned by a powerful emphasis on parental responsibility for the spiritual nurturing of the next generation.[152] Priests in training for the Elizabethan mission were instructed to underline the responsibility of Catholic heads of families to 'labour most diligently' to incline their offspring and servants to piety and zeal for the faith and to 'think badly of heretics and avoid their company', lest they 'rush headlong into all kinds of wickedness'.[153] The preface to Henry Garnet's English edition of Peter Canisius's influential catechism warned that those who ignored the Lord's 'straite charge of good education of children' placed themselves in danger of 'everlasting damnation'.[154] Translated in 1613, Francis de Sales's *Introduction to a devoute life* similarly stressed parents' duty 'to emprint the feare and love of God in their tender harts', building up their houses and extending their lineages in religion and piety like the ancient Hebrews. De Sales invoked St Monica as 'a notable lesson for Christian women', whose assiduous care in

---

[148] R. N. Swanson, *Religion and Devotion in Europe, c.1215–c.1515* (Cambridge, 1995), pp. 122–6. On Lady Margaret Beaufort, see Malcolm J. Underwood, 'Politics and Piety in the Household of Lady Margaret Beaufort', *JEH*, 38 (1987), 39–52.

[149] Maya Corry, Deborah Howard, and Mary Laven, *Madonnas and Miracles: The Holy Home in Renaissance Italy* (2017); Abigail Brundin, Deborah Howard, and Mary Laven, *The Sacred Home in Renaissance Italy* (Oxford, 2018), p. 315.

[150] See Maya Corry, Marco Faini, and Alessia Meneghin (eds), *Domestic Devotions in Early Modern Italy* (Leiden, 2018), quotation at p. 2, and Marco Faini and Alessia Meneghin (eds), *Domestic Devotions in the Early Modern World* (Leiden, 2018).

[151] Marc R. Forster, 'Domestic Devotions and Family Piety in German Catholicism', in *idem* and Benjamin J. Kaplan (eds), *Piety and Family in Early Modern Europe: Essays in Honour of Steven Ozment* (Aldershot, 2005), pp. 97–114.

[152] See Oliver Logan, 'Counter-Reformatory Theories of Upbringing in Italy', in Diana Wood (ed.), *The Church and Childhood*, SCH 31 (Oxford, 1994), pp. 275–84.

[153] P. J. Holmes (ed.), *Elizabethan Casuistry*, CRS 67 (1981), p. 103.

[154] Peter Canisius, *A summe of Christian doctrine*, trans. Henry Garnet ([Douai], 1592; STC 4571.5), sig. *3r.

striving to correct her wayward son Augustine had sown the seeds for his conversion. He hoped that her 'holie motions and affections' would instil the Catholic religion in their own offspring.[155] The decline of the medieval cult of holy motherhood in the sixteenth and seventeenth centuries may have been exaggerated.[156]

The emphasis that early modern Catholicism placed on the role of the family as a spiritual unit also sets a question mark beside John Bossy's influential claim that the Tridentine hierarchy 'seems to have taken it for granted that household religion was a seed-bed of subversion.'[157] This was a corollary of his conviction that both Reformations eroded a communal Christianity whose strength lay in its commitment to kinship in favour of an atomizing individualism. The experience of being a proscribed minority undoubtedly enhanced the familial character of the post-Reformation English Catholic community. Anthony Errington's *Catechetical discourses* (1654) were intended to be read aloud to a domestic congregation, and the translator of Cardinal Richelieu's *Christian instruction* (1662) envisaged that 'the Master of the familie' would recite these lessons to his children and servants in the absence of a priest.[158] The home took the place of the parish as the locus of Tridentine instruction. But the conditions that surrounded the practice of Catholicism in England also fostered an internal dynamic that sometimes rubbed uncomfortably against prevailing paternalist assumptions and structures. The principal way in which they did so was by appearing to carve out space for female agency within and beyond the domain of the household. The spinsters, wives, and widows who are so prominent in laudatory biographies have helped to feed the impression that Elizabethan and Stuart Catholicism was a matriarchy.[159] Contemporaries and subsequent historians have been drawn to single women like Jane Wiseman and Anne Line who took extreme risks to harbour priests and to married ones whose stalwart recusancy contrasted with the occasional or partial conformity of their ostensibly less zealous husbands. This pattern was not confined to the elite, but it seems to have been more common among the gentry and nobility.[160] Protestant magistrates and lawmakers looked upon male church papistry as 'a weak kneed evasion of patriarchal responsibility' and sought to

[155] Francis de Sales, *An introduction to a devoute life*, trans. I. Y. ([Douai], 1613; STC 11316.5), pp. 463–8. See Clarissa W. Atkinson, "Your Servant, My Mother": The Figure of St Monica in the Ideology of Christian Motherhood', in *eadem*, Constance H. Buchanan, and Margaret R. Miles (eds), *Immaculate and Powerful: The Female in Sacred Image and Social Reality* (Boston, MA, 1985), pp. 139–72, esp. pp. 152–8.

[156] Laura A. Smoller, 'Holy Mothers: The History of a Designation of Spiritual Status', in Forster and Kaplan (eds), *Piety and Family*, pp. 178–200.

[157] John Bossy, 'The Counter-Reformation and the People of Catholic Europe', *P&P*, 47 (1970), 51–70, at 68.

[158] Anthony Errington, *Catechistical discourses* (Paris, 1654; Wing E3246), 'A Preface to the reader'; Armand John du Plessis, duc de Richelieu, *A Christian instruction composed long a goe*, trans. Thomas Carre (1662; Wing R1417), sigs a6r–v, cited in Lucy Underwood, 'Catholics', in Anna French (ed.), *Early Modern Childhood: An Introduction* (2020), pp. 140–59, at p. 148.

[159] Bossy, *English Catholic Community*, p. 153, and see pp. 150–60.

[160] Sheils, 'Household, Age and Gender', pp. 139–42.

compel such men to exert better control over their unruly spouses.[161] Some couples fit this mould better than others, including Margaret Clitherow, the devout butcher's wife whose pious disobedience towards her husband was one source of the scandal that led to her being pressed to death, despite being pregnant, in 1586. John Mush's careful construction of her as a martyr further attests to the idea that the Lord sanctioned reversals of conventional family roles when the times were out of joint.[162]

Often, however, this phenomenon must be seen as 'a natural (and mutually agreed) division of labour in the management of dissent', a mechanism by which families preserved the spiritual integrity and material resources of the household simultaneously.[163] The Shireburne family of Stonyhurst in Lancashire is a case in point: Richard was a church papist, who reluctantly conformed and even signed the Protestant Association to defend Elizabeth I against her enemies in 1584, while his wife and children mostly stayed at home and never deigned to communicate.[164] The extended Throckmorton family of Coughton in Warwickshire was not a 'recusant bubble': there was a persistent tendency towards outward conformity within its male ranks.[165] The wife of James Ravenscroft of Fould Park in Middlesex was also a schismatic, but the couple conscientiously sent their sons to be educated at Douai College and ensured that their daughters were instructed in the Catholic faith. One of them, Thomasine, entered the Franciscan nunnery at Nieuport in 1647.[166]

Yet persecution and proscription could and did sow the seeds of dissension within Catholic households, as the casuistical advice sought by troubled laypeople anxious to reconcile their duty to their earthly superiors with allegiance to their father in heaven indirectly reveals. Some clergy conceded that wives could be excused for bowing to the authority of husbands who commanded them to participate in heretical activities; others said that it would 'be much better if they refused to do this sort of service'.[167] By choosing to heed the counsels of their 'ghostly fathers' over the orders of their spouses, married women not only defied patriarchal authority. The ambiguous liaisons they entered into with chaplains

---

[161] Bossy, *English Catholic Community*, p. 155.

[162] Peter Lake and Michael Questier, 'Margaret Clitherow, Catholic Nonconformity, Martyrology and the Politics of Religious Change in Elizabethan England', *P&P*, 185 (2004), 43–90; and *eidem*, *The Trials of Margaret Clitherow: Persecution, Martyrdom and the Politics of Sanctity in Elizabethan England* (2011), ch. 3.

[163] Alexandra Walsham, *Church Papists: Catholicism, Conformity and Confessional Polemic in Early Modern England* (Woodbridge, 1993), pp. 80–1.

[164] John Callow and Michael Mullett, 'The Shireburnes of Stonyhurst: Memory and Survival in a Lancashire Catholic Recusant Family', in Richard Dutton, Alison Findlay, and Richard Wilson (eds), *Region, Religion and Patronage: Lancastrian Shakespeare* (Manchester, 2003), pp. 169–85, at pp. 173–4.

[165] Peter Marshall and Geoffrey Scott (eds), *Catholic Gentry in English Society: The Throckmortons of Coughton from Reformation to Emancipation* (Aldershot, 2009), pp. 6, 11–17.

[166] P. R. P. Knell, 'A 17th Century Schismatic and his Catholic Family', *London Recusant*, 1 (1971), 57–70.

[167] Holmes (ed.), *Elizabethan Casuistry*, p. 119.

and missionary priests who had cure of their souls gave rise to rumours that they were guilty of a kind of adultery. They were cuckolding their husbands, metaphorically, if not literally.[168] The actions of 'collapsed ladies' corroded the assumption that a wife was subject to her spouse in matters of conscience and unsettled the prevailing household-state analogy.[169]

To resist the pressure exerted by Protestant parents who ordered one to commit the sin of schism was likewise not insubordination but rather a commendable form of Christian renunciation of kith and kin. In his 1593 treatise showing 'how farre it is lawfull or necessary for the love of Christ to forsake Father, Mother, wife and children, and all other worldly creatures', the Jesuit Henry Garnet told Catholic youngsters that in such circumstances it was better 'by your owne perseverance to turne away Gods wrath from your family, least he punish it for your parents faultes in you and your children to the fourth generation, than by yielding to your Parents iniquity, you damne your selves & increase their torments'.[170] What was at stake was not simply their own spiritual health but also that of their posterity.

In these respects the Catholic home did indeed appear to some to be a site of domestic subversion and political resistance as well as 'the nucleus of a closed society that taught its young to oppose the world outside'.[171] This explains why both civil magistrates and Church of England bishops and ministers claimed the right not merely to intrude into the realm of the household to arrest the priests who were perverting the monarch's subjects, but also to coerce husbands who failed to discipline their wives and to remove children into the custody of sound Protestants for re-education in the reformed religion. In the case of the recalcitrant recusant Mrs Lea, the state stepped in to fill the shoes of her husband. His protestations that he would restrain her did not convince John Piers, archbishop of York, who noted that 'the forbearinge of hir hitherto hath bene a great occasione of her disobedience and sinne'. She was 'justlie and necessarily' imprisoned for 'hir reformatione' in May 1590.[172]

Fatherly power passed to the civic and ecclesiastical authorities when men failed to live up to prevailing models of masculinity, reducing them to the status

---

[168] Laurence Lux-Sterritt, '"Virgo becomes Virago": Women in the Accounts of Seventeenth-Century English Catholic Missionaries', RH, 30 (2011), 537–53; Colleen M. Seguin, 'Ambiguous Liaisons: Catholic Women's Relationships with their Confessors in Early Modern England', Archiv für Reformationsgeschichte, 95 (2004), 156–85.

[169] Christine Peters, 'Religious, Household-State Authority, and the Defense of "Collapsed Ladies" in Early Jacobean England', Sixteenth Century Journal, 45 (2014), 631–57.

[170] Henry Garnet, A treatise of Christian renunciation... wherin is shewed how farre it is lawfull or necessary for the love of Christ to forsake father, mother, wife and children, and all other worldly creatures ([1593]; STC 11617.8), pp. 144–8.

[171] Quotation from Mary Elizabeth Perry, 'Space of Resistance, Site of Betrayal: Morisco Homes in Sixteenth-Century Spain', in Nicholas Howe (ed.), Home and Homelessness in the Medieval and Renaissance World (Notre Dame, IN, 2004), pp. 57–90, at p. 70.

[172] AAW/HIS/4/15 (copy of a letter from John Piers, 9 May 1590).

of children themselves. As we saw in Chapter 1, a similar form of coercive paternalism came into play when parents were perceived to be negligent in the religious duty of upbringing. The magistrate asserted his right to act *in loco parentis* when the spiritual welfare of their offspring was in jeopardy.[173] In situations such as this fatherhood was 'a transferable identity'. Patriarchal privilege became concentrated in the hands of the minority of men deemed fit to exercise it.[174] In Calvin's Geneva, illegitimate children were presented for baptism by Reformed Church members in the absence of their delinquent parents. As Karen Spierling remarks, in emphasizing the responsibility of fathers, the authorities here were confronted by a paradox. They simultaneously affirmed parental authority and justified its usurpation when people failed to live up to godly standards.[175]

As recent work on the Court of Wards demonstrates, in England the strategy of taking the young into care was, in fact, employed only occasionally.[176] An anti-Catholic bill of 1593 which would have transferred the children of recusants into the charge of surrogate parents at the age of 7 and imposed crippling fines on the men married to recalcitrant nonconformists was modified by MPs in the Commons in ways that underline the government's reluctance to interfere too far into family life.[177] An ordinance of 1643 adopted the indirect tactic of sequestering the goods and estates of Catholics whose children, grandchildren, and co-resident servants and dependants had been brought up in the popish religion. It was rumoured that the Cromwellian statute against recusants of 1657 would prescribe the education of their offspring 'in the doctrines of Luther and Calvin', but no such clause materialized. If 'the state never quite codified a claim to be the primary custodian of children', it also never entirely abandoned the notion that it had the right to appoint foster parents.[178] Illustrating these ambiguities, Jeremy Taylor's *Ductor dubitantium* upheld the precept that a father's authority did not

---

[173] Patricia Crawford, *Parents of Poor Children in England, 1580–1800* (Oxford, 2010), pp. 15–16 and ch. 5. See also Chapter 1 above. On masculinity, see Shannon McSheffrey, 'Man and Masculinity in Late Medieval London Civic Culture: Governance, Patriarchy and Reputation', in Jacqueline Murray (ed.), *Conflicted Identities and Multiple Masculinities: Men in the Medieval West* (New York, 1999), pp. 243–78; Shepard, *Meanings of Manhood*, esp. ch. 3.

[174] See Alexandra Shepard, 'Brokering Fatherhood: Illegitimacy and Paternal Rights and Responsibilities in Early Modern England', in Steve Hindle, Alexandra Shepard, and John Walter (eds), *Remaking English Society: Social Relations and Social Change in Early Modern England* (Woodbridge, 2013), pp. 41–63, at pp. 44, 63.

[175] Karen E. Spierling, *Infant Baptism in Reformation Geneva* (Aldershot, 2005), p. 221. On the baptism of illegitimate children, see ch. 5.

[176] Lucy Underwood, *Childhood, Youth and Religious Dissent in Post-Reformation England* (Basingstoke, 2014), ch. 4. See also *eadem*, 'The State, Childhood and Religious Dissent', in Hannah Crawforth and Sarah Lewis (eds), *Family Politics in Early Modern Literature* (Basingstoke, 2013), pp. 191–210.

[177] John Neale, *Queen Elizabeth and Her Parliaments*, vol. ii (1957), pp. 281, 293–4, 297; Bossy, *English Catholic Community*, pp. 155–7; Marie B. Rowlands, 'Recusant Women 1560–1640', in Mary Prior (ed.), *Women in English Society 1500–1800* (1985), pp. 149–80, at pp. 154–5. The Act is 35 Eliz. C. 2.

[178] Underwood, *Childhood, Youth and Religious Dissent*, pp. 102–3 and see ch. 5.

extend to 'matter of Religion' and into the 'Court of Conscience', but also said that the child of an infidel could be baptized by his believing parent. Applying a further double standard, he declared that 'in the Countries of the Roman Communion' this was practised to 'evil purposes' by disqualifying a heretic father from the right to govern his offspring.[179]

Many continued to worry that the family was a key agent in perpetuating popery and preventing its natural extinction. Hence Protestantism's consistent condemnation of mixed marriages. Probably written in the 1630s, the archdeacon of Surrey and rector of Exeter College, Oxford, George Hakewill's unpublished treatise 'The Wedding Robe' stressed the hazards that marrying idolatrous papists posed not just to the parties themselves but also to their offspring, especially when Catholicism travelled down the maternal line. Hakewill stressed the superior power of a mother of 'the right Roman stamp' to breed her infants in idolatry and superstition, especially since she regarded herself as 'not bound to yield to her husband true benevolence'.[180] A different window onto the tensions within families divided by faith is provided by an anti-Catholic pamphlet about the Hertfordshire matron Margaret Vincent, who converted to the Church of Rome around 1616 and killed her own children to save their souls from the 'blindnes and darksome errours' in which they had been brought up by order of their father. By murdering them, this 'pitilesse or Tygerous Mother' reportedly believed she had made them into martyrs and secured their place in the company of saints in heaven. She had carried out her maternal responsibility to work for their salvation.[181]

This was evidence filtered through a hostile lens, but it finds confirmation in internal Catholic sources. The response to one Caroline case of conscience warned parents that allowing their children to lodge with Protestant friends and relations was equivalent to throwing them into 'miseries for eternity, in a worse place than beasts'. The danger of their spiritual perversion was acute.[182] The conviction that mothers and fathers had a duty to propagate the true religion to their children explains the increasingly close ties of kinship that developed between Catholic families. Their growing tendency to intermarry created biological as well as spiritual links between the tight-knit body of committed believers created by England's Counter-Reformation. It turned cousins in Christ into relations linked by law and by blood.

---

[179] Jeremy Taylor, *Ductor dubitantium, or the rule of conscience in all her generall measures* (1660; Wing T324), book 3, ch. 5, pp. 369–70.

[180] Bodl., MS Jones 14, item 3, fo. 313v.

[181] *A pitilesse mother. That most unnaturally at one time, murth[ered] two of her own children at Acton within six miles of London uppon holy Thursday last 1616* ([1616], STC 24757).

[182] Peter Holmes (ed.), *Caroline Casuistry: The Cases of Conscience of Fr Thomas Southwell SJ*, CRS 84 (Woodbridge, 2012), p. 24.

Yet we should overemphasize neither the solidarity nor the endogamy of this community. Families were not immune to the internal frictions over hierarchy, governance, and mission that consumed English Catholicism in the early seventeenth century. As James Kelly has commented, they were paradoxically both 'fault-lines' within it and the 'ideological glue' that bound it together. Internal splits over whether to support the strategies of the Jesuits or the secular clergy were not uncommon: in Essex, these questions challenged the unity of the Petre and Southcote dynasties.[183] Nor were these households impermeable to Protestantism and the presence of relatives and acquaintances whose religious convictions theoretically rendered them enemies of God. This did not necessarily disturb peaceful relations. As Bill Sheils's study of Egton on the north York moors reveals, bonds between family members just as often helped to break down confessional barriers within generations as it did to cement them between the generations.[184] Kinship and friendship continued to operate unpredictably, complicating English society in ways that entrenched religious pluralism. They led to mixed marriages between Catholics and Protestants and they excused the conduct of children who cast off the traditional religion of their mothers and fathers. They enabled the development of what Norman Jones has called 'treaties of private toleration' that held together families and households whose members were fractured by faith, allowing 'the bonds of love and duty to paper over the chasms of ideology'.[185]

Spiritual Kinship

Thus far discussion has centered on the biological family and the relatives and friends who temporarily sheltered under the umbrella of the early modern household. It has privileged spatial proximity and co-residence as the criteria for inclusion in this category and reinforced the insight that any definition limited to those linked by blood effaces the omnipresence of people bound by alternative ties of obligation, patronage, and service. It has shown that the family became a critical forum in which religious renewal and resistance occurred and explored some of the ways in which the Reformation served both to cement and to complicate the potent metaphor of the Church as the family of God, an imagined community that transcended physical walls and incorporated kith as well as kin. In the remaining sections of this chapter, I turn the problem inside out and examine the theme of spiritual kinship. My aim is to investigate how fictive and artificial

[183]   James E. Kelly, 'Kinship and Religious Politics among Catholic Families in England, 1570–1640', *History*, 94 (2009), 328–43, at 329.

[184]   William Sheils, 'Catholics and Their Neighbours in a Rural Community: Egton Chapelry 1590–1780', *Northern History*, 34 (1998), 109–33.

[185]   Norman Jones, *The English Reformation: Religion and Cultural Adaptation* (Oxford, 2002), p. 199.

relationships created by ritual, theology, and liturgy shaped social interactions alongside and in conjunction with bonds of consanguinity and affinity. In the process, I shall argue that the role of England's intertwined Reformations in eroding religious kinship and sapping its power to bind communities together should be revisited. If these developments consigned some traditional forms to the scrapheap, they retained others in modified guise and created new ones.

One institution that managed to navigate the choppy waters of religious change was godparenthood. In medieval Catholicism, the appointment of godparents who vowed on behalf of the infant to forsake the Devil and all his works was an integral element of the rite of baptism by which children were cleansed of the sin they had inherited from Adam and Eve via their progenitors. As formulated by Thomas Aquinas, this practice rested on drawing a clear distinction between the natural parents who had carnally engendered them and those who took responsibility for their spiritual regeneration by presenting them for christening. This was a legacy of early Christianity in which the orthodoxy of the former could not be taken for granted. Its paradoxical consequence, however, was to treat them as effectively equivalent, to make godparents into kin, and to render it illegal for their godchildren to marry them or their blood relatives. This was technically classified as incest.[186]

Protestantism's attitude towards godparenthood was ambivalent.[187] Influenced by Luther's views on the subject, Cranmer's liturgy for the sacrament of baptism for the Book of Common Prayer retained this Christian office. The Church of England abolished the attendant impediments to marriage.[188] It emphatically denied that a state of kindred was contracted in and through baptism, which was simply a sign or seal rather than a cause of supernatural rebirth. The ecclesiastical prohibition on marrying was regarded as an invention of medieval Catholic canonists. As William Perkins commented, since all believers were 'brethren and sisters in Christ' and 'spiritually allied' in some sense, the logic of this taboo was that Christians would never be permitted to match with each other, but only with pagans and infidels.[189] The puritan authors of the 1572 Admonition to Parliament articulated the view that godparents themselves were unnecessary and that though not expressly prohibited in Scripture, this was one of the 'childishe and

---

[186] Will Coster, *Baptism and Spiritual Kinship in Early Modern England* (Aldershot, 2002), ch. 3. For Aquinas, see p. 78. See also William Coster, ' "From Fire and Water": The Responsibilities of Godparents in Early Modern England', in Diana Wood (ed.), *The Church and Childhood*, SCH 31 (Oxford, 1994), pp. 301–11. The earlier history is traced in Joseph H. Lynch, *Godparents and Kinship in Early Medieval Europe* (Princeton, NJ, 1986). See also Guido Alfani and Nicholas Gourdon (eds), *Spiritual Kinship in Europe, 1500–1900* (Basingstoke, 2012), esp. 'Spiritual Kinship and Godparenthood: An Introduction', pp. 1–43.

[187] In addition to Coster, *Baptism and Spiritual Kinship*, see David Cressy, *Birth, Marriage and Death: Ritual, Religion and the Life-Cycle in Tudor and Stuart England* (Oxford, 1997), ch. 7.

[188] Cummings (ed.), *Book of Common Prayer*, pp. 46–57, 141–50, 408–25.

[189] William Perkins, *The whole treatise of the cases of conscience, distinguished into three bookes* (Cambridge, 1606; STC 19669), pp. 322–3.

superstitious toyes' for which there was no apostolic evidence.[190] Thomas Becon
listed it among his 'reliques of Rome'; James Calfhill declared that the second-
century Pope Hyginus had 'hatched thys egge'; and Anthony Gilby included the
promises made by spiritual kin in his list of a 'hundred pointes of Poperie, yet
remayning, which deforme the Englishe reformation'.[191] The separatist Henry
Barrow roundly condemned these 'special Gossipes' (a colloquial corruption of
the word 'godsib' or sibling) among other 'fond trifling ceremonies...added to
their Sacramentes'.[192] Anabaptists wasted no breath on the subject, which their
position on paedobaptism rendered completely redundant.

At the heart of these critiques was the conviction that the duty of caring for the
physical and spiritual needs of children should be consolidated and concentrated
in the persons of their biological parents and within the nuclear family. The idea
that fathers should present their own offspring for baptism and not shift responsibility onto a proxy was a by-product of the spiritualization of the household. The
Scottish kirk saw this relationship as a mirror of that between God, Christ, and
the Church.[193] In England, the resilience of the official position that these two
roles should be separate was reflected in visitation articles enquiring whether
any persons had been admitted to serve as godfather or godmother to their own
children.[194] Richard Baxter's critical aside about 'Parents who set God-fathers at
the Font, to Vow and Promise to do the Parents part' is indicative of the puritan
conviction that they should not be distinct.[195] The only situation in which some
form of surrogate was regarded as legitimate was when a child's parents had died
or otherwise defaulted in their role as its religious tutors.

Godparents were eliminated from the liturgy for baptism in the Directory of
Public Worship in 1643, which required the father to present the infant or
'(in case of his necessary absence)...some Christian friend'.[196] But to say that
puritans were 'naturally hostile to an institution specifically designed to create links

[190] An admonition to the Parliament ([Hemel Hempstead, 1572]; STC 10847), sig. C2r–v.
[191] Thomas Becon, The reliques of Rome contayning all such matters of religion, as have in times past bene brought into the Church by the Pope and his adherents (1563; STC 1755), fo. 96r–v; James Calfhill, An aunswere to the treatise of the crosse wherin ye shal see the plaine and undoubted word of God, the vanities of men disproved (1565; STC 4368), p. 105; Anthony Gilby, A pleasant dialogue, betweene a souldior of Barwicke, and an English chaplain ([Middelburg?], 1581; STC 11888), sig. M5r.
[192] Henry Barrow, A brief discoverie of the false church ([Dort?], 1590 [1591]; STC 1517), p. 100.
[193] See Melissa Hollander, 'The Name of the Father: Baptism and the Social Construction of Fatherhood in Early Modern Edinburgh', in Elizabeth Ewan and Janay Nugent (eds), Finding the Family in Medieval and Early Modern Scotland (Aldershot, 2008), pp. 63–72.
[194] See, e.g., Advertisements partly for due order in the publique administration of common prayers and usinge the holy sacramentes (1565; STC 10027), sig. B1r; and Articles ecclesiastical to be enquired of by the church-wardens and sworne-men...in the visitation (1621; STC 10133.9), sig. B2r; Articles to be enquired of, and answered unto by the church-wardens and sworn-men in the visitation (1666; Wing C4009E), p. 4. This enquiry reflected Canon 29 of 1604.
[195] Baxter, Catechizing of families, sig. A4r. See also his A Christian directory: or, a sum of practical theologie, and cases of conscience (1678; Wing B1220), bk 3, pp. 114–15.
[196] A directory for the publique worship of God, throughout the three kingdoms of England, Scotland and Ireland (1644; Wing D1544), pp. 40, 43–4.

between members of different households, sexes and social strata' is a mistake.[197] Even in Geneva, the practice persisted, recast in a reformed guise that prioritized the educational responsibilities of godparents, in a sign of compromise with the deep-seated familial and social ties forged by the baptismal rite. John Calvin himself served as a godfather to no fewer than forty-seven children between 1550 and 1563.[198]

In England, there were hardliners, but the majority of Protestants with scruples about godparents ultimately compromised, recognizing that though the institution was not directly grounded in Scripture, it was also 'not repugnant thereunto'. Many exchanged the irksome name 'godparent' for the more neutral terms 'witnesses' or 'sureties', which removed the connotations of kinship and eliminated any hint that they had spiritual agency in the infant's symbolic admission to the church family. The whole congregation of the faithful was sufficient to attest to this, though godparents retained some utility as supplementary instructors. The Restoration divine Thomas Comber defended godparenthood more robustly, declaring that those who thought they could 'shake off this Charge...and assign it over to the Parents' was one of 'the evil Customs of this Licentious Age'. Supervisors were needed when mothers and fathers were dilatory. They thereby became 'Instruments' of their neighbours' salvation and fulfilled the biblical mandate that 'every Christian must reprove his offending Brother'.[199] The Hampshire minister John Birket drew on the precedent of St Paul, 'father to the Corinthians', saying that those who undertook the office had the same duty to bring about the 'new and spiritual Birth' of the children for whom they had been appointed as godparents. There was no residue of superstition in the use of sureties, whose presence in the Church long predated the advent of popery.[200]

In practice, there was often considerable overlap between religious kith and kin. Godparents were often blood relations of the children for whom they acted as sponsors, as the lists of them inserted in some bibles, prayer books, and other manuscripts alongside other genealogical data reveal.[201] Aunts and uncles were a popular choice of the Graham family of Norton Conyers, Yorkshire, while the witnesses to the baptism of Bathshua, daughter of the Northamptonshire puritan minister Robert Smart, who was born in 1594, were her maternal and paternal grandparents.[202] Thomas Congreve of Stretton in Staffordshire kept genealogical

---

[197] Coster, *Baptism and Spiritual Kinship*, p. 276.

[198] Spierling, *Infant Baptism*, ch. 4, citation at p. 115.

[199] Thomas Comber, *A brief discourse upon the offices of baptism, catechism and confirmation* (1677), bound with *A companion to the altar. Or a help to the worthy receiving of the Lords supper* (1678; Wing C5450A), pp. 444–50.

[200] John Birket, *The god-father's advice to his son. Shewing the necessity of performing the baptismal vow, and the danger of neglecting it* (1700), pp. 34–6.

[201] See SA, MI 1841/1 (Calcott family bible); DRO, D3850/FZ/18 (Longsdon family papers, list of godfathers and mothers). These exist alongside lists of births, marriages, and deaths: FZ/6, 7, 8, 9, 17.

[202] NYCRO, ZKZ/4/9 (Graham family bible); BL, Sloane MS 271, fo. 72v.

records of his godchildren as well as his own offspring in a memorandum book that attests to the close intersections between biological and spiritual kinship in this period. When his daughter-in-law Dorothy, née Brooke, was delivered of a baby girl in July 1608, the godparents were his wife and two of her cousins.[203] In the parish of Almondbury in Yorkshire, as many as 42.2% of those recorded in the surviving early modern parish registers were relatives; by contrast, at St Margaret's church in York, it was only 1.9%.[204] Godparenthood was one of the powerful links that connected unmarried women with their natal families and which reciprocally bound together sisters and their daughters and nieces.[205]

During the Middle Ages what anthropologists call extension rather than intensification of the web of kinship was the norm; in the *longue durée* the pattern was reversed.[206] In the post-Reformation era, godparenthood wove threads within but also beyond the conjugal family that bear out David Cressy and Naomi Tadmor's suggestions that such ties had greater significance and more latent potential than has often been claimed.[207] They created horizontal and vertical links and facilitated forms of religious and secular interaction that help to explain why the word used to describe them, 'gossip', evolved into a synonym for sociability. And if many godparents were simply sleeping partners in the task of directing the Christian young, others took their responsibilities very seriously indeed. A child who stole a chicken in seventeenth-century Essex was sharply reproved by her godmother, who said 'Thou art my goddaughter, and surelie if thy parents will not convert thee, I will' and proceeded 'then and there...[to] bete her.'[208] Six-year-old Adam Martindale received an ABC from his, given 'out of a reall

[203] SRO, D1057/O/1 A-B ('Memorandum & Manuscript of Congreves of Stretton, Staffordshire', 1580), fos 12v, 30v, 71v, 77r-v.
[204] Coster, *Baptism and Spiritual Kinship*, p. 139.
[205] Froide, *Never Married*, ch. 3, esp. p. 47.
[206] Philip Niles estimates that only about 8% of godparents came from patrilineal kin at the end of the Middle Ages: 'Baptism and the Naming of Children in Late Medieval England', *Medieval Prosopography*, 3 (1982), 95-107. Louis Haas posits a figure of 15% of godparents as blood relatives: 'Social Connections between Parents and Godparents in Late Medieval Yorkshire', *Medieval Prosopography*, 10 (1989), 1-21. For long term trends, see Guido Alfani, 'The Reformation, the Council of Trent and the Divergence of Spiritual Kinship and Godparenthood across Europe: A Long-Run Analysis', in Silvia Sovic, Pat Thane, and Pier Paolo Viazzo (eds), *The History of Families and Households: Comparative European Dimensions* (Leiden, 2016), pp. 142-67, esp. pp. 162-3, 167.
[207] Cressy, 'Kinship and Kin Interaction'; Tadmor, 'Early Modern English Kinship'. See also Miranda Chaytor, 'Household and Kinship in Ryton in the Late Sixteenth and Early Seventeenth Centuries', *History Workshop*, 10 (1980), 25-60; but cf. Keith Wrightson, 'Household and Kinship in Sixteenth-Century England', *History Workshop Journal*, 12 (1981), 151-8. See also Robert Lutton, 'Godparenthood, Kinship and Piety in Tenterden, England, 1449-1537', in Isabel Davis, Miriam Müller, and Sarah Rees Jones (eds), *Love, Marriage and Family Ties in the Middle Ages* (Turnhout, 2003), pp. 217-34; Clodagh Tait, 'Spiritual Bonds, Social Bonds: Baptism and Godparenthood in Ireland, 1530-1690', *Cultural and Social History*, 2 (2005), 301-27.
[208] Cited in Alan Macfarlane, *The Family Life of Ralph Josselin, a Seventeenth-Century Clergyman: An Essay in Historical Anthropology* (Cambridge, 1970), p. 144n.

principle of conscience to performe her promises and engagements for me at my baptisme.[209]

Sometimes godparenthood forged connections across confessional boundaries. Invitations to act in this capacity and a corresponding willingness to serve testify to the practical forms of coexistence that developed at the grassroots between Protestants and Catholics, Dissenters and Anglicans. Despite canonical rules urging minimal contact with heretics, some Jesuit casuists sanctioned this on the grounds that children were not generally educated by their godparents.[210] Some Church of England ministers hoped that such spiritual alliances might have salutary effects. The vicar of Westham in Sussex inserted an entry in his parish register recording the baptism of Margaret Thatcher, the daughter of a recusant, who 'had a good Protestante to her Godfather Mr Herbert Pelham. I pray God the Childe maye Learne of the godfather and godmother Mtrs Morley of Glyn[d]e Anno Domini 1572.'[211] The ritual could also be used to police the boundaries of ecclesiastical orthodoxy, as in the case of the Laudian minister in Oxford who refused to allow a man who would not bow at the name of Jesus to be appointed a godfather.[212] Godparenthood may only have survived the Reformation by the skin of its teeth, but the resilience and adaptability of this institution should be underlined. Its Protestant history is less a symptom of the demise of forms of Christian community in favour of individualism than an index of a wider shift towards a greater convergence between biological and spiritual kinship.[213] As I shall argue below, this was one of the unexpected side effects of the gradual eclipse of the tenacious ideal of Christian unity by grudging acknowledgement of a whole series of churches each claiming to be the ark of salvation.

One version of spiritual kinship that was a conspicuous casualty of Protestantism's doctrinal priorities was the fraternity or guild. These voluntary associations of devout people eager to join together for mutual support and to carry out charitable activity provided their members with access to indulgences, vicarious intercession, and post-mortem remembrance. They were unions of prayerful people who sought the company of fellow Christians who were not part

[209] *The Life of Adam Martindale Written by Himself*, ed. R. Parkinson, Chetham Society 4 (Manchester, 1845), p. 5.
[210] See Holmes (ed.), *Caroline Casuistry*, pp. 10–11.
[211] Brighton, East Sussex Record Office, PAR 505/1/1/1 (parish register of Westham, Sussex). I am very grateful to Christopher Whittick for this reference and for further information about the Thatcher family.
[212] Cited in Cressy, *Birth, Marriage and Death*, p. 155.
[213] Cf. John Bossy, 'Godparenthood: The Fortunes of a Social Institution in Early Modern Christianity', in Kaspar von Greyerz (ed.), *Religion and Society in Early Modern Europe 1500–1800* (1984), pp. 194–201. For its evolution in a Catholic context, see Guido Alfani, *Fathers and Godfathers: Spiritual Kinship in Early Modern Italy* (Farnham, 2009), esp. chs 4–5. He argues that the Tridentine reforms effected a greater transformation of patterns of behaviour than Protestantism, which permitted the persistence of traditional customs: 'Reformation...and the Divergence of Spiritual Kinship', pp. 158–9.

of their own circles of kin. A critical manifestation of what John Bossy calls the late medieval 'social miracle', some were extra-local and regional organizations that linked individuals unknown to each other and dispersed by physical distance. If these religious brotherhoods and sisterhoods sometimes functioned as a form of substitute kindred, their role in binding together kith from different households must also be recognized. They were societies that fostered an elaborate network of religious affection and friendship.[214] Those linked with local abbeys and priories offered their members a share in the spiritual benefit of the monks' prayers. Certificatory letters such as those issued to Edmund Mauleverer and his wife Eleanor by the Augustinian friars in 1472 and to Johanna Bigod and her husband John by the Carthusians of Mount Grace Priory in 1520 made them honorary members of the sprawling monastic families that were religious orders.[215]

Fraternities of men and women striving to accumulate merit to secure their collective salvation were an affront to the central tenets of justification by faith and God-given grace, regardless of how people behaved during their lives. They were swept away along with other institutions that embodied the theological assumption that spiritual benefits were transferable. The precept that this kind of credit could be extended vertically as well as horizontally, to dead as well as to living generations, was no less offensive to the reformers. Their disappearance represented a profound attack upon a central plank of traditional Christianity.

Discarded by Protestantism, fraternities were subject to reform by the Tridentine Church, which sought to regulate their autonomy, discipline their secular activities, and ensure that they did not provide a rival point of identity to the parochial church.[216] But these 'artificial kin groups' did not lose their social relevance in Catholic Europe. Revived and promoted by the Jesuits as a tool of spiritual intensification and an instrument of confessional identity formation, congregations devoted to the Virgin Mary proliferated and became an international movement. These Marian sodalities were imported into England by the members of the Society of Jesus who came as missionaries from the 1580s

---

[214] Bossy, *Christianity in the West*, ch. 4. See Virginia R. Bainbridge, *Gilds in the Medieval Countryside: Social and Religious Change in Cambridgeshire c.1350–1558* (Woodbridge, 1996); Gervase Rosser, *The Art of Solidarity in the Middle Ages: Guilds in England, 1250–1550* (Oxford, 2015), esp. ch. 3.

[215] NYCRO, ZFL 184 and 57. These are printed in M.Y. Aschcroft and E. A. Jones, *Monastic Charters and Other Documents Relating to Medieval Piety in the North Yorkshire County Record Office*, 2 vols (Northallerton, 2009), vol. i, pp. 440–1, 444. Another example issued to Robert and Alice Claxton in 1508 can be found in DCRO, D/Lo/F 327.

[216] For some important studies, see Louis Chatellier, *The Europe of the Devout: The Catholic Reformation and the Formation of a New Society* (Cambridge, 1989); Nicholas Terpstra (ed.), *The Politics of Ritual Kinship: Confraternities and Social Order in Early Modern Italy* (Cambridge, 1999); Christopher F. Black, *Italian Confraternities in the Sixteenth Century* (Cambridge, 2003); Lance Gabriel Lazar, *Working in the Vineyard of the Lord: Jesuit Confraternities in Early Modern Italy* (Toronto, 2005); Christopher Black and Pamela Gravestock (eds), *Early Modern Confraternities in Europe and the Americas: International and Interdisciplinary Perspectives* (Aldershot, 2006).

onwards. They were pop-up institutions well suited to the peripatetic lives of the community's priests and to an environment in which worship and devotion was of necessity clandestine and, as we have seen, often centred upon the family home.[217] Anne Dillon has investigated how recusant households such as Dorothy Lawson's in Northumberland became a locus for Catholic fellowship. Overseen by her chaplain, Lawson's was devoted to the Immaculate Conception. She not only assiduously enrolled all her children in the sodality but also recommended the admission by her 'ghostly father' of such servants and neighbours as 'she found capable of that devotion'. It helped to bind together relatives, dependants, and friends and connect them virtually, via the mechanism of prayer and meditation, with their coreligionists in England and elsewhere.[218]

This was a religious organism which the Jesuits also creatively adapted for Catholic laypeople who rarely had contact with priests and were only intermittently able to participate in the liturgy. They actively encouraged the formation of spiritual networks that connected their members through shared rituals, enhanced their spiritual knowledge, gave them access to the treasury of merit channelled through indulgences, and served as a 'safe haven' until penitents could be sacramentally absolved of their sins. As described in Henry Garnet's handbook for the *Societie of the rosarie* printed around 1593, their aim was 'to knit together in one band of mutual Societie all kind of devout Christians' and to do so under the banner of the Virgin Mary, the Mother of God. Her status as a shield against and scourge of heretics made her a natural mascot for these cells of dissident piety, from which, as Garnet stressed, none should be excluded, 'neither the husbandman in the fields, nor the travailer in his jorney, nor the labourer with his toiling, nor the simple by his unskilfulness', neither women nor men, neither young or old, neither the crippled nor blind. The only requirement was thrice weekly recitation of prayers with the aid of rosary beads. In an emergency this could be done by another on one's behalf, 'who performeth the due exercise for his brother, being either sicke or otherwise hindered'. The practice of formally recording those received into this 'holy company' in writing was to be followed, but once their names had been taken down, it was expedient and in the interests of their safety that the document be torn up.[219] This is one reason why these voluntary associations have left so little trace in the historical record: the hostile

---

[217] Anne Dillon, 'Praying by Number: The Confraternity of the Rosary and the English Catholic Community, *c.*1580–1700', *History*, 88 (2003), 451–71, esp. 468. Lisa McClain, 'Using What's at Hand: English Catholic Reinterpretations of the Rosary, 1559–1642', *JRH*, 27 (2003), 161–76.

[218] Palmes, *Life of Mrs Dorothy Lawson*, pp. 33–4. See also Anne Dillon, 'Public Liturgy Made Private: The Rosary Confraternity in the Life of a Recusant Household', in Peter Davidson and Jill Belper (eds), *The Triumphs of the Defeated: Early Modern Festivals and Messages of Legitimacy* (Wiesbaden, 2007), pp. 245–70.

[219] Henry Garnet, *The societie of the rosary. Newly augumented* (1596]; STC 11617.5), pp. 3–4, 7, 20–1. The first edition was published in 1593 or 1594. For another little booklet guiding such confraternal devotions, see *The arch-confraternity of the holy rosary of our blessed lady* (1636).

Protestant report of twelve women and three or four men discovered 'at their beads' in Bath in 1667 is an example of an elusive local phenomenon that must have helped to compensate for the absence of regular worship and functioned as a surrogate for the parish.[220] The sodality had special utility for a scattered community under the cross determined to avoid its own annihilation and conscious of being part of a universal Catholic household that was triumphantly resurgent in the early modern world.

Missionaries from other religious orders also introduced confraternities. The Franciscan confraternity of the Cord of the Passion appears to have had sufficient numbers of devotees in England to warrant the publication of a vernacular translation of its manual. Printed in 1654, this saw such congregations as an auxiliary to the family. It envisaged them as schools in which children would be instructed and by which 'the Father...is discharged of his duty'. It emphasized that 'the mutuall provocation of each other to the workes of piety & love' that followed from joining such a society was superior to what could be achieved by an individual alone. It presented the fraternity as a walled city:

> fenced against all invasions; for as corporall Brethren, living in unitie & peace, doe much advance their familie: so spirituall Brethren, joyned in charitie & devotion, doe strengthen and corroborate each other, to the great advancement of Christian perfection.[221]

The same precepts underpinned the Benedictine confraternities that sprang up in the early seventeenth century. A fragmentary printed indulgence dating from 1628 and now in Cambridge University Library is a certificate of the admission of an unnamed person to the suffrages of the order. Signed by Father Leander, the vicar general, it promises that diligent performance of prayer, examination of conscience, and penance will enable those 'thus admitted to our brotherhood' to tap into the cumulative merit of its illustrious members throughout ages, including St Benedict, St Anselm, St Boniface, St Hildegard, and St Etheldreda, 'besides others innumerable whose names wee know not, which yet are written in the booke of life'. The recipient could trust 'in the favour of above 55510 Saints' who would intercede actively for his or her salvation. Stretching across the generations, this was a very large family indeed.[222]

One such Benedictine confraternity, dedicated to Our Lady of Power, was set up in the chapel of Cardigan House in London, the home of Robert Brudenell, sometime between 1650 and 1655, and remained active until the Popish Plot,

[220] J. Anthony Williams (ed.), *Post-Reformation Catholicism in Bath*, vol. i, CRS 65 (1975), p. 37.
[221] Angelus à Sancto Francisco, *A manuell of the arch-confraternitie of the cord of the passion, instituted in the seraphicall order of S. Francis* (Douai, 1654; Wing M939), pp. 51, 53, 55.
[222] [*Letter of confraternity of the English Benedictines*] (Douai, 1628; STC Indulgence 23): CUL Broadsides B.62.18.

when it was suspended. Clearly this was a fellowship that incorporated his own close relatives and resident staff and servants, but it was also envisaged as extending to the city tradesmen and shopkeepers who lived in proximity to the Brudenell residence. This had its own handbook, which exists in two editions, one published during the Interregnum in 1657 and a second which appeared in 1663 and was dedicated to Charles II's consort Catherine of Braganza. It sailed under the flagship of the Blessed Virgin, and its title page combined images of Saints Benedict and Dominic with a touching depiction of the Holy Family (Fig. 2.6). Ringed by a rosary, Mary and Joseph bold the hands of Jesus and gaze affectionately upon the happy toddler under their care. This was a text that encouraged members of the fraternity to think of themselves as members of God's family. The preface was an extended dilation on this theme that celebrated Mary as 'the Common Mother' of all 'pious Christians' and Joseph as 'her glorious Bridegroom' and presented laypeople as the step-siblings and 'adopted brethren' of Christ. Confusingly, they were also the Virgin's grandchildren, 'the Children of her Child, by whom we are regenerated to a spirituall life'. Brudenell's introduction described the 'Mother of Power' as a refuge for sinners and a refuge from 'the tempestuous winds and billows', dangers, distresses, and difficulties of the times—in other words from the hatred and hostility to which Catholics were subjected by the heretics by which they were surrounded, which, especially in the capital, sometimes spilled out into overt violence.[223]

Such confraternities also connected Catholics who stayed in England with those who had chosen to leave and settle overseas. They were Skype-like devices for binding a lay and clerical diaspora that moved across frontiers and territorial boundaries. Embodying what Liesbeth Corens has fruitfully called 'confessional mobility', they connected blood relations and spiritual relations living both at home and in exile.[224] Enrolling members both absent and present, they overlapped with the newly founded religious houses across the Channel to provide places of asylum but also to function as a launching pad for attempts at regime change, whether through physical force or through the puissant weapon of intercessory prayer. They were part of a fabric in which ties of Catholic affinity

---

[223] A[rthur] C[rowther], *Jesus, Maria, Joseph, or, The devout pilgrim, of the ever blessed Virgin Mary, in his holy exercises, affections, and elevations. Upon the sacred mysteries of Jesus, Maria, Joseph. Published for the benefit of the pious rosarists* (Amsterdam, 1657; Wing C7410), sigs b3r, b5r, pp. 1, 17. The 1663 edition (Wing C7411) contains a dedication to Catherine of Braganza. On this confraternity, see Anne Dillon, ' "To Seek out some Comforts and Companions of his own Kind and Condition": The Benedictine Rosary Confraternity and Chapel of Cardigan House, London', in Lowell Gallagher (ed.), *Redrawing the Map of Early Modern English Catholicism* (Toronto, 2012), pp. 272–308.

[224] Liesbeth Corens, *Confessional Mobility and English Catholics in Counter-Reformation Europe* (Oxford, 2019), esp. pp. 143–9.

Fig. 2.6 A[rthur] C[rowther], *Jesus, Maria, Joseph, or, The devout pilgrim, of the ever blessed Virgin Mary, in his holy exercises, affections, and elevations. Upon the sacred mysteries of Jesus, Maria, Joseph. Published for the benefit of the pious rosarists* (Amsterdam, 1663), title page and frontispiece.

Source: © British Library Board, 699.a.44. All Rights Reserved/Bridgeman Images.

originating in the biological family intertwined with those rooted in the quasi-familial organizations that were monasteries and convents.

Monasticism is the second form of Christian kinship that the Tudor Reformation brought to an end. The Henrician suppression of the religious houses between 1536 and 1539 violently dismantled an institution that embodied both a rejection of the human family through the vows of chastity taken by monks and nuns and an attempt to create an alternative household modelled on divine relations. A central strategy of the government-sponsored propaganda that justified the dissolution was to attack the monasteries as nests of sin and vice in which celibacy was a hypocritical cloak for rampant sexual promiscuity. Stories of the illegitimate children engendered by these illicit unions became a trope of Protestant polemic, the dark underside of its celebration of the conjugal couple and its godly offspring.[225] The closure of religious houses resulted in the mass displacement of persons, some of whom returned to their families. Elizabeth Craike, a former nun of Wilberfoss in Yorkshire, evidently went back to live with her mother, who left her an annuity as well as bedding, linen, and household equipment when she died in 1548.[226] It was to Elizabeth Patrike, her friend and former sister in religion, that Elizabeth Thorne of Swine bequeathed her house in Hull, describing her as 'my well-beloved in Christ'.[227] Other former nuns assumed that the Edwardian legislation on clerical marriage applied to them and found husbands.[228] Though some pursued independent paths, male religious likewise frequently fell back on family networks, finding a new home with parents, siblings, and relatives.[229]

A few communities sought to reconstitute themselves, at least partially, in exile, including the small group of Bridgettines from Syon Abbey which was also one of only two houses to be officially revived during the reign of Mary I.[230] Beginning in the 1590s and gathering momentum in the early seventeenth century, a spirited offshore revival of English monastic life in the Low Countries, France, and the Iberian peninsula occurred. The first separate Benedictine convent was founded in Brussels in 1598, and in 1609 a discrete community of Augustinian canonesses, St Monica's, opened in Louvain. This proved so successful in attracting recruits that it spawned a daughter house in the form of the Convent of Nazareth in Bruges, which was operational from 1629. Other orders, including the Franciscans, Dominicans, Carmelites, Sepulchrines, and Poor Clares followed suit and set up their own houses for women in succession. Alongside them emerged a series of communities catering for a corresponding new spurt of male

[225] See Sophie Murray, 'Dissolving into Laughter: Anti-Monastic Satire in the Reign of Henry VIII', in Mark Knights and Adam Morton (eds), *The Power of Laughter and Satire in Early Modern England: Political and Religious Culture 1500–1820* (Woodbridge, 2017), pp. 27–47, esp. pp. 34–8. For post-Reformation examples, see Thomas Robinson, *The anatomie of the English nunnery at Lisbon in Portugall* (1622; STC 21124), esp. pp. 1–2, 7–28; Lewis Owen, *The running register, recording a true relation of the state of the English colledges, seminaries and cloysters in all forraine parts* (1626; STC 18996), pp. 100–2.

[226] Marilyn Oliva, 'Unsafe Passage: The State of Nuns at the Dissolution and Their Conversion to Secular Life', in Joan Greatrex (ed.), *The Vocation of Service to God and Neighbour: Essays on the Interests, Involvements and Problems of Religious Communities and Their Members in Medieval Society* (Turnhout, 1998), pp. 87–104, at p. 97.

[227] Mary Erler, 'Religious Women after the Dissolution: Continuing Community', in Matthew Davies and Andrew Prescott (eds), *London and the Kingdom: Essays in Honour of Caroline M. Barron*, Harlaxton Medieval Studies XVI (Donington, 2008), pp. 135–45, at p. 140.

[228] See Geoffrey Baskerville, 'The Dispossessed Religious after the Suppression of the Monasteries', in Henry W. Davis (ed.), *Essays Presented to Reginald Lane Poole* (Oxford, 1927), pp. 436–65, at pp. 460–1.

[229] James G. Clark, *The Dissolution of the Monasteries: A New History* (New Haven, CT, 2021), ch. 9, esp. p. 447.

[230] See E. A. Jones and Alexandra Walsham (eds), *Syon Abbey and Its Books 1400–1700* (Woodbridge, 2010).

religious vocations, with traditional orders vying with newly constituted ones such as the Capuchins.[231]

Some who joined these orders were people who sought to escape not merely the heat of persecution in England but also broken family relationships. Jeremy Taylor's emphatic denial that it was lawful for children to take religious vows to become priests, monks, friars, or hermits without the consent of their parents alerts us to a problem that was perceived to be commonplace.[232] The life stories enshrined in convent annals and registers likewise suggest that the decision to enter religious life often met with parental opposition or entailed abandoning beloved relatives in order to dedicate oneself to Christ. Drawn by something 'more powerfull then the love of any mortall creature', Lady Mary Roper Lovel left behind her young children to join the Benedictines of Brussels in 1608.[233] The symbolism of the rites of initiation, in which novices ready to take their final vows dressed in elaborate marriage gowns, underlined their status as his brides. Admission to these houses also coincided with abandoning heresy, a process that was itself conceived in familial terms: Anne Fenne abjured the Protestant religion and 'was received into the communion of our holy Mother the church' in the Franciscan convent of the Immaculate Conception in Paris in 1663, while a cer tain Mistress Hilda was likewise welcomed into its maternal 'Bosome' in 1677.[234] Such examples nurtured ongoing misgivings about religious spinsterhood and ensured that late seventeenth-century calls for the establishment of Protestant convents for unmarried women never came to fruition.[235]

The pattern of recruitment to these Continental nunneries was for the most part a family affair, a function of the agency of mothers and fathers, uncles and aunts, who placed young girls in their schools and encouraged them to become nuns.[236] To read the voluminous records of these institutions is to be struck by the dense and tangled web of kinship to which they attest. It is to unearth sisters like Marie and Jane Perkins, who 'took the habit' together in Brussels in 1624 and cousins such as Elizabeth, Grace, and Mary Ingleby, the granddaughters of Sir William Inglebie of Ripley and nieces of a priest martyred at York during the

---

[231] Claire Walker, *Gender and Politics in Early Modern Europe: English Convents in France and the Low Countries* (Basingstoke, 2003); Caroline Bowden and James E. Kelly (eds), *The English Convents in Exile, 1600–1800: Communities, Culture and Identity* (Farnham, 2013). The AHRC 'Who Were the Nuns?' project has transformed our understanding of English female religious houses: http://wwtn. history.qmul.ac.uk, accessed 30 May 2022. The male orders have been comparatively neglected, but see now Cormac Begadon and James E. Kelly (eds), *British and Irish Religious Orders in Europe, 1560–1800: Conventuals, Mendicants, and Monastics in Motion* (Woodbridge, 2022).

[232] Taylor, *Ductor dubitantium*, book 3, ch. 5, pp. 378–81.

[233] Cited in Walker, *Gender and Politics*, p. 36.

[234] Joseph Gillow and Richard Trappes-Lomax (eds), *The Diary of the 'Blue Nuns' or Order of the Immaculate Conception of Our Lady at Paris, 1658–1810* (1910), pp. 15, 27.

[235] Froide, *Never Married*, p. 172.

[236] See the helpful discussion in K. S. B. Keats-Rohan (ed.), *English Catholic Nuns in Exile 1600–1800: A Biographical Register*, Prosopographica and Genealogica, Occasional Publications 15 (Oxford, 2017), introduction, esp. pp. xlvi–liii.

reign of Elizabeth, who were admitted as probationers, aged 22, 25, and 26 the year before.[237] Multiple generations of the prominent Lancashire Catholic family of the Blundells resided in convents in Gravelines, Rouen, Ghent, and Louvain in the late seventeenth century, members of a clan with very long tentacles that tied its lay and religious members together despite their geographical dislocation.[238] The Benedictine monastery of St Gregory's at Douai admitted the brothers James and Christopher Anderton of Lostock in Lancashire, who professed in 1623 and 1624, respectively, while Roger Hesketh was its prior when his nephew and namesake took his vows in 1681.[239] The spiritual families created by the Counter-Reformation thus remained entangled with biological ones in significant ways. A portrait of Margaret Wake dressed as the bride of Christ before her clothing as a Carmelite in 1633 was a poignant memento of a daughter who had left behind her earthly parents and entered the religious life.[240]

Claustration did not prevent those behind the grille and veil from maintaining intimate links with their families in the outside world. Nuns kept in close contact with their relatives via letters, which were accompanied by gifts of relics, and abbesses keenly exploited networks of family patronage to draw donations that would bolster the financial security of their houses. Gentry mothers and wives often temporarily resided in religious houses where their children were being educated as pensioners, and fathers were also regular visitors. The rhythm of religious life mimicked the quasi-monastic regimes that some recusants established in their own households, including the observance of a daily horarium. It is not surprising that after losing her husband, Lady Grace Babthorpe chose to embrace the contemplative life more fully and became an Augustinian canoness at Louvain. She was clothed, together with her own granddaughter Frances, in 1621, in what must have been an emotional ceremony.[241] Other pious widows did the same: Ann Battin 'left ye world' in 1663, two years after her spouse died and she had settled her twelve children, taking her vows with two of her daughters, Elizabeth and Jonne.[242]

The ecclesiastical hierarchy remained conscious that the blood ties that bound members of these communities might interfere with their vocation, as well

---

[237] Richard Trappes-Lomax (ed.), *The English Franciscan Nuns 1619–1821 and the Friars Minor of the Same Province 1618–1761*, CRS 24 (1922), pp. 10–11.

[238] See https://wwtn.history.qmul.ac.uk, s.v. 'Blundell'. See also Walker, *Gender and Power*, p. 28.

[239] See https://community.dur.ac.uk/monksinmotion/, James and Christopher Anderton (Monk ID 372 and 370); Roger and Roger (Jerome) Hesketh (Monk ID 485 and 486).

[240] This portrait is now at Douai Abbey, Berkshire. It is discussed and reproduced in Geoffrey Scott, 'Cloistered Images: Representations of English Nuns, 1600–1800', in Bowden and Kelly (eds), *English Convents in Exile*, pp. 191–208, at p. 195 and Plate 12. Other mementos of daughters in convents were wax dolls dressed as nuns.

[241] Adam Hamilton (ed.), *The Chronicle of the English Augustinian Canonesses Regular of the Lateran, at St Monica's in Louvain (Now at St Augustine's Priory, Newton Abbot, Devon) 1548–1625*, 2 vols (Edinburgh, 1904), vol. ii, pp. 203–13. See above, p. 131.

[242] Trappes-Lomax (ed.), *English Franciscan Nuns*, p. 36.

as foster cliques that could hinder their smooth operation. Some bishops insisted that no more than two sisters could be members of the same convent. Leaving behind her siblings Frances and Elizabeth in Nazareth, Ann Webb went to settle at a sister house of the Augustinians in Liège in 1654 for this reason.[243] Biological links complicated the fictive ones that nuns and monks developed with their fellow religious. They were the source of what Daniel Bornstein calls 'a squirming hydra' and 'a perduring tension'.[244]

To this was added the problem of upholding the proper order of matriarchal and patriarchal relations in an all-female environment that technically owed deference to male bishops and confessors who were supposed to supplant their own families in the affections of the professed. In a set of 'Instructions for a Religious Superior' dated 1668, Richard White, confessor to the Augustinians in Louvain, lamented the 'want of government' in the convent and offered his advice about how to remedy these ills 'as a father', urging the abbess to discipline those under her charge as the 'Mother of the familie'. The filial honour she owed him was replicated by the respect they showed to her.[245] The frictions that seem to underpin this document contrast with 'the most tender fatherly affection' that Father James Blomfield was remembered as having displayed to the sisters of Nazareth after his death in 1658.[246]

Often the surrogate family of the religious house was a powerful substitute for a real one, as in the case of Frances Stamford, who entered Nazareth without the consent of her father and later became its abbess. She oversaw the community conscientiously, sacrificing herself to its service, and becoming 'truly a Mother to every one'.[247] Mary Bedingfield, who arrived in 1643 aged 13, struggled to convince her mother to allow her to become a member of the order, despite the fact that her aunt Helen was its superior. Forced to return home, she crept out at midnight and hastened to Bruges, where she was welcomed back joyfully. She made her holy profession in 1652 despite having no dowry or maintenance from her family.[248] Eugenia Risdon, who was orphaned as a child and lost both her sister Susan and her closest friend Dorothy in 1691, eventually found solace in the same cloister.[249] Such sisterhoods could be very forgiving. Perpetua Errington, who

[243] Caroline Bowden (ed.), *The Chronicles of Nazareth (the English Convent)*, Bruges 1629–1793, CRS 87 (Woodbridge, 2017), pp. 37–8. For these restrictions, see Laurence Lux-Sterritt, *English Benedictine Nuns in Exile in the Seventeenth Century* (Manchester, 2017), p. 57.
[244] Daniel Bornstein, 'Spiritual Kinship and Domestic Devotions', in Judith C. Brown and Robert C. Davis (eds), *Gender and Society in Renaissance Italy* (1998), pp. 173–92, at 177 and 191.
[245] Cited in Walker, *Gender and Politics*, pp. 58–9 and see ch. 2.
[246] Bowden (ed.), *Chronicles of Nazareth*, p. 44.
[247] Ibid., pp. 11–12.   [248] Ibid., pp. 28, 32, 35.
[249] Laurence Lux-Sterritt (ed.), *English Convents in Exile, 1600–1800*, vol. ii, *Spirituality* (2012), pp. 353–7.

eloped using a skeleton key in 1696, was greeted like a prodigal daughter when she returned to Nazareth eleven years later.[250]

Conventual documents are saturated with familial vocabulary. The religious spoke of each other as spiritual mothers, fathers, brothers, and sisters and gave frequent expression to the ties of charity and affection that bound them.[251] The sentimental attachment that members of monastic households felt for each other was rooted in the social and liturgical rituals they shared with each other. Reminiscent of the depictions of godly Protestant families seated around a table discussed earlier, an illustrated poem now at Douai Abbey commemorates a surprise dinner held to discuss the foundation of St Monica's in Louvain in 1609 (Fig. 2.7). The centrepiece is a massive apple pie in the process of being served out to the Mother Superior, the nuns, their father confessor and their gentleman patron, before they return to their 'happy retreat'. This is a light-hearted image of religious commensality in a sacred space that was simultaneously a locus of humble domesticity.[252] Carrying visual cues to the Last Supper, it reflects the 'complex intermeshing of the devotional and the mundane' that marked convent life in this period.[253]

The close interweaving of spiritual and natural kinship that was so characteristic of post-Reformation English Catholic monasticism perhaps finds most striking expression in tales of entire families that abandoned secular life and resolved to take vows in religious houses. The Benedictine Mary Vavasour, who professed in 1616, was the child of a recusant who had been imprisoned many times for his stubborn refusal to comply with the statutes, all of whose ten offspring consecrated themselves to God, while he himself joined the third order of St Francis. Lady Mary Crispe became abbess of the same convent in 1719 and 'by an extraordinary disposition of Divine providence...numbered her own mother among the subject children of her monastery'. Apparently, she knelt in the chapter room for her blessing before giving to the rest of the community.[254] Lady Trevor Warner and her husband Sir John converted from Protestantism in 1664, mutually agreed to forsake their married state, and went abroad to enter religious orders. She became a Poor Clare at Gravelines and he a Brother, and until her death, though separated, they maintained their close relationship by letter. Both their daughters and her sister-in-law subsequently became nuns. Lady Warner's anxieties about other friends and relatives 'yet detain'd in Schism and Heresie', including her own elderly father, are reflected in the many missives she sent to these 'misled, and

---

[250] Bowden (ed.), *Chronicles of Nazareth*, pp. xxx and 126–9.
[251] See Walker, *Gender and Politics*, pp. 61–2; Lux-Sterritt, *English Benedictine Nuns*, pp. 49–57.
[252] 'The Feast of Louvain', in Nicky Hallett (ed.), *English Convents in Exile, 1600–1800*, vol. iii, *Life Writing I* (2012), pp. 345–9.
[253] See Maryanne Kowaleski and P. J. P. Goldberg (eds), *Medieval Domesticity: Home, Housing and Household in Medieval England* (Cambridge, 2008), p. 10, and Marilyn Oliva, 'Nuns at Home: The Domesticity of Sacred Space', in Kowaleski and Goldberg (eds), *Medieval Domesticity*, pp. 145–61.
[254] Lux-Sterritt (ed.), *English Convents in Exile*, vol. ii, pp. 361, 363.

Fig. 2.7 'The Feast of Louvain': Seventeenth-century manuscript poem from the Priory of Our Lady, Kingston-near-Lewes, Sussex.
Source: Trustees of Douai Abbey, Berkshire.

unbelieving Creatures', pleading with them to consider the dangers of remaining within the Church of England if they hoped to achieve salvation. She was a stoical mistress of the passions she repressed in exchanging motherhood for religion, but could not stop weeping when she saw her two 'Angelical Children' during her

final illness.[255] The whole scenario was sufficiently familiar to have been anticipated in a pamphlet of 1642 which takes the form of a dialogue between
Orthodoxus, an imaginary Catholic gentleman, his wife Lady Gynecia, and their
three offspring. The elder daughter Caelia enters a nunnery and when she refused
to come home following the death of her only brother and heir, her worldly sister
Cosmophila is sent over to fetch her and is there persuaded to become a novice
herself, changing her name to Christophila. Upon hearing this, her parents are
at first aggrieved, but resigning themselves to the fact that their line will die out,
they subsequently swear to spend the rest of their own lives in 'a Religious
Course'. Gynecia joins the same house as her daughters and Orthodoxus becomes
a Capuchin.[256]

Such families adopted a strategy for sustaining English Catholicism that prioritized the bearing of witness in one generation over the duty of reproducing living
heirs to carry it on in the next. Parents who systematically sent their children to
convents in the Low Countries and their sons to the English Colleges in Douai,
Rome, and Valladolid engaged in a careful calculus that implicitly preferred the
creation of a dynasty of holy confessors to the creation of a cohort of laypeople
who could perpetuate the family and the faith by staying at home. Their actions
were reminiscent of the medieval practice of child oblation in which children
were dedicated to the religious life by mothers and fathers willing to sacrifice
their most precious treasure to the Almighty, transforming them into 'a consecrated offering' and transporting them into 'the domain of the sacred'.[257] In the
case of the Wisemans of Braddocks in Essex, all four daughters became nuns,
while two of their four sons died as Jesuits.[258] All three of the Fenn brothers,
Robert, John, and James, became priests; the first was 'a greater sufferer for his
religion', the second helped compile the *Concertatio Ecclesiae Catholicae* and was
confessor to the Augustinian nuns at Louvain, and the third was captured in his
native county of Somerset and executed for treason in 1584.[259] In the 1690s,
Nicholas Salvin of Croxdale, near Durham, left legacies for the maintenance of a

[255] Edward Scarisbricke, *The life of the lady Warner of Parham in Suffolk. In religion call'd Sister Clare of Jesus*, 2nd edn (1692; Wing C575), pp. 190–1, 241–5.

[256] N. N. [Lawrence Anderton], *The English nunne being a treatise wherein (by way of dialogue) the author endeavoureth to draw yong & unmarried Catholike gentlewomen to imbrace a votary and reli-gious life* ([St Omer], 1642; Wing A3109), quotation at p. 16.

[257] See Mayke De Jong, *In Samuel's Image: Child Oblation in the Early Medieval West* (Leiden, 1996), p. 224; Liesbeth van Houts, 'Orderic and His Father, Odelerius', in Charles C. Rozier et al. (eds), *Orderic Vitalis: Life, Works and Interpretations* (Woodbridge, 2016), pp. 17–36.

[258] The daughters were Jane, Bridget, Anne, and Barbara. See https://wwtn.history.qmul.ac.uk, s.v. 'Wiseman'. For the Wiseman household, see the account in Gerard, *Autobiography*, chs 5, 9. See Henry Foley, *Records of the English Province of the Society of Jesus*, 7 vols in 8 (1877–83), vol. vii/2, pp. 853–4. The Jesuit sons were William and John (died as a novice aged 21, 1592); another son Thomas was also a scholar priest.

[259] Richard Challoner, *Memoirs of Missionary Priests*, ed. J. H. Pollen (1924), pp. 89–93.

youth at the seminary at Lisbon or Douai, ideally a member of the family or one 'of nearest kindred', whom he hoped '(if God please to honour him with a vocation)' would 'consecrate himself to the service of God in the mission of England'.[260]

The impulse to train for the priesthood and become a missionary entailed weighing up the same competing imperatives. It involved choosing a path of sacred chastity and aspiring martyrdom that could denude the Catholic Church of individual members but might yield a bigger harvest of souls among schismatics and heretics to replenish them. It placed charismatic evangelism above procreation as the key to growing the Church of Rome. Like the religious, those who entered seminaries and joined the Society of Jesus abandoned claims to the material inheritance that descended to them from their parents to dedicate their lives to building a spiritual one. They cherished their fellowship with those with whom they were schooled and alongside whom they worked in the mission field. They regarded each other as brothers in battle and as fellow labourers in the Lord's vineyard.

This was especially pronounced among the small, tightly knit band of Jesuits who exercised an influence disproportionate to their actual numbers. They attracted lay disciples, like the young Suffolk gentleman George Gilbert, who formed a group of twenty-six Catholic men of birth and property without wives or offices who promised 'to content themselves with food and clothing and the bare necessities of their state, and to bestow all the rest for the good of the Catholic cause'. Gilbert himself was received into the society on his deathbed in 1583.[261] The hagiographical texts in which these men were later celebrated commonly stressed their willingness to sacrifice family ties for the greater good of returning England to allegiance to the Mother Church, but they too maintained close links with their biological relatives. The story of John Geninges, who credited his conversion to the intercession of his sibling Edmund, a priest executed in 1609, offers further insight into these intricacies. It was 'a heavenly conceipt...of his deare brother's felicity' that he experienced in the course of a vision that compelled him 'to forsake kinred and countrey' and seek out the truth of the faith for which he had died.[262] Cemented by the experience of defeat and persecution, spiritual kinship remained a critical force field within the English Catholic community, as well as one that interlocked increasingly tightly with the matrix of blood relations that bound its diverse membership together in the face of adversity.

---

[260] DCRO, D/Sa/F 26 and D/Sa/F 26:2 (Nicholas Salvin, papers regarding legacies, for maintenance of a youth at Douai, 1694–6).

[261] See *ODNB*, Thompson Cooper, rev. Thomas H. Clancy, 'Gilbert, George (d. 1583)'. See also *Miscellanea II*, CRS 2 (1906), p. 201.

[262] John Genings, *The life and death of Mr Edmund Geninges priest, crowned with martyrdome at London, the 10 day of November in the yeare M.D.XCI* (St Omer, 1614; STC 11728), pp. 99–100.

Families of Love and Societies of Friends

It was not just within Catholicism, however, that forms of religious kinship proved resilient. The process by which Protestantism entrenched itself and then splintered English society served to engender a range of new ones. In continuity with the medieval ideal of the *corpus Christianum*, the dominant ecclesiology of the Elizabethan Church of England, as enshrined in the language of the liturgy, was an inclusive one, involving the charitable assumption that every person was potentially predestined to salvation. To think of the visible church as a 'mixt company' comprising true believers and hypocrites, elect and reprobate, was to envisage a large extended family in which the small handful of the godly coexisted with so many black sheep.[263] As Calvinist theology waned in the later seventeenth century, a greater emphasis on the mercy God extended to all of its members became apparent. Richard Allestree underlined the obligations that Protestants owed to their spiritual brethren: 'tenderness and affection', willingness to bear with their infirmities and to draw them to repentance, and 'Sympathy and fellow feeling' for their misfortunes.[264]

Yet the sixteenth- and seventeenth-century Reformations also fostered the creation of gathered churches and sects that conceived of themselves as exclusive entities consisting solely of the saints, whom they claimed to be able to identify with some degree of certainty. From the beginning, the sense of intimate kinship that was integral to evangelical Protestant identity irritated their opponents and critics: Thomas More's *Apologie* (1533) is thick with sarcasm about the 'bretherne and sisters of the false fraternite' of heresy. '[T]hys newe broched brotherhed' was a perverted imitation of the vibrant brand of voluntary religion that was the religious guild.[265] These congregations and their successors drew inspiration from the Pauline epistles, in which the apostle frequently spoke to 'the household of God'.[266] Within them, the boundaries between kith and kin were very blurred indeed. Communities of faith intersected with those created by ties of flesh and blood. To adopt the phrase used by the Restoration Oxford divine Abraham Wright, people were 'Brethren by Race, or Grace'.[267] Over time, as we shall see, the two tended to converge.

We begin with the Family of Love, the mysterious fellowship inspired by the writings of Hendrik Niclaes (H. N.).[268] While outsiders were repudiated and

[263] See William Perkins, *An exposition of the symbole, or creed of the apostles*, in *Workes*, vol, i (1626; STC 19652), pp. 302–3.

[264] Allestree, *Whole duty of man*, pp. 305–11.

[265] Thomas More, *The Apology* (1533), in *The Complete Works of St Thomas More*, vol. ix, ed. J. B. Trapp (New Haven, CT, 1979), pp. 14, 15.

[266] Galatians 6:10; Ephesians 2:19.

[267] Abraham Wright, *A practical commentary or exposition upon the Pentateuch* (1662; Wing 3688), p. 204.

[268] See Alastair Hamilton, *The Family of Love* (Cambridge, 1981), esp. ch. 6; Christopher Marsh, *The Family of Love in English Society, 1550–1630* (Cambridge, 1994).

castigated as mere 'beasts', members were treated as if they were intimate blood relations and greeted as 'sisters' and 'brethren'. The language of kinship liberally deployed by H. N. helped cement the elusive and secretive network of Familists that the painstaking work of Christopher Marsh has helped to reconstitute in a group of Cambridgeshire villages. As his research reveals, these too were communities centred on the mutually supportive households in which families and neighbours met for discussion and worship. Although they were well integrated into and respected in their communities, they were also inward-looking, a tendency reinforced by the sect's endogamous marriage policy—by its insistence that its members could only marry within the bounds of the family and by the associated requirement that women in childbirth should not be assisted by non-Familist midwives. Paralleling mainstream Protestantism, H. N. and his disciples cultivated a brand of domestic piety that stressed patriarchal deference to fathers and to the elders of the sect and which was dedicated to the 'nourishing up of sound Children' , both literally and figuratively.[269] Assisted by printed ABCs, booklets, broadsides, ballads, and hymn books, Familist religion revolved around a regime of daily recitation of prayers, singing, and the saying of grace before and after meals, as depicted a the woodcut adorning II. N.'s *Benedicitie or blessinge to be saide over the table* (1575). Another depicts a domestic schoolroom in which the 'youngones' are taught the tenets of their faith in the form of an ABC (Fig. 2.8).[270]

Fierce clerical critics such as John Knewstub, William Wilkinson, and John Rogers attacked these 'monstrous and horrible' heretics vociferously, warning of the 'poyson which dayly floweth from our Lovely Familie', and calling them 'the householde of Selfelove'. The confessions extracted from those who were apprehended reinforced these prejudices, which drew on ancient stereotypes of deviance in perceiving their pious conventicles as a cover for hypocrisy and sexual impropriety.[271] These were further strengthened in satirical plays such as Thomas Middleton's *Family of love*.[272] This artificial kin group was also compared to its counterpart on the other side of the confessional divide, the Society of Jesus.[273]

[269] H[endrik] N[iclaes], *Exhortatio*, p. 207; Marsh, *Family of Love*, pp. 145–8, 179–80.

[270] H[endrik] N[iclaes], *A benedicitie or blessinge to be saide over the table* ([Cologne], 1575; STC 1858); *idem*, *All the letters of the A.BC by every sondrye letter wherof ther is a good document set-fourth and taught in ryme* ([Cologne], 1575; STC 18548.5). See Marsh, *Family of Love*, pp. 89–93.

[271] William Wilkinson, *A confutation of certaine articles, delivered unto the familye of love* (1579; STC 25665), sig. *3r and the Epistle to the Reader; John Knewstub, *A confutation of monstrous and horrible heresies, taught by H. N. and embraced of a number, who call themselves the familie of love* (1579; STC 15040), sig. xx5r. For accounts of household meetings, see the confession of two Familists in 1561, in John Rogers, *The displaying of an horrible secte of grosse and wicked heretiques, naming themselves the familie of love* (1578; STC 21181), sigs I4v–5v.

[272] [Thomas Middleton], *The famelie of love. Acted by the children of his Maiesties Revells* (1608; STC 17879).

[273] William Charke, *An answere to a seditious pamphlet lately cast abroade by a Jesuite* (1580; STC 5005), 'To the Reader'; Meredith Hanmer, *The Jesuites banner* (1581; STC 12746), sig. A3r–v; *idem*, *The great bragge and challenge of M. Champion* (1581; STC 12745), p. 3.

Fig. 2.8 Hendrik Niclaes, *All the letters of the A.B.C. by every sondrye letter wherof ther is a good document set-fourth and taught in ryme* (1575), broadsheet.

Source: By permission of the University of Glasgow Archives and Special Collections, Euing Ballad 1.

The 'holye Communialtie' that both advocated was regarded as a perversion of Christianity and a dangerous rival to the official Church.[274] The irony lying behind contemporary fear of the Familists was their embodiment of values that were shared across the ecclesiastical establishment. The 'family religion' they practised exposed its dual capacity to buttress and undermine the status quo, as well as the anxieties that periodically crystallized around private homes in which spiritual kith united in prayer with natural kin.

Similar patterns emerge when we turn to the separatists. The writings of the Elizabethan dissidents Henry Barrow, Robert Browne, John Penry, and John Greenwood, and of those who departed out of England and set up gathered churches on congregationalist lines in exile are also suffused with the vocabulary of the family and household.[275] For these radical Protestants, the idea that the

[274] H[endrik] N[iclaes], *The first epistle of H. N. A crying-voyce of the holye spirit of love* ([Cologne, 1574?]; STC 18555), sig. A5v.

[275] See, e.g., *The Writings of Robert Harrison and Robert Browne*, ed. Leland H. Carlson and Albert Peel (1953), p. 423.

visible church was a broad-bottomed ship that could accommodate both the invisible rump of the godly and the vast mass of the wicked was an Antichristian anathema. The congregations they gathered around them incorporated people whose worthiness was attested in their sound doctrine and outward behaviour alone, and excluded the unregenerate, who were beyond the pale. These too seem to have been communities in which religious and blood links were mutually reinforcing, assisted by the strong emphasis their leaders placed on marrying within the ranks of the tiny remnant that would inherit the kingdom of heaven. John Smyth insisted that members of his gathered church of Baptists should not unite with the 'profane' and 'godless people of the world'.[276] One corollary of this was acknowledgement that desertion and divorce could be sanctioned. As Robert Browne remarked, 'if by keeping togeth[e]r the one can not hould the true religion through the untowardnes of the other in a wicked and false religion…in such cases the husband may depart from the wife or the wife from the Husband'. This was not a breach of the covenant of marriage but an act taken in defence of a good conscience.[277]

These little flocks of the faithful were also fraternities that were simultaneously families. Their internal dynamic required people to exercise their responsibility to be their brothers' keepers and to restrain the wayward from error, immorality, and sin in an avuncular manner. Their rhetoric described the double duty of the godly: to estrange themselves from the profane in public worship and to bind themselves ever more tightly to those whom they recognized as fellow saints. Once again, this had the potential to create strains within the microcosm of the visible church that was the household. Henry Barrow's prescriptions for the excommunication of disobedient members required that the congregation of the faithful abstain from eating and drinking with them, except of necessity, as in the case of 'his Wife, his Children and Familie: yet these (if they be Members of the Church) are not to joyne to him in anie Spirituall exercise'.[278]

Many echoes of these tendencies can be found within the slippery and amorphous entity that was puritanism. Puritans too were people who conceived of themselves as societies of saints. They too used the language of kin to define themselves and to describe their relationships with each other. The godly thought of

---

[276] Cited in Michael Watts, *The Dissenters from the Reformation to the French Revolution* (Oxford, 1999), p. 329. For the rhetoric of fraternity in German Anabaptist communities, see Kat Hill, *Baptism, Brotherhood, and Belief in Reformation Germany: Anabaptism and Lutheranism, 1525–1585* (Oxford, 2015), ch. 6.

[277] Robert Browne, *A booke which sheweth the life and manners of all true Christians and howe unlike they are unto Turkes and Papistes, and heathen folke* (Middelburg, 1582; STC 3910.3), sig. K2v. On the marriage policy of the separatists, see R. J. Acheson, *Radical Puritans in England 1550–1660* (1990); Murray Tolmie, *The Triumph of the Saints: The Separate Churches of London 1616–1649* (Cambridge, 1977); B. R. White, *The English Separatist Tradition from the Marian Martyrs to the Pilgrim Fathers* (Oxford, 1971).

[278] [Henry Barrow], *A true description out of the word of God, of the visible church* ([Amsterdam], 1589; STC 1526.5), sig. B1r–v.

themselves as part of 'the household of faith' and addressed each other in letters and conversations as spiritual siblings. One Scottish minister even signed his letter to an 'elect Ladie' of unknown identity 'your zealous and religious bedfellow', wishing her 'christian familie' good health and faith in the Lord. The expression was not sexual in the ordinary sense.[279] The identity of puritans as fellow brethren was forged through the religious voluntarism that took them 'gadding' to sermons in other parishes and the extra-liturgical domestic devotions in which they engaged with both kith and kin. It was in considerable part an outgrowth of activities that took place in the forum of the home, from which, as we have seen, they were urged to expel the reprobate, including, on occasion, their own blood relatives. Godly friends were a substitute for those one forsook to follow Christ: John Dod 'testified from his own experience, that for the losse of one carnal Brother he had two hundred spiritual Brethren'.[280] In turn, the Lord would serve as a loving step-parent when death took away those of the flesh. Ellen Angier, wife of the nonconformist John Angier, 'bade' her 8-year-old daughter Elizabeth to 'get god for her father and mother, for she knew not how soon' her own might be gone.[281] Recollecting that her father had been orphaned at the age of 13 following the passing of her grandfather, Mary Honeywood wrote: 'he that hath God for his Guardian feeles not the want of earthly parents'.[282] The Lord's 'love to his special flock' shared a 'similitude' with the affection earthly parents lavished upon their own children.[283] A further consequence was that the godly considered themselves part of the holy family itself: 'kinship', wrote Oliver Heywood, 'grows out in process of time, and tis not much materiall what family we are of so that we be of the household of faith, and have god for our father, Ch[ris]t for our elder brother and the spirit of grace running in our best veines....'[284]

The tensions generated by the imperative to prioritize the community of the elect are summed up in an entry in the commonplace book of the Herefordshire puritan Lady Brilliana Harley: 'we must be careful of our families, of our parents, of our kindred, if they be of the household of faith, strangers if they [be] righteous; but our delightest love must only be to the saints on the Earth'.[285] If the 'holy

[279] Edinburgh, National Library of Scotland, MS Wodrow Folio XXV 1–2, fo. 3r. See Patrick Collinson, '"Not Sexual in the Ordinary Sense": Women, Men and Religious Transactions', in *idem*, *Elizabethan Essays*, pp. 119–50.

[280] Samuel Clarke, *The lives of two and twenty English divines* (1660; Wing C4540), p. 207. On religion and sibling relationships, see Capp, *The Ties that Bind*, ch. 7.

[281] *The Rev. Oliver Heywood, B.A. 1630–1702: His Autobiography, Diaries, Anecdote and Event Books: Illustrating the General and Family History of Yorkshire and Lancashire*, ed. J. Horsfall Turner, 4 vols (Brighouse, 1882), vol. i, p. 72.

[282] Bodl., MS Rawlinson D. 102 (Mistress Mary Honeywood's Life of her Father, *c*.1635).

[283] For an extended meditation on this theme dated 24 September 1624, see CL, MS I.f.2 (Spiritual Diary of Ellis Crispe, 1622–6), item 18.

[284] Heywood, *Autobiography*, ed. Turner, vol. i, p. 17. See W. J. Sheils, 'Oliver Heywood and His Congregation', in W. J. Sheils and Diana Wood (eds), *Voluntary Religion*, SCH 23 (1986), pp. 261–77.

[285] Nottingham, University of Nottingham Archives, Portland Papers, London Collection, Commonplace Book of Brilliana Harley, fo. 62r, cited in Jacqueline Eales, *Puritans and Roundheads: The Harleys of Brampton Bryan and the Outbreak of the English Civil War* (Cambridge, 1990), p. 43.

Sympathy' the godly felt for fellow believers sometimes exceeded the tenderness they felt for their natural kin, on other occasions it cemented it.[286] The terms in which Mrs Dorothy Hutton, sister to the Parliamentary general Sir Thomas Fairfax, wrote to her sibling Mary Arthington sometime in the 1640s are particularly telling: 'I should wrong my owne soul in forgetting you who is a member with me of the body of Christ, the Lord hath made us a nearer relation by grace then we are by nature.' Filled with exhortations to gratitude for God's mercies and gentle reproof of the recipient's careless security, the letters they exchanged bespeak the strong sense of obligation that compelled zealous puritans to act as their brothers' and sisters' keepers. Such 'plaine' speaking proceeded from their 'true love' for each other's souls.[287] William Perkins had played on these same themes in a revealing exposition of Galatians 6:10 in a commentary published in 1604. This described those 'nourished with the same milke of the word' as siblings and said that after one's wife and children, parents and progenitors, 'kindred in the flesh' linked 'by the bond of nature' were to be respected and relieved 'if they be of the household of faith; otherwise the Saints of God, which are neither kith nor kinne unto us, are to be preferred before them'.[288] The Venn diagram of religious and family relations such texts constructed was messy and complex.

These developments were accompanied by a corresponding emphasis on forming friendships and making matches within the same circles. It was best to 'keep company' within the circle of 'Gods Elect', since there was 'no greater enemey to the Salvation of thy Soul, than an Evil Companion'.[289] Dod and Cleaver warned against reliance on 'carnall friends', insisting that 'alliance and kindred will faile, but grace and religion will never faile'.[290] The dangers of socializing with the wicked in mundane matters were bad enough; to enter into a lifelong contract was even more perilous, and forbidden by divines such as Richard Bolton as an infringement of the biblical injunction against yoking Christ and Belial, truth and falsehood. Intimate fellowship of this kind was 'the Saints peculiar' and 'speciall passages of dearest acquaintance with prophane men, children of darkenesse, and enemies of God' should be wholly avoided.[291] Such writers extended the precept

---

[286] The phrase 'holy Sympathy' is Hinde's in *Faithfull remonstrance*, p. 185.

[287] Bodl., MS Additional A. 119 (Fairfax family letters, copied by Mary Arthington, c.1680–1700), fos 44v, 46r–47v. See also Diane Willen, ' "Communion of the Saints": Spiritual Reciprocity and the Godly Community in Early Modern England', *Albion: A Quarterly Journal Concerned with British Studies*, 27 (1995), 19–41, esp. 23–4.

[288] William Perkins, *A commentarie or exposition, upon the five first chapters of the Epistle to the Galatians* ([Cambridge], 1604; STC 19680), pp. 593–7.

[289] FSL, MS V.a.11 (Thomas Hunt, 'A Bosome Companion or The Fathers advice to his Children', 1690), pp. 43–50.

[290] John Dod and Robert Cleaver, *A plain and familiar exposition of the thirteenth and fourteenth chapters of the Proverbs of Salomon* (1609; STC 6960), p. 119.

[291] Robert Bolton, *Some generall directions for a comfortable walking with God delivered in the lecture at Kettering in North-Hamptonshire* (1638; STC 3254), p. 74.

that it was unlawful to marry idolaters to encompass merely nominal Christians as well as rank papists. The underlying trajectory of Elizabethan and Stuart puritanism seems to have been towards a form of religious, if not biological endogamy.[292] Whether or not the seeds of sectarianism can be located within it has been disputed; what can be observed is that the umbilical cord that linked puritans to the Church of England and compelled them, as a matter of principle, to remain within its maternal embrace despite its imperfections could quite easily be severed. Like the Family of Love, the covenanted 'seed' of separatists, semi-separatists and puritans was the subject of a vein of hostile polemic which exposes the inherent tensions surrounding spiritual kinship even as it underlines its vitality in post-Reformation society.

Although the Quakers did not become officially known as the Society of Friends until the late eighteenth century, from the beginning they referred to themselves using the terminology of kith and kin that came so instinctively to religious minorities that set themselves up in competition with the Church of England. The voluminous correspondence and printed literature they have left behind are filled with references to those who embraced the distinctive teachings of George Fox and underwent 'convincement' as 'Children of Light', 'the household of the seed of Abraham', and 'the church and family of the living God'.[293] George Fox's *Primmer and catechism for children* published in 1670 incorporated a long list of alternative names by which they were known, from 'the Lot of God's Inheritance' to his 'Sons and Daughters', 'Heirs', 'Brethren', and 'chosen Generation'.[294]

Setting aside Calvinist soteriology and denying the doctrine of predestination, the energetic and charismatic evangelism that drew so many to the sect in its first generation was underpinned by assumptions about the universality of Christ's promise to humankind. In a pamphlet of 1677 addressed to 'the churches of Jesus throughout the world' William Penn urged Quakers to conceive of themselves as 'one Holy Flock, Family and Household to the Lord, who hath Redeemed them from among all the Kindreds of the Earth'.[295] Like early evangelicals, 'Friends' retrospectively revelled in the fact that they had broken with parents and relatives who sought to prevent them from joining the sect. They regarded this as a superior form of obedience to their Father in heaven, as well as a validation of the biblical precept to set aside bonds of affection and consanguinity when they stood in the

---

[292] For a classic exposition of this theme, see Patrick Collinson, 'The Cohabitation of the Faithful with the Unfaithful', in Ole Peter Grell, Jonathan I. Israel, and Nicholas Tyacke (eds), *From Persecution to Toleration: The Glorious Revolution and Religion in England* (Oxford, 1991), pp. 51–76.

[293] See, e.g., George Fox, *An epistle to the household of the seed of Abraham and to every family in particular to read & practise* (1682; Wing F1812); FHL, TEMP MSS 752 (Commonplace book of Mary Penington), unfoliated. On the Quaker metaphor of the family, see Su Fang Ng, *Literature and the Politics of Family in Seventeenth-Century England* (Cambridge, 2007), ch. 7, esp. pp. 201–3.

[294] George Fox, *A primmer and catechism for children* (1670; Wing F1883B), pp. 54–5.

[295] William Penn, *To the churches of Jesus throughout the world* (1677; Wing P1387), p. 1.

way of adhering to righteousness.[296] Writing in 1666, Stephen Crisp urged Quakers to beware of family attachments: wives, children, and relations were 'instruments of Satan' who would 'lead thee into darkness'. Pity for one's loved ones was 'a subtile Enemy'.[297] For Nicholas Gates 'the Lord was more to me than my earthly father', from whom he was alienated because of his Quakerism, though he loved him dearly.[298] Such themes are also prominent in the biographies and autobiographies of women such as Margaret Lucas, Elizabeth Ashbridge, and Alice Hayes, which celebrate their resistance to aunts, uncles, fathers, and husbands and their willingness to set aside earthly ties for the sake of the inner light.[299] In turn, their enemies accused this sect in which women and young people seemed so prominent of undermining the correct order of gender and age relations and of subverting the natural respect that youth and children owed to their parents.

The new 'spiritual parents' and kin that early Quakers found within the movement took the place of the natural ones they were obliged to relinquish. Its institutional structures, including Meetings, were understood as extended families. They fostered a sense of belonging to a group that ranged beyond their blood relatives. Friendships with fellow believers found expression in missionary letters that crossed the Atlantic, helping to create a transatlantic community whose intimacy belied the tyrannies of distance. Some historians have detected a drift back in the direction of patriarchy once the movement entered its institutional phase. Feminist scholars have lamented the apparent retraction of women into the household once the enthusiasm of its initial conversionary phase—in which female prophets and preachers had been conspicuous—had passed.[300] But Naomi Pullin has recently demonstrated that the developing emphasis on perpetuating the sect within the family unit did not necessarily occur at the expense of female authority. Her work resists the tendency to denigrate domesticity and occlude its capacity to function as a mode of agency. In the guise of the revered figure of the Mother of Israel, Quakerism both retained some of its matriarchal tendencies and laid new stress on the household as a site of nurture and education.[301]

---

[296] See Chapter 1 above.

[297] Stephen Crisp, *An epistle to friends concerning the present and succeeding times* (1666; Wing C6931A), p. 11.

[298] Nicholas Gates, *A tender invitation to all, to embrace the secret visitation of the Lord to their souls* (1708), p. 27.

[299] See Sheila Wright, '"Truly Dear Hearts": Family and Spirituality in Quaker Women's Writings 1680-1750', in Sylvia Brown (ed.), *Women, Gender and Radical Religion in Early Modern Europe* (Leiden, 2007), 97–113.

[300] For example, Phyllis Mack, *Visionary Women: Ecstatic Prophecy in Seventeenth-Century England* (Berkeley, CA, 1994), esp. pp. 274–5, 412; Patricia Crawford, *Women and Religion in England 1500-1720* (1993), p. 160; Catie Gill, *Women in the Seventeenth-Century Quaker Community: A Literary Study of Political Identities, 1650-1700* (Aldershot, 2005), p. 186 and ch. 5. See also Keith Thomas, 'Women and the Civil War Sects', *P&P*, 13 (1956), 42–62.

[301] Naomi Pullin, *Female Friends and the Making of Transatlantic Quakerism, 1650-c.1750* (Cambridge, 2018), esp. ch. 1.

It reanimated and reconfigured the medieval tradition of holy motherhood alongside that of prophetic masculinity. Jane Whitehead's husband stayed at home looking after their 'five goodly Children', while she travelled to spread the truth and spent time in prison, charging them to take heed of their father.[302] By contrast, Mary Capper remained single for all ninety-one years of her life and throughout her ministry, having decided against marrying a Friend who she believed to be insufficiently committed to Quaker principles at the age of 33: 'she could never afterwards entertain the prospect of matrimony'.[303]

As time progressed, and especially in the wake of the Act of Toleration, the endogamous tendencies within what was belatedly christened the Society of Friends intensified. Fox and others placed growing emphasis on 'Gospel family-order', urging heads of household to be diligent in 'circumcising' their children and subordinates 'with the Spirit', setting up 'the Law of Love', and erecting 'the Ark of the Lord' in their hearts and homes.[304] Like puritans, Quakers warned of the dangers of being 'unequally yoked' with spouses from outside the sect.[305] Marrying fellow Friends was strongly recommended by senior figures like William Penn. Thereby, Quakers would not 'like the forgetting & unnatural world grow out of kindred & as cold as strangers but...live in the pure & fervent love of God towards one another, as becometh brethren in the spiritual and natural relation'.[306]

Once again biological kinship and spiritual kinship overlapped and converged. Bridget Fell wrote fondly to her mother Margaret in August 1660, expressing her 'dear and endless love...unto thee, who hath not only been a mother and nurse to the natural birth but hath also travailed for me in the spirit, that the life of right-eousness may be formed in me'.[307] As time progressed, the metaphorical language of parents and siblings increasingly acquired a literal edge. What had once been a sect became 'a great clan'. As we shall see in Chapter 4, Quakerism increasingly found its locus within the family, upon which its succession to future generations depended.[308] However, this was not inconsistent with maintaining cordial relations

---

[302] For Loveday Hambly, see Chapter 1 above. Theophila Townsend, *A testimony concerning the life and death of Jane Whitehead that faithful servant and hand-maid of the Lord, who was a mother in Israel, and her memorial is blessed of the Lord for ever* (1676; T1989), pp. 9, 15.

[303] *A Memoir of Mary Capper, Late of Birmingham, A Minister of the Society of Friends*, ed. Katharine Backhouse (1847), p. 73. Mary Capper was born in 1755.

[304] George Fox, *Gospel family-order, being a short discourse concerning the ordering of families, both of whites, blacks and Indians* (1676; Wing F1829), pp. 3, 7, 11. This discourse was taken down 'from the Mouth' of Fox at a men's meeting in Barbados in 1671.

[305] Richard T. Vann and David Eversley, *Friends in Life and Death: The British and Irish Quakers in the Demographic Transition, 1650-1900* (Cambridge, 1992), ch. 3, esp. pp. 83-4.

[306] FHL, MS VOL 62/5, p. 85 (transcription of William Penn's letter to his wife and children, 4 June 1682).

[307] Quoted in Bonnelyn Young Kunze, *Margaret Fell and the Rise of Quakerism* (Basingstoke, 1994), p. 39.

[308] For these trends, see Richard T. Vann, *The Social Development of English Quakerism 1655-1755* (Cambridge, MA, 1969), ch. 5, esp. pp. 164-7. See also Pullin, *Female Friends*, pp. 167-71.

with people with different religious convictions beyond its perimeters. Both developments might be seen as symptoms of the birth of a denominational society in which individual churches became more preoccupied with consolidation than with conversion and outreach.

This chapter began with the holy family; it ends with the royal family. In various ways the Tudor and Stuart dynasties were both representative and unusual: like many others in early modern England, they were families fractured by untimely death and remade through remarriage and step-parentage. The history of the English Reformations hinges in considerable part on the history of their successive generations. An official group portrait of the family of James VI and I engraved by Willem van de Passe is emblematic of the tensions engendered by religious schism and pluralization that swirled around them.[309] Entitled *Triumphus Jacobi Regis Augustaque Ipsius Prolis* ('The Triumph of King James and His Majestic Offspring'), this carries more than a faint echo of the older iconography of holy kinship. The happy vision of family unity that the picture constructs belies the frictions that simmered beneath the surface and around the Stuart household. Postdating the death of his crypto-Catholic wife Anne of Denmark Anne in 1619, who stands to the left of the monarch touching a skull, this image survives in several successive states. The first version (not reproduced here) depicts Charles as Prince of Wales as a bachelor in the foreground, with his hand resting on a bible marked '*Religione et constantia*'. His much lamented dead brother Henry hovers behind his shoulder and his siblings, Mary (who died aged 2) and Sophia (who survived just three days) are seated on the step beside him. Another lost infant Robert, who expired when he was 4 months old, is missing, together with any reference to the three miscarriages Anne suffered. On the right are Princess Elizabeth and her husband, Frederick V, King of Bohemia and Count Palatine of the Rhine and their teeming tribe of children. The picture occludes the misfortunes that befell the couple, who were ejected from their kingdom following the Battle of White Mountain in November 1620, which ended the first phase of the Thirty Years War. Intimately linked with anxiety about the future of Protestantism in Europe, the reluctance of the regime to ride to their rescue provoked criticism, until the about-turn in foreign policy in 1624 that contemporaries heralded as the 'Blessed Revolution'.[310]

The later state of this engraving (reproduced as Fig. 2.9) records the birth of a further baby to Elizabeth and Frederick, who appears at the bottom in a cradle, and the demise of her elder sister immediately beside her.[311] Charles is now

[309] Willem van de Passe, *Triumphus Jacobi Regis Augustaeque ipsius Prolis* (1622): BM 1935,0413.80.
[310] See Thomas Cogswell, *The Blessed Revolution: English Politics and the Coming of War, 1621–1624* (Cambridge, 1989).
[311] BM 1854,1113.114. See Fig. 2.9. For these and other royal group portraits, see Jonathan Goldberg, 'Fatherly Authority: The Politics of Stuart Family Images', in Margaret W. Ferguson,

Fig. 2.9 Willem van de Passe, *Triumphus Jacobi Regis Augustaeque Ipsius Prolis* (London, engraving after 1625).

Source: © The Trustees of the British Museum 1854,1113.114.

shown with his bride, the French princess, Henrietta Maria, whom he married in May-June 1625, following his coronation in February of that year. Viewers could not but be reminded of the failed match with the Spanish Hapsburg Infanta Maria which had provoked such a furore. Regarded as a victory for the Protestant cause, its collapse in 1623 was a source of public rejoicing. The overt Catholicism of Charles's consort, who was devoted to the Virgin Mary, increasingly turned the king's household into a focal point for religio-political discontent and one of the touchpapers that ignited the Civil Wars. The influence she exerted over her husband and sons made motherhood a fraught category and fostered intense distrust of the woman who was perceived to be perverting the nursing father of the English Church and people.[312] This striking set of images captures a family in

Maureen Quilligan, and Nancy J. Vickers (eds), *Rewriting the Renaissance: The Discourses of Sexual Difference in Early Modern Europe* (Chicago, 1986), pp. 3–32. For a print of the family of George III, see *The Royal Family of Great Britain* (print, c.1736–51): BM, 1866,0407.645.

[312] See the excellent discussion in Frances Dolan, *Whores of Babylon: Catholicism, Gender and Seventeenth-Century Print Culture* (Ithaca, NY, 1999), ch. 3. For the literary dimensions of these

motion, as well as one whose history both mirrored and shaped the uncertain course of religious reform in this era.

England's long Reformation was thus in multiple respects a family affair and, indeed, a family quarrel. This chapter has investigated the role of both kith and kin in the ecclesiastical developments that sundered medieval Christendom. It has shown that these served to create a brood of devout and confessionally self-conscious families and to spawn many groups that described themselves as the children of God—as societies of sisters, brethren, cousins, and friends. It has contested the suggestion that the ecclesiastical and theological developments of the sixteenth and seventeenth centuries were corrosive of horizontal ties of kinship and resisted the impulse to set godly domesticity and social friendship in opposition. The religious conflicts of the period should not be read as 'a battle between fatherhood and brotherhood'.[313] On the contrary, all these tendencies were reinforced by the advent and entrenchment of Protestantism and by the resurgence of Roman Catholicism. Far from being pared to its nuclear core, the 'family', like the household, remained a capacious structure capable of encompassing those bound by ties of faith as well as blood and law.[314] The relationships of religious mutuality and interpersonal obligation I have analysed are a critical but still neglected part of the 'connective tissue' that held together early modern society.[315] The Reformations reconfigured these in significant ways and with some curious side effects. A growing elision between natural and spiritual kinship was an unexpected legacy of the fragmentation of Christianity into an array of churches and sects and of the process by which the English gradually but partially accommodated and tolerated their presence.

This chapter has focused primarily on the living generations that coexisted at a given moment in time. Chapter 3 examines the chain of ancestors and descendants that preceded and followed them, stretching back into the past and forward into the future.

---

tensions, see Laura Lunger Knoppers, *Politicizing Domesticity from Henrietta Maria to Milton's Eve* (Cambridge, 2011).

[313] Bossy, *Christianity in the West*, p. 125.

[314] Cf. Susan Karant Nunn, 'Reformation Society, Women and the Family', in Andrew Pettegree (ed.), *The Reformation World* (2000), pp. 433–59, at pp. 433–6.

[315] Keith Wrightson, 'Mutualities and Obligations: Changing Social Relationships in Early Modern England', *Proceedings of the British Academy*, 139 (2006), 157–94, esp. his brief but underdeveloped comments on 183–4. The phrase 'connective tissue' is used by Susannah Ottaway, 'Introduction: Authority, Autonomy and Responsibility among the Aged in the Pre-industrial Past', in Susannah Ottaway, Lynn A. Botelho, and Katharine Kittredge (eds), *Power and Poverty: Old Age in the Pre-Industrial Past* (Westport, CT, 2002), p. 3.

3

Blood and Trees

No prophetic text from the Old Testament was more frequently depicted in medieval art than Isaiah 11:1: 'And there shall come forth a rod out of the stem of Jesse, and a Branch shall grow out of his roots.' Foretelling the Incarnation of Christ and situating him in the lineage of the kings of Israel, this verse provided the inspiration for a pervasive iconography that found expression in the leaves of illuminated psalters and bibles, wall paintings and floor tiles, stonework and stained-glass windows (Fig. 3.1). Often this took the form of a trunk or vine springing from the navel or side of the reclining or sleeping patriarch, from which sprout the ancestors of Christ in the guise of fruit, surrounded by tendrils of foliage. Jesse's posture alludes, in turn, to Adam, the original father of humankind, out of whose rib was created Eve. They were the first forebears of the Saviour, who, conceived by the Virgin Mary through the Holy Ghost, came into the world in order to redeem their fatal sin in the Garden of Eden. Jesus was the seed that the Lord declared would bruise the head of the evil serpent which had deceived the innocent couple he had planted in Paradise.[1]

Genealogical images such as these were common in pre-Reformation England. Some Trees of Jesse were casualties of early Protestant iconoclasm: the south transept of St Cuthbert's church in Wells contains a mutilated late fifteenth-century sculpture which was also immured in a concealing layer of plaster but has since been revealed.[2] A thirty-foot-high wooden carving on the same theme in St Mary's Priory at Abergavenny was described as 'defaced and pulled down in peeces' in the 1580s: only the recumbent Jesse survives.[3] The savage assaults to which these images were subjected should not, however, lead us to assume that the reformers sought to bury Christ's ancestry in oblivion. The main target of the iconoclasts' zeal was probably the anthropomorphic figure of Jesus, which the

---

[1] See Arthur Watson, *The Early Iconography of the Tree of Jesse* (Oxford, 1934); H. T. Kirby, 'The "Jesse" Tree Motif in Stained Glass: A Comparative Study of some English Examples', *Journal of the British Society of Master Glass-Painters*, 13 (1959–63), 313–20, 434–41; Étienne Madranges, *L'Abre de Jessé, de la racine à l'ésprit* (Paris, 2007); Susan L. Green, *Tree of Jesse Iconography in Northern Europe in the Fifteenth and Sixteenth Centuries* (New York, 2019).

[2] See Margaret Aston, *Broken Idols of the English Reformation* (Cambridge, 2016), pp. 222–3. A similar window dating from c.1340 survives in Dorchester Abbey, Oxfordshire.

[3] Thomas Churchyard, *The worthines of Wales wherein are more then a thousand severall things rehearsed* (1587; STC 5261), sig. F4r-v. See Aston, *Broken Idols*, p. 992. Three windows in the Lady Chapel of Exeter Cathedral depicting fourteen generations of Christ's descent were still present in 1635 but have since been destroyed: J. Wickham Legg (ed.), 'A Relation of a Short Survey of the Western Counties (1635)', *Camden Miscellany XVI*, CS, 3rd ser., 52 (1936), p. 48.

Fig. 3.1 Tree of Jesse from the Queen Mary Psalter (illuminated manuscript, London/Westminster or East Anglia, *c*.1310–20).

Source: © British Library Board, MS Royal 2 B VII, fo. 67v. All Rights Reserved/Bridgeman Images.

hotter sort of Protestants regarded as a blasphemous affront to his majesty. Other examples of this distinctive imagery escaped, including a striking set of five windows from the church of St Dyfnog in Llanrhaeadr-yng-Nghinmeirch, Denbighshire, installed on the very eve of the break with Rome in 1533.[4] Nor was this motif excluded from the new visual culture to which English Protestantism gave rise. It appears, for instance, on a moulded ceiling made around 1635 for a house owned by a godly fish merchant in Dartmouth.[5]

The Tree of Jesse was a classic symbol of divine genealogy that survived England's Reformations, albeit not entirely unscathed. Neatly combining several senses of the word generation, it highlights the extent to which the act of physical procreation and the progression of successive cohorts of a family through histor- ical time were closely interconnected in the early modern mind. Chapters 1 and 2 have focused on the dynamics of the relationships that developed between living generations—between youth and age and between kith and kin. In this chapter and Chapter 4, the focus shifts towards the vertical links that tied early modern people to their dead forebears and their future heirs. First I turn to ancestry and genealogy. I explore a range of manifestations of what J. H. Plumb once called 'genealogical fever' in the context of the sixteenth and seventeenth centuries.[6] While the fascination with lineage, birth, blood, and descent that was a hallmark of the Tudor and Stuart elite has hardly been neglected by scholars, its links to the religious impulses and upheavals of the era have been insufficiently scrutinised. I argue here that the biological and spiritual, dynastic and confessional dimensions of this enterprise must be assessed in tandem and that genealogical thinking stretched further downwards into English society than we have hitherto realized. In the process, a number of contemporary assumptions about sin and sex, preg- nancy and childbirth, race and heredity will be tested and tried. A further object- ive of this chapter is to underscore the value of placing theology at the heart of the social and cultural history of religion.

The Lineage of Adam and Christ

Christianity has always been obsessed with its own origins, but a growing preoccupation with human and divine ancestry is one of the less recognized effects of the Reformation. Protestants lavished renewed attention on the book of Genesis, which was itself a genealogy. As John Calvin observed in his

---

[4] See https://coflein.gov.uk/en/site/165239/images (last accessed 24 July 2022). By tradition, this largely complete window survives because it was hidden during the Civil Wars.

[5] Tara Hamling, *Decorating the 'Godly' Household: Religious Art in Post-Reformation Britain* (New Haven, CT, 2010), pp. 258–9. The house is now the Dartmouth Museum, 6 The Butterwalk, Duke Street.

[6] J. H. Plumb, *The Death of the Past* (1969), pp. 31–2.

commentary on it, it was a 'booke of the generations of Adam', set down as a record of the continual succession of his stock, kindred, and progeny.[7] Beginning with the supernatural creation of the world and its first inhabitants and proceeding to describe the eschatological and environmental disasters of the Fall and the Flood, its account of these momentous events is enveloped in an enumeration of the offspring of Adam and the patriarchs. The book records the descent of humanity from a single root and tells how the continents were populated by Noah and his three sons, Ham, Shem, and Japheth and their wives, after they came out of the Ark, in which, together with every species of bird, fish, and beast, they had been afforded safe asylum. It goes on to describe how the Lord blesses Abraham and his posterity, with whom he enters into an everlasting covenant symbolized by the rite of circumcision, and to tell the stories of his descendant Jacob and of the trials and tribulations his son Joseph suffers at the hands of his envious brothers. Revolving around God's injunction to Adam and Eve to 'increase and multiply', it traces the rise of religion as a function of reproduction and of the succession of blood. It is a recital of 'begats', of the cyclical process by which fathers and mothers engender daughters and sons. Dwelling on the themes of marriage and childbearing, fertility and barrenness, it is a text that forges an intimate link between demography and theology, between generational change and the transmission of grace.

The critical importance of Genesis for our understanding of early modern monogenetic theories of race has been delineated by Colin Kidd, while Naomi Tadmor has illuminated the role that Scripture more generally played in shaping the wider social universe within which contemporaries operated.[8] However, it is also necessary to stress its significance as a source of ideas about ancestry, procreation, and family life. Its ubiquitous presence in the schemes of interior decoration designed for Protestant homes reflects its resonance as a core narrative by which devout people came to understand their own part in Christian history. John, Lord Robartes, for instance, commissioned a remarkable thirty-six-panel plasterwork ceiling on this theme for the long gallery at Lanhydrock House in Cornwall in the 1630s.[9]

The many biblical commentaries published on Genesis in this period attest to the tricky exegetical questions that reading it served to stimulate in the minds of early modern clergy and laypeople. Among the problems that this compressed narrative posed were ones of chronology. When exactly did Adam and Eve begin to have sex—before or after they were ejected from Eden? The royal chaplain

[7] John Calvin, *A commentarie of John Calvine, upon the first booke of Moses called Genesis*, trans. Thomas Tymme (1578; STC 4393), p. 159.

[8] Colin Kidd, *The Forging of Races: Race and Scripture in the Protestant Atlantic World, 1600–2000* (Cambridge, 2006); Naomi Tadmor, *The Social Universe of the English Bible: Scripture, Society and Culture in Early Modern England* (Cambridge, 2010).

[9] Hamling, *Decorating the 'Godly' Household*, pp. 182–9, 256–7.

Abraham Ross reasoned that Cain must have been born subsequent to their expulsion, since it was unfit that any 'carnall copulation' should be committed in paradise. The three children recorded in the Bible could not have been their only offspring, he surmised.[10] William Whately, pastor of Banbury in Oxfordshire, agreed, inferring that this was a genealogy from which collateral lines must have been omitted and excised.[11] Protestant divines also speculated about the extraordinary longevity of the patriarchs and their capacity to engender children at a very advanced age. Methuselah, for instance, 'begat' Lamech at 187 and apparently continued to expand his family until his death at 969. Seth seemed to have been 105 when his first son Enos arrived and Noah 500 when Ham, Shem, and Japheth appeared on the scene. How could this be squared with the biological fact that human fertility reduces with time? Resolving these questions required some ingenious mathematical gymnastics, as well as the assertion that the sexual virility of centenarians was necessary in order to fulfil God's decree to propagate and people the earth speedily and efficiently.[12] To explain why the males mentioned in Genesis had apparently abstained from having children for many decades Protestant ministers envisaged a sliding temporal scale, in which 60 to 65 became the perfect age for generation and the prime of life. This was the age at which Adam had been created by God, declared Andrew Willet in his *Hexapla in Genesin* published in 1632, so that from 'first instant' he was in a position to beget offspring.[13] In the era of the patriarchs, 'none was sayd to come to mans estate, till hee had bin a hundred yeeres and more'.[14] The human life cycle and its milestones were thus elongated. The steady moral degeneration of mankind through the succeeding eras was the main reason why this been reversed over time, though better exercise and diet and a less polluted atmosphere were also cited. One writer believed that it was related to the rise of wet-nursing and the concomitant decline of maternal breastfeeding. The former practice was widely criticized in the period and made to take the blame for a variety of evils.[15]

Other awkward issues raised by the first book of Moses concerned polygamy and incest. Reconciling early modern ideals of faithful monogamous marriage

---

[10] Abraham Ross, *An exposition on the fourteene first chapters of Genesis, by way of question and answere* (1626; STC 21324), p. 74.

[11] William Whately, *Prototypes, or the primarie precedent presidents out of the booke of Genesis* (1640; STC 25317), p. 47; Patrick Simon, *A commentary upon the first book of Moses, called Genesis* (1695; STC P772), p. 111.

[12] See Gervase Babington, *Certaine plaine, briefe, and comfortable notes upon everie chapter of Genesis* (1592; STC 1086), fo. 26r.

[13] Andrew Willet, *Hexapla in Genesin, that is, a sixfold commentarie upon Genesis* (1632 [1633]; STC 25684), pp. 25, 65; Benjamin Needler, *Expository notes, with practical observations; towards the opening of the five first chapters of the first book of Moses called Genesis* (1655; Wing N412), p. 221.

[14] Ross, *Exposition*, p. 92.

[15] On breastfeeding, see Needler, *Expository notes*, p. 222, and see pp. 226–7. See also Simon, *Commentary*, pp. 113–14. See David Harley, 'From Providence to Nature: The Moral Theology and Godly Practice of Maternal Breast-Feeding in Stuart England', *Bulletin of the History of Medicine*, 69 (1995), 198–223.

with the stories of Abraham taking his maid Hagar as his mistress and of Jacob's two wives, Leah and Rachel (the daughters of his uncle Laban and his own cousins), proved difficult. These and other stories left the unfortunate impression that Scripture sanctioned adultery and bigamy. In his expository notes on the topic published in 1655, the London puritan minister Benjamin Needler admitted that Cain had indeed wedded his sister, saying that what was a sin under the Gospel had been unavoidable when only one family was living in the world. Incestuous intermarriage with close kin was a corollary of the mandate to multiply mankind and, furthermore, of the punishing purge that God had carried out by sending the Deluge. Needler also devoted space to associated perplexities such as the suggestion that Abraham and the patriarchs were sexually promiscuous, obviating their fault by insisting that they took additional wives not of 'a lewd minde, for the satisfying of their lust, but of a conscience not rightly informed in this point'.[16] Later ages had adopted higher and superior standards of personal morality.

More broadly, the extended families of Adam and his progeny described in Genesis were extremely dysfunctional ones. They were filled with quarrelling brothers such as Cain and Abel and Jacob and Esau, who fought and murdered each other, and with children who showed no respect for their parents. Ham had not only mocked the nakedness of his elderly father Noah but neglected to protect his dignity and cover his genitals, a crime of filial disobedience for which he and his own offspring in turn were grievously cursed. Noah's descent into drunkenness was a further embarrassment, a reminder of the inherent corruption and wickedness bequeathed by Adam, which also manifested itself in the unseemly coupling of his posterity with the brood of Cain. Protestant ministers were compelled to bend over backwards to turn this section of Scripture into a tool for teaching the religious values and upholding the social institutions they held dear and revered. The frequency with which their commentaries digress into a discussion of 'the holy knot of wedlock' and godly parenthood is a measure not merely of the challenges Genesis presented but also of the plasticity of the Bible as a cultural resource.[17] For Calvin, knowledge of Adam's genealogy was essential, because it underlined that a lineage, household, and church consisting of those who had righteously worshipped God had been continued and preserved since the beginning of time.[18] It was profitable, declared Abraham Ross, because it displayed the Lord's blessing in populating the world and refuted the fabulous legends about its origins spread by heathen philosophers and poets.[19]

---

[16] Needler, *Expository notes*, pp. 172–3, 178–90, quotation at p. 190. These questions had troubled medieval theologians too: see Peter Biller, *The Measure of the Multitude: Population in Medieval Thought* (Oxford, 2000), pp. 87–8, 113–14.

[17] Calvin, *Commentarie*, p. 160.   [18] *Ibid.*, p. 159.   [19] Ross, *Exposition*, pp. 73–4.

While other parts of the Bible also took the form of a catalogue of 'begats', including the first book of Chronicles, the Gospels of Matthew and Luke, which laid out two competing versions of the ancestry of Christ, were more crucial. The former traced the royal line of dynastic succession from David, while the latter was concerned with demonstrating his blood descent from the patriarch Abraham. Luke was concerned, in other words, with sanguinity and Matthew with institutional inheritance. Theologians seeking to refute heretics and unbelievers had wrestled strenuously with the challenge of harmonizing these accounts throughout the Middle Ages, but the task of establishing Christ's lineage became more imperative in the context of the renewed attention that humanism and Protestantism focused on the text of Scripture in its original languages and of the controversies over translation and the elimination of the errors that riddled the Vulgate. Closely entangled with the associated issue of biblical chronology, it was a topic that engaged major European reformers including Martin Luther, John Calvin, and Andreas Osiander.[20]

Unravelling the knots within the Gospels was regarded as immensely important. As the cantankerous Hebrew scholar Hugh Broughton declared in a tract of 1612, all Christians who looked for salvation by Scripture ought to have a special care to understand the genealogy of Jesus, which 'as from a fountain doth branch itself into a most pleasant variety of all God's holy proceedings'. Knowing both his legal and natural descent was critical to proving that he was indeed the promised seed who would redeem mankind and the heir of David's crown at the same time.[21] As William Cowper commented in a 'heavenly treatise' published the same year, precisely establishing the seventy-seven generations that stretched back from Christ to Abraham and the 'golden line' that connected him to his distant ancestor Adam not only demonstrated that he was the 'kinsman' of all human beings, 'nearest to us of flesh and blood'. It also had profound eschatological implications. What was ultimately at stake was Christ's identity as the awaited messiah who would break the serpent's head and the fulfilment of the prophecy about his appearance in Isaiah 11:1. What was at stake, in short, was the integrity and validity of the Bible as a canon of sacred truth.[22]

These too were issues upon which English Protestant divines expended considerable energy and ink. They did so driven by the conviction that the obscurities in divine genealogy rooted in the ostensible contradictions between the evangelists

---

[20]   See Kirsten Macfarlane, 'The Biblical Genealogies of the King James Bible (1611): Their Purpose, Sources and Significance', *The Library*, 7th ser., 19 (2018), 131–58; *eadem, Biblical Scholarship in an Age of Controversy: The Polemical World of Hugh Broughton (1549-1612)* (Oxford, 2021), ch. 3. I am indebted to Dr Macfarlane for helpful discussions of this topic. On biblical chronology, see Chapter 5 below.

[21]   H[ugh] B[roughton], *The holy genealogie of Jesus Christ both his naturall line of fathers...and his kingly line...* ([1612?]; STC 3867.9), sig. ¶1r.

[22]   William Cowper, *Three heavenly treatises, concerning Christ: 1 His genealogie. 2 His baptisme. 3 His Combat with Sathan* (1612; STC 5936), pp. 1–48, quotation at p. 10.

Matthew and Luke both deeply perturbed and seriously misled ordinary people. One way of resolving these tensions was to stress that the former wrote from the perspective of the Jews and highlighted Christ's status as the heir of David and Solomon, while the latter, by birth a Gentile, wrote to convert his erstwhile co-religionists to the new faith and so emphasized his descent from the stock of Adam. William Sympson's tract of 1619 on this topic was another attempt to measure the length of Christ's genealogy, take 'the altitude of the steps' between him and Abraham, and clear up an array of niggling questions that apparently puzzled the untrained laity. It took the form of an extended dialogue between Theophilus and Mnemon, who has woken up thoroughly troubled by the genealogical conundrums he heard 'tossed from hand to hand' at supper the previous night and seeks the counsel of his learned friend. These include why Jesus is said to have had no father and mother in Hebrews 7:5, when he was born of the Virgin, albeit not in accordance with 'the common law of generation'; the double meaning of 'begat' to denote both legal and natural succession; and the story of how Joseph was convinced not to set aside his pregnant bride-to-be Mary for cuckolding him by the timely visit of an angel. Mnemon closes by earnestly thanking Theophilus and hoping he can make 'good use of this sweete conference we have had together'.[23]

This familiar contrivance was a didactic device. Yet our instinctive scepticism that such questions were the stuff of everyday dinner-table conversation is offset by the continuing appearance of publications on this theme in the vernacular as well as in Latin. *The harmony of the old and new testament* (1682) appeared posthumously from the pen of Jean d'Espagne, minister of the French church in London. Among other issues, it considered why the lineage of Christ appeared to overturn the precept of primogeniture, because it showed that he descended from the youngest rather than the eldest of Adam and Noah's children, Seth and Shem, respectively. It also endeavoured to clarify the confusing numbering of the generations.[24] At the end of the seventeenth century, the internal discrepancies within the various accounts of the Saviour's genealogy were perceived to be one of the causes of atheism: a 1696 *Vindication* had originally been written to satisfy the doubts of a young gentleman travelling in Europe who had conceived 'an ill opinion of the Holy Scriptures' by 'conversing with bad Company'. One of the points its anonymous author made to reconcile the discordant pedigrees in Matthew and Luke was that the word generation 'doth not always relate simply to Birth or Genealogies' but often signified 'an Event that time brings forth' and a history or

---

[23] William Sympson, *A full and profitable interpretation of all the proper names that are within the illustrious and resplendant genealogie of Jesus Christ, set forth in the first chapter of S. Matthewe, conferred with the originall and best writers* (Cambridge, 1619; STC 23595), quotations at fo. ¶4r, pp. 1, 2, 39, 55–7, 60.

[24] John d'Espagne, *The harmony of the old and new testament: and the obscure texts explained* (1682; Wing E3262), pp. 14–15, 17–21.

relation of such passages. This explained why one was a less exact enumeration of the line of succession than the other, which left out some of the names recorded in the former.[25]

A further index of the sense of pastoral urgency that surrounded these problems from the early days of the Reformation onwards was the proliferation of pictorial genealogies prepared for insertion in printed bibles. Matthew Parker ensured that one was incorporated in the preliminary pages of his brainchild, the Bishops' Bible, first published in 1568, adorned with the imprimatur of his own coat of arms (Fig. 3.2). In fact, this was borrowed from the influential visual scheme devised by the twelfth-century scholastic theologian Peter of Poitiers as a tool for helping people to memorize the Bible, examples of which Parker found close to hand in his own library of medieval manuscripts. Its original format as a scroll had to be modified for inclusion in a codex-shaped book, but it retained its educational intention as a 'table that setteth out to the eye the genealogie of Adam, so passing by the Patriarches, Judges, Kinges, Prophetes, and Priestes, and the fathers of their tyme, continuyng in lineal descent to Christe our Saviour'. These were arranged in a central vertical line, surrounded by biographical notes and texts regarding the eight ages of the world, to which were added the caveat that any person or deed mentioned therein that could not be found referred to in Scripture was vouched for in ecclesiastical history.[26]

These outdated diagrams were superseded by those devised for the King James Version of 1611, the result of an unlikely collaboration between Hugh Broughton and the cartographer John Speed. As Kirsten Macfarlane has recently demonstrated, this joint enterprise was an attempt to bring the latest advances in biblical scholarship down to the level of laity who, like Speed himself, were illiterate in the sacred languages of Holy Writ. Correcting the mistakes made by Peter of Poitiers and facilitating a more accurate representation of the intricate web of kin relations laid out in Genesis and the Gospels, Broughton and Speed's genealogies sought to breach the gap between elite erudition and the unwitting ignorance of everyday readers (Fig. 3.3). They took inspiration from the developments in heraldry and secular genealogy to which we shall turn shortly. Alongside other forms of paratext such as maps of the Holy Land, illustrations, and symbols, they assisted believers in comprehending the salvation history laid out in the Old and New Testaments and in resolving their apparent inconsistencies.[27] The opening page depicts the word 'GOD' in a bolster of clouds, an image of Adam and Eve at

---

[25] *A vindication of our Blessed Saviours genealogy* (Edinburgh, 1696; Wing V487), quotations at sigs A2r, A3r.

[26] *The holie bible conteynyng the olde testament and the newe* (1568; STC 2099), sig. (iii)r. For the link with Peter of Poitier's *Compendium historiae in genealogia Christi*, see Macfarlane, 'Biblical Genealogies of the King James Bible', 141–4; *eadem, Biblical Scholarship in an Age of Controversy*, ch. 3. Parker probably borrowed the diagram from one of the manuscripts in his own library, including Corpus Christi College, MS 29, fos vi r– xi r; MS 437, fos 1r–6v.

[27] See Macfarlane, 'Biblical Genealogies of the King James Bible'.

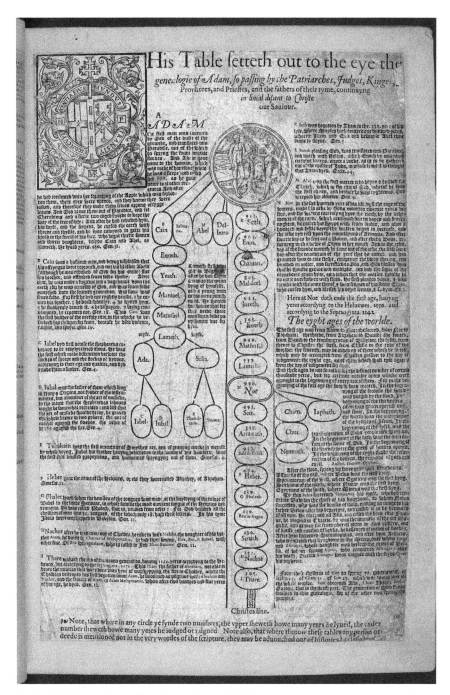

Fig. 3.2 Genealogical table in the Bishops' Bible: *The holie bible conteynyng the olde testament and the newe* (London, 1568), sig. (iii)r.

Source: © British Library Board, 1.e.2. All Rights Reserved/ Bridgeman Images.

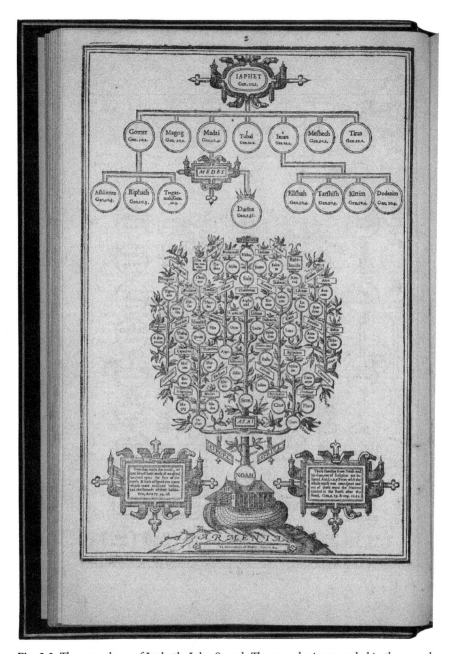

Fig. 3.3 The genealogy of Japheth: John Speed, *The genealogies recorded in the sacred scriptures according to every familie and tribe* (London, 1613?), sig. A2v.

Source: Folger Shakespeare Library, Washington DC, Bd.w.STC 2216. Folger Digital Image Collection.

the centre, and roundels containing the names of their descendants running down the sides; next is the genealogy of Japheth in the guise of a tree springing out of Noah and his ark that describes the populating of Europe, Africa, and Asia; subsequent pages detail the generations of each of the patriarchs.[28]

Published separately and bound with the Bible and the Book of Common Prayer in a range of sizes, these genealogies 'according to every family and tribe' became a highly lucrative corner of the contemporary book trade, as the numerous surviving editions reveal.[29] Although they are now synonymous with Speed, they were in essence the work of the erratic and argumentative Broughton, who approached the task of combating the 'grosse errours' some detected in the New Testament and used 'to pervert and obscure the glorious entrance of the blessed Gospel' with nothing less than missionary zeal.[30] He had already published a broadside table entitled 'Our Lord his line of Fathers from Adam...' and an alphabetical index that allowed readers to identify every individual mentioned in the Bible and their blood relations.[31] The popularity of Speed and Broughton's genealogies inspired various spin-off publications, including *A clowd of witnesses* (1616), which was designed to illustrate the spiritual and typological use of such pedigrees and to smooth out residual issues such as whether Jesus had stepbrothers and sisters via Mary or Joseph.[32] Biblical genealogy was evidently big business in Stuart England.

It also occupied an important place in puritan and Protestant piety, engendering its own offspring in the guise of elaborate manuscript copies. A set of handdrawn and written genealogical tables on folio sheets owned by the Guide family in the early seventeenth century runs from Creation to AD 902, beginning with Adam and extending beyond the birth of Christ in the 3,929th year of the world to include the baptism of Lucius, first king of Britain and the conversion of Donald, ruler of Scotland (Fig. 3.4).[33] There was also a flourishing market in prints of the pedigrees of Christ and portraits of the patriarchs. Together with a series of splendid scenes from Genesis, these were among the woodcut pictures published by the French Protestant immigrant Gyles Godet, who worked in

---

[28] *The holy bible, conteyning the Old Testament, and the New* (1611; STC 2216), pp. 1–34.

[29] John Speed, *The genealogies of holy scriptures* 1611; STC 23039, and many other editions).

[30] Broughton, *Holy genealogie of Jesus Christ*, sig. ¶2v. See also BL, Sloane MS 3927 (Hugh Broughton, 'Genealogia et chronologia sacra').

[31] Hugh Broughton, *Our Lord his line of fathers from Adam* (1595; STC 3874.5); *idem, A direction to finde all those names expressed in that large table of genealogies of Scripture* ([1595?]; STC 3859.5). See also *idem, A defence of the holy genealogies whose ignorance hath greatly hurt the Jewes, and hundred Christianitie* ([1595?]; STC 3859). Bodl., MS 950, is a set of manuscript tables of chronology and genealogy by Broughton, dated *c*.1600.

[32] John Speed, *A clowd of witnesses: and the holy genealogies of the sacred scriptures* (1616; STC 23031). For the question of whether Jesus had 'naturall brethren...either by father, or mother, or both', see Speed's tract on the genealogy of Christ, 'Jesus of Nazareth', c.1616: BL, MS Egerton 2255, fos 9r–v.

[33] See LPL, MS 766; BL, Sloane MS 2498 (Genealogical tables from Creation to AD 902, owned by the Guide family).

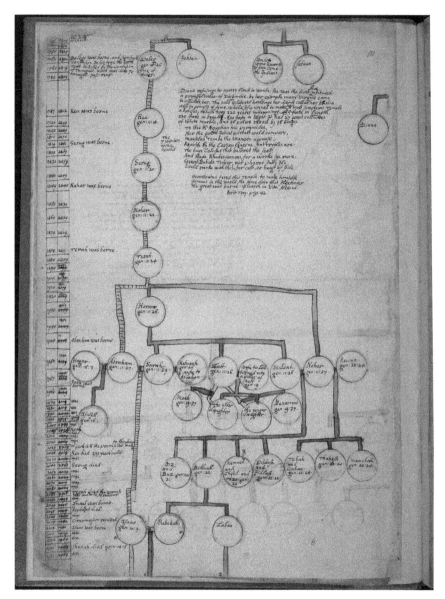

Fig. 3.4 Genealogical tables from Creation to A D 902, owned by the Guide family.
Source: © British Library Board, Sloane MS 2498. All Rights Reserved/Bridgeman Images.

London's Blackfriars until his death in 1571.[34] Their popularity is attested by the high-quality and colourful copies that Thomas Trevelyon made for the elaborate

---

[34] See Tessa Watt, *Cheap Print and Popular Piety, 1550–1640* (Cambridge, 1991), pp. 183–91. Among the items registered to Godet in the Stationers' Register was 'The geneolige or lyne of our savyour Christe as touchynge his humanyte from Noee to Davyd': ibid, p. 354.

visual commonplace book he completed around 1602.[35] They later became part of the stock of the mid-seventeenth-century bookseller Thomas Warren, who entered them in the Stationers' Register in 1656.[36] Broughton and Speed's genealogies found subsequent imitators, including the Shropshire antiquarian John Reynolds's *The Scripture genealogy beginning at Noah* (1739). As the marks of ownership in extant copies suggest, these were texts that were passed down from father and mother to daughter and son as family heirlooms.[37] They are a neglected facet of what Daniel Woolf has christened 'the genealogical imagination'.[38] Carried across the Atlantic, they also put down firm roots in New England, creating a culture permeated by an equally high degree of genealogical literacy.[39]

The Genealogical Imagination

The developing fascination with Christ's ancestry must be situated in the context of the obsession that the Tudor and Stuart gentry and nobility developed with establishing their own lineages and producing pedigrees. This was a side effect of a social order that was in massive flux and in which the traditional criterion for determining rank and status, blood, was in the process of being challenged by the wealth of the nouveau riche. It reflected the pressures that upward mobility presented to the traditional elite against the backdrop of a Reformation that sold off vast quantities of monastic property to arrivistes after 1536, as well as the eagerness of the beneficiaries of this unprecedented process of redistribution to prove or to fabricate spurious evidence of their antiquity and legitimacy. It was also a consequence of the recurrent sense of vulnerability that all families felt in the face of the genetic lottery that saw approximately a quarter of landed dynasties die out in the course of a generation.[40] Their fragility was a function of a legal system that

[35] FSL, MS V.b.232 (Thomas Trevelyon Miscellany, 1608), fo. 37r–68v. These are reproduced in *The Trevelyon Miscellany of 1608: A Facsimile of Folger Shakespeare Library MS B.b.232*, ed. Heather Wolfe (Washington DC, 2007). See Fig. 1.6.

[36] Thomas Warren entered 'The generation from Adam to Noah' in 1656: Watt, *Cheap Print*, p. 354. No copies are extant.

[37] John Reynolds, *The Scripture genealogy beginning at Noah* (Chester, 1739). See the copy in the NLW, MS 7192B, which has genealogical notes facing the main title: 'This Book was given Ewan Lloyd by Jn Reynolds of Oswestry the Father & was delivered to me by E. Lloyd a few weeks before his decease in order to present it to his nephew...as a token of his love to him...24 July 1773.' One CUL copy of Speed's *Genealogies* (1636) is annotated by a late seventeenth-century hand on p. 10: 'Elizabeth faulknour is my name and with my son i wrot thes': Syn. 5.63.5. I owe this reference to Kirsten Macfarlane.

[38] Daniel Woolf, *The Social Circulation of the Past: English Historical Culture 1500–1730* (Oxford, 2003), ch. 4.

[39] Karin Wulf, 'Bible, King and Common Law: Genealogical Literacies and Family History Practices in British America', *Early American Studies* 10 (2012), 467–502.

[40] See Mervyn James, *Family, Lineage and Civil Society* (Oxford, 1974), pp. 108–12; Lawrence Stone, *The Crisis of the Aristocracy* (Oxford, 1965), pp. 22–7. Felicity Heal and Clive Holmes, *The Gentry in England and Wales, 1500–1700* (Basingstoke, 1994), ch. 1; Woolf, *Social Circulation*, ch. 4. See also Anthony Wagner, *English Genealogy*, 3rd edn (Chichester, 1983), esp. pp. 351–75; Michael Sharpe, *Family Matters: A History of Genealogy* (Barnsley, 2011), ch. 1.

privileged patrilineal inheritance and in which titles and property passed down by the rule of primogeniture. Old families were ones in which generations of sons lived to beget male heirs. Those who had the misfortune to engender only daughters were doomed to extinction. Genealogy has an inherent gender bias that prioritizes reproductive seed and treats women largely as vessels for childbearing.[41]

The product of conscious decisions about which ancestors to remember and which to forget, it is critical in forging the family as an imagined community of kin. As Eviatar Zerubavel observes, it entails manipulations and distortions of memory, 'strategic agendas of inclusion and exclusion' that reconstruct the past with an eye to the shaping of the present and future. Constructed by the techniques of cutting, pasting, clipping, braiding, pruning, and splitting, pedigrees must be approached as creative forms of 'genealogical engineering'.[42]

Genealogy was steadily transformed by the rise of reading, writing, and print. Formerly reliant on oral transmission, in the Middle Ages it was usually only committed to paper, stone, or brass in a context of crisis, ruin, or failure that threatened the very survival of a family line.[43] Insecurity remained a significant stimulus to this form of activity, but the rich textual and material culture in which early modern genealogical instincts found expression had a momentum of its own. Possession of such objects became an end in itself. Alongside heraldry, genealogy assumed new importance as the visitations of representatives of the College of Arms became increasingly preoccupied with tracing descent. Recording this was made obligatory by a writ of 1512. Other artefacts of lineage also proliferated.[44] An adjunct science to the antiquarianism that was gripping educated laypeople across the country, as a research enterprise it involved the systematic recovery of documents from libraries and other repositories. Gradually 'a world of paper' was superimposed 'upon family experiences, communally shared memories, binding emotions, the lived reality of kinship relations'.[45]

---

[41] See Eviatar Zerubavel, *Ancestors and Relatives: Genealogy, Identity and Community* (Oxford, 2012), p. 45; Katharine Hodgkin, 'Women, Memory and Family History in Seventeenth-Century England', in Erika Kuijpers, Judith Pollmann, Johannes Müller, and Jasper van der Steen (eds), *Memory before Modernity: Practices of Memory in Early Modern Europe* (Leiden, 2013), pp. 297–313, at p. 301.

[42] Zerubavel, *Ancestors and Relatives*, pp. 16, 47, 54, 76.

[43] See Jon Denton, 'Genealogy and Gentility: Social Status in Provincial England', in Raluca L. Radulescu and Edward Donald Kennedy (eds), *Broken Lines: Genealogical Literature in Medieval Britain and France* (Turnhout, 2008), pp. 143–58.

[44] On the College of Arms, see Anthony Richard Wagner, *The Records and Collections of the College of Arms* (1952), pp. 15–20, 22–4. On heraldry and genealogy, see Anthony Wagner, *Heralds and Heraldry in the Middle Ages*, 2nd edn (Oxford, 1956); Michael Maclagan, 'Genealogy and Heraldry in the Sixteenth and Seventeenth Centuries', in Levi Fox (ed.), *English Historical Scholarship in the Sixteenth and Seventeenth Centuries* (1956), pp. 31–48; Richard Cust, *Charles I and the Aristocracy, 1625-1641* (Cambridge, 2013), ch. 1, esp. pp. 7–22; Nigel Ramsay (ed.), *Heralds and Heraldry in Shakespeare's England* (Doningon, 2014).

[45] Markus Friedrich, 'Genealogy as Archive-Driven Research Enterprise in Early Modern Europe', *Osiris*, 32 (2017), 65–84, at 83–4. See also Jan Broadway, *'No Historie so Meete': Gentry Culture and the Development of Local History in Elizabethan and Stuart England* (Manchester, 2012), ch. 5; Jost

Considerable numbers of the pedigrees drawn up by official heralds survive in record offices and national archives, and many more have been retained in private hands. The sheer length of lavishly prepared and elaborately illuminated rolls on vellum, complete with painted coats of arms, is emblematic of the longevity claimed by the families they commemorate.[46] These exist alongside an even larger body of sketchy and roughly scribbled family trees, many of which are now very fragile and fragmentary indeed.[47] While most are dominated by male heirs, some illustrate female lines too. The fourteen-foot-long pedigree of Sir Randle Brereton of Malpas in Cheshire described the issue of the four daughters he had with his wife Eleanor alongside the children and grandchildren of his ten sons.[48] Some such family trees trace lineages that were tenuous, if not spurious and fictitious. The genealogy of a Somerset woman called Elizabeth Downe, produced around 1620, claimed she was a descendant of Edmund, ancient earl of Cornwall, while the pretensions of the early eighteenth-century Chester shoemaker Roger Maddock are reflected in a pedigree that presents his wife as a descendant of the royal house of York.[49]

Funeral monuments that embodied the same aspirations in brass and stone were more durable, though some early evangelicals made them the target of vandalism, as the Elizabethan proclamation of 1560 prohibiting this reveals. It condemned such acts of iconoclasm for impairing the 'true understanding of divers families in this realm (who have descended of the blood of the same persons deceased)' and jeopardizing 'the true course of their inheritance'.[50] The creation of two and three-dimensional pedigrees of this kind gathered pace in subsequent decades. Examples include the metal plaque listing seven generations of the Beale

Eickmeyer, Markus Friedrich, and Volker Bauer (eds), *Genealogical Knowledge in the Making: Tools, Practices and Evidence in Early Modern Europe* (Berlin, 2019).

[46] For some pedigrees on vellum, see BL, Additional MS 47882 (Hopton family illuminated pedigree roll, late 17th century); BL, Additional MS 74251A (illuminated genealogy of the Weston family, c.1632–3); Devon HC, 528B/Z/1 (Pedigree of the Giffard family, c.1628); CRO, D 6120 (Pedigree of the Bruen of Bruen Stapleford family, 11th–16th centuries). The pedigree of the Bowes family (DCRO, D/St/C1/1/3) illustrates the fate of families whose heirs died without issue: the final line notes that both William and Thomas Blakiston 'died Unmarried'.

[47] For handwritten and fragmentary examples, see LLRRO, 2D31/349 (Roos family pedigree, c.1684); WAAS, 705:134 BA 1531/79/20 (Lechmere family genealogical notes, mid-17th century). On pedigree rolls, see John Baker, 'Tudor Pedigree Rolls and Their Uses', in Ramsay (ed.), *Heralds and Heraldry*, pp. 125–65.

[48] CRO, DDX 95 (Illuminated pedigree roll of the Brereton family of Malpas, Cheshire, c.1564).

[49] Somerset HC, DD/WO/63/3/1 (Pedigree of Elizabeth Downe, showing fictitious descent from Edmund, earl of Cornwall, c.1620); CRO, DDC/15/25 (The line of the House of York, or the White Rose, to Hannah, wife of Roger Maddock of Chester, shoemaker).

[50] *Tudor Royal Proclamations*, ed. P. L. Hughes and J. F. Larkin, 3 vols (1950–4), vol. ii, pp. 146–7. On funeral monuments as a vehicle for genealogy, see also Nigel Llewellyn, *Funeral Monuments in Post-Reformation England* (Cambridge, 2000), p. 42; Peter Sherlock, *Monuments and Memory in Early Modern England* (Farnham, 2008), pp. 20–8; Richard Cust, 'The Material Culture of Lineage in Late Tudor and Stuart England', in Catherine Richardson, Tara Hamling, and David Gaimster (eds), *The Routledge Handbook of Material Culture in Early Modern Europe* (2017), pp. 247–74.

family at Maidstone in Kent set up in the 1590s, which carries the Latin inscription '*quorum posteritati benedicat deus*' ('whose posterity may God bless '). Next to the enchanting triple-tiered memorial erected to Edward Fettiplace, his father William, and his grandfather Alexander at Swinbrook in Oxfordshire after 1613 is a second monument displaying three more generations dating from the later seventeenth century.[51] Completed around 1589, the memorial to the Elizabethan gentleman Sir Gawen Carew and his forebears in Exeter Cathedral was a studied attempt to preserve the memory of a declining dynasty teetering on the edge of oblivion after he had died childless.[52]

Other pedigrees took typographical form. In England there is nothing quite like the elegant etching of three Portuguese genealogies in the guise of tall trees with intertwined branches dating from 1645.[53] But broadsheet pedigrees were sometimes printed in the context of legal disputes involving contested claims of succession and lineage, especially when the last remaining blood relative expired without issue. One surviving item supports the claim of Mrs Elizabeth Sherwin to be the only surviving niece and the heir-at-law of George Monck, 'Who had the Honour & happiness of Restoring the Royal Family' to the throne in 1660 and was created Duke of Albemarle as a reward. Her own demise is indicated by the small handwritten alteration of 'is' to 'was'.[54] Such texts alert us to a social hierarchy that was increasingly dynamic and unsettled in character, not merely in its upper reaches but right across the spectrum.[55]

The 'genealogical gaze' and 'craze' of the early modern era has been extensively studied by social historians. Sterling work in uncovering its contours has been undertaken by Felicity Heal, Clive Holmes, and others.[56] But there remains a tendency to see this development as largely a secular one, in clear tension with Protestant imperatives that stressed personal election rather than inherited merit. Oliver Harris remarks that 'there was no explicitly religious dimension to the celebration of ancestry'. Heal and Holmes present Calvinist concepts of grace, alongside humanist emphasis on merit and moral virtue, as an 'intensely subversive challenge' to prevailing notions of status, though they do recognize the ways in which they were absorbed and incorporated into older schemes of descent and

[51] Sherlock, *Monuments and Memory*, pp. 109 and 17–19 respectively and see ch. 1.
[52] Oliver Harris, 'The Generations of Adam: The Monument of Sir Gawen Carew in Exeter Cathedral', *Church Monuments*, 29 (2014), pp. 40–71.
[53] BM, Q, 6. 137 (genealogical tree of the families of the Azambuia, Movras, and Cortereales families, 1645).
[54] *The pedigree of the Monkes of Potheridge* ([1684–1709]): BM, 1864, 0813.293. See also *The Earle of Carberyes pedigree: with their titles, and honourable endowments* (1646; Wing E71); *The pedigree from old Andrew Barret, Esq* (1678; Wing P1049A); [*A pedigree illustrating the claim of Sir Richard Verney to the barony of Broke*] ([1694]; Wing V242B).
[55] For a particularly important recent intervention, see Alexandra Shepard, *Accounting for Oneself: Worth, Status and the Social Order in Early Modern England* (Oxford, 2015).
[56] Heal and Holmes, *Gentry*, ch. 1; Jan Broadway, *'No History so Meete': Gentry Culture and the Development of Local History in Elizabethan and Early Stuart England* (Manchester, 2006), ch. 5. See also Eric Ketelaar, 'The Genealogical Gaze: Family Identities and Family Archives in the Fourteenth to Seventeenth Centuries', *Libraries and the Cultural Record*, 44 (2009), 9–28.

lineage.[57] The prevailing emphasis on uneasy coexistence and contradiction may, however, underestimate the extent to which the compilation of genealogies was actively shaped and inflected by faith, and particularly by the example set by the book of Genesis.

Although St Paul was on record in 1 Timothy 1:4 for saying 'Give no heede to Genealogies' and dismissing them as 'vain' and unprofitable, elsewhere Scripture provided a positive incentive for making them. The Somerset preacher Richard Bernard warmly encouraged the keeping of records 'of our Ancestours, and the increase of our posterities, to behold therein the Lords blessing, and to rejoice in our encreasing the Lords Church'. Such texts should be set down 'to shew how God registreth up his people in a booke of remembrance, as being precious in his eyes' and to demonstrate that throughout all ages he had selected 'a race of right-eous people' and 'a peculiar generation, in despite of Satans malice and all his bloody instruments'.[58] Their very format alluded to and replicated the patrilineal origin of humankind and its regeneration through the creation of the second Adam, Christ, of which they served as a telling and timely reminder.[59] Enumerating the many descendants of a family dynasty was also an act of thanksgiving for the mercies God had bestowed upon it in the guise of offspring. Marriages that gave rise to multiple children were ones that enjoyed divine favour.

Fecundity and fertility were thus sources of pride. Devout Protestants saw them as promising signs. Sterility and barrenness were accordingly surrounded by tremendous anxiety for both men and women.[60] Women who suffered from deformities or diseases that prevented them from conceiving were advised that by these 'signes of impotencie God sheweth that he calleth them to live single'.[61] Godly ladies praised the Lord for the children of their unions and prayed that they might be 'fruitful vines'.[62] Tracts written to guide them through pregnancy and childbirth such as John Oliver's *Present for teeming women* (1663) deployed the rhetorics of human and horticultural generation interchangeably, grounding

[57] Oliver D. Harris, 'Lines of Descent: Appropriations of Ancestry in Stone and Parchment', in Andrew Gordon and Thomas Rist (eds), *The Arts of Remembrance in Early Modern England: Memorial Cultures of the Post-Reformation* (Farnham, 2013), pp. 85–102, at p. 101; Heal and Holmes, *Gentry*, pp. 30, 32–3.
[58] Richard Bernard, *Ruths recompense: or a commentarie on the booke of Ruth* (1628; STC 1962), pp. 376, 471.
[59] See Gabrielle M. Spiegel, 'Genealogy: Form and Function in Medieval Historical Narrative', *History and Theory*, 22 (1983), 43–53.
[60] On male and female infertility, see Helen Berry and Elizabeth Foyster, 'Childless Men in Early Modern England', in *eaedem* (eds), *The Family in Early Modern England* (Cambridge, 2007), pp. 158–83, esp. pp. 164–5; Jennifer Evans, *Aphrodisiacs, Fertility and Medicine in Early Modern England* (2014), esp. ch. 3; Daphna Oren-Magidor, 'From Anne to Hannah: Religious Views of Infertility in Post-Reformation England', *Journal of Women's History*, 27 (2015), 86–108; eadem, *Infertility in Early Modern England* (2017), esp. chs 1, 4.
[61] Gouge, *Domesticall duties*, pp. 181–2.
[62] See Patricia Crawford, 'Attitudes to Pregnancy from a Woman's Spiritual Diary, 1687–9', *Local Population Studies*, 21 (1978), repr. in *eadem*, *Blood, Bodies and Families in Early Modern England* (Harlow, 2004), pp. 38–40.

their discussion in the mandate for the multiplication of mankind contained in Genesis.[63] As Christopher Hooke commented in a text written for young couples and expectant mothers in 1590, children were 'an inheritance, a reward, and a crowne unto us from the Lord'.[64] A sermon delivered at the funeral of a 34-year-old woman, who had borne twelve offspring and died shortly after safely delivering the last one, sharply reproved 'the wretchedness of their fault, who grudge and repine at the increase of children as a burthen'. On the contrary, this was a mechanism for building up Israel, fervently to be desired for 'the increase, and inlargement of Gods Church'.[65]

Genealogy was a natural corollary of the new emphasis on the twin vocations of marriage and procreation that followed from the reformers' repudiation of the voluntary celibacy of Catholic priests and religious.[66] It must be seen in the context of the Protestant reconceptualization of the institution of wedlock as a covenant for 'the multiplying of an holy seed' and for augmenting the company of the faithful upon earth. Lauding virginity over marriage and denying the need for further expansion of the human race, the early church father Augustine had declared that 'the coming of Christ is not served by the very begetting of children'.[67] In the post-Reformation world, by contrast, maternity and paternity acquired the status of a religious vocation. Much attention was paid to the text of 1 Timothy 2:15 ('she shall be saved by child-bearing').[68] Like the portraits that some Protestants, including William Cecil, had painted of their pregnant wives, pedigrees memorialized a state of being that echoed the original act of Creation itself and that was celebrated as a fulfilment of the Lord's will (Fig. 3.5).[69] A continuous dynasty, no

[63] John Oliver, *A present for teeming women. Or, scripture-directions for women with child* (1663; Wing O276). On the shared rhetoric of human and horticultural generation, see Mary Fissell, 'Gender and Generation: Representing Reproduction in Early Modern England', *Gender and History*, 7 (1995), 433–56; Claire Duncan, '"Nature's Bastards": Grafted Generation in Early Modern England', *Renaissance and Reformation/Renaissance et Réforme*, 38 (2015), 121–47. For Genesis, see Kathleen Crowther-Heyck, '"Be Fruitful and Multiply": Genesis and Generation in Reformation Germany', *RQ*, 55 (2002), 904–35.

[64] Christopher Hooke, *The child-birth or womans lecture* (1590; STC 13702), sig. B3r.

[65] *Death in birth; or the fruite of Eves transgression* (1639), in Daniel Featley et al., *Threnoikos. The house of mourning...delivered in XLVII sermons, preached at the funerals of divers faithfull servants of Christ* (1640; STC 24048), pp. 715–16.

[66] See Eric Carlson, *Marriage and the English Reformation* (Oxford, 1994), esp. pp. 49–66; Helen Parish, *Clerical Marriage and the English Reformation: Precedent, Policy and Practice* (Aldershot, 2000).

[67] Augustine, *Treatises on Marriage and Other Subjects*, trans. Charles T. Wilcox, ed. Roy D. Ferrari (New York, 1955), p. 159. See David Herlihy, 'The Family and Religious Ideologies in Medieval Europe', in Tamara Hareven and Andrejs Plakans (eds), *Family History at the Crossroads: A Journal of Family History Reader* (Princeton, NJ, 1987), pp. 3–17, at p. 5.

[68] Matthew Griffith, *Bethel: or, a forme for families* (1633; STC 12369), p. 223. On maternity and paternity, see Patricia Crawford, 'The Construction and Experience of Maternity in Seventeenth-Century England' and 'Blood and Paternity', both repr. in *eadem, Blood, Bodies and Families*, pp. 79–112, 113–39.

[69] See Karen Hearn, '"Saved through Childbearing": A Godly Context for Elizabethan Pregnancy Portraits', in Tara Hamling and Richard L. Williams (eds), *Art Re-Formed: Re-Assessing the Impact of the Reformation on the Visual Arts* (Cambridge, 2007), pp. 65–71.

Fig. 3.5 Pregnancy portrait of an unknown lady (oil, attributed to Marcus Gheeraerts II, *c.*1595).
Source: Tate Gallery, London, no. TO7699. Steve Vidler/Alamy Stock Photo.

less than the swelling belly of an expectant mother, was tangible proof of providential intervention. The dual emphasis on female fecundity and familial continuity that was a central feature of this culture also served as an incentive for paintings of children, which often noted their age in weeks, months, and years. Their arrival and survival testified to the divine blessings bestowed on their parents.[70] The inscription on a portrait of Baron Cobham and his family (see Fig. 6.13), surrounded by an array of fruit—grapes, apples, cherries, oranges, quinces, and pears, which symbolize the couple's fertility—reflects the same convictions:

> See here the most noble father, here the most excellent mother. Seated around them spreads a throng worthy of their father. Such was once the family of the patriarch Jacob, such the progeny gathered about the pious Job. God grant that the line of Cobham beget many offspring such as Joseph, and flourish like the

---

[70] Jane Eade, 'Portraiture', in Anna French (ed.), *Early Modern Childhood: An Introduction* (Abingdon, 2020), pp. 282–303.

seed of Job restored. Much has been given to the noble race of Cobham. Long may their joys endure. Anno Domini 1567.[71]

If a 'quiver full' of children was a gift from heaven, in turn, as William Gearing declared in a meditation on Psalm 127:3, grandchildren were a 'superadded bless-ing' and 'a treble Crown of Honour'.[72] From this perspective, creating a perman-ent record of uninterrupted family lineages facilitated by the religious matches with fellow believers that the godly were encouraged to enter into was nothing less than a pious duty. The eighteenth-century Derbyshire minister Edward Bagshaw's account of the divine deliverances vouchsafed to him not only recorded the godparents of the children born to his wife in the 1720s and 1730s but also the midwives who ('through Gods assistance') had delivered them. They too played a part in the making of godly families.[73]

The notebooks in which Oliver Heywood registered his family history provide further evidence that the early modern genealogical imagination could be a highly spiritualized one. The son of a puritan yeoman educated at Cambridge and called to the ministry in the 1650s, after his ejection in 1662 he devoted himself to serving the dissenting congregations of Yorkshire. Alongside authoring many edifying publications, he was a dedicated registrar not just of nonconformist bap-tisms, marriages, and deaths, but also of his own lineage. He was married to the daughter of the renowned godly divine John Angier, and two of his three sons became ministers, planting the seeds for a clerical dynasty. The extensive notes Heywood kept about his ancestors and relatives dwelt upon their struggles to gain assurance of salvation and the external signs they displayed of their elec-tion. 'Kinship grows out in process of time', he wrote, and 'tis not much materiall what family we are so that we be of the household of faith, and have god for our father, Ch[ris]t for our elder brother and the spirit of grace running in our best veines and acting us for god', he wrote. But if godliness rather than noble blood was what mattered to Heywood, he still could not resist speculating about his family's ancient gentry origins and connection with a local esquire who 'was wont to call my father Cozen'. The 'Genealogy, or table of the family and off-spring' of his father Richard that Heywood drew up is a document that quaintly calculates the sixty-six children who 'proceeded out of his loynes by a direct line', together with some eighty-eight or ninety from the collateral line. He proudly

[71] Susan E. James and Katlijne Van Der Stighelen, 'New Discoveries Concerning the Portrait of the Family of William Brooke, 10th Lord Cobham, at Longleat House', *Dutch Crossing: Journal of Low Countries Studies,* 23 (1999), 66–101, inscription translated at p. 83.

[72] William Gearing, *Pious fathers, the glory of children. And godly children the glory of fathers* (1669), published with John Maynard, *A memento to young and old* (1669; Wing M1451), p. 138.

[73] DRO, D5430/76/9 (Commonplace book of Edward Bagshaw, vicar of Castleton, notes on the Bible, prayers and other Christian texts and a narrative entitled 'Instances of Gods Good Providence to myself').

remarked that there were fifty then living that called him father, grandfather, or great grandfather.[74]

Similar sentiments are enshrined in Thomas Hodge's eulogistic discourse of the 'very aged and religious matron' Frances Walbank, which he dedicated to his grandfather John Morley, who had multiplied his days to 'Foure-score days and upwards' and his 'Seed to above an hundred'.[75] A commemorative engraving of the puritan matriarch Mary Honeywood aged 93 declares that she had 367 descendants in the year preceding her death in 1717 (Fig. 3.6).[76] And a note written on an eighteenth-century genealogical table states that Hester, wife of Sir Thomas Temple, who had four sons and nine daughters, died in 1737, having 'lived to see seven Hundred persons descended from her'.[77] These men and women regarded the size of their families as evidence of heavenly approbation. As Elizabeth Egerton, countess of Bridgewater, wrote in her personal meditations on Genesis around 1620, 'Fruitfulnesse is a blessing and gift that comes from the Lord'.[78] Such examples suggest that the relationship between Protestant predestinarianism and lineage was less a fraught tension than an intricate nexus.[79]

Pedigrees of legitimate descendants must also be seen as alter egos of the diagrammatic tables of unseemly and incestuous unions with close blood relatives that the Church of England, following in the footsteps of its medieval predecessor and tracing its source to Leviticus, assembled in order to condemn. Since at least the ninth century, these had taken the form of trees of consanguinity and affinity which clearly laid out what was prohibited and what was permissible.[80] Unions between people who were ritually as well as biologically related required ecclesiastical dispensation: a surviving document dating from 1535 allowing Francis Shirley to wed Dorothy Congreve, of whose child he was a godfather, is signed by none other than the archbishop of Canterbury, Thomas Cranmer.[81]

---

[74] The Rev. Oliver Heywood, B.A. 1630–1702: His Autobiography, Diaries, Anecdote and Event Books: Illustrating the General and Family History of Yorkshire and Lancashire, ed. J. Horsfall Turner, 4 vols (Brighouse, 1882), vol. i, pp. 17, 105–9.

[75] Thomas Hodges, The hoary head crowned. A sermon preached at Brackley at the funerall of Frances Walbank. A very aged and religious matron (1652; Wing H2320), sig. A2r.

[76] Mary Honeywood Aged 93 who had 367 descendants living the Year preceeding her Death (engraving, late 18th century): NPG, D28136.

[77] HEHL, Stowe Temple Personal Papers, Box 17 (Genealogy), folder 2. See also Richard Steele, A discourse concerning old-age, tending to the instruction, caution and comfort of aged persons (1688; Wing S5386), p. 16.

[78] HEHL, Rare Books 297,343 (Elizabeth Egerton, countess of Bridgewater, Manuscript meditations on the severall chapters of the Old Testament, c.1620), p. 3.

[79] On predestination, see Chapter 4 below.

[80] See the examples reproduced in Christiane Klapisch-Zuber, 'The Genesis of the Family Tree', I Tatti Studies in the Italian Renaissance, 4 (1991), 105–29, figs 9–13, 17–20; BM, 1851, 1213.95 (German Tree of Consanguinity woodcut, c.1450–1500). For a manuscript version, see BL, Arundel MS 381, fos 173v–174r.

[81] LLRRO, 26D53/2556.

Fig. 3.6 *Mary Honeywood, aged 93, who had 367 descendants living the Year preceeding her Death* (engraving, English, late 18th century).
Source: © National Portrait Gallery, London, NPG D28136.

Although the English reformers wholly rejected the Catholic proscription of marriages between spiritual kin, they retained the ban on matches between people descended from the same parents within four degrees and ordered that placards summarizing the rules be hung up in parish churches. Some of these were painted on wood; others were the products of a growing trade in bureaucratic paperwork.[82] Bishops regularly enquired about their presence as a vital piece of ecclesiastical furniture.[83] Forbidden liaisons of this kind were often denounced in treatises regarding 'domesticall duties', and the fearful consequences of incestuous liaisons with people 'neere unto us by any decree of kindred or affinitie' filled a chapter of Thomas Beard's *Theatre of Gods judgements*.[84] The Restoration divine Robert Dixon dedicated a fifty-page tract to describing and delineating the constraints on marital and sexual relationships in 1674.[85] Marriages between first cousins, or cousins-german, occupied something of a grey area. John Hales wrote a famous and influential ruling concluding that they could be sanctioned.[86] The various copies of this that survive in family archives suggest both that such connections occurred quite frequently and that they continued to be surrounded by an aura of unease and ambiguity.[87] The issue was also discussed at length in Jeremy Taylor's *Ductor dubitantium, or the rule of conscience*, which drew a distinction between marrying those 'neer of kin' and those 'neer in flesh' and concluded that 'no person ought to be affrighted with the pretences of any fierce and misperswaded person' that this was against the law of nature or the church.[88] Incest and illegitimacy were the archenemies of godly genealogy, despite the inconvenient precedents set by the patriarchs described in Genesis.

All this should compel us to reassess the powerful contemporary impulse to commission, create, and indeed invent pedigrees. The quest for evidence of the antiquity of landed families usually had the Norman Conquest as its end point: comparatively few sought out their Saxon ancestors, probably on the grounds that it was more honourable to be descended from conquerors than from a subjugated

[82] See, e.g., *An admonition to all such as shall intend hereafter to enter the state of matrimonie godly, and agreeable to lawes* (1600; STC 19287.3); *Incestuous marriages, or, relations of consanguinity and affinity hindering and dissolving marriage* (1678; Wing I128A). On the Reformation changes to these laws, see Sybil Wolfram, *In-Laws and Outlaws: Kinship and Marriage in England* (1987), pp. 21–30.

[83] See, e.g., *Articles ecclesiasticall to be inquired of... within the dioces of Hereforde* (Oxford, 1592; STC 10215.5), sig. A4v.

[84] William Gouge, *Of domesticall duties* (1622; STC 12119), pp. 185–6; Thomas Beard, *The theatre of Gods judgements revised, and augmented* (1631; STC 1661.5), bk 2, ch. 26 (pp. 383–6).

[85] Robert Dixon, *The degrees of consanguinity and affinity described and delineated* (1674; Wing D1746).

[86] John Hales, *Golden remains* (1673; Wing H271), pp. 262–72. The judgement was dated 1630. For a manuscript copy, see Bodl., MS Rawlinson D. 1345 (Theological Tracts), fos 12-6r. Another text that found in favour of it was James Durham, *The law unsealed: or, a practical exposition of the ten commandments with a resolution of several momentous questions and cases of conscience* (Edinburgh, 1676; Wing D2817), p. 216. See also Matthew Hale's *De successionibus apud Anglos, or, a treatise of hereditary descents... with a scheme of pedigrees and the degrees of parentage and consanguinity* (1700; Wing H236A).

[87] For example, among the L'Estrange papers: NRO, LEST/NE 7 ('A treaty concerneing marriages of first cozens or cozen Germans').

[88] Jeremy Taylor, *Ductor dubitantium, or the rule of conscience in all her generall measures* (1660; Wing T324), book 2, ch. 2, pp. 301–18.

race.[89] Sometimes, however, this impulse fused with a desire to identify mythical ancestors such as King Arthur or Brutus the Trojan and to track a dynasty back to remote biblical figures such as Noah and Adam. Daniel Woolf has rightly warned against exaggerating the frequency with which contemporaries made 'wild' and 'outlandish claims', but his scepticism about how seriously people took 'descents from extreme antiquity' reinforces the tendency to see them as relics of medieval credulity.[90] The boastfulness of some in this regard did become the butt of jokes, most notoriously in the case of the Catholic bibliophile John Lord Lumley, whose genealogical enthusiasm provoked this acid comment from James I in 1603: 'by my saul I did na ken Adam's name was Lumley'. Lumley's pedigrees, which traced his line back to the original inhabitants of Eden, are a reminder that an avid interest in biblical ancestry was by no means a Protestant monopoly.[91]

Nevertheless, the interest in establishing a direct link with Adam and the patriarchs that was quickened by the Reformation left a firm mark on family trees drawn up in this period. The Popham genealogy, for example, began with an illustration of Noah seated in a tiny, toy-sized ark evocative of the one depicted in the King James Bible, while, in keeping with an ancient Welsh tradition, the scroll created for an Elizabethan landlord began with 'Adam, son of God' (Adaff ap Duw).[92] In parallel columns written in Gaelic and English, Mr Timothy Sullivan of Dublin traced his pedigree, via Enoch, Lamech, Noah, and Japheth, back to 'Adam our Prothoparent' in 1682.[93] That this was a Christian commonplace does not detract from the fact that such people went to the trouble of incorporating it in the expensive documents of lineage which they commissioned. Such initiatives were also shaped by heraldic texts like John Ferne's *The blazon of gentrie* (1586), which tracked gentility itself back to biblical times and described Christ and his apostles as gentlemen of blood.[94]

Some genealogies visually mimicked the legendary tree of Jesse itself, including one produced for the godly Protestant Sir Nicholas Bacon of Raveningham Hall in Norfolk. This shows him standing at the bottom with full-length portraits of his two wives, Anne Ferneley and Anne Cooke, and their progeny living and extinct (including the young Francis Bacon and 'Bryan Dead') blossoming from

---

[89] Broadway, 'No historie so meete', p. 155.   [90] Woolf, *Social Circulation*, pp. 99, 130, 131.

[91] See Thomas Pennant, *A Tour in Scotland, MDCCLXXII: Part II* (1776), pp. 325–6. On Lumley, see Harris, 'Lines of Descent', pp. 87–90; Christian D. Liddy with Christian Steer, 'John Lord Lumley and the Creation and Commemoration of Lineage in Early Modern England', *Archaeological Journal*, 167 (2010), 191–227.

[92] The Popham pedigree is cited in Stone, *Crisis of the Aristocracy*, p. 23. For the Welsh pedigree, see Francis Jones, 'An Approach to Welsh Genealogy', *Transactions of the Honourable Society of Cymmrodorion, Session 1948* (1949), 303–466, at 305, and see 322–3.

[93] BL, Sloane MS 761, fos 1r, 13r, 23r.

[94] John Ferne, *The blazon of gentrie deuided into two parts* (1586; STC 10825), p. 2. See also Woolf, *Social Circulation*, p. 100.

flowers on the branches that stretch towards the sky.[95] Another, which is among the pedigrees collected by William Cecil, Lord Burghley, now in Lambeth Palace Library, depicts the ancestry of John Dudley, duke of Northumberland, whose illustrious career as a leading figure in the government of Edward VI came to an end with his execution in 1553 for seeking to place his daughter-in-law Lady Jane Grey on the throne. This begins with a recumbent figure named 'Roderycke' (Fig. 3.7).[96] Inverting the normal structure of genealogies that start at the top, these grow upwards from the bottom. As Christiane Klapisch-Zuber has argued, they create a flattering image that invests these family lineages with eschatological significance, showing the generations slowly ascending—both spatially and spiritually—towards heaven as they progress through time. To adopt an iconography charged with mystical and theological meaning was to lay emphasis as much on the future destiny of a dynasty as on its past history.[97]

Most surviving pedigrees prioritize the continuity of families over the various historical ruptures through which they lived. Rarely marked with dates, they are disconnected from the temporal events that occurred during the lifetimes of those whom they commemorate, including the immense upheavals inaugurated by the English Reformations. Yet genealogical activity was not uncoloured by the religious developments and confessional conflicts of the era. Its attractions for aristocratic Catholics anxious to dispel the questions about their status and loyalty raised by their decision to dissent from the Church of England have been underlined by Richard Cust and others. Lord Lumley's obsession with reviving and embellishing his ancestry and enshrining it in stone, parchment, paint, glass, and vellum was driven in considerable part by a desire to counteract the ignominy of his father's execution following the Pilgrimage of Grace against Henry VIII, as well as by his concern about the imminent demise of the family line.[98] An Elizabethan portrait of the Towneley family of Lancashire dated 1593 depicts them kneeling in prayer around a crucifix with their coats of arms hanging like fruit above them in an umbrella of vines. An inscription recalls the imprisonment and heavy fines born by the head of the household (Fig. 3.8).[99] Successive generations of the Blundells of Little Crosby in the same county were similarly determined to preserve a textual record of their forebears, and the Northumberland gentleman Sir William Swinburne viewed his ancestral pedigree as a monument

---

[95] This is reproduced in Robert Tittler, *Nicholas Bacon: The Making of a Tudor Statesman* (1976), plate 2, between pp. 128–9.

[96] LPL, MS 310 (William Cecil, Pedigrees and Historical Notes), fo. 58.

[97] Klapisch-Zuber, 'Genesis of the Family Tree', 118–23. See also *eadem*, *L'Ombre des ancêtres: Essai sur l'imaginaire médiéval de la parenté* (Paris, 2000).

[98] See Liddy with Steer, 'John Lord Lumley', 215.

[99] *The Towneley Family at Prayer* (oil on panel, 1593): Towneley Hall, Burnley Borough Council. See Robert Tittler, *Portraits, Painters and Publics in Provincial England 1540–1640* (Oxford, 2012), p. 24.

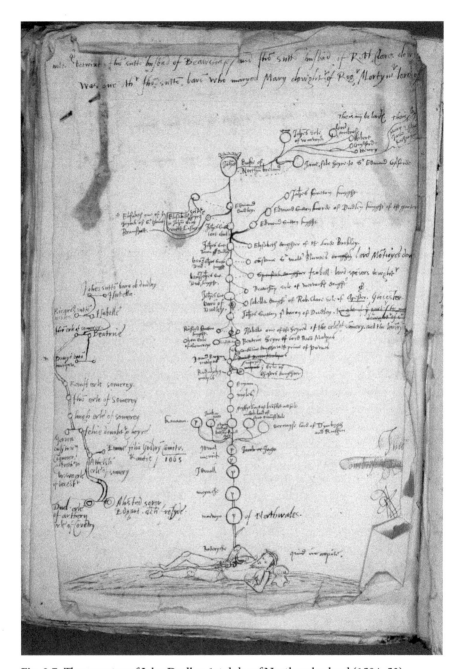

Fig. 3.7 The ancestry of John Dudley, 1st duke of Northumberland (1504–53).

Source: © Lambeth Palace Library, London, MS 310 (William Cecil, Pedigrees and Historical Notes), fo. 58r. Bridgeman Images.

Fig. 3.8 *The Towneley family at prayer* (oil, English school, 1593).

Source: © Towneley Hall Art Gallery and Museum/Bridgeman Images.

to 'the continuance of our family, with relation to the steadiness of principalls for conscience sake, by wandering through the adversity of difficult times'.[100] The roundels that decorate the seventeenth-century genealogical roll of the Draycott family of Leicestershire, which covers twenty-two generations, contain details of

[100] See *The Great Diurnal of Nicholas Blundell of Little Crosby, Lancashire*, ed. F. Tyrer and J. J. Bagley, 3 vols, Record Society of Lancashire and Cheshire (1968–72), vol. iii, p. ix. Newcastle, Northumberland County Record Office, Swinburne MS 6/95 (Sir William Swinburne, family pedigree, 1712), cited in Gabriel Glickman, 'Gothic History and Catholic Enlightenment in the Works of Charles Dodd (1672–1743)', *HJ*, 54 (2011), 351.

members of the family who were stalwart nonconformists, including John, who was 'comitted close prisoner unto the cowntar in the pultrie for recuzansi' in 1562 and his son Philip, who 'continued a parfit recusant to his deathe' in 1604.[101]

It is not surprising that Catholic genealogists were acutely conscious of the vulnerability of their lineages to extinction. The delicate balancing act in which such dynasties engaged—steering a course between preserving their bloodline through the reproduction of children and sustaining the faith through the dedication of their members to religious vocations—added a further dimension to the worry that they might disappear into oblivion over time. The Rookwoods of Stanningfield in Suffolk are a case in point. Three of the four sons of Robert and Dorothy became celibate monks or priests: Henry and Christopher joined the Franciscans and ended their lives in Lisbon and Madrid, while Robert took orders and resided with the Poor Clares at Rouen until his death, aged 82, in 1668. The second son, Ambrose, who succeeded to the family estates, was executed for complicity in the Gunpowder Plot of 1605. The pattern was mirrored in later generations. Henry, Francis, and John professed as a Jesuit, Benedictine, and Franciscan, respectively; their brother, another Ambrose, was convicted for high treason for his role in a conspiracy against William III and put to death in 1696. Several of their sisters entered Flemish nunneries and took vows of chastity. It is no wonder that the preface to the seventeenth-century family history dwelt upon 'the instabyllyttie & transitorines of all sublunary things' and 'the multitude of ancient names...[that] arre nowe cleane worne owte...what a revolution of infinite families ar now wholly extinguished'. This served as a stimulus to record-ing their descents on paper and to gathering up 'the sondry fragments of a pytty-full wracke, in a most dangerous and tempestuous sea...after they had byn washed up, with wave, wynde & tyde' for the benefit of posterity.[102]

The genealogical endeavours of the prominent recusant Sir Thomas Shirley are equally revealing. The astonishingly large pedigree created for him in 1632 is an impressively illustrated celebration of a dynasty that defiantly retained its Catholic faith despite the many temptations to conform and compromise.[103] The accompanying heraldic compilation called 'The Catholic Armorist' that he assembled for circulation among his fellow co-religionists is an extraordinary hybrid of genealogy and martyrology. Applauding the suffering and sacrifices that his own and other families made on behalf of the faith, this was suffused with the conviction that the endurance of the Shirleys through the ages bore witness to divine approval of their resolute adherence to the old religion. The dynasty had been rewarded for this by 'admirable fecunditie in the production of soe many

[101] LLRRO, DE3214/12424 (Pedigree roll of the Draycott family, 1604–1662).
[102] CUL, MS Hengrave 76/1 ('*Vetustissima Prosapia Rookewodorum de Stanningefilde, in Comitatu Suffolciae*', 17th–19th century), unfoliated. The manuscript includes a broadside of Ambrose Rookwood's scaffold speech in 1696.
[103] LLRRO, 26D53/2681 (The Great Pedigree of the Shirley family, 1632).

brave and active spirits'. Their cousins, the Iretons, who had apostatized to Protestantism and fallen into decadence and vice, by contrast, had not flourished. 'Suffering themselves to be misled by the iniquity of the tymes', they had 'miserably degenerated from theire Pious Stocke', whereby the 'Luster' of the family 'was not only obscured but the wholl Branch Ruined by the contageous Plauge of Haerisie'.[104] Linking 'the great Services his Ancestours had performed, in the Holy Land, against the Enimies of Christe' during the era of the Crusades with their noble deeds in upholding Catholicism in more recent times, 'The Catholike Armorist' concluded by encouraging later generations to emulate preceding ones, and by quoting Maccabees: 'call to remembrance what acts your fathers did in their times; so shall you receave great honour and an everlasting name'.[105]

The same assumptions were mirrored on the other side of the confessional divide. The stained-glass window showing eight generations of his family that Sir Henry Feilding, 1st earl of Denigh, of Newnham Paddox in Warwickshire had made in the 1590s also combined an emphasis on its longevity with motifs that stressed the devotion that had made it the recipient of providential blessings for so many centuries.[106] Such sentiments are repeatedly expressed in the prefaces that the fervently Protestant gentleman, Edward Dering of Kent, wrote to the various drafts of his family's history he prepared in the early seventeenth century. In one fragmentary leaf he described why he had been moved to 'memorize theire names' and preserve the deeds of his progenitors, 'inciting thereby my selfe and all theire issue living to thanke our God, first for good birth derived from a worthy race of noble auncestors, next for the vertues wherewith observably they have beene endued'. He left 'this Lieger record to my posterity' to inspire them to imitate their dead relatives.[107] In another version, quoting Proverbs 7:6 ('The glory of children are their fathers'), he declared that 'descent of bloud' was a gracious gift 'whereof with due circumstance we may and ought to preserve a thankfull remembrance'. He understood that the reformed doctrines of freely given divine grace and predestination constituted a promise 'beyond all ascentes of climing degrees, to be the Sonnes of God. But he spoke as if—and piously hoped—that salvation also passed down the generations.[108] As in Scripture,

---

[104] The several parts of this large manuscript are now in different repositories, including BL, Harley MS 4928, (see fos 127r–128r); TNA; and three volumes at The Queen's College, Oxford, MS 141–3. The final quotation here is from MS 141, p. 288. See also *Stemmata Shirleiana; or the Annals of the Shirley Family, Lords of Nether Etindon in the County of Warwick, and of Shirley in the County of Derby* (Westminster, 1873), pp. 120–35; Richard Cust, 'Catholicism, Antiquarianism and Gentry Honour: The Writings of Sir Thomas Shirley', *Midland History*, 23 (1998), 40–70, esp. 50–1.

[105] BL, Harley MS 4928, fo. 65v; TNA, SP 9/9, fo. 231, quoted in Cust, 'Catholicism, Antiquarianism and Gentry Honour', 50.

[106] Cust, 'Material Culture of Lineage', pp. 269–70.

[107] FSL, MS X.d.531, no. 16 (A fragmentary leaf from Sir Edward Dering's family history).

[108] FSL, MS Z.e.27 (Sir Edward Dering, history of the Dering family from the time of the Conquest, c.1635), unfoliated.

'successive posterity' was a sign of divine approbation and 'want of issue a curse': 'continuance of descent is expressly promised to the godly, as the rooling out of name and memory is frequently threatned unto the wicked.'[109]

Lady Anne Clifford also utilized a language of dynasty that was deeply dyed with ideas derived from the Bible, as well as with the distinctive vocabulary that ran through it like a silver thread. The Great Books of Record she wrote to assist her lawyers in fighting for her right to the Clifford titles began, in a deliberate echo of Scripture, with the words that she had been 'begotten by my valiant father and conceived with childe by my worthy mother' on 1 May 1589. Reflecting a wider female impulse to assemble genealogical information,[110] her assiduous activities in this sphere were inspired by her belief that the continuity of her line and the dual descent of blood and land were divinely contrived. In the words of the motto she had inscribed on the ornamental fireplace of her grandson Nicholas Tufton to celebrate his wedding to his cousin several times removed, Elizabeth Boyle, she was convinced that 'GODS PROVIDENCE IS MINE INHERITANCE'.[111] To this extent Protestantism not merely passively condoned but also actively promoted the impulse to make and preserve pedigrees. Following the excellent example set by the patriarchs themselves, it reflected the determination of the godly to establish the kinship that linked them with Christ himself.

Exceptions to the general rule of 'structural amnesia' that shapes early modern genealogies further reinforce this point.[112] Many, if not most pedigree rolls and associated prose documents are silent on the subject of the religious past of members of families that embraced Protestantism who had been born before the Henrician Reformation. They gloss over predecessors involved in rebellion and treason, or those who were tainted by association despite their less than heroic attempts to avoid incrimination by fence-sitting. This was comparatively easy in the case of the genealogical material gathered by Richard Weston of Staffordshire, whose grandfather had married the daughter of Ralph Neville, fourth earl of Westmorland, who had sent his young son to fight with the Pilgrims of Grace in 1536 and supplied them with their mascot, the banner of St Cuthbert, but carefully preserved himself 'from th'infection of their traitorous poison'.[113] This was merely a legal, collateral, and maternal link that could be hidden without too much difficulty.

---

[109] FSL, MS V.b. 307 (Sir Edward Dering, notes for a history of the Dering family, c.1631), p.101.

[110] On women and genealogical knowledge, see Woolf, *Social Circulation*, pp. 116–18; Hodgkin, 'Women, Memory and Family History', p. 298.

[111] See Anne Clifford, *The Memoir of 1603 and The Diary of 1616–1619*, ed. Katherine Acheson (Peterborough, ON, 2007), p. 218; and *Anne Clifford's Great Books of Record*, ed. Jessica L. Malay (Manchester, 2015), p. 797. See the excellent discussion in Antoinina Bevan Zlatar, 'Anne Clifford and Her Bible', *Studies in English Literature, 1500–1700*, 57 (2017), 157–80. The fireplace is discussed at p. 161.

[112] See J. A. Barnes, 'The Collection of Genealogies', *The Rhodes-Livingstone Journal*, 5 (1947), 48–55, at 49, 52.

[113] BL, MS Additional 74,251 A (illuminated genealogy of the Weston family, c.1632–3), esp. fo. 140v. See Keith Dockray, 'Neville, Ralph, fourth earl of Westmorland, 1498–1549', *ODNB*.

More sleight of hand was required by Laurence Cromp, the Yorkshire herald, who was the creator of a beautiful pedigree of the Boun or Bohun family of Bakewell and Hulme in Derbyshire dated *c*.1715. This highlighted their alliance with William Wickham, the Elizabethan bishop of Winchester, whose name is surmounted with a mitre, and with the Dukes of Buckingham, though it is telling that when it reaches George Villiers, no reference at all is made to his assassination by John Felton in 1628. It was probably thought best to draw a veil over the fate of this controversial court favourite.[114]

Other families subtly tweaked and adjusted the record to present their dead relatives in the best possible light or to disguise their Catholicism. The splendidly decorated pedigree created for the Taylor family of Shadoxhurst in Kent in 1665 drew explicit attention to the piety of an ancestor who had bequeathed all his lands to religious uses in 1525 and made gracious benefactions and charitable bequests for the upkeep of his parish church during his lifetime, including buying a New Testament.[115] Those descended from prominent evangelicals were keen to celebrate them in the same medium. A genealogy prepared in the mid-nineteenth century for the Tracys of Toddington in Gloucestershire depicts an incident that was central to the family's precocious Protestant credentials and heritage: the exhumation and burning of the bones of the 'Godlie Confessour' William Tracy by 'popish priests' in 1531 after his will was found to contain an overtly heretical preamble. Expounded in print by William Tyndale and John Frith, the document subsequently became a template for many other self-conscious testaments of the Protestant faith. Also included is an image of the heroic death of another relative: the 'Christian lady' martyred for her Protestant faith in 1546, Anne Askew. Both illustrations closely mimic the iconography of these episodes in the pictures incorporated in Foxe's *Actes and monuments*.[116] The symbiotic relationship between such pedigrees and longer family narratives in manuscript bears out the suggestion that contemporaries were increasingly interested in connecting their personal pasts with the collective histories of their counties and of the nation at large.[117]

The interrelationship between the genealogies drawn up by the elite and royal pedigrees also demands attention. These had proliferated in the late Middle Ages, not merely as an instrument of propaganda and power that assisted in legitimating the competing York and Lancastrian regimes, but also to satisfy a thirst for vernacular knowledge of the country's history. The very appearance of these long rolls smoothed out the fragile links and jagged breaks in the chain of hereditary

---

[114] FSL, MS V.b.155 (Laurence Cromp, Genealogy of the Boun or Bohun family, 1690).
[115] FSL, MS Z.e.41 (Pedigree of the Taylor family, Shadoxhurst, Kent, 1665).
[116] The Great Sudeley pedigree roll (compiled 1849–51) is in the possession of the Sudeley family. On the cause célèbre of Tracy's will, see John Craig and Caroline Litzenberger, 'Wills as Religious Propaganda: The Testament of William Tracy', *JEH*, 44 (1993), 415–31.
[117] Woolf, *Social Circulation of the Past*, pp. 98, 134.

succession to the English Crown.[118] They also established gratifying bonds of kinship between Jesus and the country's Saxon kings: a pedigree of c.1510 traces their mutual descent from Adam (who the accompanying narrative says 'died of the gowte') via the patriarchs and the rulers of Israel.[119]

Such documents conveyed an impression of institutional antiquity and inevitability comparable to that sought by the gentry and nobility, who in turn were eager to align themselves with and establish blood ties with the monarchy.[120] Some produced scrolls that displayed both together in parallel vertical lines punctuated by roundels reminiscent of the sacred genealogies pioneered by Peter of Poitiers and refashioned by Broughton and Speed.[121] Prefaced with the sacred letters IHS, a late fifteenth-century genealogical roll tracing the kings of England from Adam ('the firste man [who] was made of the slyme of the Erthe'), incorporates the descent of the Percy family in a separate column alongside the left margin, whose pious foundation of and benefactions to Whitby Abbey are also celebrated in an associated prose narrative.[122] Others, including the remarkable pedigree of the Poulett family of Somerset created c.1627–35 depicted the intricate interweaving of their own family trees (complete with branches and leaves) with those of the royal houses of England, France, Spain, and other nations. This genealogy begins with a series of encomiastic verses in Latin and English held by two naked figures, who appear to be Adam and a very hairy Eve (Fig. 3.9).[123]

Regal pedigrees retained their purpose as political tools under Tudor rule, concealing the violent beginning of the dynasty behind the fiction of a mythical British ancestry and supplying ammunition with which to combat the disjunctures and uncertainties attendant upon Henry VIII's marital whims. Produced at the very moment of the break with Rome in 1533-4, after the king's divorce from Catherine of Aragon and following his marriage to Anne Boleyn, Lambeth Palace Library MS 19 not only creates the illusion of an unbroken line that papers over the cracks in recent royal history. It also boldly asserts the descent of the Tudors from Adam himself and is adorned with medallions depicting the six ages of the world described in Scripture and with earlier kings including William the Conqueror. The absence of Princess Mary, the future queen, is a deliberate omission reflecting her dubious

[118] For one example, see BL, Additional MS 18002. See Olivier de Laborderie, 'A New Pattern for English History: The First Genealogical Rolls of the Kings of England', in Radulescu and Kennedy (eds), *Broken Lines*, pp. 45–61; Judith Collard, 'Gender and Genealogy in English Illuminated Royal Genealogical Rolls from the Thirteenth Century', *Parergon*, 17 (2000), 11–34.
[119] London, College of Arms, Arundel MS 53: reproduced, with various other pedigrees, in *Heralds' Commemorative Exhibition 1484–1934 Held at the College of Arms: Enlarged and Illustrated Catalogue* (1970), pp. 74–5 and plate XLIII.
[120] See the appendix listing genealogies from Henry VI to Henry VIII in Sydney Anglo, 'The British History in Early Tudor Propaganda', *Bulletin of the John Rylands Library*, 44 (1961–2), 17–48, at 41–8.
[121] See, e.g., NRO, LEST/OD 2 (Pedigree of the Le Strange family, 1655).
[122] Bodl., MS Bodleian Rolls 5 (Genealogical history of the kings of England, c.1485). See also BL, MS Stowe 72 and 73 (Genealogical chronicles of the kings of England to Edward IV, 15th century).
[123] Somerset HC, DD/BR/ba/1 (Pedigree of the Poulett family, compiled c.1627–35).

Fig. 3.9 Pedigree of the Poulett family, *c.*1627–35.

Source: Taunton, Somerset Heritage Centre, DD/BR/ba/1.

status in the wake of the annulment of her mother's marriage to Henry, which rendered her illegitimate.[124] The king's justification for this decision rested on a conviction that he was guilty of incest, according to the rules laid down in Leviticus, for taking the wife of his dead brother Arthur into his bed. This had some elements of sincerity as well as a large dollop of convenience.[125]

The Tudors were no more immune to 'genetic misfortune' than the gentry and nobility,[126] as Henry's difficulties in begetting a male heir, Edward's premature death, and Mary's infertility and phantom pregnancies attest. It was these contingencies that determined the unpredictable path of the Reformation in the 1540s and 1550s; after 1558 it was shaped by Elizabeth's stubborn refusal to marry and produce offspring and her careful cultivation of her image as a virgin queen. It is no wonder that these monarchs were so concerned to project an image of genealogical strength and stability through a range of media. Manuscript pedigrees displaying Elizabeth's ancestry using the motif of the Tree of Jesse and depicting her family tree back via Noah to Adam and Eve belie the precariousness of her regime (Fig. 3.10). They served as a smokescreen to cover up the intense anxiety about the succession felt by her closest political advisers.[127] Robert Persons' provocative book on this topic, *A conference about the next succession to the crowne of Ingland* (1595), took the liberty of adding 'a Perfect and Exact Arbor and Genealogy' of royal lineage designed to demonstrate that it should rightfully descend to a Catholic prince, in this instance the Spanish Habsburg infanta (Fig. 3.11).[128] On Elizabeth's death this headache was finally solved by the accession of James VI of Scotland, whose great-grandmother was Elizabeth's aunt. Genealogical engravings celebrating the 'happy unions' contracted between previous princes of royal blood belonging to the two kingdoms were published soon after this event.[129] Others made energetic efforts to trace James's lineage from Noah and integrated it with that of Brutus and other legendary kings of Britain and Wales.[130] The flurry of ballads and single-sheet prints delineating James's pedigree and progeny issued during his reign reflects the growth of popular interest in the genealogy of the British monarchy.[131]

---

[124] LPL, MS 19 (Descent of the Kings of England from Adam, c.1533–34).

[125] See George Bernard, *The King's Reformation: Henry VIII and the Remaking of the English Church* (New Haven, CT, 2005), pp. 17–19.

[126] Heal and Holmes, *Gentry*, p. 24.

[127] For an example, see FSL, MS V.b.375 (A Collection of Armes in Blazon, c.1585–91), p. 53. This finds an echo in the title page of John Stow's *The Annales of England* (1592; STC 356). For Adam and Noah, see Hatfield House, Cecil Papers 357, cited in Baker, 'Tudor Pedigree Rolls', p. 131.

[128] [Robert Persons], *A conference about the next succession to the crowne of Ingland* ([Antwerp], 1594 [1595]), fold-out table following p. 267.

[129] *The most happy unions contracted betwixt the princes of the blood royall of theis towe famous kingdoms of England & Scotland* (1603; STC 23039g.3): BM, 1856, 0614.149.

[130] Georg Owen Harry, *The genealogy of the high and mighty monarch, Iames, by the grace of God, king of great Brittayne, &c. with his lineall descent from Noah, by divers direct lynes to Brutus, first inhabiter of this ile of Brittayne*...(1604; STC 12872).

[131] *An excellent new ballad, shewing the petigree of our royall King Iames the first of that name in England* (1603; STC 14423); *The roiail progenei of our most sacred King James* (1619); NPG, D1370; *The progenie of the most renowned prince James king of Great Britaine France and Ireland* ([1624–35]): BM, 1849, 0315.15.

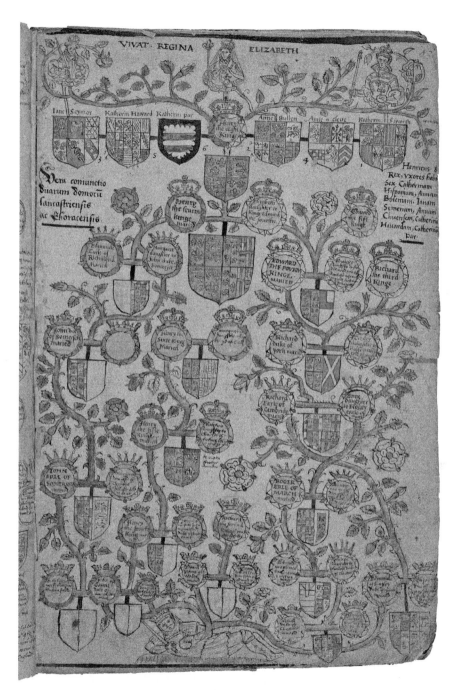

Fig. 3.10 A genealogy of Elizabeth I in a 'Collection of Armes in Blazon: Taken from an antient Booke of Ordinaries: Tricked and extracted, from Visitations & Pedigrees in the Heralds Office…Liber of Ordinaries' (*c*.1585–90).

Source: Folger Shakespeare Library, Washington DC, MS V. b. 375. Folger Digital Image Collection.

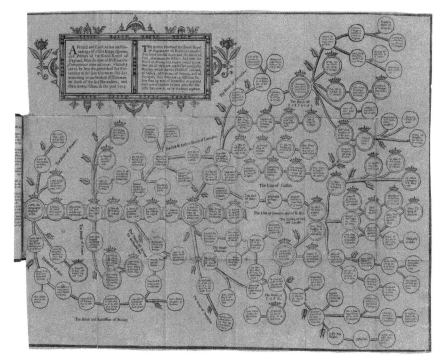

Fig. 3.11 'A Perfect and Exact Arbor and Genealogy', in [Robert Persons], *A conference about the next succession to the crowne of Ingland, divided into two partes*... ([Antwerp], 1594 [1595]), fold-out plate opposite sig. *4v.

Source: Folger Shakespeare Library, Washington DC, STC 19398 copy 1. Folger Digital Image Collection.

James I had genealogical challenges of his own, notably the death of the main focus of the advanced Protestant cause, Prince Henry of Wales in 1612.[132] Fortunately, he had a brother to step into his shoes, though James's efforts to marry his children off in an ecumenical fashion to the royal houses of Protestant and Catholic Europe in wistful pursuit of the reunion of Christendom were not appreciated by all of his subjects. Princess Elizabeth's marriage to Frederick, the Calvinist Elector of the Rhineland Palatinate, made her a celebrity among the godly, even more so when the couple and their extensive family were forced out of Bohemia into exile.[133] Several broadsides recorded their 'imperiall and princely pedegree'.[134]

---

[132] For two engraved broadsides depicting Henry's genealogy as heir, see *Iacobi I. Britannicarum insularum monarchae...eiusque uxoris...effigies* (Paris, 1604), BM, 1974, 1207.6; and a Dutch version produced in Amsterdam, c.1602–1612, BM, 1848, 0911. 271.

[133] See the portrait of this family: *Frederick Carolus Elisabeth Robertus Mauritius Louisa Hollandria Ludovicus* ([1625–60]): BM, 1877,0811.1099.

[134] James Maxwell, *The imperiall and princely pedegree of...Friderick...Prince Palatinate...sprung from glorious Charlemaigne...and...Elizabeth, Infanta of Albion* (1613; STC 17700.5).

By contrast, the attempted match between Prince Charles and the Habsburg infanta Maria was singularly ill-starred, stirring up trouble that was cathartically released in the streets of London when negotiations were abandoned in 1623. The root of the conflicts sparked off by this mixed marriage lay in concerns about the yoking of believers and unbelievers, and they replayed the arguments that had been rehearsed by John Stubbs and others in response to the proposed betrothal of Elizabeth I to the French duke of Anjou, which ultimately fell through.[135] Charles' subsequent alliance with Henrietta Maria did little to settle discontent in puritan circles, and her ostentatious Catholicism was a further affront to the sensibilities of forward Protestants. The queen's more than adequate fertility did little to lift the mood: although their first child died shortly after birth in 1629, others followed along in quick succession. The picture book of portraits of the couple with the 'Royall Progenie', combined with a compendium of their genealogies, published in 1641 lauded Charles's consort as 'a fruitfull Vine... Graced, by th'Almighties Hand'. This probably only added fuel to the flames that were then beginning to ignite and which broke out into the raging fire of civil war the following year.[136] Like their Tudor predecessors, the early Stuarts were eager to demonstrate their lineage back to the biblical patriarchs, as well as the dense web of connections between the kings of a united Britain and a subjugated Ireland with the royal houses of Spain, France, and Denmark. William Slatyer's *Genethliacon* (1630) was subtitled *Stemma Jacobi* in an arrogant, if conventional allusion to the Tree of Jesse. Its crowded tables of interconnecting ovals and lines are organized from top to bottom rather than the reverse, but they begin with God, symbolized by the Hebrew tetragrammaton.[137] The British were hardly out on a limb in this regard, as the many similar family trees produced by the royal houses of other European countries for mass consumption reveal. These include the Valois and Bourbons of France, the Spanish Habsburgs, and the Medici dukes of Florence.[138]

The rude interruption of the Stuart dynasty wrought by the regicide in 1649 only served to catalyse renewed interest in royal genealogy after the Restoration. Giles Fleming's *Stemma Sacrum* of 1660 proudly displayed the text of 2 Kings

---

[135] John Stubbes, *The discoverie of a gaping gulf whereinto England is like to be swallovwed by another French marriage* (1579; STC 23400).

[136] *The true effigies of our most illustrious soveraigne lord, King Charles Queene Mary, with the rest of the royall progenie* (1641 [1642]; Wing T2690).

[137] William Slatyer, *Genethliacon. sive, Stemma Iacobi: genealogia scilicet Regia, Catholica, Anglo-Scoto-Cambro-Britannica* (1630; STC 22633).

[138] See *Genealogie de la royale maison de Bourbon* (1589–99): BM, 1859,0514.317.1215; *Genelogia Regiae domus Borboniae* (1595): BM, 1927,1008.378; *Arbor gentilitia Henrici huius nominis 4 Regis Franciae et Navar. 3* (1595): BM, 1848,0911.588; [Genealogical Tree of the House of Habsburg] (1540): BM 1904,0723.1; *Genalogia Hassiaca a Carolo Magno Deducta* (1600–1650): BM, 1930,0516.1–3; [Medici family tree] (1761): BM, 1910, 0610.82.

19:30 on its title page ('And the remnant that is escaped of the house of Judah, shall yet again take root downward, and bear fruit upward') and showed Charles II springing from a father who was now labelled a 'Prophet and Martir' (Fig. 3.12). Ironically, his execution only reinforced the empowering link between the

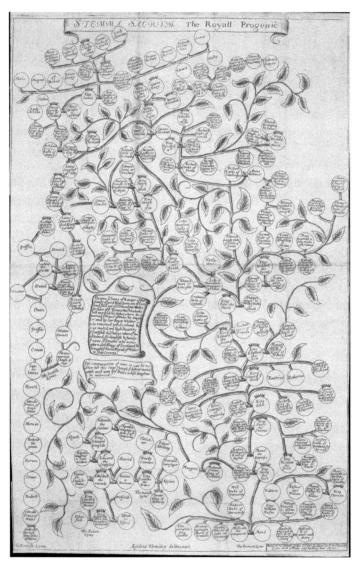

Fig. 3.12 Giles Fleming, *Stemma sacrum, The royal progeny delineated…shewing his sacred majesties royal and lawful descent to his crown and kingdoms, from all the kings that ever reigned in this nation* (London, 1660), fold-out plate.

Source: © British Library Board, E914.(1). All Rights Reserved/Bridgeman Images.

pedigree of Britain's monarchy and that of Christ.[139] It is probably no accident that one of the symbols of the restored king was the Boscobel Oak in which he was reputed to have been miraculously preserved after the battle of Worcester in 1651. Its iconography contains more than a faint echo of the Tree of Jesse.[140]

The politics of royal descent remained troubled in the reign of Charles II's Catholic brother James II. It turned in large part on questions of fecundity and paternity. The rebellion mounted by the king's illegitimate son, the duke of Monmouth, revealed that ironically some would have preferred to have been ruled by a Protestant bastard than a legal papist heir. Meanwhile, the difficulties that Mary of Modena had conceiving spurred rumours that their long-awaited son James Francis Edward was a spurious child smuggled into the birthing chamber in a warming pan.[141] The arrival of this dubious heir was an immediate cause of the Glorious Revolution of 1688, when James's daughter Mary and her Dutch husband William III were jointly invited to accept the crown in a coup that overturned the principle of propinquity of blood and made adherence to Catholicism an automatic disqualification from holding office. Once again elaborate genealogies such as *The royall Orange tree* (1691) helped to buttress the precarious constitutional legitimacy of their succession to the throne, and to present it as another act of 'mercifull Deliverance' of Britain's triple kingdom from popery.[142] Mary's three stillborn children meant that she was succeeded by her sister Anne, who became the last in the Stuart line. The history of the monarchy in the late seventeenth and early eighteenth centuries illustrates the same interweaving of religious and dynastic priorities, of fertility and faith, that shaped the genealogical imagination of the aristocracy and gentry and those snapping aggressively at their heels.

The temptation to suppose that these questions of blood and birthright were essentially an elite phenomenon—a set of imperatives confined to those of high status and to wealthy and successful merchants and tradesmen who aspired to join their privileged ranks—must be resisted. Concerns about legitimacy and lineage were widespread throughout early modern society. Growing anxiety about the problem of bastardy—which was itself sometimes observed to occur in successive generations—did not simply reflect a drive for social control.[143] It was a

---

[139] Giles Fleming, *Stemma sacrum, The royal progeny* (1660; Wing F1261). See also *idem, His Majesty's pedigree from the Saxon, Dane, Norman, and Scottish line; with an exact genealogy deliniated by their distinct families* (1664; Wing F1260A).

[140] I owe this point to John Blair.

[141] See Rachel Weil, *Political Passions: Gender, the Family and Political Argument in England, 1680–1714* (Manchester, 1999), ch. 3; Mary E. Fissell, *Vernacular Bodies: The Politics of Reproduction in Early Modern England* (Oxford, 2004), ch. 7; Patricia Crawford, 'Blood and Paternity', in *eadem, Blood, Bodies and Families*, pp. 113–39, at 123–4.

[142] *The royall Orange tree* (1691): BM, Y, 1.125. For a literary study of the nexus between politics and genealogy, see Erin Murphy, *Familial Forms: Politics and Genealogy in Seventeenth-Century English Literature* (Newark, DE, 2011).

[143] Anne Laurence, *Women in England 1500–1750: A Social History* (1994), pp. 82–3. On contemporary concerns about illegitimate children, see Patricia Crawford, *Parents of Poor Children in England, 1580–1800* (Oxford, 2013), esp. chs 1, 2, and 5.

function of shared moral values that found expression in popular ballads and cheap pamphlets recounting scandalous news of the unmarried mothers who committed the 'bloudy' crime of infanticide with a prudish disapproval that was often mistaken for the puritanism with which it loosely converged.[144] These must also partly be credited for the rising tide of business in the ecclesiastical courts associated with adultery and fornication.[145] At least some of those who bore witness against their neighbours and reported their misdemeanours to parish officials were people who had internalized the strong emphasis on sexual probity that was a hallmark of Protestant teaching on the Decalogue and that has long been recognized as a preoccupation of the magistrates and ministers who spearheaded the contemporary Reformation of manners and inflicted shame punishments on flagrant offenders.[146] More informally, others resorted to traditional rituals of humiliation such as rough music and the skimmington ride to ventilate their disapproval of those who infringed accepted codes of behaviour and illicitly had carnal knowledge of each other. Mockery of cuck-olded husbands and promiscuous wives and prejudice against children born out of wedlock are overlooked dimensions of the concerns about pedigree and parentage that exercised more elevated members of the social hierarchy. Illegitimacy was a common preoccupation: 'bad' and 'base' blood coloured atti-tudes and cast its shadow down the generations.[147] The sharp increase in litiga-tion about both male and female sexual honour and reputation in this period supplies further evidence of its centrality in everyday life.[148]

Fertility and infertility were likewise matters of pressing import to people of all sorts—better, middling, and poor. The search for solutions to this perennial problem evidently inspired many to intensify their daily piety and to utilize the special prayers that the clergy wrote for the benefit of those struggling to fulfil the

---

[144] See, e.g., T. B., *The bloudy mother, or The most inhumane murthers, committed by Iane Hattersley upon divers infants, the issue of her owne bodie* (1610; STC 3717.3). See Frances Dolan, *Dangerous Familiars: Representations of Domestic Crime in England, 1550–1700* (1994), ch.4; Laura Gowing, 'Secret Births and Infanticide in Seventeenth-Century England', *P&P*, 156 (1997), 87–115.

[145] Martin Ingram, *Church Courts, Sex and Marriage in England 1570–1640* (Cambridge, 1987), chs 7–8.

[146] See Keith Wrightson and David Levine, *Poverty and Piety in an English Village* (Oxford, 1995 edn), ch. 5; Martin Ingram, *Carnal Knowledge: Regulating Sex in England, 1470–1600* (Cambridge, 2017), ch. 10. On the Decalogue, see Jonathan Willis, *The Reformation of the Decalogue: Religious Identity and the Ten Commandments in England, c.1485–1625* (Cambridge, 2017), esp. 122–9.

[147] See Martin Ingram, 'Ridings, Rough Music, and the "Reform of Popular Culture" in Early Modern England', *P&P*, 105 (1984), 79–113; *idem*, 'Ridings, Rough Music, and Mocking Rhymes in Early Modern England', in Barry Reay (ed.), *Popular Culture in Seventeenth-Century* (1988), pp. 166–97.

[148] Ingram, *Church Courts*, ch. 10; James Sharpe, *Defamation and Sexual Slander in Early Modern England: The Church Courts at York*, Borthwick Papers 58 (York, 1980); Laura Gowing, *Domestic Dangers: Women, Work, and Sex in Early Modern London* (Oxford, 1996), ch. 3; Alexandra Shepard, *Meanings of Manhood in Early Modern England* (Oxford, 2003), ch. 6; and Bernard Capp, *When Gossips Meet: Women, Family, and Neighbourhood in Early Modern England* (Oxford, 2003), pp. 189–97, and ch. 5. See also Patricia Crawford, 'Blood and Paternity', in *eadem, Blood, Bodies and Families*, pp. 113–39, esp. pp. 124–30.

divine obligation to increase and multiply. Protestantism fostered a focus on godly procreation that did not bypass the majority of the populace. Barrenness and sterility and miscarriages and stillbirths were afflictions that linked the experiences of rich ladies and gentlemen with those of impoverished labourers. Interpreting their reproductive difficulties through the lens of providence as a punishment, trial, and chastisement, many sought and found comfort in the Bible, especially the stories of Sarah, Elizabeth, Rachel, Rebecca, and Hannah in the Old Testament, to whom the Lord had provided offspring beyond their expectation and in the face of despair.[149] The text of Scripture supplied a continuing incentive to hope that they too might overcome whatever was inhibiting generation and engender healthy children, not least by demonstrating sincere repentance. It also provided a series of compelling metaphors that compared spiritual apathy with the unfruitfulness of the barren fig tree in Christ's parable.[150] The Staffordshire minister Richard Lee paralleled the religious condition of his hearers with the infertility of Rachel in a sermon delivered in the early 1620s.[151] Such comparisons encouraged the same conflation of the religious and the physical, the gynaecological and the agricultural, which characterized the mental universe created by the book of Genesis.[152]

The many bibles and prayer books in which Tudor and Stuart people recorded family births, marriages, and deaths surviving in libraries and archives offer insight into a species of vernacular genealogy that parallels its better-studied elite counterpart and had greater social reach than has previously been recognized. The information that otherwise unknown individuals of humbler rank scribbled on flyleaves and blank pages attests to a world in which interest in divine and human ancestry and spiritual and biological kinship were interlinked. Revealingly, in a 1699 edition of the King James Version now in Dr Williams's Library a list of 'The Children God hath given Hen: & Mary Chandler' has been inserted facing the first chapter of Matthew's Gospel, which described the genealogy of Christ.[153]

---

[149] See Daphna Oren-Magidor, 'From Anne to Hannah: Religious Views of Infertility in Post-Reformation England', *Journal of Women's History*, 27 (2015), 86–108. See also *eadem, Infertility in Early Modern England* (2017), ch. 4.

[150] Thomas Adams, *The barren tree: a sermon preached at Pauls Crosse October 26, 1623* (1623; STC 106); John Bunyan, *The barren fig-tree, or, the doom and downfall of the fruitles professor…* (1673; Wing B5484). See also Nehemiah Rogers, *The fig-less fig-tree: or, the doome of a barren and unfruitful profession lay'd open* (1659; Wing R1823); Samuel Willard, *The barren fig trees doome. Or, a brief discourse wherein is set forth the woful danger of all who abide unfruitful under Gospel privileges, and Gods husbandry* (1691; W2267); Henry Pendelbury, *The barren fig-tree, or, a practical exposition of the parable, Luke 13. 6, 7, 8, 9, very useful for the awakening of those that remain unprofitable under gospel-priviledges and vineyard enjoyments* (1700; P1138).

[151] Richard Lee, *The spirituall spring. A sermon preached at Pauls, wherein is declared the necessity of growing in grace, and the goodly gaine that come thereby, etc* (1625; STC 15354), p. 9.

[152] See Crowther, '"Be Fruitful and Multiply"'; *eadem, Adam and Eve in the Protestant Reformation* (Cambridge, 2010), ch. 4.

[153] *The holy bible containing the Old Testament and the New* (1699): DWL, MS 28. 174–5. Similar examples could be multiplied.

Many also recorded miscarried fetuses and infants who had died in the womb.[154] Henry and Elizabeth Revell of Egham in Surrey, whose first child was stillborn on 10 March 1710, marked it in the flyleaf of their bible, while the genealogical notes inscribed in one belonging to the Harcourt and Skrine families of Somerset list a series of miscarriages in the early eighteenth century.[155] These failed conceptions were understood as members of their families, in the same way as babies who were delivered alive but expired prematurely. Their presence in these records raises interesting questions about early modern conceptions of personhood.

It is striking that the rise of this cultural pattern of record-keeping coincided with one of the more significant symptoms of the Tudor revolution in government, the introduction of parish registers. In due course these became an important source for early modern genealogists.[156] Lancelot Ridley confirmed the date of his own christening in 1544 from 'the churche booke of Ely', and the Eaton family derived its pedigree in part from the register of the chapel of Goostrey in Cheshire in the seventeenth century.[157] Quakers too developed an obsession with recording such information: in 1668 George Fox exhorted Friends to 'buy convenient Books for Registring the Births and Marriages and Burials, as the holy men of God did of old'.[158] All of these trends were artefacts of the reformation of the generations.

Moral Biology

The discourses and practices discussed thus far were, on the whole, positive and empowering ones. No less pervasive, though ostensibly more depressing, was the doctrine of original sin. This is not a topic to which modern scholars have been magnetically attracted, but it is vitally important for our understanding of early modern religious mentalities. The idea that after the Fall all humanity carried a

---

[154] BL, Additional MS 37127 (*The compleat history of the old and new testament: or a family bible* (1735) owned by the Smith family). Also listed are two other children who died during their births.

[155] Surrey HC, 3996/1 (Photocopy of manuscript notes in the Revell family bible, 1708–1875); Somerset HC, DD/SK/4/4/14 (Genealogical notes on the Harcourt and Skrine families taken from the family bible 1680–1894). See also the miscarried son listed among Thomas Honeywood's children in Bodl., MS Rawlinson D. 102 (Mistress Mary Honeywood's Life of her Father, c.1635).

[156] See Will Coster, 'Popular Religion and the Parish Register, 1538–1603', in Katherine L. French, Gary G. Gibbs, and Beat A. Kumin (eds), *The Parish in English Life, 1400–1600* (Manchester, 1997), pp. 94–111.

[157] BL, Additional MS 44062 (Notebook of Lancelot Ridley), fo. 18r; CRO, DCB/1363/9 (Pedigree of Eaton Family of Blackden, 1570–1674).

[158] *Canons and institutions drawn up and agreed upon by the General Assembly or Meeting of the heads of the Quakers from all parts of the kingdom at their New-Theatre in Grace-church-street in or about January 1668/9* (1669; Wing F1755), p. 10.

residue of the corruption that had induced Adam and Eve to transgress God's commandment and eat the fruit of the forbidden tree in the Garden of Eden had been at the heart of Christianity from the beginning. It was a central element in the great soteriological drama of Christ's crucifixion, a catastrophic act that set the scene for a supreme act of self-sacrifice. The reason why the Lord had sent his only son into the world to die a terrible death, it functioned paradoxically as both a cause and an effect of divine wrath and mercy.

Implicit in Scripture, the theology of original sin was not fully elaborated until the fifth century. It was Augustine who crystallized the doctrine of inherited guilt that had been transmitted to Adam and Eve's posterity through sexual lust and the conjugal act, partly in response to the Pelagian heretics, who denied that men and women were inherently evil creatures and insisted that they could take active and effective steps towards their salvation. Refined and elaborated by scholastic theologians such as Thomas Aquinas, Augustine's deep pessimism about human nature was offset by the emphasis that the late medieval Church increasingly placed on the accumulation of merit through virtuous living and on the power of the papacy to pardon sin. For medieval Christians and Tridentine Catholics alike, the concupiscence that was the consequence of Adam and Eve's transgression was a mere absence of righteousness rather than a state of ingrained depravity. Baptism cleansed Christians of this culpability as infants and through the exercise of free will adults could resist, if not overcome the impulse to sin.[159] Humanists such as Desiderius Erasmus famously ridiculed the idea that original sin was conveyed down the generations via reproduction, lineage, and blood as an absurd mystery.[160]

With Protestantism came a resurgence of the rather gloomy anthropology that was the legacy of St Augustine. A neo-Augustinian emphasis upon the intrinsic wickedness of human beings was adopted by all the principal reformers. This pessimism was a feature of the Lutheranism that shaped the first phase of the English Reformations. It left its mark on the liturgy of the Church of England, as well as upon the instructional works that the early reformers borrowed from early Protestant Europe. Thomas Cranmer's 1548 translation of the Nuremberg

---

[159] See Mathijs Lamberigts, 'Original Sin', in Willemien Otten (ed.), *The Oxford Guide to the Historical Reception of Augustine* (Oxford, 2014), vol. iii, pp. 1472–7; William E. Mann, 'Augustine on Evil and Original Sin', in David Vincent Meconi and Eleanore Stump (eds), *The Cambridge Companion to Augustine* (Cambridge, 2014), pp. 98–107. See also Elizabeth A. Clark, 'Generation, Degeneration, Regeneration: Original Sin and the Conception of Jesus in the Polemic between Augustine and Julian of Eclanum', in Valeria Finucci and Kevin Brownlee (eds), *Generation and Degeneration: Tropes of Reproduction in Literature and History from Antiquity through Early Modern Europe* (Durham, NC, 2001), 17–40.

[160] Desiderius Erasmus, *The Praise of Folly*, trans. and ed. Clarence A. Miller (New Haven, CT, 1979), p. 88.

catechism asserted that infants in their mother's wombs were inflicted with 'evyll lustes and appetites' and were thus in contravention of the Ten Commandments even before they were born.[161] As Swiss theological influences increasingly eclipsed German ones, this emphasis was reinforced further. The idea of 'original or birth sin' was a basic tenet of the Protestant faith enshrined in the 39 Articles of 1563 and discussed in more detail in an official homily on 'the misery of mankind', which dwelt on the terrible 'state of imperfection' and captivity in which people had been left by the transgression of their 'first parent' and 'great grandfather Adam' and his spouse Eve.[162]

The doctrine found particularly trenchant expression in John Calvin's influential *Institutes of Christian religion* and his commentary on Genesis, both of which were quickly translated into English. These defined original sin as a defect that had been passed down the generations to the present one in a direct line of succession. 'All of us...descending from an impure seed, came into the world tainted with the contagion of sin,' he said. 'Before we behold the light of the sun we are in God's sight defiled and polluted.' Citing Psalm 51:5 ('Behold, I was shapen in iniquity, and in sin did my mother conceive me') and Ephesians 2:3 (St Paul's insight that 'we are by nature children of wrath'), he stressed that all people were thereby made the 'bondslaves of Sathan', subject to 'everlasting malediction'. The excellent gifts of knowledge, reason, moral integrity, and religious sincerity that the Almighty had bestowed upon the first man and woman had been gravely impaired by the Fall. A living death became the destiny of humans, who would universally be doomed were it not for Christ's redemptive suffering on the Cross at Calvary. Even the regenerate were not free of its traces: those who were blessed with being born again could not entirely throw off the shackles of the old Adam within them. They remained intrinsically flawed.[163] No one was immune to this, including the Virgin Mary. The doctrine of her Immaculate Conception may have been contested within Catholic ranks, but this did not stop Protestant polemicists from using it to castigate popish errors relating to this theological precept.[164] They no less emphatically rejected any suggestion that the sacrament of baptism

---

[161] Thomas Cranmer, *Catechismus, that is to say, a shorte instruction into Christian religion for the synguler commoditie and profyte of childre[n] and yong people* (1548; STC 5994), sigs M4r–N2v.

[162] Thirty-Nine Articles, no. 9; *Certayne sermons appoynted by the quenes maiestie, to be declared and read, by all persones, vycars, and curates, euery Sondaye and holy daye in theyr churches* (1559; STC 13648.5), sigs C1r–D2r.

[163] John Calvin, *Institutes of the Christian Religion*, trans. Henry Beveridge, 2 vols in 1 (Grand Rapids, MI, 1989 edn), vol. i, pp. 214–20; idem, *A commentarie...upon the first booke of Moses called Genesis*, trans. Thomas Tymme (1578; STC 4393), pp. 212–13.

[164] Diarmaid MacCulloch, 'Mary and Sixteenth-Century Protestants', in R. N. Swanson (ed.), *The Church and Mary*, SCH 39 (2004), pp. 197–217, at pp. 210–11.

wiped the slate clean, stressing that the concupiscence that human beings retained was a lingering disease that fretted away at their inclination for goodness and induced them to commit actual sins.[165] As an illustration in a seventeenth-century picture book describing 'The Ages of Sin' suggests, original sin was envisaged as 'a foule great-Bellyed Snake', an agent of Satan that tempted men and women to transgress and which bred 'Lustfull-Thoughts' within (Fig. 3.13).[166]

Calvin's uncompromising exegesis of this theme set the tone for dozens of expositions of it by his many disciples in England. They too spoke of it as a 'bitter root' from which sprang manifold mischiefs, an 'uncleane fountaine' that had permanently contaminated humanity's initial purity, and a slow-working but toxic poison that could never be successfully counteracted. Like 'the dead flye that marreth the most precious ointment of the Apothecary', so original sin left behind an indelible mark that could not be eradicated.[167] According to the Northamptonshire puritan divine Robert Bolton, it was comparable to an innate physical trait, cleaving so 'fast to thy nature, even as blacknesse to the skinne of an Ethiopian, which cannot possibly be washed out'. The 'remnants of olde Adam' in humanity were as ineradicable as the dark colouring of the inhabitants of Africa.[168] Such discussions both fed into and flowed from the scripturally grounded concepts of race that were in the process of being forged in early modern thought.[169] As a synonym for a tribe and nation of people, race was a word that sprang frequently to the lips of the ministers and preachers who tried to unravel the mysteries of Genesis for their lay parishioners.[170] It was deployed to denote the pervasive corruption that ran through the blood of all the descendants of Adam and Eve without exception. As Richard Bernard declared, 'as wee bee of *Adams* race, so have we our children conceived in sinne, and brought forth in iniquity, and beget such as be after our owne likenesse'.[171]

---

[165] See Calvin, *Institutes*, vol. i, pp. 517–18 (bk iv, §10).

[166] *The ages of sin, or, sinnes birth & growth. With the stepps, and degrees of sin, from thought to finall Impenitencie* ([1635]; STC 15193.5), title page. This book was republished in 1655 (Wing J661A, A761) and appeared in 1675 as a broadside (Wing J661AB).

[167] Elnathan Parr, *The grounds of divinitie plainely discovering the mysteries of Christian religion, propounded familiarly in divers questions and answers* (1614; STC 19314), pp. 168, 170; James Ussher, *A body of divinitie, or the summe and substance of Christian religion* (1645; Wing U151), p. 146, and see pp. 143–4.

[168] Robert Bolton, *The carnal professor* (1634; STC 3225), pp. 49–50. This was an allusion to Jeremiah 13:23–5.

[169] See Kidd, *The Forging of Races*, pp. 25, 29, 61, 63, 65; Ian Campbell, *Renaissance Humanism and Ethnicity before Race: The Irish and the English in the Seventeenth Century* (Manchester, 2013), pp. 147–65. For a fuller discussion of these themes, see my 'Générations d'Adam: Théologie et race dans la pensée protestante anglaise', *Revue d'histoire moderne et contemporaine*, 68 (2021), 54–76.

[170] See OED, s.v. 'race'.

[171] Bernard, *Ruths recompense*, p. 414.

Fig. 3.13 *The ages of sin, or, sinnes birth & growth* (London, 1635).

One particular consequence of Protestantism's Augustinian turn was to concentrate close attention on the precise course of events that led to the Fall. Clerical interpreters of Genesis were compelled to answer a range of inquisitive questions that arose from reading this story. These included whether Adam and Eve had slept together before they were tempted by what Bishop Gervase Babington termed the latter's 'tittle tattle' with the serpent,[172] or whether this had occurred after their heinous act of rebellion in tasting the fruit of the tree. Protestant ministers agreed that only the latter could explain humanity's irreducible sinfulness. As Philip Almond has commented, to insist upon this was 'not moral timidity, but theological necessity'.[173] There was evidently also a great deal of fascination with the fact that our 'first parents' became ashamed of their nakedness and felt compelled to cover up their privy parts. How—and why—Adam and Eve made themselves aprons of fig leaves rather than those of any other tree was a topic of perennial curiosity.[174]

So was the exact mechanism by which original sin had been propagated to their offspring. The clergy were keen to suppress too much discussion of this delicate subject, frowning upon those who were excessively inquisitive about the specifics of this process. The Irish primate James Ussher warned 'wee are not to bee so curious in seeking the manner how, as to marke the matter to bee in us: even as when a house is on fire, men should not be so busie to enquire how it came, as seeing it there to quench it'.[175] Samuel Hieron, minister of Modbury in Devon in the Jacobean period, was equally concerned to discourage attempts to delve into the manner by which depravity had 'crept in upon us'. He quoted Calvin to the effect that the 'universall corruption of our nature, proceedeth not so much out of generation, as Gods ordination'.[176] This was to step back from the suggestion that the infection of the soul as well as the body was a result of the conjunction of flesh in sexual intercourse and to insist that this required supernatural intervention.[177] It was to think of it as more akin to artificial insemination than unaided fertilization. Others were more equivocal. William Perkins said that the soul was either 'infected by the contagion of the body, as a good ointment by a fustie vessel; or because God, in the very moment of creation & infusion of souls into infants, doth utterly forsake them'.[178]

These technicalities aside, the drift of English Protestant discourse on this topic was to imply that original sin had indeed descended down the generations through the loins of Adam and his posterity, via what the convert John Salkeld described as 'the matrimonial act'.[179] As Robert Bolton commented, by this means every parent became 'the channell of death to his posterity'. Thomas Wilson's popular *Christian dictionarie* said that human sinfulness was 'a prerogative gotten

---

[172] Babington, *Certaine briefe, plaine and comfortable notes*, fo. 14v.

[173] See Philip C. Almond, *Adam and Eve in Seventeenth-Century Thought* (Cambridge, 1999), pp. 167–8. For some discussions, see Willet, *Hexapla in Genesin*, p. 56; George Hughes, *An analytical exposition of the whole first book of Moses, called Genesis* (1672; Wing H3305), p. 26.

[174] e.g., Needler, *Expository notes*, p. 76.

[175] Ussher, *Body of divinitie*, pp. 145–6. This was a paraphrase of William Perkins, *A golden chaine, or the description of theologie containing the order of the causes of salvation and damnation* (Cambridge, 1591; STC 19657), p. 20.

[176] Samuel Hieron, *All the sermons…heretofore sunderly published, now diligently revised, and collected together into one volume* (1614; STC 13378), p. 420.

[177] Calvin, *Commentarie*, p. 96.   [178] Perkins, *Golden Chaine*, sig. C3r.

[179] John Salkeld, *A treatise of paradise, and the principall contents thereof* (1617; STC 21622), p. 279.

by birth, or Naturall descent and generation.[180] As in the era of Augustine, theological debates about this topic were 'grounded in culturally bound and historically determined biological understandings of reproduction'.[181] In early modern England, these physiological theories were rooted in Galenic assumptions about blood and seed. They were rooted in the idea that moral as well as physical characteristics could be passed down in ways that defy the distinctions that are now drawn between nature and culture.[182]

Many spoke and wrote of original sin as a kind of 'hereditary disease' and compared it to a range of ailments that were perceived to run in families and that seemed 'to bee intailed to one stocke'.[183] These included venereal and sexually transmitted conditions such as the pox, as well as scrofula and rickets, which were believed to be communicated from a father or mother by the generative 'seed' during gestation. Richard Rollock mentioned gall stones and other conditions 'derived from parents to children', and Elnathan Parr cited gout as a comparable example of how 'certaine incurable impassions and dispositions' were conveyed down the generations.[184] Leprosy was an even more common point of parallel. A powerful descriptor for deviance since the Middle Ages, this debilitating skin disease served as a synonym for the spiritual disfigurement wrought by the Fall. William Perkins said that original sin similarly ran 'from the crowne of the head, to the sole of the foote'.[185] David Harley has underlined the frequent overlap between the vocabularies of corporeal and spiritual sickness in this period. Such metaphors open a window onto a dynamic discourse in which the boundary between analogy and reality was indistinct.[186]

[180] Bolton, *Carnall professor*, pp. 63–4; Thomas Wilson, *A Christian dictionarie, opening the signification of the chiefe wordes dispersed generally through Holie Scriptures of the Old and New Testament, tending to increase Christian knowledge* (1612; STC 25786), p. 332.

[181] Valeria Finucci, 'Introduction: Genealogical Pleasures, Genealogical Disruptions', in *eadem* and Brownlee (eds), *Generation and Degeneration*, pp. 1–14, at p. 1.

[182] Nick Hopwell, Rebecca Flemming, and Lauren Kassell (eds), *Reproduction: From Antiquity to the Present Day* (Cambridge, 2018), esp. pt 2, including Silvia De Renzi, 'Family Resemblances in the Old Regime', pp. 242–52.

[183] See Godfrey Goodman, *The fall of man, or the corruption of nature, proved by the light of our natural reason* (1616; STC 12023), p. 443, and see p. 57; Nehemiah Rogers, *The true convert, or an exposition upon the whole parable of the prodigall* (1620; STC 21201), p. 55; William Gurnall, *The Christian in compleat armour* (1655; Wing G2251), pp. 257–8. See also Thomas Jackson, *An exact collection of the works of Doctor Jackson* (1654; Wing J89), pp. 329–32.

[184] Richard Rollock, *A treatise of gods effectuall calling* (1603; STC 21286), p. 133; Parr, *Grounds of divinitie*, p. 165.

[185] William Perkins, *The foundation of Christian religion gathered into six principles* (1591), sigs A7v–8r. See also Thomas Wilson, *A commentarie upon the most divine epistle of S. Paul to the Romanes* (1614; STC 25791), p. 306; Ussher, *Body of divinitie*, p. 142–3; Richard Baxter, *A Christian directory, or a sum of practical theologie and cases of conscience* (1673; Wing B1219), p. 518. On leprosy and deviance, see R. I. Moore, 'Heresy as Disease', in D. W. Lourdaux and D. Verhelst (eds), *The Concept of Heresy in the Middle Ages* (Louvain, 1976), pp. 1–11.

[186] See David Harley, 'Medical Metaphors in English Moral Theology, 1560–1660', *Journal of the History of Medicine and Allied Sciences*, 48 (1993), 396–435.

The frequency with which contemporaries reached for the language of inheritance to describe original sin is also striking. In claiming that its stain descended down to Adam's heirs 'hereditarily', as if by descent, they were comparing it to the way in which land and property was transmitted in accordance with blood.[187] The legal and juridical overtones of the term coexisted with other meanings, including medical ones, which have acquired more prominence since. These elements of early modern writing on original sin suggest that the neo-Augustinian elements of Protestant theology must be recognized as one of the multiple cultural domains in which current concepts of heredity were crystallized and forged. They augment and nuance important recent work by Staffan Müller-Wille and Hans-Jörg Rheinberger investigating the various 'epistemic spaces' out of which the nineteenth-century life science of genetics gradually emerged, redressing their conspicuous neglect of the pervasive biblical rhetorics and religious registers I have explored.[188] John Bossy memorably described the ethical shift within early modern Christianity from the Seven Deadly Sins to the Ten Commandments as 'moral arithmetic'.[189] Rooted in the book of Genesis and revolving directly around the multivalent notion of generation, reformed thinking on 'hereditary' sin might be described as a type of moral biology. To say that it foreshadowed aspects of how reproduction is now understood is not to fall into the seductive trap of teleology; it is simply to identify some tendencies that contributed to the prolonged and contingent process of their evolution.

Protestant ideas regarding the transmission of original sin contrast sharply with how they understood the mysteries of election and predestination. According to Calvin, if guilt came from nature, sanctification was a function of celestial grace. As we saw in Chapter 1, the most prevalent way of conceptualizing this was in terms of adoption. God selected a remnant who would be saved and then brought them to assurance of their special status as his children through an emotional and sensual conversionary experience. True Christians were made through spiritual regeneration rather than born as a result of corporeal generation.[190]

---

[187] See *OED*, s.v. 'hereditary'. Neil Kenny, *Born to Write: Literary Families and Social Hierarchy in Early Modern France* (Oxford, 2020), esp. ch.3, considers how literary works were compared to inheritable assets.

[188] Staffan Müller-Wille and Hans-Jörg Rheinberger, 'Heredity: The Formation of an Epistemic Space', in *eidem* (eds), *Heredity Produced: At the Crossroads of Biology, Politics, and Culture, 1500–1870* (Cambridge, MA, 2007), pp. 3–34; *eidem, A Cultural History of Heredity* (Chicago, 2012), esp. chs 2–3. See esp. Ohad S. Parnes, 'On the Shoulders of Generations: The New Epistemology of Heredity in the Nineteenth Century', in Müller-Wille and Rheinberger (eds), *Heredity Produced*, pp. 315–46. Müller-Wille and Rheinberger note the need for research on the contribution of theories of original sin in 'De la génération à l'hérédite: Continuités médiévales et conjonctures historiques modernes', in Maiike van der Lugt and Charles de Miramon (eds), *L'Hérédité entre Moyen Âge et époque moderne: Perspectives historiques* (Florence, 2008), pp. 355–88, at p. 388. Their importance is emphasized by Claude-Olivier Doron, *L'homme altéré: Races et dégénérescence (XVIIe– XIXe siècles)* (Paris, 2016), esp. pp. 70–7.

[189] John Bossy, 'Moral Arithmetic: Seven Sins into Ten Commandments', in Edmund Leites (ed.), *Conscience and Casuistry in Early Modern Europe* (Cambridge, 1988), pp. 214–34.

[190] See Chapter 1 above.

Nevertheless, as will be further explicated in Chapter 4, fervent Protestants weaned on a diet of Scripture that included large portions of Genesis could not forget the promises that God had made to the seed of Abraham. They could not entirely resist the temptation to understand the genealogies laid out in the first book of the Old Testament and in Luke and Matthew as a paradigm of how godliness travelled down family lines. They can be forgiven for finding the tantalizing idea that election might, in some sense, be hereditary in the Bible.[191]

Here it is worth observing the intriguing visual similarities between the diagrammatic tables of the order of salvation and damnation prepared by William Perkins and John Bunyan and the divine and secular pedigrees that proliferated in early modern England. The dual and parallel lines they trace to heaven and hell through a series of stages of awakening and degeneration are too reminiscent of those in the family trees we have already discussed to be merely accidental. The impression of inexorable succession conveyed by these 'ocular catechisms' and 'mapps' was the same as the unbroken continuity implied by genealogical rolls and codices. Bunyan's begins, moreover, with the Trinity of God the Father, Son, and Holy Spirit, from whom proceed not only Adam and his offspring Abel and Cain but the lines of Grace and Justice leading to election and reprobation (Fig. 3.14).[192]

Protestant teachings on predestination and original sin had, in any case, always been inseparable twins. This explains why reformed theologians were so sensitive to the dangers of Pelagianism and why they thought of themselves as engaged in a renewed battle against an ancient heresy that appeared to be resurgent and, like a hydra, to be able to regenerate its multiple heads. One of these forms of 'patched Pelagianism' was obviously Catholicism, but in the course of the sixteenth and seventeenth centuries the label was also applied to denounce Arminians and Quakers.[193] The emergence of anti-Calvinism within some circles of the church in the early seventeenth century brought alternative ideas about predestination and original sin from the edges into the mainstream. Arminian divines played down the irrevocable taint conveyed from Adam to his posterity and emphasized

[191] See Chapter 4 below.

[192] Fold-out table in William Perkins, *A Golden Chaine*, in *Workes* (Cambridge, 1608; STC 19649), following sig. B2r; John Bunyan, *A mapp shewing the order & causes of salvation & damnation* ([1691]; Wing B5554A). See Peter Titlestad, 'From Beza to Bunyan: The Pilgrim Road Mapped', *Bunyan Studies*, 13 (2008–9), 64–81; Lori-Anne Ferrell, 'Page Techne: Interpreting Diagrams in Early Modern English "How to" Books', in Michael Hunter (ed.), *Printed Images in Early Modern England* (Farnham, 2010), pp. 113–27, esp. pp. 121–5.

[193] See Theodore Beza, *An evident display of popish practises, or patched pelagianisme. Wherein is mightelie cleared the soueraigne truth of Gods eternall predestination* (1578; STC 2018.5); William Prynne, *The church of Englands old antithesis to new Arminianisme. Wherein...opposite Arminian (once popish and Pelagian) errors are manifestly disproved...* (1629; STC 20457); Joseph Carly, *The doctrines of the Arminians & Pelagians truly stated and clearly answered* (1651; Wing W2006); Richard Blome, *The fanatick history: or an exact relation and account of the old Anabaptists, and new Quakers* (1660; Wing B3212), p. 132.

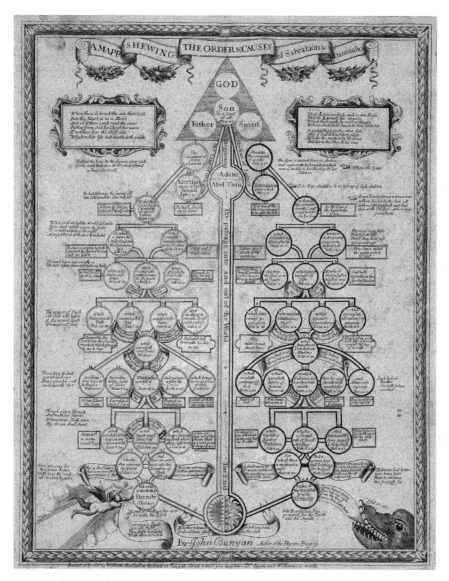

Fig. 3.14 'A mapp shewing the order & causes of salvation & damnation', in John Bunyan, *The works of that eminent servant of Christ, Mr. John Bunyan* . . . (London, 1692), fold-out plate.

Source: Folger Shakespeare Library, Washington DC, B5479. Folger Digital Image Collection.

the abundance of grace Christ had poured out for humanity's salvation. The Essex minister Samuel Hoard's 1633 treatise disproving God's absolute decree of damnation strongly countered the precept that the Adam's transgressions wholly corrupted the nature of his heirs. Arguing that this sin was 'not by generation . . . but by Gods own voluntary imputation', he was particularly concerned to refute the claim that children were guilty of the iniquities of their parents. 'Miserable would [their] case bee on whom the ends of the world are come,' he wrote, if they were held accountable for their 'Ancestors prevarications'.[194]

In this context it is not surprising that the Westminster Assembly of Divines strongly reaffirmed traditional doctrine in its 1646 confession of faith, stating that depravity had descended 'by ordinary generation' to the progeny of Adam and Eve, rendering them utterly incapable of and opposite to good.[195] But although Presbyterians such as Anthony Burgess firmly reiterated the precept that human beings were irredeemably polluted, the tide was turning among the learned towards a more optimistic anthropology and, by association, towards a doctrine of salvation in which there was more room for human volition and will. Jeremy Taylor and other ministers had little sympathy for the forbidding view of God they accused Calvinists of creating: a deity who punished Adam's posterity for a crime that they themselves had not committed and assumed that the fault of 'our first parents' completely compromised the innocence of their children.[196] In the second half of the seventeenth century, the reformed Protestant doctrine of inherited guilt gradually retreated as the emotional tenor of piety shifted.[197] To puritans, this was dismaying further evidence of the resilience of the old Pelagian heresy that Augustine had tried so hard to slay in the fifth century. For their part, they continued to reiterate the precept that original sin and the 'old man' of concupiscence had withered humanity's beauty and purity and made it 'deformed in God's eyes'.[198]

Convinced that most people must have found the doctrines of predestination and original sin inherently alienating, an earlier generation of historians of the English Reformation tended to characterize popular piety as irrepressibly Pelagian. Drawing on the evocative picture of 'countrie divinitie' painted by

---

[194] Samuel Hoard, *Gods love to mankind manifested, by dis-proving his absolute decree for their damnation* (1633; STC 13534.5), pp. 63 and 53–5.

[195] For the confession, see *Creeds of the Churches*, ed. John H. Leith (Richmond, VA, 1963), pp. 201–2. See also *The Minutes and Papers of the Westminster Assembly, 1643–1652*, ed. Chad van Dixhoorn and David F. Wright, 6 vols (Oxford, 2012), vol. iv, p. 528 and vol. v, p. 326. For the mid-seventeenth-century debates about original sin, see William Poole, *Milton and the Idea of the Fall* (Cambridge, 2005), chs 3–5.

[196] Anthony Burgess, *A treatise of original sin...shewing what original sinne is and how it is communicated* (1658; Wing B5660), 1, 4; Jeremy Taylor, *Unum necessarium: or, the doctrine and practice of repentance* (1655; Wing T415) and *Deus justificatus, or, a vindication of the glory of the divine attributes in the question of original sin* (1656; STC T311), esp. pp. 7, 35–6, 38.

[197] Michael Heyd, 'Original Sin, the Struggle for Stability, and the Rise of Moral Individualism in Late Seventeenth-Century England', in Philip Benedict and Myron P. Gutmann (eds), *Early Modern Europe: From Crisis to Stability* (Newark, DE, 2005), pp. 197–233; idem, 'Changing Emotions? The Decline of Original Sin on the Eve of the Enlightenment', in Penelope Gouk and Helen Hills (eds), *Representing Emotions: New Connections in the Histories of Art, Music and Medicine* (Aldershot, 2005), pp. 123–36; Matthew Kadane, 'Original Sin and the Path to the Enlightenment', *P&P*, 235 (2017), 105–40.

[198] Thomas Watson, *A body of practical divinity consisting of above one hundred seventy six sermons on the lesser catechism composed by the reverend assembly of divines at Westminster* (1692; Wing W1109), p. 82.

writers such as George Gifford and Arthur Dent, they mistook the disillusionment that was an occupational hazard of Elizabethan and early Stuart clergymen
for the more complex pastoral situation that they encountered on the ground.[199]
Yet as Peter Lake, Arnold Hunt, and others have shown, the revisionists arguably
underestimated the extent to which reformed tenets about salvation penetrated
the religious culture and outlook of the early modern laity.[200]

The same might be said about 'hereditary sin'. Discussion of it was not confined to dusty tomes of systematic theology. It was also pervasive in a wide range
of vernacular texts to which ordinary people were constantly exposed and which
shaped their thinking in various ways: catechisms, sermons, and works of practical divinity such as John Downame's influential *Guide to godlynesse* (1622). This
contains a morning prayer designed for family use that meditates on the corruption and guilt 'we have derived from our first parents' and humbly admits to
the 'cursed fruits of actuall transgressions' that spring from the 'roote of original
sinne'.[201] These ideas found pictorial form in the illustrations of the temptation of
Adam and Eve incorporated in bibles, including the Geneva version, and in the
genealogies that prefaced the King James Version.[202] They were also embodied in
domestic wall paintings that adorned farmhouses no less than town and manor
houses. A surviving example from Monks Risborough in Buckinghamshire is
dated c.1627, while a wooden panel produced in Plymouth in the first half of the
seventeenth century was probably made for a prosperous middling sort home
(Fig. 3.15).[203] Even cottagers could afford broadside pictures, and published
engravings had an afterlife in manuscript facsimiles and copies like those created
by Thomas Trevelyon.[204]

The doctrine of original sin was also enshrined in material objects, from
embroidered bookbindings, samplers, lace mats, overmantels, and chairs to
bedheads and hangings. The images of Adam and Eve that appeared on such
items served as a warning that while conjugal relations within wedlock were
divinely ordained, they also posed a threat to the immortal soul. Eating the forbidden fruit at the behest of the serpent was widely understood as emblematic of

---

[199] George Gifford, *A briefe discourse of certaine points of the religion which is among the common
sort of Christians, which may bee termed the countrie diuinitie* (1582; STC 11845); Arthur Dent, *The
plaine mans path-way to heauen* (1601; STC 6626). Christopher Haigh, *English Reformations: Religion,
Politics, and Society under the Tudors* (Oxford, 2003), pp. 280–4; idem, *The Plain Man's Pathways to
Heaven: Kinds of Christianity in Post-Reformation England* (Oxford, 2007), part II; Patrick Collinson,
The Religion of Protestants: The Church in English Society 1559-1625 (Oxford, 1982), pp. 191, 201–2;
Ian Green, *Print and Protestantism in Early Modern England* (Oxford, 2000), p. 497.
[200] See Peter Lake, 'Deeds against Nature: Cheap Print, Protestantism and Murder in Early
Seventeenth-Century England', in Kevin M. Sharpe and Peter Lake (eds), *Culture and Politics in Early
Stuart England* (1994), pp. 257–83; Arnold Hunt, *The Art of Hearing: English Preachers and Their
Audiences, 1590-1640* (Cambridge, 2010), ch. 7.
[201] John Downame, *A guide to godlynesse or a treatise of a Christian life* (1622; STC 7143), p. 899.
[202] See above, pp. 178–9.
[203] Watt, *Cheap Print*, p. 201; V&A, W.39–1914 (Adam and Eve oak panel, oil, c.1600).
[204] See FSL, MS V.b.232, fos 40v–41r.

Fig. 3.15 Wooden panel of the Temptation of Adam and Eve (oil on oak panel, Plymouth, early 17th century).

Source: © Victoria and Albert Museum, London, W.39-1914.

the perils of sexual lust. Some such pieces of furniture and linen were marriage gifts or items commissioned by a couple to commemorate their union.[205] So too

---

[205] Hamling, *Decorating the 'Godly' Household*, pp. 143, 152–3, 159–60, 170–2, 186–8, 204–5, 231–3, 260–1; Catherine Belsey, *Shakespeare and the Loss of Eden: The Construction of Family Values in Early Modern Culture* (Basingstoke, 1999), ch. 3. See also Andrew Morrall, 'Regaining Eden: Representations of Nature in Seventeenth-Century English Embroidery', in Andrew Morrall and Melinda Watt (eds), *English Embroidery from The Metropolitan Museum of Art, 1580–1700: 'Twixt Art and Nature* (New Haven, CT, 2008), pp. 79–97. For two examples, see V&A, T.17–1909 (lace panel, 1600–1650); Fitz., T.33–1945 (embroidered panel, *c.*1625–75).

were the many decorated delftware plates and chargers that survive in museums: the Glaisher Collection in the Fitzwilliam in Cambridge alone contains twenty-four specimens with this design, many of which must once have been family heirlooms. Displayed in rooms in which food was consumed, these pieces of moralistic pottery must be seen as forms of embodied theology which instructed people in the dangers of gluttony and promiscuity simultaneously (see Fig. 5.12).[206] Their iconography both attested to and helped to spread knowledge of Genesis and the distinctive renderings of it embedded in English translations of Scripture.

Many of the mass-produced Adam and Eve plates manufactured in the late seventeenth and early eighteenth century are snapshots of the moment at which the pair became aware of their nakedness and cover their genitals with fig leaves. In one made by the Norfolk House pottery c.1705–30, they resemble oversized three-leaf clovers. In another produced in Bristol during the same period, the aprons they were said to have created look like tutus. In a third, they have the appearance of the breeches invoked in the Geneva translation.[207] While the reception of these texts, images, and artefacts is difficult to gauge, their ubiquity is suggestive of the ways in biblical discourses of generation and original sin infiltrated the daily lives of ordinary people. Bearing witness to a vigorous strain of popular Augustinianism, they reinforce calls for a social and cultural history of religion that is alive to the potency of Protestant theology in shaping lived experience. Without it, we are in danger of perpetuating a vision of the Reformation akin to a doughnut: with a hole in the middle or with the jam missing.[208]

Original sin, then, was not a recondite or rarefied topic; it must be located close to the centre of reformed piety. Together with the closely associated notion that all were conceived in sin and 'shapen in iniquity', the story of the primal transgression of 'our first parents' preoccupied members of both sexes. Elizabeth Hastings, countess of Huntingdon, meditated upon Adam and Eve's transgression in one of her commonplace books. It can also be found in the voluminous notebooks of the London artisan Nehemiah Wallington, who reflected on the 'miserable condition' in which this event had left posterity and prayed for God's mercy in counteracting the corrupt nature he had inherited.[209]

---

[206] See Alexandra Walsham, 'Eating the Forbidden Fruit: Pottery and Protestant Theology in Early Modern England', *Journal of Early Modern History*, 24 (2020), 63–83. For an earlier discussion, see Malcolm MacTaggart, 'English Delft Adam and Eve Chargers: Their Earliest Dating and Derivation', *The Connoisseur Year Book* (1959), 58–63.

[207] See Fitz., C. 1619-1928 (charger, Norfolk House pottery, Lambeth [?], c.1705–30); C. 1618-1928 (charger, unidentified Bristol pottery, c.1725–1735); C. 1629-1928 (charger, unidentified Bristol pottery, c.1720–1740).

[208] See Alexandra Walsham, 'Afterword', in Jonathan Willis (ed.), *Sin and Salvation in Reformation England* (Farnham, 2015), pp. 259–76, esp. 262–4; Jonathan Willis, *The Reformation of the Decalogue: The Ten Commandments in England, c.1485-c.1625* (Cambridge, 2017), esp. pp. 10–11.

[209] HEHL, MSSHM 15369 (Commonplace book of Elizabeth Hastings, countess of Huntingdon), fo. 14v; FSL, MS V. a. 436 (Notebook of Nehemiah Wallington, 1654), pp. 1, 152, 372.

In particular, original sin critically inflected how early modern people understood pregnancy and childbirth.[210] The whole process of generation, from conception to delivery, was a stark reminder of the Fall. The intense pains women suffered during labour were the bitter legacy of the punishment God had inflicted upon their 'grandmother Eve'. The memory of her transgression hung heavily upon those awaiting the arrival of the infants growing inside them. Reinforced by the liturgies for baptism and the churching of women incorporated in the Book of Common Prayer,[211] this was disseminated through the prayers that divines like Samuel Hieron and John Oliver composed for 'teeming women' in 'travail'.[212] Daniel Featley's immensely influential 'hand-maid to private devotion', *Ancilla pietatis* (1626) contained a similar set of petitions, which acknowledged the sorrows that befell the female sex for the transgressions of Eve, 'the Mother of the living', though, 'remembring mercy', God had also sanctified them to the propagation of his Church.[213] By contrast, there is no reference to original sin in two prayers for pregnant women written by the Laudian divine John Cosin.[214]

Expectant mothers often seem to have internalized these precepts. A prayer attributed to Lady Frances Abergavenny, for instance, humbly accepts these 'bitter pangs' as 'the rod of thy correction', 'justlie pronounced against me, and the whole generation of Adam' for 'the gilt and transgression of my progenitors'.[215] But if the ancestral curse upon Eve coloured attitudes to maternity among literate and pious people who recorded their emotions and feelings in diaries, it also coloured the outlook of their social inferiors. It was at the heart of 'the popular theology of reproduction' to which David Cressy refers.[216]

These were beliefs that came even more acutely into focus when mothers gave birth to imperfect and disabled infants. While a variety of explanations for such defects circulated—medical, diabolical, astrological, and providential—some divines explicitly listed such unnatural conceptions as among the judgements the Lord had visited upon the female sex for Eve's fatal transgression. Abraham Ross cited Augustine himself to this effect, and these were assumptions that many

---

[210] See Crawford, 'Construction and Experience of Maternity'; Leah Astbury, 'Breeding Women and Lusty Infants in Seventeenth-Century England' (PhD thesis, University of Cambridge, 2016). Anna French's forthcoming study, *Born in Sin: The Spirituality of Pregnancy, Birth and Infancy* promises to develop these themes in more detail.

[211] Cummings (ed.), *Book of Common Prayer*, pp. 144, 175–6.

[212] Samuel Hieron, *A helpe unto devotion containing certain moulds or forms of prayer* (1608; STC 13406.3), pp. 161–3; Oliver, *A present for teeming women*, p. 53.

[213] Daniel Featley, *Ancilla pietatis: or, the hand-maid to private devotion* (1626; STC 10726), p. 600, and see pp. 595–9.

[214] John Cosin, *A collection of private devotions in the practice of the ancient church, called the houres of prayer* (1627; STC 5816), pp. 202–4.

[215] Thomas Bentley (ed.), *The monument of matrons* (1582; STC 1892), pp. 95, 106, and see also 101–2, 197.

[216] David Cressy, *Birth, Marriage and Death: Ritual, Religion, and the Life-Cycle in Tudor and Stuart England* (Oxford, 1997), 16.

Protestants absorbed.[217] Blurring the hereditary sin derived from Adam with the trespasses she and her husband had committed during their lives, Elizabeth Egerton, countess of Bridgewater, prayed to God that her child would be born perfect and 'without any deformity, so that I and it's Father may not be punish't for our sinnes, in the deformity of our Babe'.[218]

The same tendency is apparent in the many ballads and pamphlets about monstrous births that flooded from presses, which also bear telltale marks of the reformed theology of the effects of the Fall. As well as drawing lessons about the egregious sins that such monsters were sent to chastise, they too quote the key biblical texts discussed in clerical commentaries on Genesis and treatises on original sin. Thus, a misshapen child born in the Isle of Wight in 1564 was said to have been 'conceyved in sin', and an infant without lips and an anus delivered near Dorchester in 1613 provoked its reporter to comment that 'the filth of sin remaineth still within us because their wanteth true Repentance in us'.[219] The monster that was the product of 'incestuous copulation' between unmarried first cousins in Herefordshire in 1600 prompted not only a prose sermon on the church's law regarding consanguinity but also the observation that 'by original guiltynes, we are subject to all sinne whatsoever'.[220] The anonymous authors of these ephemeral texts may have been ministers, but others were the work of ballad-mongers who mimicked their moralistic messages. Both offer indirect evidence of the propensity of contemporaries to interpret such monsters as a form of divine vengeance visited upon their parents for contravening the Ten Commandments, and especially the seventh regarding adultery. Even as they castigated the 'common custome' of accusing the progenitors of such infants of hidden crimes, defending their integrity and insisting that God's purpose in sending these pitiful creatures cannot be searched, they inadvertently perpetuated these uncharitable rumours.[221] Others could not pass up the chance to denounce whoredom, inferring that their fathers and mothers had committed fornication or broken the sacred bond of matrimony. Margaret Mere, who was delivered of a monster in Maidstone in 1568, for instance, was said to have 'played the naughty packe' and to have had sex promiscuously (Fig. 3.16).

[217] Ross, *Exposition*, 68. See Augustine, *Of the citie of God with the learned comments of Io. Lod. Viues*, trans. I. H. (1610; STC 916), bk xxii, ch. 19.

[218] BL, MS Egerton 607, fo. 33v, and see also fos 22v–27v, 28v, 39r, 47r. See also Bentley (ed.), *Monument of Matrons*, pp. 132–3, for a prayer that the child may come forth 'sound and perfect, without all deformitie'. On what would have been the birthday of her dead son on 1 February 1695, Lady Anne Halkett rejoiced in remembering 'the mercy the Lord shewed to mee in giving a Living Child withoutt blemish or deformity in his body'; see Suzanne Trill (ed.), *Lady Anne Halkett: Selected Self-Writings* (Aldershot, 2007), p. 172.

[219] *The true description of a monsterous chylde borne in the Ile of Wight* (1564; STC 1422); John Hilliard, *Fire from heaven. Burning the body of one John Hittchell* (1613; STC 13507.3), sig. B8v.

[220] I. R., *A most straunge, and true discourse, of the wonderfull judgement of God* (1600; STC 20575), pp. 3, 8–9, 12. On this case, see Robert Hole, 'Incest, Consanguinity and a Monstrous Birth in Rural England, January 1600', *Social History*, 25 (2000), 183–99.

[221] Quotation from *The true discription of two monsterous children borne at Herne in Kent* ([1565]; STC 6774).

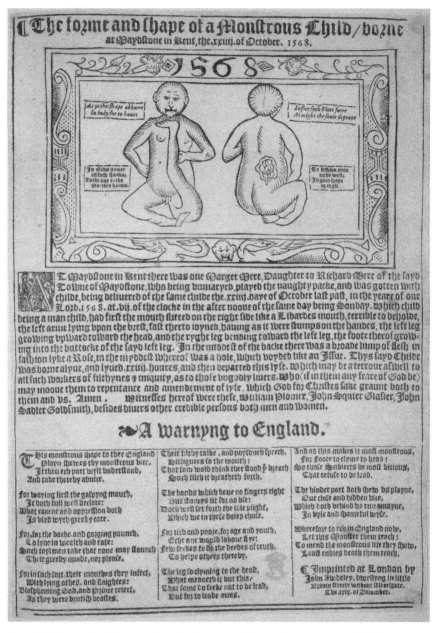

Fig. 3.16 The fruit of fornication: *The forme and shape of a monstrous child, borne at Maydstone in Kent, the.xxiiij. of October. 1568* (London, 1568).

Source: © British Library Board Huth 50.(38). All Rights Reserved/Bridgeman Images.

The Lancashire preacher William Leigh who reported the 'strange news' of conjoined twins born in Adlington in Lancashire in 1613 did not flinch from declaring that the father of these Janus-faced children was a man of 'very lewde carriage and conditions', while their mother was bastard. Her own illegitimacy was mirrored in that of her offspring in what Leigh saw as a patent demonstration of God's promise in several places in the Old Testament to punish flagrant sinners down to the third and fourth generations.[222]

Painted on the walls of some parish churches, the relevant passages in Exodus 20:4–5, Numbers 14:18, and Deuteronomy 5:9 were themselves very familiar.[223] Although sometimes read as a description of original sin, they were more frequently understood as referring to God's determination to exact revenge not merely upon the wicked but also their offspring. Richard Bernard's *Common catechisme* (1630) was one of many that drilled children in this precept:

Q. What a one is he?
A. A jealous God.
Q. What will his jealousie make him to doe?
A. To visite.
Q. What will he visite?
A. Sinnes.
Q. Whose sinnes?
A. The sinnes of the Fathers.
Q. Upon whom?
A. Upon the children.
Q. How farre?
A. To the third and fourth generation.[224]

As Calvin himself had admitted some laypeople were 'sadly perplexed' by these texts. The frequency with which the whole question of why 'the fathers smarte devolved to their posterity' and how just it was for the Lord's wrath to fall on the heads of both an individual and 'all his lineage' was addressed by the clergy suggests that it remained a contested topic.[225] One reason for this was the contradictory pronouncements found in other parts of Scripture, especially Ezekiel 18:20 ('The son shall not bear the iniquity of the father, neither shall the father bear the iniquity of the son.') and John 9:3, where Jesus tells his disciples that the blind

---

[222] *The forme and shape of a monstrous child, borne at Maydstone in Kent, the.xxiiii. of October. 1568* ([1568]; STC 17194); William Leigh, *Strange newes of a prodigious monster, borne in the township of Adlington in the parish of Standish in the countie of Lancaster* (1613; STC 15428), esp. sig. A4r–v.

[223] e.g., at All Saints parish church, Aston, near Sheffield, where they still survive.

[224] Richard Bernard, *The common catechisme, with a commentarie thereupon, by questions and answers* (1630; STC 1929), sig. B3v.

[225] Calvin, *Institutes*, vol. i, pp. 330–3; John King, *Lectures upon Jonas delivered at Yorke in the yeare of our Lorde 1594* (Oxford, 1600; STC 14978), pp. 131–5.

man to whom he restores sight suffers not for his own sins or those of his parents, but so that the glory of God might be revealed. These verses implied that retributive justice did not extend to either previous or subsequent generations.

Reconciling these discordant notes in the Bible exercised many. Calvin said that it was 'no absurditie' that the Almighty punished reprobate children for the wickedness of their parents, but necessary to demonstrate the grievousness of their sins.[226] The Hertfordshire divine Andrew Willett explained that such temporal chastisements were 'medicinall corrections' inflicted upon the great-grandchildren of sinners 'because so long the impietie of the fathers may be had in remembrance'. He also defended it with reference to traitors whose surviving relatives were legitimately deprived of the goods and honours they were due as heirs and insisted that it was a privilege 'peculiar to God' to extend his judgements to the tenth generation, as in the case of the posterity of Canaan.[227] Preaching at Grantham in Lincolnshire in 1621, Robert Sanderson offered an extended exposition of the issue, insisting that the punishments God inflicted were temporal and outward rather than spiritual and inward. If He removed the candlestick of the Gospel from a nation or people 'for the sinnes and impieties of their Ancestors in some former generations', this did not affect their eschatological fate individually. The lesson he hoped his adult hearers would learn from this was the danger of passing sin down by nature, example, and education 'from the father to the son, and so downeward, by a kind of lineall descent from predecessours to posterity'.[228] In *Religio domestica rediviva* (1655), Philip Goodwin warned that though 'prophane prayerlesse families' might flourish for a generation or two, in the third and fourth 'Gods furie' would inevitably find them out, 'pouring out plagues upon their posterities' with 'the full Vialls of his vengeance'.[229] William Gearing similarly dismissed the 'false and foolish conceits' of those who resisted this precept, insisting that 'Fathers in sinning, do not only sin in their own destruction, but to the destruction of the Children that are yet unborn'.[230]

Anxiety that the sins of the fathers would indeed to be visited on daughters and sons seems to have been most deeply felt in relation to the cardinal offences of idolatry and sacrilege. The centrality of the first in Reformation thought has been exhaustively investigated by Margaret Aston, but the worry that this offence would be punished not merely in the present but also in the future

---

[226] Calvin, *Commentarie*, p. 231.

[227] Andrew Willet, *Hexapla in Exodum, that is a sixfold commentary upon the second booke of Moses called Exodus* (1633; first publ. 1608; STC 25684), pp. 282–5; Willet, *Hexapla in Genesin*, pp. 91–2.

[228] Robert Sanderson, *Ten sermons preached I. Ad clerum. II. Ad magistrum. III. Ad populum* (1627; STC 21705), pp. 371–5, 378–80.

[229] Philip Goodwin, *Religio domestica rediviva: or, Family-religion revived* (1655; Wing G1218), pp. 136–8. For Henry Garnet's deployment of this text to warn against heresy, see Chapter 2 above.

[230] Gearing, *Pious fathers*, pp. 179–80.

deserves further emphasis.[231] It is significant that these scriptural warnings were issued in the context of the proscription against making and worshipping images. They were admonitory elements of the Decalogue, a moral code that the Protestant Reformation elevated to new importance and within which idolatry became not only pre-eminent but a shorthand for all ten commandments.[232] Robert Allen responded robustly to the objection that this form of hereditary retributive justice was 'unequal' by saying that it was rather a 'wonderfull mercie, that he doth so graciously limite and restraine the curse: seeing he might justly withdraw his grace from the whole posteritie of the Idolaters, as from an illegitimate and bastardly seede' and by stressing that those who forsook the sin of their fathers and worshipped God truly would escape this inherited punishment.[233]

At least some people whose lives spanned the chasm opened up by the break with Rome and whose families were riven by it were haunted by these biblical passages threatening inherited judgements. As an anguished letter sent by an unknown elderly man to his son Harry in the Elizabethan period reveals, it weighed heavily on the minds of Protestant children whose parents persisted in the Catholicism in which they had been baptized and raised. He wrote, 'you cry out to me soe pittyfully and begging me soe kindely that I should not…cause god to punnish them for my sinnes', because it is written in the Scriptures 'I will lay the fathers sinnes upon the children unto the third and fowerth generation'. Harry's passionate plea that his father abandon papistry and embrace the faith of the Church of England seems to have been driven not only by concern for the latter's soul but also by the fear that he himself would be judged for the false religion to which his parent still, albeit rather eccentrically, clung. It sprang from a settled conviction that the Lord is 'a jealous God' who righteously visits the evils committed by men and women upon their descendants.[234] These assumptions also coloured the outlook of Edward Harley, who interpreted the destruction of the family's seat at Brampton Bryan in Herefordshire during the Civil Wars as a punishment 'for the sins and iniquities of my forefathers, who were idolaters and sinners'. He saw the incineration of the castle and church as an indictment of the popery professed by his ancestors.[235]

Increasingly, however, it seems to have been less the sin of idolatry than of sacrilege that troubled contemporaries. For some this took the form of the blood guilt associated with the mass murder of the Marian martyrs. In the 1640s,

---

[231] Margaret Aston, *England's Iconoclasts* (Oxford, 1988); Aston, *Broken Idols*.

[232] See Bossy, 'Moral Arithmetic'; Willis, *Reformation of the Decalogue*, esp. pp. 192–8 on idolatry.

[233] Robert Allen, *A treasurie of catechisme, or Christian instruction* (1600; STC 366), pp. 71–2.

[234] Bodl., MS Rawlinson D. 1345 (Theological Tracts), fos 33v, 36v, 56r. I am grateful to Alison Shell for drawing my attention to this manuscript.

[235] Jennifer Heller, 'Reading "Wrecks of History" and the Harley Family Narrative', *The Seventeenth Century*, 32 (2017), 139–59, at 152.

leading puritans called for this to be acknowledged and avenged, lest divine judgement be visited upon the land. As Karl Gunther has shown, it inspired impassioned calls for action 'to resolve events that had happened long before they were born'.[236] However, as time progressed, it was the violent iconoclasm carried out in the mid-sixteenth century in the name of purification that caused most trepidation in this respect. Ironically, these were not people who had witnessed or participated in the upheavals of the 1530s, 1540s, and 1550s; they were their children and grandchildren. Deploring the excessive contempt for sacred space that the dissolution of the monasteries seemed in hindsight to represent and the tendency of the crusade against idols to tip over into outright profanation, Protestants became preoccupied with the fate of those who had committed sacrilege in the first age of the Reformation.

Writing in the 1590s, Michael Sherbrooke worried that its effects were still being felt: 'Such is the Providence of God to punish Sinners in making themselves Instruments to punish themselves, and all their Posterity, from Generation to Generation.'[237] Using the tools of genealogy and history, Clement and Henry Spelman traced the disasters that had befallen families who had purchased monastic lands and saw the curtailment of their pedigrees and lineages as proof that the Lord was slow to forgive this most heinous of sins. Sir Thomas Gresham, owner of Malsingham Abbey, for instance, had died suddenly in his kitchen without male issue. A whole range of other misfortunes were similarly linked causally with sacrilege, including lunacy, murder, and execution for treason. The family of Henry Somerset, Lord Herbert, earl of Worcester, who had helped pass the legislation, was more fortunate than most, 'for their lineal descent remains entire and without blemish, having at this day many Noble Branches'. But it too had not entirely escaped the hand of God, with one son slaughtered in battle and another beheaded at York.[238] It is indicative of the sea change in opinion that accompanied the passage of the generations that Spelman and others also detected these processes at work in the dying out and 'extinguishment' of the Tudor dynasty itself. Henry VIII's own trouble producing an heir was mirrored in

[236] Karl Gunther, '"Not Revenged, nor Repented of": Martyrs and England's Long Reformation', *Reformation*, 24 (2019), 138–150, at 150.
[237] Michael Sherbrook, 'The Falle of Religiouse Howses, Colleges, Chantreys, Hospitalls, &c', in A. G. Dickens (ed.), *Tudor Treatises*, Yorkshire Archaeological Society Record Series 125 (Leeds, 1959), p. 125.
[238] Clement Spelman, *A letter from Utercht [sic], to the Assembly of Divines at Westminster: shewing the conversion of church-lands to lay-uses, to be condemned…as a detestable sacriledge before God, and provoking his heavy judgements* (1648; Wing S4915); Henry Spelman, *The history and fate of sacrilege, discover'd by examples of scripture, of heathens, and of Christians; from the beginning of the world, continually to this day* (1698; Wing S4927), ch. 7, citations at pp. 262 and 211. On sacrilege, see Michael Kelly, 'The Invasion of Things Sacred: Church, Property and Sacrilege in Early Modern England' (PhD thesis, University of Notre Dame, 2013).

in the childlessness of his offspring.[239] The unruly elements of England's early Reformation had come home to roost in the premature death and infertility of the king's heirs.

The Descent of Dissent

These developments raise the associated question of whether contemporaries thought that the religious crimes that had pulled down divine anger upon the heads of successive generations were themselves hereditary. Did particular forms of actual sin, like original sin, run in families? In particular, did the religious dissidence that many believed to be inflaming God's ire in the wake of the sixteenth-century Reformation have an ancestral dimension? The etymology of the word heresy, which derives from the Greek for choice, partially inhibited this, as did the discourse surrounding it, which stressed the voluntarism of the heretic.[240] But there were moments when early modern people talked about heresy and popery as if they were inherited characteristics. They moved beyond the traditional convention of describing them as forms of cancer and gangrene to thinking about them as conditions that descended lineally. The patterns of familial heterodoxy and domestic dissent explored in Chapter 2 provoked attention and comment. Some officials spoke of Lollardy in terms that implied that it was transmitted from father to son by blood. The abjured heretic William Bocher of Steeple Bumpstead in Essex was noted to have come from 'vicious stock' and to be the grandson of a man who had been executed for heresy. When John Browne of Ashford in Kent was burnt at the stake in 1512, 'one Chilton, the baily-arrant, bade cast in Browne's child also, for they would spring, said he, of his ashes'.[241] Such episodes suggest that polemical Catholic rhetoric that denounced heretics as the spawn of Satan shaped perception of its adherents at the grassroots. Denunciations of the 'sons of iniquity [who] are trying to introduce into this country of ours the old and accursed Wycliffite heresy and its foster child the Lutheran heresy' like those embedded in the licence to read prohibited books that Cuthbert Tunstall issued to Thomas More in 1528 had local repercussions.[242] They arguably predisposed people to look for family connections and resemblances, though when these were noticed, they were often presumed to be the product of immersion, contact, emulation, and indoctrination. In other words, they were generally thought to be the

---

[239] Spelman, *History and Fate*, pp. 191–3. See also Ephraim Udall, *Noli me tangere is a thing to be thought on* (1647; Wing U11), p. 10.

[240] See *OED*, s.v. 'heresy'.

[241] Shannon McSheffrey, *Gender and Heresy: Women and Men in Lollard Communities 1420–1530* (Philadelphia,PA, 1995), ch. 4, at pp. 97–8.

[242] *English Historical Documents*, vol. v, *1485–1558*, ed. C. H. Williams (1995), p. 828.

consequence of nurture (human and diabolical) rather than nature. The sin of heresy was not thought of as genealogical in the same way as original sin, let alone understood as what we would now call a congenital condition. Nevertheless the potential for slippage and hermeneutic ambiguity was ever-present.

Similar phraseology was applied to describe Catholicism. Protestant propagandists often alleged that it was transmitted in a manner comparable to infant breastfeeding. The official homily on idolatry, for instance, said that the 'rablement' of the Popish Church 'drunk' this heinous sin in 'almost with their Mothers Milk'. This was echoed by the Protestant convert Thomas Clarke, who described, in the course of his recantation at Paul's Cross, how he had been brought up in the seminary at Rheims: 'to this mother of errors and nurse of Idolatry did I repayre being from my childhoode in some sort fostered with hers or the like poysoned milke'. In a biblical commentary published in 1618, William Attersoll similarly reproved 'sottish and ignorant Recusants' who had 'sucked in their superstition and impiety', whereby their religion had 'continued from father to sonne for manie hundred yeeres'. The 'horrible abhomination wherein they haue bene nuzled' from birth was one of the reasons why popery had proved so hard to eradicate.[243]

Such expressions materially affected—and were affected by—social developments that were occurring on the ground. Officials charged with detecting and apprehending the networks of church papistry and recusancy that flummoxed the Elizabethan government's attempts to eradicate resistance to the Reformation were attuned to the fact that these centred on the household and implicated successive generations of people linked by ties of consanguinity and affinity. The 'petigrew' [pedigree] of the Fitzherbert family drawn up by a spy in 1594 was a device for representing the religious loyalty of its members, who include priests, outlawed fugitives, and imprisoned dissidents. Each circle enclosing a name is a locus of suspicion, beneath which are written short tags such as 'trator', 'daungerous', and 'very badd'. Connected by arrows and lines of inheritance, this genealogical diagram illustrates the perceived link between blood ties and religio-political dissent. Interestingly, the one relative who is a 'good subject' sits apart from it in splendid isolation as the only worthy heir of his popish uncle's estates, and thereby the progenitor of a Protestant family (Fig. 3.17).[244]

By the late seventeenth century, the virulent strain of anti-Catholicism to which this pedigree attests seemed to some Catholics to be a generational

---

[243] *Certain sermons or homilies appointed to be read in churches in the time of Queen Elizabeth of famous memory and now reprinted for the use of private families, in two parts* (1687 edn; Wing C4091I), p. 197; Thomas Clarke, *The recantation of Thomas Clarke* (1593; STC 5366), sigs B1v–2r; William Attersoll, *A commentarie vpon the fourth booke of Moses, called Numbers* (1618; STC 893), p. 586.

[244] TNA, SP 12/235/88. See the discussion of this document in Julian Yates, 'Parasitic Geographies: Manifesting Catholic Identity in Early Modern England', in Arthur F. Marotti (ed.), *Catholicism and Anti-Catholicism in Early Modern English Texts* (Basingstoke, 1999), pp. 63–84, at pp. 72–4.

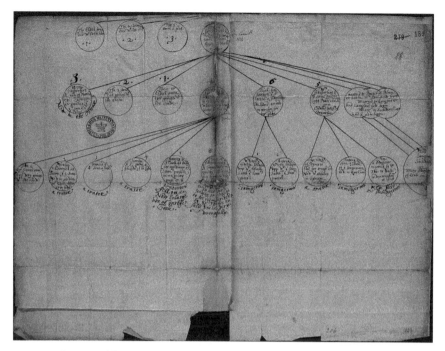

Fig. 3.17 'Petigrew' [pedigree] of the Fitzherbert family drawn up by a spy in 1594.
Source: The National Archives, Kew, State Papers Domestic 12/235, fo. 189.

tendency itself. In a memoir of the 'popish plot' fabricated by Titus Oates published in 1685, one Protestant declared that 'the frenzy of our Fathers' in this
respect was 'hereditary': 'the extravagant Apprehensions of the Danger of Popery
being that natural imperfection that the generality of English men are as much
born to, as men are to a Club-Foot, or a Hunch-back, or any other Deformity; and
really, which they are almost as hardly to be cured of'.[245] In an earlier pamphlet,
in a similar vein, the Whore of Babylon is made to complain that boys and youths
'have suckt in your Enmity against Me, with your Mothers Milk.[246]

Witchcraft was viewed through the same lens and seen as a skill that travelled,
especially but not exclusively, down the matrilineal line, in an inversion of the
patriarchal order and of primogeniture that befitted this demonic crime. Legal
records and news reports reveal that mothers and daughters were frequently
caught up in a whirlpool of accusation and rumour, as in the case of Goodwife
and Mistress Champnes in Canterbury in 1571, who were identified as working
together to bewitch their neighbours' child. But victims and witnesses implicated

[245] *The memoires of Titus Oates written for publick satisfaction* (1685; Wing M1674), p. 14.
[246] Jeremy Taylor, *The last speech, and confession of the whore of Babylon, at her place of execution,
on the fifth of November last* (1673; Wing L505), p. 1.

sons, sisters, and cousins too. The offspring of suspected witches were at high risk, because it was popularly supposed that the science of sorcery and the gift of inflicting maleficia ran in families. In the Maidstone trials in 1652 spectators called for a witch's body to be burnt to ashes because this would prevent her blood 'from becoming hereditary to her Progeny in the same evill'.[247] Others supposed that witchcraft was transmitted by instruction and tradition and that co-resident relatives, friends, and servants were carefully nurtured in the black arts by their kith and kin. The Scottish witch Agnes Sampson confessed that she had learnt her skill and her spell-like prayer from her father.[248]

As in Germany, where entire dynasties were prosecuted, such episodes were underpinned by concerns about godly upbringing, poor parenting, and patriarchy that reflect the impact of the texts on 'domesticall duties' and household religion discussed in Chapter 2.[249] Demonological literature fed the impression that there was a connection between motherhood and diabolism, not least in the guise of the witch's familiar. The pet demons that she suckled with her blood represented a form of what Deborah Willis has aptly described as 'malevolent nurture', while Lyndal Roper has taught us to be alert to the role of anxieties about fertility and maternity in fuelling the Continental witch craze.[250] Like other enemies of God, witches were entangled in the spidery webs woven by the early modern genealogical imagination. In discussing the drive to restrain and eradicate them, we should be as attentive to generation as to gender.

The same tendencies are detectable in connection with the sprawling sects that seemed to contemporaries to be generating spontaneously in the middle years of the seventeenth century. Alongside the age-old impulse to describe them in terms of disease that found its most passionate expression in Thomas Edwards' *Gangraena* ran a perennial instinct to see them as perversions bred in the nest of the family and household.[251] However we interpret the genealogical commonplaces

---

[247] Malcolm Gaskill, 'Witchcraft in Early Modern Kent: Stereotypes and the Background to Accusations', in Jonathan Barry, Marianne Hester, and Gareth Roberts (eds), *Witchcraft in Early Modern Europe: Studies in Culture and Belief* (Cambridge, 1996), pp. 257–87, at pp. 277–8. For the Maidstone episode, see H. F., *A prodigious & tragical history of the arraignment, tryall, confession, and condemnation of six witches at Maidstone in Kent* (1652; Wing G13), p. 5. See also Clive Holmes, 'Women: Witnesses and Witches', *P&P*, 140 (1993), 45–78, at 51.

[248] See William Perkins, *A discourse of the damned art of witchcraft* (Cambridge, 1608; STC 19697), pp. 202–3; Richard Bernard, *A guide to grand-jury men, divided into two books* (1629 edn; STC 1944), pp. 206–7. For Agnes Sampson, see Lawrence Normand and Gareth Roberts (eds), *Witchcraft in Early Modern Scotland* (2000), p. 143.

[249] Alison Rowlands, 'Gender, Ungodly Parents and a Witch Family in Seventeenth-Century Germany', *P&P*, 232 (2016), 45–86.

[250] Deborah Willis, *Malevolent Nurture: Witch-Hunting and Maternal Power in Early Modern England* (Ithaca, NY, 1995), esp. ch. 2; Lyndal Roper, *Witch Craze: Terror and Fantasy in Baroque Germany* (New Haven, CT, 2004).

[251] Thomas Edwards, *Gangraena: or a catalogue and discovery of many of the errours, heresies, blasphemies and pernicious practices of the sectaries of this time, vented and acted in England in these four last years* (1646; Wing E228). See Ann Hughes, *Gangraena and the Struggle for the English Revolution*

that pervade polemical literature, they offer insight into a mental universe within which it made sense to perceive religious deviance as something that ran in the blood.

The preceding paragraphs provide a fresh perspective on Margaret Spufford's contested theory regarding the 'descent of dissent'. The efforts of Spufford and some of her students to test the hypothesis that nonconformity was a phenomenon that carried across from one generation to the next, mutating from Lollardy to evangelical Protestantism, separatism, and Quakerism as it did so, are not without their methodological problems, as Patrick Collinson and others have pointed out. Even where techniques of family reconstitution suggest continuities they are far from conclusive. They may tell us more about the influence of environment than about inherited patterns of radical religious dissidence. It is doubtful that 'telling case-histories of godliness begetting godliness over the generations' can be placed on a 'scientific basis' and demonstrated beyond doubt to be true.[252]

It remains intriguing that some contemporaries anticipated the Spuffordian suggestion that sectarian dissent had a clearly ancestral dimension. The link they drew between religious deviance and lineage prompts reflection and invites comparison with unsettling developments elsewhere in Europe. It resonates with the preoccupations about spiritual purity that led to the emergence of the blood laws (*estatutos de limpieza de sangre*) in fifteenth- and sixteenth-century Spain and Portugal, though it is only a faint echo of the animus these inflamed against religious minorities there. An obsession with identifying new converts to Christianity from Judaism who 'still held on their lips the milk of their ancestors' recent perversity' was a *raison d'être* of the Inquisition and gathered momentum to include the blood descendants of the condemned. Cementing the connections between reproduction, faith, and heredity, it laid the foundations for a form of discrimination that fused religious prejudice with emerging assumptions about immutable human differences.[253] It provoked a virulent literature in which Catholics condemned 'Christians only in name' as 'sons of iniquity', denigrated conversos for returning to their original vomit, and stressed their utter inability to escape the

(Oxford, 2004); David Loewenstein, *Treacherous Faith: The Specter of Heresy in Early Modern English Literature and Culture* (Oxford, 2013), ch. 5.

[252] Margaret Spufford, 'The Importance of Religion in the Sixteenth and Seventeenth Centuries', in *eadem* (ed.), *The World of Rural Dissenters 1520–1725* (Cambridge, 1995), pp. 23–40; and Nesta Evans, 'The Descent of Dissenters in the Chiltern Hundreds', ibid., pp. 288–308, and Appendix B, pp. 401–11. Patrick Collinson's comments are made in the course of his 'Critical Conclusion', ibid., pp. 388–96, at p. 393. See also Michael Questier, 'Catholicism, Kinship and the Public Memory of Sir Thomas More', *JEH*, 53 (2002), 476–509, at 478–9.

[253] See Gregory B. Kaplan, 'The Inception of *Limpieza de Sangre* (Purity of Blood) and its Impact in Medieval and Golden Age Spain', in Amy Aronson-Friedman and Gregory B. Kaplan (eds), *Marginal Voices* (Leiden, 2010), pp. 19–41. In the later sixteenth century, these ideas infiltrated and also transformed the admission policy of the Society of Jesus itself: Robert Aleksander Maryks, *The Jesuit Order as a Synagogue of Jews: Jesuits of Jewish Ancestry and Purity-of-Blood Laws in the Early Society of Jesus* (Leiden, 2010), quotation at p. 30.

taint of their Jewish heritage. David Nirenberg has argued that this was the outcome of a process of conflict in which lineage became a newly meaningful way of thinking about both Christian and Jewish identity in the Iberian peninsula.[254] Imported across the Atlantic, these 'genealogical fictions' coalesced with questions of colour in ways that shaped and complicated relations with people of indigenous descent in colonial contexts that were increasingly preoccupied with the issue of miscegenation.[255]

As we shall see in more detail in Chapter 4, a tendency for genealogy and grace to become entangled was also one of the repercussions of the English Reformations. Protestant biblicism was a crucible in which the idea that salvation might be inherited coexisted uneasily with the precept that parents had no control over the fate of their children. This was ultimately governed not by education and love but by the mysterious double decree of predestination and reprobation.

Polemical Pedigrees

Genealogy had another role in the unfolding drama of England's protracted religious revolution. It was a powerful weapon in inter- and intraconfessional controversy and an established mode of heresiography. The sixteenth and seventeenth centuries saw the publication of many satirical pictures showing the pedigrees of heresy and popery. These often took the form of family trees, the branches and leaves of which represented fissiparous tendencies and breakaway movements. Here exuberant growth was not a form of fertility that signalled divine approbation but rather a symbol of the chaotic and uncontrolled plurality that threatened the still cherished ideal of Christian unity. It represented the fragmentation of truth that was the chief but unintended consequence of the European Reformations. It is an iconography that further highlights the extent to which the debates that divided people by faith turned on the question of generation, human and botanical.

Genealogy was a device for denouncing heresy that had ancient roots. Closely linked with the assumption that it was fathered by the Devil, both literally and metaphorically, it had long been wielded as a rhetorical tool in the battle against heterodoxy. Its reappearance in response to Lollardy and Lutheranism in early

---

[254] David Nirenberg, 'Mass Conversion and Genealogical Mentalities: Jews and Christians in Fifteenth-Century Spain', *P&P*, 174 (2002), 3–41, at 24. See also *idem*, 'Was there Race before Modernity? The Example of Jewish Blood in Late Medieval Spain', in Miriam Eliav-Feldon, Benjamin Isaac, and Joseph Ziegler (eds), *The Origins of Racism in the West* (Cambridge, 2009), pp. 232–64; Jonathan M. Elukin, 'From Jew to Christian? Conversion and Immutability in Medieval Europe', in James Muldoon (ed.), *Varieties of Religious Conversion in the Middle Ages* (Gainesville, FL, 1997), pp. 171–89.

[255] María Elena Martínez, *Genealogical Fictions: Limpieza de Sangre, Religion, and Gender in Colonial Mexico* (Stanford, CA, 2008), esp ch. 2, pp. 46–54; Stuart Schwartz, *Blood and Boundaries: The Limits of Religious and Racial Encounter in Early Modern Latin America* (Waltham, MA, 2021).

and mid-sixteenth-century England was predictable. Both the vocabulary and the trope flourished in this environment. We only have second-hand knowledge of a Catholic broadside entitled 'Genealogy of Heresye', via the characteristically vituperative denunciation of it published by the former Carmelite friar John Bale in Geneva in 1545, during the final reactionary years of Henry VIII's reign. Printed in 1542, two editions of this ballad by John Huntingdon circulated so widely 'amonge the common people in a wonderfull nombre of copyes' that Bale felt to compelled to counteract its 'wycked blasphemyes'. The text was compiled by an 'olde pestilent Papyst' and 'Romyshe rybalde' under the pseudonym Ponce Pantolabus, whose subsequent repentance and conversion from a wolf into a lamb did nothing to ameliorate Bale's indignation. This 'abhomyable Jest' apparently attacked Protestantism and its faithful witnesses as a monstrous birth that gave rise to a diabolical lineage. The ballad ingeniously deployed the biblical language of 'begat' to locate the satanic origins of the upstart new religion, trace its descent through 'blynde obstynacye', 'myschaunce', and 'dame ignoraunce', and delineate its unseemly children—'stryfe', 'ambycyon' and 'supersticyon'. Concluding by exhorting its readers to pray for Prince Edward, it must be seen as a political intervention aimed at securing a conservative and pro-Catholic succession and settlement.[256]

While no example of this ephemeral text survives, the polemical strategy it deployed remained very attractive to those seeking to reverse the break with Rome and reunite England with the Mother Church. Thomas Stapleton's 1565 translation of a work of controversy by the German theologian Fridericus Staphylus contains a fold-out plate entitled 'A show of the Protestants Petigrew', which attacks 'its first founders and fathers'. Itself borrowed from a Continental prototype, in this woodcut Protestantism springs out of the trunk of the 'arch heretics' Martin Luther and his wife Katharina van Bora, while from its three main branches (Bernard Rotman, Philip Melanchthon and Ulrich Zwingli) sprout a host of sects, illustrating the unholy diversity engendered by the Reformation. Below, the figure of the monk calf, a deformed creature with a flap of skin like a cowl, whose birth was itself harnessed for confessional ends, symbolizes the evil life and doctrine of the Wittenberg reformer.[257] It is an image that derives added edge from the fact that Protestantism defended clerical marriage and celebrated sexual relationships between laymen and women within the bonds of wedlock.

---

[256] John Bale, *A mysterye of inyquyte contayned within the heretycall genealogye of Ponce Pantolabus, is here both dysclosed & confuted* (Geneva [Antwerp], 1545; STC 1303). Quotations are taken from the preface: sigs A1v–A3r, fos 1v, 4r, 84v–86r. On Huntingdon, who himself later converted to reformist views, see *The Gospel and Henry VIII: Evangelicals in the Early English Reformation* (Cambridge, 2003), p. 75, 101–2.

[257] Fridericus Staphylus, *The apologie of Fridericus Staphylus*, trans. Thomas Stapleton (Antwerp, 1565; STC 23230), fold-out plate following p. 254. On the monk calf, see R. W. Scribner, *For the Sake of Simple Folk: Popular Propaganda for the German Reformation* (Oxford, 1994 edn; first publ. 1981), pp. 127–32.

The age-old connection between heresy and lechery upon which this print plays
was itself a genealogical trope, and one that was frequently rearticulated to attack
the Reformation. Peter Frarin's *Oration against the Unlawfull Insurrections of the
Protestants of our Time* appeared in English in 1566 and contains a series of illustrations depicting the sexual promiscuity of Luther and Calvin.[258]

For some Elizabethan and Jacobean Catholics, anti-Protestant pedigrees provided a pictorial focal point for religious resistance. An elaborate two-volume
polemical commonplace book associated with the Tresham family incorporates
another version of this visual genealogy. Labelled 'The tree of apostacie or Roote
of Deathe', its iconography is clearly based on the one in the Staphylus text, but it
has been adapted and improvised in ways that make it even more overtly hostile
to heresy (Fig. 3.18). It begins with the union of 'a filthy Whore and wicked
Nunne' and the 'Apostata frier that all theise sturres beganne', from whose academic successor Melanchthon emerge three burgeoning shoots, one of which is
inscribed with the words 'Disorderly and unruly Lutherans'. This 'fayre figure' is a
personal device for cultivating hatred of the licentious and dastardly heretics
whose doctrine has destroyed the true religion in England.[259] In a German variation
on this theme entitled *Delineatio Malae Arboris Lutheranae* published in 1589,
the central figure is a seven-headed Luther. The print also drives home the point
that Protestantism springs from a form of spiritual incest: above the deformed
reformer on the trunk of the insect-infested tree is a scroll with the words '*soror,
mea sponsa*' (my sister, my spouse).[260]

This was a method of discrediting Protestantism that seventeenth-century
Catholic propagandists continued to deploy. Laurence Anderton's 1633 tract, *The
progenie of Catholicks and Protestants* performed the double task of proving 'the
lineal Descent of Catholicks...from the Primitive Church' and exposing the shal-
low ancestry of a 'novel sect' that arrogantly boasted its antiquity.[261] It appeared in
the same year as a treatise entitled *Puritanisme the mother, sinne the daughter*,
written by a Catholic priest with the initials B. C., which exposed the 'flagitious
Lives' of the principal Protestant doctors—Beza, Calvin, Ochinus, Zwingli, and
Luther—alongside the theological doctrines that led their English disciples
into the thickets of 'Vice, Sinne, and Impiety'. The occasion for writing it was the

---

[258] Peter Frarin, *An oration against the unlawfull insurrections of the protestantes of our time, under
pretence to refourme religion*, trans. [John Fowler] (Antwerp, [1566]; STC 11333). This was reprinted
in Douai in 1607/8.
[259] Bodl., MS Eng.th.b.1–2, vol.1, p. 798.
[260] Abraham Nagel, *Delineatio Malae Arboris Lutheranae* ((Ingoldstat, 1589).
[261] Lawrence Anderton, *The progenie of Catholicks and Protestants. Whereby on the one side is
proved the lineal descent of Catholicks, for the Roman faith and religion, from the holie fathers of the
primitive Church...and on the other, the never-being of Protestants or their novel sect during al the fore-
sayd time* (Rouen, 1633; STC 579).

Fig. 3.18 'The tree of apostacie or Roote of Deathe', springing from Katharina von Bora and Martin Luther.

Source: Bodleian Library, Oxford, MS Eng.th.b.1-2, p. 798.

incident in which the Welsh puritan Enoch ap Evan had killed his own brother and mother with an axe, a murder story about a family destroyed by the adherence of one of its sons to Protestant extremism.[262]

Genealogy was too effective as a piece of confessional ammunition for Protestants to allow their Catholic opponents to monopolize it. Taking a leaf out of the book of Luther, evangelicals exploited it from the early days of the English Reformation to undermine popery and associated enemies. Attributed to Miles Coverdale, *The original & sprynge of all sectes & orders* (1537) was a translation of a Dutch work describing the various species of monasticism engendered by the Bishop of Rome, together with the rival Christian churches of Greece, Russia, Armenia, and elsewhere that it failed to recognize and the different factions of Jews and Hebrews. These run from 'barefooted freres' and the Brethren of Jerusalem to the Pharisees and Sadducces.[263] In the preface to his 'Mysterye of inyquyte' confuting Ponce Pantolabus, Bale approvingly quoted Paul's admonition to his disciples Titus and Timothy to spurn genealogies as fabulous and vain. Yet his own book is itself a kind of pedigree of the Antichrist, whose kingdom it describes as 'a false, fylthye, fleshlye, whoryshe, preposterouse, prostybulouse, promiscuouse, and abhominable generacion'. It operates, in a diabolical inversion of the normal order, with the child begetting his father and grandfather '& all in the femynine gender'. Accusing Catholicism of 'stinkynge sodomitycall' sexual perversity, his book denounces the sensual appetites of St Dunstan, the scandal of nuns' bastards, and episcopal brothels and stews. Alluding to the 'carnall chyldren' of biblical sinners such as Ham, Esau, Manasses, and Herod, it sees popery as one of the offspring begotten by the Devil himself.[264] John Barthlet's *Pedegrewe of heretiques* (1566) is another text in the same vein, an encyclopedic taxonomy of colourful varieties of Catholic error from 'Metamorphistes' and 'Mice feeders' to 'Bread Spoylers' and 'Hallowers' who baptize their children by belching upon them. Attached to it is 'This poysonous tree planted in Rome', a parody of the sacred Tree of Jesse (Fig. 3.19). Its roots lie in Simon Magus and Judas and are fertilized by the world's wealth and watered by ignorance, and its double trunks grow upwards from Gratian and Peter Lombard into the leaves of religious orders and a succession of popes. At the top is the Lutheran answer to the monk calf, the

[262] B. C., *Puritanisme the mother, sinne the daughter. Or a treatise, wherein is demonstrated from twenty severall doctrines, and positions of puritanisme; that the fayth and religion of the puritans, doth forcibly induce its professours to the perpetrating of sinne, and doth warrant the committing of the same* ([St Omer], 1633; STC 4264), sig. *7r, *8r–v. For this case, see Peter Lake, 'Puritanism, Arminianism and a Shropshire Axe-Murder', *Midland History*, 15 (1990) 37–64.

[263] *The original & sprynge of all sectes & orders by whome, whan or were they beganne*, trans. [Miles Coverdale?] ([Southwark], 1537; STC 18849).

[264] Bale, *Mysterye*, fos 1v, 2r, 2v, 19v–20r, 20v, 75r, 2v. According to the OED, 'prostibulous' means 'relating to or suggestion of a prostitute, meretricious'. The word is now obsolete.

Fig. 3.19 'This poysonous tree planted in Rome', in John Barthlet, *The pedegrewe of heretiques* (1566), fold-out plate.

Source: Folger Shakespeare Library, Washington DC, STC 1534. Folger Digital Image Collection.

papal ass supposedly discovered in the Tiber in Rome in 1496, a hybrid creature, part donkey, part dragon, part woman, which Protestants interpreted as an apocalyptic portent.[265]

These tactics continued to be used by later anti-Catholic controversialists.[266] Lewis Owen's 1628 *Unmasking of all popish monks, friers and Jesuits* is a reworking of the books by Coverdale, Bale, and Barthlet already discussed, updated and supplemented with discussion of the Society of Jesus and its founder, 'the halting holy-hee Mid-wife' Ignatius Loyola, and the English convents established overseas, including the Bridgettine house in Lisbon.[267] This had been the subject of an equally distasteful dissection or 'anatomie' by Thomas Robinson in 1623, the title page of which literally pulled aside the curtain concealing the naughty and incestuous liaisons between the sisters and brothers of this double monastery.[268] Both emerged in a context in which scurrilous broadsides, including *A nest of nunnes egges, strangely hatched*, readily found Protestant buyers.[269] Rechristened a *Genealogie* when it was republished in 1646, Owen's tract was a warning to Great Britain and Ireland to take heed of the 'Romish Locusts' who were gathering once more.[270] The idea that the popish Antichrist was 'lineally descended from the divell' was encapsulated more concisely in various pamphlets and ballads reprinted at moments of anti-Catholic crisis and Protestant triumph. In describing the Church of Rome's diabolical lineage and its 'first risening and ripening', their authors once again made abundant use of the term 'begat' and of the interconnected vocabularies of procreation and agriculture.[271]

In turn, Protestants mobilized the ancient device of equating religious deviants with the offspring of Satan to combat the radical sectarians who seemed to proliferating on the extreme left wing of the Church of England, assisted by the collapse

[265] John Barthlet, *The pedegrewe of heretiques. Wherein is truely and plainely set out, the first roote of heretiques begon in the Church, since the time and passage of the Gospell, together with an example of the ofspring of the same* (1566; STC 1534), fos 57r–v, 58r–v, 55r, 48r–v. See Scribner, *For the Sake of Simple Folk*, pp. 127–32. Philipp Melanchthon and Martin Luther's tract on this topic appeared in English in 1579: *Of two wonderful popish monsters*, trans. John Brooke (1579; STC 17797).

[266] See, e.g., CUL, MS Gg.iv.13, fo. 239, a satirical mock genealogy which is an adaptation of a passage in Martin Luther's *Table Talk* regarding the identification of the Pope as the Antichrist.

[267] Lewis Owen, *The unmasking of all popish monks, friers, and Jesuits. Or, A treatise of their genealogie, beginnings, proceedings, and present state* (1628; STC 18898), quotation at p. 99.

[268] Thomas Robinson, *The anatomie of the English nunnery at Lisbon in Portugall: dissected and laid open by one that was sometime a yonger brother of the co[n]vent* (1623; STC 21124).

[269] *A nest of nunnes egges, strangely hatched, with the description of a worthy feast for joy of the brood* ([1680?]; Wing N467). This was originally published for John Trundle before 1626.

[270] Lewis Owen, *A genealogie of all popish monks, friers, and Jesuits, shewing their first founders, beginnings, proceedings, and present state in 1646* (1646; Wing O828), title page.

[271] See *A true and plaine genealogy or pedigree of antichrist, wherein is cleerely discovered that hee is lineally descend from the diuell* (1634; STC 674); *The Popes pedigree, usurpation, & abominable pride; the fore-runner of His Holiness down-fall. Briefly declaring the first rising, and the ripening of popery* (1664; Wing K22); *The pedigree of popery; or, the genealogie of antichrist* (1688; Wing P1050); *The popes pedigree: or, the twineing of a wheelband, shewing the rise and first pedigrees of mortals inhabiting beneath the moon* ([1685?]; Wing P444); *The lineage of locusts or the popes pedegre beginning with his prime ancestor the divell* (1641; Wing C5499).

of censorship and the church courts in the 1640s. Groups like the Anabaptists, Ranters, and Familists, who became the subject of anti-sectarian propaganda such as Daniel Featley's *Dippers dipt* (1645), Ephraim Pagitt's *Heresiography* (1647), Robert Baillie's *Anabaptism, the true fountaine of Independency, Brownisme, Antinomy, Familisme* (1647), and Samuel Rutherford's *Survey of the spirituall antichrist* (1648) were themselves seen as Catholics in disguise, mutant species that all sprang from the same root, whatever dissembling cloak they wore on the outside. Anchored in the idea of Lucifer as the father of all heresies and lies, '*sperma diaboli*', they too are suffused with horror at these sects' antinomian indulgence in sexual pleasure and flagrant nudity.[272] Published at a time when both patriarchy and paternity seemed under fire, such texts were obsessed with the themes of copulation and conception, as well as with the grotesque and aberrant offspring engendered by the proponents of the pretended new reformations that rivalled the Presbyterian one many of these writers desired. *A nest of serpents discovered* (1641) damns the Adamites for encouraging their members to 'goe, increase and multiply' and for describing the products of the free love they supposedly preached as the 'true children of God' and 'heires of paradise'. It sees their creed as one in which deviance was indeed passed down consanguineally as an ancestral sin.[273] Perceived as 'kin to the Antinomians in many things', the Quakers were another target of genealogical polemic. Salacious stories about men, women, and children who went to bed together naked circulated, reanimating ancient stereotypes of heretical promiscuity, and polemical pamphlets 'laid open' their pedigree to 'publick view'. This was one of the roots of the commonplace that Quakerism was 'first Hatcht by the JESUITES', a popish plot that cracked open to bring forth a sectarian chick. Quakers retorted by saying that this was itself a Jesuitical ruse.[274]

The mid-seventeenth-century victims of this venomous discourse appropriated it for their own purposes. Christopher Feake's *The genealogie of Christianity and of Christians* (1650) was a sermon delivered by a Fifth Monarchist who later

[272] Daniel Featley, *The dippers dipt, or, the anabaptists duck'd and plung'd over head and eares, at a disputation in Southwark* (1645; Wing F585A); Ephraim Pagitt, *Heresiography: or, a description of the heretickes and sectaries of these latter times* (1645; Wing P174); Robert Baillie, *Anabaptism, the true fountaine of Independency, Brownisme, Antinomy, Familisme, and the most of the other errours, which for the time doe trouble the Church of England, unsealed* (1647; Wing B452A); Samuel Rutherford, *A survey of the spirituall antichrist* (1648 [1647]; Wing R2394). The quotation is from John Taylor, *An Exact description of a roundhead, and a long-head shag-poll* (1642; Wing E3638), p. 6. See the excellent discussion in Kirsten Poole, *Radical Religion from Shakespeare to Milton: Figures of Nonconformity in Early Modern England* (Cambridge, 2000), ch. 5.
[273] *A nest of serpents discovered, or, A knot of old heretiques revived, called the Adamites wherein their originall, increase, and severall ridiculous tenets are plainly layd open* (1641; Wing N470).
[274] James Browne, *Antichrist (in spirit) unmasked: or, the leaven of the Sadduces (lately lying hid amongst the Ranters, and Quakers) laid open to publick view* (Edinburgh, 1657; Wing B5022A), p. 39; *The Quakers pedigree: or, a dialogue between a Quaker, and a Jesuit, who at last become reconciled, as (holding in a great measure) the same principles* (1674; Wing Q28), title page. For the response, see J[ohn] M[oon], *A Jesuitical designe discovered: in a piece called, The Quakers pedigree* ([1674]; Wing M2524B). See also Edward Cockson, *The Quakers pedigree trac'd: or, some brief observations on their agreement with the church of Rome, both in their principles and practices* (1703).

joined the Baptists. His tract is only incidentally interested in tracing a lineage and uses the term in its title to castigate a generation of renegades, backsliders, atheists, and apostatized professors –'Unchristian' and 'Antichristian' Christians who would be consumed when Christ came, as he soon would, to deliver his final judgement.[275] These perceptions and prejudices once again took pictorial and diagrammatic form. *The true emblem of antichrist: or, schism display'd* ([1654?]) was an anti-puritan production directed at Oliver Cromwell, 'the chief Head of the Fanaticks and their Vices Supported by Devils'. He sits at the top, engendering Anti-Christ and Pride, who then unite in marriage, giving birth to a brood of evil forces, from Blasphemers, Arians, Deists and Muggletonians to Enthusiasts, Impostures, Self-conceit and Vain-glory. Out of these spring Presbytery, Ignorance, Persecution, and Fanaticism, whose marriage to Profaneness yields seven daughters: Wrath, Strife, Sedition, Envy, Rebellion, Discord, and Civil-War. A further and final generation consists of Oppression, Contention, Tumults, Murders, Regicides, Confusion, and Beggary. As Kirsten Poole has very perceptively commented, like its textual counterparts it 'undermines its apparent intent of indicating schismatic lineage'. The family tree it produces is a contorted and inconclusive one that fails in its aetiological purpose and is unable to locate the source of error clearly. The lines of familial descent it traces are highly incestuous, similar to those depicted in the Church's tables of consanguinity and affinity. The products of these ungodly sibling relationships are accordingly monstrous births.[276] Reissued in the early eighteenth century, this print became a touchstone for remembering the most dreadful bastard offspring of the Reformation, the Great Rebellion (Fig. 3.20).[277]

The rash of pseudo-news pamphlets about deformed infants that emerged from the presses in the same period must be seen in the light of these perverted genealogies. If some opportunistically exploited real events, others, like the 1648 tract describing *Mistris Parliament brought to bed of a monstrous childe of Reformation*, aided by Mrs Schisme, Mrs Privilege, Mrs Ordinance, Mrs Universall Toleration, and Mrs Leveller, her gossips, was an ingenious allegorical fiction.[278] Deployed by journalists on both sides of the Civil War divide, this polemical trope is another artefact of the generational politics that flourished in revolutionary England and of a universe in which the boundaries between signs and signifiers, reality and representation, were fluid.[279]

---

[275] C[hristopher] F[eake], *The genealogie of Christianity and of Christians* (1650; Wing F570), sig. C1r.

[276] *The true emblem of antichrist: or, schism display'd* ([1654?]; Wing T2693A). See Poole, *Radical Religion*, p. 135.

[277] *A genealogy of Anti-Christ: Oliver Cromwel triumphant, as head of the fanaticks and their vices, supported by devils* ([c.1700–1769]): BM, 1851,0614.15.

[278] Mercurius Melancholius, *Mistris Parliament brought to bed of a monstrous childe of Reformation* (1648; Wing M2281).

[279] See Fissell, *Vernacular Bodies*, ch. 6.

Fig. 3.20 *A genealogy of Anti-christ: Oliver Cromwel triumphant, as head of the fanaticks and their vices, supported by devils* (London, [1700–69]; first publ. 1651).

Source: © The Trustees of the British Museum 1851,0614.15.

The Roots of Reformation

The foregoing discussion must be situated in the context of the determined efforts made by Catholics, Protestants, and sectarians to demonstrate their own unbroken institutional continuity from the time of Christ onwards. Reformation historiography was a type of genealogical narrative. As Gabrielle Spiegel has commented, the human process of procreation and filiation has operated as a metaphor for historical change since the medieval era, and such texts are mimetic of the creation of life itself. The principle of hereditary succession that underpins them is a succession that stands as much for the passing of time as for a legal notion of transference or inheritance.[280]

Protestantism's quest to demonstrate that it was not an upstart religion lately invented by a renegade monk and that it had a venerable pedigree began in the early phases of the evangelical movement. The need to develop a convincing response to the Catholic taunt, 'Where was your church before Luther?' provided the stimulus for a large body of historical writing and scholarship. Part of a wider revival of sacred history, it inspired the efforts of Matthias Flaccius Illyricus and the Magdeburg Centurians in Germany and of John Bale and John Foxe in England, whose influential works set out to establish an unbroken line of descent from the apostolic Christianity of the primitive Church to the Protestant faith born in their own era. Identifying a hidden brotherhood of persecuted believers who had defied the papacy and kept the candle of the Gospel alight through the 'dark' ages was critical to this task. It had the well-known side effect of elevating a succession of medieval heretics—from the Cathars and the Waldensians to the Lollards and Hussites—onto a pedestal as the precursors of Martin Luther and the Swiss reformers.[281] A further consequence was eager pursuit of evidence that the Christian faith had been planted in the British Isles in apostolic times. Here Joseph of Arimathea, said to have landed near Bristol and settled at Glastonbury in AD 63, was the key link: a figure with impeccable scriptural credentials whose role in burying the body of Jesus was attested in all four of the canonical Gospels.[282] Others strenuously gathered evidence that the ideological priorities of

---

[280] Spiegel, 'Genealogy', p. 50.

[281] See Bruce Gordon (ed.), *Protestant History and Identity in Sixteenth-Century Europe*, 2 vols (Aldershot, 1996); S. J. Barnett, 'Where Was Your Church before Luther? Claims for the Antiquity of Protestantism Examined', *Church History*, 68 (1999), 14–41; Mark Greengrass and Matthew Phillpott, 'John Bale, John Foxe, and the Reformation of the English Past', *Archiv für Reformationsgeschichte/Archive for Reformation History*, 101 (2010), 275–87; Rosamund Oates, 'Elizabethan Histories of English Christian Origins', in Katherine van Liere, Simon Ditchfield, and Howard Louthan (eds), Sacred History: Uses of the Christian Past in the Renaissance World (Oxford, 2012), pp. 165–85. For heretics as forerunners of the Reformation, see Euan Cameron, 'Medieval Heretics as Protestant Martyrs', in Diana Wood (ed.), *Martyrs and Martyrologies*, SCH 30 (Oxford, 1993), pp. 185–207. See also Chapter 1, above, pp. 39–41.

[282] e.g., Thomas Fuller, *The church-history of Britain* (1655), pp. 6–8. See Glanmor Williams, 'Some Protestant Views of Early British Church History', in *idem*, *Welsh Reformation Essays* (Cardiff, 1967), pp. 207–19; Felicity Heal, 'What Can King Lucius Do for You? The Reformation and the Early British

the reformed Church of England had Anglo-Saxon precursors, notably Archbishop Matthew Parker and the members of his scholarly circle. The battles over its true descent and its degeneration in which Protestant writers engaged with Thomas Stapleton, the translator of Bede, were themselves genealogical ones.[283]

This was an enterprise that lost none of its relevance in the seventeenth century. A series of treatises devoted to demonstrating the perpetual visibility of the true Church and to delineating the 'cloud of witnesses' who had confessed it openly in defiance of the papacy and priesthood appeared. These included Richard Bernard's *Looke beyond Luther* (1623), which advertised itself as another answer to the question 'so insultingly proposed by our adversaries'. Bernard gathered arguments from Scripture, the fathers, and his own Catholic adversaries, as well as citing the testimonies of the blessed martyrs and establishing England's conversion to Christianity long before the arrival of Augustine in the sixth century in the days of King Lucius.[284] Samson Lennard's *Luthers fore-runners* (1624) was a more extensive discussion of the 'originall beginning', 'puritie', and persecution suffered by the Protestant religion translated from a French text by Jean Paul Perrin, to which was added a history of the Waldensians and Albigensians.[285] The interest of Thomas James, the first Bodleian librarian, in this ongoing project is reflected not only in the frieze that adorns the Upper Reading Room but also in his *Apologie for John Wickliffe* of 1608. This repolished the image of the fourteenth-century Oxford don compelled to retire to Lutterworth and posthumously condemned as a heretic and presented him as the 'morning star of the Reformation'.[286] It depicted Wyclif as a premature infant born before the rest of English society was ready to acknowledge the gospel he taught.

These were some of the many ripostes to the continuing attacks on Protestantism as a novel heresy by Catholic controversialists, notably the Jesuit Robert Persons in his voluminous *Treatise of three conversions* (1603–4).[287] On the wider European

Church', *EHR*, 120 (2005), 593–614; Sarah Scutts, 'Sixteenth- and Seventeenth-Century Perceptions of Joseph of Arimathea', (MA thesis, University of Exeter, 2006).

[283] Timothy Graham and Andrew G. Watson (eds), *The Recovery of the Past in Early Elizabethan England: Documents by John Bale and John Joscelyn from the Circle of Matthew Parker* (Cambridge, 1998); Benedict Scott Robinson, ' "Darke Speech": Matthew Parker and the Reforming of History', *SCJ*, 29 (1998), 1061–83; idem, 'John Foxe and the Anglo-Saxons', in Christopher Highley and John N. King (eds), *John Foxe and his World* (Aldershot, 2002), pp. 54–72.

[284] Richard Bernard, *Looke beyond Luther: or An answere to that question, so often and so insultingly proposed by our adversaries, asking us; where this our religion was before Luthers time?* (1623; STC 1956.7).

[285] Jean Paul Perrin, *Luthers fore-runners: or, A cloud of witnesses deposing for the Protestant faith. Gathered together in the historie of the Waldenses*, trans. Samson Lennard (1624; STC 19769.3). This is a reissue of *The bloudy rage of that great antechrist of Rome and his superstitious adherents, against the true church of Christ and the faithfull professors of his gospel* (1624; STC 19768.5).

[286] J. N. L. Myres, 'Thomas James and the Painted Frieze', *Bodleian Library Record*, 4 (1952–3), 30–51; Thomas James, *An apologie for John Wickliffe, shewing his conformitie with the now Church of England* (Oxford, 1608). See Margaret Aston, 'John Wyclif's Reformation Reputation', repr. in *eadem*, *Lollards and Reformers: Images and Literacy in Late Medieval Religion* (1984), pp. 243–72.

[287] Robert Persons, *A treatise of three conversions of England from paganisme to Christian religion* ([St Omer], 1603–1604; STC 19416).

stage, leading theologians such as Cesare Baronius retaliated by placing renewed emphasis on the institutional continuity of the Church of Rome from the time of Christ and by tracing the origins of the papacy to the apostle St Peter.[288] In its distinctive English guise this narrative was given compelling expression in the series of murals that adorned the walls of the English College in Rome, which located the victims of the Henrician purges and the missionary martyrs of Elizabeth's reign in a single glorious lineage that stretched back to St Alban and other indigenous early Christian evangelists.[289]

History as genealogy was also an instrument that helped to splinter Protestantism from within. In castigating the presbyterian model of church government advocated by Thomas Cartwright and his colleagues, Richard Bancroft's vicious *Survey of the pretended holy discipline* (1593) cast doubt on its claim to be of 'very great antiquitie' with the following scathing comment:

> The Herroldes at armes they say, can do verie much, in a mans pedigree. Though peradventure his Gentilitie be not of fiftie yeares standing: yet if neede require, *William Conquerours* time is nothing: they will fetch it from *Adam*... And even suche a like course is taken, for the *Geneva Discipline*. She must needes be a Lady, of an auncient stocke.... To leape over a thousand and five hundred yeares, at the first skippe, over almost two thousand yeares at the next, and in a manner to *Noahs* Arke at the third: is but a small matter with them. There was never poore gentlewomans credite more sought to be set foorth: with the smoakie images of her worm-[e]aten auncestors, then hers is. The *Geneva* platforme to be reckoned so late a devise, as that maister *Calvin* should be the first author of it; they cannot abide it.[290]

In short, declared Bancroft, Presbyterianism itself had a counterfeit pedigree. He castigated the strategy of assimilating early English Protestantism to the puritan cause recently analysed by Karl Gunther in *Reformation Unbound*.[291]

By the 1630s, the temperature of the Church of England's quarrels with its Roman Catholic adversary was declining. Simultaneously, the traditional genealogical spats between them lost some of their ferocity. This was a consequence of the mellowing of attitudes to the medieval church that accompanied the rise of Laudianism. As Anthony Milton has shown, antagonism towards Rome as a horn of the beast was overshadowed, at least in the circles of those who supported

---

[288]   See Giuseppe Antonio Guazzelli, 'Cesare Baronius and the Roman Catholic Vision of the Early Church', in Van Liere, Ditchfield, and Louthan (eds), *Sacred History*, pp. 52–71.

[289]   On which, see Anne Dillon, *The Construction of Martyrdom in the English Catholic Community, 1535–1603* (Aldershot, 2002), ch. 4.

[290]   Richard Bancroft, *A survey of the pretended holy discipline* (1593; STC 1352), p. 71.

[291]   Karl Gunther, *Reformation Unbound: Protestant Visions of Reform in England, 1525–1570* (Cambridge, 2014), esp. ch. 7.

Laud's rediscovery of the beauty of holiness, by greater willingness to acknowledge her not merely as a flawed but still essentially true church, but also as in some sense English Protestantism's own mother. In other words, they relocated the ecclesiastical institution begotten by the reforms of Henry VIII in a line stretching back through, rather than bypassing, the medieval episcopacy. The corollary of this shift in opinion was a corresponding cooling of affection for the sister churches on the Continent with which early evangelicals had felt such an affinity— a loosening, if not severing of the ties of spiritual kinship that had bound England's reformers with the brethren who made up the Calvinist international across the Channel.[292]

Unease about these trends formed part of the backdrop for the confrontations that led to the wars of religion that broke out in 1642. Disputes regarding the genealogy of the English Reformation were part of the climate in which revolution grew. And once the advantage had shifted towards the puritans once more, polemical histories tracing Protestantism's lineage re-emerged from the shadows. Daniel Featley's *Roma ruens* published in 1644 combined a 'succinct' account of the antiquity and uninterrupted succession of believers through the ages—'even in the most obscure times, when it seemed to be almost totally eclipsed'—with a graphic emblem of a seven-headed Whore of Babylon. Its frontispiece depicted the Tower of Babel and identified Rome as the place described in Apocalypse 18.7 as 'the habitation of devils, and the hold every foule spirit, and a cage of every uncleane and hatefull bird'.[293] The resurgence of this rhetoric at the time of the Civil Wars was a response to Caroline attempts to suppress it as politically incorrect and to the Laudian censorship that had muzzled its voice and, in the eyes of the godly, mutilated and distorted that of Foxe's *Actes and monuments* itself.[294] Repeatedly revived in the second half of the seventeenth century, it gave expression to the ongoing struggle to define the ancestry of what was belatedly baptized as 'Anglicanism'.

Finally, Catholicism too built upon the long tradition of utilizing genealogy as a historiographical device. Medieval religious orders such as the Franciscans had often represented their histories arboreally, deploying the iconography of the family tree as a mnemonic tool that conjoined the past with an eschatological perspective upon the future.[295] In a pictorial pedigree of the Benedictines preserved in Roger Dodsworth and William Dugdale's *Monasticon Anglicanum*, the main trunk ascends in a straight line from St Benedict to God in heaven,

[292] Anthony Milton, *Catholic and Reformed: The Roman and Protestant Churches in English Protestant Thought, 1600–1640* (Cambridge, 1995), esp. chs 6 and 8.
[293] Daniel Featley, *Roma ruens Romes ruine* (1644; Wing F592).
[294] Damian Nussbaum, 'Appropriating Martyrdom: Fears of Renewed Persecution and the 1632 Edition of *Actes and Monuments*', in David Loades (ed.), *John Foxe and the English Reformation* (Aldershot, 1997), pp. 178–91.
[295] Marianne P. Ritsema van Eck, 'Genealogy as a Heuristic Device for Franciscan Order History in the Middle Ages and Early Modernity: Texts and Trees', *Franciscan Studies*, 77 (2019), 135–69.

represented by a triangle and tetragrammaton, with the branches on either side bearing groups of brothers kneeling piously in prayer.[296] Chroniclers of the English convents in the Low Countries adopted the same strategy. A 1652 relation of the foundation of the Sepulchrines at Liège, for instance, traced its roots back to St James the Apostle and declared that the institution of religious canonesses had 'proceeded from the very first birth of the Church'. An account of the establishment of the Augustinians of Louvain listed the successive Mothers Superior of the house from its foundation, in 1609, as a daughter house of St Ursula's in the same Flemish town, beginning with Mary Wiseman. In each case, the writer highlighted the prioress's natural ancestry before noting her spiritual offspring. Magdalene Throckmorton, who died in 1668, had professed thirty-eight religious, twenty-eight nuns, one conversa, and nine lay sisters; Marina Plowden, who expired in 1715, had professed twenty-three religious, twenty-five nuns, and seven lay sisters.[297]

This was a device that was readily embraced by the English Jesuits. Turning the tables on satirical counter-genealogists like Lewis Owen, they too harnessed the ancient motif of the Tree of Jesse to celebrate their role in sustaining the Catholic faith in Protestant England. The eighteenth-century painting in the refectory at Stonyhurst College is a spectacular explication of this theme: Ignatius Loyola takes pride of place at the base of the trunk, while his spiritual offspring (starting with a company of bishops and cardinals) sit in serried ranks on its branches bearing placards inscribed with their names that have the appearance of leaves (Fig. 3.21).[298] Similar pedigrees could be found in religious houses throughout Latin America, including examples produced for the Mercedarian Order.[299] The hereditary successions these images and texts recorded gave expression to genealogies of faith and profession rather than blood.

This chapter has explored the previously under-investigated interconnections between biblical, secular, and polemical genealogy. It has demonstrated that the narratives of biological and institutional descent by which contemporaries were so fascinated were the products of social conventions and of selective memory. Early modern interest in lineage was not simply a function of concerns about hierarchical rank and status; it was rooted in and inflected by the content of Scripture. Religious preoccupations were a key feature of the environment in which the early modern English genealogical imagination flourished, and they

---

[296] Roger Dodsworth and William Dudgale, *Monasticon Anglicanum, sive, Pandectae coenobiorum Benedictinorum, Cluniacensium, Cisterciensium, Carthusianorum a primordiis ad eorum usque dissolutionem* (1655; Wing D2484), vol. 1, sig. c5r.

[297] *A brief relation of the order and institute of the English religious women at Liège* (Liège, 1652), pp. 6–16; BL, MS 5813, fos 31r–33r (An Account of the Nunnery of St Monica in Louvain).

[298] I thank Jan Graffius for supplying information about this painting.

[299] *Genealogical Tree of the Mercedarian Order* (Bolivia, mid-18th century): Carl and Marilynn Thoma Collection (Art Institute of Chicago). I am grateful to Andrew Spicer for drawing this to my attention.

Fig. 3.21 'The Jesuits' family tree' (oil, 18th century).
Source: Stonyhurst College, Lancashire.

stretched beyond the gentry and aristocracy to shape the outlook of ordinary people. So too did the ideas about ancestry and heredity embedded in Genesis and revitalized by the neo-Augustinian Protestant doctrine of original sin. Never simply the subject of abstruse academic debate, these permeated everyday experience and piety, colouring contemporary views of fertility and barrenness, sex and pregnancy, marriage and childbirth. They helped to forge discourses in which embryonic ideas about genetics and race would coalesce and crystallize more fully in later centuries. They also emphasize the need for a social and cultural history of religion that is alive to the influence and force exerted by theology.

Chapter 4 turns from blood and trees to generations and seed. It examines the perplexing and pressing questions that confronted devout people of all religious complexions about the spiritual fate of their dead relatives and about the salvation of their children and grandchildren.

4

Generations and Seed

'What is meant by this word Generation, which is so often used in Scripture?' asked Abraham Ross, chaplain to Charles I and preacher to the parish of St Mary's near Southampton, in a commentary on the book of Genesis published in 1626. The list of eight definitions he supplied illustrates the many connotations of this pervasive word in early modern culture. Signifying origin, nativity, and history, as well as genealogy, posterity, and lineage, it was also employed to describe an age or period of time and the people living in it.[1]

As explained in the Introduction to this book, academic historians have largely approached the concept of generation as a social cohort. The idea that groups of coevals bound by a sense of common identity and purpose forged by shared formative experiences play a critical role in the unfolding of history has its roots in the work of Auguste Comte, François Mentré, Karl Mannheim, and José Ortega y Gasset. For these writers, generations offered insight into revolutionary events that were perceived to be the midwife of a reconceptualization of history itself as linear, forward-looking, and progressive. Shedding the teleological assumptions that shaped the perspective of these early theorists, more recent studies see the generation as a set of relationships between self and society determined by a shared location in time, as well as a conceptual matrix and a framework for individual agency and collective action. They analyse it as both a passive and active category, and as one marked by fluidity and flexibility, malleability and mutability, complexity and ambivalence.[2]

This chapter builds upon this scholarship, but it also departs from it in two principal respects. First, it rejects the lingering assumption that the concept of generation had 'a precarious existence prior to modernity' and that the forms of generational consciousness that result from rapid and tumultuous changes in political structures, social relations, and cultural codes were less acute in the sixteenth and seventeenth centuries than in later ones.[3] Secondly, rather than detaching the concept of generation from genealogy and biological reproduction,

---

[1] Abraham Ross, *An exposition on the fourteene first chapters of Genesis, by way of question and answere* (1626; STC 21324), second pagination, pp. 72–3. See also Thomas Wilson, *A Christian dictionarie* (1616; STC 25787), pp. 223–4.

[2] See Introduction, pp. 8–9.

[3] Judith Burnett, *Generations: The Time Machine in Theory and Practice* (Farnham, 2010), p. 25. Peter Burke drew similar conclusions in an unpublished paper entitled 'Generation: Strengths (and a Few Weaknesses) of the Concept', delivered to the Comparative Social and Cultural History Seminar in Cambridge in 2013.

it remains alert to its close links with kinship and blood. It contends that horizontal senses of generational identity were a significant by-product of the English Reformations and the creative, yet disorderly religious impulses they brought into being. It also seeks to delineate some of the complicated ways in which these were interconnected with concerns about ancestry and family. A further topic of investigation is the role that the advent of Protestantism played in transforming vertical relationships between past, present, and future generations, between the living and the deceased, and between parents and their children.

In pursuing these themes, this chapter probes a series of delicate transactions between theology, experience, emotion, and language that muted, softened, and subtly transformed the reformed doctrines of salvation and damnation as they were applied and played out in daily life. It builds on Norman Jones's suggestion that to understand England's evolving Reformation we must pay careful attention to how it was absorbed and navigated by different generations and probe the 'generational *mentalités*' that these processes served to engender and cement.[4] In developing these arguments, it will be necessary to take several trips across the Atlantic to New England.

Past Generations: The Fate of the Dead

In medieval Christianity, the dead were what Natalie Zemon Davis called an 'age group', still present in the social imaginary despite the fact that they had passed from the earthly realm into the afterlife.[5] The extended family and household stretched across the barriers erected by time and mortality to encompass past generations. The possibility of converse between the quick and the dead was widely accepted. If the former could intercede to speed the path of relatives through purgatory to paradise via the mechanism of prayer, the latter, safely ensconced in heaven, had the capacity to intervene for those trapped in the temporal world by persuading God the Father, Christ the Son, and his mother the Virgin Mary to exercise mercy towards their sinful relatives and friends. Although A. N. Galpern memorably described pre-Reformation religion as 'in large part a cult of the living in the service of the dead', this may be to place too much emphasis on traffic in one direction.[6] The Catholic economy of salvation

---

[4] Norman Jones, 'Living the Reformations: Generational Experience and Political Perception in Early Modern England', *HLQ*, 60 (1999), 273–88, esp. 274.

[5] The phrase was first used by Natalie Zemon Davis, 'Some Tasks and Themes in the Study of Popular Religion', in Charles Trinkaus and Heiko Oberman (eds), *The Pursuit of Holiness in Late Medieval and Renaissance Religion* (Leiden, 1974), pp. 327–8; and see *eadem*, 'Ghosts, Kin and Progeny: Some Features of Family Life in Early Modern France', *Daedalus*, 106 (1977), 87–114, esp. 92, 94. Since then it has entered into the early modernist's lexicon.

[6] A. N. Galpern, *The Religions of the People in Sixteenth-Century Champagne* (Cambridge, MA, 1976), p. 20, and see ch. 2.

was a reciprocal one in which strings could be pulled by kith and kin on either side of the eschatological divide. It was a system of continuous and busy exchange between those who had departed this life and those who remained, who would meet again at the Last Judgement.

A number of doctrines and practices buttressed this comforting vision in which ties of consanguinity and affinity bridged the gap opened up by death and mitigated the threat of eternal torment. The belated emergence and codification of the theologies of purgatory and limbo in the thirteenth century were partly a pastoral response to popular fears about the fate of the dead.[7] In turn, the presence of an official halfway house in which people could work off the accumulated punishment incurred by their moral transgressions helped to give birth to the cult of indulgences. Whether obtained through pilgrimages, penitential prayers, or the purchase of ecclesiastically endorsed pieces of paper, such pardons were a form of passport or insurance policy that could be acquired vicariously by loved ones on behalf of kith and kin who had died.[8] The recitation of benefactors listed on bede rolls and the masses that testators requested be said for their own and their ancestors' souls, and for which their families and acquaintances paid, gave further expression to the assumptions about intergenerational collaboration that sustained late medieval Catholic soteriology. They illustrate that purgatory both depended upon and reinforced the spiritual dimensions of kinship and the centrality of natural and supernatural bonding between the living and the dead. It was a place that devout Catholics like Thomas More imagined to be teeming with 'spouses, companions, play felowes & frendes', piteously calling for help in releasing them from the pains they suffered for their sins.[9] The imperative to take care of lost relatives left a clear imprint on funeral monuments and brasses that read 'ora pro nobis', inviting spectators to intercede for the souls of those they commemorated. Transcending the divide between the generations, social and biological, a memorial dated 1491 in St Benet Gracechurch in London carried the words: 'Prey for the saulygs [souls] of Henry Denne, and Joan his wyf, theyr fadyrs, theyr modyrs, Bredyrs, and good frendys, and of all Christian saulygs Iesu have mercy, Amen, who

---

[7] Jacques Le Goff, *The Birth of Purgatory*, trans. Arthur Goldhammer (Aldershot, 1984). For different claims about the chronology of its emergence, see R. W. Southern, 'Between Heaven and Hell', *Times Literary Supplement* (18 June 1982), 651–2.

[8] R. N. Swanson, *Indulgences in Late Medieval England: Passports to Paradise?* (Cambridge, 2007).

[9] *The Workes of Sir Thomas More knyght sometime lorde chancellor of England* (1557; STC 18076), p. 288. See Joel T. Rosenthal, *The Purchase of Paradise: Gift Giving and the Aristocracy 1307–1485* (1972); Bernard B. McGuire, 'Purgatory, the Communion of Saints, and Medieval Change', *Viator*, 20 (1989), 161–82; Eamon Duffy, *The Stripping of the Altars: Traditional Religion in England 1400–1580* (New Haven, CT, 1992), ch. 10, esp. pp. 348–54; Peter Marshall, *Beliefs and the Dead in Reformation England* (Oxford, 2002), pp. 33–41; and the sensitive discussion in Susan E. James, *Women's Voices in Tudor Wills, 1485–1603: Authority, Influence and Material Culture* (Farnham, 2015), ch. 1, esp. pp. 32–40.

departyd this lif.'[10] A note inserted into a pre-Reformation primer evokes the same comforting image of solidarity and inclusion:

> Pray for John Iwardlby & sanetie his wife eldest daug. Of Nicholas Carru of Bedington in Surrey &...of his heires for their children, freinds & wellwishers; & for the soule of Katherine late wife of the said John, daug. Of Edward Nevill Lord Burgeyne & for the soules of John & Edward sonns of the said John & Katherine, & for the soules of ye Fat[her]s, mot[her]s, alliances & friends of all them above rehearsed & for all Xtens.[11]

The belief that the living could assist the dead also underpinned two other institutions that occupied a key place in traditional religion on the eve of the Reformation: chantries and confraternities. Foundations dedicated to improving the spiritual welfare of the dead through acts of liturgical and sacramental intercession, chantries have aptly been described a form of lineage or kinship community. The rituals carried out by the priest for the benefit of specific individuals testified to bonds of attachment that were neither broken by the grave nor confined to blood relations. Thus, the founder of a London chantry established in 1521 gave instructions for the singing of the Mass for his friends as well as himself, while the prayer stipulated by William Whaplode of Chalfont St Peter extended to his father, mother, brothers, sisters, wives, relatives, friends, and benefactors ('*patris, matris, fratrum, sororum, uxorum, consanguineorum, amicorum, et benefactorum*').[12] In the late fifteenth century, the Norwich alderman Robert Thorp had similarly paid for a priest to 'sing perpetually' for his soul and those of his three successive wives, Elizabeth, Emme, and Agnes, his son John, and 'his kindryd Sowls, frends Sowls, and al cristen Sowls' in the church of St Michael, Gosney.[13] 'Family feeling', Joel Rosenthal writes, 'may have been the strongest single ligature' binding together philanthropic activity in this period.[14]

Parish fraternities and confraternities too were mutual benefit societies in which the fortunes of biological and social generations were connected by lines of

[10] John Weever, *Ancient funerall monuments within the united monarchie of Great Britaine, Ireland and the ilands adjacent; with the dissolved monasteries therein contained* (1631; STC 25223), p. 416.
[11] Bodl., MS Wood D 7 (2) (Assorted notes of Ralph Sheldon, 17th century), fo. 37. This was a transcription of an item in the family's library.
[12] See K. L. Wood-Legh, *Perpetual Chantries in Britain* (Cambridge, 1965), p. 290. See also John Bossy, 'Blood and Baptism: Kinship, Community and Christianity in Western Europe from the Fourteenth to the Seventeenth Centuries', in Derek Baker (ed.), *Sanctity and Secularity: The Church and the World*, SCH 10 (Oxford, 1973), pp. 129–43, at p. 136.
[13] Weever, *Ancient funerall monuments*, p. 803.
[14] Rosenthal, *Purchase of Paradise*, p. 124. See also Barbara J. Harris, *English Aristocratic Women and the Fabric of Piety 1450-1550* (Amsterdam, 2018); Sally Badham, 'The Robertsons Remembered: Two Generations of Calais Staplers at Algakirk, Lincolnshire', in Caroline M. Barron and Clive Burgess (eds), *Memory and Commemoration in Medieval England: Proceedings of the 2008 Harlaxton Symposium* (Donington, 2010), pp. 202–17.

duty and dependence woven through the dimension of time. They were communities bound together vertically as well as horizontally. The services to which their members had access were strategies for rescuing parents, siblings, colleagues, and companions from their purgatorial trials and facilitating their passage to everlasting happiness. The registers in which they were inscribed when they became members were annotated after they died, which ensured that they were held in perpetual memory.[15] A remarkable list relating to the guild of St Chad in Lichfield Cathedral dating from 1532–3 contains 51,000 names and is neatly arranged in family groupings, including deceased wives, husbands, and children, mothers, fathers, grandparents, and other relatives—a genealogy of spiritual beneficiaries as well as blood ancestry.[16] The spiritual charity of one's 'soul-brothers and sisters' created an obligation that would be repaid in kind in the afterlife.[17] This was a form of investment in the future that could also be secured retrospectively. By the fifteenth century, in a measure of the mixture of anxiety, affection, and guilt felt by the laity, some English guilds and brotherhoods were even admitting dead persons on payment of a posthumous entry fee.[18]

The Reformation brought an abrupt end to the lively forms of cross-generational religious communication that had flourished in medieval Catholicism. It fundamentally altered relationships between the living and the dead, sharply dividing the inhabitants of these two realms and throwing away the ladders between them. It firmly repudiated the efficacy of prayer as a method of salvific remembering and insisted that the souls of the deceased were beyond the help of those they had left behind. They were either already enjoying heavenly glory or suffering the endless agony of the damned in hell. No one lingered in the hallway and escape hatch that was purgatory, a place that Protestants vehemently dismissed as a popish invention designed to deceive the ignorant and credulous and to fill the coffers of the Church of Rome with filthy lucre. One corollary of its exposure and elimination as a prime example of diabolical delusion and forgery was the

---

[15] This was prescribed by Ordinances of c.1400 for one guild: see A. G. Rosser, 'The Guild of St Mary and St John the Baptist, Lichfield: Ordinances of the Late Fourteenth Century', *Collections for a History of Staffordshire*, 4th series, 13 (1988), 19–26. See also H. F. Westlake, *The Parish Gilds of Medieval England* (1919); Caroline Barron, 'The Parish Fraternities of Medieval London', in eadem and Christopher Harper-Bill (eds), *The Church in Pre-Reformation Society* (Woodbridge, 1985), pp. 13–37; Virginia Bainbridge, *Gilds in the Medieval Countryside: Social and Religious Change in Cambridgeshire, c.1350–1558* (Woodbridge, 1996), esp. ch. 4; Philip Morgan, 'Of Worms and War: 1380–1558', in Peter C. Jupp and Clare Gittings (eds), *Death in England: An Illustrated History* (New Brunswick, NJ, 1999), pp. 119–46.

[16] See A. J. Kettle, 'A List of Families in the Archdeaconry of Stafford 1532–3', *Collections for a History of Staffordshire*, 4th ser., 8 (1978), pp. xvi–xix.

[17] See Galpern, *Religions of the People*, p. 52.

[18] John Bossy, *Christianity in the West 1400–1700* (Oxford, 1985), p. 61.

abolition of the chantries and confraternities and 'the stemming of that endless upward flood of intercessory prayer'.[19]

Another was to render it both unnecessary and absurd for the dead to return to seek the aid of their surviving relatives in the guise of ghosts, who were thereby peremptorily ejected from the reformed universe.[20] In theory, Protestantism thus had the effect of demoting past generations from their status as an age group.[21] It denied them agency in human affairs and placed them behind an impenetrable veil and an insurmountable wall. It not merely made their descendants incapable of changing their ultimate destiny; it also justified a degree of disinterest in it. As Keith Thomas comments, 'Protestant doctrine meant that each generation could be indifferent to the spiritual fate of its predecessor.'[22]

Those who remained loyal to the proscribed Church of Rome reacted to these developments by vigorously reasserting the continuation of spiritual concourse between the generations in this world and the next. Its clerical leaders and controversialists robustly defended the power of the keys and of prayer. They continued to emphasize the ability of the faithful to tap into the treasury of merit accumulated by the good works done by the heroic dead now residing in heaven and channelled to the living through relics and other sacred objects. William Allen's tract on this topic sharply condemned Calvin's 'unkind haeresy', whereby '[s]uch lacke of compassion is driven into oure heads, that we feel not the wo of our owne felowes, oure kinne, oure brethren, and our owne membres'. In response, he emphatically upheld 'the unitye and knotte of that holy felowship' in which the souls of those already 'happely promoted to the joye of Christes blessed kingdom...perpetually praye for the doubtfull state, of theyr owne fellowes benethe' and 'the carefull condition of the membres belowe, [who] continually crieth for helpe at theire handes in heaven above'. The 'happy community' and 'socyety' Allen evoked was a transgenerational one, bound together by 'mutuall agreement', compassion, and love.[23]

---

[19] Marshall, *Beliefs and the Dead*, p. 312 and chs 2–3. See also Bruce Gordon and Peter Marshall (eds), *The Place of the Dead: Death and Remembrance in Late Medieval and Early Modern Europe* (Cambridge, 2000); Philip Lindley, ' "Pickpurse" Purgatory, the Dissolution of the Chantries and the Suppression of Intercession of the Dead', *Journal of the British Archaeological Association*, 164 (2013), 277–304. For the dissolution of institutions, see Peter Cunich, 'The Dissolution of the Chantries' in Patrick Collinson and John Craig (eds), *The Reformation in English Towns, 1500–1640* (Basingstoke, 1998), pp. 159–74. For a European perspective, see Craig Koslofsky, *The Reformation of the Dead: Death and Ritual in Early Modern Germany, 1450–1700* (Basingstoke, 1999).

[20] On ghosts, see Keith Thomas, *Religion and the Decline of Magic: Studies in Popular Beliefs in Sixteenth- and Seventeenth-Century England* (Harmondsworth, 1973 edn), ch. 19; Peter Marshall, 'Deceptive Appearances: Ghost and Reformers in Elizabethan and Jacobean England', in Helen L. Parish and William G. Naphy (eds), *Religion and Superstition in Reformation Europe* (Manchester, 2002), pp. 188–208; idem, *Beliefs and the Dead*, ch. 6.

[21] Davis, 'Ghosts, Kin and Progeny', 95.

[22] Thomas, *Religion and the Decline of Magic*, p. 721.

[23] William Allen, *A defense and declaration of the Catholike churchies [sic] doctrine, touching purgatory, and prayers for the soules departed* (Antwerp, 1565; STC 371).

The Jesuit James Mumford was driven to publish on this subject by his conviction that too many did 'passe over this important busines of praying for the dead so coldly, as they think they do inough to help their owne year Christs own, Brother, if they do but say God rest his soule'. This was a most unmercifull manner of proceeding'. Contemporaries were lamentably 'forgetfull' about the distressed souls' languishing in purgatory. Vigorously defending intercessory prayer and indulgences, he encouraged his readers to meditate on the gratitude that would be extended to them by 'their friends, acquaintance, & kindred, their Angel-guardians, and Patrons, yea all the whole Court of heaven; seeing that there is that perfect charity among the Blessed'.[24] In the eyes of these writers, Protestants were guilty of an unnatural cruelty to their ancestors. But those who abandoned their allegiance to Rome were quite capable of projecting the same criticism back against their erstwhile co-religionists. The Jacobean convert James Wadsworth, who spent his childhood in a seminary in the Spanish Netherlands, recalled that when his Catholic teachers heard of the decease of his grandfather and other relatives, 'they charged me not to wish a requiem to their soules because they were heretickes, and so consequently are damned in hell'.[25] One's obligations to dead family members did not extend to those who had wilfully separated themselves from the mother Church.

Confraternities remained a vital resource, especially for those members of the Catholic community who had irregular access to the sacramental grace dispensed by missionary priests, for whom they served as a surrogate, and for those separated from their families by the geographical distance of exile. The sodalities they established at home and abroad recreated bonds of belonging that epitomized the mobility of the English Counter-Reformation and the umbilical links it maintained with the faithful in the towns and cities in which it found refuge. The confraternity of the rosary established at St Gregory's, Douai, extended its privileges to English students and 'any friends from England living there', while the Jesuit house at Watten allowed Flemish residents to join, growing to 700 members by 1710.[26] Catholics clung defiantly to the idea that past and present generations were not irrevocably severed from each other and re-established the machinery of intercession abolished by the Protestant reformers as far as they could in a context of persecution. Indeed, their status as a beleaguered minority served as a powerful incentive to cross-generational cooperation in the collective labour of prayer for England's return to the spiritual safe haven of Rome and for the souls of those who had resisted the lure of heresy and suffered stoically the discrimination that followed from doing so.

[24] [James Mumford], *A remembrance for the living to pray for the dead* ([St Omer], 1641; Wing M3069), p. 5, sig. A2r–v, p. 85.
[25] James Wadsworth, *The English Spanish pilgrime* (1629; STC 24926), p. 77.
[26] See Chapter 2 above; Liesbeth Corens, *Confessional Mobility and English Catholics in Counter-Reformation Europe* (Oxford, 2019), ch.5, at p. 145.

Meanwhile, within reformed circles, as Peter Marshall has shown, the profound ruptures wrought by Protestant theology in theory were attenuated and tempered in practice by persisting ambiguities. Eager to console grieving relatives, Elizabethan and Jacobean preachers of funeral sermons held out the hope that the living would ultimately be reunited with their families in heaven. They catered for the continuing interest of laypeople in 'the estate of the dead', recharting the territory of the hereafter in the aftermath of the violent excision of purgatory, and developing an affective rhetoric that fostered the idea that the living would indeed see their kin and kith again. In short, they implied that death was not the final goodbye.[27]

In a sermon delivered in Constantinople following the death of Lady Anne Glover in 1616, William Ford encouraged his hearers to envisage the welcome they too would receive in paradise, painting a picture in which 'an infinite number of acquaintance expect us there: our parents, our brethren and sisters, our children, our kindred, our friends, that are already secure of their own immortalities, but yet solicitous for our safetie, what joy, what comfort will it be to see, to imbrace them'.[28] It was a message replicated by many other Protestant clergymen. Pastoral compassion prompted them to imply that earthly bonds of affinity and sociability would be reconstituted in the next life against the more alienating precept that the dead were completely oblivious of the needs, concerns, and cares of the living. If some spoke of the compensation of exchanging natural parents and siblings for intimate ties with Christ and 'the children in heaven', others had no qualms about evoking an image of the amicable gatherings of blood ancestors and spiritual kin that the godly would rejoin when they reached heaven. In the 1630s, the puritan divine Samuel Rogers optimistically imagined the afterlife as a place where he would 'sit downe in companye, with Abraham, Paul, my grandfather, and all other blessed saints, and angels'.[29] This was an assembly in which religious and natural lineage converged and in which the ancient patriarchs and biblical apostles comingled with his own revered progenitor, himself a renowned minister.

The bestselling devotional writer John Andrews described a similarly heartwarming scene of the neighbours, friends, and family members meeting with the newly departed, with 'cryes and shouts', 'clapping of hands and sweete embracements'.[30] William Gearing's treatise on the 'happiness of the saints', *A prospect of*

---

[27] Peter Marshall, 'The Company of Heaven: Identity and Sociability in the English Protestant Afterlife, c.1560–1630', *Historical Reflections/Réflexions Historiques*, 26 (2000), 311–33; idem, *Beliefs and the Dead*, pp. 214–20.

[28] William Ford, *A sermon preached at Constantinople, in the Vines of Perah, at the funerall of the vertuous and admired Lady Anne Glover* (1616; STC 11176), p. 62.

[29] *The Diary of Samuel Rogers, 1634–38*, ed. Kenneth Shipps and Tom Webster, Church of England Record Society 11 (Woodbridge, 2004), p. 44.

[30] John Andrews, *A celestiall looking-glasse: to behold the beauty of heaven* (1621; STC 592), pp. 27–8.

heaven (1673), was no less sanguine, insisting that people would be 'dearer to their Parents, Children, Relations, then now they are' and inviting his readers to contemplate the 'most pleasant spectacle' of 'their sweet Familiarity with one another' there.[31] When Thomas Aldersey wrote to his brother Robert in April 1690 to send his condolences following a recent bereavement, he stressed that 'Children are not lost but gone before, whither he shall (in the wise & good Gods best time) follow after, and where he shall be happy with God, & Christ, & ye saints, & all his blest Relations'.[32] Young people facing early death also took comfort in the promise that they would meet their loved ones in the next life. Susannah Bicks looked forward to being reunited with her dead brother Jacob and little sister in 1664, and in 1679 Isaac Archer told his gravely ill 6-year-old daughter Frances that she was on her way to join the siblings who had died in infancy.[33]

Post-mortem reunion was hardly a novel theme. It had parallels in both medieval and Tridentine piety, not least in the work of the Jesuit Robert Persons, who, quoting the church father Cyprian, wrote of souls that would joyfully be reunited in heaven with their 'familiares, with kynred, with acquayntance'.[34] This was probably one reason why some fervent Calvinists felt queasy about upbeat homiletic treatments of this topic, which seemed to gloss over the fact that only a tiny minority had been elected to receive saving grace. Samuel Gardiner warned laypeople not to waste time speculating about such idle questions, saying 'let our care be to knowe whether wee shal come to heaven, then to know whether we shall know one another in heaven'.[35] While Robert Bolton did not doubt that there would be 'familiar acquaintance' in the next life, he was perturbed by 'the curious *Quaere* of carnall people' who nurtured 'presumptuous conceipts with golden dreames, and vaine hopes of many future imaginary felicities in the world come'.[36] To such ministers, it seemed no less difficult to wean ordinary people away from the idea that generational ties were not irrevocably broken by death than to dissuade them from the notion that salvation was firmly within the reach of all devout and well-intentioned people. Many dismissed this assumption as a telltale symptom of church papistry and Catholic survivalism, but it arguably found some of its moorings in the Book of Common Prayer. As puritan critics of

---

[31] William Gearing, *A prospect of heaven: or, A treatise of the happiness of the saints in glory* (1673; Wing G437), p. 239.

[32] CRO, ZCR 469/422 (Draft letter from Thomas Aldersey to his brother Robert, offering consolation on the death of a child, 1690).

[33] See Hannah Newton, *The Sick Child in Early Modern England, 1580–1720* (Oxford, 2012), pp. 217–18.

[34] Robert Persons, *The first booke of Christian exercise appertayning to resolution* ([Rouen], 1582; STC 19353), p. 175.

[35] Samuel Gardiner, *Doomes-day booke: or, an alarum for atheists, a watchword for worldlinges, a caveat for Christians* (1606; STC 1065), p. 107.

[36] Robert Bolton, *Mr. Boltons last and learned worke of the foure last things death, judgement, hell, and heaven* (1632; STC 3242), p. 149.

Cranmer's liturgy pointed out, the burial rite appeared to promise eternal redemption to all without exception, whether 'Papist, or Atheist, Heretique, Usurer, or Whoremonger, good or badde'.[37] It committed the body of deceased persons to the ground 'in sure and certein hope of resurrection to eternall lyfe', and it ended with a prayer that, notwithstanding the conditional tense in which it was constructed, left the impression that they were already on their way to 'perfect conssumacion and blisse'.[38] It embodied the tacit assumption that all members of the national Church of England numbered among the small remnant of the saved. This was both a source of strength and the root of enduring internal tension.[39]

A similar soteriological confidence came to suffuse the inscriptions carved on some post-Reformation funeral monuments. These ceased to invoke those who viewed them to pray for the souls of deceased and dwelt instead on the exemplary qualities for which they should be remembered and which surviving friends and relatives should seek to emulate. As in sermons preached to mark their passing, theological orthodoxy was squared with the imperative to console and succour the bereaved by drawing upon the tradition of the *ars moriendi*.[40] Deploying the distinctive vocabulary of predestination itself, some monuments went so far as to proclaim that their subjects were assured of salvation and were already triumphant in paradise. A brass erected in the parish church of Ufton in Warwickshire in memory of Richard Woddomes, who died in 1587, for instance, ended with the assertion that his 'Soule restethe with God', while another dating from after 1617 to the dedicated Protestant pastor Francis Bunny, who became archdeacon of Northumberland, included a ventriloquized verse to the effect that 'my barke' had 'wonne the haven' and 'my home is heaven'.[41]

To echo Peter Marshall, such epitaphs freely attempted to 'accommodate the ineluctable doctrine of election to a deep-seated impulse to think well of the dead', though they did not entirely dispel the underlying worries that exercised the most pious.[42] Peter Sherlock goes further in stressing the dominant note of optimism on late sixteenth- and early seventeenth-century memorials and tombs, which celebrated the liberation of past generations from grief, pain, and fear and implied that relatives merited heavenly reward because of the virtuous lives they had led on earth.[43] The epitaph on a memorial to Thomas Edgecombe, a Hertfordshire

---

[37] Albert Peel (ed), *The Second Parte of a Register: being a calendar of manuscripts under that title intended for publication by the Puritans about 1593, and now in Dr William's library, London*, 2 vols (Cambridge, 1915), i. 201.

[38] Cummings (ed.), *Book of Common Prayer*, pp. 171–4.

[39] See Patrick Collinson, *The Elizabethan Puritan Movement* (Oxford, 1990 edn; first publ. 1967), p. 25.

[40] Leif Dixon, *Practical Predestinarians in England, c.1590–1640* (Farnham, 2014), ch. 7, esp. p. 305.

[41] For both examples, see Peter Sherlock, *Monuments and Memory in Early Modern England* (Aldershot, 2008), p. 111.

[42] Marshall, *Beliefs and the Dead*, p. 197.

[43] Sherlock, *Monuments and Memory*, ch. 4, esp. 127.

boy who died on 22 May 1614, was particularly upbeat, presenting him as 'an Infant, born of Gentile Race' who would surely gain 'eternal Bliss' as part of 'God's faithful Seed'. Urging his parents not to mourn him, it reminded them that 'ye procreate to Number Gods Elect': 'Angels and Souls alike pure Essence be, And new born Babes are pure in next Degree.'[44] Mothers and fathers told each other that though 'remov'd...from our present Sight', their beloved offspring were 'yet...in the Bosome of God, and we shall find them on[e] day made perfect in Glory'.[45]

In these ways English Protestantism overcame the epistemological problem of distinguishing the elect from the reprobate at the point of death and attenuated some of the harsher consequences of reformed theology for intergenerational relations. Complicating the stark realities of predestinarian soteriology, it condoned tendencies that pushed back against the view that people could neither assist beloved family members and friends nor communicate with them once they had died. The continuing propensity of contemporaries to see apparitions of their dead kith and kin may be interpreted in the same light. In the early days of the Reformation such visions were largely dismissed as hangovers from the popish past—as evidence of the stubborn resistance of some sectors of the populace to the evangelical precept that such revenants were a Machiavellian device of the Antichristian priesthood and papacy which had been vanquished by the advent of the Gospel. But as time progressed, it became necessary to accommodate their ongoing presence in the Protestant imagination and to account for their remarkable cultural resilience. Insistent that the dead were unable to return to the earthly realm, minsters systematically redefined these experiences as optical illusions created by God or Satan, in short as celestial helpers or diabolical fiends. In doing so they implicitly accepted that spectres, particularly those of beloved blood relatives, could not easily be expelled from the invisible world.[46]

It evidently remained commonplace for ghosts to appear in the likeness of immediate family members and other kinsfolk. Thomas Nashe acknowledged this in his treatise on the *Terrors of the night* published in 1594, explaining that the devil adopted this disguise because he knew that unwary believers would most easily be seduced by 'those shapes which hee supposeth most familiar unto us', and to which 'wee are inclined...with a naturall kind of love'.[47] In the process, he attested indirectly to the bonds of tender affection and the channels of interaction

[44] Henry Chauncy, *Historical antiquities of Hertfordshire* (1700; Wing C3741), pp. 167b-168a.

[45] Bodl., MS Rawlinson D. 1308 (Lady Mary Carey's Meditations and Poetry, transcribed by Charles Hutton), p. 8 (written to her husband George Payler in anticipation that she might die delivering her fourth child, 1653).

[46] Marshall, *Beliefs and the Dead*, ch. 6; *idem*, 'Deceptive Appearances'. See also Bruce Gordon, 'Malevolent Ghosts and Ministering Angels: Apparitions and Pastoral Care in the Swiss Reformation', in Gordon and Marshall (eds), *The Place of the Dead*, pp. 87–109.

[47] Thomas Nashe, *The terrors of the night, or a discourse of apparitions* (1594; STC 18379), sig. B3r.

between the living and the dead that Protestantism proved unable, despite its best attempts, to dissolve, and which it evolved organically to assimilate once more. Troublesome phantoms that, like their medieval precursors, returned to ensure that their testamentary instructions were carried out, to correct unrepented wrongs, to counsel husbands, wives, and children, and to set unfinished affairs in order were not simply a feature of the first few confused generations of the Reformation. The spectre around which the action revolves in Shakespeare's tragedy *Hamlet* is indicative. A menacing father who haunts his son, urging him to take revenge for his untimely demise, this ghost is best seen less as a measure of the playwright's religious conservatism than of a society and culture flexible enough to incorporate ostensibly dissonant elements.[48]

Ghosts grew and proliferated in number as the period progressed, assisted by the gradual lessening of heated confessional quarrels about purgatory and by the rise of unbelief. The celebrated story of Old Mother Leakey of Minehead in Somerset revolved around her disruptive posthumous reappearance to her daughter-in-law. She was also credited with whistling up winds to sink her son's ships and strangling her grandchild: this was a malevolent ghost which returned to settle scores with the succeeding generations.[49] To echo Caroline Callard's observation about early modern France, the appearance of these 'familiar ghosts' underlines the new authority they assumed 'as arbiters in matters of inheritance in families where the fading of genealogical memory required dead relatives to act'.[50]

The apparent resurgence of Sadduceeism gave ghosts a new lease of life as weapons in the war to uphold Christianity against atheism and deism. It is not surprising that stories of revenants who appeared in the guise and 'similitude' of dead relatives featured in texts such as the Cambridge Platonist Henry More's *Immortality of the soul* (1659) and Joseph Glanvill's celebrated *Sadducismus triumphatus* (1681) The latter told the story of the Wiltshire weaver Thomas Goddard, who saw an apparition of his father-in-law in 1674, which he recognized because he was wearing the same clothes, hat, stockings, and shoes in which he had typically been attired during his life. The ghost proceeded to ask after his offspring and to give Thomas 20 or 30 shillings to send to the daughter he had neglected, before revealing the murder he had secretly committed and covered up forty years before. Glanvill concluded that this was no 'imposing phansy', 'voluntary invention', or trick devised by a 'ludicrous goblin': it was a real supernatural being.[51]

---

[48] William Shakespeare, *Hamlet*, I. v. See Stephen Greenblatt, *Hamlet in Purgatory* (Princeton, NJ, 2013 edn).

[49] See Peter Marshall, *Mother Leakey and the Bishop: A Ghost Story* (Oxford, 2007).

[50] Caroline Callard, *Le Temps des fantômes: Spectralités de l'âge moderne (XVIe–XVIIe siècle)* (Paris, 2019), pp. 131–70, at p. 143. The quotation is from the translation: *Spectralities in the Renaissance: Sixteenth and Seventeenth Centuries*, trans. Trista Selous (Oxford, 2022), p. 120 and see ch. 5 passim.

[51] Henry More, *The immortality of the soul, so farre forth as it is demonstrable from the knowledge of nature and the light of reason* (1659; Wing M2663), p. 296, Joseph Glanvill, *Sadducismus triumphatus, or, full and plain evidence concerning witches and apparitions* (1681; Wing G822), pp. 209–19.

In the eighteenth century, as Sasha Handley has shown, ghosts were even more ubiquitous as an index of both the long tentacles of emotion that connected people separated by death and the festering problems within families and households that such spectres so often came back to fix. They appeared frequently to admonish dilatory heirs and executors and to confess to hidden crimes, including murder and infanticide—to domestic felonies that fractured already dysfunctional households that were the alter egos of the little churches and bethels described in Chapter 2. They were instruments for resolving bitter intergenerational conflicts that had continued beyond the grave. The undead open a window into the history of what people remembered and how those memories continued to haunt them.[52] The social and emotional dynamics of incidents in which ghosts appeared were closely connected with the process of grieving and with the troubling interfamilial tensions that often surrounded inheritance. They also reflected pressing questions about salvation, predestination, and providence that continued to preoccupy laypeople.[53]

The lasting deposit that such stories left in later collections of folklore should be seen not as a symptom of pagan or popish 'survivalism' but of the creativity with which the long Reformation adapted to the pastoral dilemmas and challenges faced by ordinary people—people eager to believe that they were not cut completely adrift from their dead loved ones and that they could still engage in dialogue with them. As Natalie Zemon Davis astutely observed in a seminal essay, 'paradoxically, in trying to lay all ghosts forever, Protestants may have raised new ones'.[54] In the long run, the Reformation did not strip religion of intimacy with the dead, who remained a continuing, if intangible presence.[55]

For those who were born in the middle decades of the sixteenth century, there was an additional problem. This was the issue of what had happened to their Catholic ancestors. Were they doomed by virtue of their adherence to a false religion? Was it really the case that all one's forebears who had lived in the dark centuries of popery now burnt in hell? Or might past generations have been excused and forgiven by God because they had sinned in ignorance? This was a controverted issue that troubled people from the beginning of the Henrician schism onwards, as it did elsewhere on the Continent.[56] According to a tract by Pierre

---

[52] Sasha Handley, *Visions of an Unseen World: Ghost Beliefs and Ghost Stories in Reformation England* (2007), esp. p. 15.

[53] See Laura Sangha, 'The Social, Spiritual and Personal Dynamics of Ghost Stories in Early Modern England', *HJ*, 63 (2020), 339–59.

[54] Davis, 'Ghosts, Kin and Progeny', 96.

[55] For a study of this theme in nineteenth-century America, see Erik R. Seeman, 'The Presence of the Dead among US Protestants 1800–1848', *Church History*, 88 (2019), 381–409 and *idem, Speaking with the Dead in Early America* (Philadelphia, PA, 2019).

[56] See Judith Pollmann, 'A Different Road to God: The Protestant Experience of Conversion in the Sixteenth Century', in Peter van der Veer (ed.), *Conversion to Modernities: The Globalization of Christianity* (New York, 1996), pp. 47–64, at p. 57. For England, see Marshall, *Beliefs and the Dead*, pp. 205–10; Woolf, *Social Circulation*, pp. 82–3.

Viret translated from French in 1579, questions 'touching the salvation or damp-naction of our predecessors which have lived in errour' were raised 'dayly'.[57] Early evangelicals who tackled them were reluctant to reach the conclusion that all such individuals were utterly lost. Some simply refused to discuss it and to pass clear judgement. In the course of a sermon preached at Stamford in 1550, Hugh Latimer urged his listeners to set aside this 'vain and unprofitable question' and concentrate on the fate of their own souls, trusting that God had reserved 'our forefathers in so perlouse times, more graciouslye then we can think...leve them & comend them unto gods mercy, who disposeth better for them then we can wysshe'.[58] Many preferred to err on the side of charity and persuade themselves that thousands of those who had lived and died with the 'wals' of the Church of Rome had found mercy at the hands of God, because their persistence in popish superstition was misguided rather than wilful. In a sermon delivered in 1585, Richard Hooker did not doubt that the Lord 'hath most compassion over them that sinne for want of understanding'. This was by no means an uncommon response to a complex problem, but the ardent Presbyterian Walter Travers, who preached in refutation of this claim the very same afternoon, took a much harder line, horrified by the idea that Catholics might escape the eternal punishment that they deserved.[59]

These internal tensions provided welcome ammunition to their confessional adversaries, who took advantage of this area of vulnerability and contradiction in reformed thinking. One of the polemical demands listed by the Douai professor Richard Bristow in his handy guide to debating with Protestants was this: 'they will say, that all our and their fathers & mothers grandfathers and grandmothers, and other Anncestors, Kinsefolke & Countreimen, and all others that haue gonne so long for Christian men, are all damned in Hell'. The exceptions for revered church fathers such as St Augustine whom the heretics made to their own rule underlined the inconsistency with which this position was riddled.[60] Some Protestants came to see this issue as 'the greatest barre and hinderance' to con-verting papists to the true religion. Thomas Morton wrote that the 'Honour and love, which man naturally oweth to his Parents and Progenitors, is felt in every

[57] Pierre Viret, *The Christian disputations*, trans. John Brooke (1579; STC 24776), fo. 273v.

[58] Hugh Latimer, *A sermon of Master Latimer, preached at Stamford the. ix. day of October. Anno. M.cccc. and fyftie* ([1550]; STC 15293), sigs F2v–4r.

[59] Richard Hooker, *A learned discourse of justification, workes, and how the foundation of faith is overthrown* (Oxford, 1612; STC 13708), esp. pp. 22, 64; idem, *The answere of Mr. Richard Hooker to a supplication preferred by Mr Walter Travers to the HH. Lords of the Privie Counsell* (1612; STC 13706), p. 25. For the theological complexities behind this dispute and the wider issue, see Richard Bauckham, 'Hooker, Travers and the Church of Rome in the 1580s', *JEH*, 29 (1978), 37–50, at pp. 45–7; Anthony Milton, *Catholic and Reformed: The Roman and Protestant Churches in English Protestant Thought, 1600–1640* (Cambridge, 1995), pp. 285–7.

[60] Richard Bristow, *Demands to be propounded of Catholickes to the heretikes* (1623 edn; STC 3801.5), pp. 108–9.

mans heart, as a forcible motive to draw on a conceite in the Child, both of their godlinesse, and also of their after-blessednesse; and consequently to inforce an inclination to adhere to their Religion, whatsoever it was'.[61]

As time progressed, emphasis on the magnanimity of God towards medieval ancestors who had been born and died in the bosom of Rome settled into a consensus. This softer stance was partly polemically motivated. It was a manoeuvre in the continuing game of chess in which Protestants were engaged with their Catholic opponents and in the ongoing struggle to win over the apathetic and undecided, who seem to have constantly kicked back against claims that their forebears were guilty of 'superstition', especially in rural areas poorly served by godly preachers. It was easier to excuse relatives many centuries removed in time than those who had lived during the turbulent early days of the Reformation. Sincere papists who had never had the opportunity to embrace the Gospel were less culpable than individuals who had defiantly stood against the tide. Their sins were not so grievous, 'because they h[e]ard not the word of the Lord'. In a revealing extended passage on this subject written in 1589, Francis Trigge used it to castigate the religious indifference of so many of his contemporaries and to urge them to forsake the 'Romish Babylon…and all his trumperie'. He responded robustly to the Catholic charge that 'we condemne our forefathers' by saying that had they 'lived now in this great light', they would surely have denounced 'the great blindnesse of many of their children' and their obstinacy in refusing the goodness of God. They would, in short, have scolded them for their stupidity in resisting the truth. He also claimed that though many during those days had trusted in good works and called upon saints, on their deathbed it was the Lord alone whom they had in their mouths, and so their salvation could be surmised.[62] From this it was but a short step to taking pity on one's living as well as dead Catholic friends and piously hoping, with the Elizabethan gentlewoman Lady Grace Mildmay, that despite their misguided opinions they too might be part of the household of faith.[63] A degree of tolerance to papists extended across the generations. The death of purgatory did not spell the end of the close ties and interchanges that bound together people in the past with those who lived in the present. It reconfigured them, curtailing intercession for the deceased in favour of a firmer focus on the task of remembrance for its own sake.[64]

[61] Thomas Morton, *The grand imposture of the (now) Church of Rome manifested in this one article of the new Romane creede* (1626; STC 18186), p. 365.

[62] Francis Trigge. *An apologie or defence of our dayes, against the vaine murmurings & complaints of manie* (1589; STC 24276), pp. 38–41.

[63] Linda Pollock, *With Faith and Physic: The Life of a Tudor Gentlewoman: Lady Grace Mildmay: 1552–1620* (1993), pp. 64–5, 90–1.

[64] Sherlock, *Monuments and Memory*, p. 126. See also Chapter 6 below.

Rising Generations: Saving the Children

This is a thesis we shall revisit in Chapter 6, but it is necessary now to turn to another pressing issue that perturbed contemporaries: the soteriological status of their children and grandchildren. What, if anything, could be done to ensure that the rising generation found a resting place in heaven? Medieval scholastic theology was predicated on the assumption that human beings could take initiatives that would materially advance their own and others' chances of reaching paradise. They could earn approbation in the eyes of God through the good deeds they did during their lives, while their devotion to the sacraments and prayer would help to counterbalance the sins that, like all men and women, they were prone to commit. The concomitant of Catholic emphasis on free will was a mitigated sense of how far humanity's capacity for righteousness had been compromised by the Fall. Rejecting the Augustinian view that the depravity inherited by infants was ineradicable, Catholics understood baptism as a rite that remitted the guilt and wiped away the essence of original sin. The natural concupiscence or inclination to err that remained in infants could not fatally injure them or 'hinder their entrance into heaven', if they 'manfully' resisted it.[65] As James Wadsworth (father of the Protestant convert quoted earlier) wrote in an apologia for his own dramatic decision to abandon the Church of England, through this sacrament children were 'quite forgiven' and freed from the fault of Adam until they actively committed transgressions of their own.[66] Accordingly, Catholics viewed childhood as a state of innocence during which their parents and godparents could actively work to combat their proclivity to wickedness through religious education and training. They believed in the ability of careful nurture to overcome the inherent frailties of human nature.

One index of these convictions is the energetic programme of catechesis that Catholics launched from the mid-sixteenth century.[67] Another is the wider effort of the missionary priests to engage with the young delineated by Lucy Underwood. This manifested itself not merely in the many schools that they set up on the Continent but in their stress on the duty of parents to act both as allies of and substitutes for the community's comparatively small contingent of priests. In the preface to his edition of Peter Canisius's *Summe of Christian doctrine*, Henry Garnet emphasized 'the most straite charge of good education of children'

---

[65] *The Canons and Decrees of the Council of Trent*, ed. H. J. Schroeder (Rockford, IL, 1978 edn), p. 23, and see pp. 53–4. See also John Brereley, *Sainct Austines religion* (1620), pp. 68–70.

[66] James Wadsworth, *The contrition of a Protestant preacher, converted to be a Catholique scholler conteyning certayne meditations upon the fourth penitentiall psalme, Miserere* ([St Omer, 1615]; STC 24924.5), pp. 41–4, and Meditation IIII.

[67] On catechizing, see Chapter 1 above. Lucy Underwood; *Childhood, Youth and Religious Dissent in Post-Reformation England* (Basingstoke, 2014), ch. 3. See also Alexandra Walsham, 'Wholesome Meat and Strong Milk: Catholic Translations of Peter Canisius's Catechisms and the Conversion of Protestant Britain', *BCH*, 32 (2015), 293–314.

given by God, sharply reproving those 'who as though they had by carnall generation brought into this world brute beastes, whose onely end is to live here, without any end of heavenly blisse: do not seeke for their children the meanes of their
salvation, onely providing for them earthly riches, not caring for heavenly'. He
drew an unfavourable comparison between the Turk or Jew who, perceiving their
offspring to have been present at Christian ceremonies:

> would not sticke to embrew his handes in that which he begotte. And yet he
> which professeth himself a Catholike, by sending his child, or permitting his
> childe to be sent to such things as are indispensably forbidden by God himself:
> doth unnaturally deprive his innocent sonne of that which he could not
> give him.[68]

The cases handled by Elizabethan casuists, meanwhile, highlight the intense
anxieties that devout laypeople felt about the spiritual fate of their children and
servants. Did one sin by allowing one's offspring and employees to go freely to
Church of England services and sermons? Was it permissible to leave a legacy to a
heretical daughter or son, or should they be deprived of their inheritance? The
casuists advised against the latter strategy for fear that this might cause 'a tragic
outbreak of persecution against Catholics', but they condemned the negligence
that allowed so many young people to 'rush headlong into all kinds of wickedness' and insisted that parents who did not make every endeavour—from pleas
and promises to presents and bribes—to stop their children from attending heretical worship sinned mortally.[69]

As the clerical hierarchy increasingly recognized, creating a generation of committed believers was vital for the survival and future of this beleaguered religion.
The optimism that buoyed them up in their battle to retain and win souls sprang
from the belief that it was eminently possible to mould the soft wax and pliable
plant of children's minds and successfully bring them to knowledge of the truth.[70]
The exemplary young people celebrated in missionary memoranda and martyrologies provided compelling evidence that those of tender years could be inspired
to lead holy and sanctified lives, whether with the assistance of their mothers and
fathers or indeed in defiance of their natural kin.[71] As the community turned
inwards and became more endogamous, it concentrated increasing attention on
cultivating and bringing up good Catholic offspring who would carry on the fight

---

[68] Peter Canisius, *A summe of Christian doctrine*, trans. Henry Garnet (1592; STC 4571.5), sig. *3r.
[69] P. J. Holmes (ed.), *Elizabethan Casuistry*, CRS 67 (1981), pp. 103–5.
[70] Underwood, *Childhood*, esp. ch. 6. See also Lucy Underwood, 'Recusancy and the Rising
Generation', *RH*, 31 (2013), 511–33.
[71] Alison Shell, 'Furor Juvenilis: Post-Reformation English Catholicism and Exemplary Youthful
Behaviour', in Ethan H. Shagan (ed.), *Catholics and the 'Protestant Nation': Religious Politics and
Identity in Early Modern England* (Manchester, 2005), pp. 185–206.

to restore their faith to dominance and reverse the Reformation. The salvation of those who followed closely in the footsteps of their ancestors was never really in doubt. As Francis de Sales wrote in his influential *Introduction to a devoute life*, translated into English in 1613, parents who took due care 'to emprint the feare and love of God in their tender hearts' once they reached the years of discretion contributed to 'the bwilding up of a house', and to the making of a 'race' and 'generation' of the faithful.[72]

For Protestants, by contrast, the task of saving one's children was very much more complex. There were two obvious reasons for this. The first was the renewed stress on the deep and hereditary corruption of all human beings that was the legacy of the reformed neo-Augustinianism examined in Chapter 3. Accompanied by the assumption that the taint of original sin lingered in children after they were christened, this laid a considerable burden of responsibility on Protestant parents. It was incumbent upon them to do all they could for the progeny to whom they had directly passed down this depravity, as their own progenitors had done in an unbroken chain extending back to Adam and Eve. The very fact that offspring 'drew contagion from their parents' should be an incentive to bring them to be 'washed with the water' of holy baptism.[73] In his *Grounds of divinitie*, Elnathan Parr similarly commented that 'as they are Instruments of their generation, and also of their conception and guiltinesse, conceyved by the same', so they were under an obligation to endeavour to 'become instruments by their good Education and Discipline of their regeneration by the Spirit of God'.[74]

The second, closely associated reason why this was intrinsically difficult had to do with the doctrine of predestination that dominated the theology of the Church of England until the 1620s and continued to exert a powerful influence for many decades thereafter.[75] Technically, this ruled out the possibility that parents could do anything to prevent the damnation of their daughters and sons and to stop their souls from descending to hell if that was God's will. All decisions about who would be saved and who would be damned had been made at the beginning of time, long before such children were even a twinkle in their parents' eyes and without any reference to how they might behave during their earthly lives. The logic of the intertwined processes of election and reprobation was to deny that godliness could descend down the generations.

---

[72] Francis de Sales, *An introduction to a devout life*, trans. I. Y. ([Douai], 1613; STC 11316.5), pp. 464–5.

[73] William Gouge, *Of domesticall duties* (1622; STC 12119), p. 520.

[74] Elnathan Parr, *The grounds of divinitie plainely discovering the mysteries of Christian religion, propounded familiarly in divers questions and answeres* (1614; STC 19314), p. 150. See also Anna French, 'Raising Christian Children in Early Modern England: Salvation, Education and the Family', *Theology*, 116 (2013), pp. 93–102.

[75] See Peter Lake, 'Calvinism and the English Church 1570-1635', *P&P*, 114 (1987), 32–76; Nicholas Tyacke, *Anti-Calvinists: The Rise of English Arminianism, 1590-1640* (Oxford, 1990); Dixon, *Practical Predestinarians*.

'Can a man hope for a holy posteritie?' asked the Cambridgeshire divine Richard Greenham.[76] Even as they highlighted the inexorable transmission of original sin via the primal act of sexual intercourse, he and his colleagues were bound to admit that true religion did not and could not run down family lines. As the Devonshire minister Samuel Hieron declared in the early years of the seventeenth century, people were not made children of the Lord as a result of 'reall descent or propagation' but rather by adoption and imitation—by a process of rebirth that was itself dependent on the infusion of providential grace via the Holy Spirit and through the hearing of the Word. Christians were 'born not of blood' but engendered through the work of God alone. This resembled a form of horticulture—the grafting of a branch onto a different stock to create a new plant. This explained why 'holy children have issued out of god-lesse parents, as *Abraham*, out of the loines of idolatrous *Terah* and wicked children have branched out of gracious progenitors, as *Hophni* and *Phineas* out of *Eli*, *Ammnon & Abshalom* out of *David*'.[77] If one's sons and daughters became a blessed generation, remarked a series of ministers from Andrew Willet and James Ussher, this had less to do with the gifts they gained through their 'carnall' generation than those they acquired through their spiritual rebirth: 'Unles they become new born, they have no good thing in them.'[78] As Matthew Griffith wrote in *Bethel, or, a forme for families* (1633), godly persons did not beget their children as saints. Saving faith did not pass down the generations by inheritance but by divine blessing.[79]

This widely made observation was, however, in tension with the lesson that many Protestants derived from the text of Genesis 17:7, which described the everlasting covenant that God established with Abraham and his seed for generation after generation without end. Also containing the Lord's promise that he would make the patriarch 'exceeding fruitful' and the father of kings and nations, this chapter went on to describe how circumcision of the foreskin of male children would serve as a token of this binding contract. It implied that salvation was a birthright bestowed upon an entire lineage of people and, inverting the classic formula

---

[76] Richard Greenham, *The works of the reverend and faithfull servant of Jesus Christ M. Richard Greenham, minister and preacher of the word of God*, ed. H. H (1599; STC 12312), pp. 159–68 ('Of the Good Education of Children'), at p. 159.

[77] Samuel Hieron, *All the sermons...heretofore sunderly published, now diligently revised, and collected together into one volume* (1614; STC 13378), pp. 314, 422, 410. See also Chapter 1 above, p. 71.

[78] James Ussher, *A body of divinitie, or the summe and substance of Christian religion* (1645; Wing U151), p. 145; Andrew Willet, *Hexapla in Genesin, that is, a sixfold commentarie upon Genesis* (1632 [1633]; STC 25684), p. 64. The final quotation is from Greenham: Kenneth L. Parker and Eric J. Carlson (eds), 'Practical Divinity': The Works and Life of Revd Richard Greenham (Aldershot, 1998), p. 172.

[79] Matthew Griffith, *Bethel: or, a forme for families* (1633; STC 12369), p. 392. See also Benjamin Needler, *Expository notes, with practical observations; towards the opening of the five first chapters of the first book of Moses called Genesis* (1655; Wing N412), p. 107.

of Tertullian, that Christians were not made but born.[80] In contrast with the statements quoted above, it presented grace as a genealogical trait that passed from parents to children. It assimilated the congregation of the faithful to the family and tribe of the patriarch, which by virtue of this pledge had been separated from the rest of the world, as light from darkness, and as a household of people predestined to salvation.

A trace of such sentiments can be detected in the work of some early evangelical writers, including Thomas Becon, whose voluminous catechism published in the 1560s included the comment that 'God is now no less the God of the Christians and of their children, than he was in times past the God of the Jews and their children.'[81] These were also an undercurrent in the theology of Calvin, who heralded the young as 'the heritage of the Lord' and inferred that they were full members of the covenant.[82] His willingness to do so reflected his belief in the unknowability of the identities of those saved and damned by the double decree. As Dennis Austin Britton has argued, what this reading of Genesis constituted was a 'racialisation of salvation' that was somewhat hard to reconcile with the idea that the elect were saved only through Christ. It sat awkwardly alongside Calvin's repudiation of those who 'dream of some seed of election implanted in their hearts from their very birth.'[83]

Nowhere did these apparent contradictions become more apparent than in the context of baptism, which was understood as a type of the Hebrew rite of circumcision. Rejecting the notion that the sacraments had efficacy as conduits and agents of grace, reformed theology reduced them to memorials and seals. Christening did, however, nominally confer on infants the status of heirs of Christ. It was a rite that incorporated them into the Christian community.[84] In the context of renewed emphasis on original sin, the baptismal ceremony may even have acquired greater significance: the iniquity in which children were conceived made them 'theologically vexed and soteriologically uncertain creatures.'[85] The ambiguities that hovered around Protestant thinking about this sacrament

[80] 'Christians are made, not born': Tertullian, *Apology, De Spectaculis*, trans. T. R. Glover; Minucius Felix, *Octavius*, trans. Gerald H. Rendall (Cambridge, MA, 1931), p. 91 (18.4).
[81] *The Catechism of Thomas Becon, with Other Pieces*, ed. John Ayre, PS (Cambridge, 1844), p. 208.
[82] See Barbara Pitkin, '"The Heritage of the Lord": Children in the Theology of John Calvin', in Marcia J. Bunge (ed.), *The Child in Christian Thought* (Grand Rapids, MI, 2001), pp. 160–93.
[83] Dennis Austin Britton, *Becoming Christian: Race, Reformation, and Early Modern English Romance* (New York, 2014), p. 48, and ch. 1. John Calvin, *Institutes of the Christian Religion*, trans. Henry Beveridge, 2 vols in 1 (Grand Rapids, MI, 1989 edn), vol. ii, p. 249.
[84] See E. Brooks Holifield, *The Covenant Sealed: The Development of Puritan Sacramental Theology in Old and New England, 1570–1720* (New Haven, CT, 1974), chs 1 and 3; Will Coster, *Baptism and Spiritual Kinship in Early Modern England* (Aldershot, 2002), chs 2–3; John Whelan Riggs, *Baptism in the Reformed Tradition: A Historical and Practical Theology* (Louisville, KY, 2002); Karen E. Spierling, *Infant Baptism in Reformation Geneva* (Aldershot, 2005), esp. ch. 2.
[85] Anna French, '"All Things Necessary for their Salvation?" The Dedham Ministers and the "Puritan" Baptism Debates', in Tali Berner and Lucy Underwood (eds), *Childhood, Youth and Religious Minorities in Early Modern Europe* (Cham, 2019), pp. 75–98, at pp. 87, 91.

were encapsulated in the temporally confusing language of the liturgy, which moves between *hoping* that the infant will in due course be awoken in faith and become fully incorporated into the body of Christ's congregation and the invisible church of the saved on earth and *implying* that this process may have already occurred. It swings seamlessly between seeing baptism as a sign of a promise that might be fulfilled in the future and as an indication that they had indeed been chosen to receive eternal glory.[86] This was certainly how it was possible for people to interpret the words said over the babies that godparents brought to be baptized in church and those whose fragile health necessitated that laypeople conduct an emergency christening.[87]

The text of Genesis 17:7 also consoled those grieving for children who had died before there was time to christen them by implying that they too were encompassed under the Abrahamic covenant. William Hubbock devoted an entire sermon to proving this precept by 'the revealed will of God'. In the preface to the published version, which appeared in 1595, he asked 'is his compassion shut up from the seed of Christians?'[88] Some years earlier John Hooper had drawn a similar comparison to the ancient Jews, inferring that, like those who perished prior to their circumcision, these children too would be saved by the faith of their progenitors.[89] In the 1620s, the London pastor George Scarborough spoke of such infants as 'the holy branches of believing Parents'.[90] In his account of the 'holy life' of his late wife Elizabeth, who had borne eleven children, the Essex rector Anthony Walker implied that the external rite was almost unnecessary: 'if ever Children were Baptized in their Mothers Belly (excuse the Expression) doubtless hers were so'.[91] This trope had often been invoked by fifteenth-century Lollards under investigation for heresy. The Norfolk women Hawisia Moone and Margery Baxter were among those who denied that babies born of Christian parents required neither christening nor confirmation, since they received the blessing of the Holy Spirit in the uterus.[92]

[86] Cummings (ed.), *Book of Common Prayer*, pp. 141–50.
[87] See Anna French, 'Disputed Words and Disputed Meanings: The Reformation of Baptism, Infant Limbo and Child Salvation in Early Modern England', in Jonathan Willis (ed.), *Sin and Salvation in Reformation England* (Farnham, 2015), pp. 157–72, esp. pp. 166–7.
[88] William Hubbock, *An apologie of infants in a sermon: proving, by the revealed will of God, that children prevented by death of their baptisme, by Gods election, may be saved* (1595; STC 13898), 'To the Reader'.
[89] John Hooper, *A briefe and cleare confession of the Christian faith*, printed in John Baker, *Lectures ... upon the xii. Articles of our Christian faith briefely set forth for the comfort of the godly, and the better instruction of the simple and ignorant* (1581; STC 1219), sig. Ff2v.
[90] George Scarborough, *The summe of all godly and profitable catechismes, reduced into one* (1623; STC 21806.5), sig. B11r.
[91] Anthony Walker, *The holy life of Mr Elizabeth Walker, late wife of A.W. D.D., rector of Fyfield in Essex* (1690; Wing 305), p. 61.
[92] See J. Patrick Hornbeck II, '"A Prophane or Hethyn Thing": English Lollards on Baptism and Confirmation', *Mediaeval Studies*, 74 (2012), 283–306, at 299, 301–2.

In the context of the tragic loss of a child, it is entirely understandable that pastors wished to give surviving relatives the impression that salvation was in some sense a birthright. In a world in which the concept of limbo no longer existed, Protestants instinctively fell back on God's promise to Abraham to ease the pain of those who were victims of the high rates of infant mortality characteristic of early modern English society. This also provided reassurance to expectant mothers anxiously waiting for their labour to begin.[93] Prayers of thanksgiving for a safe delivery alluded to it in calling upon God to bless the infant and by imploring him to demonstrate that the child was one of 'the number of them, with whom thou hast made the pretious covenant, I will be thy God, and the God of thy seed'.[94]

The frequency with which Protestants invoked these passages in Scripture brought them into conflict with Anabaptists on the one hand and Catholics on the other. Although the logical consequence of their own position was that infant baptism was not strictly necessary for salvation, they strongly repudiated the idea that conscious belief had to precede it. They consequently found themselves on the receiving end of accusations of creating a church by means of what John Smyth, the exiled leader of a gathered congregation in the Netherlands, dismissed as 'carnall genealogie'. To continue the spiritual succession of true believers by this means was to build religion on a false and sandy foundation. True baptism could only take place when people had become 'new born babes in Christ' through the process of spiritual conversion; false baptism of infants 'borne after the flesh' was a mark of the Beast.[95] In *The smoke in the temple* (1646), John Saltmarsh declared 'Baptism is not to be received by Generation now, as Circumcision was, but by Regeneration or visible Profession, as at first: Nor are the carnall seed now any more children of Abraham, but the Faithful'.[96] He wrote in a tradition of puritan thinking that, according to John Coolidge, 'positively militates against the historical extension of the Church beyond a single generation of converts to Christ' and within which there was an enduring antithesis between generation and regeneration.[97]

Albeit from a different perspective, Catholics also castigated the Church of England's teaching on baptism for suggesting that grace was passed down from parents to children. Eager to uphold the salvific efficacy of the sacrament itself, in his *Confutation* of 1565, Thomas Harding mocked Jewel's observation that 'the issue which commeth of faithfull parents, is borne holy, and is a holy progenie,

[93]   See, e.g., John Oliver, *A present for teeming women* (1663; Wing 276), p. 4.
[94]   Ch[ristopher] H[ooke], *The child-birth or womans lecture* (1590; STC 13702), sig. D3v.
[95]   John Smyth, *The character of the beast, or, the false constitution of the church discovered in certayne passages...concerning true Christian baptisme of new creatures, or new borne babes in Christ, and false baptisme of infants borne after the flesh* ([Middelburg], 1609; STC 22875), pp. 61, 62. This echoed Romans 9:7–8.
[96]   John Saltmarsh, *The smoke in the temple* (1646; Wing S498), p. 9.
[97]   John S. Coolidge, *The Pauline Renaissance in England: Puritanism and the Bible* (Oxford, 1970), ch. 4, at pp. 78, 84.

and that the children of such being yet enclosed in the wombe before they drawe breath of life, be never the lesse chosen into the covenant of life everlasting'.[98] Writing in 1620, John Brereley was likewise dismissive of the 'ordinary opinion' among Protestants that infants 'borne of faithful parents dying without Baptisme may be saved', declaring this a 'cruel and uncharitable practise' that doomed them to near certain damnation.[99] The theme continued to find a place in works of controversy directed against Protestant doctrine, including John Heigham's *Touch-stone of the reformed gospel*, which cited various biblical texts contradicting the opinion that 'the children of the faithful are sanctified' and which was still being reissued in 1676.[100]

These radical and conservative critics of the magisterial English Reformation had a valid point. The inclusive ecclesiology to which it was committed obliged its leaders to imply that baptism was a seal and pledge of the election of all its members, despite the unlikelihood that everyone born into it had been predestined to salvation. It fostered a willing suspension of disbelief that the odds were stacked against this. Echoed in the resonant words of the Magnificat said or sung at evening prayer, the mercy that the Lord had 'promysed to our forefathers, Abraham and his sede for ever' seeped into the consciousness of England's Protestants and predisposed them to be hopeful about the eschatological prospects of their children.[101]

It is telling that the language of the Prayer Book, particularly the service for baptism, was one of the weapons that avant-garde conformists and Laudians used to contest Calvinist claims about predestination. If the liturgy provided support for the doctrine of election, it also offered ammunition to an emerging body of churchmen sympathetic to a more Arminian theology of grace, including Richard Montagu and Edmund Reeve. Critical of puritan presumption in prying into the secrets of divine will, Laudians were more inclined to shroud these in mystery and to play up the latitude of God's promise of mercy to humankind. Baptized children, Reeve argued, had 'all things necessary for their salvation and are undoubtedly saved'. 'Every Infant baptized is justified and made a member of Christ, a child of God, and an inheritour of the kingdom of heaven.' Scrutiny of the double decree was deemed to be more fit for the schools than the pulpit or practical divinity, but when it suited them, ministers of this disposition could deploy the potent terminology of the Old Testament. Thus, in a tract defending paedobaptism, Jeremy Taylor spoke of the 'holy seed' created by the sacrament.[102]

---

[98] Thomas Harding, *A confutation of a booke intituled An apologie of the Church of England* (Antwerp, 1565; STC 12762), fo. 67v.

[99] Brereley, *Sainct Austines religion*, p. 71.

[100] John Heigham, *The touch-stone of the reformed gospel* (1676 edn; Wing H1370E; first publ. 1634), pp. 89–90.

[101] Cummings (ed.), *Book of Common Prayer*, p. 112.

[102] See Edmund Reeve, *The communion booke catechisme expounded* (1635; STC 20830), pp. 62–3; Jeremy Taylor, *A discourse of baptisme, its institution, and efficacy upon all believers* (1652; Wing

Such statements remind us of the 'bizarre parallels, echoes, cross-overs and borrowings among the different traditions of English religion'. These belie an overly polarized picture of ecclesiastical developments in this period, even as they highlight the elements of tension and divergence that emerged in the struggle for possession of the Church of England.[103]

In the handbooks about household management they prepared, godly ministers encouraged their readers to believe that their offspring would inherit their own spiritual worth like the posterity of Abraham. William Gouge's influential *Domesticall duties* declared that 'though God doe reserve in himselfe a freedome to order his blessings as it pleaseth him, and to bestow them upon whom he will...it is a very usuall course with him to extend his blessing (according to his promise) to the children of the righteous'. Testifying to 'his great good liking' and 'high approbation' of their efforts to serve him, this was a reward for their piety. Although Gouge added the caveat that divine grace itself was 'not communicated to children' and did not descend by 'naturall propagation from the parent', the tenor of his discussion left the impression that blessings could in some sense be inherited.[104]

Despite the genealogical overtones of the passage in Genesis to which Protestant ministers repeatedly alluded, they themselves were clear that if godly parents did breed zealous children, this was not because they were actually engendered with these virtues, but because their upbringing induced them to mimic their mothers and fathers. 'Should not the Fathers graces provoke children to goodnesse?' asked Richard Bernard, commenting in response that 'good children will not degenerate from good Parents'.[105] Through their honest care, wise oversight, and constant guidance, declared another divine, 'in their posteritie true religion and godlines may continue and never cease, so as their children may be Gods children until all generations'.[106] There was 'no more effectuall meanes' to provoke the Lord to look benignly upon their offspring than for parents to obey his voice, wrote Gervase Babington. He urged adults to ensure that their assiduous attendance at church, hearing of the word, and receiving of the sacraments would bear fruit in the next generation, sealing the favour of the Almighty 'not onely to your selves, but to your children after you, to a thousand desents'. In turn, it should be a source

T315). Stephen Hampton discusses shifting opinion within the Church of England in 'Confessional Identity', in Anthony Milton (ed.), *The Oxford History of Anglicanism*, i: *Reformation and Identity, c.1520–1662* (Oxford, 2017), pp. 210–42, esp. 225. On the Laudians and predestination, see Peter Lake, *On Laudianism: Piety, Polemic and Politics during the Personal Rule of Charles I* (Cambridge, forthcoming), esp. Part 4.

[103] Anthony Milton, *England's Second Reformation: The Battle for the Church of England 1625–1662* (Cambridge, 2021), pp. 510, 512.

[104] Gouge, *Domesticall duties*, pp. 502–3.

[105] Richard Bernard, *Ruth's recompence: or a commentarie upon the booke of Ruth* (1628; STC 1962), p. 451.

[106] *The office of Christian parents shewing how children are to be gouerned throughout all ages and times of their life* (1616; STC 5180), p. 16.

of comfort to the young to note that when God 'loved the stock', he would 'not cast away the branch, but graciously respect him'.[107] In such texts, the benefits of example and education were silently elided with election—or at least so it must have seemed in the eyes of laypeople eager to believe that they could indeed save their children.

Such statements provide compelling evidence of the pastoral flexibility of second-generation Protestantism, as well as of a form of wishful thinking. Once the initial phase of evangelical conversion to the new religion had passed, as we have seen, the salutary effects of nurture, instruction, and discipline acquired fresh importance. According to Gouge, parents' conscientious performance of their duty to act as 'watchmen over their children' was 'an especiall meanes of propagating true religion from age to age, and from generation to generation'. By teaching, catechizing, and reading them Scripture, they were exposing their offspring to experiences that might germinate the seed of election that they earnestly hoped, if not presumptuously supposed lay dormant in their souls. Serving as instruments of both their second birth and their first, they were working towards their regeneration as the adopted sons and daughters of God.[108] 'Thus will children sucke in religion with learning,' as they did their mother's milk, commented Gouge, deploying a metaphor of lactation that must have further complicated perceptions of this mysterious process. If all were diligent in this regard, 'as there is a succession of children, and thereby a preservation of mankinde, so there would be a succession of those that feare God, and thereby a preservation of true religion'.[109] By rearing them diligently, parents were also actively building, preserving, and perpetuating God's church for the future. They were establishing an unbroken lineage stretching far into the future.

These were precepts that laypeople such as Grace Mildmay internalized. Her diary contains earnest reflections on the need for parents to instruct and inculcate virtue in their children in order 'to preserve goodnesse in them, as an holy seed for generation to generation'.[110] Elizabeth, countess of Lincoln, even extended this logic to supply an argument for maternal breastfeeding, insisting that by this means the child '(... perhaps one of Gods very elect...) might finde food of syncere milke, even from Gods immediate providence'. In turn, the very act of suckling an infant showed that the mother was one of 'his new borne Babes, by your earnest desire after his word; & syncere doctrine thereof'.[111] Other circumstances were also conducive to confidence in the promise extended to the posterity of

[107] Gervase Babington, *Certaine plaine, briefe, and comfortable notes upon everie chapter of Genesis* (1592; STC 1086), fos 106r–v, 128v.
[108] See Samuel Doolittle, *The righteous mans hope at death consider'd and improv'd for the comfort of dying Christians* (1693; Wing D 1879), sig. a3r; Joseph Waite, *The parents primer and the mothers looking glasse* (1681; Wing W222), p. 71.
[109] Gouge, *Domesticall duties*, pp. 538–9.   [110] Pollock, *With Faith and Physic*, p. 29.
[111] Elizabeth Clinton, *The Countess of Lincolnes nurserie* (Oxford, 1622; STC 5324), pp. 17, 20.

Abraham. George Scarborough flattered his patron, Lady Anne Sackville, countess of Dorset, dedicating the catechism he had written for 'weaker Christians, who are as yet babes in Christ' to her 'to testifie hereby unto the world my unfained estimation of those saving graces and truth of Religion, which hereditarily from your childhood, & from your noble Tribe, dwelleth in you'.[112] Timothy Rogers chose his words carefully when consoling the bereaved son of 95-year-old Martha Hasselborn, praying that 'the pure and constant faith that was in your mother is passed unto you; not by a propagation of Blood, but of Spirit; not of Nature, but of Grace'.[113] The constant slippage between religion and reproduction, faith and inheritance apparent in such utterances is, nevertheless, indicative of the influence that the story of Abraham's seed exerted on family life and domestic piety. Notwithstanding the forbiddingly random logic of predestination, generational thinking lay at the heart of reformed soteriology in practice.

The immense popularity of the iconographical motif of Abraham and the angel that averted him from sacrificing his infant son Isaac (Genesis 22) as a theme of the material culture of the devout household offers further evidence of the extent to which these ideas filtered into and shaped daily experience. Adorning cushion and bible covers, prints, plasterwork, wooden panels, and ceramic plates, such imagery served as a reminder that the patriarch's willingness to obey God's command and kill his child was rewarded by a renewed promise that the Lord would bless and multiply his seed forever (Fig. 4.1). If it served as a typological parallel of the Almighty's own sacrifice of Christ for the redemption of all humanity, it was also a symbol of the everlasting covenant into which he had entered with the Hebrew patriarch and which extended down the generations. The scene is depicted, for instance, on a charger dated *c*.1665 and on the carved wooden overmantel of a fireplace in a town house built for the Oxford apothecary John Williams in 1613, beneath which is a lengthy inscription, which begins:

BEHOLD THE FATHER OF THE FAITHFULL SEEDE
WAS HEERE APPROVED TO BE SOUND INDEEDE.[114]

Such texts and objects are symptomatic of the shifts of emphasis that accompanied the transformation of the Tudor Reformation from a charismatic protest

[112] Scarborough, *Summe*, sig. A3r.

[113] Timothy Rogers, *The happiness of a quiet mind, both in youth and old age, with the way to attain it in a discourse occasioned by the death of Mrs. Martha Hasselborn who died March 13th, 1695/6, in the 95th year of her age* (1696; Wing R1851), sig. A3r.

[114] See V&A, C.73-1951 (dish, *c*.1665); Tara Hamling, 'Reconciling Image and Object: Religious Imagery in Protestant Interior Decoration', in *eadem* and Catherine Richardson (eds), *Everyday Objects: Medieval and Early Modern Material Culture and Its Meanings* (Farnham, 2010), pp. 321–34, at p. 32; and *eadem, Decorating the 'Godly' Household: Religious Art in Post-Reformation Britain* (New Haven, CT, 2010), pp. 151–2, 218, 238–45. Hamling emphasizes the episode as a type of Christ's crucifixion. The sacrifice of Isaac was the most common biblical subject in decorative art in the period.

Fig. 4.1 English embroidery of Abraham and the sacrifice of Isaac (Genesis 22) dated 1673.

Source: © Ashmolean Museum, University of Oxford: WA.OA414. Bridgeman Images.

movement into the ecclesiastical bastion of the establishment. By the 1580s, becoming (as opposed to being) Protestant was less a consequence of the unpredictable workings of the Holy Spirit than of the biological fact of reproduction combined with diligent upbringing. For those born after 1558, the reformed religion was indeed a birthright, but also one that depended upon pious parenthood.

These references to seed cannot easily be disentangled from Aristotelian theories of generation, which understood conception as the result of the mingling of male and female seed in the womb (Fig. 4.2). Some credited men's seed with sole responsibility for the creation of a new human being, but others stressed the physiological contribution of both fathers and mothers in engendering children. The Virgin Mary's immaculate conception of Jesus was a miraculous act: Christ came of her flesh but of supernatural rather than natural seed. For the rest of humanity procreation was a process comparable to the cultivation of crops in agriculture.[115]

---

[115] On theories of generation, see Thomas Chamberlyne, *The compleat midwifes practice, in the most weighty and high concernments of the birth of man containing perfect rules for midwifes and nurses* (1656; Wing C1817C); Levinus Lemnius, *A discourse touching generation* (1667; Wing L1043B), esp.

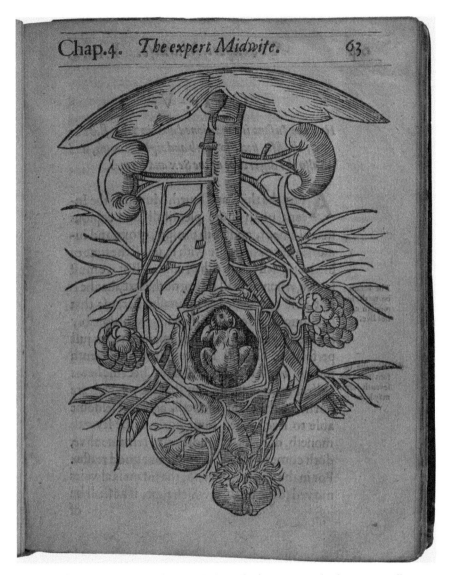

Fig. 4.2 The generation of children: Jakob Rüff, *The expert midwife, or an excellent and most necessary treatise of the generation and birth of man* (London, 1637), p. 63.
Source: Folger Shakespeare Library, Washington DC, STC 21442. Folger Digital Image Collection.

The silent transpositions between the figurative and the literal that characterized Protestant invocations of God's covenant with Abraham and his offspring in
Genesis 17:7 are indicative of how the literary forms in which complex religious
doctrines are discussed affect their meaning. At one level, these are examples of
what Maria Devlin has helpfully called 'rhetorical theology'. They are instances of
the voluntarist language that suffused sermons and works of practical divinity, as
it did the drama of the period—a language that implied that people were not quite
as helpless to shape their fate as an assessment of high Calvinist dogma might
lead one to believe and that fervent piety and sincere repentance in the real time
of their earthly lives could just make a difference with regard to their place in the
afterlife. This required suspending a regime of temporality that insisted that the
key events in an individual Christian's history had already happened in favour of
one that stressed the conditionality of divine decrees.[116] Such texts attest to the
empathy and care with which preachers and ministers balanced the calculus of
divine omnipotence and human responsibility in order to combat inertia and
despair, even if this introduced ostensible inconsistencies into Protestant thinking. These subtleties were probably lost on some ordinary laypeople, especially in
the emotionally charged contexts in which they struggled and strove to protect
the bodies and souls of their children.

Such transactions have always been a feature of Christian piety. But they also
need to be situated against the backdrop of organic evolutions in predestinarian
theology that were themselves responses to the experience of trying to translate
its tenets into a template for everyday existence. Driven by the impulse to gain
assurance and find evidence of where one stood in the scheme of salvation, the
forms of experimental and practical predestinarianism that developed in late
Elizabethan and Stuart England (and indeed in Dutch Calvinism) offered a degree
of solace to those seeking a thread of soteriological certainty.[117] In what Leif
Dixon calls 'the culture of predestinarian communication', the double decree of
election and reprobation did not necessarily foster intense spiritual anxiety; on

chs 6 and 20; *Aristoteles master-piece, or, the secrets of generation diplayed in all the parts thereof* (1684;
Wing A3689). See also Mary E. Fissell, *Vernacular Bodies: The Politics of Reproduction in Early Modern
England* (Oxford, 2004), pp. 187, 199–201.
    [116] Maria Devlin, '"If it were made for Man, 'Twas thde for Me": Generic Damnation and
Rhetorical Salvation in Reformation Preaching and Plays', in Jonathan Willis (ed.), *Sin and Salvation
in Reformation England* (Farnham, 2015), pp. 173–89.
    [117] See R. T. Kendall, *Calvin and English Calvinism to 1649* (Oxford, 1979), esp. p. 9. Kendall's
bifurcation between the intellectualism of Calvin and the voluntarism of his successors has been criticized. See J. G. Moeller, 'The Beginnings of Puritan Covenant Theology', *JEH*, 14 (1963), 46–67;
Richard A. Muller, *The Unaccommodated Calvin: Studies in the Foundation of a Theological Tradition*
(New York, 2000). For the Netherlands, see Freya Sierhuis, *The Literature of the Arminian Controversy:
Religion, Politics and the Stage in the Dutch Republic* (Oxford, 2015), p. 168. As in England, much
turned on the status of young children: see Erik A. De Boer, '"O, Ye Women, Think of Thy Innocent
Children When They Die Young": The Canons of Dort (First Head, Article Seventeen) between
Polemic and Pastoral Theology', in Aza Goudriaan and Fred van Lieburg (eds), *Revisiting the Synod of
Dort (1618–1619)* (Leiden, 2011), pp. 275–90, at p. 261.

the contrary, as presented to born-and-bred Protestants, it could inspire a degree of optimism and confidence. Systematic and pastoral theology coexisted in 'a connective relationship'.[118]

In such an atmosphere, it is scarcely surprising that the notion that true believers were part of a two-way covenant with God took hold or that fervently Protestant parents found in the text of Genesis 17:7 a locus of hope about the fate of their beloved offspring. This crucial passage underpinned the Staffordshire Presbyterian minister Thomas Blake's *Birth-priviledge, or, covenant-holinesse of beleevers and their issue in the time of the Gospel* (1644), which described faith as a heritable right and insisted that nothing could exclude the seed of a believer from the sacrament of baptism. The charter made with Abraham had not been abrogated by the coming of Christ, who was himself a branch of the stock of this 'holy root'. The holiness in question was not a 'fruit of nature' but a consequence of the covenant of free grace which entitled one's offspring to its outward privileges. Moving seamlessly between the languages of spiritual and biological ancestry, Blake declared that it was 'the greatest of our comforts, that posteritie, our little ones, and those that shall be born, are bound up of God in the same promise'. All those within the covenant, he concluded, could be confident that their children would enjoy bliss in the next life.[119] The targets of Blake's remarks were those who denied the infants of erring and unregenerate parents the right to baptism.

During the Civil Wars and Interregnum the exclusion of the children of those who were 'grossly ignorant', 'scandalous in their conversation', 'scoffers at godliness', and resistant to church discipline became a touchstone for sectarian dispute and a focal point for recrimination. In 1652 Daniel Cawdrey, the Presbyterian pastor of Great Billing in Northamptonshire, felt compelled to provide a 'sober answer' and to publish a series of animadversions to the assertions and actions of those, including Giles Firmin and Thomas Hooker, who refused to christen the infants of delinquent mothers and fathers. Clinging desperately to the endangered concept of an inclusive national church, Cawdrey thought that debarring this seal and ordinance to the offspring of such parents was not merely a recipe for making its congregations 'little better than infidels', but more fundamentally a contravention of the promise made to Abraham. However profane their progenitors, as long as they professed belief in Jesus Christ, they were part of the seed: 'The truth is, as I conceive, that relation of Christians one to another, is...after a sort, natural; and flowes as natural from the Covenant of Christianity, or Regeneration, as that of father and child, brother and brother, from generation.'[120]

[118] Dixon, *Practical predestinarians*, esp. pp. 254, 24.

[119] Thomas Blake, *The birth-priviledge, or, covenant-holinesse of beleevers and their issue in the time of the Gospel together with the right of infants to baptisme* (1644; STC B3142), pp. 6–8, 13–14, sig. A2r, p. 33.

[120] Daniel Cawdrey, *A sober answer, to a serious question... Whether the ministers of England are bound...to baptise the children of all such parents, which say, they believe in Jesus Christ* (1652; Wing C1636), quotations at sigs A2v, A4r.

It is a curious irony that such ideas assumed even greater significance for those who steadily gravitated out of the Church of England into gathered churches consisting solely of the self-proclaimed elect and of the visible saints. In the guise of Congregationalism, the Old Testament convergence of family and sect, tribe and church, had the capacity to become a reality once more.[121] The laboratory in which these developments can most easily be analysed is colonial New England. Those who first migrated there formed congregations composed of people who had made a profession of faith and repentance, believing they had experienced the saving grace of inner regeneration. But as they engendered families of their own, not all of whom shared their intense piety, strains began to emerge. These both threatened the purity of the communities and necessitated a reassessment of the criteria for membership. The question of who came under the covenant of grace God had extended to Abraham and his seed, and by which he had adopted them as his 'peculiar people', was a tricky one. John Cotton wrote in 1647 that 'The faith of the Parent doth bring the Children and houshold of a Christian, even now in the days of the new Testament, under a Covenant of salvation, as well as the faith of Abraham brought his houshold of old under the same covenant.' But when he addressed this issue in a series of sermons delivered in Boston, he was careful to distinguish between the outward blessings afforded to the 'carnal seed of Christian parents' and the 'inward fellowship' of those who were given access to the 'kernel' of the Gospel. The former benefited from God's bounty and patience, but like Ishmael and Esau, some ultimately despised, repudiated, and forfeited their birthright. The offspring of the godly should not be complacent that they would be saved by their parents' piety, whose own diligent performance of family duties could not prevent them from being 'discovenanted'. Degenerate children had no one to blame but themselves, and 'their bloud shall be upon their own heads'. While the elect did emanate from 'the loyns of Abraham' in one sense, salvation was not in fact a biological prerogative. Every family contained members who were doomed to damnation.[122] At the same time the temptation to interpret the text of Genesis 17:7 in a literal sense was an ever-present one: mothers, fathers and pastors colluded in a process that glossed over the exegetical complexities of this topic and implied that godliness was inherited.

The difficulties and tensions that had been lurking in the puritan conception of the church from the beginning increasingly came to the fore. As the Congregational experiment ran into problems in its second and third generations,

---

[121] The classic account is Geoffrey F. Nuttall, *Visible Saints: The Congregational Way 1640–1660* (Oxford, 1957). See also Edmund S. Morgan, *Visible Saints: The History of a Puritan Idea* (Ithaca, NY, 1963); E. Brooks Holifield, *The Covenant Sealed: The Development of Puritan Sacramental Theology in Old and New England, 1570–1720* (New Haven, CT, 1970), esp. pp. 169–96.

[122] John Cotton, *The grounds and ends of the baptisme of the children of the faithfull* (1647 [1646]; Wing C6436), p. 48; idem, *A treatise of the covenant of grace, as it is dispensed to the elect seed, effectually unto salvation* (1659; Wing C6465), pp. 218–31, quotations at 220, 226, 218. Brooks Holifield, *Covenant Sealed*, chs 5–6 is particularly insightful on these debates in the context of New England.

the clergy found themselves on the horns of a dilemma: should they compromise and allow the church to be populated by the unregenerate offspring of church members or should they stand firm and risk condemning it to eventual oblivion? What was at stake was its very survival. Jonathan Mitchell, pastor at Cambridge, expressed the issue succinctly: 'The Lord hath not set up churches onely that a few old Christians may keep one another warm while they live, and then carry away the Church into the old grave with them when they dye.' He had done so with the intention that they might be continued down the generations.[123]

Most recognized the danger of extinction and embraced the so-called 'Half-Way Covenant' devised by the Synod of 1662, which accepted that the privileges of baptism extended to the children of church members, but confined the second sacrament of communion to those who publicly professed their evangelical con-version when they came of age.[124] This condition was itself frequently unfulfilled, with the consequence that the miniature new Jerusalems established in the wil-derness reverted by default to versions of the promiscuous mixture of godly and ungodly, sheep and goats, from which the initial immigrants had symbolically withdrawn when they left England. In the words of Edmund Morgan, the church ceased to be company of the faithful and became 'a genealogical society' of their descendants. 'The tangle of problems created in time by human reproduction' pushed puritanism back in the direction of a kind of parish system. These precipi-tated theological and ecclesiological developments that facilitated the emergence of a kind of 'hereditary religious aristocracy', even as they created conditions in which this spiritual elite inevitably mixed with the reprobate.[125] Some, including John Davenport, first minister of New Haven in Connecticut, resisted the trend to make the right of baptism conferred by family lineage the basis for church mem-bership, saying that this was 'not capable of being propagated and continued, in a lineal succession by natural generation'.[126] But many defended it by harking back

[123] Jonathan Mitchell, 'An Answer to the Apologetical Preface', in [Richard Mather], *A defence of the answer and arguments of the synod met at Boston in the year 1662* (Cambridge, MA, 1664; Wing M1271), p. 45.

[124] See Robert G. Pope, *The Half-Way Covenant: Church Membership in Puritan New England* (Princeton, NJ, 1969); Herbert W. Schneider, 'A Changing Sense of Sin', in David D. Hall (ed.), *Puritanism in Seventeenth-Century Massachusetts* (New York, 1968), pp. 92–8; Stephen Foster, *The Long Argument: English Puritanism and the Shaping of New England Culture, 1570–1700* (Chapel Hill, NC, 1991), pp. 180–9; Anne S. Brown and David D. Hall, 'Family Strategies and Religious Practice: Baptism and the Lord's Supper in Early New England', in David D. Hall (ed.), *Lived Religion in America: Towards a History of Practice* (Princeton, NJ, 1997), pp. 41–68; Holly Brewer, *By Birth or Consent: Children, Law and an Anglo-American Revolution in Authority* (Chapel Hill, NC, 2005), ch. 2; Michael P. Winship, 'North America to 1662', in Milton (ed.), *Oxford History of Anglicanism*, vol. i, pp. 266–79.

[125] Edmund S. Morgan, 'The Half-Way Covenant Reconsidered', in Hall (ed.), *Puritanism*, pp. 99–107, at pp. 107, 105 (repr. from Morgan's *Visible Saints*, 125–36); idem, *The Puritan Family: Religion and Domestic Relations in Seventeenth-Century New England* (New York; 1966 rev. edn; first publ. 1944), ch. 7 ('Puritan Tribalism'), esp. p. 174.

[126] See John Davenport, *Another essay for investigation of the truth in answer to two questions* (Cambridge, 1663; Wing D356), p. 6. Davenport insisted that there was a distinction to be drawn

to the promise made to Abraham and his seed, though precisely who was encompassed in that category was a source of dispute. Most ministers insisted that it extended only to the natural offspring of 'immediate Parents' and not to their grandchildren. However, some thought adopted children and servants enjoyed the same benefits because they were subjected to the government of the household patriarch.[127]

Whether we see the Half-Way Covenant as a symptom of the dilution of principle and zeal or as an honest attempt to square the circle between biology and ecclesiology, strategies for family preservation and a pristine vision of the gathered church, its effect was to locate salvation in the lines of descent that connected the generations. It was to engender what Kathy Cooke has called a 'sexceptional' society—a society in which physical procreation and spiritual fecundity became intertwined and which 'birthed its elect'.[128] The overall trend finds especially eloquent expression in the writings of Increase Mather, which are littered with variations on one particularly striking phrase: 'God hath seen good to cast the line of Election so, as that it doth (though not wholly, and only, yet) for the most part, run through the loins of godly Parents.' Caveats, qualifications, and stark realities aside, in his sermons and tracts the idea, derived from Genesis, that salvation was a birthright perhaps came to its fullest flowering. As he declared in *A call from heaven to the present and succeeding generations* in 1679, the covenant of grace was so strong and lasting that even where God skipped over the immediate seed, he remembered his commitment to succeeding ones as a chosen race of religious children. While Mather emphasized that God was free in disposing his sanctifying grace and allowed that some of the elect were not born of predestined parents, the impression he left was that true Christianity was a genealogical phenomenon. It was a seed sown in mankind by God, brought forth by human reproduction, and watered and fertilized by moral instruction and learning. The longer that a family continued in holiness, the more gracious the Lord would be to its posterity. The promise made in Isaiah 49:25 ('I will save thy children') had been fulfilled in 'these dayes of the Gospel, by giving heaven to the children of beleivers as their everlasting inheritance'.[129]

---

between the church under the law and under the Gospel: the former had been a 'domestical' institution; the latter was a congregational one.

[127] Richard Mather, *A disputation concerning church-members and their children* (1659; Wing M1271A), pp. 19–20.

[128] Kathy J. Cooke, 'Generations and Regeneration: "Sexceptionalism" and Group Identity among Puritans in Colonial New England', *Journal of the History of Sexuality*, 23 (2014), 333–57, esp. 338, 340.

[129] Increase Mather, *Pray for the rising generation, or, a sermon wherein godly parents are encouraged, to pray and believe for their children* (Cambridge, MA, 1678; Wing M1238), p. 13; *idem, A call from heaven to the present and succeeding generations or a discourse wherein is shewed, that the children of godly parents are under special advantages and encouragements to seek the Lord* (Boston, MA, 1679; Wing M1190), quotations at pp. 5, 9. The same point is reiterated in *idem, The duty of parents to pray for their children* (Boston, MA, 1719), pp. 14–15, and *idem*, 'Advice to the children of Godly Ancestors' in *idem, A course of sermons on early piety* (Boston, MA, 1721), pp. 5–6.

It is not, therefore, surprising that historians have perceived puritan New England as a space in which a compelling nexus between race and redemption was forged. As Rebecca Anne Goetz has argued in relation to Virginia, the dark side of the notion that Protestant Christianity passed down the generations was the concept of 'hereditary heathenism'. Although this coexisted uneasily with the ongoing hope that indigenous Americans might be converted, in the guise of the curse of Ham's posterity, the book of Genesis lent weight to the belief that they were a race that had been 'shut out from grace'. This had profound consequences for the indigenous people the settlers encountered and with whom, in due course, they interbred. The idea that faith ran in the blood legitimized enslavement and contributed to the emergence of racial thinking.[130]

The same enticing link between religion and genealogy can be found in English puritanism, especially after the Restoration when it was forced into nonconformity. In a tract defending the right of infant baptism, the Presbyterian Richard Baxter wrote optimistically:

> We have no reason…to think that love and grace are so much less under the Gospel to the members of Christ, than under the Law to the members or seed of *Adam*, as that then all the seed should have partaked with the same blessings with the righteous Parents, and now they shall all be turned out of the society, whereof the Parents were members…God gives us himself the reasons of his gracious dealing with the children of the just.[131]

In a tract entitled *The best entail, or Dying parents living hopes for their surviving children* published in 1693, Oliver Heywood likewise invoked the idea of God's covenant with his elect to suggest that their seed probably numbered among the saved and that they too were the 'rightful heirs of all Gospel-priviledges'. While it was true, he said, that grace came not by succession, yet it came 'oft in succession'. The line of the covenant reached to many generations, and the more numerous one's pious predecessors were, the greater the shower of blessings a family could expect. Dedicated parenting was, therefore, essential to the spiritual welfare not merely of one's own offspring but the chain of posterity stretching far into the future.[132] Exploiting the same resonant vocabulary of genealogy, Joseph Waite's *The parents primer and the mothers looking glasse* (1681) urged his readers to:

---

[130] See Richard A. Bailey, *Race and Redemption in Puritan New England* (New York, 2011), esp. ch. 1; Rebecca Anne Goetz, *The Baptism of Early Virginia: How Christianity Created Race* (Baltimore, MD, 2012).

[131] Richard Baxter, *More proofs of infants church-membership and consequently their right to baptism, or, A second defence of our infant rights and mercies in three parts* (1675; Wing B1312), pp. 112–13.

[132] Oliver Heywood, *The best entail, or, dying parents living hopes for their surviving children grounded upon the covenant of Gods grace, with believers and their seed* (1693; Wing H1761), p. 28, sig. A3r.

lay a very solemn Injunction upon your children, to teach Their children. Thus leave an Inheritance to your childrens Children. Make your practice profitable to Posterity, to convey conversion from Generation to Generation: that Religion may run in a Blood, and flourish in your Families throughout All generations.

Diligent nurture, he implied, could have the effect of creating an enduring pedigree of godliness.[133]

The space that such writers devoted to the corruption that could break out even in godly families, as it had in those of the biblical patriarchs, is a measure of the anguish that later seventeenth-century puritans experienced about children who failed to follow the example set by their godly elders. Heywood wrote feelingly of the 'gray hairs with Sorrow' by which wayward offspring had brought some servants of God to their graves prematurely.[134] Dedicated to his six sons and three daughters, the deprived Shropshire minister Edward Lawrence's *Parents groans over their wicked children* (1681) discussed the issue of black sheep in some detail, observing that it was 'ordinary' for religious parents to have foolish and impious children, just as it was not uncommon to find 'trees of righteousness' growing within otherwise unregenerate families. As the 'doleful' cases of Cain and Ham, the sons of Adam and Noah revealed, such a 'calamity' could not be entirely averted, but it could be minimized by prudent choice of a 'yoke fellow' and by the faithful educational efforts they carried out together.[135]

In turn, some devout men and women worried that the habits instilled in them by this means might be the sole 'root and chiefe branch of their religion', a deceptive substitute for the real seed of election. This was evidently the occasion of many 'sad disputes and questionings about her state' by Heywood's own mother, herself the daughter of a noted puritan minister. She frequently mentioned 'the grounds of fear' experienced by those who were 'trained up under godly parents'. Her son, by contrast, took the view that 'she was sanctified from the womb, or had the seeds of holiness instilled into her heart with her mothers milke'.[136] This was the overscrupulousness of an intensely pious woman, but it too underlines how central the question of inherited godliness became in dissenting circles, especially in the context of the Clarendon Code when the boundaries between household and conventicle became very blurred. Matthew Henry's *Church in the house* warned that the 'entail' of the covenant of grace could be forfeited if care was not taken to transmit the means to realize it to the next generation.[137]

---

[133] Waite, *Parents primer*, p. 110.   [134] Ibid., sig. A6v.

[135] Edward Lawrence, *Parents groans over their wicked children. Several sermons on Prov. XVII, 25, published for the benefit of all, but especially of good parents and their children* (1681; Wing L654), quotations at pp. 4, 11, 12, 20–1, 54.

[136] *The Rev. Oliver Heywood, B.A. 1630–1702: His Autobiography, Diaries, Anecdote and Event Books: Illustrating the General and Family History of Yorkshire and Lancashire*, ed. J. Horsfall Turner, 4 vols (Brighouse, 1882), vol. i, pp. 59–60.

[137] Matthew Henry, *A church in the house. A sermon concerning family-religion* (1704), p. 19.

His own posterity, meanwhile, appears to have demonstrated the success of such efforts. In his old age, he often blessed the Lord that his twenty-four grandchildren 'were all the sealed ones of the God of Heaven, and enrolled among his Lambs'.[138] On his deathbed in 1715, the young puritan Joseph Jacob was comforted by his grandmother, who said 'child you had the happiness of being born of Covenanting Parents, that set you apart, and sealed you for God in your infancy'.[139] Such sentiments gave a fillip to the 'family religion' that became such an insistent puritan refrain in this period. They also helped to foster the endogamous marriage patterns that developed within Dissent in the eighteenth century. Once again, the tendency for religion to become an inherited legacy became increasingly pronounced.

In some respects the rise and growth of sects that espoused alternative soteriological ideas was a function of and response to the same set of personal anxieties and pastoral concerns about salvation. The practice of adult baptism rested on resisting the easy elision between the natural and spiritual offspring of Abraham that became a hallmark of puritanism and on insisting that only those who demonstrated religious discretion and understanding were entitled to receive this rite of incorporation into God's church, regardless of their blood lineage. Just as the infant seed of the Jews had enjoyed a right to circumcision, so too could the children of believing parents claim the 'new Seal of the Covenant', christening. This was a lasting ordinance that had not been abrogated by the Gospel.[140] It is revealing that some committed Baptists who spurned the 'sprinkling' of infants continued to worry about their newborn babies. They developed the practice of praying in the homes of their mothers and writing the names of their children in a church book as the seed of the faithful.[141] The patterns of intermarriage between Baptists in the period to 1750 provide further evidence that, despite its insistence that divine grace was not a form of birthright given according to the flesh, the family became a vital forum for sustaining this denomination too. In Sussex, for instance, some 96% married within their own communion.[142] Fuelled by love and affection, the impulse to save one's children was universal and powerful.

The same preoccupation with the 'rising generation' also shaped the Quaker movement. Forged in the crucible of rejection of the Calvinist doctrines of original sin and predestination, the Children of Light or, as they later became

---

[138] *Diaries and Letters of Philip Henry, M.A. of Broad Oak, Flintshire A D 1631–1696*, ed. Matthew Henry Lee (1882), p. 332.

[139] CL, MS I.i.13 (Commonplace book of Joseph Jacob), unfoliated.

[140] See Michael Harrison's spirited repudiation of anti-paedobaptism: *Infant baptism God's ordinance: or, a clear proof that all the children of believing parents are in the covenant of grace* (1694; Wing H905).

[141] Rachel Adcock, *Baptist Women's Writings in Revolutionary Culture, 1640–1680* (Farnham, 2015), p. 122.

[142] See John Caffyn, *Sussex Believers: Baptist Marriage in the Seventeenth and Eighteenth Centuries* (Worthing, 1988), p. 187.

known, the Society of Friends, erased the distinction between the elect and the reprobate and believed that all individuals held the kingdom of God and the potential for redemption within their own hearts. The energetic evangelism of the earliest Quakers convinced that the Lord would illuminate the souls of every-one who opened their hearts to him left little time for considering the fate of their children. In any case, during the first decade many Friends were people who had abandoned their families and set aside their blood ties with mothers, fathers, wives, husbands, and siblings.[143] However, parenthood and upbringing soon emerged as a preoccupation of the movement. Ideas about human perfectibility and the innate goodness of children disposed Quakers to emphasize the poten-tially salutary effects of education. Although convincement remained a supernat-ural process of personal revelation, the crop of primers and catechisms produced by George Fox and his colleagues were designed to help the young to recognize the inner light within, indoctrinate them in the principles of the sect, and equip them with useful knowledge of spelling and arithmetic.[144] The purpose of Humphrey Smith's tract entitled *To all parents of children upon the face of the whole earth* was to show the former how to train up the latter, so that 'iniquity may not be received by tradition from Parents to Children, and so from one Generation to another'.[145]

This trend intensified as the expansive proselytizing phase of the sect gave way to the task of nurturing its faithful members and preventing the haemorrhage of their offspring. Ironically, this was fostered by the religious freedom the Quakers gained as a result of the Act of Toleration of 1689. Paradoxically, its evolution into an inward-looking and endogamous sect that relied on generational transmission coincided with the end of the official persecution from which it had gained so much kudos in the preceding decades. Tellingly, by the end of the first century of Quakerism around 1750, some 80–90% of Quakers were themselves the children of Friends.[146] In turn, this was closely linked to the growing tendency of Friends to seek marriage partners within the sect: a developing emphasis on 'marrying within…so as it be without the bounds forbidden in God's law', in order to create 'a truly natural & christian stock'. This was the recommendation made by William

[143] See Chapter 1 above.
[144] G[eorge Fox]. and E[llis] H[ookes], *A primmer and catechism for children* (1670; Wing F1883B); George Fox, *A catechisme for children* (1657; Wing F1756); William Smith, *A new primmer wherein is demonstrated the new and living way, held forth by way of question and answer, as from a child's enquiry after truth, to be informed by the father* (1662; Wing S4321). See Alexandra Walsham, 'Nature and Nurture in the Early Quaker Movement: Educating the Next Generation of Friends', in Morwenna Ludlow, Charlotte Methuen, and Andrew Spicer (eds), *The Church and Education*, SCH 55 (2019), pp. 161–76. See also Chapter 1 above.
[145] Humphrey Smith, *To all Parents of Children upon the Face of the Whole Earth* (1660; Wing S4077), title page.
[146] Richard T. Vann, *The Social Development of English Quakerism 1655–1755* (Cambridge, MA, 1969), p. 166, and see ch. 5. See also Naomi Pullin, *Female Friends and the Making of Transatlantic Quakerism, 1650–c.1750* (Cambridge, 2018), esp. ch. 1.

Penn in his famous letter to his wife and children, which ended with a prayer that his posterity might be made part of God's 'celestial family' and serve him with an upright heart 'from Generation to Generation'.[147]

As the movement matured, the future of Quakerism was increasingly seen to lie in the children of believing parents. Abigail Fisher's *Salutation of true love* of 1690 deployed the familiar metaphors of fruit and seed, describing the offspring of faithful Friends as 'the natural branches of such who have been grafted into the true vine' and praying that they might be 'as a second spring on the same ground'. They were the offshoots 'in this our day' of the 'root of Jesse'.[148] An epistle written by John Banks two years later provided similar words of good counsel and wholesome advice, urging adult Quakers to do their utmost to beget in their sons and daughters a love of the Truth.[149] John Hands's *Seasonable epistle* of 1705 included a section addressed specifically to 'those that are Friends by Education, but not by Conversion', seeking to rouse them to a true realization of the seed within them.[150] The Welsh schoolmaster John Kelsall noted in his diary many meetings at which the matter of bringing up the 'young generation...in the service of the truth' was stressed as an imperative. Visiting Quaker ministers, both women and men, lamented how frequently parents fell short of their obligations to their children, who were regarded as 'the heritage of the Lord'.[151]

The minutes of the London Yearly Meetings reflect a growing preoccupation with the religious nurture and education of the younger generation by fathers and mothers, whose duty to keep them unspotted by the surrounding world was underlined. In 1767 the Meeting called upon Quaker parents to take every opportunity to impress 'a sense of the Divine being' upon their children in 'their tender years', saying that 'though virtue descendeth not by lineal succession, nor piety by inheritance, yet we trust the Almighty doth graciously regard the sincere endeavours of their parents, whose early and constant care is over their offspring for their good; who labour to instruct them in the fear of the Lord'.[152] In some cases, Quaker ministry passed down matrilineally, with mothers providing 'spiritual apprenticeships' to their daughters.[153]

---

[147] William Evans and Thomas Evans (eds), *The Friends' Library: Comprising Journals, Doctrinal Treatises, and Other Writings of Members of the Religious Society of Friends*, 14 vols (Philadelphia, PA, 1837–50), vol. v, pp. 166–9. This is transcribed in FHL, MS 62/5, item 38, quotation at p. 85. See Chapter 2 above, p. 166.

[148] Abigail Fisher, *A salutation of true love to all faithful friends, brethren and sisters in the fellowship of the blessed truth with an addition of tender love to all younger convinced friends in and about London &c* (1690; Wing F986), pp. 13–14, 5.

[149] John Banks, *An epistle to Friends shewing the great difference between a convinced estate and a converted estate* (1692; Wing B652), pp. 16–20.

[150] John Hands, *A seasonable epistle to believing parents, and their children* (1705), pp. 5–7.

[151] FHL, MS S 185 (Transcript of John Kelsall's diary), vol. i (1701–12), pp. 65, 11; see also pp. 14, 26–7, 31, 39, 41, 67, 101, 104–5, 118–19, 139.

[152] See *Extracts from the Minutes and Advices of the Yearly Meeting of Friends held in London, from its First Institution* (1783), pp. 77–9.

[153] Pullin, *Female Friends*, p. 72.

In 1675 the leading Quaker apologist Robert Barclay commented acidly that when men became Christians 'by birth and education, and not by conversion, and renovation of Spirit', then 'Christianity came to be lost', 'and nothing remained but a shadow and image'. By the eighteenth century this was being widely reiterated.[154] Friends such as John Crook issued warnings regarding the superficiality of merely inherited faith, calling upon the children and servants of believing parents and masters to examine themselves and assess whether they had derived their religion simply 'by Tradition, only because of your outward Relations', rather than by the 'inward Work of God' upon their souls.[155] And, in an echo of objections to the Half-Way Covenant, the schismatic Meeting founded by the dissident Quaker George Keith and his followers in New England required children to declare a real convincement. Their parents were required to register the dates of their 'Spirituall Birth' as well as their 'outward birth' in the Monthly Meeting register.[156] Yet there is no denying that membership of this society of spiritual kin largely became a privilege of biological lineage over time. In 1737, the London Yearly Meeting formalized the status of the children of Quakers as Friends.[157] Although Quakers repudiated the exclusivist doctrine of election and reprobation that underpinned Congregational ecclesiology, they too drifted towards the view that faith could be passed down the generations. The metaphorical language of kinship that had come so naturally to the movement in its early years became a description of the real ties of blood that increasingly bound together its members.

Chosen Generations: The Seed of God

From past and future generations, we must now turn to living ones. How far did early modern people perceive and describe themselves as members of a particular generation? The ubiquity of the language of generation in the vernacular Bible and in everyday discourse must be underscored. Its appearance in contemporary

---

[154] Robert Barclay, *An apology for the true Christian divinity, as the same is held forth, and preached, by the people, called in scorn, Quakers* (1678 edn; Wing B720), p. 184. See also idem, *Truth triumphant through the spiritual warfare, Christian labours, and writings of that able and faithful Servant of Jesus Christ* (1692; Wing B740), p. 406.

[155] John Crook, *The design of Christianity* (1701), pp. 319–20.

[156] J. William Frost, *The Quaker Family in Colonial America: A Portrait of the Society of Friends* (New York, 1973), p. 68; George Keith, 'Gospel Order and Discipline', *Journal of the Friends Historical Society*, 10 (1913), 70–6, at 73–5. For Keith's critique of puritan covenant theology, which incorporated the children of believers into the visible church, see idem, *The Presbyterian and Independent Visible Churches in New-England and Else-where, Brought to the Test* (1689; Wing K190), pp. 84–6. On Quakerism and the family in North America, see Barry Levy, *Quakers and the American Family: British Settlement in the Delaware Valley* (New York, 1988).

[157] This was in the context of the drawing up of rules about removal and settlement: *Extracts from the Minutes and Advices*, p. 214. See also Walter Joseph Homan, *Children and Quakerism: A Study of the Place of Children in the Theory and Practice of the Society of Friends, Commonly Called Quakers* (Berkeley, CA, 1939), ch. 4; Vann, *Social Development*, pp. 143–4.

dictionaries, concordances, commentaries, and religious texts of all kinds is a further measure of its centrality in the 'social universe' of Scripture, as well as its hermeneutical complexity.[158] Applying the techniques Naomi Tadmor has used to illuminate the words 'friends' and 'neighbours', 'marriage' and 'wives', 'slaves' and 'servants', 'prince' and 'lord', to 'generation' yields further insight into the ways in which the Bible was domesticated and anglicized as it was translated. 'Generation' too provides an illustration of the dialectical manner in which Bible translations both responded to and shaped culture and society. They supplied a blueprint for living and a prism through which people viewed current affairs and comprehended their own place in history. And they did so in a context in which the Bible was understood as a timeless canon of sacred truth whose two component parts, Hebrew and Christian, were not discrete but typologically linked.

Contemporaries drew liberally on this vocabulary to brand their enemies and to give expression to a sense of group identity derived from the fact that they lived during the same period of time. This binary process can be detected at work from the first stages of the English Reformation. Exhorting their followers to be steadfast in the face of oppression from the jails in which they were incarcerated in the 1550s, evangelicals frequently spoke of their Catholic persecutors and adversaries as members of a 'viperous', 'prophane', 'monstrous', 'perverse', and 'crooked generation'. From prison, George Marsh urged the 'faithfull brethren' to whom he wrote in the manner of St Paul to 'Save your selves from this untoward generation', while John Bradford compared the 'children of this world', who followed the devil, with the 'children of light in their generation'.[159] Writing in 1555, Robert Smyth roused his spiritual friends to stand firm and not shrink, knowing that God was on their side and that those ranged against them were none but 'the marked men of the Beast, the offspring of the Pharisees, the congregation malignant, the generation of Vipers, murtherers, as theyr father the devil hath bene from the beginning'.[160] Early Protestants attacked monks and priests as a 'shaven generation', vehemently denouncing the 'shameles practises of that lying generation' of papists which had pulled the wool over the eyes of the unlearned laity. They lambasted Bonner and other bishops at the forefront of the drive to eradicate heresy as members of a 'bloudy' and 'wolvishe generation'.[161] They also used the word to indicate their

[158] Naomi Tadmor, *The Social Universe of the English Bible: Scripture, Society and Culture in Early Modern England* (Cambridge, 2010). For other contemporary dictionary definitions, see Richard Huloet, *Huloets dictionarie newelye corrected, amended, set in order and enlarged*, ed. John Higgins (1572; STC 13941), s.v. 'generation'; Elisha Coles, *An English dictionary explaining the difficult terms that are used in divinity, husbandry, physic, philosophy, law, navigation, mathematicks and other arts and sciences* (1677; Wing C5071), s.v. 'generation'.
[159] John Foxe, *Actes and monuments* (1570 edn; STC 11223), pp. 1741, 1833.
[160] John Foxe, *Actes and monuments* (1583 edn; STC 11225), p. 1700.
[161] Foxe, *Actes and monuments* (1570 edn), pp. 673, 966, 2259.

determination to resist the temptation to conform, bow to Baal and become nicodemites and 'mass gospellers', and to reprehend the 'faythles generation' that was ashamed openly to confess the Gospel.[162] From the King's Bench, John Philpot defiantly declared, 'I will lye all the dayes of my lyfe in the stockes (by goddess grace) rather then I will consent to the wicked generation.' He was eager to set an example to those who condescended to have fellowship with the workers of darkness.[163]

Prefaced by an array of hostile adjectives, the word served as a shorthand for the passionate conviction that popery was the accursed religion of the Antichrist which inspired these men to embrace death at the stake so bravely. It suffused the correspondence they sent to console those left behind, fostering antagonisms that may be seen as precocious signs of confessional identity formation. This process had a more positive side too. Filled with allusions and references to the covenant that God had made with Abraham and his seed, the letters of martyrs also helped to forge bonds of solidarity between Protestants and to strengthen their sense of affinity with both the early Christians and the ancient Hebrews. The parallels they discerned between their tribulations and those of the godly generations described in the Bible convinced them that its prophecies were being played out in their own time.[164]

Recent work suggests that we should see Elizabethan Catholicism in the same terms. Although apocalypticism has often been regarded as a mode of exegesis largely monopolized by Protestantism, as Coral Stoakes has demonstrated, some late sixteenth-century English Catholics also believed that they were living in the last days of the world and on the edge of time. Common experiences of persecution and marginalization, resentment and danger fused to create a collective commitment to reversing the Reformation and defeating heresy, whether through violent rebellion or through the 'militant passivity' of martyrdom. Connecting individuals who went into exile in the Low Countries, Italy, and Spain with those who stayed at home, the antipathy to Protestantism that welded the Elizabethan and Stuart Catholic community together was itself a form of generational mentality. It stimulated a stalwart commitment to recusancy and to the alternative strategy for resistance that was calculated church-papistry, and it drew strength from the sacrifices made by missionaries and laypeople executed as traitors by the state.[165]

---

[162] Foxe, *Actes and monuments* (1583 edn), p. 1636.
[163] Foxe, *Actes and monuments* (1563 edn; STC 11222), p. 1605.
[164] See, e.g., Foxe, *Actes and Monuments* (1583 edn), p. 1528.
[165] Coral Stoakes, 'English Catholic Eschatology, 1558–1603' (PhD thesis, University of Cambridge, 2016), esp. ch. 6.

This corporate consciousness left a variety of linguistic traces in contemporary texts—from the 'consolatory epistles' Catholics sent to their followers and the memoranda that Jesuits and seminary priests wrote for their superiors and for each other to the prolific devotional and polemical literature that poured from foreign and secret presses from the 1560s onwards. Catholics too utilized the distinctive vocabulary of generations to engage with heretics. Ventriloquizing their own translation of the Latin Vulgate,[166] they condemned the clergy and laity of the Church of England as a 'perverse and incredulous generation' for refusing to believe points of doctrine consecrated by tradition but not explicitly referred to in the pages of the Bible.[167] Writing in 1603, Richard Broughton displayed conventional contempt for Protestants as a 'blasphemous', 'impious', 'godless', and 'beastly generation' which had 'brooded up' a host of heresies and absurdities.[168] A few years later William Bishop adeptly turned reformed libels against Catholics as a 'vipers broode, a malecontented Samaritan generation' back against his eminent Protestant enemies William Perkins and George Abbot, declaring that these 'grievous and malicious slanders' better fitted 'men of your own coate and profession'. Were not heretics the 'cosen germans, or very near kinsmen' of the ungodly nations described in the Old and New Testaments?[169] Philip Woodward's refutation of the Protestant convert Thomas Bell's scurrilous *Triall of the new religion* (1608) was mainly concerned with counteracting his arguments, but he could not resist indulging in a sideswipe against the puritans, whom he called 'the Geneva generation of the mocking Martinists'.[170] A controversial tract of 1621 that milked the genealogical metaphors discussed in Chapter 3 vehemently condemned the 'pestiferous writings' of various sectaries, including William Whitaker and William Fulke, whom it accused of condoning the 'triple generation of prodigious broods' of the Novations, Pelagians, Donatists, Wycliffites, and Hussites out of which the 'hideous monster' of Protestantism had sprung.[171]

Catholics were less apt than their Protestant rivals to deploy the term generation to articulate their collective identity as faithful adherents of the old religion and loyal children of the Mother Church of Rome. They drew inspiration less from

---

[166] See *The New Testament of Jesus Christ, translated faithfully into English, out of the authentical Latin*, trans. Gregory Martin (Rheims, 1582; STC 2884).

[167] T. T., *The whetstone of reproofe. A reproving censure of the misintituled safe way* (Catuapoli [Douai], [1632]; STC 23630), p. 268. See also B. D., *Controversial discourses relating to the church being an answer to Dr Sherlock's discourse concerning the nature, unitie, and communion of the Catholick Church* ([Douai, 1697]; Wing R1741), p. 63.

[168] Richard Broughton, *The first part of the resolution of religion devided into two bookes, contayning a demonstration of the necessity of a divine and supernaturall worshippe* (1603; STC 3897), pp. 80–2, 154.

[169] William Bishop, *A reproofe of M. Doct. Abbots defence, of the Catholike deformed by M. W. Perkins* (1608; STC 3098), p. 21.

[170] Philip Woodward, *Bels trial examined that is a refutation of his late treatise, intituled the trial of the newe religion* (Rouen [Douai], 1608; STC 25972.2), p. 138.

[171] S. N., *The guide of faith, or, a third part of the antidote against the pestiferous writings of all English sectaries* ([St Omer], 1621; STC 18659), p. 14.

the Hebrew Scriptures than from medieval hagiography and ecclesiastical history. The community of which they imagined themselves a part was a company of saints and confessors continuously connected through the ages by the threads of mutual intercession and accumulated merit. When they spoke of seed, it was more often with reference to Christ, the prophesied seed of the Virgin Mary who had crushed the serpent's head, the church he had engendered, or the blood of the martyrs than the offspring of Abraham as described in Genesis.[172] The Church was an institution rooted in the concept of the apostolic succession of priests and bishops, consecrated in their vocation by the ordination ritual of the laying on of hands.

Proponents of the project to restore the beauty of holiness within the Caroline Church of England were similarly reticent about using the rhetoric of generations to give expression to their own identity as an ecclesiastical party or coalition. They rarely invoked this word to rally themselves or others to action and often employed it generically or neutrally. By contrast, they energetically harnessed the term as a vehicle of their vicious anti-puritanism. It proved a versatile tool for lumping together the 'factious brethren' whom they accused of introducing unwarranted novelties in doctrine, practice, and discipline. In 1637, James Buck, vicar of Stradbroke in Suffolk, compared puritans to the scribes and pharisees, 'a generation of vipers, for that they taught pestilent opinions, that destroyed their mother-Church, and poysoned their follower, yet that had a righteousnesse, and very bewitching and popular shewes of godlinesse'.[173] A year earlier, the scourge of sabbatarianism, John Pocklington, had been similarly uncompromising about the 'generation' of 'vipers' that had 'eaten out' the bowels of the Church by plotting:

> the casting downe of Crownes and Scepters, and lawes of the Land, and the Professours thereof, as for the trampling under their feet of Miters and corner'd Caps, Bishops and such as exercise jurisdiction under them, together with our Booke of Common Prayer, and Canons Ecclesiasticall.[174]

Once the Civil Wars were under way, the term became a handy label for castigating a range of unsavoury tendencies unleashed by the collapse of control and censorship. The editor of the sermons of Robert Sanderson, late bishop of Lincoln,

---

[172] For Christ as the prophesied seed of the woman, see John Heigham, *A devout exposition of the holie Masse with an ample declaration of all the rites and ceremonies belonging to the same* (Douai, 1614; STC 13032), p. 72. On the church as the seed of Christ, see Theophilus Higgins, *The first motive of T. H. Maister of Arts, and lately minister, to suspect the integrity of his religion which was detection of falsehood in D. Humfrey, D. Field, & other learned protestants, touching the question of purgatory, and prayer for the dead* ([Douai], 1609; STC 13454), p. 42. On martyrs as the seed of the church, see, e.g., George Leyburn, *An epistle declaratorie, or manifest written by G. L. to his brethren residing in England* ([Douai], 1657; Wing L1937), pp. 15. 37.

[173] James Buck, *A treatise of the beatitudes or Christs happy men* (1637; STC 3998), pp. 230–1. On Laudian anti-puritanism, see Lake, *On Laudianism*, part II.

[174] John Pocklington, *Sunday no sabbath* (1636; STC 20077), p. 41.

spoke of 'the late-sprung-up generation of Levellers, whose Principles are so destructive of all that Order and Justice by which publick societies are supported', who 'do yet style themselves as by a kinde of peculiarity, *The Godly*'.[175] The preface to a 1659 edition of Lancelot Andrewes's liturgy for the consecration of churches and chapels decried the 'Sacrilegious generation' that defiled God's dwelling places by iconoclasm.[176] But the polemicist who most frequently wielded this label against the puritans was Peter Heylyn. Echoing the denunciatory adjectives appended to it in the New Testament, he condemned the 'faithlesse', 'froward' and 'perverse', 'stubborn and untractable', 'proud and refractory Generation' of non-formists and Genevans who, since the settlement of 1558, had striven to plant the 'seeds of Calvinism' in England. His animosity towards 'the rabble of Mar Prelates in Queen Elizabeths time, to whom there never was the like generation of railing Rabshakehs since the beginning of the world' was insatiable.[177] After the Restoration, the 'lust and delusions' of this 'Generation' of 'restless' and 'Godless-men', as well of the more recent 'Covenanting Generation', continued to be dilated by way of exorcising these evils.[178] The self-styled 'hotter sort of Protestants' had no monopoly on this derogatory idiom.

The mid-seventeenth-century sects were even more active in brandishing the biblical language of generation and its heavily weighted synonym, seed. A critical component of the rhetoric they devised to define themselves and the role they believed they had been appointed to play in ushering in the millennium, it appears countless times in the manuscript letters, tracts, and pamphlets by which Friends bound together the body of the faithful and engaged in combat with their mainstream Protestant opponents. From the outset of the Quaker movement in the 1650s, its founders and leading figures, including George Fox, James Naylor, Edward Burrough, William Dewsbury, Margaret Fell, and William Penn, spoke of themselves and greeted each other as the 'seed' of the Lord and the 'first born in England, in the latter age and Generation'.[179] This was in keeping with their belief

---

[175] Robert Sanderson, *Fourteen sermons heretofore preached* (1657; Wing S605), sig. B1v.

[176] *The form of consecration of a church or chappel...exemplified by...Lancelot late lord-bishop of Winchester* (1659; Wing A3126), sig. A6r.

[177] Peter Heylyn, *The parable of the tares expounded & applied* (1659; Wing H1729), p. 323; idem, *Cyprianus anglicus, or, the history of the life and death of the most reverend and renowned prelate William, by divine providence lord archbishop of Canterbury* (1668; Wing H1699), p. 49–50; idem, *Certamen epistolare, or, the letter-combate* (1659; Wing H1687), p. 51. See also idem, *A full relation of two journeys* (1656; Wing H1712), pp. 336, 371.

[178] From the life of Hooker prefacing *The works of Mr Richard Hooker...in eight books of ecclesiastical polity* (1666; Wing H2631), pp. 11, 15; Matthew Wren, *An abandoning of the Scottish covenant* (1662; Wing W3674), p. xxxix.

[179] For example, George Fox, *A visitation of love unto all people...for the deliverance and freedom of the righteous seed* (1659; Wing F2018); Edward Burrough, *To the beloved and chosen of God in the seed elected particularly in London and elsewhere* (1660; Wing B6036); William Dewsbury, *To all the faithful brethren [sic] born of the immortal seed* (1661; Wing D1276); Margaret Fell, *A call to the universall seed of God, throughout the whole world* (1665; Wing F625A); Margaret Askew Fell Fox, *A call unto the seed of Israel, that they may come out of Egypts darkness, and house of bondage* ([1668?]; Wing F626); William Penn, *To the children of light in this generation, called of God to be partakers of eternal life in*

that God had selected them to bear witness to and bring about great events that would advance the cause of the Gospel and open the way for all to see and feel the inner light that the Almighty had planted in every heart. In labelling themselves the Children of God, they were laying claim to be 'A chosen Generation'.[180] These were men and women conscious of having been called 'in the morning and breaking forth of that blessed and everlasting day in this our Age: in short of being present at the dawn of new phase of Reformation.[181] The 'loving', 'dear', and 'tender salutations' they issued to the 'risen and immortal seed' and 'despised remnant' who had already been convinced and who were now the target of anger, violence, and outrage make constant reference to Genesis, which they read as a mirror of their own age.[182] Thus, William Smith sent out a 'holy kiss of peace' to 'the seed of life' in 1660.[183] John Higgins's affectionate 'greeting' to 'the Christian people of God (Often in scorn called Quakers)' published three years later bolstered their morale by stressing that though 'none of the Sons of Bondage' recognized 'the Royalty of your Birth and Generation', 'those of the same Off-spring and Linage' assuredly would.[184] Friends revelled in their personal sufferings in the same terms. In *Davids enemies discovered* (1655), Christopher Atkinson signed himself as 'one who for the captivated seeds sake suffers now in outward bonds'.[185]

Celebrating the rebirth and germination of the truth in and through those who received it, such texts also reflect the rapidity with which Friends embraced the nickname 'Quaker' and made it their own. They show how quickly a polemical tag coined by their enemies was taken up as a form of self-description, helping the movement to cohere and crystallize within less than a decade of its inception and investing it with a self-consciousness that was both a consequence and cause of the intense animosity it stirred. Fox's own 1682 *Epistle to the household of the seed of Abraham* is at once a charismatic address to the entire sect and to the individual spiritual and biological families of which it was made up. The

---

Jesus Christ, the lamb of God & light of the world (1678; Wing P1386). The quotation is from the title page of John Higgins, *A Christian salutation and greeting unto all the true Christian people of God (often in scorn called Quakers) who are the true church of Christ, the first-born in England, in this latter age and generation* (1663; Wing H1952).

[180] See the list of 'names the Children of God are called by': Fox and Hughes, *Primmer*, pp. 54–5.

[181] *The memory of the righteous revived being a brief collection of the books and written epistles of John Camm & John Audland* (1689; Wing C390), sig. A2v.

[182] Margaret Fell, *A loving salutation to the seed of Abraham among the Jewes where ever they are scattered up and down upon the face of the earth* (1656; Wing F634); George Keith, *A salutation of dear and tender love to the seed of God arising in Aberdeen* ([Aberdeen?], 1665; Wing K202); Charles Marshall, *A second epistle being a tender salutation to the seed of Jacob* (1673; Wing M742); Roger Crab, *A tender salutation or the substance of a letter... to the despised remnant and seed of God, in the people called the Quakers* (1659; Wing C6738).

[183] William Smith, *An holy kiss of peace, sent from the seed of life, greeting all the lambs and little ones with a tender salutation with a few words, entituled, relief sent forth into the camp of Israel* (1660; Wing S4307).

[184] Higgins, *A Christian salutation*, p. 4.

[185] Christopher Atkinson, *Davids enemies discovered* (1655; Wing A4126), title page.

'holy seed' to whom he writes are simultaneously all the Children of Light and the children of the believing parents to whom this was designed to be read and rehearsed out loud. Used in conjunction with the phrase 'a suffering people' in the 1660s and 1670s, both words helped to make a movement that lay in the minds of its disciples as well as in the eye of the beholder.[186]

'Generation' was also widely used in Quaker books to denounce those who opposed the true 'seed' of the Lord. It was a way of disowning the Reformation of the sixteenth century as a false dawn and its adherents and heirs as self-deluded deceivers. It was an instrument for warning the 'hypocrites' who stubbornly refused to accept the truth and the 'false teachers' who fed innocent people corrupt doctrine.[187] It was a weapon in the war against enemies—Anabaptists, Independents, Presbyterians, Levellers, and Ranters—and other members of the 'faithlesse generation of the world' that the Friends fought during the Interregnum.[188] It assisted in exposing the priests and persecutors who punished the lambs of God as 'Caines bloudy race' and in issuing threats of divine vengeance to 'prophane' and 'unruly rulers' under the veil of 'a word of pitty'.[189] In 1654, a syndicate of Independent ministers led by Thomas Weld poured out vitriol on 'that generation of men called Quakers', laying open their blasphemies, equivocations, lyings, raylings, and other 'detestable principles and practices'; in 1659 Alexander Parker boldly presented a testimony on behalf of those who are 'by the scorners of this generation called Quakers against the many lyes and slanders which the devil is the chief author of'.[190] If Quakerism, like puritanism, was 'one half of a stressful relationship',[191] it was one that explicitly conceived of itself in generational terms. Against the backdrop of a teeming array of sects all claiming to be the sole possessors of divine truth, Friends never had a moment's

---

[186] George Fox, *An epistle to the household of the seed of Abraham and to every family in particular to read & practise* (1682; Wing F1812). On the process by which the Quakers embraced their nickname, see Kate Peters, *Print Culture and the Early Quakers* (Cambridge, 2005), ch. 4.

[187] John Swinton, *One warning more to the hypocrites of this generation* ([Scotland?, 1663]; Wing S6285); Margaret Abbott, *A testimony against the false teachers of this generation* ([1659?]; Wing A70A).

[188] George Fox and James Nayler, *A word from the Lord unto all the faithlesse generation of the world, who know not the truth, but live in their own imaginations* (1654; Wing F1992); William Smith, *Some queries propounded to this professing generation the people called Baptists* (1659; Wing S4331).

[189] Anthony Hutchins, *Caines bloudy race known by their fruits, or, a true declaration of the innocent sufferings of the servants of the living God, by the magistrates, priests and people in the city of Westchester* (1657; Wing C208A); Andrew Robesen, *A word of pitty to the prophane and to the unruly rulers in this generation* ([1662]; Wing R1623).

[190] Thomas Weld, *A further discovery of that generation of men called Quakers by way of reply to an answer of James Nayler to The perfect Pharisee* (1654; Wing W1268); Alexander Parker, *A testimony of truth given forth…on the behalf of the despised servants, and professors, of truth…who are by the scorners of this generation called Quakers* (1659; Wing P386).

[191] Patrick Collinson, *The Birthpangs of Protestant England: Religious and Cultural Change in the Sixteenth and Seventeenth Centuries* (Basingstoke, 1988), p. 143. See also *idem*, 'A Comment: Concerning the Name Puritan', *JEH*, 31 (1980) 483–8; *idem*, 'Antipuritanism', in John Coffey and Paul C. H. Lim (eds), *The Cambridge Companion to Puritanism* (Cambridge, 2008), pp. 19–33.

hesitation in believing that they alone were the special and chosen generation foreshadowed in Scripture. Initially sharpened by evangelical zeal, as time passed this congealed into an ingrained habit and a self-affirming custom.

Generation Work

There is a further dimension of the surge in generational consciousness that seems to have reached its peak in the 1650s, when England was a country without a king, a precarious republic initially overseen by a parliament of self-styled saints, and a society charting a path through the treacherous waters of Cromwellian martial rule, chronic political instability, and unprecedented religious pluralism. This was the rising chorus of calls issued to contemporaries to carry out the 'generation work' God had appointed to those who lived in this turbulent age. This compound was a recent coinage: as one preacher remarked, with more than a modicum of sarcasm, it was a 'newfound word'.[192] It was closely associated with the most impassioned manifestation of the millenarian fever that broke out during these decades: the Fifth Monarchy Men. This group took its name from the prophetic dream of Nebuchadnezzar recounted in the Book of Daniel predicting the four world empires that would precede the kingdom of Christ (Babylonian, Persian, Greek, and Roman) and which looked forward to the imminent end of all human government and the arrival of the feted Messiah. Many believed that this would take place in 1666, the year incorporating the number of the Beast.[193]

In 1653, John Tillinghast, minister at Great Yarmouth in Norfolk published the first instalment of *Generation-work* (Fig. 4.3). This was followed by two further parts the following year in which he expounded at great length the biblical prophecies that were the source of Fifth Monarchist millenarianism, especially the seven vials described in Revelation 16, which he identified respectively with Luther's reforms, the abolition of episcopacy, the execution of Charles I, the collapse of the Holy Roman Empire, the destruction of the Church of Rome, the conquest of the Ottoman Turk, and the battle of Armageddon. But it is the opening volume that demands attention here. Dedicated to Parliament, this took the form of 'A Brief and Seasonable Word' to 'the Saints and people of God in this

---

[192] Edward Boteler, *The worthy of Ephratah presented in a sermon at the funerals of the Right Honorable Edmund earl of Mulgrave, Baron Sheffield of Botterwic* (1659; Wing B3804), p. 17.

[193] The definitive account of the Fifth Monarchists is still Bernard Capp, *The Fifth Monarchy Men: A Study in Seventeenth-Century English Millenarianism* (1972). See also *idem*, 'The Fifth Monarchists and Popular Millenarianism', in J. F. McGregor and B. Reay (eds), *Radical Religion in the English Revolution* (Oxford, 1984), pp.165–89.

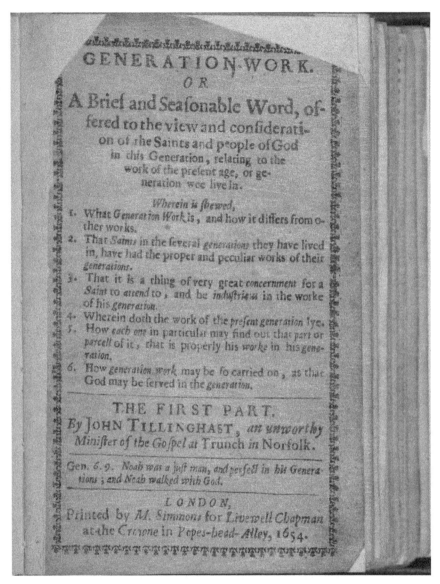

Fig. 4.3 John Tillinghast, *Generation-work. Or a briefe and seasonable word, offered to the view and consideration of the saints and people of God in this generation, relating to the work of the present age, or generation wee live in* (London, 1654), title page.
Source: © British Library Board 1471.e.44. All Rights Reserved/Bridgeman Images.

Generation', outlining the responsibilities that fell to them at this extraordinary juncture in history. Tillinghast began by delineating the principle that every generation had 'its proper and peculiar Work', a special mission or task pertaining to the transactions of God in the age in which it lived, which was distinct from an individual's social station, vocational calling, and place in the partriarchal order.

He went on to analyse biblical personages who had been eminent for their 'generation work': Noah, the constructor of the ark in which his own family and the animals were saved from the Flood and 'by which he preached a real Sermon for one hundred and twenty years to the Old World'; Moses and Aaron, David and Solomon, who had built the great temple; Ezra, Nehemiah, and other major and minor prophets. Looking to the New Testament, he said that John the Baptist's 'generation work' was to be the forerunner and harbinger of Jesus, the redeemer of mankind, while the Apostles Peter and Paul had been commissioned to go forth and publish the glad tidings of salvation. Advancing into his own era, he highlighted the role played by Martin Luther and other worthies in recovering 'the precious truths of Christs Priestly Office, the glorious Doctrine of our justification by Christ, which was well nigh swallowed up by the Antichristian innovations of Masses, Crosses, Pennance, Purgatory, Vowes, Pilgrimages, solitary and single life, with other inventions of humane wisdom'. Since then the saints had striven to reveal the regal office of Christ and prise it from the mist cast over it by the Antichrist and his followers.[194]

Generation work, declared Tillinghast, was both the most important and the most neglected work of all: 'Of all the sins we read in Scripture, we find not any more provoking to the Lord, and falling so heavy upon the head of the sinner, as offences and neglects in the work of their Generation.' Too many excused themselves by thinking that others should and would do it, contenting themselves with industriously performing their common duties as saints. This was a heinous sin, which provoked the Lord to wrath like no other, as the chilling precedent of the Jews, whom God had abandoned for shirking the great work allocated to their generation, revealed. When other responsibilities stood in the path of generation work it was the duty of the Christian to omit them. Those who excelled in carrying out their divinely ordained duties would be crowned with glory. He felt compelled to point out 'the never to be forgotten proceedings of the Army of England', whom the Lord had 'eminently owned, beyond belief, and to admiration' because they had followed the work of their generation.[195]

Turning to his own times, Tillinghast declared that the appointed work of the present generation was to convert the Hebrews and Gentiles, redeem Israel, unite the squabbling saints, pull down those in high places, establish justice and righteousness, and finally to exalt Christ as supreme king of all the earth. He saw promising signs that these tasks were well under way in the arrival of the

---

[194] John Tillinghast, *Generation-work. Or, a briefe and seasonable word offered to the view and consideration of the saints and people of God in this generation relating to the work of the present age, or generation wee live in* (1654; Wing T1173); idem, *Generation-work: the second part wherein is shewed, what the designs of God abroad in the world, may in all likelihood be, at this present day, and in the dayes approaching* (1654; Wing T1176). There were several other editions in these heady years: (1654; T1174), (1655, T1175 (pt. 1), T1177 (pt. 2), T1178 (pt 3)). Quotations from the 1655 edn: part 1, pp. 3, 10, 13.

[195] Ibid. (Wing T1173), pp. 18 [*vere* 17], 20.

Portuguese Rabbi Menasseh ben Israel to negotiate the readmission of the Jews, the initiatives to propagate the Gospel in Wales, Ireland, and the East and West Indies, and the collapse of royal and episcopal power, though he had to confess 'with grief' that the breaches within the puritan camp remained both deep and wide. Yet even this could not depress his confident expectation that the prophecies of old were about to be fulfilled. One further 'rule of discovery' that things were proceeding apace was the observation that 'the pulses of the most spiritual enlightened Saints [were] beating this way'.[196]

Lastly, Tillinghast provided guidance to those eager to know the 'particular part or parcel' that was their own generation work, urging them to humble themselves, pray, and consider the inclination of the spirit within. Anyone, he said, could be the bearer of the 'new light' that beamed forth in each age, advancing the cause of truth, despite the resistance of learned 'retarders' and 'the tumultuous confused rabble'. Tillinghast concluded by urging the saints not to be discouraged by 'the littlness and lowness' of the beginning of their generation work and to take heed of procrastinating this business 'under a pretence that the time of doing it is not yet come, neither are things ripe for it'. With these trenchant and empowering words, he sought to rouse millenarians to usher in the expected Second Coming. He sought to galvanize them to the sacred task of making history itself.[197] The generational consciousness of the Fifth Monarchy movement was orientated less towards the past than towards the present and future. Sharpened by the unwavering conviction that the prophesied millennium would soon dawn and wrapped up in the intoxicating rhetoric in which they specialized, it had a distinctly eschatological and prospective quality.

'Generation work' rapidly became a catchphrase and watchword of the Fifth Monarchists. Those 'waiting for the visible appearance of Christ's kingdome' on earth were firmly persuaded that the prophecies of Revelation would shortly be accomplished and that the 'time for the doing thereof, is at the door'. Writing from prison in Windsor and inspired by his reading of Tillinghast's books, Christopher Feake urged his 'Brethren in the Lord, throughout all the Churches of Saints, who are spirited for Generation-work' to put their hands to the wheel.[198] John Canne's exposition of the seven vials likewise underlined the necessity for the 'waiting Saints' to enquire after their 'generation work', to consider whether they were special instruments raised up by 'a more particular Call...to ruine the Whore' and to yearn to be among the 'brave Champions' who would achieve the

---

[196] Ibid., pp. 30–47, esp. 43–4, 47. On the campaign for the readmission of the Jews, see David S. Katz, *Philo-Semitism and the Readmission of the Jews to England, 1603–1655* (Oxford, 1982).

[197] Ibid., pp. 48, 62, 65, 68, 75. On Tillinghast, see Richard L. Greaves, 'Tillinghast, John (bap. 1604, d. 1655), Fifth Monarchist', *ODNB*; Capp, *Fifth Monarchy Men*, pp. 192–3.

[198] Christopher Feake, *The oppressed close prisoner in Windsor-Castle, his defiance to the father of lyes, in the strength of the God of truth* (1654; Wing F572), p. 70.

'Generation-victory' of trampling the Beast.[199] The word was also adopted by the outspoken prophetess Anna Trapnel and appeared in several of the pamphlets recounting her apocalyptic visions and the pronouncements she made before assembled politicians at Whitehall. On a journey to Cornwall in 1654, she had prayed in spirit with the congregation of the saints in All Hallows in London, her thoughts being 'very seriously intent upon generation-work', by which she meant the restoration of the kingdom of Israel.[200] Another Fifth Monarchist, John Rogers, told of his sufferings for the cause in a tract that anticipated the return of Christ to rule in fulfilment of Isaiah's prophecy that a male child would be born to save the world: 'Like as a woman with child that draweth near the time of her delivery…in pain…so are we in they sight O Lord'. Sion was now in the last stages of labour before this long-awaited second birth. This was generation work in a double sense of the term.[201]

So closely was the phrase connected with the movement that its opponents used it as a stick with which to beat them. One polemicist denounced 'these frenzy–conceited men', accusing them of seeking to 'involve these Nations again in bloud and misery', under the pretence of doing the work of their generation. Contemptuous mockery of the 'Monarchical generation Workmen' who sought to pull down Christ from his throne in heaven and set him up on earth was a measure of the real fear that the puritan majority felt about the extremism of this radical sect, which they believed would stop at nothing to bring their crazy vision for the future to fruition. They 'would save the Devil a great deal of labour, if they could but beat down Ministry and Magistracy', which had been Satan's design from the beginning.[202] Written in the wake of Thomas Venner's disastrous rising of 1661, John Tombes's scathing attack on the 'Quinto-Monarchians', *Saints no smiters* (1664) condemned the generation work of destroying civil authority itself as a damnable doctrine, together with the murderous violence they meted out to all who reviled them.[203] It is no accident that the first person executed for the regicide was Major Thomas Harrison. Taking revenge for the generation work of

---

[199] John Canne, *Truth with time, or certain reasons proving that none of the seven last plagues or vials are yet poured out* (1656; Wing C443A), pp. 15, 55, 72.

[200] Anna Trapnel, *The cry of a stone. Or A relation of something spoken in Whitehall, by Anna Trapnel, being in the visions of God* (1654; Wing T2031), p. 63; eadem, *Anna Trapnel's report and plea, or, a narrative of her journey into Cornwal* (1654; Wing T2033), p. 7; and see eadem, *A legacy for saints; being several experiences of the dealings of God with Anna Trapnel, in, and after her conversion* (1654; Wing T2032), p. 50.

[201] John Rogers, *Jegar-Sahadvtha. An oyled pillar. Set up for posterity, against the present wickednesses, blasphemies, persecutions and cruelties of this serpent power (now up) in England (the our-street of the beast)* (1657; Wing R1809), p. 65, quoting Isaiah 26:17–18.

[202] *The downfall of the fifth monarchy. Or, The personal reign of Christ on earth, confuted* (1657; Wing D2092), title page, esp. pp. 6, 10.

[203] John Tombes, *Saints no smiters, or, Smiting civil powers not the work of saints* (1664; Wing T1816), p. 49.

killing an anointed monarch was one of the first priorities of the restored
Stuart regime.

Fifth Monarchism gradually withered away, but the concept of 'generation
work' did not. Some Restoration writers attached it to the Quakers, including the
author of a character published in 1671. Subtitled *The clownish hypocrite anatom-
ized*, this was a vehicle for castigating religious enthusiasm and 'phanaticisme'
more generally, which bundled together traits from a range of sects into one.
Combining conventional anti-puritanism with allegations of sexual deviance, its
colourful taxonomy of the Quaker included the comment that 'he is very diligent
in his *Generation-worke*, and may therefore have many children but no heirs; for
his issue comes into the World out-law'd, and can no more boast to be born in
lawful Wedlock, then the Kinchin-cove of a Gypsie got under a hedge by a strav-
ling Tinker'.[204] It was a pun that played cleverly on the dual biological and historical meaning of this rich and complex word.

Friends did, in fact, deploy this term to describe their own ambitious plans for
transforming the English nation and spreading the message of the inner light to
people farther afield. A Quaker tract entitled *Plantation work* published in 1682
argued that the settlement of North America and its reclamation from Christian
ignorance was an eminent part of the generation work of the day. Bringing the
true Christian faith to the natives of the New World was as vital an enterprise in
the late seventeenth century as the zealous labours of the biblical patriarchs and
the heroic sacrifices made by the Protestants persecuted in Queen Mary's reign.
Like Tillinghast, its author, William Loddington, provided a roll call of the Lord's
'spirited servants' in past ages, from Noah, Moses, and Joshua to Paul, before
describing the 'passive Generation Work' of suffering carried out 'against that
particular Sillicism of Popery' by the martyrs burnt in the 1550s. In his own century, the priority had to be expansion and cultivation accompanied by energetic
proselytism.[205]

An index of both discontent and zeal, the term was also deployed by other
nonconformists. In 1660, Henry Adis, who described himself as 'a Baptized
Believer, undergoing the Name of a Free-willer', regarded it 'a part of my
Generation work, to speak a word in season' to the recently restored Charles II.
A fannaticks mite was a trenchant warning that unless the king took steps to
repress abomination, stamp out vice, and show himself worthy of his office, the
wrath of God would be visited upon him and the whole kingdom.[206] The ejected

[204] R. H., *The character of a Quaker in his true and proper colours, or, The clownish hypocrite anat-
omized* (1671; Wing A4256), pp. 10–11.
[205] William Loddington, *Plantation work the work of this generation written in true-love to all such
as are weightily inclined to transplant themselves and families to any of the English plantations in
America* (1682; Wing L2804), p. 5.
[206] Henry Adis, *A fannaticks mite cast into the kings treasury being a sermon printed to the king
because not preach'd before the king* (1660; Wing A581), sig. B2v.

Independent minister Christopher Ness made repeated reference to the 'generation work' of both biblical and contemporary figures—from Hezekiah and David to the Parliamentary general Sir William Waller. 'Sedulous attendance' upon this public duty, he said, was no less pleasing to God than private devotion. Interestingly, this was an activity that he aligned with the middle and later phases of the Christian life cycle and with adulthood: 'a fresh and vigorous Ability for Generation-Work in Old Age' was 'a singular gift of God'. It was also one, he implied, that both signalled and contributed to the ageing process: 'we have our White Hairs after our Fruit-bearing to God in our Generation-work'.[207]

The puritans of the New England colonies, meanwhile, were preoccupied with generation work of their own. They too saw this as a solemn duty essential to the prosperity and success of the experiment of settlement and church-building. But whereas the objective of the Fifth Monarchists was the dismantling of earthly institutions and structures of government in preparation for the reign of the returning Saviour, for the early American colonists the imperative was the propagation of faith to the 'rising generation'—a project that, as we have seen, was as much genealogical as it was evangelical. In 1671, a posthumous book by another member of the illustrious Mather clan, Eleazar, the former pastor of Northampton in Massachusetts, appeared. Addressed to the children of the godly rather than the unregenerate, his *Serious exhortation* summarized a series of sermons he had preached to his congregation calling upon its members and their heirs to do their utmost to ensure that the Lord's name was remembered and that his presence would continue to their posterity. The generation work for which he called was the work of breeding godly families worthy of the covenant of grace that God had bestowed upon Abraham and his seed forever. What was at stake was the very survival of the Reformation that the colony's forefathers had crossed the ocean to perfect and its uninterrupted succession in subsequent generations. Lamenting the 'backsliding times' of great degeneracy and apostasy in which he lived, Mather warned in no uncertain terms of disaster if this work was neglected. Even as he acknowledged that it was 'too heavy for the shoulders of any Angel in heaven to bear' and incapable of being achieved by human beings without divine assistance, he underlined the catastrophic consequences of failing in this weighty affair. Adopting the mantle of Jeremiah, Jonah, Hosea, and Amos, he prophesied that the Lord would surely forsake this 'carnal unsavoury Generation' that did not bear fruit, cutting it off like a dead branch from the tree of Jesse.[208] In the preface, Eleazar's brother and editor, Increase Mather, cemented this sinister prediction

---

[207] Christopher Ness, *A Christians walk and work on earth* (1678; Wing N443), sig. A3r, pp. 7, 82–3; idem, *A compleat and compendious church-history* (1680; Wing N446), p. 212; idem, *A compleat history and mystery of the Old and New Testament* (1696; Wing N449), p. 526; idem, *A divine leagacy bequeathed unto all mankind* (1700; Wing N454), pp. 267, 289, 347.

[208] Eleazar Mather, *A serious exhortation to the present and succeeding generation in New-England* (Cambridge, MA, 1671; Wing M1179), pp. 14–15, 19, 27, 30.

further, stressing that unless the current generation put its hand to the wheel, New England would turn from a 'Goshen' into 'the darkest place under Heaven' and cease to be a Bethel and become a Beth-aven. Ultimately, God would remove the very candlestick of the Gospel itself. The *Serious Exhortation* was a poignant legacy, which Increase published not merely in memory of his brother but also of his father, who own dying counsel to his son had been to 'seriously endeavour the good of the Rising Generation in this Country'. It was a painful irony that Eleazar had been taken by God in the very act of performing the generation work that was his religious vocation.[209]

A sense of foreboding about the future of Massachusetts was widespread. Speaking before the General Assembly in 1670, Samuel Danforth, pastor of Roxbury, was concerned that the initial fervour of the godly errand into the wilderness had waned into a 'Laodicean lukewarmness' and that the 'radical disease' of 'declension' had overtaken too many professors. He called for an urgent review and a 'holy', 'brotherly', and 'thorough-Reformation' and admonished magistrates and ministers to 'declare themselves loyal to Christ in their Generation-work' in the fight against 'Sceptical Indifference', 'Reed like Vacillation', and 'wilful Opposition to the Doctrine and Way of the first Fathers and Founders'.[210] Three years later Samuel Arnold, 'Teacher of the Church of Christ' at Marshfield, preached an equally heartfelt sermon to the general court of New Plymouth on election day. Taking up the text of Acts 13:36, he took the story of David falling asleep in the Lord after diligently serving his generation to exhort his hearers to imitate his faithfulness and zeal. Men in public life had a special responsibility in this respect. The welfare of the community at large lay upon their shoulders, a colony-cum-church that was 'our Masters Family', over which God ruled as a patriarch. Encompassing near relations by blood as well as the spiritual kin of fellow saints, the generation whose secular and eschatological future they were charged with securing would owe them the same debt of gratitude that they in turn owed to their worthy ancestors. These were men and women who had been 'mighty wrestlers with God', standing in the gap to keep his judgements at bay. But Arnold's sermon was one of reprehension as well as instruction—reprehension of the unprofitable, useless, and idle persons who did nothing for the benefit of the others, 'meer Drones' whose apathy provoked the deep displeasure of God and pulled down his wrath upon all the rest.[211]

---

[209] Ibid., sigs A2r–4r. Increase Mather explained that Eleazar had intended to include another sermon directed to the 'Rising Generation' to spell out the steps they should take to assure that God's gracious presence would be 'successively continued' but that the author's death had deprived the world of those meditations: p. 30.

[210] Samuel Danforth, *A brief recognition of New-Englands errand into the wilderness* (Cambridge, MA, 1670; Wing D175), sig. A2v.

[211] Samuel Arnold, *David serving his generation, or, A discourse wherein is shewed that the great care and endeavour of every Christian ought to be that he may be serviceable unto God and to the present generation* (Cambridge, MA, 1674; Wing A3732), quotations at pp. 4, 7, 6. See also W. J., *A*

The mood of the godly at the end of the seventeenth century was sombre. The generation work of their predecessors looked as if it might go completely to waste. The series of funeral sermons that celebrated earnest magistrates and ministers who had served their generations with integrity as latter-day Davids and laboured unceasingly to transmit the religious privileges they enjoyed to their posterity should not deceive us.[212] The presence of the regenerate might delay punishment, but it could not prevent it. The seed of God seemed a dwindling remnant.

Lost Generations: Pious Precursors

The forms of generational consciousness analysed thus far were contemporaneous ones. They reflected a profound sense that people living through the long English Reformation of the sixteenth and seventeenth centuries were witnessing critical events in the history of the Church and nation and that the present was simply the prelude to a more marvellous future. But generations are also made retrospectively, in the realm of memory.[213] They are entities forged by the subjective and interlinked processes of remembering and forgetting, by individuals and communities looking back at past experiences with the benefit of hindsight and by subsequent generations recalling those of previous ones. At certain moments these tendencies converge to create conscious forms of 'generational identity'.[214] The imagined communities thus engendered are also emotional communities which draw upon inherited vocabularies and traditions which they in turn rework and bequeath to their successors. In Barbara Rosenwein's words, they are 'generations of feeling'.[215]

I begin by briefly anticipating a theme that will be explored at greater length in Chapters 5 and 6: that the Tudor Reformation was a project that entailed a concerted attempt to remake the memory of the Middle Ages and of the men, women, and children who had lived in this time of 'superstition' and 'darkness'. Its public discourse encouraged Protestants to reimagine their Catholic predecessors as an undifferentiated bloc of credulous papists, a misguided generation that had fallen prey to the wiles of Satan and the Antichrist. The response on the other side of the confessional divide was to recollect the pre-Reformation era as one marked by piety, philanthropy, and good cheer and to remember those who had had the

---

remembrance of former times for this generation; and our degeneracy lamented (Boston, MA, 1697; Wing J444).

[212] See, e.g., Ebenezer Pemberton, *A true servant of his generation characterized, and his promised state of refreshment assigned. A sermon preached on the death of the honourable John Walley Esq.* (Boston, MA, 1712).

[213] See Foster, *Vivid Faces*, pp. 7, 289–325.

[214] See Fulbrook, *Dissonant Lives*, esp. pp. 6–7, 11–12.

[215] Barbara H. Rosenwein, *Generations of Feeling: A History of Emotions, 600–1700* (Cambridge, 2016), esp. pp. 9, 12, 320–1.

good fortune to be born prior to the break with Rome with a degree of nostalgia. The rose-tinted spectacles through which they viewed the generations that had inhabited Catholic England had the same homogenizing effect: squeezing out any hint of disagreement or dissent and airbrushing away incriminating rumours of corruption and immorality, it envisaged a body of people who were almost wholly innocent of heresy. It projected an image of a dedicated clergy and a devoted laity that had no wish to throw off the shackles of the old religion.

Protestantism itself proved no less vulnerable to the distorting effects of individual and collective memory. The psychological difficulty that it had 'coming to terms with victory', to adopt Andrew Pettegree's phrase, became apparent quite early.[216] Discomfited by circumstances that had catapulted them into the position of representatives of the official religion, some Edwardian Protestants looked back more than a little wistfully to the first stages of the Reformation when they had been the standard-bearers of an embattled creed. Bereft of the trials and tribulations that validated their status as the true children of God, some yearned to be a 'poor persecuted little flock' once more. The idea of being a repressed minority that was integral to their self-image as a covenanted generation was partly a product of remembering a time when they had been one.[217] The cauterizing scars of suffering were empowering. Many found it hard to relinquish them despite the change in their objective situation. Evangelicals such as Richard Finch and Anthony Gilby keenly grasped at evidence that the lambs of God were still under the thumb of the 'monstrous beast' and 'troden under the fote with stinking Goates'. They contrasted the purity of their predecessors with the plague of 'carnal gospellers' that infiltrated the current generation.[218] The Christian nominalism they perceived all around them only sharpened their sense that their precursors had been men and women of superior zeal. It intensified the doubts and anxieties about their own identity fostered by the bewildering setbacks of the period between 1549 and 1554, including the fall of Edward Seymour, duke of Somerset, from power. The memory of these experiences paradoxically helped to foster a newly positive sense of purpose and self-esteem. It enhanced the siege mentality

---

[216] Andrew Pettegree, 'Coming to Terms with Victory: The Upbuilding of a Calvinist Church in Holland, 1572–1590', in *idem*, Alastair Duke, and Gillian Lewis (eds), *Calvinism in Europe, 1540–1620* (Cambridge, 1996), pp. 160–80, at p. 160.

[217] Catharine Davies, '"Poor Persecuted Little Flock" or "Commonwealth of Christians": Edwardian Protestant Concepts of the Church', in Peter Lake and Maria Dowling (eds), *Protestantism and the National Church in Sixteenth-Century England* (1987), pp. 78–102; *eadem*, *A Religion of the Word: The Defence of the Reformation in the Reign of Edward VI* (Manchester, 2002), ch. 5.

[218] Richard Finch, *The epiphanie of the church* (1590; written 1550; STC 10877.5), sig. D3v; Anthony Gilby, *A commentarye upon the prophet Mycha* (1551; STC 11886), sig. D2v. See also Thomas Lever, *A sermon preached the thyrd Sonday in Lent before the kynges Maiestie, and his honorable counsell* (1550; STC 15547), sig. A4r.

which they elevated into an art, especially after the accession of Mary, when real pyres upon which to burn heretics were built once more.[219]

Elizabethan Protestants likewise constantly glanced back to the traumas suffered by those who had refused to bow to Baal between 1553 and 1558. From the position of relative peace and stability that the reformed faith had attained by the 1580s, they could not help but remember the immense sacrifice made by the Marian martyrs, which made their own piety seem weak and feeble. The demise of a whole cohort of reformers in the fires of Smithfield in the 1550s had an impact akin to the loss of the tens of thousands of young men slaughtered in the trenches between 1914 and 1918.[220] It left a lasting imprint on the outlook of later Protestants, one symptom of which was a kind of survivor guilt. If Mary's Counter-Reformation destroyed a generation, it also created one.

As those who had escaped into exile or ridden out the storm by strategic displays of conformity themselves died their children and heirs began to feel a peculiar regret for the passing of a time when faith had been whetted by the sword of persecution. The typological title page that adorned editions of the Geneva Bible showing the exodus of the Israelites and the parting of the Red Sea helped some Protestants to imagine themselves as honorary members of that lost generation.[221] Alec Ryrie has evoked the efforts of others to cultivate an artificial sense of crisis in their devotional lives, and I have discussed elsewhere how puritans repeatedly sought to recreate the happiness of suffering vicariously.[222] Laypeople secretly hoped to be compelled to follow in the footsteps of their forefathers. The godly London matron Elizabeth Juxon was said to have been 'very mindfull of the fiery trial which might come upon us: and she for her part looked for it, and prepared for it: Yea, she was minded rather to burne at a stake, then ever to yeeld to Poperie, or to betray the truth of the Gospell'.[223] She echoed the words of the elderly lady in Essex who had declared to her minister Richard Rogers on her deathbed in

---

[219] Davies, *Religion of the Word*, p. 198. See also Joy Shakespeare, 'Plague and Punishment', in Lake and Dowling (eds), *Protestantism and the National Church*, pp. 103–23; Scott Lucas, 'Coping with Providentialism: Trauma, Identity, and the Failure of the English Reformation', in Yvonne Bruce (ed.), *Images of Matter: Essays on British Literature of the Middle Ages and Renaissance* (Newark, DE, 2005), pp. 255–73.

[220] See J. M. Winter, *The Great War and the British People* (1985), ch. 3.

[221] *The bible and holy scriptures conteyned in the Olde and Newe Testament* (Geneva, 1560; STC 2093), title page.

[222] Alec Ryrie, *Being Protestant in Reformation Britain* (Oxford, 2013), pp. 416–27; Alexandra Walsham, 'The Happiness of Suffering: Adversity, Providence and Agency in Early Modern England', in Michael Braddick and Joanna Innes (eds), *Happiness and Suffering in Early Modern England: A Festschrift for Paul Slack* (Oxford, 2017), pp. 45–64.

[223] Stephen Denison, *The monument or tombe-stone, or, A sermon preached at Laurence Pountnies church in London, Novemb. 21. 1619. at the funerall of Mrs. Elizabeth Juxon* (1620; STC 6604), p. 111.

1588 that if she was sentenced to death in this way, 'she should set light by it, for the hope of the glory which was set before her.'[224]

Contemplating martyrdom was also a pastime of the young. *Spirituall experiences, of sundry beleevers* includes the story of the 7-year-old girl who found herself tempted to deny her faith and asked herself 'what wouldest thou doe … if thou shouldest be … called to suffer for his sake, as some of thy kindred were in Queen Maries time?'[225] She was just one of those who wished that she been part of the seed and household of God that had displayed supreme courage in the 1550s. Anxious anticipation and a vivid historical imagination were key ingredients of the generational consciousness of late sixteenth- and seventeenth-century Protestants. In the absence of actual persecution, they revelled in more mundane troubles as tests of faith.

A further manifestation of this mentality was the constant complaint that preachers made about the shocking indifference and inexcusable ingratitude of those who now freely enjoyed the light of the Gospel. This contrasted with the reverence in which it had been held, like a precious jewel, in the first generation of the Reformation. One example among hundreds must suffice: the Oxford divine Lancelot Dawes, who delivered a sermon on *Gods mercies and Jerusalems miseries* from the public outdoor pulpit at Paul's Cross in 1609, drawing a depressing parallel between 'the faithless and stubborne generation' of the Jews and the English people and threatening that unless there was mass and heartfelt repentance, they too would find themselves punished down to the third and fourth generation, if not completely destroyed. The incineration of ungodly Sodom typologically foreshadowed the desolation of Jerusalem.[226] Predictions that God would take away his candlestick and inflict a famine of the word on the nation may have become a tedious refrain in the late Elizabethan and Jacobean era, but they too attest to the pervasive sense that those who had planted the infant Church of England were a religious generation that had set an exceptionally high standard for their heirs.[227]

The Civil Wars and Interregnum brought a repeat of the same cycle of exultation, trepidation, self-castigation, and dismay. In their aftermath, people harked back to the glory days of the revolution of the saints. The experience of defeat etched the temporary achievements of the 'generation workers' of the 1640s and 1650s in the memories of their successors, even if also fostered a good deal of convenient amnesia about the extreme lengths to which some went to build

---

[224] *Two Elizabethan Puritan Diaries by Richard Rogers and Samuel Ward*, ed. M. M. Knappen (Chicago, 1933), p. 83.

[225] *Spirituall experiences, of sundry beleevers* (1653; Wing P3095), p. 162.

[226] Lancelot Dawes, *Gods mercies and Jerusalems miseries A sermon preached at Pauls Crosse, the 25. of June. 1609* (1609; STC 6388), sigs A4v, B4r.

[227] See, e.g., Samuel Buggs, *Davids strait A sermon preached at Pauls-Crosse, July 8. 1621* (1622; STC 4022), p. 40. See also Alexandra Walsham, *Providence in Early Modern England* (Oxford, 1999), ch. 6, esp. pp. 299–304.

Christ's kingdom on earth and bring in the millennium, and above all about the execution of Charles I as a 'man of blood'.[228] The silver lining in the cloud of persecution that puritans and the sects suffered under the Clarendon Code was a renewed and affirming sense of worthiness. Alluding to Hebrews 12:6, they consoled themselves that those whom the Lord loved, he chastened and scourged as sons. The Restoration reinforced their conviction that they were members of the family and household of God and the seed of Abraham. It helped them to think of themselves as a generation.

Dissenters continued to invoke the pattern and example of King David in commemorative texts. A 1666 broadside memorial to Thomas Glass entitled *A mite from three mourners* heralded the noble 'Generation-Work' he had done, in tandem with his colleague John Wiggan, a fellow 'witness to the cause of Christ'.[229] The same praise was ladled onto John Vernon after his death the following year in *Bochim. Sighs poured out by some troubled hearts* in a series of elegiac verses and acrostic poems composed by his grieving friends and admirers.[230] The phrase was also invoked in sermons marking the departure of 'painful labourers in the Lords vineyard' such as the godly minister James Sharp, honourable citizens of London like William Hiett, and devout ladies such as Mary Wilson of Crosfield in Cumberland.[231] The impression one gains is less of a cohesive cohort of spiritual kin and co-religionists working together towards a common goal than of scattered individuals operating at the level of particular families, communities, and congregations. The high point of public-spirited generation work had passed. As prosecution and discrimination were tempered by indulgence and then toleration, the impulse to undertake it on behalf of the church and commonwealth at large lessened. The Glorious Revolution dimmed and diluted it further, turning nonconformists away from outward-facing initiatives towards inward-facing ones, especially the task of saving their children and preventing them from becoming entangled in worldly temptations. The journey that John Bunyan's *Pilgrim's Progress* immortalized in literature found its counterpart in life: Christian and Faithful escape from the abuse, vilification, and danger of death in Vanity

---

[228] The allusion is to Christopher Hill, *The Experience of Defeat: Milton and Some Contemporaries* (1984).

[229] A. C., *A mite from three mourners: in memorial of Thomas Glass a pattern of faith and patience in the churches, naturally caring for their state, who died in the lord, the 30th day of the Seventh month, 1666. being the same day twelve-month that the beloved John Wiggan (his fellow-labourer, and witness to the cause of Christ) was taken from the evil to come* ([1666]; Wing C8).

[230] *Bochim. Sighs poured out by some troubled hearts, and tendred towards continuing the precious savour of the good name of the late worthy man of God, John Vernon who having faithfully served his generation and finished his testimony, by the will of God, fell asleep the twenty ninth day of the third month, 1667* ([1667]; Wing B94A).

[231] See Nicholas Blake, *Brauch's work finished a sermon preached at the funeral of that painful labourer in the Lords vineyard, Mr. James Sharp* (1681; Wing B3135), p. 17; Thomas Lye, *Death the sweetest sleep, or, a sermon preach't on the funeral of Mr. William Hiett, late citizen of London* (1681; Wing L3531), pp. 26–8; S. A., *The virgin saint, or, A brief narrative of the holy life and Christian death of Mary Wilson with some memorable passages, and occasional speeches a little before her death added thereunto* (1673; Wing A28A), pp. 61–2.

Fair only to reach 'a delicate plain, called Ease', where they are beset with hesitation, doubt, and greed.[232]

Reflecting on the first decades of Quakerism in the later seventeenth century, William Penn remembered the Friends as 'an exercised People...Care for others was much upon us, as well as for ourselves, especially the Young Convinced, often had we the Burthen of the Lord to our Neighbours, Relations & Acquaintance, and Sometimes Strangers'. He added with an audible sigh:

> I cannot forget the Humility and Chaste Zeal of that day. Oh! How Constant at Meetings, how Retired in them, how firm to Truth's life, as well as Truth's Principles; and how entire & United in our Communion, as Indeed became those that progress one Head, even Christ Jesus the Lord.

The best of generations had passed, leaving a selfish and lukewarm one in its place.[233] This was a sentiment that later Friends shared. Writing to his brethren in 1703, John Whitehead was:

> sensible how that Generation which did see the Wonders of the Lord, and were upheld by his might power, is passing away...and another Generation that hath heard more, but seen and experienced less, both of the Wiles of Satan, and the operation of God's Power, that discovers and breaks his Snares, are entering.[234]

Quakers too were conscious that their predecessors had excelled them in the intensity and ardour of their piety.

The same strain of disillusionment and disappointment became an insistent theme of preaching in later seventeenth- and early eighteenth-century New England. The perceived declension of religious zeal since the days of the early Pilgrim Fathers that was the subject of so much hand-wringing by the puritan ministry has attracted extensive analysis by historians from Perry Miller to David Hall. Whether the jeremiads in which it was enshrined reflected real decline or forged and purveyed a powerful myth need not detain us here.[235] What does bear emphasis, however, is the powerful undercurrent of generational thinking that it

---

[232] John Bunyan, *The Pilgrim's Progress*, ed. Roger Sharrock (Harmondsworth, 1968 edn), p. 144.

[233] FHL, MS 62/5, pp. 207–8.

[234] John Whitehead, *The written gospel-labours of that ancient and faithful servant of Jesus Christ, John Whitehead* (1704), p. 231. I owe this reference to the late and lamented Clive Holmes.

[235] Perry Miller, 'Declension in a Bible Commonwealth', *Proceedings of the American Philosophical Society*, 51 (1942), 37–94; idem, *The New England Mind: From Colony to Province* (Cambridge, MA, 1953) and idem, *Errand into the Wilderness* (Cambridge, MA, 1956). For different assessments, see Edmund Morgan, 'New England Puritanism: Another Approach', *William and Mary Quarterly*, 18 (1961), 241–2; Robert G. Pope, 'New England versus the New England Mind: The Myth of Declension', *Journal of Social History*, 3 (1969), 95–9; David D. Hall, *The Faithful Shepherd: A History of the New England Ministry in the Seventeenth Century* (Williamsburg, VA, and Chapel Hill, NC, 1972), ch. 8; idem, *Worlds of Wonder, Days of Judgement: Popular Religious Belief in Early New England* (Cambridge, MA, 1989); idem, *The Puritans: A Transatlantic History* (Princeton, NJ, 2019), pp. 145–7, 338–40.

carried with it. To many preachers, the epidemic of irreligion and worldliness sweeping early America represented not merely a betrayal of the ideals of the original founders of the colonies, but also monstrous ingratitude for their exemplary role in preserving a pristine version of Protestantism for their posterity. It became a commonplace to say that the Pilgrim Fathers had left the old world for the sake of their children.[236] This not only carried with it an idealization of the colony's founders on a par with scriptural heroes. As David M. Scobey has argued, it also recalibrated the puritan sense of the past and their successors' place in the trajectory of historical change. It projected authority 'back across the divide onto their dead parents, with obsessive force and urgency'.[237]

Increase Mather's *A call from heaven* was an extended attempt to prick the consciences of young New Englanders. It described in graphic detail the consequences of collective degeneration and apostasy as laid out in the Bible: the 'discovenanting' and 'unchurching' of Jews and their disinheritance as irredeemable and bastard children. He looked back to the worthies who had planted New England as Abrahams, Davids, and 'eminent Reformers'. 'Let me speak freely', he said, '(without offence to any) there never was a Generation that did so perfectly shake off the dust of Babylon, both as to Ecclesiastical and civil Constitution, as the first Generation of Christians, that came into this Land for the Gospels sake.' Mather twisted one more emotional screw, telling his hearers that 'it was for your sakes especially that your Fathers ventured their lives upon the rude waves of the vast Ocean'. In those days, America had been the seat of the true new Jerusalem. But now, just as in Scripture, sin had set in and engendered an unconverted generation that God would surely cast off. He called for all to take up the work of reformation once more, urging governors to emulate the godly magistrates Zerubbabel and Shealtiel who had assisted the prophets Haggai and Zachariah, as well as the rulers who had supported Luther in Wittenberg, Calvin in Geneva, Zwingli in Zurich, and Oecolampadius in Basel. The renewal of the covenant in his own age also required an earnest commitment to the task of conversion, and to re-establishing families as the nurseries of the Church and nation. Their disorder was 'the great wound and misery of New-England'. Declension and divine judgement could only be counteracted and reversed if people concentrated attention on bringing up the young in the image of the pious predecessors who had first planted this new Eden.[238]

By 1700 the idea that these pioneers had left the Old World in the interests of the next generation had settled into accepted tradition. So had the gloomy opinion that Protestant New England was a 'dying world', as Increase's Mather's son Cotton described it in a sermon delivered in 1715. This jeremiad was a

[236] See Morgan, *Puritan Family*, pp. 168–9.
[237] David M. Scobey, 'Revising the Errand: New England's Ways and the Puritan Sense of the Past', *William and Mary Quarterly*, 3rd ser, 41 (1984), 3–31, at 22.
[238] Mather, *A discourse concerning the danger of apostasy, especially as to those that are the children and posterity of such as have been eminent for God in their generation*, part of *A call from heaven*, pp. 46, 55–6, 31, 80, 91.

meditation on the passing of time and of the successive generations. It likewise urged the imitation of godly ancestors, sounded alarm bells about the 'vile apostasy' of Cotton's age, and called upon the worthies and governors of Massachusetts to save New England from 'a Sett of Degenerate Grand-Children'.[239] He spoke with a feeling born of personal experience of what he saw as an outbreak of youthful male rebellion. His own son Increase, the namesake of his prodigiously pious father, was himself so wayward that he could not be dissuaded from spending time in the company of 'detestable rakes', and rumours circulated that he had begotten a harlot with a bastard. He nevertheless clung to the hope that the afflicting hand of God would inspire penitence and renew the spiritual health of early American society, not least by bolstering the practice of godly child-rearing.[240] A proclivity to perceive declension and apathy was not merely an occupational hazard; in this instance it was also a hereditary characteristic.

The Generations of the English Reformations

The last section of this chapter examines a final index of the generational identities that were by-products of England's extended and messy Reformations: contemporary representations of cohorts of people bound together by their commitment to a common religious cause. Taking both textual and visual form, the group biographies and portraits of individuals born in the same era I shall describe supply further evidence of the horizontal ties that connected men, women, and children and fostered an awareness of their status as distinct and chosen generations.

First, there are the collected lives of the Protestants burnt during the reign of Mary I, at the forefront of which stands John Foxe's *Actes and monuments*, first published in 1563 and augmented and reissued in several more editions during and after its compiler's lifetime. Although these comprise only part of Foxe's immense anthology of documents and commentary, the significance that the victims of the Catholic queen's fires acquired in early modern culture dwarfed the rest of his lengthy history. Colloquially known as *The Book of Martyrs*, it left a mark on the Protestant imagination second only to that of the Bible and Prayer Book. Its well-known title page incorporated contrasting cartouches of the adherents of truth listening intently to an evangelical preacher with the aid of personal copies of the Bible and the superstition of the inattentive members of a popish

---

[239] Cotton Mather, *Successive generations. Remarks upon the changes of a dying world, made by one generation passing off, and another generation coming on* (Boston, MA, 1715), p. 36.

[240] David Setran, '"Declension Comes Home": Cotton Mather, Male Youth Rebellion, and the Hope of Providential Affliction in Puritan New England', *Religion and American Culture: A Journal of Interpretation*, 26 (2016), 31–73, at 37. See also Glenn Wallach, *The Discourse of Youth and Generations in American Culture, 1630–1860* (Amherst, MA, 1997).

congregation fingering their rosary beads. Above them, on the left and right, respectively, the martyrs bound to the stake sound their trumpets to heaven before receiving their crowns, while their popish rivals kneeling in idolatrous worship to the transubstantiated Mass do so to the hideous devils who await them in hell. This series of snapshots was an emblem of the ongoing war between the faithful and wicked generations throughout history. Foxe's book also incorporated many woodcuts of steadfast Christians strung together with rope as they are marched off to prison and consoling and encouraging each other as their bodies are consumed by the hungry flames.[241] Its popularity and expense led to a handy abridged edition compiled by Timothy Bright and a flock of 'little foxes' in which the heroic lives and deaths of the martyrs were so compressed that they became little more than a mere list of Protestant saints, a telescoped genealogy.[242] Engraved pictures of this lost generation, such as *Faiths victorie in Romes crueltie*, published by Thomas Jenner in the 1620s, continued to be issued at moments of crisis and tension: to stiffen the resolve of those feeling renewed pressure to cling fast to their faith and as a reminder of the sacrifice made by Latimer, Ridley, Cranmer, and all the rest of the cloud of witnesses put to death by the vicious papists (Fig. 4.4).[243] Other surviving versions of this print date from the era of the Popish Plot, during which the memory of the 'blessed martyrs' of the Reformation was revived to stir up anti-Catholic prejudice once more.[244] Such images and texts helped the children and grandchildren of those who had been eyewitnesses and victims of the Marian persecutions to recognize them as a special generation and to gain reflected glory as their posterity.

The corporate identity of the post-Reformation Catholic community was also catalysed by a cohort of sufferers. This began with Thomas More, John Fisher, and the Carthusian monks executed for denying royal supremacy under Henry VIII in the 1530s and stretched forward into the seventeenth century to the missionary priests and laypeople executed for treason. Together with scribally circulated and printed martyrologies, the engravings published by the Antwerp-based exile Richard Verstegan's *Theatrum crudelitatum* and in the *Ecclesiae Anglicanae trophaea* were a pointed riposte to the woodcuts in Foxe (Fig. 4.5). They helped to provide Catholics with a rallying point for resistance to the Reformation and a focus for their identity as a beleaguered minority up to and beyond Emancipation in 1829.[245] Although their deaths cover a more prolonged period than those of the

[241] Foxe, *Actes and monuments*, title page.
[242] John Foxe, *An abridgement of the booke of acts and monumentes of the Church*, ed. Timothy Bright (1589; STC 11229). On the small-format editions, see David Scott Kastan, 'Little Foxes', in Christopher Highley (ed.), *John Foxe and his World* (Aldershot, 2002), pp. 117–29.
[243] *Faiths victorie in Romes crueltie* (c.1620s): BM, 1855,0512.317. See Malcolm Jones, *The Print in Early Modern England: An Historical Oversight* (New Haven, CT, 2010), pp. 58–60.
[244] The edition in the FSL (ART 265962 (size M)) dates to the 1670s.
[245] Richard Verstegan, *Theatrum crudelitatum haereticorum nostri temporis* (Antwerp, 1592); Giovanni Battista de Cavalleriis, *Ecclesiae Anglicanae trophaea* (Rome, 1584). See Anne Dillon, *The*

Fig. 4.4 *Faiths victorie in Romes Crueltie* (engraving, London, *c.*1620–30).
Source: © The Trustees of the British Museum, 1855,0512.317.

Protestants who died between 1553 and 1558, they too came to be envisaged as a cohesive and more or less contemporaneous group united in their defiance of Protestant heresy and universally innocent of the charges of political disloyalty of which they were convicted. While their posthumous reputations were the subject of internecine and intraconfessional conflicts and the causes for their canonization protracted and fraught, collectively they represented a cohort of saintly heroes revered for the sacrifices they had made on behalf of the faith. The biographical bent of Catholic memory well into the twentieth century may be seen as a measure of the legacies of the sense of generational identity forged at Tyburn and other locations during the era of the penal laws.[246]

Construction of Martyrdom in the English Catholic Community, 1553–1603 (Aldershot, 2002), chs 4–5; Christopher Highley, 'Richard Verstegan's Book of Martyrs', in *idem* and John N. King (eds), *John Foxe and his World* (Aldershot, 2002), pp. 183–97.

[246] The journal of the Catholic Record Society was launched by Anthony Allison and David Rogers in 1951 as *Biographical Studies 1534–1829: Materials towards a Biographical Dictionary of Catholic History in the British Isles from the Breach with Rome to Catholic Emancipation*. It was renamed *Recusant History* in 1957 and *British Catholic History* in 2014.

Quod S. Romanæ Ecclesiæ fidem tenerent, ac prædicarent in Anglia multi Sacer=
dotes, et laici, hoc mortis genere occisi sunt anno 1582.1583. Inter quos hi fuerūt
Sacerdotes, Ioannes Shertus, Lucas Kirbeius, et Gulielmus Hartus, huius Ro=
Collegij alumni. Robertus, et Laurentius Ionsoni, Gulielmus filbeius, Kircmannus,
Threlkelus, et Hudsonus Collegij Rhemensis alumni. Thomas Cottamus, Ioannes
Paynus, Thomas fordus, Gulielmus lactus.   Complures etiam in singulis Regni
prouincijs iam condemnāti, talem mortem in horas expectant.
35

Fig. 4.5 The English missionary priests executed in 1582–3: Giovanni Battista de
Cavalleriis, *Ecclesiae Anglicana Trophaea* (Rome, [1584]), plate 35.

Source: Folger Shakespeare Library, Washington DC, BR 1607.C7 1584 Cage. Folger Digital Image
Collection.

The bestselling collections of the lives of godly divines gathered together and published by Samuel Clarke, preacher of St Bennet Fink in London, in the 1650s and 1660s also constructed a group biography of puritanically inclined clergy 'famous in their generations for learning, prudence, piety and painfulnesse in the work of the ministry'. This glossed over fractious divisions and subversive tendencies in order to present a carefully constructed image of Aristotelian moderation.[247] Clarke's works had a competitor and counterpart in Thomas Fuller's *Abel redevivus* (1651), 'a magazeen of religious patterns', in which leading lights of the European Reformation rubbed shoulders with English worthies. Among the 'moderne divines' it incorporated, there was rather heterogeneous mixture of ministerial styles, but also a good smattering of bishops, including Parker, Jewel, and Whitgift and lesser clergy of a conformist, not to say avant-garde conformist complexion, such as Lancelot Andrewes. Fuller's vision of those who were 'eminent' in their generation was rather different from Clarke's.[248] Both involved the selective amnesia that is always an element in the making of generational identities.

The turbulent decades of the mid-seventeenth century triggered and shaped these in other ways too. The golden age to which an alliance of Presbyterian, Congregationalist, and Baptist divines looked back during the Interregnum was one populated by past puritans. 'The good old Puritans in former times' became a benchmark and model for legitimation and emulation. Different groups competed to claim kinship with the Elizabethan and Jacobean heroes whose sufferings bore a resemblance to their own.[249] Shared experiences of deprivation and sequestration during the Civil Wars brought together ministers of the disestablished Church of England in the 1650s. They cast a long shadow upon individual lives and continued to rankle, even after the Restoration, eventually finding collective expression in John Walker's *Sufferings of the clergy*, compiled with the aid of questionnaires in the early eighteenth century. A compendium of largely second-hand information, it recounted their afflictions mostly through the mediated memories of their friends and relatives, wives and children.[250]

---

[247] See Samuel Clarke, *The lives of two and twenty English divines eminent in their generations for learning, piety, and painfulnesse in the work of the ministry, and for their sufferings in the cause of Christ* (1660; Wing C4540); idem, *A collection of the lives of ten eminent divines famous in their generations for learning, prudence, piety, and painfulness in the work of the ministry* (1662; Wing C4506); idem, *The lives of thirty-two English divines famous in their generations for learning and piety, and most of them sufferers in the cause of Christ* (1677; Wing C4539). See Patrick Collinson, ' "A Magazine of Religious Patterns": An Erasmian Topic Transposed in English Protestantism', in idem, *Godly People: Essays on English Protestantism and Puritanism* (1983), pp. 499–525; Peter Lake, 'Reading Clarke's Lives in Political and Polemical Context', in Kevin Sharpe and Steven N. Zwicker (eds), *Writing Lives: Biography and Textuality, Identity and Representation in Early Modern England* (Oxford, 2008), pp. 293–318.

[248] Thomas Fuller, *Abel redevivus, or, The dead yet speaking the lives and deaths of the moderne divines* (1652 edn; Wing F2401), sig. A2v.

[249] See Milton, *England's Second Reformation*, pp. 369–72.

[250] John Walker, *An attempt towards recovering an account of the numbers and sufferings of the clergy of the Church of England, Heads of Colleges, Fellows, Scholars, &c. who were sequester'd, harrass'd, &c. in the late times of the Grand Rebellion* ([1714]). On Walker's *Sufferings*, see Fiona McCall, *Baal's*

Walker's book was a response to Edmund Calamy's *Account* of the noncon-formist ministers ejected from their livings en masse in 1662, another event that both scarred a generation and simultaneously summoned it into being.[251] As John Seed has argued, it was in recounting these testimonies of the founding events of its history 'that Dissent became the oppositional historical community that bears this name'. The preface to Calamy's *Continuation* situated the dissenters of the 1720s in continuity with their predecessors and insisted that each gener-ation in succession stood witness to the path that had not, but should have been taken in the English Reformation. Key precepts about Scripture, private judge-ment, and liberty of conscience 'were chief Principles of the old Puritans. They were the principles of our Fathers; and they are also ours.'[252]

The sheer number of reprints of the omnibus editions of the farewell sermons preached by puritan pastors to their parish congregations attests, albeit indirectly, to a sense of outrage that was widely felt. These incorporated their final prayers, in which they took pride in standing straight 'in the midst of a crooked and per-verse generation'. The frontispieces to these tracts, which take the form of a patch-work of portraits of godly divines silenced at the height of their oratorical powers and in the prime of their careers, assisted in cementing their status as a cloud of witnesses and a host of martyrs (Fig. 4.6).[253] Their offspring and successors recalled 'Black Bartholomew's Day' with bitterness but also with defiance. William Tong's biography of Matthew Henry, the son of one of those expelled, said that even then God was busy 'making Provision for another Generation, a Seed to serve him in the Ministry, for whom he had appointed fairer and more peaceful Days', such as 'we have now enjoy'd for Eight and Twenty Years'.[254]

The Quakers were assiduous creators of a record of their sufferings from the outset, and their compilations of accounts of the trials and tribulations of perse-cuted Friends imprisoned for running naked for a sign and refusing to pay tithes likewise contributed to creating the intense sense of solidarity that was one of the keys to the astonishing success of the movement. The most influential expression

Priests: The Loyalist Clergy and the English Revolution (Farnham, 2013), esp. chs 2 and 5; *eadem*, 'Children of Baal: Clergy Families and Their Memories of Sequestration during the English Civil War', *HLQ*, 76 (2013), 617–38. See also Chapter 6 below.

[251] Edmund Calamy, *An abridgment of Mr. Baxter's History of his life and times. With an account of many others of those worthy ministers who were ejected, after the Restauration of King Charles the second* (1702). This was later published separately as *The nonconformists memorial*.

[252] John Seed, 'History and Narrative Identity: Religious Dissent and the Politics of Memory in Eighteenth-Century England', *JBS*, 44 (2005), 46–63, at 53; Edmund Calamy, *A continuation of the account of the ministers, lecturers, masters and fellows of colleges and schoolmasters, who were ejected and silenced after the Restoration in 1660*, 2 vols (1727), p. xv.

[253] Edmund Calamy, *An exact collection of farewell sermons preached by the late London-ministers* (1662; Wing C241), pp. 306, 308. See also *The London-ministers legacy to their several congregations being a collection of farewel-sermons* (1662; Wing L2905A). See also Lazarus Seaman et al., *The Second and last collection of the late London ministers farewel sermons* (1663; Wing S2257). See David J. Appleby, *Black Bartholomew's Day: Preaching, Polemic and Restoration Nonconformity* (Manchester, 2007).

[254] William Tong, *An account of the life and death of the late reverend Mr Matthew Henry* (1716), p. 5.

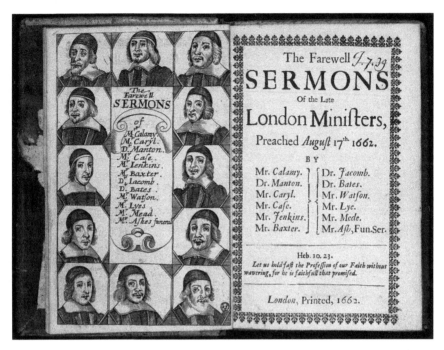

Fig. 4.6 The generation of Black Bartholomew's Day: *The farewell sermons of the late London ministers* (London, 1662), title page and frontispiece.

Source: Trinity College, Cambridge, I.3.40. By permission of the Master and Fellows.

and important conduit of the Quakers' sense of being a 'suffering people' was Joseph Besse's *Collection* of accounts (written down and registered at their meetings) of Friends who had patiently born punishment for 'the testimony of a Good Conscience' between 1650 and 1689. This appeared in two folio volumes in 1753.[255] Looking back from Bunyan's 'plain called Ease', Besse composed a composite image that smoothed over differences and occluded the antinomian enthusiasm that had scandalized contemporaries in the first phase of the sect and which had become an embarrassment to a denomination that had carefully rebranded itself as sober and industrious. His book became a touchstone for quickening Quaker identity and for sharpening later Friends' sense that they too were the children of light and the risen seed of Lord.

The collective biographies and group portraits discussed above were naturally biased towards generation workers of indigenous origin. But it would be wrong to suggest that the spiritual households and social cohorts with which contemporaries

[255] Joseph Besse, *A collection of the sufferings of the people called Quakers*, 2 vols (1753).

identified themselves were entirely insular ones. Foxe was fully alive to the Continental dimensions of the religious developments that he narrated and celebrated, and Fuller and Clarke's galleries of divines included heroes of the German, Swiss, and French Reformations. So did the cheap pamphlet pastiches produced by profit-seeking booksellers such as Nathaniel Crouch. His *Martyrs in flames, or Popery … displayed* (1693) contained hastily stitched summaries of past persecutions, including those of the Protestants in Piedmont, France, and Savoy who had become the latest victims of 'that bloody generation of Antichristians'.[256]

The point that English people envisaged themselves as part of a pan-European Protestant family is made even more compellingly by another print created and marketed by Thomas Jenner, known as 'The Candle is Lighted' (Fig. 4.7). This is an image of all the major reformers—Luther, Melanchthon, Calvin, Beza, Zwingli, Bullinger, Bucer, and Zanchius—seated around a table on which stands a candlestick. Reproduced and updated frequently in a range of media and formats, it is an image in which home-grown figures such as John Wyclif, Hugh Latimer, Thomas Cranmer, Nicholas Ridley, William Perkins, James Ussher, and

Fig. 4.7 The family of reformers: *The candle is lighted, we cannot [it] blow out* (etching, London, c.1620–40).

Source: © The Trustees of the British Museum, 1907,0326.31.

---

[256] R. B. [Nathaniel Crouch], *Martyrs in flames, or, Popery (in its true colours) displayed … published for a warning to all Protestants, … what they must expect from that bloody generation of Antichristians* (1693; Wing C7344A).

the Scottish firebrand John Knox sit as equals alongside their European partners and neighbours. Below, from the shadows, a quartet consisting of the Pope, a cardinal, a monk, and a bishop or a devil desperately but unsuccessfully attempt to blow the flame out. Alluding to the gatherings from which Luther's famous *Table talk* emerged, this happy extended family is itself an emanation of patriarchal household religion. It evokes the domestic assemblies of kith and kin which the Reformation elevated into a sacred institution. But the impression of harmonious agreement that the picture conveys is deceptive. It forgets the violent disputes about the Eucharist that divided Luther from the Swiss reformers, and it completely excludes the radicals, Andreas Carlstadt, Thomas Munster, and others against whom the magisterial reformers so violently turned. And although the personalities depicted here were not in fact contemporaneous and spanned two generations, the timeline has been shortened and they are presented as if they are one.[257]

As the ingenious research of Joke Spaans has recently shown, this remarkable group portrait continued to be adapted and copied for a variety of polemical purposes into the nineteenth century. Although it draws on an earlier Continental iconography, its prototype appears to have originated in England. A rare example of a successful British export, it spread to the Netherlands, Bohemia, France, Germany, and Moravia and crossed back and forth across the confessional divide.[258] If its travels supply insight into how the Reformation was repeatedly reconceptualized in different contexts and circumstances, they also illuminate its role in creating both a discourse and an iconography of generations. In the guise of oil-painted panels, book illustrations, and even ceramic plates, it helped to spread awareness of the English Reformation as a branch of a European movement (Fig. 4.8). The presence of Wyclif, the so-called morning star of the Reformation, adds an element of self-congratulation, but this is not at the expense of a spirit of collaboration and alliance in the fight against the Roman Antichrist.[259]

It is, nevertheless, significant that at the very moment that Jenner issued this print, attitudes were beginning to shift. England's commitment to a foreign policy that backed international Protestantism was under strain, and the following years saw a further cooling of relations between the sister churches on the Continent with which the English Church had once enjoyed close kinship.[260] With Laudianism, these sibling affinities weakened. But the long afterlife of Jenner's motif and its derivatives offsets any suggestion that the more insular vision of the first Reformation promoted by the Laudians was dominant

[257] *The candle is lighted, we cannot blow [it] out* (c.1620s): BM, 1907, 0326.31. On this print, see Alexandra Walsham, 'Domesticating the Reformation: Material Culture, Memory and Confessional Identity in Early Modern England', *RQ*, 69 (2016), 566–616. See also Chapter 5 below.
[258] Joke Spaans, 'Faces of the Reformation', *Church History and Religious Culture*, 97 (2017), pp. 408–51.
[259] On Wyclif, see Margaret Aston, 'John Wycliffe's Reformation Reputation', *P&P* 30 (1965), 23–51.
[260] Milton, *Catholic and Reformed*, esp. 270–321.

Fig. 4.8 *The Protestant Reformers* (oil, English school, after 1662).
Source: Society of Antiquaries of London.

in later seventeenth- and eighteenth-century England. It is true that one late version of the print peremptorily expels all the European reformers to concentrate on the Marian martyrs, Hooper, Ridley, Latimer, Cranmer, Bradford, and Taylor.[261] But in many others the whole European family remains present. Possessing such images gave expression to a vision of Protestant internationalism that remained resilient, perhaps especially in dissenting circles. In the 1670s and 1680s, the Leeds nonconformist and antiquary Ralph Thoresby devoted many days to transcribing the lives and hand-copying the pictures of Luther, Zwingli, Calvin, Beza, and all the rest, pasting the latter into a book 'according to their several generations'.[262]

And so we come, finally, to an important point that has been implicit throughout the preceding analysis: contemporaries understood the Reformation as a process that progressed in a series of generational phases. The historiography of European Protestantism has long recognized the utility and value of thinking of its evolution over time in these terms and the concept of a second Reformation is well entrenched in the literature. Historians of England have been slow to follow suit. Anthony Milton's major new study of the battle for the Church's identity between 1625 and 1662 deploys the phrase more loosely, to characterize a second sustained wave of attempted reforms divided from the first by more than a

---

[261] V&A, no. 29719.2, press mark GG 51. My thanks to Joke Spaans for drawing my attention to this item.
[262] *The Diary of Ralph Thoresby, F.R.S. Author of the Topography of Leeds (1677–1724)*, 2 vols, ed. Joseph Hunter (1830), p. 74, and see pp. 8, 9–10, 83.

century.[263] There are strong arguments for suggesting that this way of conceptualizing the Reformation was rooted in the early modern period itself.

Contemporaries too seem to have had a linear view of history in which Christian truths unfolded incrementally. They saw it as a historical development that had different stages and that had changed as it aged. The whole question of whether the ignorance of dead ancestors born before the arrival of the Gospel could be excused presumed this. The very structure of Foxe's *Actes and monuments* was teleological, and the story of progressive enlightenment he told compared the partial knowledge of Wyclif in the fourteenth century with the more advanced insights afforded to Luther in the sixteenth century, whose understanding was in turn imperfect. The Lollards only had a glimmering of the light, and though Luther was without doubt a great theologian and seer, his ideas about the real presence in the Eucharist seemed very backward to Foxe, who condescendingly urged his reader not to be too exercised by 'one small blemish, or for a little stoupyng...in the Sacrament'.[264]

The same outlook can be found in Francis Trigge's *Apologie or defence of our dayes* (1589), which described how, when Wyclif and Hus had preached, the light was dim 'in the middest of most thicke Popish darkenesse'. By the time of Erasmus and Luther, it had increased 'as in the dawning, or in the daye breake', and when Calvin, Bucer, and Bullinger arrived on the scene, 'it was spread farre and wyde'. Another thirty years on, it had 'entred into every chinke' and 'lightned all the ayre'. That it continued to become brighter and clearer was a 'most certaine signe' that Christ's second coming drew near.[265] The idea that religious revelation was an open-ended process in which earlier reform efforts were eclipsed by later ones continued to be articulated. Preaching at St Mary Aldermanbury in London during the 1630s, John Stoughton declared that there was 'more light in these times, then there was an hundred yeares agoe, at the beginning, at the dawning day of reformation'.[266] Speaking in other contexts, his fellow puritans would soon be more inclined to worry that the candle was about to be snuffed out by disturbing ecclesiastical developments. The language of progressive reformation was, however, a flexible tool which Laudians themselves sometimes deployed to give expression to their own agenda. Like both 'generation' and 'reformation', it was a multivalent discourse that could carry competing meanings.[267]

---

[263] Anthony Milton, *England's Second Reformation: The Battle for the Church of England 1625–1662* (Cambridge, 2021), esp. pp. 4–5.

[264] Foxe, *Actes and monuments* (1570 edn), pp. 992–3. On the theme of progressive enlightenment in Foxe, see Susan Royal, *Lollards in the English Reformation: History, Radicalism, and John Foxe* (Manchester, 2020), esp. pp. 29–31, 211–13.

[265] Trigge, *Apologie*, p. 4.

[266] John Stoughton, *A forme of wholesome words* (1640; STC 23307.5), p. 63.

[267] Milton, *England's Second Reformation*, pp. 49–50, 63, and see pp. 159–62. See also Chapter 5 below.

In other hands, this historical scheme acquired a more eschatological inflection. An extended elaboration of it can be found in John Tillinghast's book *Generation-work*. He too charted the gradual discovery of the light by successive generations of reformers, showing how 'the fogs of Antichristianism' had steadily disappeared as time passed, so that Luther was in some respects more in the dark than Calvin, and both were less advanced than those who had succeeded them. To say so was 'no disparagement to them, who did worthily in their Generations', and it was no cause for 'exaltation to our selves, who have nothing but free Grace to boast of'.[268] As another Fifth Monarchist pamphlet proclaimed in 1659, 'Jesus Christ...works us up age after age to a further Reformation, to more light and holiness.'[269] By contrast with our tendency to regard Luther's legendary protest against the Church of Rome in 1517 as a revolutionary juncture and a major milestone, many English Protestants evidently thought of it as merely 'the first Reformation', as the initial stage in an ongoing, incremental, open-ended, and incomplete process. As Captain Henry Bell wrote in the preface to the first English translation of Luther's *Table talk* (1652), it could not 'rationally be expected that at that first dawning of the Gospel of light, all Spiritual Truths should be known in that perfection whereunto God hath brought the knowing professors of this Age'.[270] The millenarian moment in which Tillinghast and Bell wrote was one in which excitement was growing that the Reformation would soon reach its final destination and in which time itself would end.

It is to temporality and other topics that Chapter 5 turns. But it is necessary to close this one by drawing out a few salient themes. The first is that one of the more significant consequences of the English Reformation was to alter how people perceived and understood the relationship between the generations, past, present, and future. In the abstract, its theology had the effect of cutting off the living from the dead and reconfiguring the capacity of human beings to influence their fate in the afterlife. It nevertheless proved flexible enough to react compassionately to concerns about the soteriological status of those who had died, to keep open the possibility of communication and reunion with them in heaven, and to offer hope to parents that their children might indeed number among the elect and be the chosen seed. The concept of generation was a powerful resource in this culture. Wrought by emotion, shared experience, and memory, it was a vehicle for thought and action and a vital lens and discourse through which people viewed and talked about their world. The traces

---

[268] Tillinghast, *Generation-work*, p. 62.

[269] *The fifth monarchy, or kingdom of Christ, in opposition to the beasts* (1659; Wing F890), p. 6.

[270] Martin Luther, *Dris Martin Lutheri colloquia mensalia: or Dr Martin Luther's divine discourses at his table, &c*, ed. and trans. Henry Bell (1652; Wing L3510), sig. a4v.

it has left in contemporary speech, records, and texts belie the lingering assumption that generational consciousness has no history before the modern era. They also highlight how tightly interwoven notions of social generation were with genealogy, family, lineage, and kinship. In early modern England, generations were reproduced as well as remembered.

5

History and Time

Lambeth Palace Library MS 66 is an early sixteenth-century manuscript chronicle of the world from the Creation to 1525 written in English. Contrary to expectation, the page for Anno Mundi 6715 and Anno Domini 1517 is blank: apparently there was nothing worth recording for this date. A void pregnant with meaning, it reflects the vagaries of remembering but also, perhaps, a strategic act of forgetting. This conspicuous omission not only highlights how far historical events are the belated products of hindsight. It may also encode active resistance to recalling a development that the conservative compiler of this chronicle seemingly lamented.[1]

By contrast, everyone now knows what happened in 1517. It was the year in which, on 31 October, an obscure German monk by the name of Martin Luther launched his famous protest against the corruptions of the Church of Rome by posting his 95 theses against indulgences and the papacy's power to pardon sin on the door of the castle church in the small university town of Wittenberg. Marking the birth of the movement we call the Reformation, this possibly apocryphal episode has entered into the annals of legend as a turning point in Western history, a fork in the path of our civilization, and a pivotal date in the making of the modern world. Although images of Luther brandishing his pen as a weapon against the Pope did circulate in the early years of the reform movement, it was not until much later that his famous act of defiance at Wittenberg acquired enduring visual form in the guise of the print known as the dream of Frederick the Wise, which appeared at the time of the first centenary of the Reformation in 1617.[2] As Scott Dixon and Peter Marshall have shown, its invention as a watershed is a comparatively recent phenomenon.[3] Shaped by processes of retrospection, historical events have no independent ontological status or intrinsic meaning. They are not happenings that exist to be narrated but, in the words of the sociologist Philip

---

[1] LPL, MS 66 (A chronicle of the world from the Creation to 1525), fos 312v–313r. See https://exhibitions.lib.cam.ac.uk/reformation/artifacts/the-absence-of-1517/, accessed 4 June 2022.

[2] For Luther using his pen as a weapon, see *The husbandman. Doctor Martin Luther. The pope. The cardinall* ([1550?]; STC 14008.5): Magdalene College, Cambridge: Pepys Library Ballads I: 16–17. For the dream of Frederick the Wise, see *Göttlicher Schrifftmessiger, woldenckwürdiger Traum, welchen der Hochlöbliche*...(Leipzig, 1617): BM, 1880,0710.299. See Brian Cummings, 'Luther and the Book: The Iconography of the Ninety–Five Theses', in R. N. Swanson (ed.), *The Church and the Book*, SCH 38 (Woodbridge, 2004), pp. 222–32.

[3] C. Scott Dixon, 'Luther's Ninety-Five Theses and the Origins of the Reformation Narrative', *EHR*, 132 (2017), 533–69; Peter Marshall, *1517: Martin Luther and the Invention of the Reformation* (Oxford, 2017).

Abrams, happenings 'to which cultural significance has been assigned'.[4] Like generations themselves, they are, in large part artefacts of imagination and memory. They must be studied over the *longue durée*, in the process of their 'becoming' and as they evolve over time.[5]

Generations were one of the ways in which contemporaries conceptualized historical development. In the sixteenth and seventeenth centuries, the pervasive scheme of the seven ages of man referred not merely to stages in the human life cycle; it was also a shorthand for a process of temporal progression. Just as 'age' was deployed to denote both the number of years people had lived on earth and a particular phase or period in time, so generation was used simultaneously as a synonym for 'a history or narration of things' and as a moment within it, especially of origin, beginning, and genesis.[6] This chapter examines the intersections between the religious upheavals of the era, the arts of history, and the sciences of time. It traces how the protracted and pluralistic phenomenon that was the English Reformation came to be recognized as a historical event and conceptualized as a unit of historical chronology. It argues that the end product of this process was not a single unitary vision but rather many conflicting ones that corresponded with the several frames of temporal reference, synchronic and diachronic, that coexisted in this culture. Fraught with ambiguity about when (and if) the Reformation had started and ended, these competing accounts were the catalysts of ongoing controversies that have left a lasting legacy in prevailing models of historical periodization.

The discussion that follows avoids becoming embroiled in the debates about the 'historiographical revolution' that have long animated intellectual historians. With David Womersley, it firmly resists the assumption that the emergence of history as an academic discipline entailed 'its steady self-emancipation from the bondage of religion'.[7] It builds on the emerging consensus that erudition and confessionalism, scholarship and faith, were intricately and reciprocally linked and that theology and piety were not enemies to critical method and empirical rigour; instead they were its principal stimuli.[8] Similarly, this chapter is only incidentally

---

[4] Philip Abrams, *Historical Sociology* (Shepton Mallet, 1982), p. 191.

[5] See Marek Tamm, 'Introduction: Afterlife of Events: Perspectives on Memory History', in *idem* (ed.), *Afterlife of Events: Perspectives on Mnemohistory* (Basingstoke, 2015), pp. 1–23, esp. pp. 6–8. See also François Dosse, 'Historical Event between Sphinx and Phoenix' and Nikolay Koposov, 'Events, Proper Names and the Rise of Memory', in this volume, pp. 27–43 and 44–61 respectively.

[6] See OED, s.vv. 'age' and 'generation'; Thomas Wilson, *A Christian dictionarie* (1612; STC 25786), p. 223.

[7] David Womerseley, 'Against the Teleology of Technique', in Paulina Kewes (ed.), *The Uses of History in Early Modern England*, special issue of *HLQ*, 68 (2005), 95–108, at 98. For paradigms that stress secularization, see F. Smith Fussner, *The Historical Revolution: English Historical Writing and Thought 1580–1640* (1962); F. J. Levy, *Tudor Historical Thought* (San Marino, CA, 1967); Peter Burke, *The Renaissance Sense of the Past* (1969), esp. ch. 4. For a more nuanced account of developments, see Daniel Woolf, 'From Hystories to the Historical: Five Transitions in Thinking about the Past, 1500–1700', in Kewes (ed.), *Uses of History*, 33–70.

[8] See, e.g., Simon Ditchfield, *Liturgy, Sanctity and History in Tridentine Italy: Pietro Maria Campi and the Preservation of the Particular* (Cambridge, 1995); Anthony Grafton, *The Footnote: A Curious*

concerned with the claim, most closely associated with Reinhart Koselleck, that a heightened awareness of change and of the rapid acceleration of time is a hallmark of modernity.[9] It steps back from the temptation to read the birth of linear and teleological schemes back into the early modern era and to identify an acute consciousness of discontinuity as the defining feature of its historical sensibility.[10] Drawing inspiration from the Judith Pollmann's recent work on memory, it approaches early modern England as a society alive to the 'virtues of anachronism' and capable of adopting a variety of perspectives on the relationship between the past and the present simultaneously. Multiple modes of temporality overlapped and complemented each other. Allegory, typology, and analogy retained their vitality alongside chronology.[11] Experiences and conceptions of time continued to be shaped by the cycle of the Christian liturgy and by notions of divine periodicity.[12] This chapter is also alert to the creative uses to which competing visions of the future—imaginative constructs integrally linked to different perspectives on history—were put in sixteenth- and seventeenth-century Europe.[13]

Particular attention will be focused on how perceptions of the Reformation as a moment of rupture evolved as the generation that had personally experienced the religious upheavals of the 1540s, 1550s, and 1560s was succeeded by people whose memory of them was inherited from their parents and grandparents.

History (Cambridge, MA, 1997); Irena Backus, Historical Method and Confessional Identity in the Era of the Reformation (1378-1615) (Leiden, 2003); Arnoud S. Q. Visser, Reading Augustine in the Reformation: The Flexibility of Intellectual Authority in Europe, 1500-1620 (Oxford, 2011); Dmitri Levitin, 'From Sacred History to the History of Religion: Paganism, Judaism, and Christianity in European Historiography from Reformation to "Enlightenment"', HJ, 55 (2012), 1117–60; idem, Ancient Wisdom in the Age of the New Science: Histories of Philosophy in England, c.1640-1700 (Cambridge, 2015); Katrina Olds, Forging the Past: Invented Histories in Counter-Reformation Spain (New Haven, CT, 2015); Jan Machielsen, Martin del Rio: Demonology and Scholarship in the Counter-Reformation (Oxford, 2015); Nicholas Hardy, Criticism and Confession: The Bible in the Seventeenth-Century Republic of Letters (Oxford, 2017); Dmitri Levitin and Nicholas Hardy (eds), Confessionalisation and Erudition in Early Modern Europe: An Episode in the History of the Humanities, Proceedings of the British Academy 225 (Oxford, 2019).

[9] Reinhard Koselleck, Futures Past: On the Semantics of Historical Time, trans. and intro. Keith Tribe (New York, 2004; first publ. in German 1979). See also François Hertog, Regimes of Historicity: Presentism and Experiences of Time, trans. Saskia Brown (New York, 2015).

[10] On a new sense of change and discontinuity, see Daniel Woolf, The Social Circulation of the Past: English Historical Culture 1500–1730 (Oxford, 2003), ch. 19. For the rise of linear treatments of time, see John C. Sommerville, The Secularization of Early Modern England: From Religious Culture to Religious Faith (New York, 1992), ch. 3.

[11] Judith Pollmann, Memory in Early Modern Europe 1500–1800 (Oxford, 2017), esp. ch. 2. See also the incisive discussion of this topic by Margreta de Grazia, 'Anachronism', in Brian Cummings and James Simpson (eds), Cultural Reformations: Medieval and Renaissance in Literary History (Oxford, 2010), pp. 13–32. Peter Burke is the most emphatic exponent of its emergence as a hallmark of modernity: see his 'The Sense of Anachronism from Petrarch to Poussin', in Chris Humphrey and W. M. Ormrod (eds), Time in the Medieval World (Rochester, NY, 2001), pp. 157–73.

[12] Étienne Bourbon, 'Temporalities and History in the Renaissance', Journal of Early Modern Studies, 6 (2017), 39–60.

[13] Andrea Brady and Emily Butterworth (eds), The Uses of the Future in Early Modern Europe (New York, 2010).

A further theme is the intertwining of senses of historical and liturgical time with the rhythms of biological reproduction and the life cycle. Generations, it will be suggested, are a neglected domain in which the social circulation of the past took place. In the process, this chapter engages critically with Daniel Woolf's contention that 'an increasingly homogenized and chronologically rigorous' narrative of English history steadily displaced other historical traditions, even as it develops his suggestion that in the course of the seventeenth century a more intimate connection between the familial and national pasts emerged.[14] It does so by exploring the manner in which public remembering of England's long Reformation became entangled with personal memory and genealogy.

Prophecy and Eschatology

It is now well established that the writing of sacred history underwent a significant revival as a consequence of Europe's plural Reformations. In a context in which all the actors believed that they were the sole possessors of the truth taught by Christ in the first century AD, the onus fell on each to prove this. Protestants urgently sought to locate their genealogical roots in the apostolic era and to trace an unbroken but invisible brotherhood of true believers who had defied the papacy and priesthood throughout the Dark Ages. Questions of institutional continuity were critical for Roman Catholics too, and recovering the textual and material traces of early Christianity lay at the heart of the historical scholarship of Tridentine and Jesuit giants such as Cesare Baronius. Ecclesiastical history in the mode of Eusebius became the handmaiden of religious controversy. Alongside this, its sister disciplines of hagiography, martyrology, bibliography, archaeology, and geography flourished anew. The chief battleground on which the wars of words ignited by the Reformation were waged was the past, both immediate and distant.[15]

One of the principal consequences of this flurry of historical activity was the erection of a sharp divide between the Middle Ages and the Reformation era. Implicit in humanism's conviction that the glories of classical civilization had been eclipsed by the aridity of scholastic learning, the idea that the medieval centuries were a period of ignorance and credulity, obscurantism and pedantry, was harnessed and reinforced by the Protestant reformers. Alongside the Renaissance, the Reformation played a key role in reconfiguring what Eviatar Zerubavel has called the 'time map' of the past. It created a new 'social scalpel' for carving up

---

[14] Woolf, *Social Circulation of the Past*, pp. 274, 98.

[15] Katherine van Liere, Simon Ditchfield, and Howard Louthan (eds), *Sacred History: Uses of the Christian Past in the Renaissance World* (Oxford, 2012). For Catholic approaches, see Christopher Highley, *Catholics Writing the Nation in Early Modern Britain and Ireland* (Oxford, 2008). See also Chapters 1 and 3 above.

this imagined space and for correlating it with both the present and the future.[16] Yet it did not do so at the expense of older modes of historical thinking.

One of these was eschatology. Feverish apocalyptic expectation grew in the early sixteenth century, fed by renewed attention to the biblical prophecies of Daniel, Esdras, and Revelation. It was in this climate of increasing anticipation of the Second Coming that Martin Luther's own view of church history was forged, a vision that was at once cosmic and historical, atemporal and linear. For Luther, history was above all the everlasting story of the salvation of mankind wrought by a gracious God, but it was also a gripping drama that took place in real time. Premised on the idea that the end was imminent, Luther's theocentric vision accentuated the looming gulf between the fallen society he saw all around him and the perfection of the eternal kingdom he expected soon to be erected on earth. It drew strength from the traditional commonplace that the world was sinking into old age and terminal decline. Luther, Melanchthon, and their disciples believed that they were living in the last times and in the dregs of Christian civilization, the principal index of which was the appearance and unmasking of the Antichrist.[17] Protestantism's bold and insistent identification of the Seven-Headed Beast and the Whore of Babylon with the Church of Rome collapsed prophecy and history into one and invested the associated task of gnosis with urgency. Andreas Osiander's Conjectures of the ende of the worlde (1544) stoked speculation regarding the End, and the millenarian periodization of the Middle Ages as an era of declension was embodied in Matthias Flaccius Illyricus's Catalogue of witnesses to the truth (1556) and enshrined in the mammoth Magdeburg Centuries, whose preparation by a team of Protestant scholars he coordinated between 1559 and 1574.[18]

Lutheran history grafted the events of the sixteenth century onto the scheme of the four world monarchies (Babylonian, Persian, Greek, and Roman) and the steady degeneration of Christianity across the millennium and a half since the time of the apostles. It saw the advent of the Gospel as a prelude to the Apocalypse

---

[16] Eviatar Zerubavel, *Time Maps: Collective Memory and the Social Shape of the Past* (Chicago, 2012), p. 96, and see ch. 4. On the Middle Ages as 'a terminological creation of Renaissance humanism', see Donald R. Kelley, *Faces of History: Historical Inquiry from Herodotus to Herder* (New Haven, CT, 1998), p. 130 and ch. 6, and see ch. 7 ('Reformation Traditions'). See also Mark Greengrass and Matthias Pohlig (eds), 'Themenschwerpunkt/Focal Point: The Protestant Reformation and the Middle Ages', *Archiv für Reformationgeschichte*, 101 (2010), 233–304.

[17] This finds compelling expression in the remarkable altarpiece Lucas Cranach painted for the Stadtkirche in Wittenberg in 1548. See John M. Headley, *Luther's View of Church History* (New Haven, CT, 1963); Markus Wriedt, 'Luther's Concept of History and the Formation of an Evangelical Identity', in Bruce Gordon (ed.), *Protestant History and Identity in Sixteenth-Century Europe*, 2 vols (Aldershot, 1996), vol. i, pp. 31–45.

[18] Robin Bruce Barnes, *Prophecy and Gnosis: Apocalypticism in the Wake of the Lutheran Reformation* (Stanford, CA, 1988); Andrew Cunningham and Ole Peter Grell (eds), *The Four Horsemen of the Apocalypse: Religion, War, Famine and Death in Reformation Europe* (Cambridge, 2000), ch. 2. Andreas Osiander, *The conjectures of the ende of the worlde*, trans. George Joye ([Antwerp, 1548]; STC 18877).

and thought of it as a candle whose eventual and certain extinction would be preceded by a great burst of illumination. It broadly divided history into three stages: the early Church, the era of Antichrist, and the end times. Superimposed over this tripartite scheme was a binary one consisting of two phases: one of gradually descending darkness and the other of progressive enlightenment. In simplified form, this became a potent metaphor for the Reformation itself, which was commonly compared to the dawning of a new day and to the banishment of the black night brought about by the diabolical duo of Satan and the papacy.[19]

Popularized by Johannes Sleidan's short textbook outlining the trajectory of world history,[20] these ideas were also disseminated by Johannes Carion's bestselling *Chronicle*, which was first published in English in 1550, but also circulated widely in manuscript. One version dated *c*.1600 makes reference to Luther's 95 theses being 'fastened unto the churches gate, which toucheth the Castle of Wittemberg, on the last day of October'.[21] Contemporaries were quick to integrate the events of their own time into the ancient schema of universal history, which envisaged the future as a stage of superior spiritual development. Walter Lynne's *Beginning and endynge of all popery* (1548) was an allegorical exposition of medieval prophecies and of Paul's premonition of the downfall of the man of sin in 2 Thessalonians 2 sponsored by Lord Protector Somerset.[22] Spurred by the accession of Queen Mary I in 1553, Henry Bullinger's commentary on the Apocalypse was dedicated to the English Protestant exiles who had clustered in Zurich.[23] John Bale's *Image of bothe churches* (1541–8) likewise expounded it figuratively in order to decipher the true meaning of the 'ages, tymes, and seasons' of history and unveil the mystery of Catholic iniquity. The scheme of the seven seals also underpinned John Foxe's *Actes and monuments of these latter and perillous dayes*, initially published in 1563.[24] Such texts effected 'a dramatic change in the

[19] On the language of light and darkness, see Craig Koslofsky, *Evening's Empire: A History of the Night in Early Modern Europe* (Cambridge, 2011), ch. 2, esp. pp. 19–23. See also Alain Cabantous, *Histoire de la nuit: Europe occidentale XVIIe-XVIIIe siècles* (Paris, 2009).

[20] This was printed in both Latin and English in Elizabeth's reign. Later editions appeared under the titles *The key of historie. Or, a most methodicall abridgement of the foure chiefe monarchies...being a general and compendious chronicle from the flood* (1627; STC 19850) and *The general history of the Reformation of the Church, from the errors and corruptions of the Church of Rome: begun in Germany by Martin Luther, with the progress thereof in all parts of Christendom, from the year 1517, to the year 1556* (1689; Wing S3989).

[21] LPL, MS Sion L40.2/E49: Johann Carion, 'Chronicon' (*c*.1600), fo. 347v. This translation appears to have been made from Simon Goulart's French edition of the *Chronicon Carionis* of 1595. For the first English translation in print, see Johannes Carion, *The thre bokes of cronicles* ([1550]; STC 4626).

[22] Walter Lynne, *The beginning and endynge of all popery, or popishe kyngedome* ([1548?]; STC 17115).

[23] Henry Bullinger, *A hundred sermons upo[n] the Apocalips of Jesu Christe, reveiled in dede by thangell of the Lorde: but seen or receyved and written by thapostle and Eva[n]gelist S. John* (1561; STC 4061).

[24] John Bale, *The image of bothe churches after the moste wonderfull and heavenly Revelacion of Sainct John the Evangelist, contaynyng a very frutefull exposicion or paraphrase upon the same* ([1548?]; STC 1297; 1570, STC 1301), quotation at sig. A4r; John Foxe, *Actes and monuments of these latter and perillous dayes* (1563; STC 11222). See Avihu Zakai, 'Reformation, History, and Eschatology in English Protestantism', *History and Theory*, 26 (1987), 300–18.

meaning of the present', causing 'a jolt in historical consciousness for the first generation of Protestants by marking the Reformation as a break with the past'.[25]

Replicating the pattern of steady corruption and decline in Lutheran histories,
Bale and Foxe discerned some remaining glimmers of light in the Anglo-Saxon
era, followed by a sharp downturn after the Norman Conquest. Charting the
same epic struggle between the forces of light and darkness, Foxe celebrated the
hidden minority of heretics from the Cathars and Waldensians to the Lollards
and Hussites who had kept the candle alight. He glossed over their theological
heterodoxy and airbrushed out sectarians who diverged inconveniently from the
mainstream in the interests of projecting a vision of harmony and unity. He presented the sixteenth-century Reformation inaugurated by Henry VIII and his
Protestant heirs as the beginning of a new era in England, but he also devoted
considerable space to delineating concurrent developments on the Continent, not
least Luther's protest in the autumn of 1517. Repeating a mistake of dating resulting from the mistranslation of Melanchthon's life of the reformer, he implied that
this had occurred on the day after rather than the day before the feast of All
Saints—in other words on 2 November.[26] Pan-European and internationalist,
Foxe's historical vision had features in common with John Knox's *Historie of the
reformation of the Church of Scotland*, which described the 'generation of
Antichrist' throughout time and traced the re-emergence of the truth following
its near universal desertion before the era of Luther.[27] It described a militant
movement fuelled by divinely inspired revolutionary zeal. The instinct of the
authors of apocalyptically inflected histories was to see the Reformation less as a
distinct event than as a process that would culminate in the Second Coming.[28]

The eschatological impatience of the reformed tradition was less pronounced
than within Lutheranism, though the commentaries on Revelation and Daniel
that emanated from Geneva and Zurich converged with those that emerged from
Wittenberg in identifying the papacy as the implacable enemy of Christ's church
foretold in these prophecies.[29] However, apocalypticism remained a significant

---

[25] See Adam Morton, 'Remembering the Past at the End of Time', in Alexandra Walsham, Bronwyn
Wallace, Ceri Law, and Brian Cummings (eds), *Memory and the English Reformation* (Cambridge,
2020), pp. 80–97, at p. 81.

[26] Foxe, *Actes and monuments* (1563 edn), p. 455. This was repeated in subsequent versions. The
initial mistake was made in Henry Bennet's translation of Philip Melanchthon's *A famous and godly
history, contaynyng the lyves & actes of three renowmed reformers of the Christia[n] Church, Martine
Luther, John Ecolampadius, and Huldericke Zvinglius* (1561; STC 1881), sig. C1v. On Foxe's editorial
practices, see Patrick Collinson, 'Truth and Legend: The Veracity of John Foxe's Book of Martyrs', in
A. C. Duke and C. A. Tamse (eds), *Clio's Mirror: Historiography in Britain and the Netherlands*
(Zutphen, 1985), pp. 31–54. To emphasize the internationalism of Foxe's vision is not to deny that in
the hands of his readers his book may have nurtured the seeds of jingoism and ethnocentrism.

[27] John Knox, *The historie of the reformation of the Church of Scotland containing five books* (1644;
Wing K738), pp. 104, 143. See also *idem*, 'Appellation', p. 3 (bound with this and separately paginated).

[28] See Susan Royal, 'English Evangelical Historians on the Origins of "the Reformation"', *Études
Épistémè*, 32 (2017), doi: 10.4000/episteme.1859.

[29] See Irena Backus, *Reformation Readings of the Apocalypse: Geneva, Zurich, and Wittenberg*
(Oxford, 2000).

strand in English Protestant thinking about history and time. It colours William Watkinson's translation of the Freiburg rector Johann Rivius's *Notable discourse of the happiness of this our age, and of the ingratitude of men to God for his benefites* (1578), the dedicatory epistle of which lays out ecclesiastical history in a Foxeian fashion and shows how the very beginning of Antichrist's kingdom was laid in the Apostles' time and how the darkness that grew up 'by degrees' had eventually drowned the world entirely. Ventriloquizing Rivius's own celebration of the dispelling of 'the thicke cloudes of errours' by the heavenly light of the Gospel and the 'sundrie learned Divines' from Luther, Zwingli, and Calvin to Latimer, Hooper, Bradford, Jewell, and Foxe whom God had raised up to 'conduct us out of the land of Aegypt', Watkinson's upbeat preface heralded his own times as a 'golden age' in which the God's truth shone more clearly than in any former one. It also spoke of the English as more blessed than any other nation 'under the Sunne' and prayed that they would be duly grateful for these '*Halcionii dies*'.[30]

Infused with an ebullient strain of patriotic pride, eschatological thinking entailed a concept of linear progress that regarded the present as an improvement on the past. As Katharine Firth, Paul Christianson, and William Lamont have shown, Thomas Brightman carried forward the mantle of the Protestant apocalyptic historical tradition into the later sixteenth and seventeenth centuries, using it as an exegetical tool to castigate the insufficient zeal of the Church of England and to urge further Genevan-style reform. He also went further than his predecessors in declaring that the last trumpet had already sounded, in dating this to 1558, and in making the millennium an attainable historical goal.[31] Joseph Mede's *Clavis apocalyptica*, first published in Latin in 1627 and translated, after his death, into English in 1643 was another straw in the wind. The preface by William Twisse stressed the 'excellency' of Mede's exegetical method in explicating recent history:

> Not onely in respect of the great Reformation wrought in this Westerne part of the world an hundred yeeres agoe and more: God awaking as it were out of a sleep, and like a gyant refreshed with wine: and the Lord Christ awaking, and stirring up his strength for the raising up of *Jacob*, and restoring the desolations of *Israel*, and blessing us with a resurrection of his Gospel, and discovering the

---

[30]   John Rivius, *A notable discourse of the happinesse of this our age, and of the ingratitude of men to God for his benefites*, trans. William Watkinson (1578; STC 21064.5), sigs A2v–B2v.

[31]   Thomas Brightman, *A revelation of the Apocalyps, that is, the Apocalyps of S. Iohn illustrated with an analysis & scolions: where the sense is opened by the scripture, & the events of things foretold, shewed by histories* (Amsterdam, 1611; STC 3754). William Lamont, *Godly Rule: Politics and Religion in England 1603–1660* (1969); Richard Bauckham, *Tudor Apocalypse: Sixteenth-Century Apocalypticism, Millenarianism and the English Reformation: from John Bale and John Foxe to Thomas Brightman* (Oxford, 1978); Paul Christianson, *Reformers and Babylon: English Apocalyptic Visions from Reformation to Civil War* (Toronto, 1978); Katharine R. Firth, *The Apocalyptic Tradition in Reformation Britain 1530–1645* (Oxford, 1979).

man of sin, and blasting him with the breath of his mouth. But also opening the mysterie of the slaughter of the Witnesses, which we have just reason to conceive to have beene on foot divers yeares, not by judiciall proceedings only in the Martyrdom of Gods Saints; but by the sword of war, First in the *Low-Countries*, then in *France*, after that in *Bohemia*, then in *Germany*... and now amongst us, First in *Ireland*, then in *England*, and that by the Antichristian generation, with so manifest opposition unto truth and holinesse under a Protestant Prince, as I thinke the like was never known since the beginning of the world.[32]

Unfolding events across Europe, which were now engulfing Britain, powerfully reinforced the sense that the future would look back on the present as a prophetic fulfilment of the resonant prophecies of Revelation.

Millenarianism reached a new pitch during the Civil Wars and Interregnum, notably among the Fifth Monarchists. As we saw in Chapter 4, this was the context in which an especially intense form of generational consciousness emerged, when contemporaries convinced themselves that they had a vital part to play in ushering in the Second Coming. Seeped in the prophecies of the apocalyptic scriptures, the Fifth Monarchy Men waited with bated breath for the rule of Christ and the saints to begin. Disillusionment with false dawns, repeated delays, and betrayals dimmed the enthusiasm of all but a few by 1660. Venner's rebellion the following year was a last-ditch attempt to bring this shimmering utopia to fruition by violent means. The printed manifesto of this insurrection, *The door of hope*, proffered a diagnosis and proposed a radical cure. Indicting 'the wicked Apostacy of O[liver] C[romwell]' and his 'unfaithful servants', who had abandoned 'the work of their Generation: whereby they have made themselves unmeet for any place of Power and Trust', it called upon 'the persevering Remnant' to 'gird on a Sword for Christ' and 'become Souldiers in the Lambs Army', however lowly in social status. Quoting Psalm 45:16, it evoked a tantalizing image of a world in which youth would displace age: 'instead of thy Fathers, shall be thy Children (a second Generation) whom thou mayest make Princes in all the Earth'. The 'true spiritual Seed, the legitimate Heirs' of the Lord's promises, had both a duty and a warrant 'to rise up against the carnal, serpentine, accursed seed, who are the destroyers of the Earth' and to make history. *The door of hope* had no doubt that Christ's kingdom could arise 'out of a poor, obscure, illitterate, and (such as the world calls) Fanatick People'.[33]

As Warren Johnston has demonstrated, this mentality did not wane after the Restoration. Ever adaptable to new circumstances, it remained a powerful lens

---

[32] Joseph Mede, *Clavis apocalyptica ex innatis et insitis visionum characteribus eruta et demonstrata* (Cambridge, 1627; STC 17766); idem, *The key of the Revelation, searched and demonstrated out of the naturall and proper charecters of the visions* (1643; Wing M1600), sig. b2r–v.

[33] *A door of hope; or, a call and declaration for the gathering together of the first ripe fruits unto the standard of our Lord, King Jesus* (1661; Wing D1908), pp. 3–4.

through which contemporaries viewed events such as the Popish Plot and the Glorious Revolution.[34] The 'prophetical history' published by the Congregationalist minister Thomas Beverley in 1689 predicted that the 1260 years allowed to the 'Beastian Kingdom, or to the Roman Apostasie' were nearing their end and eagerly anticipated the 'great re-reformation' that would coincide with Christ's return to earth, which he predicted would occur in 1697. Beverley addressed his endeavours to the ecclesiastical commissioners and bishops assembled at Westminster, upon whose weighty shoulders the religious fate of the nation now lay. He urged them 'to Remember the first principles of the Reformation, convey'd in the Thunders; to Strengthen the Things, that Remain to be done'. He dissected 'the Types of the Estoppage of the Kingdom of Christ amongst us', under both popish and Protestant princes, before explicating the 'Hieroglyphical Figures' of the churches of Thyatira, Sardis, and Philadelphia, which were symbols of the truly reformed churches that England should mimic.[35] For Beverley, like the Baptist Benjamin Keach, the 'late great revolution in this nation' was a new stage in the victory of English Protestantism over the Beast.[36]

As the work of Denis Crouzet on the religious wars in France, Ottavia Niccoli on Italy, and Coral Stoakes on England makes clear, apocalypticism was not a Protestant monopoly. Catholics too developed a counter-narrative of the past in which the break with Rome was understood as an ominous sign, the historical identity of Protestants as forerunners of Antichrist was a live issue, and Elizabeth I herself was perceived as a Jezebel, not to say the fabled Whore of Babylon. These ideas were forced to the surface by the papal excommunication of the queen in 1570, by the execution of Mary Stuart of Scotland in 1587, and by the Gunpowder Plot of 1605. Convinced that they were instruments of divine will, some of those behind these conspiracies believed that God had appointed them as human agents to change the course of history and to effect regime change, if necessary by force.[37]

In exile in Louvain, the former lawyer of the Middle Temple Richard Hopkins prepared *Of prayer, and meditation,* a translation of a work by Luis de Granada.

---

[34] Warren Johnston, 'Revelation and the Revolution of 1688–1689', 48 (2005), 351–89; *idem, Revelation Restored: The Apocalypse in Later Seventeenth-Century England* (Woodbridge, 2011); *idem,* 'Radical Revelation? Apocalyptic Ideas in Late Seventeenth-Century England', in Ariel Hessayon and David Finnegan (eds), *Varieties of Seventeenth- and Early Eighteenth-Century English Radicalism in Context* (Farnham, 2011), pp. 183–204.

[35] Thomas Beverley, *The prophetical history of the reformation; or the reformation to be reform'd; in that great re-reformation: that is to be 1697* (1689; Wing B2169), sigs b1v, a2r–4v.

[36] Thomas Beverley, *The late great revolution in this nation: argued according to Rev. 17.16, 17* (1689; Wing B2160); Benjamin Keach, *Antichrist stormed; or mystery Babylon the great whore, and great city, proved to be the present church of Rome* (1689; Wing K44).

[37] Denis Crouzet, *Les Guerriers de Dieu: La Violence au temps des troubles de religion, vers 1525–vers 1610,* 2 vols in 1 (Paris, 1990); Ottavia Niccoli, *Prophecy and People in Renaissance Italy,* trans. Lydia Cochrane (Princeton, NJ, 1990); Coral Stoakes, 'English Catholic Eschatology, 1558–1603' (PhD thesis, University of Cambridge, 2016).

This was first published in 1582, with a dedicatory epistle to his former colleagues at the Inns of Court that bespoke an intense belief in the imminence of the arrival of Antichrist and the Last Judgement. Hopkins's literary mission to rehabilitate the mystical Spanish Dominican was integrally linked with his role as an agent of Cardinal William Allen in negotiations for foreign intervention to restore his native country to the Roman fold. He read the temptations and persecutions to which the faithful were subject and the 'horrible sects and heresies' that abounded in all parts of Christendom as evidence of Satan's envy and malice in the last days of the world, singling out the 'counterfaite pure gospellers' called 'puritans' as a particular manifestation of the devil's 'wyly deceitefull devises' to prepare the way for his earthly reign. Together with the pandemic of iniquity, infidelity, and atheism that was spreading apace, this foretold that 'the terrible time approcheth nowe verie neare at hande, which our Sauiour forewarned us in the gospell'. Hopkins interpreted contemporary events as telling evidence that the apocalypse was nigh.[38] He was part of a generation of Catholic activists prepared to contemplate armed resistance, invasion, and regicide to overthrow heretical tyranny.[39]

A medieval intellectual tradition reanimated by the vigorous scripturalism of the early modern era, apocalyptic conceptions of history and time that blurred the boundary between the allegorical and the literal, between the sacred drama of salvation and unfolding developments in the secular realm, intensified on both sides of the Reformation divide in the sixteenth and seventeenth centuries. The historical texts that were the products of this outlook in its most ardent and radical forms were less about recording the past so that it could be remembered by posterity than about prophesying the impending end of the world. They envisaged a future in which history itself would be unnecessary and the temporal disconnection between eternity and the here and now would disappear.

History and Providence

The models of periodization encouraged by eschatological approaches to the past coexisted with a different mode of understanding God's role in history: providentialism. This too was invigorated by the Reformations. Helping to lay the foundations for Protestant myths of English nationhood rooted in the identification of England with ancient Israel, it was a template that operated within and above time simultaneously. It diminished the distance between biblical time and the

---

[38] Luis de Granada, *Of prayer, and meditation. Wherein are conteined fowertien devoute meditations for the seven daies of the weeke*, trans. Richard Hopkins (Paris, 1582; STC 16907), sigs a2r–b2v; G. Martin Murphy, 'Hopkins, Richard', *ODNB*.

[39] Peter Lake, *Bad Queen Bess? Libels, Secret Histories, and the Politics of Publicity in the Reign of Queen Elizabeth I* (Oxford, 2016), esp. chs 6 and 12.

present day by promoting analogical thinking, but it also enabled contemporaries to recognize different stages, and indeed generations, in recent religious history. These historical generations aligned closely with royal and biological ones: with the dynastic succession of the Tudor monarchy from Henry VIII down to his son Edward and his childless stepsisters Mary and Elizabeth, and then sideways, tracing a collateral line in the family tree, to James VI of Scotland and his Stuart offspring.

Protestant periodization by monarch found its taproot in Foxe's *Actes and monuments*, in which the progression of the English Reformation by reign was loosely reconciled with the broader apocalyptic timeline around which the book was organized. A strategy involving subtle sleights of hand, selective forgetting and remembering, and a heavy dollop of typology, its effect was to telescope the twists and turns of ecclesiastical and political history into a focus on particular moments, which were crystallized in the emblematic images that accompanied the text. In the case of Henry VIII, it was the break with Rome in 1534 that he and others in Matthew Parker's circle eagerly dug out of medieval records. Foxe presented this episode as a reversal of papal usurpation of royal sovereignty and a reinstatement of the Erastianism *avant la lettre*. A counterpart to illustrations of Pope Alexander treading on the neck of the Emperor Frederick Barbarossa, the picture of Henry VIII stamping the vicar of Rome underfoot that prefaced the account of his reign became a visual shorthand for his claim to be supreme head of the Church as well as the realm.[40] It skimmed over the king's own ambiguous theological outlook, the pendulum swings of official policy led by court faction, the greedy land grab that was the suppression of the monasteries, and Henry's earlier record of executing heretics in favour of concentrating on the declaration of the Royal Supremacy in 1534. Textually and iconographically, Foxe's book invented this as a defining event of the jumble of incomplete initiatives we now call the English Reformation.

Edward's short reign was likewise concertinaed into three cartoon-like images: the young king enthroned; a frame portraying the purging of the 'temple', the burning of idols, and the rickety ship of the Romish church shipping away the papists' 'paltry' (or rubbish) overseas; and the interior of a reformed ecclesiastical building with a preacher in the pulpit and representations of the two Protestant sacraments of Communion and baptism. These are pictures that play a series of temporal and spatial tricks. Editing out the conservative rebellions and sectarian radicalism that challenged his regime, they turn the interval between 1547 and 1553 into a highpoint of the evangelical drive to restore the Gospel in England.[41]

Foxe's account of Mary was inevitably dominated by the 300 Protestants she burnt on the pyres of Smithfield and elsewhere, whose heroic deaths collectively

---

[40] Foxe, *Actes and monuments* (1570 edn; STC 11223), pp. 263, 1201.   [41] Ibid., p. 1483.

constitute the icon event of her reign. Some of the graphic woodcuts of their incineration in the *Actes and monuments* were individualized; others were generic, repeatedly recycled across its pages with the consequence that particular victims became blurred with their fellow believers. The process of chronological concentration gathered pace over time and takes tangible form in Thomas Jenner's *Faiths victorie in Romes crueltie*, in which the most prominent Marian Protestants expire together on a monster-sized bonfire in a compelling image of a lost generation (see Fig. 4.4).[42] In turn, Foxe's own self-described 'universal history' became synonymous with the sacrifices made by these heroic evangelicals, acquiring the colloquial name *The Book of Martyrs*. It was both an agent and an index of the steady advance of Protestant periodization.

Compressed into the opening initial, the image of Elizabeth that begins the book about her reign depicts the queen as a female Constantine.[43] As Tom Freeman has shown, like the narrative it accompanies, this carries an 'icy undercurrent' of criticism of a monarch who had failed to live up to Foxe's own expectations and cleanse the Church of England of the remaining vestiges of popery. 'A pill of prescriptive medicine under a sugar coating' in which adulation and praise shaded into reprimand and shame, it urged her to imitate the example of her precocious dead brother, whose youth and premature death facilitated his emerging reputation as a reincarnation of King Josiah in the Bible.[44] It bears comparison with the remarkable historical painting of 'Edward VI and the Pope' brilliantly analysed by Margaret Aston in *The King's Bedpost*, which was another attempt to persuade Elizabeth to grasp the nettle of further reform by manipulating the timeline of history.[45] It is ironic that an image that evoked the recent past was mistaken for a piece of royal propaganda produced in Edward's reign for so long. This is a measure of its success in deploying the art of visual archaism.

The alternative versions of Reformation history prepared by Nicholas Harpsfield and Nicholas Sander turned this empowering providential narrative on its head, presenting these monarchs not as benevolent instruments of a Protestant God but as tyrants sent by a Catholic one to scourge and punish an apostate people. *Historia Anglicana ecclesiastica* and *De origine ac progressu schismatis Anglicani* told the story of disastrous events directed, with divine permission, by the Devil, who was the puppeteer of egotistical figures driven by mercenary motives and blatant ambition. Here they had in their sights evil

---

[42] Thomas Jenner, *Faiths victorie in Romes crueltie* (c.1630): BM, Satires Series 11. See also Chapter 4 above.

[43] Foxe, *Actes and monuments*, 'To the Right Vertuous, most Excellent and Noble Princesse, Queene Elizabeth'.

[44] Thomas Freeman, 'Providence and Prescription: The Account of Elizabeth in Foxe's "Book of Martyrs"', in Thomas S. Freeman and Susan Doran (eds), *The Myth of Elizabeth* (Basingstoke, 2003), pp. 27–55, at p. 47.

[45] Margaret Aston, *The King's Bedpost: Reformation and Iconography in a Tudor Group Portrait* (Cambridge, 1993).

counsellors such as Thomas Cromwell, whose recent rehabilitation by Hilary Mantel would have enraged Sander, who declared him 'rude' and 'savage'. Nor did they hesitate to indict the kings and queens who had presided over the destruction of English religion. They described Henry VIII's wanton assault on the religious houses and Edward's on the chantries alongside the stripping of the altars and the rape and pillage of church interiors as vicious acts of sacrilege, as well as the perfidious Elizabethan campaign against missionary priests and recusants, who were mislabelled and executed as traitors. In turn they did their own forgetting, in particular by occluding the Marian persecution.[46] Understanding why this lamentable development had taken place appears to have been more of a priority than pinpointing precisely when.[47] This was another convenient form of amnesia that allowed Catholics to pretend that the Reformation was an aberration that might yet be permanently reversed.

Echoing earlier writers, Sander located the genesis of Henry VIII's Reformation in his lustful loins, in his desire to divorce Catherine of Aragon in order to marry his mistress Anne Boleyn. As a consequence of his earlier sexual indiscretions with her mother, he insisted, Anne was in fact the king's own daughter, making him guilty of incest as well as bigamy. English Protestants, Sander wrote sarcastically, honoured this illicit and unholy alliance as 'the wellspring of their gospel, the mother of Church, and the source of their belief'. Henry's subsequent decision to condone heresy and pursue a break with Rome won not divine approbation but displeasure in the eventual extinction of his own lineage and the Tudor dynasty. Henry's providential punishment was a genealogical one. His bastard daughter Elizabeth, who was guilty of no less heinous crimes and had rightly been excommunicated by Pius V in 1570, loomed large in this account. Resorting to typology, he likened Henry to Solomon, undone by his idolatrous foreign wives, and Elizabeth to a panoply of evil women in Scripture. Her accession marked not the start of enlightenment but rather a total eclipse of the sun: 'Then came the hour of Satan, and the power of darkness took possession of the whole of England.' The death of Mary and Cardinal Pole was the beginning of the end, and the end times.[48]

---

[46] Nicholas Harpsfield's *Historia Anglicana ecclesiastica* was written in the 1560s and 1570s but not published until 1622; Sander's *De origine ac progressu schismatis Anglicani* appeared posthumously and was edited and extended by Edward Rishton and published in Cologne in 1585. Quotations from Sander are from *Rise and Growth of the Anglican Schism Published* A.D. *1585*, trans. David Lewis (1877). On Sander, see Christopher Highley, '"A Pestilent and Seditious Book": Nicholas Sander's *Schismatis Anglicani* and Catholic Histories of the Reformation', in Paulina Kewes (ed.), *The Uses of History in Early Modern England*, HLQ, 68 (2005), 151–71. On Catholic histories of the Reformation, see Eamon Duffy, 'From Sander to Lingard: Recusant Readings of the Reformation', in *idem*, *Reformation Divided: Catholics, Protestants and the Conversion of England* (2017), pp. 287–324; Katy Gibbons, 'When Did the Schism Begin, and Why? Views on the English Reformation amongst Catholic Polemicists', *Études Épistémè*, 32 (2017), doi: 10.4000/episteme.1859.

[47] See Gibbons, 'When Did the Schism Begin'.

[48] Sander, *Rise and Growth*, quotations at pp. 100, 233.

This rival Catholic mode of carving up history found visual expression in Richard Verstegan's influential picture book *Theatrum crudelitatum*, a theatre of the Calvinists' cruelties in England, France, and the Netherlands (1587). Verstegan's image of 'the first fruits of the new religion' engages in the familiar strategy of manipulating the chronology of events to suggest that the destructive public iconoclasm that had characterized the Edwardian and later phases of England's stop-start Reformation had begun earlier. As Margaret Aston has remarked, it inserts 'an unhistorical Zwinglian and Calvinist leaf into Henry's book of sacrilege', backdating the onset of Swiss-style reform to present a simpler, more dramatic picture of England's inexorable descent into heresy.[49] It edits out the prevarications that marked the 1530s, when the regime steered an unsteady course between mandating the removal of 'monuments of superstition', defending images that had not been abused, and punishing evangelical zealots who took the law into their own hands to eliminate abominable idols.

The battle over the possession of the recent Reformation past continued, but the growing longevity of the Protestant settlement gave the ecclesiastical establishment a natural advantage in claiming that the hand of God was on its side. This occurred alongside another curious process closely linked to the passage of the generations. The death of the monarchs who were the linchpins in this contested narrative had two contrary effects. On the one hand it enabled more overt critique of their actions; on the other it encouraged contemporaries to see them through a more flattering lens. It facilitated, for instance, a distinct cooling of opinion regarding Henry VIII: the sycophantic praise of him as David and John the Baptist to which some had stooped during his lifetime gave way to recognition of his misuse of power and his rapaciousness. In 1548, Anthony Gilby spoke of the late king as a man appointed to 'beate down' idolatry. By 1558, under the influence of John Knox, he condemned him as a 'monstrous bore'. Alec Ryrie comments that the easiest way of dealing with the problem of Henry was 'to pretend that he was merely a martial hero, and to efface his Reformation entirely'.[50] In fact, his own propagandists did their best to bury the dissolution of the monasteries in oblivion. As time progressed, his memory came to rest in large

---

[49] Richard Verstegan, *Theatrum crudelitatum haereticorum nostri temporis* (Antwerp, 1587; 1592), pp. 22–3. Margaret Aston, *Broken Idols of the English Reformation* (Cambridge, 2016), p. 778. See also Alexandra Walsham, 'The Art of Iconoclasm and the Afterlife of the English Reformation', in Antonina Bevan-Zlatar and Olga Timofeeva (eds), *What Was an Image in Medieval and Early Modern England?*, Swiss Papers in English Language and Literature 34 (Tubingen, 2017), pp. 81–115, at pp. 100–2.

[50] Alec Ryrie, 'The Slow Death of a Tyrant: Learning to Live without Henry VIII, 1547–1563', in Mark Rankin, Christopher Highley, and John N. King (eds), *Henry VIII and His Afterlives: Literature, Politics and Art* (Cambridge, 2009), pp. 75–93, at p. 90. Gilby is quoted ibid, pp. 86–7. On associated shifts in the memory of Thomas Wolsey, who was similarly a dramatic foil for shifting perceptions of the origins, merits, and significance of the Reformation, see J. Patrick Hornbeck II, *Remembering Wolsey: A History of Commemorations and Representations* (New York, 2019), esp. chs 1–2.

part on his reputation for dismantling the religious houses, which was regarded as a criminal act of profane expropriation.[51]

Views of Elizabeth were likewise reorientated after 1603. The disillusionment of the nasty 1590s gave way to yearning for the halcyon days during which she had ruled and to favourable comparisons with Deborah, the biblical heroine who had previously been held up to her admonishingly as a pattern for emulation.[52] Just as Edward haunted the reign of his sister, so too did her ghost stalk those of her Stuart successors. The consequence of the ongoing cycle of generational change was to turn the kaleidoscope to create yet another set of images of the English Reformation. To change the metaphor, the usable past was remoulded in accordance with contemporary politics into new plasticine shapes. These transposed the Virgin Queen into a convenient paragon of reformed piety, forgetting the foibles and hesitations that had infuriated forward Protestants throughout her reign.

Meanwhile, the Foxeian framework proved flexible, expanding to absorb a host of new deliverances, including the many assassination plots and invasion scares of Elizabeth's reign, from the Northern Rebellion in 1569 to the Babington and Throckmorton conspiracies, and the Spanish Armada launched in the 'climacterical' year of 1588, which itself was the focus of much apocalyptic speculation. The queen's passive victimhood did much for her credentials as a providential monarch; indeed, this cautious and reluctant reformer largely had the Catholics and Spanish to thank for her status as a godly ruler.[53] The seamless assimilation of the Stuart dynasty into this scheme was sealed after the Gunpowder treason of 5 November 1605, which was instantaneously heralded as a new icon event.[54] In each of these cases, the temptation to deploy the tactic of creatively resequencing history to enhance its polemical effect proved hard to resist. Accompanying this was a tendency to locate pockets of ignorance in remote regions of the realm, 'dark corners of the land' deprived of sound preachers and populated by papists and atheists who were little better than the heathens of the new world. Religious backwardness was translated from time into space in a manner that brought the biblical past into a present that fell short of the exacting standards by which the godly judged the success of the Reformation.[55]

---

[51] Harriet Lyon, *Memory and the Dissolution of the Monasteries in Early Modern England* (Cambridge, 2021), ch. 1.

[52] See Alexandra Walsham, '"A Very Deborah?" The Myth of Elizabeth I as a Providential Monarch', in Freeman and Doran (eds), *Myth of Elizabeth*, pp. 143–68. On the 1590s, see John Guy (ed.), *The Reign of Elizabeth I: Court and Culture in the Last Decade* (Cambridge, 1995). For James I's attempts to combat this, see Julia Walker, 'Bones of Contention: Posthumous Images of Elizabethan and Stuart Politics', in *eadem* (ed.), *Dissing Elizabeth: Negative Representations of Gloriana* (Durham, NC, 1998), pp. 252–76. John Watkins contests and qualifies the extent of this nostalgia in 'Old Bess in the Ruff: Remembering Elizabeth I, 1625–1660', *English Literary Renaissance*, 30 (2000), 95–116.

[53] Walsham, '"A Very Deborah"', p. 151.   [54] Cressy, *Bonfires and Bells*, ch. 9.

[55] The classic exposition is Christopher Hill, 'Puritans and the Dark Corners of the Land', *TRHS*, 13 (1963), 77–102.

The emphasis that was steadily developing on recalling and recording divine deliverances is a measure of the passing of the generation that had witnessed and participated in the turbulent events of the 1530s, 1540s and 1550s and of the swelling sense that England had declined from the high point of zeal it had reached during these ordeals. In a sermon of 1599 Edward Topsell declared that recounting the Lord's wonderful works in previous ages was one of the solemn responsibilities of parenthood. Taking up text of Joel 1:3 ('And tell your children of it, and let your children shewe to their children, and their children to another generation'), he urged mothers and fathers to follow the example of the patriarchs, who had handed down the memory of God's doings by word of mouth before it was enshrined in holy writ. Teaching one's offspring Protestant history was 'the verie conduit pipe or kings highway whereby all religion, all fear of God, and the uniforme profession of the truth is preserved'.[56] Remembering the English Reformation and giving thanks for the 'great and admirable' things the Lord had done for his seed and for the Church and nation at large, especially within living memory, became an important aspect of family religion.[57] Godly parents such as the Essex vicar's wife Elizabeth Walker took pride in ensuring that holy histories such as Foxe's *Actes and monuments* and English chronicles were read aloud to their children and servants.[58] As Daniel Woolf observes, 'affective ties in the present provided a lens through which history could be "domesticated"'.[59]

This is the setting in which we should envisage popular texts such as George Carleton's *Thankfull remembrance of Gods mercy* (1624) and Christopher Lever's *Historie of the defendors of the catholique faith* (1627) being read. Carleton's book recorded how the Lord had established the truth of his word 'by his owne hand' and dispelled the 'darkness' and 'the shadow of death' under which the country had languished for so long. It spoke not of Reformation but of the 'planting' of true religion under Elizabeth, identifying her accession as the date from which the Gospel began to flourish. The title page typologically recalled Elizabeth as Deborah and James as Solomon and compared the deliverance 'by water' in the Armada year to the salvation of Noah's family in the ark. Its lessons were encapsulated pictorially in a broadside clearly intended for purchase by Protestant householders.[60]

[56] Edward Topsell, *Times lamentation: or an exposition on the prophet Joel, in sundry sermons or meditations* (1599; STC 24131), esp. pp. 51 and 51–65.

[57] William Gouge, *Of domesticall duties* (1622; STC 12119), p. 541.

[58] Anthony Walker, *The holy life of Mrs. Elizabeth Walker, late wife of A. W., D.D., rector of Fyfield in Essex* (1690; Wing W305A), p. 71.

[59] See D. R. Woolf, 'A Feminine Past? Gender, Genre, and Historical Knowledge in England, 1500–1800', *AHR*, 102 (1997), 645–79, at 655.

[60] George Carleton, *A thankfull remembrance of Gods mercy. In an historicall collection of the great and mercifull deliverances of the Church and state of England, since the Gospell began here to flourish, from the beginning of Queene Elizabeth* (1624; STC 4640), p. 417.

By contrast, Lever's *Historie* started with the reign of Henry VIII, claiming that England had been the first nation to dare to cast off the yoke of obedience to Rome. Lever celebrated the 'invincible spirit' of sprit of the king who had 'put his Princely hand to Ruine the walls of Babylon' and inflict upon the Church of Rome an initial 'mortall wound'. At the end of his reign, however, religion in England was a mere 'Farrago'. Doing what had been left undone by his parent, Edward VI had cast Henry's 'remisse and colde proceeding in the worke of reformation' into stark relief. Mary's reign was one of misery and the return of blindness, though it had led God to raise 'a holy generation out of the ashes of his holy Martyrs'. Elizabeth was praised in extravagant terms as the Lord's 'Angell' and a 'Phoenix', a Judith who had cut off the head of Holofernes, and James was remembered as a doughty defender of the faith. Lever presented his book to Charles I as a timely and not entirely unmenacing reminder of how far the Protestant religion had been advanced by his predecessors.[61]

Michael Sparke's *Thankfull remembrances of Gods wonderfull deliverances of this land* was another roll call of providential interventions on behalf of England, beginning with its release from the grip of Catholic error and tyranny. Filled with allusions to Lot's deliverance from Sodom and Noah's salvation from the Flood, it celebrated the end of 'The night of Popish superstition' following 'The returne of the Gospells light' in a fold-out plate. This incorporates miniatures of the Marian martyrs burning (including the notorious case of the Guernsey woman whose newly born infant was thrown into the flames in a calculated attempt to extinguish a lineage of heretics) and Elizabeth handing out the Bible to a kneeling line of suitably bearded and venerable ministers (Fig. 5.1). Her accession to the throne becomes the critical moment at which the switch was flipped. Sparke's book was also a warning that sinfulness would extinguish the lamp and cause God to remove his candlestick.[62] The metaphors of darkness and enlightenment it deployed were becoming commonplace. In a sermon preached in Oxford in 1613, Arthur Lake, dean of Worcester, celebrated the 'double day' of Church and commonwealth that England had enjoyed in the successive reigns of Elizabeth and James. Glancing back to the early and mid-Tudor era, he described Queen Mary's time as 'a spirituall Night' and Edward VI's as 'a Spirituall and a Civil day'. Henry VIII's forty-eight years on the throne, by contrast, were a murky twilight: 'neither Night nor Day'.[63]

[61] Christopher Lever, *The historie of the defendors of the catholique faith. Discoursing the state of religion in England, and the care of the politique state for religion during the reignes of King Henrry 8. Edward. 6. Queene Marie. Elizabeth* (1627; STC 15537), quotations at pp. 25, 32, 110, 61, 197, 254, 334.

[62] Michael Sparke, *Thankfull remembrances of Gods wonderfull deliverances of this land*, bound with *The crums of comfort with godly prayers* (1628; STC 23016). This is the first extant edition and is labelled the eighth edition.

[63] Arthur Lake, *Sermons with some religious and divine meditations* (1629; STC 15134), p. 299.

Fig. 5.1 'The night of Popish superstition' and 'The returne of the Gospells light', in Michael Sparke, *Thankfull remembrances of Gods wonderfull deliverances of this land* (1627), bound with *Crums of comfort* (London, 1628 edn), fold-out plate.

Source: © British Library Board, C.65.i.7.(2.). All Rights Reserved/Bridgeman Images.

Cementing the importance of the icon events around which collective Protestant memory was crystallizing, such texts and images also underline the point that their meanings were mutating, multiplying, and becoming ever more disputed. This is underlined by the controversy surrounding one of a number of two-dimensional paper 'monuments' designed for display in the godly home. This is Samuel Ward's famous 1621 engraving of the 'Double Deliverance' from the Armada and Powder Treason, which caused a furore in the context of the negotiations for the Spanish Match, against which this three-part cartoon was directed. In the centre, the Pope sits with the Habsburg infanta's father Philip in a dinner table cabal at which the Devil is also present.[64] This scene of commensality is a diabolical parody of the decorous depictions of devout families discussed in Chapter 2. In the similar triptych that appeared following the Blackfriars accident in 1623, when the upper room of the French ambassador's residence in which a Jesuit was preaching collapsed, killing dozens of Catholics and provoking unprecedented scenes of sectarian violence against the survivors, different temporal frames are again deftly juxtaposed to prompt pious remembrance, fan the flames of prejudice, and make a political point about the dangers of tolerating, not to mention marrying papists.[65] In this way Reformation history infiltrated the realm of the household and was passed down to the next generation.

Anxiety and pride were always intermingled in providential historiography, which became increasingly politicized as civil war approached, so much so that the Laudian regime sought to muffle the memory of the red letter days in the reformed calendar.[66] On its eve, a similar publication began its account of the Reformation with Elizabeth, who had brought England out of Egypt, saying that Henry's was 'but in art' and Edward's had been interrupted. It called for renewed efforts to extirpate popery (among which the author included the demand that Catholic children be educated by Protestant schoolmasters) lest God send punishments.[67] Once the conflict had broken out, supporters of Parliament such as John Vicars lost no time in slotting its military victories into the same typological matrix. John Vicars repolished the emblem of Catholic malice that was 5 November and described the Irish rebellion in the same light as the Marian persecutions and the 1572 St Bartholomew's day massacre in France. He also chronicled the landmarks in the second 'blessed Reformation' that was taking

---

[64] Samuel Ward, *Deo trin-uni Britanniæ bis ultori in memoriam classis invincibilis submersæ proditionis nefandæ detectæ disiectæ. To God, in memorye of his double deliveraunce from ye invincible navie and ye unmatcheable powder treason* (Amsterdam, 1621; STC 25043). On this print, see Alexandra Walsham, *Providence in Early Modern England* (Oxford, 1999), pp. 255–8; Helen Pierce, *Unseemly Pictures: Graphic Satire and Politics in Early Modern England* (New Haven, CT, 2008), ch. 2, esp. pp. 39–47.

[65] On these prints, see Alexandra Walsham, '"The Fatall Vesper": Providentialism and Anti-Popery in Late Jacobean London', *P&P*, no. 144 (1994), 36–87.

[66] Walsham, *Providence*, pp. 249–50.

[67] G. B. C, *Plots conspiracies and attempts of domesticke and forraigne enemies of the Romish religion against the princes and kingdomes of England, Scotland and Ireland* (1642; Wing C34), pp. 3, 5.

shape before their eyes, surpassing the first, which many now dated to the beginning of Elizabeth's reign.[68] But this was a chronology also shared by his rivals. Defending his actions in the 1630s in the face of the charges levelled against him, the Laudian bishop Matthew Wren likewise looked back to Edward and Elizabeth's reigns as 'the blessed Times of Reformation'.[69] It was the significance of this auspicious event that remained contested.

In puritan circles, preserving an account of the 'Lords Work of building up of his Church' for the next generation was regarded as an imperative task, not just for families and individual congregations but also in the forum of Parliament itself. Preaching in the wake of the decisive battle of Naseby in June 1645, Stephen Marshall urged the House of Commons to keep a 'sacred record' of God's providential interventions on behalf of England and Scotland 'since the beginning of our troubles' as an 'eternall monument' to show posterity what He had done to advance true religion.[70] As Imogen Peck has recently shown, the theological imperative to remember these events was in constant tension with the competing impulse to preserve peace and seek reconciliation through the technique of oblivion.[71] Writing in 1659, Nathanael Whiting lamented that his contemporaries did not follow the lead of Moses in preserving memorials of recent divine blessings for 'the children then unborn' or the inhabitants of Geneva, who had stamped coins with the inscription *post tenebras lux* ('after darkness, light'), 'in memory of the reformation begun among them'. The Swiss had also engraved the day and year when the Gospel arrived on a pillar, in letters of gold. 'Have not our Ancestors taken care to perpetuate the memorial of eighty eight, and the fifth of November?' Would the present generation be surpassed in thankful remembrance by its predecessors?[72] Remembering, though, was inextricably linked to forgetting. The Plymouth minister George Hughes recalled the passage in Exodus 17 in which God commanded a memorial to be made of the wiping and blotting out of the whole race of the wicked Amalekites from under heaven. Committing such mighty victories to writing 'to be a future memorandum' was a solemn obligation.[73]

---

[68] John Vicars, *November the 5. 1605. The quintessence of cruelty, or, master-peice of treachery, the popish pouder-plot, invented by hellish-malice, prevented by heavenly-mercy* (1641; Wing H1602); *Englands remembrancer, or, a thankfull acknowledgement of Parliamentary mercies to our English-nation* (1641; Wing V302 and V303); *God in the mount. Or, Englands remembrancer* (1641; Wing V307); *Jehovah-jireh. God in the mount. Or, Englands parliamentarie-chronicle* (1644; Wing V313); *Magnalia Dei Anglicana. Or, Englands Parliamentary-chronicle* (1646; Wing V319).

[69] *Parentalia: or, memoirs of the family of the Wrens*, ed. Stephen Wren (1750), p. 99.

[70] Stephen Marshall, *A sacred record to be made of Gods mercies to Zion: a thanksgiving sermon preached to the two houses of Parliament...June 19.1645* (1645; Wing M773), esp. pp. 2, 31, 22. My thanks to Ann Hughes for this reference.

[71] Imogen Peck, *Recollection in the Republics: Memories of the British Civil Wars in England, 1649–1659* (Oxford, 2021), ch. 1, esp. p. 36.

[72] Nathanael Whiting, *The saints dangers, deliverances, and duties personall, and nationall practically improved in severall sermons on Psalm 94. ver. 17. useful, and seasonable for these times of trial* (1659; Wing 2021A), pp. 103–4.

[73] George Hughes, *An analytical exposition of the whole first book of Moses, called Genesis* (1672; Wing H3305), p. 865.

There was, however, little consensus about the nature and chronology of the Reformation. Written in the shadow of the episcopalian Church of England's disestablishment and partly as a riposte to Catholic historians, the royalist Thomas Fuller's *Church-history* (1655) is not easy to pigeonhole. In response to papists who said that the English 'should blush at the babe, when they behold its parents, and should be ashamed of their Reformation, considering the vitious Extraction therof', it defended Henry VIII from the charge of schism and said that his actions, though spurred by bad inclinations, were still overseen by providence. Edward's reign was a turning point. No sooner had he come to the throne than 'a peaceable dew refreshed Gods inheritance in England, formerly parched with persecution', though his reign also coincided with the beginning of 'doleful divisions' about matters of liturgical conformity. The 'slow but sure pace of Reformation' in Elizabeth's reign won Fuller's approval, though he excluded from this those 'violent Spirits, [who] impatient to attend the leisure (by them counted the lazinesse) of authority, fell before hand to the beating down of superstitious Pictures and images'.[74] The passionate purging of idols celebrated by earlier writers was beginning to smack of unholy excess to some Protestants as well as Catholics, who continued to harp on the theme of Henry VIII's 'sacrilegious avarice and insatiable lust'.[75]

Nothing summed up the sentiment that the early Reformation had been disfigured by profaneness better than Roger Dodsworth and William Dugdale's *Monasticon Anglicanum*, the first volume of which appeared during the Interregnum. It also signalled a mellowing view of the Middle Ages, one consequence of which was to soften the caesura with the Catholic past. Laudians had already downplayed the Foxeian vision of England's frenzied flight from Babylon and presented it as a reluctant step brought about by contingent events.[76] Francis Osborne's 1658 account of Elizabeth's reign saw her own renewed break with Rome as forced upon her by a Pope who had branded her a bastard. He presented her religious settlement as a model of moderation.[77] The associated repudiation of the notion that the Catholic Church was Antichrist had one particularly important effect: by severing human from salvation history it helped to bring the Reformation as a distinctly *past* event into being.

[74] Thomas Fuller, *The church-history of Britain; from the birth of Jesus Christ, untill the year M.DC. XLVIII* (1655; Wing F2416), 1st pagination, pp. 195, 371, 401; 2nd pagination, p. 51. See Brown Patterson, *Thomas Fuller: Discovering England's Past* (Oxford, 2018), chs 6–7.

[75] See M. W. F, *A manifest touching M.W.F. aversion from the Protestant congregation* (1650; Wing P85A), sig. a3r.

[76] Roger Dodsworth and William Dugdale, *Monasticon Anglicanum sive pandectæ cænobiorum, Benedictinorum Cluniacensium, Cisterciensium, Carthusianorum; a primordiis ad eorum usque dissolutionem*, 3 vols (1655–73; Wing D2484-6). See Anthony Milton, *Catholic and Reformed: The Roman and Protestant Churches in English Protestant Thought, 1600–1640* (Cambridge, 1995), ch. 6.

[77] Francis Osborne, *Historical memoires on the reigns of Queen Elizabeth, and King James* (1658; Wing O515).

This interpretation of the origins of English Protestantism took most influential form in Peter Heylyn's *Ecclesia restaurata* of 1661. Obsessed by a hatred of 'fanatical' Calvinists reminiscent of Richard Bancroft's visceral aversion to Elizabethan Presbyterianism, Heylyn presented Henry's reign as a mere preamble compromised by his blunderbuss approach and mercenary motives. He regarded Edward's accession as the moment at which 'the *Epoche* of a *Reformation*' had really begun, albeit one perverted by seditious foreign influences and stained by the sin of tumultuous destruction. Heylyn went so far as to say that his death could not be reckoned an 'Infelicity to the Church of England'. After the disastrous interlude of the Marian persecution, Elizabeth had steered the Reformation back onto a happier course halfway between Geneva and Rome. Heylyn oscillated between revering the first Edwardian Prayer Book and the 1559 settlement as the original source and epitome of the Church of England's unique moderation. In the hands of Heylyn, the Reformation was remodelled as an indigenous *via media* and, to adapt Anthony Milton's apt phrase, massaged to make it speak with 'a Laudian accent'.[78] His book contributed to establishing the enduring legend about the origins of Anglicanism that Diarmaid MacCulloch has traced into the nineteenth-century, when it underwent a fresh reinvention.[79] It was part of the wider polemical manoeuvre that produced the illusion of the Tudor Reformation as 'a stable and measured process working towards a calm equipoise'.[80]

Heylyn's High Church view of the birth of Protestantism was not uncontested. The 1670s and 1680s saw the vigorous resurgence of the strand of Protestant providentialism against which *Ecclesia restaurata* reacted. In the spirit of Samuel Clarke's *Englands remembrancer* (1657), the stories of older deliverances and their pictorial shorthands were revived for the benefit of Restoration readers.[81] Published in the wake of the Popish Plot, *The Protestant tutor* (1679) (Fig. 5.2) was an anti-Catholic catechism directed at parents and schoolmasters, replete with crude woodcuts of key episodes of Romish tyranny and cruelty. A primer in prejudice as well as in reading and spelling, its aim was 'to strengthen and confirm this young generation in Protestant Principles' and 'to Create in them an Abhorrence of Romish Idolatry at the same time, which being infused in their green and tender years, may leave an Impression in their Minds to the End of

---

[78] Peter Heylyn, *Ecclesia restaurata; or, The history of the reformation of the Church of England* (1661; Wing H1701), quotations at sigs a1v, a4v. See Anthony Milton, 'Licensing, Censorship and Religious Orthodoxy in Early Stuart England', *HJ*, 41 (1998), 625–51, at 647. See idem, *Laudian and Royalist Polemic in Seventeenth-Century England: The Career and Writings of Peter Heylyn* (Manchester, 2007), see esp. pp. 83–7, 197–213.

[79] Diarmaid MacCulloch, 'The Myth of the English Reformation', *JBS*, 30 (1991), 1–19.

[80] Anthony Milton, *England's Second Reformation: The Battle for the Church of England 1625–1662* (Cambridge, 2021), p. 3.

[81] Samuel Clarke, *Englands remembrancer, containing a true and full narrative of those two never to be forgotten deliverances: the one from the Spanish invasion in Eighty eight: the other from the hellish Powder Plot: November 5. 1605* (1657; Wing C4510).

Fig. 5.2 Anti-popish pedagogy: Benjamin Harris, *The Protestant tutor* (London, 1679), title page and frontispiece.

Source: © British Library Board, G.19992. All Rights Reserved/Bridgeman Images.

their Lives'. It repolished the memory of popish malice and cruelty, from the 'Smithfield Fires…wherein our Grandfathers suffered Martyrdome' and the 'blood Massacres' of the godly in Piedmont, Poland, and other places, to the recent murder of Sir Edmund Berry Godfrey.[82] Similar mnemonic images were emblazoned on playing cards, and the canonization of Pius V in 1713 inspired fresh calls for commemoration of Elizabeth's accession as 'the birthday of the Gospel'.[83] Loyalty to the Stuart monarchy ensured that its own restoration to the Crown after the catastrophe of the regicide was absorbed into this temporal scheme as a further salvific miracle. In due course it embraced the 'Glorious Revolution' itself, a constitutional coup that was retrospectively celebrated as a mechanism by which the heritage of the Reformation had been preserved for posterity. William's arrival on these shores on the same day as the deliverance of 1605, 5 November, was regarded as providentially engineered.[84] Preachers and apologists hailed this as a fresh manifestation of God's mercy to Protestant England and a new stage in its struggle to extricate itself from popish tyranny. They repeated the fractal and

[82] Benjamin Harris, *The Protestant tutor. Instructing children to spel and read English, and grounding them in the true Protestant religio[n], and discovering the errors and deceits [o]f the papists* (1679; Wing P3843), sigs A3v, A5v, A6v–7r. This went through multiple editions.

[83] For some surviving packs, see BM, 1896, 0501.915.1–52; V&A, 2-366: 1–52. For the calls for commemoration at the time of the canonization of Pius V, see John Brand, *Observations on the Popular Antiquities of Great Britain*, ed. and enlarged Henry Ellis, 3 vols (1890 edn), vol. i, pp. 185–6.

[84] Cressy, *Bonfires and Bells*, ch. 11.

symmetrical patterns by which its history had been characterized since the sixteenth century.[85]

Infused with a powerful strain of apocalypticism and providentialism and envisaged as rebuttal of both Heylyn's *Ecclesiastica restaura* and Nicholas Sander's *Schismatis anglicani*, Gilbert Burnet's influential *History of the reformation* recast old commonplaces for a new age.[86] Celebrating the conquest of light over darkness, it reasserted its European dimensions, and averred that had Protestantism 'been longer a hatching under the heat of persecution', it might have 'come forth perfecter than it was'. It insisted that 'the Reformation, was rather conceived than brought forth' in Henry VIII's reign, the prey of factions and parties that in the last eighteen years of his rule were, like antagonistic twins, 'strugling in the Womb'. Merely embryonic in the 1530s and 1540s, it had not truly emerged into the world until 1553, when the 'mire and filth' only partially removed by his father as 'the Postilian of the Reformation' had been cleared away by his son, whose reforms had further purged it of the 'alloy' of corruptions by which it remained contaminated. Correcting the perceived 'defects' of Foxe himself, Burnet sought to set historical study of the Reformation on a more rigorous footing.[87] This was a task taken up by John Strype in his *Annals* and *ecclesiastical memorials* (1709), which adopted the strategy of preserving an archive of documents that no one could accuse of being blemished by confessional bias.[88]

Protestations of unadulterated erudition did not, however, stop rival versions of the Reformation past from circulating, ironically in the case of Charles Dodd, in the same guise of Enlightenment impartiality.[89] By contrast, the Catholic

[85] Tony Claydon, *The Revolution in Time: Chronology, Modernity and 1688-1689 in England* (Oxford, 2020), ch. 3.

[86] Gilbert Burnet, *The history of the reformation of the Church of England. The first part. Of the progess made in it during the reign of K. Henry the VIII* (1679; Wing B5797); idem, *The second part, of the progess made in it till the settlement of it in the beginning of Q. Elizabeth's reign* (1681; Wing B5798A). A French translation of Sander had recently been printed. On Burnet's apocalypticism, see Tony Claydon, 'Latitudinarianism and Apocalyptic History in the Worldview of Gilbert Burnet, 1643-1715', *HJ*, 51 (2008), 577-97.

[87] Burnet, *History of the reformation*, preface to Part 2, sig. d1v; preface to Part I, sig. (c)1r, (c)2r. Tony Claydon argues that it gave rise to a new division of the past, inventing the Restoration itself as a distinct period of British history: 'Gilbert Burnet: An Ecclesiastical Historian and the Birth of the English Restoration Era', in Peter Clarke and Charlotte Methuen (eds), *The Church on its Past*, SCH 49 (2013), pp. 181-91.

[88] John Strype, *Annals of the Reformation and establishment of religion, and other various occurrences in the Church of England; during the first twelve years of Queen Elizabeth's happy reign* (1709); idem, *Ecclesiastical memorials*, 3 vols (1721). Ironically, he was one of those taken in by the notorious fictions and ingenious forgeries of Robert Ware of Dublin. See Diarmaid MacCulloch, 'Foxes, Firebrands, and Forgery: Robert Ware's Pollution of Reformation History', *HJ*, 54 (2011), 307-46. See also Eamon Duffy, *The Reformation and the Grand Narrative: The Archive and the Writing of the English Reformation*, The Eoin MacNeill Lecture 2012 (Dublin, 2013).

[89] Charles Dodd, *The church history of England, from the year 1500, to the year 1688. Chiefly with regard to Catholicks:...In eight parts* (Brussels [London], 1737-42). On Dodd, see Gabriel Glickman, 'Gothic history and Catholic Enlightenment in the works of Charles Dodd (1672-1743)', *HJ*, 54 (2011), 347-69.

convert Thomas Ward's poem *Englands Reformation* (1710) invested traditional accusations with an acerbic twist, including the old genealogical chestnut that the 'maggot' of the Reformation had emerged from 'old Harry's monstrous cod-piece'. From this organ, Protestants traced their 'Pedegree' and their 'Blessed Race'.[90] The non-juror Jeremy Collier's *Ecclesiastical history* (1708–14) overturned conventional tropes by describing the Royal Supremacy as an innovation and vindicating aspects of English Protestantism that others saw as residues of Catholicism, while the keynote of the histories written by the nonconformists Daniel Neal and John Oldmixon was the claim that England had betrayed the spirit of the Swiss Reformation by only half-heartedly embracing it.[91]

By the early eighteenth century there was little agreement about when the Reformation had begun, let alone ended; who or what had most contributed to its creation; or what it meant. Ideas of historical periodization were similarly unstable and plural. The result was a shimmering and deceptive mosaic. There was not one myth about the Reformation in circulation, but many. The preacher who insisted in 1700 that 'the present duty of this generation' was the 'Reformation of manners' and called for 'holy zeal against sin' gave expression to the perception that the process was still incomplete, especially in the spheres of morality and personal conduct.[92] If some were in no doubt that the Reformation was an historical event that deserved the imprimatur of a capital R and the definite article, others still placed it firmly in the future.[93]

Naming the Reformation

For much of the early modern period, then, the Reformation was not recognized by contemporaries as a discrete or temporally bounded entity. The word 'reform' was used less as a noun than as a transitive verb and 'reformation' was correspondingly described as a process rather than an event. This practice had a long lineage: in the Middle Ages the term *reformatio* was repeatedly deployed to describe an

---

[90] Thomas Ward, *Englands Reformation from the time of King Henry the VIIIth to the end of Oates's plot* (Hambourgh [St Omer], 1710), pp. 1–2.

[91] Jeremy Collier, *An ecclesiastical history of Great Britain, chiefly of England: from the first planting of Christianity, to the end of the reign of King Charles the second*, 2 vols (1708–14); Daniel Neal, *The history of the Puritans or Protestant non-conformists, from the Reformation to the death of Queen Elizabeth* (1732); John Oldmixon, *The critical history of England, ecclesiastical and civil: wherein the errors of the monkish writers, and others before the reformation, are expos'd and corrected. As are also the deficiency and partiality of later historians* ([1724]). See Tony Claydon, *Europe and the Making of England, 1660–1760* (Cambridge, 2007), ch. 2.

[92] J. E., *Holy zeal against sin, shewn to be an acceptable and seasonable duty: in a sermon preached at Lyme Regis, in the county of Dorset, Sept. 4th. 1700. At a quarterly lecture appointed for the promoting the reformation of manners* (1700; Wing E14B), esp. p. 1.

[93] As Tony Claydon has recently argued in 'The Reformation of the Future: Dating English Protestantism in the Late Stuart Era', *Études Épistémè*, 32 (2017), doi: 10.4000/episteme.1831.

ongoing cycle in which institutional and spiritual life underwent revitalization. In particular, it was a piece of nomenclature intimately linked to conciliar discourse. However, it remains necessary to ask when and why the particular manifestation of this impulse that occurred in the sixteenth century formally acquired its name.[94] In tackling this question, I take inspiration from Patrick Collinson's classic exposition of the linguistic invention of puritanism and Peter Marshall's inspiring work on the 'intricately transactional patterns of identity formation' involved in the 'naming of Protestant England'. In both cases, what began as a derogatory epithet and a calculated insult eventually settled into a mode of self-description.[95] Far from a passive reflection of evolving social realities, language itself forges relationships and effects change. It is an activating agent in the elusive and multidimensional cultural process that scholars call religious confessionalization.

These are insights that help us to understand how 'Reformation' entered into contemporary nomenclature as a proper noun and evolved into an instantly recognizable abbreviation for the disruptive events by which England was engulfed in the sixteenth and seventeenth centuries. Like 'Protestant', it was first used sarcastically by Catholics, to denigrate the simulacrum of religious *reformatio* that the heretics had initiated to wreak havoc in the Church and state. This was a pseudo-'reformation' that sprang not from sincere motives but from wicked ones. Thus, in his 1531 account of the 'orygynall ground of these Lutheran faccyons', William Barlow satirized the 'mervelouse zele' and 'fervent spyryt' by which the Wittenberg monk had seduced the common people to acknowledge him as a prophet appointed to carry out 'a dewe reformacion of the hole world'.[96] Ninian Winzet, John Rastell, and William Bishop likewise spoke of the 'praetentit [pretended] reformation' or 'deformation' inaugurated by the European reformers and their disciples in England, comparing this unfavourably with the Church of Rome's own efforts to bring about renewal via the Council of Trent.[97]

---

[94] This section was written prior to reading Benjamin M. Guyer's *How the English Reformation Was Named: The Politics of History, c.1400–1700* (Oxford, 2022), which also tackles this theme. There are points of similarity but also some differences in our analyses. I am very grateful to Dr Guyer for allowing me to read his text in advance of publication.

[95] Patrick Collinson, 'A Comment: Concerning the Name Puritan', *JEH*, 31 (1980), 483–8; Peter Marshall, 'The Naming of Protestant England', *P&P*, 214 (2012), 87–128, at 91. For a similar approach, see Kate Peters, *Print Culture and the Early Quakers* (Cambridge, 2005), ch. 4. An earlier version of the arguments presented here can be found in Alexandra Walsham, 'History, Memory and the English Reformation', *HJ*, 55 (2012), 899–938, at 919–24.

[96] William Barlow, *A dyaloge descrybyng the orygynall ground of these Lutheran faccyons, and many of theyr abusys* ([1531]; STC 1461), sig. d4v.

[97] Ninian Winzet, *Certain tractates together with the book of four score three questions and a translation of Vincentius Livinensis*, ed. James King Hewison, Scottish Text Society, 2 vols (1888), vol. i, p. 67; John Rastell, *The third booke, declaring by examples out of auncient councels, fathers, and later writers, that it is time to beware of M. Jewel* (Antwerp, 1566), fo. 58v; William Bishop, *A reformation of a Catholike deformed* (1604; STC 3096), sig. *iv r. For the Council of Trent's call for 'christen reformation', see *Newes concernynge the general cou[n]cell, holden at Trydent*, trans. John Hollybush (1548[1549]; STC 24266), sig. A3v.

The word was also used to refer to the reform and refoundation of old monastic orders such as the Discalced Carmelites by saintly visionaries such as Teresa of Avila.[98] When priests such as John Floyd wrote of 'the Protestant Reformation' they did so with invisible quotation marks that indicated their withering contempt for the arrogance of their opponents.[99] Such contests were closely connected with the struggle to appropriate 'Catholic' as the exclusive badge of the adherents of the true faith in a society that believed that this had only one institutional manifestation on earth.

Only in the heat of battle were evangelicals such as John Bale driven to deploy 'reformation' to rebuff the 'blasphemies' of the 'franticke papysts'. Turning the tables, he boasted in 1550 that 'the most christen reformacyon of England' was 'a wurthie spectacle' to other nations, which 'they very turkyshely deride & mocke'.[100] By contrast, never one to choose the path of discretion, in a tract published in 1558 John Knox mimicked his enemies in declaring that there had been 'no reformation, but a deformation in the tyme of that tyrant and lecherous monster', Henry VIII. Stressing his 'beastlynes' and suggesting that he was 'no better then the Romishe Antichrist' were hardly calculated to endear Knox to Henry's daughter Elizabeth.[101]

Constituent episodes in this drama were likewise christened by their opponents and detractors, including the 'Dissolution' or 'Suppression of the Monasteries'. As Harriet Lyon has shown, initially this was a label resonant with lament and pity for the destruction of a whole way of life and its magnificent material heritage, and weighed down with overtones of the biblical deluge that God had sent as a judgement upon the iniquitous human race in Genesis. Ironically, it too owed its belated appearance as a critical juncture in history more to its critics than to its friends.[102] The invention of 'Kett's rebellion' in 1549 as a discrete event, by contrast, was the work of the Tudor state, the artefact of a strategic attempt to erase rival memories of the 'commotion time' that had blighted Edward's reign.[103]

[98] St Teresa of Avila, *The flaming hart, or, The life of the glorious S. Teresa foundresse of the reformation, of the order of the all-immaculate Virgin-Mother, our B. Lady, of Mount Carmel* (Antwerp, [1642]; Wing T753); Richard Crashaw, *Steps to the temple; The delights of the muses; and, Carmen Deo Nostro* (1670; Wing C6839), p. 61.
[99] See John Floyd, *The overthrow of the Protestants pulpit-Babels convincing their preachers of lying & rayling, to make the Church of Rome seeme mysticall Babell* ([St Omer, 1612]; STC 11111), pp. 103, 294, 300. On the 'Name of Protestants', see Richard Bristow, *A briefe treatise of diverse plaine and sure ways to finde out the truthe in this doubtful and dangerous time of heresie* (Antwerp, 1574; STC 3799), pp. 10–12.
[100] John Bale, *An expostulation or complaynte agaynste the blasphemyes of a franticke papyst of Hampshyre* ([c.1550]; STC 1294), sig. A3r.
[101] John Knox, *The appellation of John Knoxe from the cruell and most injust sentence pronounced against him by the false bishoppes and clergie of Scotland* (Geneva, 1558; STC 15063), fo. 69v, 70r.
[102] Lyon, *Memory and the Dissolution of the Monasteries*, ch. 1.
[103] See Andy Wood, *The 1549 Rebellions and the Making of Early Modern England* (Cambridge, 2007), esp. pp. 229–30, 237.

On the whole, the term 'Reformation' appeared belatedly in the vocabulary of those who strove to bring it about. If the phrase was rarely used in the first generation of England's religious revolution, this was largely because those caught up in it could be certain of neither its permanency nor its outcome. Paradoxically, only after it had grown to maturity and adulthood could its birth be discerned. Secondly, its identity as a distinct moment was impeded by the widely shared opinion that it had yet to achieve its final consummation. This was not simply a function of the dizzying array of reversals and interruptions it encountered between 1534 and 1558; it was also a projection of growing concern that this hiatus was of human making. Mary was obviously the chief culprit here, but a radical and politically charged vision of 'reformation unbound' was also present under Henry and Edward.[104]

As the idea that the English Church was 'but halfly reformed' gathered pace during Elizabeth's reign, impatience with the queen's hesitation erupted into frustration and anger that she was being deliberatively obstructive. In a letter written to Frederick, Prince Elector Palatine around 1567, George Withers lamented that, despite the best efforts of 'prince Edward of pious memory', the reformation now lay in a 'wretched' and 'unsightly state', 'prostrate, and...on the very brink of destruction'.[105] As puritan petitions and admonitions to Parliament fell on deaf ears, demands for a 'thorow and speedy Reformation' gained further urgency, spilling out from private correspondence into the emergent public sphere. The 'reformation' for which Thomas Cartwright and others called ever more overtly was a Genevan-style presbyterian one, the blueprint for which lay in Scripture.[106] An aspiration rather than an achievement, it remained an elusive goal. Elizabethan puritans never celebrated it as something that had happened in the past; for them it always remained frustratingly out of reach in the future. It was a mantra and a mission statement rather than a signal development that had occurred within living memory. In the late sixteenth century, it was 'a rhetorical exhortation rather than a historiographical category'.[107]

The godly glanced enviously at Scotland, where the grass appeared to be greener, but the expectations raised by the accession of James I were dashed at the Hampton Court Conference of 1604. The superior 'Reformation' of the Scottish kirk continued to irk English puritans, and their northern brethren were not

---

[104] As recent work by Karl Gunther has shown: *Reformation Unbound: Protestant Visions of Reform in England, 1525–1590* (Cambridge, 2014).

[105] Hastings Robinson (ed.), *The Zurich Letters (Second Series) [1558–1602]*, PS (Cambridge, 1845), pp. 162, 157.

[106] W. H. Frere and C. E. Douglas (eds), *Puritan Manifestoes: A Study of the Origin of the Puritan Revolt with a Reprint of the Admonition to Parliament and Kindred Documents, 1572* (1954), p. 19; John Udall, *A parte of a register, contayninge sundrie memorable matters, written by divers godly and learned in our time, which stande for, and desire the reformation of our Church, in discipline and ceremonies, according to the pure word of God, and the lawe of our lande* ([Middelburg], 1593; STC 10400).

[107] Guyer, *How the English Reformation was Named*, p. 73.

above rubbing salt in the wound. Archibald Johnston, Lord Wariston's 1638 'advertisement' to the ministers of the Church of England came from a 'hearty Well-wisher to both kingdomes' but the note of condescension was clear: a 'Reformation' worthy of the name had yet to occur south of the border.[108]

The advent of the Long Parliament and the establishment of the Westminster Assembly seemed to promise the long-awaited fulfilment of puritan dreams. The early 1640s were filled with the heady rhetoric of the 'blessed reformation' that now seemed within reach. One effect of this optimistic mood was to foster fond memories of the earlier ones presided over by the young Josiah Edward and the 'glorious Deborah', Elizabeth, a further phase of forgetfulness about her temperamental stubbornness having set in.[109] Another was to tip the balance away from thinking in terms of a glass half-empty towards a glass half-full. 'Our happy deliverance out of Babylon by the blessed Reformation of Religion begun amongst us, some good number of yeeres by past' was invoked in the very first fast sermon delivered to the House of Commons by Cornelius Burges in 1641 and reiterated by subsequent preachers to stir their hearers to carry it through to completion. In another delivered in the same year, Burges contrasted the 'infant-Reformation' begun under Henry VIII with its more mature phases. Edmund Calamy stressed that under Edward VI it was still clothed in garments that smelt 'a little of the Dungeon from whence we came' and had proved abortive. There remained much work to be done.[110] Sir Edward Dering agreed that there had been 'a happy and blessed reformation of our Church' but prayed God to send a 'better, and a more severe' one, or else it would be 'in danger to be deformed again'.[111] Anticipation that the faults of the first phase of reform would soon be rectified induced the godly to admit, albeit grudgingly, that some kind of key juncture had occurred in 1558, if not earlier under Elizabeth's precocious half-brother.[112]

Hebrews 9:10 ('until the time of reformation') became a topical text for exposition, prompting discussion of what exactly constituted a true one, as well as a review of previous phases of its life cycle in England. Both the meaning of the

---

[108] Archibald Johnston, Lord Wariston, *A short relation of the state of the Kirk of Scotland since the reformation of religion, to the present time for information, and advertisement to our brethren in the Kirk of England, by an hearty well-wisher to both kingdoms* ([Edinburgh], 1638; STC 22039).

[109] See, e.g., *The reformation of Christian religion by Josiah* (1641; Wing R742). This was originally published *c.*1590 as *The reformation of religion by Josiah*. On Josiah, see also Stephen Marshall's *Reformation and desolation* (1642; Wing M770). David Loewenstein discusses Milton's exploration of Edward VI and Josiah in 'Milton and the Creation of England's Long Reformation', *Reformation*, 24 (2019), 165–80.

[110] Cornelius Burges, *The first sermon, preached to the honourable house of commons now assembled in Parliament at their publique fast* (1641; Wing B5671), p. 40; *idem, A sermon preached to the honourable house of commons assembled in Parliament at their publique fast* (1641; Wing B5683), pp. 38, 48; Edmund Calamy, *England's looking-glasse, presented in a sermon* (1642; Wing C236), p. 47.

[111] Edward Dering, *A collection of speeches made…in matter of religion* (1642; Wing D1104), pp. 50, 74, 136.

[112] See also Ann Hughes, 'Preaching the "Long Reformation" in the English Revolution', *Reformation*, 24 (2019), 151–64.

term and the event and process to which it referred were ambiguous and hotly disputed. They were the subject of struggle between the multiple parties— Laudian, episcopalian, Presbyterian, and Congregationalist—competing for possession of the Church of England and its complex legacy and unstable heritage.[113] Preaching on this passage at the church of Savoy in 1643, Thomas Fuller confessed that the reforms inaugurated under Henry and Edward had been 'but partiall and imperfect'. He flatly denied the 'uncivill' charge that Queen Elizabeth had swept the Church but 'left the dust behind the Doore', but insisted that her 39 Articles were 'all gold' and had no 'drosse in them'. In calling for a 'thorough reformation' but an orderly one undertaken 'with all due and Christian moderation', his sermon indicated the cracks that were beginning to appear within the campaign for ecclesiastical reform.[114] By contrast, when the New Model Army chaplain William Dell tackled this verse in 1646, he lashed out against the 'carnall Reformation' carried out by 'worldly power' with which too many of his Presbyterian contemporaries seemed to be preoccupied and called instead for an 'inward' 'Gospel Reformation' of the heart and spirit brought about by Christ 'dwelling and living in us'.[115]

Writing a year earlier, Sir Simonds D'Ewes had lamented the 'many distractions' that were impeding the 'blessed Reformation' which seemed 'so neere the birth' from coming forth.[116] The obstetric metaphor he employed was a popular one, which Stanley Gower's *Things Now-a-doing: or, The churches travaile of the child of reformation now-a-bearing* (1644) milked for all it was worth (Fig. 5.3). This apocalyptically flavoured fast sermon on Daniel 12:10 underlined the prolonged labour and birth pangs in which the Churches of the Saints were engaged, predicting that out of its current trials and tribulations a 'man-Child of Reformation' would yet emerge. The 'delivery' this biblical prophecy foretold would be worth the wait, and members of Parliament would be able to take pride in being the 'midwives' to its arrival in the world. They would be honoured by their posterity, just as Luther, Elizabeth, and the renowned king of Sweden Gustavus Adolphus had been in their own times.[117] This was generation work in a double sense. In applying the language of childbirth to describe England's protracted religious troubles, Gower pipped Christopher Haigh and Patrick Collinson to the post by 350 years.[118]

---

[113] Milton, *England's Second Reformation*, esp. pp. 5–6, 159–62.

[114] See Thomas Fuller, *A sermon of reformation. Preached at the church of the Savoy, last fast day, July 27, 1643* (1643; Wing F2461), pp. 9–11.

[115] William Dell, *Right reformation: or the reformation of the Church of the New Testament, represented in gospell light* (1646; Wing D927), esp. pp. 4, 5, 6, 7, 9, 11.

[116] Simonds D'Ewes, *The primitive practise for preserving truth* ([1645]; Wing D1251), sig. A3r–v.

[117] Stanley Gower, *Things now-a-doing: or, The churches travaile of the child of reformation now-a-bearing* (1644; Wing G1462), quotations at sigs A2r–v, pp. 25, 26.

[118] Christopher Haigh, 'The English Reformation: A Premature Birth, a Difficult Labour and a Sickly Child', *HJ*, 33 (1990), 449–59; Patrick Collinson, *The Birthpangs of Protestant England: Religious and Cultural Change in the Sixteenth and Seventeenth Centuries* (New York, 1988).

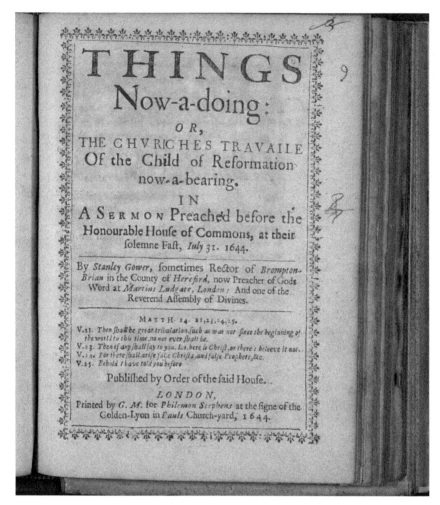

Fig. 5.3 Stanley Gower, *Things now-a-doing: or, the churches travaile of the child of reformation now-a-bearing* (London, 1644), title page.
Source: Trinity College, Cambridge, I.10.122[9]. By permission of the Master and Fellows.

The phrase 'blessed Reformation' became ever more contentious as the decade progressed. What had once been a rallying call to unity and an emblem of hope took on an increasingly sour and discordant note. Its appropriation by the prolif-erating 'sectaries' attracted the scorn of the Presbyterian Thomas Edwards, author of *Gangraena* (1646), who lashed out against the 'Master-builders' of 'an Hell-bred conspiracy'.[119] Indicative of the way in which Protestant apocalyptic rhetoric itself

---

[119] Thomas Edwards, *The first and second part of Gangraena: or a catalogue and discovery of many of the errors, heresies, blasphemies and pernicious practices of the sectaries of this time, vented and acted in England in these last four yeers* (1646; 3rd edn; Wing E227), p. 10.

was splintering, John Vicars's *The great Antichrist* took aim at the 'Hypocrites' who 'pretended Reformation must be done in a day, not considering the divers gradations' by which it had developed in the Old Testament, and who were daring to suggest that the monarchy itself was a human institution that could be removed.[120] After Charles I's execution, the term became a shorthand for the regicide, which was denounced as the calamitous consequence of radical puritanism. The act issued by the Rump Parliament for a day of humiliation on 19 April 1649 called upon the populace to pray that God, who had 'through a Wilderness of Temptations brought us even to the entrance of a Canaan, and to the hope of a blessed Reformation', would at last ensure its completion.[121] Like the Second Coming itself, this event was continually—and ever more desperately—projected forward into the future.

Royalists, meanwhile, vented their spleen against the misplaced zeal of 'peevish Elves' who itched against the king and bishops with such chaotic and catastrophic results: 'Behold your blessed Reformation!'[122] If this sarcastic slur was one product of the religious experimentation that marked the Civil War decades, as Benjamin Guyer has argued, another was the entry of the very concept of '*the English Reformation*' into the historical lexicon. It was adopted by some apologists to justify the moderate, monarchical style of religious reform overseen by the Tudors against the unruly, rebellious, and Scottish one for which they supposed their puritan opponents yearned. They utilized it in approving contrast to the violent version that had sparked off armed conflict and culminated in the heinous act of regicide. This species of 'reformation' remained cloaked in 'a hermeneutic of suspicion'.[123] As John Evelyn recorded in his diary on 28 August 1653, 'that holy Martyr' John Hewett, the former chaplain to Charles executed for treason by the Cromwellian regime, had preached 'threatning the Extinction of his Gospel light for the prodigious impiety of the age'.[124] The blowing out of the candle of Protestantism was not only a puritan theme.

After 1660, the derogatory epithet 'blessed Reformation' was repeatedly invoked to condemn the aberration that was the Great Rebellion. Those eager to bury their worst horrors in oblivion or at least cover them under a concealing veil called them the 'late troubles'.[125] But if, for some, the Restoration marked the failure of the heady mid-seventeenth-century puritan experiment in religious reform

---

[120] J[ohn] V[icars], *The great Antichrist*, bound with *A discovery of the rebels* (1643; Wing V301), pp. 41–2.

[121] *An act of the Commons of England assembled in Parliament for the keeping a day of humiliation upon Thursday the 19 day of April, 1649* (1648[9]; Wing E2505).

[122] *A new ballad, called a review of the rebellion* (1647; Wing N555).

[123] Guyer, *How the English Reformation Was Named*, ch. 4 and p. 81. Guyer's description of these figures as 'Anglican apologists', however, may be disputed.

[124] *The Diary of John Evelyn*, ed. E. S. de Beer, 6 vols (Oxford, 1955), vol. iii, p. 88.

[125] See, e.g., William Dugdale, *A short view of the late troubles in England...* (Oxford, 1681; Wing D2492), pp. 44, 241, 574.

and thereby placed it in the past, others continued to strive to make it a present and future reality. Writing in the wake of the Fifth Monarchist uprising of 1661, Thomas Marriot, chaplain to the East India Company, admitted that 'Reformation is indeed a faire word,' but warned that disobedience of all kinds 'sheltered' under its 'wing' and that it was too often used as 'a *Stalking-horse* to mens wicked designes'.[126]

The fetid religious politics of the latter part of Charles II's reign served to fragment and destabilize this discourse yet further, not least by denouncing the 'follies' and 'villanies' that had been practised in the name of 'Thorough Reformations' since the break with Rome as both 'popish' and 'fanatical'. This was the burden of Edward Pettit's *Visions of the reformation* (1683), which set out to demonstrate that puritan attempts to bring in 'strict Presbyterianism' and the perfidious endeavours of the Jesuits to overturn Protestantism were two sides of the same coin. The title page showed a Janus-faced presbyter defacing the royal coat of arms by overpainting it with the shield of the Commonwealth with the Pope toppling the crown on the right.[127] Pettit's insistence that radical dissent was Catholicism in disguise is reminiscent of Sir Roger L'Estrange's famous 1680 print *The committee; or popery in masquerade*, which itself includes a banner proclaiming 'A Thorough Reformation'.[128] A Catholic text of 1687 adopted the similar strategy of suggesting that 'the spirit of M[artin] Luther and the original of the Reformation' sprang from Satan and compared his 'change of Religion' to that of another false prophet, 'Mahomet' [Mohammed].[129]

The relativization of the rhetoric of Reformation, like that of anti-popery and demonology, to which such texts and images attest both reflected and fostered the demise of the ideal that religious truth was singular and indivisible. It helped to create a climate in which 'toleration' emerged as an unsatisfactory solution to ineradicable pluralism. It was one by-product of an environment in which the status of this event as a historical landmark had become firmly established, even as it had lost any trace of coherence. It is telling that J. S.'s *Ecclesiastical history epitomiz'd* (1682) labels the familiar group portrait of the reformers seated around the table as 'The Reformation'. Incorporating Wyclif, Tyndale, Latimer, Cranmer, Bradford, Ridley, and Perkins, as well as Luther, Calvin, and other leading lights in Germany and Switzerland, this fictitious gathering of several different

---

[126] Thomas Marriot, *Rebellion unmasked or a sermon preached at Poplar in the parish of Stepney... upon occasion of the late rebellious insurrection in London* (1661; Wing M717), p. 22.

[127] Edward Pettit, *The visions of the reformation: or, A discovery of the follies and villanies that have been practis'd in popish and fanatical thorough reformations, since the reformation of the Church of England* (1683; Wing P1895).

[128] Roger L'Estrange, *The committee; or popery in masquerade* (1680; Wing L1226). See BM, 1849,0315.82.

[129] R. H., *Two discourses. The first, concerning the spirit of Martin Luther, and the original of the Reformation. The second, concerning the celibacy of the clergy* (Oxford, 1687; Wing W3460), esp. pp. 93–6.

generations of reformers compresses a movement stretching across two centuries into a single moment in time.[130] An emblem of the 'Glorious Dawns of Reformations Day', this image, which also symbolized English Protestantism's membership of a wider European family, was frequently republished as 'necessary to be set up in every house and family'.[131] While recognizing this event as a tangible turning point, it is strikingly vague about when it began and when it ended. Late seventeenth-century commentators similarly spoke of it as a movement that started 'in the last age' or 'at the time of our forefathers'. The Reformation had become part of the way that contemporaries defined and periodized the past, but its boundaries and parameters remained both relative and fluid.[132]

Dating the Reformation

From naming the Reformation, we must turn to the question of dating it. The chronological imprecision with which the term was deployed contrasts with the extraordinary fascination contemporaries developed with pinning down the exact dates on which the world had begun and when it would end. Biblical chronology was not a new science; it had its roots in the days of Eusebius, and before that in Scripture and Hellenistic culture. The difficulty of synchronizing the timelines in the Old and New Testaments gave rise to it in the first place, and like its conjoined twin, genealogy, it gained a new lease of life in the post-Reformation era. Scholars had long sought to calculate the age of the earth by adding up the lifespans of the patriarchs, as well as to work out the interval between the Creation and the Incarnation of Christ. One of the solutions they adopted to resolve the awkward discrepancies in the Hebrew and Greek versions of the Septuagint was to date the events of ancient history backwards from Jesus as well as forwards from the divine formation of the world. But the art of numbering the years BC and AD and of fixing the exact dates of scriptural events such as Noah's Flood and the building of Solomon's Temple became a growing preoccupation, assisted by developments in mathematics, numismatics, and astronomy.[133]

---

[130] J[ohn] S[hirley], *Ecclesiastical history epitomiz'd* (1682; Wing S3504B), frontispiece to 'An Epitome of Ecclesiastical History', Part II. Copies of this in print collections include NPG, D23051. BM Satires, British Supplementary 1720 Unmounted Roy does not include the title.

[131] *A true account of the rise and growth of the Reformation, or the progress of the Protestant religion* (1680; Wing T2398).

[132] See Claydon, *Revolution in Time*, pp. 103–6.

[133] See James Barr, 'Pre-Scientific Chronology: The Bible and the Origin of the World', *Proceedings of the American Philosophical Society*, 143 (1999), 379–87; Jeremy Hughes, *Secrets of the Times: Myth and History in Biblical Chronology* (Sheffield, 1990); Anthony Grafton, 'Chronology and its Discontents: The Vicissitudes of a Tradition', in Diane Owen Hughes and Thomas R. Trautmann (eds), *Time: Histories and Ethnologies* (Ann Arbor, MI, 1995), pp. 139–66; *idem*, 'Dating History: The Renaissance and Reformation of Chronology', *Daedalus*, 132 (2003), 74–85; Jeffrey Hopes, 'Dating the World: The Science of Biblical Chronology', *Revue de la Société d'Études Anglaises et Américaines des*

Revolutionary less in exploiting pagan classical texts alongside biblical ones than in according them independent authority, the French Huguenot scholar Joseph Scaliger's *De emendatione temporum* (*On the emendation of chronology*) (1583) was critical here. Among other things, it utilized the word 'anachronismus' to describe an error or mistake in the computation of time.[134] Another notable figure was the Calvinist professor Johann Heinrich Alsted, whose *Treasury of chronology* of 1628 relied partly on analysis of astrological conjunctions. Representing this complex body of knowledge involved reliance on an older technology of columns arranged horizontally to align the events described in biblical narratives with the stories of other societies, so as to bring it within a single time frame. Alongside it as the vertical axis was a downward-descending line like those drawn by genealogists. Family trees and temporal schemes were, in any case, related species. Daniel Rosenberg and Tony Grafton have memorably described such diagrams as a kind of 'chronological *Wunderkammer*, presenting Christian world history in many small drawers'.[135]

The chronological craze, if it may be so called, was also nurtured by the eschatological fever of the era. As we have seen, apocalypticism could encourage both linear and typological thinking about time and collapse the distinction between salvation and secular history. Like it, chronology was closely tied up with the intertwined tasks of prophecy and gnosis. Luther's *Supputatio annorum mundi* (1541) was an attempt to reckon the relative times of events in which scriptural and historical exegesis mutually informed each other. It not merely stitched Old Testament events such as the sacrifice of Isaac and the promise to Abraham's seed together with the birth of Christ, but also (somewhat presumptuously) assigned his own protest against Rome, 102 years after Jan Hus predicted the appearance of a swan, a place in this temporal scheme.[136] Zwingli's successor in Zurich, Bullinger, busied himself with similar calculations, convinced that the historic struggle with the papacy taking place in the sixteenth century was foreshadowed in Scripture and analogically tied to historical developments in the centuries since.[137]

XVIIe et XVIIIe siècles, 71 (2014), 65–83. Euan Cameron is currently preparing a monograph entitled *Cosmic Time and the Divine Plan: Biblical Exegesis, Biblical Chronology, and the Historical Imagination in Western Christianity 1250-1750* (Oxford, forthcoming). In the interim, see *idem*, 'Cosmic Time and the Theological View of World History', *Irish Theological Quarterly*, 77 (2012), 349–64.

[134] See Anthony T. Grafton, 'Joseph Scaliger and Historical Chronology: The Rise and Fall of a Discipline', *History and Theory*, 14 (1975), 156–85; *idem, Joseph Scaliger: A Study in the History of Classical Scholarship*, 2 vols (Oxford, 1983–93).

[135] Daniel Rosenburg and Anthony Grafton, *Cartographies of Time: A History of the Timeline* (New York, 2010), p. 17. On Alsted, see pp. 60, 62; Cameron, 'Cosmic Time', pp. 359–60; and esp. Howard Hotson, *Paradise Postponed: Johannes Heinrich Alsted and the Birth of Calvinist Millenarianism* (Dordrecht, 2001).

[136] Martin Luther, *Supputatio annorum mundi* (Wittenberg, 1541).

[137] See Cameron, 'Cosmic Time', 356.

English Protestants shared the avid interest of their Continental brethren in these challenging questions. As Thomas Pie wrote in the preface to his *Houreglasse* (1597), a computation from the beginning of time to Christ, chronology was the 'right eye' of divine and human history as geography was the left one.[138] In the irascible Hebraist Hugh Broughton's *Concent of Scripture* ([1587–91]) this commonplace was enshrined cartographically in a circular fold-out map of time, in which the continents form the frame for a visual explication of the prophecy of Daniel and the story of the dispersal of Noah's sons, Ham, Shem, and Japheth.[139] Other learned works dedicated to reconciling the temporal contradictions in Scripture appeared, notably John Lightfoot's *Harmony* of 1647. Vice chancellor of Cambridge and a member of the Westminster Assembly, Lightfoot dated Creation to 3929 BC.[140] This figure was revised upwards by seventy-five years by the most famous chronologer of the Church of England, the Irish primate and archbishop of Armagh James Ussher, whose *Annales veteris testamenti*, first published in Latin in 1650 famously surmised that it had occurred at dusk on 23 October 4004 BC. This conclusion was reached by painstaking philological analysis and calculation of the timing of ancient equinoxes, alongside detailed scrutiny of the ages and generations of Adam and his offspring. This body of esoteric scholarship was popularized in the tables appended to English bibles: Ussher's were a standard feature of editions after 1701.[141] This was not simply a reformed phenomenon: the Douai Old Testament of 1609–10 also incorporated its own chronology.[142] Concern about dating the world and forecasting events in the future crossed confessional lines.

Chronology was integrally linked to the writing of universal histories like those compiled by Carion and Sleidan, which took the story from Creation up to their

---

[138] Thomas Pie, *An houreglasse containing a computation from the beginning of time to Christ by X. articles* (1597; STC 19900), sig. A3r. For another example, see *A briefe chronologie of the holie scriptures, as plaine and easie as may be, according to the extent of the severall historicall bookes thereof* (1600; STC 14).

[139] Hugh Broughton, *A concent of Scripture* ([1587–91]; STC 3850), fold-out plate.

[140] John Lightfoot, *The harmony, chronicle and order of the Old Testament* (1647; Wing L2056). See also R. D., *Sacred chronologie, drawn by scripture evidence al-along that vast body of time, (containing the space of almost four thousand years) from the creation of the world, to the passion of our blessed Saviour* (1648; Wing D2131); William Nisbet, *A scripture chronology, wherein the principall periods of time from the creation of the world to the death of Christ, are included* (1655; Wing N1172); Thomas Allen, *A chain of Scripture chronology; from the creation of the world to the death of Jesus Christ* (1659; Wing A1048).

[141] James Ussher, *Annales veteris testamenti, a prima mundi origine deducti* ([1650]; Wing U147A). The first English edition was published in 1658 as *The annals of the world. Deduced from the origin of time, and continued to the beginning of the Emperour Vespasians reign, and the totall destruction and abolition of the temple and common-wealth of the Jews* (Wing U149). On Ussher, see James Barr, 'Why the World Was Created in 4004 BC: Archbishop Ussher and Biblical Chronology', *Bulletin of the John Rylands Library*, 67 (1985), 575–608; D. P. McCarthy, 'The Biblical Chronology of James Ussher', *Irish Astronomical Journal*, 24 (1997), 73–82; Alan Ford, *James Ussher: Theology, History and Politics in Early Modern England and Ireland* (Oxford, 2007).

[142] *The holie bible faithfully translated into English, out of the authentical Latin* (Douai, 1609[–10]; STC 2207).

own time, adding current events as they occurred, like beads to a thread. It was also intimately connected with the recording of prodigies, portents, and omens, which contemporaries read in a manner akin to Morse code, as cryptic messages from heaven warning of the end of the world.[143] The voluminous German anthologies of wonders assembled by Job Fincelius and Conrad Lycosthenes fed into English texts such as Stephen Batman's *Doome warning all men to the judgemente* (1581), a translation of Lycosthenes augmented with material drawn from his own reading and experience or sent to him by friends. The tales of comets, apparitions, monstrous births, and earthquakes Batman assembled also signalled his unease about developments that seemed to be jeopardizing the integrity of the English Reformation, especially the proposed alliance between Elizabeth and the French Catholic duke of Anjou. In Batman's *Doome*, history, prophecy, and polemic coalesce.[144] Laboriously copied and expanded over the years, the Essex minister William Harrison's 'Great English chronology', attests to his intensely providentialist and eschatological world view. His search for clues and patterns in the fabric of time was part of a quest to second-guess God's plans for the invisible church of the elect, as well as the future fate of earthly monarchies and commonwealths.[145]

This was a task that evidently occupied many clergy and laypeople in their spare hours. The lawyer Michael Dalton drew up a similar breviary of the state of the Western Church and Empire in 1634. It tracked the steady decay of true religion, the rise of superstition and the unchaining of the Devil, through to the discovery of Antichrist by Martin Luther in 1517, at the very moment when the grievances and abuses of the Church of Rome were so heavy 'that all the world groaned under the burthen of them'. Its ninety-nine chapters juxtaposed an account of European emperors, kings, popes, and heretics through the centuries, concluding that the Reformation begun under Luther had returned Christianity, full circle, to the doctrines taught by Jesus and the Apostles in the first age of the world. Dalton wrote that Henry VIII, with the consent of Parliament, had 'happily abolished the Popes jurisdiction' in 1533 and that the 'alteration of Religion' here had been 'effected by degrees'. It was ongoing in the reign of the current sovereign Charles I, who, like his predecessors, had maintained the Church in the purity of its primitive precursor.[146]

---

[143] See Barnes, *Prophecy and Gnosis*, esp. ch. 2.

[144] Stephen Batman, *The doome warning all men to the judgemente* (1581; STC 1582). For Batman's concerns about the French match, see Cambridge, Massachusetts, Harvard University, Houghton Library, MS Eng. 1015. See also John McNair's introduction to Stephen Batman, *The Doome: Warning all Men to the Judgement: A Facsimile Reproduction* (Delmar, NY, 1984), pp. iii–xii.

[145] Glyn Parry, 'William Harrison and Holinshed's Chronicles', *HJ*, 27 (1984), 789–810; idem, 'Harrison's "Chronology" and Descriptions of Britain', in Paulina Kewes, Ian W. Archer, and Felicity Heal (eds), *The Oxford Handbook of Holinshed's Chronicles* (Oxford, 2013), pp. 93–110.

[146] FSL, MS V.a.427 (Michael Dalton, 'A Breviary of the state of the Roman (or Westerne) Church and Empire, the decay of true Religion; and the rising of the Papacy; from the tyme of our Lord and Saviour Jesus Christ, till Martin Luther', 1634), chs 93, 97, and 98. The MS is unfoliated.

By contrast, in the list of 'occurrents' up to 1635 compiled by the conservative merchant John Steynor there is no entry relating to Luther's protest in 1517, though the legislation facilitating England's own schism from Rome is duly recorded, alongside the penal laws passed against recusants under Elizabeth and James. The name of the Wittenberg monk is only mentioned in the context of the condemnation of his teachings by the Council of Trent. In this text, the birthday of the Reformation has no status as a historic event. Its omission is an act of deliberate amnesia, like that of the defeat of the Spanish Armada: a reference to the outcome of this 'great fight by sea' was only inserted later by another writer.[147]

Harrison, Dalton, and Steynor's chronologies never reached print, but a similar compilation by John More, the so-called 'Apostle of Norwich', did appear posthumously, edited by the Suffolk puritan Nicholas Bownd, to whose 'whole care and disposition' More's papers had fallen 'by a certaine hereditary right' to publish as he saw fit. He presented this 'childe', after its 'fathers death', as a monument to his memory and he hoped that it would be of use to such as 'travyale in the knowledge of histories'. Like others, this ruled table opened with the Creation, before listing the births of Adam and Eve's son Seth and subsequent generations as recorded in Genesis (Fig. 5.4). More then paused to point out the arithmetical impossibility that Shem could have been born when his father was 500, because two years after the Flood he was 'said to be but an hundred yeeres olde...when his father Noah was six hundred and two'. Such genealogical problems did not admit easily of mathematical solutions. When this chronology reaches the sixteenth century, its hot Protestant credentials become clear. As well as noting that in 1516 'LUTHER began to teach' and charting the progress of reform in Switzerland, Scotland, Germany, and France, it lists the persecutions of the Waldensians in Piedmont in 1562 and the evangelicals hauled up before the Inquisition in Spain. An entry under the year 1550 counts the cost in lives as well as the passage of time: 'IN 30. Yeares above 150000 in divers countries have suffered for the GOSPEL.' He exaggerated the number of victims of Mary's fires, saying that 'above 500' had been burnt besides Ridley, Latimer, Cranmer, and Bradford. Nor could More resist recording some choice gossip about successive popes, such as the incestuous sexual liaisons of Paul III, the 'ribald' sodomy of Julius V, and the equally scandalous life led by Paul V, who 'kept openlie a Gentlemans wife, used to eate snailes and a strong wine Magagnerra for lust, [and] dyed in bed with his whore'.[148]

The various stages in England's Reformation were also enrolled in the table. Oddly, there is no mention of the Royal Supremacy, but the Pilgrimage of Grace,

[147] WAAS, 009:1/BA 2636 parcel 11, fos 155–159. Associated with this is a pedigree tracing the English kings back to Adam. This is transcribed and edited in Diarmaid MacCulloch and Pat Hughes, 'A Bailiff's List and Chronicle from Worcester', *Antiquaries Journal*, 75 (1995), 235–53.

[148] John More, *A table from the beginning of the world to this day*, ed. Nicholas Bownd ([Cambridge], 1593; STC 18074).

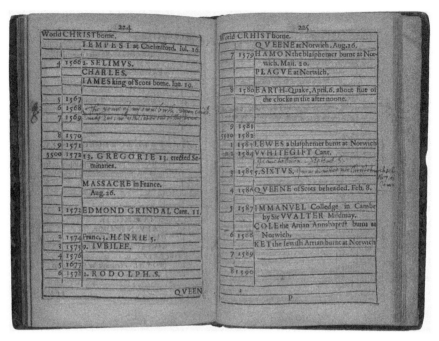

Fig. 5.4 Protestant chronology: John More, *A table from the beginning of the world to this day* (London, 1593), pp. 224–5, annotated by Samuel Burton with notes of his personal biography.

Source: Folger Shakespeare Library, Washington DC, STC 18074 copy 1. Folger Digital Image Collection.

the order for placing English bibles in churches, and the Six Articles are incorporated alongside Henry's multiple marriages and his establishment of colleges, including Trinity in Cambridge (allegedly in 1542, four years earlier than it occurred). Mary's banishment of the Gospel and Elizabeth's reversal of her stepsister's Counter-Reformation are noted, together with the beheading of Mary, Queen of Scots, in February 1587. The last entry is the burning of the 'Jewish Arian' Francis Kett at Norwich in 1588: More evidently had no sympathy for radical heretics and 'blasphemers' of this kind. The table extends forward into the future to 1631, its empty spaces inviting the book's readers to continue the chronicle for another forty years. This was done by the owner of one surviving copy in the Huntington Library, who records the taking of Cadiz in 1596, the journey of Prince Charles to Madrid to negotiate the Spanish match and the burning of Thomas Scott's provocative tract against it, *Vox populi*, in 1623, and the crowning of the new king in 1625. An earlier Protestant annotator occupied himself in transcribing the printed text on facing blank pages with which it was interleaved and supplementing them with further details about the martyrs, drawn largely from Foxe.[149]

---

[149] Ibid. The HEHL copy is shelfmark 2829. For a later item in a similarly anti-Catholic vein, see *A chronology of the rise and growth of popery: from vanity to superstition, thence to worse than heathen idolatry* (1680; Wing C3976).

Chronological knowledge of this kind passed back and forth across the porous boundary between script and print. It can be found scribbled into the commonplace book of the Brigden family along with biblical and personal genealogies, a note of the four monarchies, and the foundation of the English universities.[150] Similar material appears in a vellum volume kept by William Boules, intermingled with accounts of his estate, land transactions and leases, 'remarkable transactions' from the Norman Conquest to Henry III, and records of the birth of his children, for which he gave thanks to God for his 'infinite mercy'. 'See This Booke be keept safe 1680,' he wrote on the cover.[151] The miscellaneous papers of the Somerset MP who stirred trouble in the Caroline House of Commons, Sir Robert Phelips, also include chronological jottings and calculations for the end of the epoch of Antichrist written around 1622.[152] Keeping track of time and unravelling its eschatological significance was not simply an arcane science studied by scholars. It was a vernacular practice that could serve as a tool for political rumination. The chronological annotations that one seventeenth-century reader added to blank spaces in his copy of Robert Persons' *Conference about the next succession* (1594) turned it into an exercise book for calculating the arithmetic of history and forming a distinctively recusant perspective upon the events of the preceding century.[153]

Chronology was closely connected with the chronicle tradition, the continuing vitality of which should be underlined. Criticized as primitive forms of 'scissors and paste' history, chronicles have been regarded as one of the principal casualties of the 'historiographical revolution'. But the steady demise and alleged death of the genre have been exaggerated.[154] Chronicles were a tried and tested method of recording the passing of the generations and God's actions in the temporal realm, and the revitalization of eschatology and providentialism that was a side effect of the religious upheavals of the era contributed to the durability of chronicle. By fossilizing the flow of events at a particular moment in time, its shift from manuscript into print also played a part in inventing the Reformation as a historic event.

Shaped across its two editions by figures with quite sharply diverging religious opinions—from ardent reformers such as William Harrison, John Hooker, and

---

[150] BL, Additional MS 34,660 (Commonplace book of the Brigden family), fos 37v–41v.

[151] Somerset HC, DD/EN/115 (Notebook begun by William Boules in the late 17th century, with notes on chronology and the Bible).

[152] Somerset HC, DD/PH/221 (Letters and drafts of letters of Sir Robert Phelips; Literary Extracts; Miscellanea, *c*.1583–1706).

[153] Bodl., MS Vet. B1 f.115, discussed in Christopher Archibald, 'Calculating History: A Mid-Seventeenth-Century Reader of Robert Persons' *A Conference about the Next Succession* (1594/1595)', *The Review of English Studies*, 71 (2019), 272–91.

[154] Fussner, *Historical Revolution*, p. 230. On the decline of the chronicle, see Daniel R. Woolf, 'Genre into Artefact: The Decline of the English Chronicle in the Sixteenth Century', *SCJ*, 19 (1988), 321–54; idem, *Reading History in Early Modern England* (Cambridge, 2000), ch.1. For a partial corrective, see Alexandra Walsham, 'Chronicles, Memory and Autobiography in Reformation England', *Memory Studies*, 11 (2018), 36–50.

Abraham Fleming to the Catholic Richard Stanishurst and the conservative John Stow—the account of England's conversion into a Protestant nation offered by Raphael Holinshed's *Chronicle* was miscellaneous, inconsistent, and as unsettled as Elizabeth's own settlement.[155] The neutral persona Stow himself adopted in his own *Annales*, *Chronicles*, and *Summarie* has served to eclipse the extent to which these texts provide a less than enthusiastic perspective upon aspects of the Reformation, including the suppression of the religious houses, which he depicts as 'a pitiful thing'. In this respect it partakes of some of the nostalgia that has been identified as a feature of his topographical *Survey of London*.[156] Like the chronologies and tables already discussed, it entails strategies of selective remembering and proactive forgetting of events of which he had been an eyewitness.

Continued after his death by Edward Howes, Stow's chronicle was refashioned again for a new generation. The preface to the 1631 edition contains a striking revisionist rethinking of the traditional periodization of English history. Dividing this into five hundred year blocks, each inaugurated by a moment of 'revolution' and change, Howes identifies five, starting with the arrival of Brutus and the Trojans, moving on to England's absorption into the Roman Empire, its conquest by the Saxons, invasion by the Danes, and then the Normans. The final 'Alteration of time', 'farre milder and more peaceable' than those preceding it, is the ecclesiastical one inaugurated in the reign of Henry VIII and extending through to the end of the Tudor dynasty and the peaceful and 'triumphant' succession of James. Indicative of the metamorphosis of attitudes that occurred as the early Reformation moved out of communicative into cultural memory, Howes is critical of Henry VIII, whose prodigality he finds distasteful and offensive, recalling how he had ruled through fear and terror, overthrown the monasteries, and waxed fat and slothful in his old age, requiring engines to lift his monstrous body and move him around. Under Edward, who here is no young Josiah, the Church was 'fleec't againe', 'bishopricks cut and pared' to the bone, the chantries suppressed, tombs defaced, and parish churches spoiled. Commended for her 'milde nature, and gentle disposition', Mary gets off lightly by comparison with some earlier Protestant accounts, while Elizabeth is applauded for her excellent gifts and even-handed ministration of justice. The frustrations she caused to the exponents of further reform receive no mention at all. In Howes's version of Stow's chronicle,

---

[155] See Barrett L. Beer, 'John Stow and the English Reformation, 1547–1559', *SCJ*, 16 (1985), 257–71; Peter Marshall, 'Religious Ideology', in Kewes, Archer, and Heal (eds), *Oxford Handbook of Holinshed's Chronicles*, pp. 411–26.

[156] Harriet Lyon, '"A Pitiful Thing"? The Dissolution of the English Monasteries in Early Modern Chronicles, *c.*1540–*c.*1640', *SCJ*, 49 (2018), 1037–56; Patrick Collinson, 'John Stow and Nostalgic Antiquarianism', in Julia F. Merritt (ed.), *Imagining Early Modern London: Perceptions and Portrayals of the City from Stow to Strype, 1598–1720* (Cambridge, 2001), pp. 27–51.

the disputed developments that he did not call the Reformation became not merely a watershed; they also inaugurated an entire historical epoch.[157]

As these events passed from living memory into the realm of inherited history, their sequencing was quietly reordered for various purposes. Sometimes unfortunate errors crept in. The chronicles with which the clergy and laity filled their notebooks were often disorganized. The 'chronological relation of extraordinary events' compiled by the Church of England clergyman Samuel Carte and left by his son Thomas to the Bodleian Library in the early eighteenth century gathers together political, dynastic, ecclesiastical, and meteorological facts in a haphazard fashion. Ranging wildly from biblical times to 1700 and jumbling together stories of the advance of Protestantism in England and Europe from Luther's attack on Tetzel to the landing of William of Orange at Torbay in 1688, it is also horribly muddled in places. At one point Henry VIII's desire for a divorce and the ensuing break with Rome is said to have occurred after the birth of Prince Edward, and not before.[158] The genealogical knots that lay behind England's Reformation proved difficult to unravel two centuries on.

Timing the Reformations

The primary unit for measuring the passage of time and for organizing historical information in chronologies and chronicles was the year. But months, days, and hours were also caught up in the religious turmoil of the era. The chief mechanisms for keeping track of these were almanacs, calendars, chronometers, dials, and clocks. These too were technologies and techniques that both shaped and were shaped by the Reformations. They were less agents of disenchantment than instruments for recalibrating the spirituality of daily life. In a culture in which time was personified as an elderly man and in which people spoke of 'the age of the day', temporal awareness was tightly entangled with generational thinking.[159]

Configured and calculated for a range of local meridians, almanacs remind us that until the introduction of Greenwich Mean Time in 1847, England was a country with multiple time zones. Clerical attitudes towards these pre-eminent vehicles of astrological knowledge were ambivalent. On the one hand, astrological prognostication was a dangerous rival to the doctrine of providence; on the other,

---

[157] John Stow, continued by Edmund Howes, *Annales. or a general chronicle of England... continued and augmented with matters foraigne and domestique* (1631; STC 23340), sig. ¶2r–8v, quotations at ¶6r, 7r–v. See also Lyon, *Memory and the Dissolution of the Monasteries*, pp. 110–14.

[158] Bodl., MS Carte 251 (Samuel Carte, 'Chronological relation of extraordinary events... from the earliest times to the beginning of 1700'), esp. fo. 31r.

[159] See, e.g., BM, 1948,0410.4.171, 172, 173, 174 (Gerard de Jode, *Four Allegories of Time*, 1531–90); BM, 1873,0614.113 (Crispijn van de Passe the elder, *Father Time/Deliciarum Juvenilium Libellus*). For the 'age of the day', see *OED*, s.v. 'age', P2b.

tracking the movement of the planets and stars was a valuable tool for preaching repentance before the impending apocalypse.[160] Some disguised didactic treatises under the cloak of this popular genre. 'Faithfully Calculated by the course of holy Scripture', John Monipennie's *Christian almanacke* of 1612, was not a conventional almanac at all, but rather an exhortation to its readers to redeem the time, lest, like the foolish virgins in the Bible, one might be 'lulled a sleepe with ease & prosperity' and miss the arrival of the bridegroom. It included chapters meditating on God's government of the world, the blessings of fruitfulness and the curse of dearth, the sickness and diseases of sin, the evils of strife and trouble, the responsibilities of princes and superior powers, and guidance on how to be a 'Child of light, and escape the horrible darkeness of the wicked'.[161] Patrick Ker's *The map of man's misery: or, The poor man's pocket-book: being a perpetual almanack of spiritual meditations* aligned the seven days of the week with the seven ages of man, using this as an excuse for delivering standard advice about childhood, youth, manhood, old age, death, judgement, and eternity, along with some 'precious Remedies against Satan's Devices'. Here the spiritual and biological life cycles are superimposed upon quotidian time.[162] The Baptist Henry Jessey went one step further in his *Scripture calendar* (1649), which mimicked the structure of its astrological rivals but remodelled it in line with the Bible, providing a prophetic diagram of Daniel's prophecy of the fifth monarchy and a pedigree of the generations from Adam to Christ. Twinning biblical chronology with sacred genealogy, his was an almanac for the self-professed Saints.[163]

Almanacs were portable compendia of an assortment of useful information, almost all of it tied in some way to the passing of time. They conventionally included schedules of fair days, tides, movable ecclesiastical feasts and legal terms alongside the figure of zodiac man, with indications of which stars ruled over particular parts of the body, so that people could make informed decisions about when it was most propitious to undertake particular activities, from journeys,

---

[160] The irreconcilability of astrology and Christian religion and its marginalization as a vulgar science by the end of the seventeenth century have been overstated. For the latter, see Patrick Curry, *Prophecy and Power: Astrology in Early Modern England* (Cambridge, 1989). For more subtle expositions of the relationship between astrology and Protestant teaching, see C. Scott Dixon, 'Popular Astrology and Lutheran Propaganda in Reformation Germany', *History*, 84 (1999), 403–18; Robin B. Barnes, *Astrology and Reformation* (Oxford, 2016). The classic work on almanacs remains Bernard Capp, *Astrology and the Popular Press: English Almanacs 1500–1800* (1979). On almanacs and religion, see ch. 5.

[161] John Monipennie, *A Christian almanacke. Needefull and true for all countryes, persons and times. Faithfully calculated by the course of holy Scripture, not onely for this present yeere 1612, but also for many yeeres to come* (1612; STC 18019), sigs A4r, C5r.

[162] Patrick Ker, *The map of man's misery: or, The poor man's pocket-book: being a perpetual almanack of spiritual meditations: or compleat directory for one endless week* (1690; Wing K340).

[163] Henry Jessey, *1649, the Scripture calendar used by the prophets and Apostles, and by our Lord Jesus Christ, paralleld with the new stile, and our vulgar almanac* (1649; Wing A1835). For one computation of the generations from Adam to Christ, see Henry Jessey, *A calculation for this present yeer, 1645. Not only according to the English and beyond-sea accounts, but also according to the word of God* (1645; Wing A1833aA), p. 29.

business deals, and bloodletting to the religious duty of conceiving children. Tables of the 'age of the moon' were another regular feature. Many also incorporated short chronologies of 'memorable accidents' which reduced the timelines worked out by erudite scholars to 'one page of compressed plagiarism'. Beginning with the Creation, the compilers of these summaries galloped through Genesis to the birth of Christ, before listing the most significant landmarks of modern times. Most had a patriotic bias, alighting upon legendary events such as Brutus's entrance to this island, the first planting of Christianity by Joseph of Arimathea in AD 63, the conversion of King Lucius, and the Norman Conquest of 1066, followed by the invention of guns and the advent of printing. When it came to recent history, military victories and natural disasters were recorded alongside dynastic deaths and royal accessions. The Reformation, although it was almost never labelled as such, was also a prominent but not universal theme. Most almanac compilers concentrated on its evolution in England, referring to the appearance of Wyclif, the break with Rome and the end of papal jurisdiction, Elizabeth's accession, the Armada and the Gunpowder Plot, sometimes with the Blackfriars accident (or the 'fatal vesper') and the return of Prince Charles from Spain unencumbered by a Catholic bride thrown in. Later seventeenth-century almanacs added the execution of Charles I, the restoration of his son, the ejection of James II, and the accession of William and May in 1689.[164] Such texts contributed to the construction of the present and the immediate past. Selectively reported in the partisan productions that flooded the unregulated presses, the bloody conflicts and 'accidents' of the 1640s and 1650s similarly cemented themselves in a social memory that was not homogeneous but both heterogeneous and highly fragmented.[165]

Sometimes the recording of history merged with hope for the future. Jessey's *Scripture almanacke* of 1646 recalled Wyclif as 'the first Restorer of Religion after the grossest darknesse of Popery', duly acknowledged Henry VIII's role in putting down papal supremacy and the monasteries, celebrated the young Josiah as the first protector of 'persecuted strangers', and praised the 'present Parliament' for rooting up prelacy and engaging itself 'for a Reformation according to the Word of God', beginning 3 November 1640.[166] If almanacs contributed to fixing the

---

[164] Capp, *Astrology*, pp. 215–24, p. at 215.

[165] See Imogen Peck, 'A Chronology of Some Memorable Accidents: The Representation of the Recent Past in English Almanacs, 1648–1660', *Historical Research*, 92 (2019), 97–117; and Kevin Birth, 'Calendars: Representational Homogeneity and Heterogeneous Time', *Time and Society*, 22 (2013), 216–36. On the construction of the present, see Daniel Woolf, 'News, History and the Construction of the Present', in Brendan Dooley and Sabrina Baron (eds), *The Politics of Information in Early Modern Europe* (New York, 2001), pp. 80–118. For the role of calendars in shaping memory in France, see Philip Benedict, 'Divided Memories? Historical Calendars, Commemorative Processions and the Recollection of the Wars of Religion during the Ancien Régime', *French History*, 22 (2008), 381–405.

[166] Henry Jessey, *1646. A Scripture almanacke, or a calculation according to the English account, and the Word of God* (1646; Wing A1833A).

chronology of religious change in England, they played a part in confusing it too. Twinned with prognostications that predicted the unfolding of time still to come, they also sought to make prophecies come true.

Such texts became increasingly belligerent as carriers of reformed sentiment and providential memory, prompting Catholics to issue their own versions as rejoinders. The 'Useful Chronology of things since the REFORMATION' incorporated in the *Calendarium Catholicum* (1689) begins with the Henrician Royal Supremacy. The rest of its milestones, dated by reference to this event, rather than the Creation of the world, as was more conventional, include the beheading of the 'most unfortunate Princess' Mary Stuart, 'the Horrid Powder Plot suspected to be Politicly contriv'd by [Robert] Cecil', the 'barbarous murder' of Charles I, the death of the 'late religious Usurper, Rebel, and Regicide' Oliver Cromwell, the 'pretended Popish Plot', and finally the auspicious birth of the Old Pretender.[167] An earlier text by the recusant Thomas Blount began with the arrival of the papal envoy St Augustine and the conversion of the Anglo-Saxons in 597, recorded the first use of the royal touch by Edward the Confessor, and pointedly preceded its entries on the dismantling of the Church of Rome in England by noting that Henry VIII had been given the title Defender of the Faith by Leo X for writing against the 'Apostate Friar' Martin Luther.[168] Others skipped over religious change altogether, rendering the arrival of Protestantism a non-event, unworthy of remembrance.

The historical vision encapsulated in astrological almanacs was not, however, entirely insular. Reference was frequently made to the emergence of Martin Luther. Philip Ranger's almanac calculated for York in 1618 noted that it was 111 years since 'D. Luther detected Popish falshoods', 94 since 'H.8. crushed the Popes power in Engl.', and 70 since the start of the 'bles[sed] Q. Elizabeths raigne'. It also singled out the rebellion of the northern earls and 'dolefull Massacre in France by Papists' on St Bartholomew's Day 1572.[169] The list of 'memorable things' incorporated in John Woodhouse's Dublin almanac for 1644 included 'Martin Luther opposed the Pope', but not Henry VIII's schism.[170] John Booker's *Bloody Irish almanac* for 1645 expanded this into a prose narrative, which declared that Luther had started 'to write against the Pope' 100 years after John Hus and that 'Reformation began in his time', despite the efforts of the Devil, Pope, Holy

---

[167] *Calendarium Catholicum, or, an almanac for the year of our Lord, 1689* (1689; Wing A1386A), sigs A2v–6r.

[168] Thomas Blount, *A new almanack after the old fashion for 1663, the 3d after leap-year with memorable observations and an exposition of all the festival dayes in the year* (1663; Wing A1324), sigs A2r–3v.

[169] Philip Ranger, *A new almanacke and prognostication, for the yeare of our redemption, 1618, being the yere of the worlds creation, 5580, and the second from the leape-yeare* (1618; STC 502.4), 'A Compendious Chronologie or Computation of Yeeres'.

[170] John Woodhouse, *Woodhouse. Almanack for the year of our Lord God 1644. Being bissextile or leap-yeare, and since the creation of the world 5593* (Dublin, 1644; Wing A2830A).

Roman Emperor, and almost all the Christian world to destroy him 'by open force and secret fraud'. Yet 'God miraculously preserved him for about thirty yeers space' and allowed him to die peacefully in his bed. Calvin, 'a most reverend, orthodox man' had flourished around 1535, around which time new heresies and divisions sprung up, but none of them exceeded those of the Roman Antichrist. In any case most Anabaptists, Antinominans, Socinians, Ubiquitarians, and Arminians were papists and Jesuits underneath.[171] Booker's almanac was unusually prolix, but it is an accurate barometer of the confessionalization and politicization of the genre. The chronology drawn up by Sir George Wharton in the late 1650s was a piece of Royalist propaganda, spiked with contempt for 'Geneva trash', admiration for 'Rev'rend Laud's' refurbishment of St Paul's Cathedral, lament for the sacrifice of 'learned Stafford's Blood', regret at the 'fatal blow' of the defeat of the king's army at Naseby, and pride that Charles I had been 'made truly great and glorious' by his martyrdom in 1649. Its entry on the Reformation read 'Since Protestants (by *Luther*) first so nam'd', erroneously imply-ing that this derogatory nickname was a label of self-ascription coined in 1517. Subsequent, post-Restoration editions refused to recognize the hiatus in royal rule between 1649 and 1660, dating Charles II's reign from his father's death, thereby casting the memory of the republican Commonwealth into oblivion.[172]

Explicitly presented as 'a looking-glasse for papists, wherein they may see their own sweet Faces', another self-styled 'Protestant Almanack' said that it was the corruptions of Leo X, 'a profest Atheist' who had 'accounted the Gospel a Fable', that had induced God 'to open Luther's eyes, whence insued some Reformation'. In England, events began with the raising of rebellion in Lincolnshire 'to set up their old Mumpsimus', followed by the 'knocking down' of the Pope's supremacy and the 'plucking down' of the 'Nests of Abbots, Priors, Moncks, Fryars and Nuns; for their Pride, Covetousness, Laziness, Treachery, Gluttony, Ignorance, Luxury, Fornication, Adulteries, and Sodomies'.[173] Calculated 'for the Meridian of Babylon, where the Pope is elevated an hundred and fifty degrees above all Reason, Right and Religion', a later edition reduced Christian history to just eight events: the Creation, Incarnation, England's conversion by King Lucius in AD 190, Luther's protest against the papacy, Elizabeth's accession, the Gunpowder Plot, the Great Fire of London, and 'our Second Deliverance from Popery' by

---

[171] John Booker, *A bloody Irish almanack, or, Rebellious and bloody Ireland, discovered in some notes extracted out of an almanack, printed at Waterford in Ireland for this yeare 1646* (1646 [1645]; Wing B3723A), p. 18.

[172] George Wharton, *The works of that late most excellent philosopher and astronomer, Sir George Wharton, Bar. Collected into one entire volume*, ed. John Gadbury (1683; Wing W1538A), pp. 358–63.

[173] William Winstanley, *Speculum papismi: or, A looking-glasse for papists, wherein they may see their own sweet faces being the second part of the Protestant Almanack for this year 1669* (Cambridge, 1669; Wing S4851), sig. H3r–v. On the emergence of 'mumpsimus' to describe a traditional custom obstinately adhered to, see Peter Marshall, 'Mumpsimus and Sumpsimus: The Intellectual Origins of a Henrician *Bon Mot*', *JEH*, 52 (2001), 512–20.

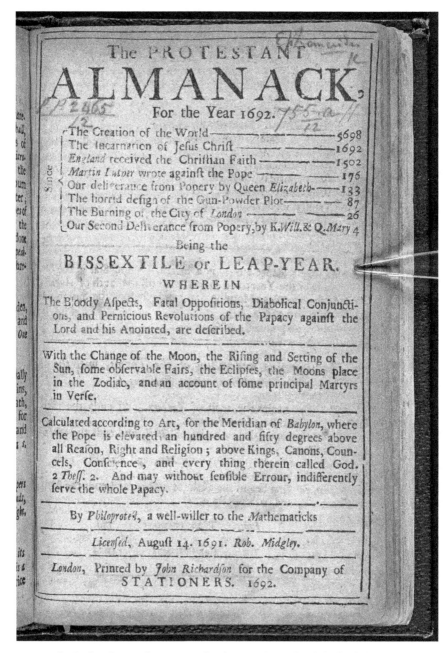

Fig. 5.5 'Calculated according to Art, for the Meridian of *Babylon*': Philoprotest
[William Winstanley], *The Protestant almanack* (London, 1692), title page.
Source: © British Library Board, P.P.2465 (1692). All Rights Reserved/ Bridgeman Images.

William and Mary (Fig. 5.5).[174] Almanacs not merely helped to entrench the Protestant reperiodization of the past around the rupture of the Reformation; by dating events with reference to each other and to the present they reinforced the figurative and synchronic dimensions of early modern temporality.[175] They also attest to the ongoing capacity of time to carry sacred meaning in Protestant culture.[176]

Alongside the Book of Common Prayer, almanacs also served as critical agents of the reformation of the calendar. They reflected the severe pruning of holy days—from 125 to 27—that lay at the heart of liturgical reform. This savage assault upon medieval Catholic memory cast a host of traditional worthies out of the pantheon, not least St Thomas Becket—the twelfth-century archbishop who, in a pre-emptive riposte to the Royal Supremacy that put Henry VIII's nose out of joint, had defended papal sovereignty against overweening royal power. His murder in Canterbury Cathedral had led to his canonization as a political martyr. Many surviving missals, litanies, processionals, and primers attest to the attempt to expunge him from collective remembrance.[177] The purging of the ecclesiastical calendar was insufficient for radical Protestants, who lamented that the Prayer Book remained 'full of the rubbish of Romish relics' and, according to the Cheshire puritan William Hinde, continued to 'smell hugely of the vessels of Judaisme, Paganisme, and Papisme'.[178] Some of these offensive vestiges, including Christmas were finally removed in the 1640s, but others persisted. In 1648, John Brinsley called upon the House of Commons to change the names of the days of the week and the months of the year, on the grounds that they perpetuated a form of 'superstition' by which people unwittingly did 'homage to strange Gods, to heathenish and abominable Idols' and 'dunghill dieties [sic]'. The Quakers replaced them with numbers, but what Brinsley called the 'Paganish Liverie' in which the vocabulary of time was dressed was not abolished by order of the state.[179]

England's resistance to adopting the Gregorian calendar is a further reflection of how time was fractured and confessionalized by the Reformation. Luther acknowledged that there were terrible 'rents' in this ancient garment but thought it would survive long enough to see Christ's second coming. Elizabeth's regime

[174] William Winstanley, *The Protestant almanack for the year from the incarnation of Jesus Christ, 1669* (1692; Wing A2223).

[175] I owe this point to Bronwyn Wallace, to whom I am grateful for stimulating discussions.

[176] Cf. Alison A. Chapman's claim that 'by lending a vertical significance to time and place, almanacs run counter to early modern Protestantism, which suggested that place and time have no inherent sacred significance': 'Marking Time: Astrology, Almanacs, and English Protestantism', *RQ*, 60 (2007), 1257–90, at 1257.

[177] See Aude de Mézerac Zanetti, 'Liturgical Changes to the Cult of Saints under Henry VIII', in Peter Clarke and Tony Claydon (eds), *Saints and Sanctity*, SCH 47 (Woodbridge, 2007), pp. 126–43. For a particularly striking example, see *Missale ad usum insignis ac preclare ecclesie Sar[um]* ([Paris, 1533]): CUL, Peterborough.W.13, sig. B6v. This is reproduced at https://exhibitions.lib.cam.ac.uk/reformation/artifacts/forgetting-the-saints/, accessed 6 June 2022.

[178] William Hinde, *A faithfull remonstrance of the holy life and happy death of Iohn Bruen of Bruen-Stapleford, in the county of Chester, Esquire* (1641; Wing H2063), p. 91.

[179] John Brinsley, *Calendar-reformation. Or, An humble address to the Right Honorable the Lords and Commons assembled in Parliament, touching dayes and moneths, that they may be taught to speak such a language as may become the mouth of a Christian* (1648; Wing B4709), sig. A2r, p. 7.

held out against the Gregorian scheme for anti-Catholic reasons, dismissing John Dee's earnest petition for 'needful Reformation of the Vulgar Kalendar' and his importunate plea that the queen take 'the most bewtifull flower of Opportunity to…ymbrace the veritie…for the true Reformation of the Civile yere is thus to her Majestie left and offered (as it were) from God, to do hym service withall, before all other Christian Princes'.[180] Sometimes the resulting gap of eleven days between reformed and Catholic countries played into Protestants' hands, notably when it was observed that the Blackfriars accident of 1623 had occurred on 5 November 'new style', a coincidence that the godly interpreted as a providential response to the failed Gunpowder Plot.[181] The new calendar was only officially embraced in 1752. For nearly 180 years, Protestant and Catholic time was out of kilter. Recusant families whose children were at school and college and whose relatives were in exile in the Low Countries, Italy, and Spain were temporally as well as spatially dislocated from their loved ones. This was another sense in which the Reformation severed the vertical and horizontal connections between the generations.

Ultimately, like Cranmer's liturgy, the English calendar remained immersed in a culture of time-reckoning based on the medieval Christian year. Transplanted into it were the icon events of England's providential deliverances, notably Elizabeth's accession and the discovery of the Gunpowder Plot, which were typologically linked with events in the Bible including the parting of the Red Sea and the destruction of Pharaoh's host. The thwarted conspiracy on 5 November and Charles I's execution on 30 January both generated occasional liturgical forms that infiltrated prayer books in the later seventeenth century and commemoration of these ultimately displayed greater longevity than 17 November, Elizabeth I's accession day.[182] Although the Henrician official Richard Morison had suggested instituting an annual holiday to commemorate the king's triumph over the Pope with bonfires, processions, feasts, and prayers as a liberation from bondage similar to Passover, this failed to take off. Mary's regime established 30 November as a thanksgiving for the country's reconciliation to Rome, but it

---

[180] For Dee, see Bodl., MS Ashmole 1789, quotations at pp. 49–50. See Robert Poole, *Time's Alteration: Calendar Reform in Early Modern England* (1998), esp. ch. 4; Charlotte Methuen, 'Time Human or Time Divine? Theological Aspects in the Opposition to Gregorian Calendar Reform', *Reformation and Renaissance Review*, 3 (2001), 36–50. Luther is quoted on p. 42. For the earlier history of calendrical reform, see C. Philipp E. Nothaft, *Scandalous Error: Calendar Reform and Calendrical Astronomy in Medieval Europe* (Oxford, 2018).

[181] See Alexandra Walsham, "The Fatall Vesper": Providentialism and Anti-Popery in Late Jacobean London', *P&P*, 144 (1994), 36–87.

[182] See David Cressy, *Bonfires and Bells: National Memory and the Protestant Calendar in Elizabethan and Stuart England* (1989); idem, 'God's Time, Rome's Time, and the Calendar of the English Protestant Regime', *Viator: Medieval and Renaissance Studies*, 34 (2003), 392–406. For the special liturgies and prayers, see Natalie Mears, Alasdair Raffe, Stephen Taylor, and Philip Williamson (with Lucy Bates) (eds), *National Prayers: Special Worship since the Reformation*, vol. i, *Special Prayers, Fasts and Thanksgivings in the British Isles, 1533–1688*, Church of England Record Society 20 (Woodbridge, 2013), pp. 182–90, 261–5, 647. For the Prayer Book versions, see *The book of common prayer and administration of the sacraments and other rites and ceremonies of the Church, according to the use of the Church of England* (1675; Wing B3642), sigs F8r–10r.

was short-lived.[183] The Act of Royal Supremacy did not become a recognized watershed in England's protracted Protestantization. This was partly because Henry's role in this process was so ambiguous and coloured by recollections of his tyranny and greed, but also because the whole purpose of the regime was to insist upon the continuity of the Church of England with the Christian past. It had no interest in commemorating its own act of novelty and rupture. If the silence of the liturgy on the subject of the early Reformation is resounding, the focus it developed on Elizabeth's reincarnation of it is equally revealing.[184] This had the effect of strengthening the tendency to regard the dynastic event of his second daughter's succession to the throne on 17 November 1558 as the birthday of the Gospel, even though it had occurred a generation after the break with Rome. English Protestantism was chronically confused about the date of its own inception, its parentage, and its numerical age.

Nor did the anniversary of Luther's protest on All Souls' Day 1517 ever receive formal liturgical recognition, though the calendars that prefaced some editions of the Geneva Bible, including a large folio of 1583, did record the date on which the famous Augustinian monk 'gave his propositions in the universitie of Witemberg, against the Popes pardons', 'Ci yerres after the death of John Hus', as well as the day on which he was born, 10 November 1483. It also noted the translation of his body, in a manner comparable to a saint's relic, to its final resting place in the town in which he had become famous. Other pages juxtapose biblical and historical events, including the reform of religion 'according to Gods expresse trueth, in the most renoumed Citie of Geneva' in 27 August 1535, and the death of Edward VI, 'the Josias of our age' on 6 July 1553.[185] Here the secular history of the Reformation and the life history of its founder are intertwined with the chronology and genealogy of Scripture.

The jubilee of the centenary of the nailing of Luther's 95 theses in 1617 gave rise to celebrations in Germany, according new coherence to the varied pattern of commemoration that had developed in different cities and territories over the years on an assortment of days, including (as in Hamburg) St Martin's Day, the date of Luther's baptism. By fixing upon 31 October, it served to confirm this date as the starting point of the Reformation. Ironically, given that these festivities seem to have been partly modelled on the developing calendrical tradition in Protestant Britain,[186] this passed largely unnoticed in England, though a translation

---

[183] See Sydney Anglo, 'An Early Tudor Programme for Plays and Other Demonstrations against the Pope', *Journal of the Warburg and Courtauld Institutes*, 20 (1957), 176–9.

[184] See Alec Ryrie, 'The Liturgical Commemoration of the English Reformation, 1534–1625', in Walsham, Wallace, Law and Cummings (eds), *Memory and the English Reformation*, pp. 422–38.

[185] *The Bible. Translated according to the Ebrew and Greeke, and conferred with the best translations in divers languages. With most profitable annotations upon all the hard places, and other things of great importance, as may appeare in the epistle to the reader* (1583; STC 2136.5), sigs ¶3r–6v.

[186] Ruth Kastner, *Geistlicher Rauffhandel: Form und Funktion der illustrierten Flugblätter zum Reformationsjubiläum 1617 in ihrem historischen und publizistischen Kontext* (Frankfurt am Main, 1982); R. W. Scribner, 'Incombustible Luther: The Image of the Reformer in Early Modern Germany', in *idem*, *Popular Culture and Popular Movements in Reformation Germany* (1987), pp. 323–53, at pp. 339–46; Charles Zika, 'The Reformation Jubilee of 1617: Appropriating the Past through Centenary

of Johann Georg's ordinance for Saxony did appear the following year, prepared by a minister of the Dutch stranger church in London. The preface to this text was a hymn to international Protestantism. It called upon the English 'to solemnize the remembrance of their manumission from the thraldome of Antichrist, by the hand of God upon Luther' together with their German brethren and to pray for the prosperous success of the Gospel, which it equated with the deliverance of the Israelites out of 'Ægiptian bondadge'. Catholics might 'looke for an evanishing of that Doctrine' and persuade themselves it was only a passing aberration, but its endurance for a century suggested otherwise and deserved to 'be written for the generations to come'. The pamphlet closed with a timeline of Protestant events from 1517 to 1617 in which the shaking off of 'the Popes Yoake' by Henry VIII in 1533, Edward VI's abrogation of the Mass and removal of images from the temple, and Elizabeth's reception of the Gospel for 'the second time' feature alongside developments in Germany, France, Scotland, Denmark, Poland, Bohemia, Hungary, and the Netherlands.[187] The comparatively subdued reception of the centenary may be read as a testimony to what Alec Ryrie has called 'the strange death of Lutheran England'.[188] But it is also a telling reminder that commemorations are always less about the past than a projection of the present's priorities. Indeed, they efface the distinction between them.

Protestant liturgical time nonetheless remained built on the bedrock of the monastic offices. Cranmer's *Book of Common Prayer* was a palimpsest, under the surface of which lay the Sarum use, from which it borrowed its fundamental structure and rhythms. The 'revolution in ritual theory' inaugurated by Protestantism redefined the Eucharist as a memorial and denied that it entailed a recurrent miracle.[189] Significantly, in the guise of the doctrine of predestination, it also insisted that salvation was an event that had occurred in the past rather than something coterminous with the present which one could strive to achieve in the future. In the words of the seventeenth-century polymath Thomas Browne, it was 'no prescious determination of our estates to come, but a definitive blast of his will already fulfilled'.[190] As James Simpson has observed, for Protestants 'the key

---

Celebration', in D. E. Kennedy (ed.), *Authorized Pasts: Essays in Official History* (Melbourne, 1995), pp. 75–112, esp. p. 77. A key figure in initiating this was Frederick V of the Palatine, who was married to Elizabeth Stuart: see p. 83. See also Thomas Albert Howard, *Remembering the Reformation: An Inquiry into the Meanings of Protestantism* (Oxford, 2016), esp. ch. 1.

[187] Johann Georg I, *The Duke of Saxonie his jubilee with a short chronologie. Both shewing the goodnesse of God, in blessing the Gospel of Christ, since Luther first opposed the Popes pardons* (1618; STC 14656), sigs A2r–3v, A4v, pp. 8–17.

[188] Alec Ryrie, 'The Strange Death of Lutheran England', *JEH*, 53 (2002), 64–92. On the memory of Luther's protest in the English Reformation, see Peter Marshall, 'Nailing the Reformation: Luther and the Wittenberg Door in English Historical Memory', in Walsham, Wallace, Law and Cummings (eds), *Memory and the English Reformation*, pp. 49–63.

[189] Edward Muir, *Ritual in Early Modern Europe* (Cambridge, 1997), ch. 5 and p. 181.

[190] Thomas Browne, *Religio medici* (1682; Wing B5178), p. 23.

events of history have, in a profound sense, already happened.[191] Technically, neither the liturgy nor the sacraments made any difference to the decisions that God had reached, before and outside time, about the fate of human beings in the afterlife.

Yet many Protestants must have continued to experience the liturgy synchronically. In the same way as biblical events were both unique and irreversible, cyclical and typological, so were religious rituals at once a representation of history and a living ladder or staircase to the next world.[192] 'Pious behaviour and soteriological anxiety subsisted together for most people,' writes Jessica Martin. 'The relationship between the religious dynamics of conversion and the disciplines of habit is delicate, and not necessarily inimical.'[193] Supplying the ceremonial template for the rites of passage that marked the human life cycle—baptism, marriage, and burial—the liturgy remained, in W. H. Auden's resonant words, a 'link between the dead and the unborn'.[194] In short, it served as an umbilical cord between people separated in time from each other. Nowhere is this more neatly encapsulated than in the Magnificat, in which Mary thanks God that she has been selected to be the mother of Christ: 'beholde, from henceforth all generacions shal cal me blessed'. A hymn of thanksgiving that had been part of the liturgy since the sixth century, it at once foretells a lifesaving future event and commemorates the blessings that God 'remembring his mercie...promised to oure fathers, Abraham and his seede for ever'. Poised between hope and assurance, it speaks to and for the family of the faithful that the Lord has called out of darkness and into the light and knowledge of his word.[195] Absorbed into the reformed Prayer Book, it is emblematic of the complex, fertile, and multivalent concept that is at the heart of this book.

The rhetoric of preachers replicated the sense of dynamic simultaneity that was essential to combat the potential for despair inherent in the precept that human effort was irrelevant to salvation. Both implied that not merely was apprehension of the gift of divine grace subject to the constraints of the calendar, but so too was the gift itself temporal.[196] God's decision about one's ultimate fate had been made

---

[191] James Simpson, 'Grace Abounding: Evangelical Centralisation and the End of *Piers Plowman*', *Yearbook of Langland Studies*, 14 (2000), 49–73, at 59.

[192] Gabrielle M. Spiegel, 'Memory and History: Liturgical Time and Historical Time', *History and Theory*, 41 (2002), 149–62, at 152.

[193] Jessica Martin, 'Early Modern English Piety', in Anthony Milton (ed.), *The Oxford History of Anglicanism*, vol. i, *Reformation and Identity, c.1520–1662* (Oxford, 2017), pp. 395–411, at p. 403.

[194] W. H. Auden, letter to J. Chester Johnson, 6 July 1971: quoted in Edward Mendelson, *Later Auden* (1999), p. 518.

[195] Brian Cummings (ed.), *The Book of Common Prayer: The Texts of 1549, 1559, and 1662* (Oxford, 2011), p. 15 (1549 edition).

[196] See Maria Devlin, '"If it were made for man, 'twas made for me": Generic Damnation and Rhetorical Salvation in Reformation Preaching and Plays', in Jonathan Willis (ed.), *Sin and Salvation in Reformation England* (Farnham, 2015), pp. 173–89; Karen Bruhn, '"Sinne Unfoulded": Time, Election and Disbelief among the Godly in Late Sixteenth- and Early Seventeenth-Century England', *Church History*, 77 (2008), 574–95.

outside the matrix of time, by a being for whom both past and future were eternally present. The very idea that he had a memory was an oxymoron.[197] But this did not mean that one's soteriological state was static and fixed. Faith was organic and prone to be overcome by moments of doubt and desolation, which were themselves impermanent and reversible. Experimental predestinarianism was an art of remembering quotidian events that paradoxically offered evidence that one would be saved in the fullness of time. If Protestantism literally put the past behind it and encouraged the pious to look forward to the afterlife, it also concentrated attention on sanctifying the continuous cycle of experience on earth.[198] The temporality of Quakers who repudiated predestination had a different character. It collapsed chronology and eternity into one; the idea of the indwelling light was a doctrine of continuous presence in which the end time was always now.[199] The role of the long Reformation in facilitating the drift towards a more linear and chronological temporality was, therefore, complicated and must not be overstated.[200]

Like ecclesiastical time, domestic time was increasingly regulated by mathematical sundials, hourglasses, clocks, and watches in ways that shaped an emerging culture of record-keeping and diary-writing.[201] The proliferation of handy devices for telling the time extended down the social scale. Those unable to afford expensive objects could resort to more ephemeral ones. At least one mid-seventeenth-century almanac incorporated instructions for making 'a perfect Sun-Diall' using the fingers of one's hand, though this relied on the sun shining.[202] Where older narratives thought of this 'horological revolution' as an agent of the disenchantment

[197] For a stimulating reflection on the question of divine memory, see Karis Riley, 'God's Memory: Why have we Forgotten it?', https://remref.hist.cam.ac.uk/research/gods-memory-why-have-we-forgotten-it.html, accessed 3 April 2021.
[198] See James P. Walsh, 'Holy Time and Space in Puritan New England', American Quarterly, 32 (1980), 79–95, esp. 79; Max Engammare, On Time, Punctuality and Discipline in Early Modern Calvinism, trans. Karin Maag (Cambridge, 2010), esp. pp. 244–5.
[199] On Quaker temporality, see Hilary Hinds, George Fox and Early Quaker Culture (Manchester, 2011), ch. 4.
[200] I have benefited from discussing this topic with David Hillman, whose article 'Salvation and Salutation in Early Modern Theology', RQ, 73 (2020), 821–65, speaks to these themes, with a subtle difference of emphasis from my own reading.
[201] The spread of clocks and other devices in both urban and rural early modern English society is documented by Paul Glennie and Nigel Thrift, Shaping the Day: A History of Timekeeping in England and Wales 1300–1800 (Oxford, 2009); see esp. ch. 6. On timepieces and diary-writing, see Stuart Sherman, Telling Time: Clocks, Diaries and the English Diurnal Form, 1660–1785 (Chicago, 1996); Rudolf Dekker, 'Watches, Diary Writing and the Search for Self-Knowledge in the Seventeenth Century', in Pamela H. Smith and Benjamin Schmidt (eds), Making Knowledge in Early Modern Europe: Practices, Objects and Texts, 1400–1800 (Chicago, 2007), pp. 127–42; Molly McCarthy, 'The Diary and the Pocket Watch: Rethinking Time in Nineteenth-Century America', in J. Arianne Baggerman, Rudolf M. Dekker, and Michael James Masusch (eds), Controlling Time and Shaping the Self: Developments in Autobiographical Writing since the Sixteenth Century (Leiden, 2011), pp. 121–45.
[202] W. Knight, Pleiades, hoc est prognosticon septennium. Or, an almanack and prognostication for seven years (1652; Wing A1857aA), 'A perfect Sun-Diall'. A copy of this almanac survives in CRO, DBW/P/J/9 and has been used as a diary by Roger Wilbraham, 1643–76. See below, pp. 508–9.

of time, more recent work has pushed back against easy assumptions about secularization.[203] It has also stressed the plurality of temporalities that prevailed in this era. In both rural and urban England, quotidian senses of time and patterns of work, rest, and play were shaped by the presence of material and mechanical timepieces.[204]

Time remained both subjective and deeply spiritualized. Timekeeping devices of all kinds retained a vital place in the religious imagination. In a discussion of the Christian householder, Thomas Gouge, for instance, compared the sins of private men to 'the errours of a Pocket watch, which usually misleads only the keeper of it. But the sins of a Master of a Family are like the errours of an house-clock, which is apt to mislead the whole Family.'[205] More generally, timepieces served as emblems of divine omnipotence and wisdom, as well as of human mortality. Christina Faraday has described them as potent symbols of the reformed theology of salvation by faith and predestination. In paintings and portraits, they both figured and facilitated the pursuit of evidence of where one stood in an opaque eschatological scheme predicated on decisions made by the Almighty before the world began.[206] Like other household possessions, such items sometimes bore moralistic and biblical imagery and confessionally charged iconography and inscriptions.[207] One striking table clock now in the British Museum even carries the Calvinist motto: '*post tenebras lux*'. Here a mechanism for marking the passage of daily time simultaneously serves as a reminder of the myth of historical periodization invented by the Reformation.[208]

[203] On the so-called 'horological revolution', see David S. Landes, *Revolution in Time: Clocks and the Making of the Modern World* (Cambridge, 1983); Gerhard Dohrn-van Rossum, *History of the Hour: Clocks and Modern Temporal Orders*, trans. Thomas Dunlap (Chicago, 1996); idem, 'Time', in Hamish Scott (ed.), *The Oxford Handbook of Early Modern European History, 1350–1750*, vol. i, *Peoples and Places* (Oxford, 2015), pp. 145–64. For the argument that Reformation effected 'a partial disenchantment of time', see Robin Barnes, 'Reforming Time', in Ulinka Rublack (ed.), *The Oxford Handbook of the Protestant Reformations* (Oxford, 2017), pp. 64–82. By contrast Matthew Champion argues that clock measurement coexisted with more subjective senses of temporality in *The Fullness of Time: Temporalities of the Fifteenth-Century Low Countries* (Chicago, 2017), p. 61.
[204] See Keith Wrightson, 'Popular Senses of Time Past: Dating Events in the North Country, 1615–1631', in Michael J. Braddick and Phil Withington (eds), *Popular Culture and Political Agency in Early Modern England and Ireland: Essays in Honour of John Walter* (Woodbridge, 2017), pp. 91–107; idem, 'Past Times: Temporalities in Early Modern England', in Edward Town and Angela McShane (eds), *Marking Time: Objects, People, and their Lives, 1500–1800* (New Haven, CT, 2019), pp. 19–29; Mark Hailwood, 'Time and Work in Rural England, 1500–1700', *P&P*, 248 (2020), 87–121.
[205] Thomas Gouge, *A word to sinners, and a word to saints* (1670; Wing G1379), p. 255.
[206] See Tiffany Stern, 'Time for Shakespeare: Hourglasses, Sundials, Clocks, and Early Modern Theatre', *Journal of the British Academy*, 3 (2015), 1–33; Christina Faraday, 'Tudor Time Machines: Clocks and Watches in English Portraits, c.1530–c.1630', *Renaissance Studies*, 33 (2019), 239–66.
[207] BM, 1888, 1201.204 (English verge watch, the dial of which is engraved with a depiction of Christ and the woman of Samaria, c.1625–35).
[208] BM, 2015, 8041.5 (striking clock, European, 17th century). On this object, see Karis Riley, 'The Sound of the Reformation', https://remref.hist.cam.ac.uk/ research/sound-reformation.html, accessed 24 July 2022.

If some Protestants were preoccupied with regulating and regimenting time, this was a by-product of their impulse to sacralize everyday life. A distinctive by-product of the Genevan 'spirituality of time' delineated by Max Engammare was 'the invention of punctuality', which was conceived as a remedy for human frailty, laziness, and forgetfulness.[209] Reformed piety revolved around the keeping of the Sabbath, the profanation of which by forms of labour or leisure was a sin against the Decalogue. The disputes that arose within puritan circles about what could be sanctioned on Sundays in the name of necessity reflect the pool of sanctity that still surrounded temporality. In Calvinist Glasgow, the Kirk session felt obliged to define that the Sabbath day ran from sun to sun and did not end at midnight.[210]

Christian vigilance in the face of worldly temptation was regarded as a vital duty, necessary to prevent descent into apostasy and decay in grace, and to advance 'our daily growth in Christ'. Regular and conscientious attention to the task of self-examination was intricately linked with the process of gaining assurance that one was 'a child of God'. It was tied to the idea of the spiritual life cycle, which in turn was often compared to the internal movement of a clock. John Brinsley's bestselling book *The true watch, and rule of life* was dedicated to Henry, Lord Hastings, earl of Huntingdon, whom he urged to spend an hour each week 'vewing your selfe in this Christal glasse, desirous to clense your spottes hereby'. Its title alluded both to the ancient art of watching as a devotional exercise and to the mechanical objects that an increasing number of sixteenth- and seventeenth-century people kept about their persons.[211] Some of these, including a surviving specimen in the British Museum dating from *c*.1645–55, doubled as calendars and almanacs, measuring not merely the turning of the hours but also the progression of the days of the month (Fig. 5.6).[212] Material reminders that time was ticking away and that repentance should not be delayed, they were utilitarian items and meditational aids at the same time. The diary of the Dissenter Ralph Thoresby reveals that on 1 November 1680 he entered into a resolution to curtail the wasted hours he spent in bed and to purchase an alarm to rouse him by 5 a.m. each morning to a regimen of reading, writing, and prayer.[213] Nehemiah Wallington filled many journals and notebooks with pages of

---

[209] Steven Engler, 'Time, Habit, and Agency in English Puritanism', *Method and Theory in the Study of Religion*, 19 (2007), 301–22. See also Engammare, *On Time*, esp. 7–9, 205, 243–7; Alec Ryrie, *Being Protestant in Reformation Britain* (Oxford, 2013), pp. 445–6.

[210] See Kenneth Parker, *The English Sabbath: Study of Doctrine and Discipline from the Reformation to the Civil War* (Cambridge, 1988); Daniel MacLeod, 'Making Time Protestant in Early Modern Glasgow', *Reformation and Renaissance Review*, 20 (2018), 168–84, esp. 175–9.

[211] John Brinsley, *The true watch, and rule of life* (1606; STC 3775), title page, p. 1, and sig. A2v. This book went through multiple editions and engendered three sequels. See STC 3776–86. *OED*, s.v. 'watch'.

[212] BM, 1862,0801.1.

[213] *The Diary of Ralph Thoresby, F.R.S. Author of the Topography of Leeds (1677–1724)*, ed. Joseph Hunter, 2 vols (1830), vol. i, pp. 72–3.

Fig. 5.6 Calendar watch made by William Bunting, 1645–1655, with 'IOANNI MILTONI 1631' engraved on the face. This spurious inscription was probably added in the nineteenth century.

Source: © The Trustees of the British Museum, 1862,0801.1.

introspective scrutiny of his shortcomings and sins in the hours he reclaimed by rising, before the rest of the household, at three or four o'clock, but he came to see this as an obsessive addiction that he should strive to overcome. Although he repeatedly vowed 'to give over writing and goe to practizing that which I have written of Gospel Conversation', fearing that it was also hindering his calling, it was an impulse that he clearly found almost impossible to resist.[214]

Worries about idleness as Satan's gateway to the soul and the misuse of legitimate leisure time were no more the preserve of the godly than personalized timepieces. The sanctification of everyday life through habituated action had Catholic manifestations as well as reformed ones, as the daily routine of the convents in exile and the devout, quasi-monastic observation of religious offices by recusant widows such as Dorothy Lawson reveal. From waking to sleeping, she was engaged in litanies and oblations, in an effort to ascend, as if via Jacob's Ladder, to heaven.[215] St Francis de Sales compared the inner life of the devout believer to the workings of a clock and said that everyone with 'a true care of his soule, should wind it up to God evening and morning' by the spiritual exercises he prescribed and oil it with the sacraments of confession and the holy Eucharist to prevent its mechanism from becoming rusty. For de Sales it was an apt metaphor for the perpetual regeneration of the human soul. The German Jesuit Jeremias Drexelius's *Angel-guardian's clock* was another Tridentine guide to private devotion, teaching its readers to live, die, and pray in lessons corresponding to the twelve segments of the night and day.[216] An elaborately illustrated recusant manuscript dating from the late seventeenth century owned by one Mary Caryll includes a twenty-four hour 'Clock of our Blessed Saviours Passion'. Explicitly envisaged as a mechanism for measuring the spiritual growth and welfare of the soul, it too liberally exploits horological metaphors.[217] The doctrine of purgatory itself was predicated on a distinctive understanding of divine time in which sinners redeemed themselves by a stint in this place of trial and torment that was measured by the quantity of their iniquities.[218] Part and parcel of a 'culture of temporal devotion' that had late medieval precedents, such texts were descendants of the new 'technology of time' that was the book of hours.[219]

---

[214] FSL, MS V. a. 436 (Nehemiah Wallington, notebook, 1654), pp. 322, 323, 333, 537. See also the extracts in *The Notebooks of Nehemiah Wallington, 1618–1654: A Selection* (Aldershot, 2007).

[215] For Dorothy Lawson, see William Palmes, *The Life of Mrs Dorothy Lawson, of St Anthony's, near Newcastle-upon-Tyne*, ed. G. Bouchier Richardson (Newcastle upon Tyne, 1855), pp. 33–5.

[216] Francis de Sales, *An introduction to a devoute life*, trans. I. Y. ([Douai], 1613; STC 11316.5), 2nd pagination, pp. 88–9; Jeremias Drexel, *The angel-guardian's clock translated out of Latin into English* (Rouen, 1630; STC 7234).

[217] FSL, MS V.a.666 (Mary Caryll of North, recusant devotional text, c.1680–1700?).

[218] Robert Mills, 'God's Time? Purgatory and Temporality in Late Medieval Art', in Gerhard Jaritz and Gerson Moreno-Riaño (eds), *Time and Eternity: The Medieval Discourse* (Turnhout, 2003), pp. 477–98.

[219] Champion, *Fullness of Time*, pp. 25, 199.

Protestantism did not discard this species of devotional literature in the wake of the Tudor Reformation. The popularity of primers demanded their adaptation rather than abandonment by the regimes of Edward VI and Elizabeth I, which issued reformed versions that were still indebted to their Sarum predecessors. The continuing attraction of the format is reflected in John Day's *Booke of Christian prayers* (1578). Adorned with woodcuts reminiscent of early sixteenth-century printed hours, it was, nevertheless, in Eamon Duffy's words, a 'Trojan Horse, harnessing the old forms to smuggle in the new religion', including belligerent prayers against the Pope.[220]

Private prayer books of this kind underwent a revival in the 1620s, when the royal chaplain Daniel Featley produced his *Ancilla pietatis*. Deliberately designed to counter the temptation of Catholic devotional manuals, which he regarded as 'bleare-eyed with superstition', this provided prayers for morning and evening for each day of the week, as well as the feasts of Christ's Nativity, Circumcision, Epiphany, Resurrection, Ascension, and Pentecost, and the fasts of Ash Wednesday and Good Friday. Insisting that there was 'no inherent holinesse' in times or seasons, it nevertheless defended their use as a prerogative of Christian liberty, except where they 'savour of Romish superstition, whereof they are a gaudy Relique'. Steering clear of saints' days, Featley found precedents for his compilation in 'the antient Primitive Church'.[221]

The storm that broke following the publication of John Cosin's *Collection of private devotions* was symptomatic of the aura of sensitivity that began to surround the 'ghostly exercise' of the 'houres of prayer' in the context of the Laudian reorientation of ceremonial priorities. Cosin defended this as a part of the 'ancient Piety' practised by 'olde godly Christians', but this did not convince his fierce puritan critics, who found the 'verie beautifull distinction of the Dayes and Seasons' that structured the book, as well as its inclusion of medieval bishops, virgin martyrs, and monastic founders, highly distasteful.[222] William Prynne denounced these 'couzening devotions' as a blatant device for reintroducing the virulent 'poyson' of popery and saw the IHS on the book's title page as a sign of its Jesuitical origin.[223] Henry Burton's 'tryall' or 'diall' was dedicated to 'the Church

---

[220] John Day, *A booke of Christian prayers* (1578; STC 6429); and see *idem, Christian prayers and meditations* (1569; STC 6428). See Helen C. White, *Tudor Books of Private Devotion* (Madison, WI, 1951) and Eamon Duffy, *Marking the Hours: English People and Their Prayers, 1240–1570* (New Haven, CT, 2006), esp. pp. 167, 171–4.

[221] Daniel Featley, *Ancilla pietatis: or, the hand-maid to private devotion* (1626; STC 10726), sig. A6r, pp. 401–2, 409, 416.

[222] John Cosin, *A collection of private devotions in the practice of the ancient church, called the Houres of prayer* (1627; STC 5816), sigs A2v, A4v, A8v, B1r. William Laud's manuscript 'officium quotidianum', which appeared posthumously, mimicked the monastic office: *The daily office of a Christian being the devotions of the most reverend father in God Dr William Laud, late archbishop of Canterbury* (1683; Wing L583). This fourth edition is the first extant edition.

[223] William Prynne, *A briefe survey and censure of Mr Cozens his couzening devotions* (1628; STC 20455), sig. ¶2v.

of England, my deare Mother'. It urged her in her 'reverend old Age' not to display 'a too motherly indulgence' towards her rebellious 'younger Sonnes' who sought to reunite her with Rome and to betray 'the first Reformation' during which she had rightly separated from 'Babylon'. Branding 'this idle Apish Booke' a form of 'Baby-devotion', he dismissed the argument that it was justified by its Elizabethan precedents on the grounds that this had been a concession to 'the weaknesse of the time'. What had been 'winked at in the infancy of the church' was 'not 'tolerable in her riper age': 'Were it not absurd and ridiculous for a man growne, to fall to his old childish sports and toyes againe?' Invoking the notion of progressive enlightenment, he charged Cosin with encouraging backsliding: 'After the cleare meridian Sun-shine of the Gospell, would he reduce us to those duskish dawning shadowes'?[224] The outrage of these firebrands is a measure of the appeal that they feared the book would have for unwary laypeople. Intertwining polemic and piety, the daily cycle of prayer and devotion was deeply implicated in the confessional struggles that animated England's fractious and unstable Reformations.

We must, therefore, envisage several intersecting systems of religious time, orientated around different spindles and pivots. Serving simultaneously as chronometric machines and as contemplative aids, the various devices for time-keeping present in this society provided a tool for meditating on the journey from cradle to grave travelled by every generation. As the illustrations in some primers reveal, the progression of the ages of man was closely linked with the yearly cycle of the seasons.[225]

Nowhere is this demonstrated more compellingly than in the genealogical notes carefully inscribed in bibles, prayer books, almanacs, and other printed and manuscript texts. The precision with which contemporaries recorded the timing of the births and deaths of their children and relatives not merely testifies to the spread of 'clock time' in early modern England; it also highlights the astrological and spiritual significance people attached to recording the particular month, day, and hour at which their loved ones arrived and departed from this earth. The children of Graham family of Norton Conyers in Yorkshire were recorded as having been born 'about' a particular hour in the morning, afternoon, or evening (see Fig. 6.14).[226] Others indicated that deliveries had occurred between adjacent ones.[227] As attested by his diary, Samuel Jeake's father made an 'Aestimate time' of his birth in Rye on Sunday 4 July 1652, '1/4 past 6 a Clock in the morning' using

[224] Henry Burton, *A tryall of private devotions, or, a dial for the houres of prayer* (1628; STC 4157), sigs ¶2r–v, B3v, D1r–3r.

[225] See, e.g., Bodl., MS Rawlinson Q.f.1 (copy of *This prymer of Salisbury use* (1552) with obits and notes of the Ramsay family and the kings of Scotland).

[226] NYCRO, ZKZ/4/9 (Family bible with entries of Graham births, deaths, marriages, 1650–present).

[227] e.g., DRO, D1689/1 (Geneva bible belonging to the Taylor family with inscriptions concerning family births); LRO, 920 MAT (Mather family bible, 1770).

a horizontal sundial.[228] As clocks and watches became widespread, it became possible to be even more exact. Nicholas Okeford's copy of a 1701 edition of the King James Bible is annotated with memoranda of the birthdays of his five children: John was born 22 July 1706 'att 15 minutes past ten', Ann on 12 September 1707 'att 10 minutes past 6', Nicholas on 11 February 1709 'att 20 minutes pas seven', Stephen on 5 February 1712 'at 35 minuts past four', and 'Stephen ye second' on 8 April 1716 'about 45 minutes past twelve att noon'.[229] Accuracy of this kind was vital for ascertaining the sign of the zodiac that would rule infants' lives, and some inserted this after their names.[230] Listing the sons and daughters with which a marriage had been graced was also regarded as a pious parental duty mandated by Scripture, the repeated perusal of which was another feature of Protestant temporality. The early seventeenth-century earl of Moray used the front leaves of his bible for genealogical data and the back to record the dates that he began rereading the Old and New Testaments over a period of nearly twenty years.[231]

Such instincts assisted in forging a conscious link between the history of individual families and the history of the communities—villages, towns, cities, and the nation at large—of which they were a part. The list of the seven children (Nathaniel, John, Elisha, Bathshua, Mary, Daniel, and Ithiell) with which God had blessed Robert Smart, puritan minister of Preston Capes, Northamptonshire, and his wife Katherine not only includes the approximate hour as well as day of their birth, together with the regnal as well as regular year. Smart also notes that his son Ithiell was born on the same day as the earl of Essex was beheaded for treason in the Tower of London.[232] The chronology of events that Matthew Wren wrote in Latin in the pages of his copy of Pond's almanac for 1652 is similarly a mixture of the personal and public. It combines career highlights like his appointment as deacon of Windsor and Wolverhampton in 1628 and his ordination as bishop of Hereford in 1634 with domestic landmarks like the death of his father in October 1624, the births and baptisms of his children, including a stillborn infant ('*infantula exanimis edita*') at 7 a.m. on 12 March 1640, and the day the 'loving soul' of his wife Elizabeth 'flew away' six years later ('*Ad Christ. evolavit pia anima. conjugis E.*'). It records his tribulations in being violently arrested and thrown into

---

[228] See Thrift and Glennie, *Shaping the Day*, pp. 246, 265–6. For Jeake, see Hunter and Gregory (eds), *Astrological Diary*, p. 85.

[229] DWL, 112.P.7(2): flyleaf preceding *The New Testament* (Cambridge, 1659).

[230] For examples, see CL, MS I.h.52 (Memorandum book with contemporary records of births, marriages, and deaths in the Mitchell, Crosby, Moody, Ingby, and Robinson families, 1646–1739); SRO, 4714/1 (Photocopies of pages in a bible owned by the Semple family of Northern Ireland, with entries of births, marriages, deaths, and other memoranda, 1630–1787), FSL, MS V.a.437 (Sermon book of Dorothy Phillips, 1616–17, with births, marriages, and deaths relating to the Hanmer family of Selattyn, Shropshire, 1588–1722).

[231] NLS, RB. s.2166 (4) (*The holy bible* (1627), bound with the *Book of Common Prayer*, belonging to the Stewart family, the earls of Moray).

[232] BL, Sloane MS 271, fo. 72r.

prison in the Tower of London alongside the arrival of the future Charles II in April 1632 and the fatal day on which the regicide took place (*à sanguinibus, ô Deus!*).[233]

The same intertwining of the private and patriotic is observable in the memoirs of the Royalist gentlewoman Alice Thornton. She recorded that the marriage of her daughter had occurred on a key anniversary, 5 November 1668:

> being that day in which Almighty God did shew His miraculous deliverances of all our soules and bodies, with the whole Church of God in the Christian world from that Gunpowder Plott of the bloody papists, for our utter ruine and sub-vertion when we had cause to rejoyce.

Alluding to the story of Abraham's seed, she hoped that the exchange of vows on this 'most eminent day' would bode well for the:

> establishment of the truth and light of God's gospel…in this my family and blood, and shall be confirmed in me and mine as long as the world indureth, and for the salvation of all the soules that spring from my deare husband and myself, which will be the great blessing I humbly crave of God, for the Lord Jesus Christ His sake. Amen.[234]

The temporal lenses through which contemporaries understood their own lives were varifocal. Life cycle events were instinctively refracted through the prism of Protestant history and vice versa. Family memory and confessional memory were inextricable.

The Life Cycle of the Reformations

The concluding section of this chapter extends these observations by exploring further ways in which evolving senses of the Reformation past became inter-twined with personal time. It charts the process by which the temporal milestones whose formation I have placed under the spotlight converged with the creation and transmission of generational memory. Tamara Hareven has commented that families often follow their own time clocks and that their histories do not fit neatly into established models of historical periodization. Individual lives syn-chronized with these chronologies in unpredictable ways, reflecting the resilience of relative timelines and the tendency of emotion to play mischievous tricks with

---

[233] *Parentalia*, ed. Wren, pp. 133–4.
[234] *The Autobiography of Alice Thornton, of East Newton, co. York*, ed. Charles Jackson, Surtees Society (Durham, 1875), pp. 229–30.

the memory, as well as to foster forms of amnesia.[235] The alignment of historical events with significant points in the life cycle affects perceptions of both, and these subjective experiences are passed down from parents to children in a kind of 'ripple effect'. Hareven's insights illuminate how family history became interlaced with the liturgy and with the public transcripts of early modern historiography.[236] They help us to trace the manner in which the ambiguous, plural, and competing accounts of recent history engendered by the Reformation were assimilated and internalized by ordinary people. The material analysed in the following pages suggests that remembrance of this contested past was inseparable from remembrance of private or domestic events.

Evidence of this interactive process can be found in the very printed and manuscript texts upon which this chapter has been built, and in the copies of them that still survive in libraries and archives. A particularly striking example is Francis Western's transcription of Thomas Heywood's *Englands Elizabeth*, prepared when he was aged 11 around 1700 (Fig. 5.7). First published in 1631, the book he copied out was a narrative of the Virgin Queen's life and troubles 'from the Cradle to the Crown', notably during the reign of her sister, when she had lamented to see 'how Bethel lay in the dust unregarded, and Babel onely exalted, true Religion dejected, and Superstition advanced' and had barely escaped death herself. Based on Foxe and embellished with poetic licence, it presented her as a quasi-martyr who had been brought up alongside her illustrious younger brother Edward and survived her own 'fiery trial' to swim through 'a sea of sorrow' to the throne in 1558. Closing with a rousing peroration of how she had progressed 'from misery to Majesty, from a Prisoner to a Princesse', it was a patriotic text that lent itself well to a pedagogic exercise. Written in a neat italic hand and probably preserved by his mother as a tender reminder of her son's school days, the manuscript is suggestive of how children absorbed the providential story of England's Reformation that had embedded itself at the centre of this culture.[237]

Nor did the compiling of chronicles and chronologies of world history occur in isolation from life cycle events, which sometimes erupted into them. Stephen Batman's *Doome warning all men to the judgemente* (1581), for instance, contains an extraordinary autobiographical digression. Sandwiched between descriptions

---

[235] Tamara K. Hareven, 'Synchronizing Individual Time, Family Time, and Historical Time', in John Bender and David E. Wellbery (eds), *Chronotypes: The Construction of Time* (Stanford, CA, 1991), pp. 167–82; Daniela Koleva, 'Daughters' Stories: Family Memory and Generational Amnesia', *Oral History Review*, 36 (2009), 188–209. On the persistence of relative chronology, see also Diana E. Greenway, 'Dates in History: Chronology and Memory', *Historical Research*, 72 (1999), 127–39.

[236] See also Katie Barclay and Nina Javette Koefoed, 'Family, Memory, and Identity: An Introduction', *Journal of Family History*, 46 (2021), 3–12.

[237] FSL, MS V. a.22 (Francis Western's copy of 'Englands Elizabeth her life and Trobles, during her minoritie, from the Cradle to the Crown', c.1700). The book he copied was Thomas Heywood, *Englands Elizabeth: her life and troubles, during her minoritie, from the cradle to the crowne* (1631; STC 13313).

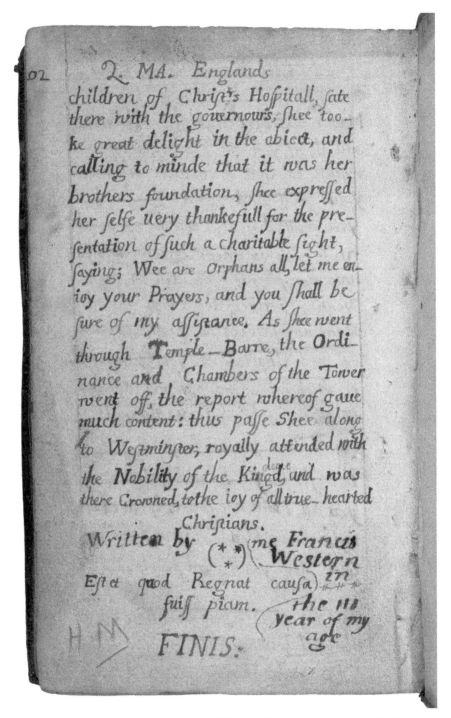

2. MA. Englands children of Christ's Hospitall, sate there with the gouernours, shee tooke great delight in the abiect, and calling to minde that it was her brothers foundation, shee expressed her selfe uery thankefull for the presentation of such a charitable sight, saying; Wee are Orphans all, let me enioy your Prayers, and you shall be sure of my assistance. As shee went through Temple—Barre, the Ordinance and Chambers of the Tower went off, the report whereof gaue much content: thus passe Shee along to Westminster, royally attended with the Nobility of the Kingdome, and was there Crowned, to the ioy of all true—hearted Christians.

Written by (*.*) me Francis Western

Est et quod Regnat causa) 277
fuiss piam. the 11o
year of my age

H M FINIS.

Fig. 5.7 Francis Western's transcription of Thomas Heywood's *Englands Elizabeth* (1631), 'written . . . in the 11th year of my age', c.1700.

Source: Folger Shakespeare Library, Washington DC, MS V. a. 22, p. 202. Folger Digital Image Collection.

of a flotilla of spectral ships seen off the coast of Cornwall in May 1580 and a wild tempest that killed two geldings and uprooted four elm trees in July of the same year is a compelling passage describing the divine deliverances vouchsafed to Batman since his youth. These include his 'miraculous' preservation from drowning at the age of 21: a close shave that precipitated a conversion experience; the strange glowing light that appeared at the end of his bed when he lived at Leeds in Kent, which he feared might be a diabolical illusion; and his narrow escape from a malicious false accusation and from assassination. He also describes the burning of his house to the ground and the retributive judgement that befell the 'double-dealing' men who turned against him, one of whom was 'stroocken blind' while another succumbed to dropsy. Batman also tells of the 'pining sickness' that afflicted him and further tribulations at the hands of people who resented his open reproof of their 'shameless Epicureanism' and sought his undoing. The whole passage is peppered with earnest religious exhortations of the kind more commonly found in puritan diaries like those of Samuel Ward, Nehemiah Wallington, and Ralph Josselin: 'The Lord is one my side, I will not feare what man doth unto me, the Lorde taketh my part with them that helpe me.' 'The Lord hath chastened and corrected me; but hee hathe not given me over unto death.' Bespeaking the distinctive language of experimental predestinarianism, this is a moment of private introspection in the midst of an account of ominous public events. At once political and spiritual, cosmic and intimate, his *Doome* sheds light on the capacity of the chronicle genre to create space for compilers to recall and record their own lives at a turbulent time. It forges a link between collective eschatology and individual soteriology, between the *chronos* of the terrestrial calendar and the *kairos* of his own particular story of salvation, a story that operates both within and beyond humanly comprehensible temporal boundaries.[238]

The publishers of such texts both expected and encouraged their readers to engage with them in similar ways. People filled the chronologies they purchased with additional information, personalizing them, and turning them into hybrids of script and print. This was actively facilitated by the inclusion of blank spaces and interleaved pages, as in Paul Eber's Latin *Calendarium historicum*, published in Wittenberg in 1550, which left ample room for book-owners to comment on current events and record personal notes of their own, intertwining chronology with genealogy and enabling the creation of individual cartographies of time.[239] Publishers of English chronological tables did the same. Inscribed with the name of its owner, Samuel Burton, and the date on which it was purchased in 1595, the Folger Shakespeare Library's copy of John More's *Table* (1593) includes added entries noting his birth on Candlemas Eve 1569 (which falls in between the birth of James VI and I in 1566 and the erection of the Catholic seminaries by Gregory

---

[238] Batman, *Doome*, pp. 410–11. On similar tendencies in Ralph Josselin's diary, see Ronald Bedford, Lloyd Davis, and Philippa Kelly (eds), *Early Modern English Lives: Autobiography and Self-Representation 1500–1660* (Aldershot, 2007), pp. 34–5.

[239] Rosenberg and Grafton, *Cartographies of Time*, pp. 74–5.

XIII in 1572), his arrival in Oxford on 3 September 1584, and his admission to Christchurch school on 7 January (in the same year as Sixtus V began his pontificate). He records the Essex rebellion and Robert Devereaux's condemnation and execution as a traitor in late February 1601. More's Protestant chronology has become a register of signal moments in Burton's life history, which are described using the intimate first person pronoun (see Fig. 5.4).[240]

Some copied out the contents of printed calendars and chronicles into manuscript books of their own. Organized chronologically from 1 January to 31 December, a late seventeenth-century yearbook compiled by Robert Le Wright combines a digest of historic and current events with memoranda of an autobiographical kind. The page for 18 January includes the foundation of Lund University in 1667 and the burial (in a dunghill) of his 'Perfidious wife', Gratiana, who deserted him in 1674. Under 21 March, Le Wright recorded both the martyrdom of Thomas Cranmer at Oxford in 1556 and the death of his 'little ward' Teresia Searle of plague in 1660. A later addition notes the demise of the Irish primate and chronologer James Ussher. Under 22 October 1517, Le Wright writes: 'Reformation of Religion first began by Martin Luther'; under 31 October 1517, we find 'Martin Luther gave his Propositions in Wittenburg, against the Popes pardons; which was 101 yeares after the death of John Hus'. Another testament to the instinct to correlate the events of past and present, this too is a text that reflects both faulty memory and chronic uncertainty about when exactly Protestantism had first emerged.[241]

No less striking is the private chronology prepared by Denis Bond of the Isle of Purbeck in Dorset in the late 1630s. Beginning with the synod of 1100 at which Archbishop Anselm of Canterbury decreed that priests should not marry, this similarly intermixes family memorials with the annals of a distinctly Protestant-tinged history. The births, marriages, and burials of four generations, including his wife's delivery of a stillborn son in 1617, sit cheek by jowl with notes about Luther's protest against indulgences in 1517, the declaration of the Royal Supremacy in 1533, the banishing of the Gospel by Queen Mary in 1553, the death of John Calvin in 1564, Pope Gregory's reform of the calendar in 1582, the founding of Emmanuel College in 1587, and 'the falle of Blackffriers' in 1623. Copied and continued by his descendants until the twentieth century, this chronology has been corrected by one of its later transcribers, who has marked certain

---

[240] John More, *A table from the beginning of the world to this day* ([Cambridge], 1593; STC 18074): FSL, STC 18074 copy 1. See pp. 224–6. See also Robert Nicolson's annotated copy of Lodowick Lloyd, *The first part of the diall of daies* (1590; STC 16621; Bodl., 4° Rawlinson 140 (1)), which has been used to compile a historical chronology, register, or commonplace book. On p. 304 he notes that on 31 October '101 yeares after the death of Jhon Hus Martin Luther gave his propositions in Wittemberg against the Popes Pardons. A° D° 1517'. Also included are occasional notes for 'my owne remembrance only' (p. 70g).

[241] BL, MS Additional 33,747 (Robert Le Wright yearbook), fos 23r, 87r, 303r, 312r.

entries with an asterisk and the word 'wrong'.[242] Such practices were not confined to learned gentleman but can be found among people of more modest rank and means, including tradesmen. They too kept chronicles for the benefit of family members and future heirs in which grand events coexisted with local and personal records as a form of 'makeshift archiving' for the future.[243]

Similar patterns of personalization have left telling traces in the handful of examples of erasable writing tables that have been preserved in libraries. These items, which were designed to serve as reusable calendars, were produced on a significant scale in the late sixteenth century.[244] Feeding the burgeoning practice of commonplacing, some of these tiny (often sextodecimo) notebooks had no accompanying printed content. Others, however, included calendars, notes about the phases and epacts of the moon, handy multiplication tables, charts of coins, weights and measures, and mileage between London and notable towns. A further component was a miniature description of England and Wales together with a brief chronology of notable dates since the Norman Conquest probably derived from Holinshed's chronicle. These were vehicles for a highly abbreviated version of Reformation history incorporating Henry VIII's divorce, the banishing of the authority of the Bishop of Rome, the suppression of the religious houses, the Pilgrimage of Grace, the Edwardian purging of churches 'for the avoiding of idolatrie' and introduction of the English liturgy, the short reign of Lady Jane Grey, Wyatt's rebellion and the 'great persecution and crueltie' carried out under the 'cruell government' of Queen Mary, the restoration of the Gospel by Elizabeth I, the Northern Rising, and the 'wonderfull great reioysing of all the Godly', accompanied by bonfires and bells, that had followed the beheading of Mary, Queen of Scots. People carried around in their pockets a *vade mecum* of the seminal religious and political events of their time. The biblical and genealogical iconography of their title pages highlights once more the analogies and typologies between past and present to which contemporaries were always alive. Tellingly, these books also contain 'Godly exercises of Prayer, to bee used Morning and Evening of every housholder in their houses, or of any other privatelie'.[245] Aids to

---

[242] Dorset HC, D 53/1 (A Private Chronology of Denis Bond ESQre of Lutton in the Isle of Purbeck Made A.D. 1636 & 1640, with notes by Thomas Bond of Tyneham. Copied from his transcription by Lilian Mary Garneys Bond, 1919, with entries added by her), fos 1r, 4r, 5r, 6r, 10r, 19r, 21r.

[243] See Brodie Waddell, 'Writing History from Below: Chronicling and Record-Keeping in Early Modern England', *History Workshop Journal*, 85 (2018), 239–64, at 254.

[244] See Peter Stallybrass, Roger Chartier, J. Franklin Mowery, and Heather Wolfe, 'Hamlet's Tables and the Technologies of Writing in Renaissance England', *Shakespeare Quarterly*, 55 (2004), 379–419. Sixteen extant editions are recorded in the STC. They are also listed in the English Stock of bestsellers registered to the Stationers' Company in 1603. These competed with versions imported from the Continent and appear alongside them in provincial and metropolitan booksellers' lists.

[245] See, e.g., Frank Adams, *Writing tables with a kalender for xxiiii. Yeeres, with sundry necessarye rules* (1601; STC 26050.2); Robert Triplet, *Writing tables with a kalender for xxiiii. yeeres, with sundry necessarie rules* (1604; STC 26050.6); John Hammond, *[Writing tables with a kalender for xxiiii. Yeeeres]* ([after 1625]; STC 26050.16).

Figs. 5.8 and 5.9 Writing tables owned by Alicia Gardiner and later her son William, silver filigree binding and page with genealogical notes, late 17th century.
Source: Folger Shakespeare Library, Washington DC, MS V.a.531. Folger Digital Image Collection.

family religion and personal piety, they became particularly associated with puritans, who used them to take down shorthand sermon notes.[246]

Some surviving copies bear traces of individual lives on their paper pages and erasable vellum and graphite leaves. The Folger's copy of Frank Adams's 1580 *Writing tables* includes notes of the death of two relatives of William Deller of Royston in Hertfordshire in 1763 and 1804. Another example printed in 1598 and now kept in a dark blue leather folding case incorporates a transcription of a catechism dated 20 June 1610 and a two-page genealogy of the Cholmeley family

---

[246] Stallybrass et al., 'Hamlet's Tables', 403.

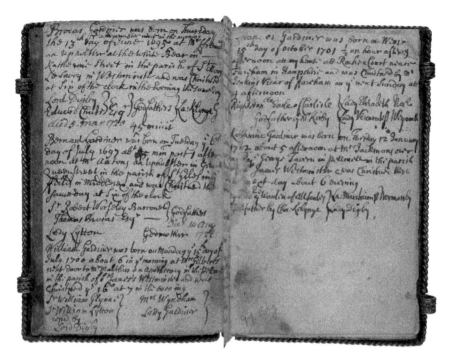

Figs. 5.8 and 5.9 Continued

between 1580 and 1601.[247] Dating from the late seventeenth century, a third copy, which still has its original stylus and is bound in exquisite silver filigree, has been used for recording the births and deaths of Alicia Gardiner's children between 1695 and 1702, together with the names of their godparents (Figs 5.8 & 5.9). She also records that her 'dear Mother departed this Life aged eighty three' and her own act of inscribing the book 'with a Pen, made with an Eagle Quill on Sunday the 9th August 1724'. Later notes by her son William include verses and death notices, notably that of his wife on 24 July 1747 at precisely '14 past 7 in the Evening'.[248] Another octavo tablet bound in leather with gold tooling is a miniature register of the Mitchell, Crosby, Moody, Ingby, and Robinson families between 1646 and 1739, the entries in which provide a poignant record of these interrelated dissenting dynasties and their living and stillborn children. One erasable page is a memorial to 'Ann Michel my Wife departed this life upon the 5 day of October 1667 & was buried the 9 day in ... the [45?] yeare of her age'.[249] These are clearly artefacts that have passed down the generations. As Peter Stallybrass and Heather Wolfe observe, they 'materialise the opposition between memory and forgetfulness', permanence and oblivion. They preserve touchingly ephemeral

---

[247] FSL, MS V. a. 480 (Writing tables, 1580?); Frank Adams, *Writing tables with a kalender for xxiiii yeeres: with sundry necessarye rules* (1598; STC 26050): FSL copy, STC 26050.

[248] FSL, MS V.a.531 (writing tables owned by Alicia Gardiner and her son, late 17th century).

[249] CL, MS I.h.52.

traces of personal lives on surfaces that could so easily have been quite literally wiped clean.[250]

Almanac-makers also left blank spaces for their purchasers to fill. Thomas Purfoot's perpetual almanac of 1566 was explicitly designed to serve as a 'memoriall' and Thomas Hill's 1571 almanac advertised itself as 'a book of memory, necessary for all such as have occasion daylie to note sundry affairs'. Others followed suit, hopeful that their products would become 'a sociable companion for evere mans pocket'.[251] As the inspiring work of Adam Smyth has shown, many were used as journals and turned into spaces in which we can see 'a culture of life-writing whose very inclusivity and taxonomical strangeness' requires us to revisit our assumptions about the nature and shape of 'autobiography' in this period. In Smyth's words, such texts thus invited their annotators and readers to 'consider, construct, and foreground their own relationship to temporality'.[252] The puritan Richard Steel turned his into a register of his sins and of the prayer meetings he had attended—a record that was subsequently used to prosecute him under the Conventicle Act.[253] The astrological diary of the Rye nonconformist Samuel Jeake was similarly annotated, though he eventually abandoned this practice 'considering that God hath blotted out as a thick Cloud my Transgressions... why should I give occasion to Man to revive the memory of that which God will remember no more'. He sanctioned his own forgetfulness by invoking the benevolent amnesia of a forgiving deity. The running list of 'material Accidents' he kept in his almanacs was part of an attempt to correlate personal events with the heavenly movements of the planets and stars and thereby discern their spiritual and eschatological significance.[254] The diary that the Presbyterian Philip Henry kept for twenty-two years in interleaved copies of Goldsmith's almanacs was written with a crow quill.[255] The eminent Independent minister of Worcester, Chewning Blackmore, used the flyleaf of his to record the dates of birth and baptism of his seven living children and one stillborn son in the 1690s and 1700s.[256]

Such impulses can found across the ecclesiastical and political spectrum. Thomas Colepeper kept a journal in his copy of George Wharton's *Calendarium*

---

[250] Stallybrass et al, 'Hamlet's Tables', p. 413.

[251] Thomas Purfoot, *A blancke & perpetuall almanack, serving as a memoriall, not only for al marchautes and occupiers...but also for any other that will make & keepe notes of any actes, deedes, or thinges that passeth from time to time (worthy of memory, to be registred)* ([1566?]; STC 401); T[homas] H[ill], *An almanack published at large, in forme of a booke of memorie necessary for all such, as have occasion daylie to note sundry affayres, eyther for receytes, payments, or such lyke* (1571; STC 454). Quotation from Thomas Bretnor, *Bretnor 1615. A newe almanacke and prognostication for the yeare of our lord God 1615* (1615; STC 420.5), 'To the courteous Reader'

[252] Adam Smyth, *Autobiography in Early Modern England* (Cambridge, 2010), pp. 1, 28, and ch.1.

[253] Capp, *Astrology*, pp. 61–2.

[254] *An Astrological Diary of the Seventeenth Century: Samuel Jeake of Rye, 1652–1699*, ed. Michael Hunter and Annabel Gregory (Oxford, 1988), pp. 98, 185.

[255] On Philip Henry, see Bedford, Davis, and Kelly, *Early Modern English Lives*, p. 30.

[256] DWL, MS 12.40, item 138.

Carolinum (1665). The image of Charles II with the words 'The 29th of May is the Restoration of the Royal Family' pasted inside it clearly indicates his political inclinations.[257] Isabella Twysden's annotations in John Booker's *Mercurius Coelicus* and other almanacs yield insight into the Civil War experiences of a gentlewoman whose husband's estates were sequestered in 1643 and include household accounts and family births and deaths. Intermingled with the military and political news of these tumultuous years, including the regicide, are notes of the babies with which she and her sister-in-law were 'brought to bed', the wet nurses she employed to suckle her infants, the son put into breeches at the age of 6, and the friends, relatives, and servants who 'left this life, for a better' one in heaven. The private rites of passage that mark her life cycle sit alongside tables of 'memorable times' from the Creation to Noah's Flood and beyond that preface the printed calendars in which she writes.[258] The modes of juxtaposition and correlation we find in Twysden's almanac diaries set a question mark beside claims that men and women date events differently and distinctively and that the latter remember the past primarily by private and domestic developments rather than public ones. The evidence assembled in this chapter suggests that contemporaries of both sexes experienced time in comparable ways. Personal occurrences were consistently apprehended in the context of current affairs.[259]

Preserved by their descendants as literary remnants, these books have defied the fate of the vast majority of almanacs, which were used to line pie dishes, light tobacco, stop mustard pots, thrown down the privy, or simply discarded. Individual memory and genealogy are repeatedly grafted onto national history in a manner that perpetuates rather than erodes habits of relative chronology and underscores the subjective and plural quality of temporality in early modern society.[260] Such texts illustrate the insight that different modes of telling time are 'not hermetically sealed but contaminate one another'.[261]

Liturgical books likewise became canvases upon which people inscribed accounts of their lives. Books of hours had long been used for this purpose, and the practice of inserting records of family births and deaths in the calendars that

---

[257] FSL, MS V.a.474 (diary for 1665, kept in interleaved copy of George Wharton, *Calendarium Carolinum* (1665; Wing A2656)).

[258] BL, Additional MS 34,169–72 (Diary of Isabella, wife of Sir Roger Twysden). Each almanac is separately foliated. See Booker, *Mercurius Coelicus* (1647), citations at fos 3r, 4r, 4v, 7r, 28r, 32r, 36r; *Pond's almanac for the yeare of our Lord Christ 1648*, fo. 24r; *Uranoscopia. Or an almanac and prognostication, being a prospective glasse for the yeare of Christ, 1649. And from the Creation, 5642* (1649), fos 3r, 8v, 17r, 29r; George Wharton, *Hemeroscopeion: a meteorological diary and prognostication for the yeere of Christ 1651* (1651), fos 12r, 14r. See also Smyth, *Autobiography*, pp. 42–54.

[259] For a discussion emphasizing how the lives of women were shaped by clock time, see Anu Korhonen, '"The Several Hours of the Day Had Variety of Employments Assigned to Them": Women's Timekeeping in Early Modern England', *Journal of Early Modern Studies*, 6 (2017), 61–85.

[260] On subjective temporality, see David Houston Wood, *Time, Narrative and Emotion in Early Modern England* (Farnham, 2009).

[261] Peter Burke, 'Reflections on the Cultural History of Time', *Viator*, 35 (2004), 617–26, at 625.

prefaced primers persisted after the break with Rome.[262] If conservatives and recusants continued to use them as family registers, so did people who became Protestants. Relieved of references to the Pope and Becket, they remained powerful touchstones of the memory of ancestors whom they piously hoped had escaped damnation despite their adherence to popery. Bridging the divide wrought by the Reformation, one late fourteenth-century illuminated book of hours manufactured in Bruges includes the birthdates and obits of members of the Roberts family of Middlesex inserted by successive generations between the years 1508 and 1531 and 1550 and 1574. It illustrates how this dynasty navigated the religious revolution and gradually made the transition to the Protestant faith.[263]

Another item in which liturgical and personal timelines are blurred is a Sarum primer of *c*.1500 owned by the Yorkshireman Thomas Wakefield, first Regius Professor of Hebrew at Cambridge, who took his BA in 1523 and was instituted to this chair in 1540. Like the slippery master of Peterhouse, Andrew Perne, Wakefield seems to have been a conformist who clung covertly to the Catholic faith until his death in 1575. Into the calendar he has inserted various bits of genealogical information, including the birth of his father on the eve of the nativity of the Blessed Virgin 1500, of himself, his sister Alisia, and his son Thomas in November, as well as the death of his wife Anna. This book successfully navigated religious change, just like its owner.[264] A further revealing survival is a printed Salisbury primer produced in Paris in the very year of the proclamation of the Royal Supremacy, 1534. Dutifully censored, with its indulgences struck out, but still retaining its stitched-in, hand-coloured woodcuts, it contains scattered memoranda relating to the Constable family of the East Riding of Yorkshire, which suffered much for its recusancy in the later sixteenth and seventeenth centuries (Fig. 5.10).[265] The practice of using prayer books to record life cycle events persisted in the late Stuart Catholic community. York Minster Library's copy of William Clifford's *Little manual of the poor mans daily devotion*, combined with the *Jesus Psalter* (1687), was once owned by a certain William Brown, who noted his marriage on 9 May 1699 and prayed that God would send him and his wife 'Both Long Life' and the ability to 'live contentedly together'. He hoped that 'when the belle tolls for him', the Lord would 'have mercy oon his sowll'. A liturgical guide to the private devotions that Catholics were compelled to

---

[262] For one among many examples, see BL, MS Harley 935 (Latin book of hours, with notes and prayers in English in the margins, written by John Brygandyn, including details of his two marriages *c*.1537 and 1546).

[263] CUL, MS Ii.vi.2 (The 'Roberts Hours', Flemish, late 14th/early 15th century), esp. fo. 109v. On the Roberts family and their books, see Margaret Connolly, *Sixteenth-Century Readers, Fifteenth-Century Books: Continuities of Reading in the English Reformation* (Cambridge, 2019).

[264] FSL, MS V. a. 228 (Book of hours, Sarum use, *c*.1500), fos iir–v, ivr, 1r, 4v, 6r.

[265] *Thys prymer of Salysbury use* (Paris, 1534; STC 15985): LPL, [ZZ] 1534.46.

Fig. 5.10 Devotional woodcut of the Virgin breastfeeding the infant Jesus stitched into *Thys prymer of Salysbury use* (Paris, 1534), owned by the Constable family of the East Riding of Yorkshire.

Source: © Lambeth Palace Library, London, [ZZ] 1534.46. Bridgeman Images.

conduct in the comparative safety of their homes, this text is another archive of memory and prayer.[266]

Books of Common Prayer were frequently annotated in similar ways. In a quarto edition of 1603 the Gloucestershire man Robert Adeane and his children and grandchildren have entered records of their offspring in the margins of the liturgies for baptism and matrimony extending from *c.*1640 to 1779 (Fig. 5.11). Next to the order for burial is a catalogue of mortality listing the deaths of seven of Matthew Adeane's nine children, including two infant sons, both named Robert, four years apart in 1740 and 1744.[267] A later post-Restoration edition of 1675 contains notes by Thomas, Lord Pelham, of the births of his ten children, the last of whom, Margaret, born in 1700, inherited it in 1712. Continuing the tradition, she recorded on the flyleaf her mother's death, her marriage in 1753, and the birth of two sons, and later the arrival of five grandchildren (Arthur, Cranley,

---

[266] W[illiam] C[lifford], *A little manual of the poor mans daily devotion, collected out of several pious and approved authors. In which are added, the Jesus Psalter, with a Litany of our Saviours passion; as also A treatise of the devotion of the beads and rosary…* (4th edition, 1687; Wing C4714A): York Minster Library, East Harsley 183. For an inspiring study, see Virginia Reinburg, *French Books of Hours: Making an Archive of Prayer, c.1400–1600* (Cambridge, 2012).

[267] *The booke of common Prayer* (1603; STC 16325 or 16326): YML shelfmark XVII/3.C.24. See also https://exhibitions.lib.cam.ac.uk/reformation/artifacts/common-prayer-the-time-of-the-living/, accessed 6 June 2022, and https://exhibitions.lib.cam.ac.uk/reformation/artifacts/common-prayer-a-catalogue-of-mortality/, accessed 6 June 2022.

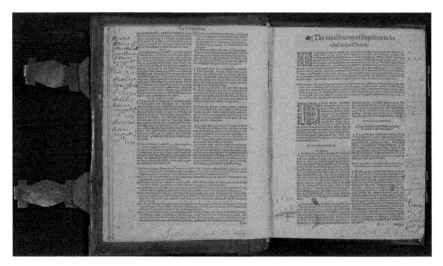

Fig. 5.11 Family notes of the Adeane family in the margins of the liturgy for baptism in *The boke of common praier* (London, 1603).
Source: York Minster Library XVII/3.C.24.

Manwaring, Harriet, and Georgina) between 1777 and 1783.[268] In a Geneva bible which belonged to the Morgan family of Rhymney in Monmouthshire family in 1775 genealogical notes are found on the blank page preceding the New Testament, the margins of which include scribbled references to John Wyclif ('an Eminent Divine'), John Hus ('A Famous Person among the Reformers'), and John Bunyan ('a Great Writer Author of Pilgrims Progress when in a prison'). At the end has been written a chronological account of events before the birth of Christ, which trawls through familiar scriptural landmarks before noting 'Martin Luther first Confutes Popery 1517' and 'England Seperates from the Church of Rome 1536.'[269] Once again these are texts in which individual and collective memory and biblical, religious, and family time merge. Reflecting the dual biological and historical meanings of the word 'generation' in early modern culture, they underline the interconnections between the idea of the ages of man and the concept of the ages of the world.

If prayers books and bibles became portable repositories of individual and social memory, so could other volumes that were treasured in Protestant homes. Mark Rankin has recently discovered a remarkable copy of Foxe's *Actes and monuments* which was turned into a Reformation miscellany by successive

---

[268] *The book of Common Prayer, and administration of the sacraments, and other rites and ceremonies, of the Church of England* (Oxford, 1675; Wing B3644): CUL, SPCK.4.1675.1.

[269] *The holy Bible, containing the Old Testament and the New with annotations and parallel Scriptures: to which is annex'd the harmony of the Gospels: as also, the reduction of the Jewish weights, coins and measures, to our English standards: and a table of the promises in Scripture by Samuel Clark* (1690; Wing B2354): NLW, Additional MS 1120E. The annotations regarding the reformers are on sigs N2r, Rr2r, Ss3r.

members of the Graile family for the benefit of their posterity. Preserving genealogical records alongside prose and verse transcriptions and engraved prints, the
material appended to it updates the Foxean narrative of martyrdom and providential deliverance to include the Blackfriars accident and the puritan triumvirate
of Prynne, Bastwick, and Burton. Largely the work of Edmund Graile, a
Gloucester physician, it memorializes the godly zeal of his father, who bought the
book in 1584 for 40 shillings, and glosses over the 'superstitious superscription'
on the tomb of his great-grandfather Thomas requesting intercessions for his soul.
It brings together history and biography, remembering and forgetting, to create a
malleable textual artefact that serves as a vehicle for the transmission of memory.[270]

One last sphere in which these processes can be detected at work is the realm
of material culture. Things not only have life cycles and social lives but are themselves biographical in the sense that they help to tell stories about people and
their experiences through time. Forging and synchronizing relationships within
and across generations, objects further illuminate the recurrent entangling of
evolving narratives about the distant and recent religious past with genealogy and
piety. Janet Hoskins situates them on a continuum that extends from gifts to commodities and sees them as possessions that are saturated with the histories of the
people who owned, used and then bequeathed them to their children and
grandchildren, brothers, sisters, nieces, nephews, and cousins. Roberta Gilchrist
writes of the 'distinctive agency that stems from their interactions with life course
rituals' and of the emotional recollections and temporal responses that they
evoke: 'a memory of the past, but also a sense of belonging in the present and a
connection to the future'. In the process, they come to be perceived as having 'a
blood relationship' to the specific family group with which they are linked.[271]

The many dated objects that survive from this period materialize the multiple
temporalities this chapter has examined. From earthenware vessels bearing the
message 'FAST AND PRAY 1650' to pieces of bespoke furniture, they offer insight
into how men and women experienced the passage of time. They encouraged
regimes of daily penitence and reminded people of life cycle events that their construction commemorated. Linked to seasonal and ecclesiastical rituals, such as
the giving of presents at New Year and to mark christenings and nuptials, their
diachronic movement through time, as they passed down the generations, helped
prompt awareness of the connections between past, present, and future.[272] They

[270] Mark Rankin, 'The Ridley Hall Foxe (1583) as a Reformation Miscellany', *Transactions of the Cambridge Bibliographical Society*, 16 (2018), 371–400.
[271] Janet Hoskins, *Biographical Objects: How Things Tell the History of People's Lives* (New York, 1998); Roberta Gilchrist, *Archaeology and the Life Course* (Woodbridge, 2012), pp. 11–13, 242–51, quotations at 243–4, 248.
[272] See the excellent work of Sophie Cope, 'Marking the New Year: Dated Objects and the Materiality of Time in Early Modern England', *Journal of Early Modern Studies*, 6 (2017), 89–111; *eadem*, 'Women in the Sea of Time: Domestic Dated Objects in Seventeenth-Century England', in Merry E. Wiesner-Hanks (ed.), *Gendered Temporalities in the Early Modern World* (Amsterdam, 2018), pp. 47–68. On the temporality of objects, see also George Kubler, *The Shape of Time: Remarks on the*

charted the turn of the life cycle as well as the linear progression of years. Some even celebrated events that were subsequently buried in oblivion, including an unusual brass warming pan dating from the era of the English Republic inscribed 'GOD BEE ON OUR SIDE AMEN 1651'.[273]

Ceramic cradles are among the items by which births and baptisms were marked, while a girdle decorated with part of the text of Proverbs 31 and dated 1698 celebrates the role of women as faithful mothers, wives, and keepers of the household. This was worn by the Quaker Rebecca Egleton and probably given to her on her wedding day.[274] Many delftware chargers painted with the popular scriptural motif of the Temptation of Adam and Eve bear the initials of the couples whose marriages they commemorated (Fig. 5.12). A plate decorated with the story of the Prodigal Son was made to mark the wedding of Robert Gray and Anne Law in St Saviour's Southwark on 23 January 1659/60.[275] Other inherited objects served as remembrancers of the dead people who had created them: relatives of Dame Dorothy Selby, the 'Dorcas' whose nimble fingers stitched a sampler showing Samuel Ward's *Double deliverance* print, had the same scene incised in slate on the funeral monument erected in Ightham parish church in Kent following her death in 1641. In turn the needlework itself became a carrier and vessel of religious sentiment and memory.[276] The identity of the A W whose initials appear on the base of a delftware wall panel depicting the monument erected to the Great Fire of London of 1666 cannot now be ascertained, but this artefact fuses recollection of a personal event with recollection of a public one widely supposed to have been a dastardly act of Catholic arson (Fig. 5.13). It connects an individual rite of passage with an episode in the unfolding saga of the English Protestant state.[277]

A final item depicting a simplified version of 'The Candle is Lighted' print discussed in Chapter 4 is of Dutch provenance. Here a quartet of reformers (Luther, Calvin, Wyclif, and Beza) watch the Pope and his minions try to blow out the candle of the Gospel to envelop the world in darkness once again. The generation that ushered in the Reformation has been reduced to a foursome. On the back are inscribed the names Jan van Dieninge and Jannetie van Wynbergen and the year 1692, together with the tools of their trades as a tailor and a button-maker. Probably made to commemorate the twelfth anniversary of their marriage in

---

History of Things (New Haven, CT, 1962); Jonathan Gil Harris, 'Shakespeare's Hair: Staging the Object of Material Culture', *Shakespeare Quarterly*, 52 (2001), 479–91.

[273] Malcolm Jones, 'Inscriptions Recorded on English Seventeenth-Century Brass Warming Pans', *Journal of the Antique Metalware Society*, 25 (2020), 90–103, at 92.

[274] Town and McShane (eds), *Marking Time*, pp. 112, 115, 381.   [275] BM, 1888,1110.17.

[276] This item is now preserved in preserved in a private collection in Cardiff, but reproduced in J. L. Nevinson, 'English Domestic Embroidery Patterns of the Sixteenth and Seventeenth Centuries', *Walpole Society*, 28 (1939–40), 10 and pi. VI (b). Edward R. Harrison, *The History and Records of Ightham Church* (Oxford, 1932), 16–18. A drawing of the incised slab is reproduced at the back. See also Walsham, *Providence*, pp. 261–2.

[277] Fitz., C.1368–1928. See Michael Archer, *Delftware in the Fitzwilliam Museum* (Cambridge, 2013), p. 343.

Fig. 5.12 Delftware dish depicting the temptation of Adam and Eve, probably commissioned as a marriage gift (Pickleherring pottery, 1635).
Source: © Victoria and Albert Museum, London, C.26-1931.

1680 or perhaps his election as an officer of his Amsterdam guild, it intertwines private remembrance of an important personal event with public remembrance of an international movement that permanently ruptured medieval Christendom.[278] Bringing the past into the present, it is an object that establishes a tangible link between the people it commemorates and those to whom it was surely bequeathed as an heirloom.

---

[278] BM, 1891,0224.3. On this item, see Alexandra Walsham, 'Domesticating the Reformation: Material Culture, Memory and Confessional Identity in Early Modern England', *RQ*, 69 (2016), 566–616.

Fig. 5.13 Delftware wall panel depicting the Monument to the Great Fire of London 1666, dated 1738, with initials A W (London, 1738).
Source: © The Fitzwilliam Museum, Cambridge, C.1368–1928.

Relative, elastic and flexible, 'generation' was a vital piece of vocabulary for describing the unfolding of time in early modern England. This chapter has sought to interrogate the connections between the Reformation, the practice of history, and ideas about chronology and temporality. It has traced the process by which the religious revolution of the sixteenth century came to be classified as a watershed event and as an epoch in its own right and argued that its recognition as a distinct stage in human history helped not merely to forge conscious senses of generational identity but also to create models of periodization that still prevail today. These processes occurred alongside others that pulled in different directions. We need to see them in a context in which the word 'Reformation' carried multiple meanings and in which ambiguity regarding both its birthdate and its end point was as persistent as it was resilient. This chapter has investigated when and why the Reformation acquired its name and the ways in which religious change fostered eschatological and providential, linear and analogical thinking about time and about the relationship between the past, the present, and the future simultaneously. It has also begun the task of examining how people in early modern England perceived the theological and cultural upheavals in which they were embroiled and the complex and unpredictable ways in which these were remembered, reinvented, and recounted in subsequent generations. It has shown how historical and liturgical temporalities continued to coexist and how these were entangled with the idiosyncratic timelines created by private recollection. Chapter 6 further investigates the relationship between the family, cultural memory, and the libraries, museums, and archives in which the materials for writing the history of the English Reformations now reside.

6

Memory and Archive

Memory is central to the making of generations. Created retrospectively through processes of selective recollection and strategic amnesia, they are artefacts of an imagined past. Simultaneously, however, they are projections of hopes and dreams about the future. Forged by intense experiences of change and rupture, they serve to crystallize distinctive social identities, which twist and turn as they travel through time. Chapter 5 traced how England's dynamic, erratic, and protracted Reformation was publicly recognized as a historic event and became entwined with personal recollection of key junctures in the human life cycle. Reversing the angle of vision, this chapter explores how contemporaries remembered its successive phases and how they recorded and conveyed these memories to their posterity. It combines discussion of the manner in which previous generations were commemorated with investigation of the imperatives that led people to leave oral, written, and material legacies for their heirs. It investigates the changing memory of the Reformations alongside the way in which the Reformations themselves decisively remoulded memory.[1]

Generations are prime examples of what Pierre Nora famously called '*lieux de mémoire*': they are sites 'where memory secretes itself and blocks the work of forgetting'.[2] In the words of Astrid Erll, they serve as 'a kind of switchboard between individual memory and larger frames of collective remembrance'.[3] How historical actors remember is ineluctably shaped by their cultural environment. But the stories and scripts this engenders also become part of the repertoire of discourses, practices, and expectations of the communities of which they are members, in a process of continuous interplay and cross-fertilization.[4] The

---

[1] See Peter Sherlock, 'The Reformation of Memory in Early Modern Europe', in Susannah Radstone and Bill Schwarz (eds), *Memories: Histories, Theories, Debates* (New York, 2011), pp. 30–40; Bruce Gordon, 'History and Memory', in Ulinka Rublack (ed.), *The Oxford Handbook of the Protestant Reformations* (Oxford, 2016), pp. 765–86; Alexandra Walsham, Bronwyn Wallace, Ceri Law, and Brian Cummings (eds), *Memory and the English Reformation* (Cambridge, 2020), esp. Introduction.

[2] Pierre Nora, 'Between Memory and History: Les Lieux de mémoire', *Representations*, 26 (1989), 7–24, at 7.

[3] Astrid Erll, 'Locating the Family in Cultural Memory Studies', *Journal of Comparative Family Studies*, 42 (2011), 303–18, at 315. See also Maurice Halbwachs, 'The Collective Memory of the Family', in idem, *On Collective Memory*, trans. Lewis A. Coser (Chicago, 1992), ch. 5; Bradd Shore and Sara Kauko, 'The Landscape of Family Memory', in Brady Wagoner (ed.), *Handbook of Culture and Memory* (Oxford, 2018), pp. 85–116.

[4] Within a large literature, the following may be highlighted: Maurice Halbwachs, *The Collective Memory*, trans. Francis J. Ditter and Vida Yazdi Ditter (New York 1980); idem, *On Collective Memory*; James Fentress and Chris Wickham, *Social Memory* (Oxford, 1992); Barbara A. Misztal, *Theories of*

discussion that follows builds upon Jan and Aleida Assmann's influential work on the shift from communicative to cultural memory, a process spanning the eighty to a hundred years in which three generations coexist.[5] It probes how remembrance of religious developments mutated as the testimony of eyewitnesses who told stories to their children and grandchildren was gradually superseded by inherited recollections stored in traditions, texts, and objects handed down as heirlooms. In placing these practices under the microscope, I contest the suggestion that memory settles into abstract, institutionalized patterns as it passes from the realm of first-hand knowledge and lived experience. On the contrary, I emphasize the many ways in which successive generations maintained intimate connections with their dead ancestors and their unborn descendants, partially repairing the rupture in the fabric of time wrought by the Tudor Reformation.[6]

A further aim is to contribute to the surge of recent work on the history, genealogy, and ethnography of the archive. As we shall see, families of faith and blood were deeply implicated in ensuring the survival of the corpus of books, manuscripts, and artefacts historians use to reconstruct the early modern past and to analyse the 'long shadow' it casts.[7] Agents of erasure and oblivion as well as conservation, generations, understood as both biological units and social cohorts, were critical actors in the formation of our understanding of the immediate impact and complex repercussions of the English Reformations.

Commemorating the Departed

We begin with the vexed question of commemorating the dead. The Henrician, Edwardian, and Elizabethan Reformations involved a concerted assault on traditional memorial cultures. By repudiating the existence of purgatory and rejecting the efficacy of post-mortem prayer, Protestantism not only severed the lines of communication between this world and the next; it also demoted memory from its traditional status as a salvific act. Dismissing intercession for family and friends as pointless and futile, it eliminated the sense of collective responsibility

Social Remembering (Maidenhead and Philadelphia, PA, 2003); Geoffrey Cubitt, History and Memory (Manchester, 2007), chs 2–3; Astrid Erll, Memory in Culture, trans. Sara B. Young (Basingstoke, 2011); Judith Pollmann, Memory in Early Modern Europe (Oxford, 2017), esp. ch. 1.

[5] Jan Assmann, 'Collective Memory and Cultural Identity', trans. John Czaplicka, New German Critique, 65 (1995), 125–33; idem, 'Communicative and Cultural Memory', in Astrid Erll and Angsar Nünning (eds), Cultural Memory Studies: An International and Interdisciplinary Handbook (Berlin, 2008), pp. 109–18. See also the critical discussion in Erll, Memory in Culture, pp. 28–33. This distinction was also implicit in Karl Mannheim, 'The Problem of Generations', in idem, Essays on the Sociology of Knowledge: Collected Works, ed. Paul Keeskemeti, vol. v, (1952), p. 296.

[6] For a similar line of argument, see Rachel L. Greenblatt, To Tell Their Children: Jewish Communal Memory in Early Modern Prague (Stanford, CA, 2014), pp. 190–1.

[7] Aleida Assmann, Der lange Schatten der Vergangenheit: Erinnerungskultur und Geschichtspolitik (Munich, 2006).

for speeding the path of departed souls to the afterlife that had underpinned the medieval Catholic arts of memorialization. Institutions dedicated to ritually and liturgically remembering them—monasteries, chantries, guilds and confraternities—were dismantled, leaving behind a vacuum. At a stroke, the dead were consigned to an absent past to which grieving relatives no longer had access.[8]

Against this backdrop, the meaning and purpose of commemorating the dead was fundamentally recalibrated. Ubiquitous on pre-Reformation brasses and tombstones, the Latin and English invocations '*ora pro nobis*' ('pray for us'), '*orate pro anima*' ('pray for the soul') and '*cuius anime propicietur deus*' ('on whose soul may God have mercy') became regarded as dangerous invitations to idolatry. Monuments that offered indulgences were particularly provocative embodiments of 'popish' doctrine, and the ecclesiastical authorities ordered the obliteration of these formulae. The many memorials that survived the onslaught, however, demonstrate that the campaign to eradicate them was neither systematic nor comprehensive. One mid fourteenth-century monument in Yorkshire takes the form of a tree of Jesse celebrating the union of John de Heslerton and Margery de Lowthorpe, as well as the chantry priests commissioned to sing for their souls. Their tonsured heads sprout from its branches alongside those of their offspring in an unusual illustration of the bond of charity that linked the living and the dead.[9] A large altar tomb constructed at Cookham in Berkshire around 1510 called upon bystanders to show compassion towards Robert Pecke, the former Master Clerk of the royal spicery, and his spouse Agnes. Above their engraved effigies God the Father sits in the guise of an old man holding Christ crucified, with a hovering dove completing the Trinity. The touching plea that emanates from the mouth of Agnes is '*Virgo dei digne... esto benigna*' ('Virgin worthy of God... be kind').[10] The fact that many medieval monuments omit the date of death has been interpreted as evidence that the deceased were perceived as still being present, albeit now on a journey to another place.[11] Parish churches remained 'a complex indoor landscape of memory' within which traditional incentives to the perpetual remembrance of Catholic ancestors and predecessors lingered for decades.[12]

Elizabeth I's proclamation of 1560 condemned the 'barbarous disorder' of those who mutilated such structures because it 'extinguished' and 'darkened' the honour of the noble and gentry families they commemorated. It legitimated the role of memorials as vehicles of genealogy, even as it decried the 'false feigned

---

[8] See Chapter 4 above, pp. 258–60.

[9] Jessica Barker, 'Invention and Commemoration in Fourteenth-Century England: A Monumental "Family Tree" at the Collegiate Church of St Martin, Lowthorpe', *Gesta*, 56 (2017), 105–28.

[10] H. T. Morley, *Monumental Brasses of Berkshire (14th to 17th Century)* (Reading, 1924), p. 87.

[11] See Jonathan Finch, 'A Reformation of Meaning: Commemoration and Remembering the Dead in the Parish Church, 1450–1640', in David Gaimster and Roberta Gilchrist (eds), *The Archaeology of the Reformation 1480–1580* (Leeds, 2003), pp. 437–49, at p. 441.

[12] Eamon Duffy, 'The End of it All: The Material Culture of the Late Medieval Parish and the 1552 Inventories of Church Goods', in *idem*, *Saints, Sacrilege and Sedition: Religion and Conflict in the Tudor Reformations* (2012), pp. 109–29, at p. 110.

images' that led the unwary astray. It walked the precarious tightrope between acceptable memory and soul-destroying error created by the English Reformation. An Edwardian statute dated January 1550 similarly exempted from the mandate for removing 'monuments of idolatry' any picture 'set or grave upon any tomb' serving to remember 'a king, prince, nobleman or other dead person, which hath not been commonly reputed and taken for a saint', saying that they could 'stand and continue in like manner and form as if this act had never been...made'.[13] Memorial brasses on which promises of pardons have been neatly crossed out, leaving the portraiture intact, are emblematic of the dilemmas surrounding the commemoration of past generations that confronted those who lived through the tumultuous decades of the mid-sixteenth century.

Determined to preserve vestiges of the past they feared might be lost, an emerging breed of antiquaries lamented the casualties of mid-Tudor iconoclasm. John Stow's laborious *Survey of London* (1598) partly functions as an inventory of the epitaphs to the city's worthies encased in its ecclesiastical buildings. He prudently omitted inscriptions that the onset of Protestantism had rendered theologically offensive, but he could not hide his regret about monuments that had been 'utterly defaced' and 'plucked up', whether 'of a preposterous zeale' or 'a greedie minde', including the 'faire Tombe' of his own godmother, Margaret Dickson, at St Michael's Crooked Lane. He excluded the names of people who had 'bin the defacers of the monuments of others' from his catalogue, thinking them 'worthy to be deprived of that memory whereof they have injuriously robbed others'.[14] Those who defamed the honourable dead deserved to be erased from the written record themselves.

John Weever's *Ancient funerall monuments* (1631) was the most ambitious attempt to salvage this threatened cultural heritage. This textual mausoleum was filled with transcriptions and depictions of traditional memorials, which he anticipated 'some may say might have beene as well left out of my booke, as they are in many places scraped out of the brasse'. Among them was the monument to Katerin and Thomas Semar, Walter Coke, and Roger Pirke, founders of a chantry at Saffron Walden, for whose 'soulys' parishioners were requested to 'sey a Pater noster and an Ave'. In the case of Stoke by Nayland in Suffolk, he reproduced the void left after the figures had been 'impiously stolen away', though the incriminating petition surrounding them, '*Orate pro animabus*', remained.[15]

[13] Paul L. Hughes and James F. Larkin (eds), *Tudor Royal Proclamations*, 3 vols (New Haven, CT, 1964–9), vol. ii, pp. 146–7. For the Act, see 3 & 4 Edward VI, c. 10.

[14] John Stow, *A survey of London contayning the originall, antiquity, increase, moderne estate, and description of that citie, written in the yeare 1598* (1598; STC 23341), pp. 350–1, 153–4, 167, 162; John Bruce (ed.), *Diary of John Manningham, of the Middle Temple, and of Bradbourne, Kent, barrister-at-law, 1602–1603*, CS, OS 99 (1868), p. 103. Many more inscriptions were included in the 1633 edition of the *Survay*.

[15] John Weever, *Ancient funerall monuments with in the united monarchie of Great Britaine, Ireland and the islands adjacent* (1631; STC 25223), p. 51, sig. A2r, pp. 54, 625, 773.

Some took pre-emptive action to protect their memory from thieves and enraged radicals: the will of Archbishop Samuel Harsnett required that his monumental brass be 'riveted and fastened clear through the stone, as sacrilegious hands may not render off the one without breaking the other'.[16] Meanwhile, the spasms of holy violence carried out by William Dowsing and Parliamentary soldiers in the early 1640s reflected ongoing anxiety that material structures were obstacles to the internalization of reformed teaching regarding death and salvation. 'Superstitious letters' on brasses were specifically targeted for erasure in this period.[17] In turn, antiquaries renewed their efforts 'to continue the remembrance of the defunct to future posteritie' by retrieving the splinters that had survived the 'shipwreck' of the Reformation and Revolution, together with the depredations wrought by time, which itself was understood as an iconoclast.[18] Peter Marshall suggests that such books served as 'almost a surrogate for those unpronounceable prayers' banned by the reformers a century before.[19]

Protestants were reluctant to cut themselves off from relatives who had lived in the dark time of popery. As we saw in Chapter 4, sentiment inspired a process of benevolent forgetting that sanitized the memory of misguided forebears and posthumously baptized them into the select ranks of those predestined to be saved. Some physically translated monuments into locations less compromised by their connection with the defunct institutions of the monastery and chantry. After the break with Rome the brass of the pious Bristol merchant Geoffrey Barbur, who died in 1417, was relocated from the local abbey to St Helen's, Abingdon.[20] Aristocratic women played a key role in 'the sepulchural musical chairs provoked by the Dissolution': Agnes Howard, dowager duchess of Norfolk was the driving force behind the shift of the family mausoleum from Thetford Priory to Framlingham and Lambeth.[21] Others devised new epitaphs in keeping with a new ideological climate hostile to vicarious prayer. The memory of the Catholic dead was reconfigured to enable the living to continue to recall them with love and pride and to reconstitute families fractured by the Henrician schism.

As Norman Jones has remarked, 'Every family tree was full of people who had lived in times of superstition, duped by the Devil and Antichrist into following

[16] Cited in Nigel Llewellyn, *Funeral Monuments in Post-Reformation England* (Cambridge, 2000), p. 261.

[17] Trevor Cooper, 'Brass, Glass and Crosses: Identifying Iconoclasm outside the Journal', in *idem*, (ed.), *The Journal of William Dowsing: Iconoclasm in East Anglia during the English Civil War* (Woodbridge, 2001), pp. 89–106, at pp. 101–5.

[18] Weever, *Ancient funerall monuments*, 'The Author to the Reader'. On time as an iconoclast, see Philip Schwyzer, 'Fallen Idols, Broken Noses: Defacement and Memory after the Reformation', *Memory Studies*, 11 (2018), 21–35, at 29.

[19] Marshall, *Beliefs and the Dead*, p. 308.   [20] Morley, *Monumental Brasses of Berkshire*, p. 19.

[21] Nicola Clark, 'The Gendering of Dynastic Memory: Burial Choices of the Howards, 1485–1559', *JEH*, 68 (2017), 747–65, at 760. On women as agents of family commemoration, see also Stephanie Thomson and Katie Barclay, 'Religious Patronage as Gendered Family Memory in Sixteenth-Century England', *Journal of Family History*, 46 (2021), 13–29.

the damnable Catholic religion.'[22] Ways had to be found to accommodate those who had entered religious orders and invested in traditional mechanisms for saving their souls. Gentlemen were loath to exclude generous benefactors from their lineages. The pedigree of the Roos family of Leicestershire records a fourteenth-century pilgrim who died en route to Jerusalem at Paphos, while a genealogical account of the Brydges family describes the 'extraordinary Devotion and Piety' of an eleventh-century forebear with striking equanimity, noting that he had founded the Abbey of St Peter and Paul in Shrewsbury and three other houses in Normandy and been 'shorne a Monk' before his death in 1094. Details of the trental and obit endowed for the spiritual welfare of a sixteenth-century ancestor and his wife, parents, and children, were supplied, together with the bequests of vestments and linen he made to his parish church at Dymock in the Forest of Dean in 1530.[23] Dating from the 1630s, the elaborately illustrated Lyte family tree includes drawings of the funeral monument of Dame Joan Wadam, who died in 1557, replete with the rosary beads that adorned her effigy. Also depicted is the memorial to one of her children, Anthony, a gentleman usher at the court of Elizabeth I, 'whome God graunt a joyfull Resurrrection', inscribed 28 January 1579. Prioritizing continuity of blood over purity of religion, this impressive document shows how one dynasty managed the memory of its passage into the post-Reformation era.[24]

Families adapted their memorial strategies in response to the official abolition of purgatory. The memorial erected to Elizabeth Cheyne of Chesham Bois, Buckinghamshire, who expired in 1516, called for intercession for her soul. The plate added below in memory of her husband Robert, who lived until 1552, reflected a shift in objective and mood: it asked 'All Christian people' to 'gyve thanks' for his 'godly dep[ar]ture' and commended his spirit to 'Gods infinite marcy'.[25] The adjacent monuments to the two Thomas Garrards of Lambourne in Berkshire, who died in 1530 and 1619, illustrate the same transition. The former is designed to stimulate spiritual compassion; the latter records the erection of the marble tomb as a retrospective act of remembrance by a grieving son.[26]

Other funeral monuments reflect the impact of the Renaissance quest for fame and their transformation into vehicles for crafting post-mortem reputation. They

[22] Norman Jones, *The English Reformation: Religion and Cultural Adaptation* (Oxford, 2002), p. 42, and see also pp. 40–50.
[23] HEHL, Stowe Temple Brydges papers, Personal Box 10, folder 8, pp. 5, 10.
[24] Somerset HC, DD/X/LY/1 (Pedigree of the Lyte family, 13th–16th centuries). See above, pp. 200–1.
[25] Cited in Peter Sherlock, *Monuments and Memory in Early Modern England* (Aldershot, 2008), p. 105. On the function of post-Reformation monuments as exemplars for the living, see Richard Rex, 'Monumental Brasses and the Reformation', *Transactions of the Monumental Brass Society*, 14 (1990), pp. 376–94; Nigel Llewellyn, 'Honour in Life, Death and in the Memory: Funeral Monuments in Early Modern England', *TRHS*, 6th ser., 6 (1996), 179–200; *idem, Funeral Monuments in Post-Reformation England* (Cambridge, 2000), esp. ch. 5.
[26] Morley, *Monumental Brasses of Berkshire*, p. 149.

attest to the process by which the medium was decontaminated of 'the asbestos dust of intercessory prayer' and remodelled to articulate the eschatological beliefs of the reformed Church of England.[27] Inscriptions ceased to be pleas for mercy to past sinners and became '*curriculum vitae* of rewarding and industrious lives.'[28] Protestantism redirected attention from the task of safeguarding the fate of the dead towards upholding them as models for emulation. Some celebrate the 'true justifying faith' that will allow the departed loved one to ascend to heaven and abide 'in blisse... with Prophets & with Patriarkes, in faithfull Abram's brest'. The verse on a brass to Elizabeth Bligh of Finchampstead dated 1635 reads: 'I know that Chris Jesus my Redemer liveth by whose meritts & abundant mercies towards me I have an assured hope of everlasting salvacion.'[29] This is the vocabulary of justification by faith and predestination.

People of humbler means had to find other ways of commemorating their kith and kin. Scratched inscriptions on the limewashed walls of parish churches perpetuate a medieval tradition of 'prayers made solid in stone'. Surviving graffiti enables us to hear the lost voices of ordinary people mourning dead children, relatives, and friends, determined to prevent them from being forgotten. Some provide a simple record of names; others take the form of miniature gravestones with dates and initials. At Stansfield in Suffolk a neatly written sentence that wraps itself around one of the pillars declares 'J F Died the forst day of February 1708.' These ad hoc epitaphs are a neglected dimension of the early modern arts of remembrance.[30]

Such memorials provide evidence of the emotional ties that continued to bind the living and the dead. They compel us to rethink the prevailing paradigm of divorce and consider the implications of this couple 'continuing to live under the same roof'.[31] Sculptures of husbands and wives surrounded by their children kneeling devoutly in prayer not merely fossilize the ideals about the spiritualized household explored in Chapter 2 (Fig. 6.1); they also illustrate the fertility of particular lineages. A prominent seventeenth-century monument to Sir Amyas Bampfylde in North Molton in Devon incorporates his mourning widow and seventeen offspring.[32] Others reconstitute complex stepfamilies. In many examples husbands are reunited with their first and second wives in an arrangement that

---

[27] Marshall, *Beliefs and the Dead*, p. 265.   [28] Finch, 'Reformation of Meaning', p. 443.

[29] Morley, *Monumental Brasses of Berkshire*, pp. 165, 235, 115.

[30] Matthew Champion, *Medieval Graffiti: The Lost Voices of England's Churches* (2015), pp. 194–6, 202–3, 209–10, 214. See also Juliet Fleming, *Graffiti and the Writing Arts of Early Modern England* (2001), p. 36.

[31] Sherlock, *Monuments and Memory*, ch. 4, esp. pp. 126–7; Marshall, *Beliefs and the Dead*, ch. 7, at p. 294.

[32] I owe my knowledge of the Bampflyde monument to Claire Donovan. On these monuments, see M. Bryan Curd, 'Constructing Family Memory: Three English Funeral Monuments and Patriarchy in the Early Modern Period', in Rosalynn Voaden and Diane Wolfthal (eds), *Framing the Family: Narrative and Representation in the Medieval and Early Modern Periods* (Tempe, AZ, 2005), pp. 273–92; Peter Sherlock, 'Patriarchal Memory: Monuments in Early Modern England', in Megan

Fig. 6.1 Lineage in stone: Monument to Sir George Manners and family, after 1623.
Source: All Saints church, Bakewell, Derbyshire. Celuici/Creative Commons CCO 1.0. Universal Public Domain Dedication.

smacks ever so slightly of bigamy, even as it highlights the enduring presence of former spouses in the minds of those who survived them (Fig. 6.2).[33] A brass erected in remembrance of Simon Burton, wax chandler and citizen of the parish of St Andrew Undershaft in London, by his 'loveing daugter' Alice Coldock in 1593 portrayed both his two spouses, Ann and Elizabeth, and their issue.[34] Widows often chose to be buried with their first husbands or the father of their first child or son.[35] Some monuments commemorated mothers who perished in childbirth, occasionally in the very beds in which they took their last breath, as in

Cassidy-Welch and Peter Sherlock (eds), *Practices of Gender in Late Medieval and Early Modern Europe* (2008), pp. 279–300.

[33] For the monument to Sir William Gee, 1611 see https://exhibitions.lib.cam.ac.uk/reformation/ artifacts/o-bright-example-for-the-future-age-a-funeral-monument-to-sir-william-gee-1611/, accessed 7 June 2022.

[34] London Metropolitan Archives, rubbing of 1593 brass to Simon Burton in the church of St Andrew Undershaft, made *c.*1820: https://www.alamy.com/brass-rubbing-from-the-church-of-st-andrew-undershaft-leadenhall-street-image60097943.html, accessed 7 June 2022.

[35] See Barbara J. Harris, 'The Fabric of Piety: Aristocratic Women and the Care of the Dead, 1450–1550', *JBS*, 48 (2009), 308–35, at 328–30.

Fig. 6.2 Remembering remarriage: Monument to Sir William Gee and his two wives, 1611.

Source: York Minster.

the case of that erected to the memory of Anne Leighton, who expired delivering her thirteenth child in 1634, at Lydiard Tregoze in Wiltshire. These tombs, which frequently include the infant wrapped tightly in swaddling clothes, defy the more general tendency to present the female body as 'a mute vehicle for the perpetuation of patrilineage'.[36] The frequent inclusion of the deceased's progeny, both those who had died in infancy and those still alive, underlines the capacity of the family to transcend temporal barriers.

Symbols of dynastic continuity, such memorials assured that a family's memory would extend to subsequent generations. Sir William More's monument in St Nicholas's church, Guildford, was set up by his son George after his death in 1600, 'for a testimonye of his dutie to those his good Parents' and 'to stir upp' those who remained to follow the godly lives of this 'zealous Professor of true Religion' and his 'faithfull wife, carefull of her familie, bountifull to the Poore & religious

---

[36] Chris Laoutaris, 'Speaking Stones: Memory and Maternity in Shakespeare's *Antony and Cleopatra*', in Kathryn M. Moncrief and Kathryn R. McPherson (eds), *Performing Maternity in Early Modern England* (Aldershot, 2007), pp. 143–69, at p. 161.

towards God'.[37] The octagonal pillar Lady Anne Clifford had erected by a road-side in Cumbria in 1656 as a monument to her 'good and pious Mother' in time became a memorial to the countess herself.[38] Merging public with private commemoration, this imposing structure was a vector of multigenerational remembrance.

Other examples illustrate the intertwining of memory of individual lives with memory of the recent past. The plate that adorned the tomb of the Protestant printer John Day in Bradley Parva church in Suffolk united celebration of his long partnership with John Foxe in the task of memorializing the martyrs with a verse biography of his two marriages and the twelve children each of his wives had borne him before he died in 1584. Highlighting his role in dispersing the 'popish fogges' that had overcast 'the sun of the Gospel', it fused the patriotic with the personal.[39] The stained glass window which Nicholas Crispe bequeathed to the church of St Mildred Bread Street similarly linked the history of his family with the recent history of the English Reformation. It combined depictions of the donor and his wife and children with images of the providential deliverances of 1588 and 1605, Queen Elizabeth as the restorer of true religion, and the plague of 1625.[40] Ironically, such commemorative strategies replicated elements of the medieval memorial culture that they displaced.[41]

Elizabethan Catholics determined to bury their dead in parish churches were obliged to settle for monuments that excluded traditional intercessory formulae. The brass to the recusant Roger Martyn, author of a wistful account of the pre-Reformation ceremonies and fixtures of the magnificent wool church at Long Melford, is a simple record of his death on 3 August 1615 'in the 89th yeare of his age' (Fig. 6.3).[42] Unable to express their prohibited faith overtly on public monu-ments, some resorted to writing. The written word became a substitute for the liturgical recitation of the names of the dead in the bede roll. Intended to be kept 'for the memorie of future ages to the glorye of God and the good of the Catholike Churche', a lengthy obituary in English and Latin prepared to mark the Warwickshire gentleman Sir Thomas Throckmorton's passing in the middle of James I's reign has a distinctly polemical, anti-Protestant edge.[43] Copied out by

[37] Surrey HC, LM/1654 (Loseley manuscripts), fo. 93r.

[38] Edward Rainbowe, *A sermon preached at the funeral of the right honorable Anne Countess of Pembroke, Dorset and Montgomery* (1677; Wing R142), p. 22.

[39] Transcribed in HEHL 283000: Richard Bull, *Extra-illustrated Biographical History of England, from Egbert the Great to the Revolution* (1769–74), vol. iii, pt 3, fo. 155r.

[40] John Stow, *The survey of London*, ed. Anthony Munday et al. (1633), pp. 859–60.

[41] See Ian Archer, 'The Arts and Acts of Memorialisation in Early Modern London', in J. F. Merritt (ed.), *Imagining Early Modern London: Perceptions and Portrayals of the City from Stow to Strype 1598–1720* (Cambridge, 2001), pp. 89–113.

[42] Roger Martyn, 'The State of Melford Church as I…Did Know It', in William Parker, *The History of Long Melford* (1873), pp. 70–3.

[43] Cited in Peter Marshall, *Faith and Identity in a Warwickshire Family: The Throckmortons and the Reformation*, Dugdale Society, Occasional papers, 49 (Stratford-upon-Avon, 2010), p. 32.

Fig. 6.3 Memorial brass to Roger Martyn, d. 1615.
Source: Parish church of Holy Trinity, Long Melford, Suffolk.

successive generations as acts of filial piety, such texts supplied the place of crypts and sarcophagi for this beleaguered minority.[44]

Perpetuating the memory of preceding generations of Catholic believers was not merely a demonstration of family loyalty; it was also a signature of confessional identity and a soteriological necessity. In the absence of local chantries, devout recusants eager to leave legacies for the health of their souls frequently relied upon the convents in exile. A bequest left in the will of Margaret Parker, a servant of the Salvin family of Croxdale near Durham, following her death in 1734 paid for an anniversary Mass on 'that day, on which it shal Please Almighty God to call me out of this World' and distributed sums to the English nunnery at Pontoise for further intercessory services.[45] Displaced into the domain of the home and religious houses overseas, the fraternal practice of salvific remembering remained alive and well long after the Reformation officially ended it.

On the other side of the religious divide, commemorative strategies were also shifting, assisted by the spread of literacy and the technology of print.[46] Paper and

---

[44] See Gerard Kilroy, *Edmund Campion: Memory and Transcription* (Aldershot, 2004), pp. 36, 86.

[45] DCRO, D/Sa/F 144–5 (Salvin Papers). See also Liesbeth Corens, *Confessional Mobility and English Catholics in Counter-Reformation Europe* (Oxford, 2019), ch. 5.

[46] Andrew Gordon, *Writing Early Modern London: Memory, Text and Community* (Basingstoke, 2013), esp. p. 5. For an extended development of this theme, see Simone Hanebaum, 'Textual Monumentality and Memory in Early Modern England, 1560–*c.*1650' (PhD thesis, University of Cambridge, 2019).

parchment were declared to be better preservatives of memory than rock, and the very meaning of the word monument migrated to encompass the manuscript and printed codex.[47] Two-dimensional memorials proliferated. Often bearing the iconography of the memento mori, broadside epitaphs such as Abraham Fleming's tribute to the Elizabethan London alderman and philanthropist William Lambe were conceived as typographical sepulchres to the memory of the worthy dead.[48] Paradoxically, such black-letter texts presented themselves as 'living remembrances', their ephemerality contrasting with the solidity of the stone and marble monuments they mimicked.[49] 'Printed in Meeter to perfume his Name', the poetic commendation of Thomas Wadsworth, a 'Pious and Reverend Minister of the Gospel' who 'changed this Life for a better' in October 1676, concluded with the exhortation to remember his blessed face, 'And pray his Death may Preach now he is Dead'. This broadside presented itself as a posthumous continuation of Wadsworth's own vocation.[50] Bound in leather and tooled in gold with two angels playing trumpets on the cover, a specially commissioned 'funeral teare' for Sir John Moore, a former Lord Mayor of London, praised his bountiful generosity to the poor and envisaged him joining 'Englands first Reforming Edward [VI]' in his 'starry Throne' with a 'chaplet' of his own.[51] Verse epitaphs have been interpreted as another way of compensating for 'the breaking of the sacred connection between the generations envisaged by Catholic theology'.[52]

Longer works served the same purpose. The 'monument' erected by the 'sorrowfull husband' of Mrs Elizabeth Crashawe, who perished in childbirth aged 24, was constructed of words 'in assurance of Her glorious Resurrection'. This book of elegies was a memorial both to the passing of a 'matchlesse' woman and to the solemn spectacle of her burial, at which James Ussher, then bishop of Meath, had

---

[47] See, e.g., Weever, *Ancient funerall monuments*, p. 3. *OED*, s.v. 'monument', senses 3 and 4.

[48] Abraham Fleming, *An epitaph, or funerall inscription, upon the godlie life and death of the right worshipfull Maister William Lambe esquire* (1580; STC 11038) and idem, *A memorial of the famous monuments and charitable almesdeedes of the right worshipfull Maister William Lambe esquire* (1580; STC 11047).

[49] See *A living remembrance of Master Robert Rogers* (1601; STC 21224), discussed in Gordon, *Writing Early Modern London*, pp. 5–6. Other examples include [Henry Petowe], *An honorable president for great men by an elegiecall monument to the memory of that worthy gentleman Mr John Banckes, citizen and mercy of London* ([1630]; STC 19807.3); *A memorial to preserve unspotted to posterity the name and memory of Doctor Crispe* (1643; Wing M1696).

[50] *The memory of the just is blessed…A most useful (pithy and deserved) commendation of (that pious and reverend minister of the Gospel) Mr Thomas Wadsworth* (1676; Wing M1702A).

[51] LLRRO, DE5833/2 (Manuscript elegy to Sir John Moore, written by Elkanah Settle, 1702).

[52] See Joshua Scodel, *The English Poetic Epitaph: Commemoration and Conflict from Jonson to Wordsworth* (Ithaca, NY, 1991), p. 21. See also Claire Bryony Williams, 'Manuscript, Monument, Memory: The Circulation of Epitaphs in the 17th Century', *Literature Compass*, 11 (2014), 573–82; Harriet Phillips, 'Old, Old, Very Old Men: Nostalgia in the Early Modern Broadside Ballad', *Parergon*, 33 (2016), 79–95, esp. 82–8.

preached so eloquently that it was said there was scarcely a dry eye in the house.[53] Stephen Denison's funeral oration for the godly matron Elizabeth Juxon appeared in 1620 as *The monument or tombe-stone*, dedicated to her spouse and five children, John, Thomas, Elizabeth, Sarah, and Mary. When the widower himself died six years later, Denison published his eulogistic address as *Another tombe-stone*.[54]

It was a commonplace that the best monument to a godly person was not a costly physical edifice but remembrance of their righteous conduct: 'Good menne need not to have their names written in marble, whose actiones live in the Memories of men.'[55] The subjects of the 'lean-to' lives appended to funeral sermons were accordingly conceived to be their own lasting memorials. The 'walking monument in paper' Nathaniel Shute constructed in honour of the London mercer Richard Fishbourne was a mere shadow of the 'mirrour of charitie' he had been while he was alive and of the enduring mark his friend had made in his heart.[56] Mrs Dorothy Shawe, whose 'tomb-stone' was published by her beloved husband and 'yok-fellow', preacher at Kingston upon Hull, to comfort his six daughters in 1658, was said to have been a 'living epistle' and 'lively transcript of Religion'. She was a tender mother, model wife, 'twice born' Christian, and 'precious servant of the Lord' whose zeal for family religion, preaching, and bible-reading made her life 'a continual Sermon'.[57]

Parish registers became a forum for recording the lives of those too impoverished to afford more concrete monuments, partly filling the gap left by now banished obits and bede rolls.[58] Their clerical compilers were sometimes explicit about the commemorative intentions of their endeavours, though they recognized the disjuncture between their own inclusive lists of the 'names of mortall men' and the Book of Life 'wheare Godes elect for ever are inrolde', a mystery beyond human comprehension. The register of St Peter's Cornhill is prefaced with the words 'Though in the grave mens bodies soone bee rotten, yet heare theyr

---

[53] *The honour of vertue. Or the monument erected by the sorrowful husband...to the immortal memory of that worthy Gentle-woman Mrs Elizabeth Crashawe* (1620; STC 6030), sig. A3r–v. See also Nicholas Guy, *Pieties pillar: or, a sermon preached at the funerall of mistresse Elizabeth Gouge, late wife of Mr William Gouge, of Black-friers, London* (1626; STC 12543).

[54] Stephen Denison, *The monument or tombe-stone: or, a sermon preached...at the funerall of Mrs Elizabeth Juxon* (1620; STC 6603.7); idem, *Another tombe-stone, or a sermon preached...at the celebration of the funerall of Mr John Juxon* (1626; STC 6598). The title pages of both quoted Proverbs 10.7 ('The memorial of the just shall be blessed, but the name of the wicked shall rot.').

[55] YML, MS 122 (Commonplace book of the family of Marmaduke Rawdon), p. 98a. See also Sampson Price, *The two twins of birth and death. A sermon preached in Christs Church in London, the 5. of September. 1624* (1624; STC 20334), sig. A2v.

[56] Nathaniel Shute, *Corona charitatis: the crowne of charitie* (1626; STC 22426), title page and sig. A2r.

[57] John Shawe, *Mistris Shawe's tomb-stone, or the saints remains* (1658; Wing S3029), sig. b5r, 'To the Christian Reader' (sig. b8v–11v) and pp. 11, 16.

[58] See Will Coster, 'Popular Religion and the Parish Register, 1538–1603', in Katherine L. French, Gary G. Gibbs, and Beat A. Kumin (eds), *The Parish in English Life, 1400–1600* (Manchester, 1997), pp. 94–111; Marshall, *Beliefs and the Dead*, pp. 291–4; Adam Smyth, *Autobiography in Early Modern England* (Cambridge, 2010), ch. 4, esp. pp. 192–8; Hanebaum, 'Textual Monumentality', pp. 209–20.

names will hardlie bee forgotten'.[59] The register of Ardingley in Sussex included brief tags indicating the stage that the parish dead had occupied in the human life cycle. Dorothie Tullie, buried on 12 May 1633, was 'a widowe of middle age', William Brooker 'a new borne Child', and Richard Hayward 'an ancient man'.[60] Even stillborn bastards sometimes found a place in their pages, including the child begotten by a London harlot called Jacamine Sadler and a lighterman by the name of Purret born in November 1584.[61]

Others incorporated concise biographies. Robert Leband, the Elizabethan vicar of Rolleston in Nottinghamshire, composed short pen portraits of those under his charge, from bonesetters and shepherds to cottagers and swineherds. Nicholas Darwin, 'a tall man but crooked throughe age beeinge foure-score & tenne at the least' was remembered as 'a painefull labourer in ditching, mowinges & other laborious woorkes'. Written in Latin, some entries also passed judgement on the moral and spiritual status of the individuals in question. Leband's epitaph for Ralph Swifte, who died in 1601, was *probus is quidem et meo iudicio deum timens senex* ('indeed an honest and in my judgement a God-fearing old man'). The 70-year old fisherman Humphrey Parke was *frugi et laboriosus* ('honest and industrious'). More damningly, he remembered William Forrest as a cunning fellow *fide pusillum, spei aeternae… minimum* ('small in faith, with very little hope of eternal life'). By contrast, the entry relating to his own father, a husbandman who died on Whit Monday 1588, articulated the hope that he would enjoy heavenly bliss (*caelestibus spero ut gaudiis frueretur*).[62] The register of Great Amwell in Hertfordshire kept by Thomas Hassall in the early seventeenth century lauded those who were good servants to the church and indicted others, including Philip Winchly, who was labelled 'an owlde notorious bedlam roge'.[63] Such texts are understudied forms of early modern life-writing.

The relatively belated reappearance of full-blown biography was a function of lingering ambivalence about its potential to idolize the dead. Radical Protestants worried about the roots of the funeral sermon in pagan eulogy and medieval hagiography. Many puritan preachers kept references to the deceased to a minimum, turning funerals into occasions for salutary instruction. An omnibus volume of forty-seven sermons, *Threnoikos. The house of mourning* named only a

---

[59] G. W. G. Leveson Gower (ed.), *A Register of all the Christninges Burialles & Weddinges within the Parish of Saint Peeters upon Cornhill*, Harleian Society Registers 1 (1877), p. iv.

[60] Gerald W. E. Loder (ed.) *The Parish Registers of Ardingly, Sussex, 1558–1812*, Sussex Record Society 17 (1913), p. 151.

[61] Gower (ed.), *Register*, p. 132.

[62] K. S. S. Train, 'Extracts from the Paper Book of Robert Leband, Vicar of Rolleston, 1583–1625', trans. T. M. Blagg, *Thoroton Society Record Series*, 14 (Nottingham, 1951), pp. 1–20, quotations at 5, 16, 12, 10, 3.

[63] S. G. Doree (ed.), *The Parish Register and Tithing Book of Thomas Hassall of Amwell*, Hertfordshire Record Publications 5 (1989), p. 95.

handful of the 'divers faithfull servants of Christ' they commemorated.[64] Over time these anxieties faded and the genre of godly lives became a lucrative sector of the book trade. The anthologies compiled by Samuel Clarke were read avidly alongside accounts of precociously pious children who died prematurely and exemplary elders whose remarkable longevity and spiritual wisdom imitated that of the biblical patriarchs. Passed through the sieve of Scripture and classical panegyric, the people who populate such volumes are largely free of individual faults and foibles, cardboard cut-outs behind which hide the more opaque inner lives of those they describe.[65] These encomiastic discourses are likewise testimonies to the unreliability of human memory.

Consciously and unconsciously, relatives and friends reinvented their ancestors in line with their own religious priorities and the inspiring narratives embedded in Foxe's *Actes and monuments*. Clarke's biography of Thomas Gataker, the godly rector of Rotherhithe and member of the Westminster Assembly, resembles a Russian doll. Nested inside it is an account of how his father had been so horrified by the fires he eyewitnessed at Smithfield and so impressed by the constancy of the Protestant martyrs that he forsook his family to follow Christ, happily accepting penury rather than compromise his conscience when his allowance was revoked and subsequently entering the reformed ministry.[66] Viewed through the flattering prism of familial memory, the elder Gataker became a confessor himself, his life narrative acquiring the distinctive colouring of one of the dominant templates of Protestant culture.

Often described as 'relics', the written residues left behind by eminent divines and devout laypeople bear witness to the elastic expansion and subtle transmutation of this category in the course of the sixteenth and seventeenth centuries.[67] The family members, friends, and admirers who prepared their literary remains for publication envisaged themselves as both midwives to their rebirth and mechanisms for their resurrection via the medium of text. They commonly invoked Hebrews 11:4 ('being dead yet speaketh') to justify their strenuous efforts to bring the words of their authors to life once more. Set forth by his spouse and executrix Anne following his death in January 1634, William Austin's *Certaine devout,*

---

[64] See Frederic B. Tromly, '"Accordinge to Sounde Religion": The Elizabethan Controversy over the Funeral Sermon', *Journal of Medieval and Renaissance Studies*, 13 (1983), 293–312; Ralph Houlbrooke, *Death, Religion and the Family in England, 1480-1750* (Oxford, 1998), p. 297 and see ch. 10. *Threnoikos. The house of mourning* (1640; STC 24049).

[65] Samuel Clarke, *The lives of thirty-two English divines* (1677; Wing C4539). On Clarke's lives, see Patrick Collinson, '"A Magazeen of Religious Patterns": An Erasmian Topic Transposed in English Protestantism', in idem, *Godly People: Essays on English Protestantism and Puritanism* (1983), pp. 499–525; Peter Lake, 'Reading Clarke's *Lives* in Political and Polemical Context', in Kevin Sharpe and Steven N. Zwicker (eds), *Written Lives: Biography and Textuality, Identity and Representation in Early Modern England* (Oxford, 2008), pp. 293–318. See also Chapter 1, p. 66, above.

[66] Clarke, *Lives of thirty two divines*, pp. 248–9.

[67] See *OED*, s.v. 'relic'. For example, *Misery is virtues whet-stone. Reliquiae Gethinianae, or, some remains of the most ingenious and excellent lady, Grace Lady Gethin, lately deceased* (1700; Wing G626).

godly, and learned meditations was designed to be a perpetual monument to his memory.[68] Others were tokens of attachment to religious mentors. George Vineing was motivated to edit Daniel Featley's sermon *The faithfull shepard* by his reverence for the 'Deceased spiritual Father' who 'begat him out of blinde Popery from dumb'd and dead Idols' and brought him into 'the clear light, to serve the true and living God'. He thereby 'revived' the agent of his evangelical conversion to the reformed faith.[69]

This trope was deployed across the ecclesiastical spectrum. When William Laud and John Buckeridge edited the *XCIV sermons* of the late bishop of Winchester, Lancelot Andrewes, for publication in 1629, they anticipated the charge that would in due course would be levelled against them: that 'after printing...the living may make the dead speake as they will' and 'contrarie' to themselves. Their edition of these texts was a 'polemically aggressive' attempt to co-opt the dead bishop to buttress the Laudian programme to remodel the Church of England, to resurrect him as a spokesman for their provocative agenda.[70] The title page of Thomas Fuller's anthology of clerical biographies, *Abel redivivus* depicts a tomb housing a skeleton, the canopy of which is ingeniously built out of books. It was a monument of conformist commemoration.[71] The 'living testimonies' of fellow Friends assembled by Quaker editors were also gramophone-like devices for ensuring that the voices of the deceased continued to resound beyond the grave.[72] A mode of posthumous speech, they too helped to breach the rigid divide that the Reformation theoretically erected between past and present generations.

A further way in which people remembered departed relatives was through the baptismal names they chose for their children. Carriers of affect as well as markers of lineage, their deployment is another index of the vitality of the family as a theatre of memory.[73] William Perkins commended the custom of calling sons and daughters after their parents and kindred 'if there be any good

[68] Wiliam Austin, *Devotionis Augustinianae flamma, or, certaine devout, godly, and learned meditations* (1637; STC 973).

[69] Daniel Featley, *Dr Daniel Featley revived, or the faithfull shepheard*, ed. George Vineing (1661; Wing F580), sig. A2r.

[70] Lancelot Andrewes, *XCVI sermons* (1629; STC 606), sig. A2v. See Peter McCullough, 'Making Dead Men Speak: Laudianism, Print, and the Works of Lancelot Andrewes, 1626–1642', *HJ*, 41 (1998), 401–24, at 402, 410, 423–4.

[71] Thomas Fuller, *Abel redivivus, or the dead yet speaking* (1651; Wing F2400). See also Jessica Martin, *Walton's Lives: Conformist Commemorations and the Rise of Biography* (Oxford, 2001), esp. ch. 3.

[72] e.g. *The last words and testimonies of and for William Allen, late of Cowen in Essex, a faithfull servant of the Lord* (1680; Wing A1065B); *Living testimonies concerning the death of the righteous. Or the blessed end of Joseph Featherstone and Sarah his daughter* (1689; Wing F576B); *Several living testimonies given forth by divers friends to the faithful labours and travels of that faithful and constant servant of the Lord, Robert Lodge...also, two general epistles, written by himself long since to the believers in Christ* (1691; Wing S2782).

[73] Amy Harris, *Siblinghood and Social Relations in Georgian England: Share and Share Alike* (Manchester, 2012), p. 37. See also Donald Lines Jacobus, 'Early New England Nomenclature', *New England Historical and Genealogical Register*, 77 (1923), 11–20.

example in the ancestors that the child may follow'.[74] As William Gouge observed, this was 'an ancient practise even among Gods people', much to be preferred over the 'heathenish, idolatrous, and ridiculous names' too many gave to their off-spring.[75] The widespread tendency to reuse the names of dead siblings similarly served as a prophylactic against forgetting them. Medieval Christians had often added the child's name saint to the roll of godparents, enlarging the family to encompass these heavenly patrons.[76] The tendency to name children after their 'gossips' declined after the Reformation in favour of naming them after their par-ents, who, as we saw in Chapter 2, were now regarded as having primary respon-sibility for their religious education. But traditional naming patterns remained resilient, reflecting the intimate ties of spiritual kinship that continued to bind children to their sponsors and witnesses at the baptismal font.[77] Whatever names were chosen, declared William Jenkyn in the course of a sermon published in 1652, they 'ought to be such as may prove remembrancers of duty', for 'a good name is as a thread tyed about the finger, to make us mindfull of the errand we came into the world to do for our Master'.[78]

These patterns must be analysed in the context of the Catholic practice of call-ing children after saints and the Protestant proclivity for adopting the names of Old Testament heroes and heroines, as well as the curious formulations, such as Repent, Flee-Sin and Praise-God, favoured by puritans.[79] The sons of the early evangelical merchant John Johnson were called Evangelist and Israel and his daughters, Charity, Rachel, and Faith; his brother Otwell also christened his male heir Israel, 'whose sede multiplied lyke the sand of the see', beseeching God to 'blesse him and his posteritie'.[80] Elizabeth Juxon's daughter Sarah was so named to encourage her to emulate the wife of Abraham, while Nehemiah Wallington's father hoped that he would exhibit the zeal of his scriptural namesake.[81] Two of John Bruen's sons were baptized Calvin and Beza, in honour of the Genevan reformers.[82] Others selected forenames that would remind their bearers of the

---

[74] William Perkins, *A direction for the government of the tongue* (1603; STC 19690), p. 44.

[75] William Gouge, *Of domesticall duties* (1622), pp. 525, 522–3.

[76] John Bossy, *Christianity in the West 1400–1700* (Oxford, 1985), p. 17. See Will Coster, *Baptism and Spiritual Kinship in Early Modern England* (Aldershot, 2002), ch. 6.

[77] See Scott Smith-Bannister, *Names and Naming Practices in England, 1538–1700* (Oxford, 1997), chs 2–3.

[78] William Jenkyn, *An exposition of the epistle of Jude (the first part)* (1652; Wing J639), pp. 6–7.

[79] See Nicholas Tyacke, 'Popular Puritan Mentality in Late Elizabethan England', in Peter Clark, A.G.R. Smith, and Nicholas Tyacke (eds), *The English Commonwealth 1547–1640: Essays in Politics and Society Presented to Joel Hurstfield* (Leicester, 1979), pp. 77–92; Patrick Collinson, 'Dudley Fenner and the Peculiarities of Puritan Nomenclature', in Kenneth Fincham and Peter Lake (eds), *Religious Politics in Post-Reformation England: Essays in Honour of Nicholas Tyacke* (Woodbridge, 2006), pp. 113–27.

[80] Danae Tankard, 'The Johnson Family and the Reformation, 1542–52', *Historical Research*, 80 (2007), 469–90, at 476.

[81] Denison, *Monument*, sig. A4r–v; FSL, MS V. a. 436, p. 216.

[82] See https://www.geni.com/people/John-Bruen/6000000006979363766, accessed 7 June 2022.

heartbreaking circumstances in which they were born. In New England, Benoni was reserved for boys whose mothers died in childbed and Ichabod assigned to posthumous sons.[83]

The names assumed by young Catholic women who took their vows of profession in Low Countries convents testify to similar strategies of family solidarity and memorialization. Helen Smith perpetuated remembrance of her sister, who had died in 1710, by choosing the same name in religion, Mary Lucy, when she professed in 1718. Both the daughter and granddaughter of Ursula Daniel, the wife of a doctor of Bury St Edmunds, adopted her forename, while the niece of Frances Mechtildis Poulton took that of her aunt.[84] Binding people separated by space and divided in time, this practice 'drew a connecting line between past and present, establishing tradition and belonging' within the imagined communities created by the English Reformations.[85]

Finally, we must attend to the mnemonics of the body. So ingrained did the memory of the Marian martyrs become in their descendants that it sometimes manifested itself somatically, as well as in posture, gesture, and action. At the very moment she was exorcised of an unclean spirit, 14-year-old Mary Glover repeated the words uttered by her grandfather Robert, the Somerset Herald, when he was burnt as a heretic in Coventry in 1555: 'The comeforter is come. O Lord thow has delivered me.' She commemorated her illustrious forebear by assimilating her own inner turmoil to his physical torments. Current affliction and historic suffering, possession and martyrdom, adolescent and ancestor were collapsed into one.[86] Susan Leyburne, who died at St Monica's in Louvain in 1624 after many years of troubling illness, mirrored the holy patience of her father James, who had been executed in Lancaster in 1583 for denying the queen's supremacy: 'being a martyr's daughter... [she] herself suffered a long martyrdom'. Her own infirmities were evidently a constant reminder of the cruelties he had suffered for his prohibited faith.[87] Here remembrance of the dead was 'sedimented in the body' itself.[88]

---

[83] David Hackett Fischer, 'Forenames and the Family in New England: An Exercise in Historical Onomastics', in Robert M. Taylor and Ralph J. Crandall (eds), *Generations and Change: Genealogical Perspectives in Social History* (Macon, GA, 1986), pp. 215–41, at p. 224.

[84] K. S. B. Keats-Rohan, *English Catholic Nuns in Exile 1600–1800: A Biographical Register*, Prosopographica et Genealogica Occasional Papers 15 (2017), pp. li–lii.

[85] See the sensitive discussion in Kat Hill, 'The Power of Names: Radical Identities in the Reformation Era', in Bridget Heal and Anorthe Kremers (eds), *Radicalism and Dissent in the World of Protestant Reform* (Göttingen, 2017), pp. 53–68, at p. 67.

[86] Stephen Bradwell, 'Mary Glovers late woeful case, together with her joyfull deliverance', in Michael MacDonald (ed.), *Witchcraft and Hysteria: Edward Jorden and the Mary Glover Case* (1991), p. 115, and pp. xxxvii–xxxix; John Swan, *A true and breife report of Mary Glovers vexation* (1603; STC 23517), p. 47. For Foxe's account of her grandfather, see *Actes and monuments* (1583 edn), pp. 1709–15.

[87] Adam Hamilton (ed.), *The Chronicle of the English Augustinian Canonesses Regular of the Lateran, at St Monica's in Louvain... 1548 to 1625*, 2 vols (1904), vol. i, p. 265.

[88] See Connerton, *How Societies Remember*, esp. pp. 74, 72.

Leaving Legacies

These were just some of the ways in which Englishmen and women maintained diachronic links with previous generations and left legacies for their posterity. This section extends the insight that the task of remembering past predecessors was closely connected with concern about instructing one's present and future heirs. It examines the powerful imperative that so many contemporaries felt to transmit wisdom and piety across the divide created by death.

One instrument for doing so was the last will and testament. As many historians have shown, will preambles became an important device for giving expression to evolving religious identities. While many borrowed conventional scribal formulae, others were more distinctive theological statements. In trusting that their souls would be saved by the merits of Christ alone or through the intercession of the whole company of saints, testators were transmitting an example of faith to the children and grandchildren who assembled to hear these documents read. Admitting that they were ailing in body but insisting that they were 'sound' and 'perfect in memory', men and women on the eve of departing from life passed on traditions of piety as well as movable goods. Drawn up in their final hours and delivered orally in the presence of witnesses, nuncupative wills were an extension of the *ars moriendi*, the art of dying well.[89]

The ancient custom of imparting wisdom on one's deathbed was not disrupted but reanimated by England's successive Reformations. The verbal pronouncements made by those in the liminal zone between this life and the next continued to be revered. Terminally ill children were accorded an authority and gravity beyond their tender years. On the threshold of death, the exclamations of pious young people like the Suffolk schoolboy William Withers acquired a quasi-prophetic quality.[90] The remarkable speech made by the Devonshire maid Damaris Pearce in her final hours in December 1679 was taken down in shorthand by a bystander and circulated among her relations and acquaintance as well as some 'strangers' before being printed, together with the text of her own composition she left to her brothers and sisters.[91] Late seventeenth-century Quakers likewise revered the precocious pronouncements of children such as 8-year-old Sarah Camm, from whose mouth sprang eloquent praise of the Lord before she

---

[89] See J. D. Alsop, 'Religious Preambles in Early Modern English Wills as Formulae', *JEH*, 40 (1989), 19–27; Christopher Marsh, 'In the Name of God? Will-Making and Faith in Early Modern England', in G. H. Martin and Peter Spufford (eds), *The Records of the Nation: The Public Record Office, 1838–1988* (Woodbridge, 1990), pp. 215–50. See also Houlbrooke, *Death, Religion and the Family*, chs 4–6.

[90] Hannah Newton, *The Sick Child in Early Modern England, 1580–1720* (Oxford, 2012), esp. ch. 6; Anna French, *Children of Wrath: Possession, Prophecy and the Young in Early Modern England* (Farnham, 2015), ch. 5. For William Withers, see Chapter 1 above, p. 67.

[91] *A present for youth, and example for the aged. Or the remains or Damaris Pearse* (1683; Wing P969C).

perished of smallpox in August 1682.[92] The 'last expressions' of Hannah Hill, a young Friend from Philadelphia who died in 1714, were also published as *A legacy for children*. She left these as 'Fruits of Love and Good Will to her dear Relations, tender Companions and Young People... That it might have the blessed Effect of exciting Children, To Remember their CREATOR in the days of their Youth'. Although she was 'green' in years, her compelling words carried almost as much weight as the testimonies of the venerable Mothers and Fathers of Israel the sect celebrated as it steadily matured into adulthood.[93]

In this gerontocratic society, the usual pattern of transmission, however, was from the older generation to its successor. The practice of passing on moral and spiritual direction had long been regarded as one of the formal obligations of parenthood. The benedictions fathers and mothers bestowed on their offspring were modelled on those given by the biblical patriarchs and their wives. Depictions of the elderly Isaac blessing Jacob were a popular iconographical theme.[94] The sayings of the dying were explicitly conceived as a way of conveying religious and family values to the young. Demonstrating 'Providence for Posterity' in this way was part of 'the work of old age'. 'Ten lines discreetly written, would prevent ten thousand lines when you are dead', wrote Richard Steele in 1688.[95] Conscious that the grim reaper might take them by surprise, many took the precaution of preparing them in advance, especially as they progressed in years and passed milestones in the human life cycle.

In a culture of inheritance that revolved around primogeniture, fathers felt a particular imperative to guide their immediate heirs in writing. Humanism as well as Protestantism helped to regenerate the ancient tradition of setting down pithy precepts for the instruction of eldest sons when they entered the state of manhood.[96] William Cecil, Lord Burghley, wrote ten directives for 'the well ordering and carriage of a mans life' as a literary legacy for his son Robert.[97] Henry Percy, ninth earl of Northumberland, prepared a set of counsels for his

---

[92] *The admirable and glorious appearance of the eternal god... in and through a child, of the age of betwixt eight and nine years* (1684; Wing C394).

[93] *A legacy for children, being some of the last expressions and dying sayings of Hannah Hill... aged eleven years, and near three months* (Dublin, 1719), pp. 19, 29.

[94] See, e.g., the many examples in the collections of the BM, including Matthäus Merian I, Isaac blessing Jacob, 1857,1212.75.

[95] Richard Steele, *A discourse concerning old-age, tending to the instruction, caution and comfort of aged persons* (1688; Wing S5386), pp. 287–92.

[96] See Felicity Heal and Clive Holmes, *The Gentry in England and Wales 1500–1700* (Basingstoke, 1994), pp. 243–7; R. C. Richardson, 'The Generation Gap: Parental Advice in Early Modern England', *Clio*, 32 (2002), 1–25 For one fifteenth-century precursor, see Charlotte D'Evelyn (ed.), *Peter Idley's Instructions to his Son* (1935).

[97] This was later printed. William Cecil, *The counsell of a father to his sonne, in ten several precepts* (1611; STC 4900.5) and *idem, Certaine precepts or directions, for the well ordering and carriage of a mans life* (1617; STC 4897). For manuscript copies, see FSL, MS X.d.212; BL, MS Egerton 2877 (Commonplace book of Gilbert Freville), fos 66v–67v ('Ten precepts left as a legacy by a father unto his son').

male heir in the mid-1590s and Walter Raleigh composed his own instructions while imprisoned in the Tower of London between 1603 and 1616.[98] Beginning with an exhortation to obey God, these didactic documents typically supplied advice on choosing a wife, estate and household management, land transactions, charity, hospitality, social relations, and personal conduct, including warnings about gluttony and drunkenness. While the tone of some was more practical than pious, others closely echo godly guides to 'domesticall duties'. Sir Richard Grosvenor's letter to his son, written between 1628 and 1636, urged:

> Make your house a Bethel, a house of God by calling your whole family together twice every day to pray unto God for his blessings and praise him for his favours...Furnish yourself with true and sound knowledge that you be not shaken in these wavering and backsliding times with any example or counsel of such as wander from the true faith...Abhor popery. It is a mock religion patched together of men's traditions and vanities without a ground of scripture or colour of truth to any but to such as the god of this world hath blinded.[99]

Set down in 'the winter of his age', Henry Hastings' early seventeenth-century injunctions to his son Ferdinando were similarly designed for his use when he reached his 'ripe years'. Cultivating anti-Catholicism alongside loyal devotion to the established Church of England, they also recalled the divine judgement that had galvanized him to keep the Sabbath strictly after his own youthful indulgence in card-playing to demonstrate the necessity of observing it punctiliously.[100] Thomas Hunt's 'bosome companion' to his children, composed in 1690, includes a list of the forty-one marks of a child of God and the twelve signs of an unregenerate believer, together with some 'characters' whereby a godly person might be discerned from a 'Hippocrate' and gain assurance of their election.[101] This textual legacy was a device for assessing whether or not one had experienced a true conversion and a second birth.

Archives and libraries abound with letters and books of advice that fathers prepared for their offspring, gave them when they went away to school or came of age, and bequeathed to them as they lay dying. The first letter that Sir Henry Sidney wrote to his son Philip, a pupil at Shrewsbury around 1565, opened by encouraging him to begin each day by 'the liftinge up of your minde to almightie

---

[98] *Advice to his Son by Henry Percy, ninth earl of Northumberland*, ed. G. B. Harrison (1930); *Sir Walter Raleighs instructions to his sonne: and to posteritie* (1632; STC 20642.5).

[99] Richard Cust (ed.), *The Papers of Sir Richard Grosvenor, first Baronet, 1585–1645*, Record Society of Lancashire and Cheshire 134 (1996), pp. 30–1 ('Letters of Advice to his Son').

[100] HEHL, Hastings Personal Papers, Box 15, folder 8 ('Certaine directions for my sonne to observe in the course of his life', c.1613).

[101] FSL, MS V.a.11 (Thomas Hunt, 'A Bosome Companion or the Fathers advice to his Children', 1690).

god by hearty prayer'.[102] Commending his text as 'a perpetuall remembrancer' of better efficacy than spoken words 'which are too easy forgotten or neglected', the father of one late seventeenth-century law student charged him to 'read out this page once in a weeke'.[103] The occasion on which Nathaniel Bladen compiled his advice to his heir in 1694 was his entry to adulthood: 'the Theatre of the World, where every one must act his part'. Among other instructions, he advised him to learn the arts of memory: to 'keep an exact dyary of all your actions & of the most memorable passages you hear or meet with' each night before going to sleep.[104]

This parental duty often fell to the older generation when their own offspring predeceased them. Aware of his own impending mortality, in September 1599 Thomas Egerton implored his own father (whom he would shortly exchange for a 'heavenly' one) to look after his wife and daughters: 'as deeply as a Deade sonne maye charge his father, I charge you be carefull of there educacion, & fortune'. He bestowed this responsibility together with 'some small remembrances' to be distributed among his friends.[105] Sometimes the task was undertaken by grand-parents as a substitute for oral instruction. Separation and solitude inspired Sir Charles Cornwallis to compose a collection of improving precepts for his name-sake in 1614. His aim was to instruct a grandson who had passed his 'Infancy' and 'Puerility' and begun his 'Entry into the Spring' of youth: 'to say unto you by my Lines those Thinges that were I with you continually my self I would deliver by Wordes'.[106] By contrast, the lawyer and merchant James Ravenscroft had 'noe other legacy' to leave his deceased daughter Tomasin, who had entered the Franciscan convent at Nieuport aged 17 in 1647 and died in 1680, than the brief 'grateful memoriall' of her 'holie life and happie death' he incorporated in his own will the following year. Although cut off from the foreign cloister in which she had resided for more than three decades, he could not 'but lament the losse of the comfort of soe good a child, whose virtues and goodness made her most deare unto me'.[107]

If the leaving of oral and scribal legacies was a manifestation of patriarchal masculinity, it was also an extension of commonly held assumptions about mater-nal responsibility. Mothers too had a duty to nurture and succour the young, from drilling them in the ABC and catechism in their early years to steering them towards virtuous living as they advanced towards sexual maturity and marriage.

---

[102] FSL, MS V.a.233 (Letter of Sir Henry Sidney to his son Philip, copy c.1600).

[103] BL, Egerton MS 2884, no. 10, fo. 21 (Anonymous advice of a father to his son, late 17th century).

[104] FSL, MS V.a.346 (Nathaniel Bladen, advice to a son, 1694). See also NRO, LEST/NE 2 and 2/1 (Sir Nichols Le Strange, 'Short notes for my sons profit', 1669).

[105] HEHL, Ellesmere MSS, Box 1, 77 (Letter to Lord Ellesmere from his son Thomas, 7 September 1599).

[106] FSL, MS X.d.539 (Sir Charles Cornwallis, precepts to his grandchild, 7 November 1614). See also Philip Taverner, *A grand-father's advice. Directed in special to his children; and published for the common good* (1681; Wing T247A).

[107] TNA, PROB 11/411/89. See 'Who Were the Nuns?' (https://wwtn.history.qmul.ac.uk/, accessed 7 June 2022): Tomasin Ravenscraft, in religion Mary Francis (BF203). I owe my knowledge of this will to Katharine Keats-Rohan.

Offering guidance on the chastity, temperance, humility, and modesty that befitted a good woman and wife, these texts embodied another medieval topos that remained resilient in reformed piety.[108] Written around 1606, Elizabeth Ashburnham's instructions for her four daughters explicitly evoked the precedent of the Old Testament, which laid down the duty of passing on knowledge of the Lord down the generations. She articulated her conviction:

> that as god hath made me a meanes for the life of their bodies, so I may discharge the care that is comitted to me…for the good of their soules, that they may both lie, and die, in the feare & favour of God, and may injoye after death, a blessed inheritance amongst the saintes of god in his kingdome of glorie; whose salvation wilbe an unspeakable comforte to me, and everlasting felicity to themselves.

She envisaged an audience of spiritual kith as well as biological kin. Godly meditations 'worthy to be remembered' sit alongside prayers for her 'parents and kinsfolkes' and 'the howsehould and the whole churche of god'.[109] Surviving in its original vellum binding, tooled with the letters E.A., this manuscript was self-consciously written for a family that stretched outwards in space and forward in time. Belatedly published in 1645, this was a 'motherly remembrance', testifying to her earnest travail 'for the new birth of your soules' and transformation into God's 'adopted children'.[110] Strictly speaking, English Protestants could do nothing to save their children. Yet, as we saw in Chapter 4, they firmly believed that they could bring them to awareness that they were members of the elect.

In an era of high maternal mortality, women felt a strong imperative to instruct their offspring posthumously. Many composed such texts during pregnancy. The ever-present perils of childbirth inspired them to pen missives to the infants they felt quickening in their wombs, for fear that they might not survive their delivery. Lady Anne Halkett's prolific manuscript remains incorporate 'The Mothers Will to her unborne child' (Fig. 6.4). Writing on the very day that she first became 'sencible' of the presence of the fetus, 26 November 1656, she set down advice on prayer, bible-reading, hearing sermons, and receiving the sacrament, as well as bridling the tongue and avoiding ostentation, pride, slander, and backbiting.

---

[108] For a medieval precursor republished in the Elizabethan period, see *The northern mother's blessing… written nine years before the death of G. Chaucer* (1597), in *Certaine worthye manuscript poems of great antiquitie reserved long in the studie of a Northfolke gentleman*, ed. J. S. (1597; STC 21499).

[109] FSL, MS V.a. 511 (Elizabeth Ashbornham, Instructions for my children, or any other Christian), fos 2r, 73r. A manuscript copy of her prayers given to her eldest daughter, Elizabeth Cornwallis, in 1635 is in Brighton, East Sussex Record Office, ASH 3501.

[110] This was published after she had remarried and become Elizabeth Richardson, Baroness Cramond: *A ladies legacie to her daughters* (1645; Wing R1382), p. 6. On this text, see Michelle M. Dowd, 'Structures of Piety in Elizabeth Richardson's Legacie', in *eadem* and Julie A. Eckerle (eds), *Genre and Women's Life Writing in Early Modern England* (Aldershot, 2007), pp. 115–30.

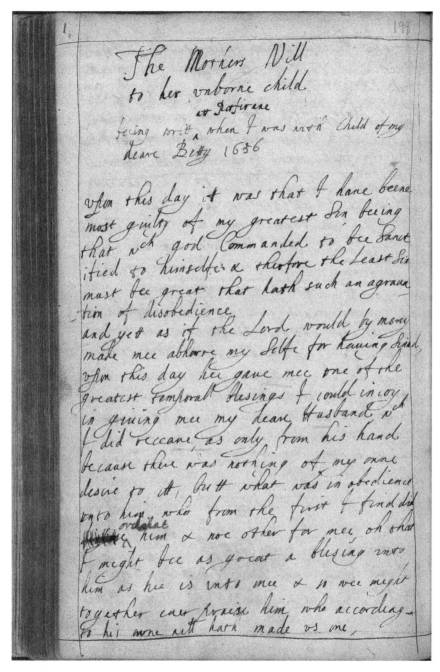

Fig. 6.4 'The Mothers Will to her unborne child', in Lady Anne Halkett, 'Meditations'.
Source: National Library of Scotland, Edinburgh, MS 6489, p. 198.

She hoped it would live to see Stuart monarchy 'made nursing fathers & mothers to preserve the puritty of the church which is now rent & devided by Scisme her- esy & error'. Nine months later, when she gave birth to a healthy girl, she jotted down an effusive thanksgiving for this mercy, which had 'turned my mourning into joy'. Sadly, little Betty died of smallpox, aged just 3, in November 1660, 'tear- ing a great peace of my soule from mee'.[111]

As these examples attest, the leaving of legacies was a social convention and a settled rite of passage, shaped by inherited scripts and formulae. But it was also an intimate personal and familial experience that took place in the domain of the closet and bedchamber. The steady migration of the legacy from speech and script into the public sphere of print turned it into a literary commonplace, but this did not prevent it from looping back and inflecting lived experience. The sixteenth and seventeenth centuries saw a proliferation of publications purporting to be parental legacies, from single sheets and three-halfpenny pamphlets to bulky treatises and tracts in a range of formats. One of the best-selling ballads of the period was *A hundred godly lessons*, which summarizes the proverbial advice dis- pensed by a dying mother to her soon to be orphaned children as they assembled around her bedside, including the danger of transgressing the sixth command- ment: 'The Ravens shall pick out their eyes, that do their Parents curse'. It ends: 'Print well in your remembrance, / the Lessons I have shown, / Then shall you live in happy state, / when I am dead and gone' (Fig. 6.5).[112] A later variation on the same theme, *The old gentlewomans last legacy*, concludes:

> My Children, I'll bid you adieu
> These words I speak pray bear in mind,
> Love one another, and to God to be true
> Then you need not fear what Man is unkind,
> And obey Gods Word and his Command,
> Then he'll bless all things you take in hand.[113]

These stylized representations of the process of generational transmission per- petuated a trope that was centuries old. The appetite for affordable didactic advice about how to live and die well among humble and middling-sort buyers was fed by stationers such as John Trundle, whose matching books for fathers and mothers supplied conventional guidance for teaching their offspring to 'keepe

[111] NLS, MS 6489 (Lady Anne Halkett's Meditations), pp. 198–256 ('The Mothers Will to her unborne child'), quotation at 201. She wrote an equally detailed manual of instructions for her son Charles, which can be found in MS 6492 (Occasional Meditations and Select Contemplations). The latter was later published: Anne Halkett, *Instructions for youth* (1701). For her meditations on Betty's death, see MS 6491, pp. 1–2.

[112] *A hundred godly lessons, that a mother on her death-bed gave to her children* ([1674–9]; Wing H3726A).

[113] *The old gentlewomans last legacy to her sons and daughters upon her death-bed* ([1670–96]; Wing O203).

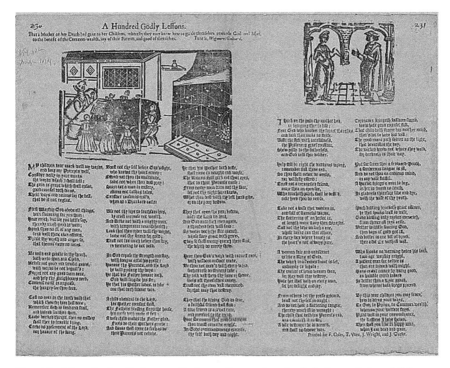

Fig. 6.5 *A hundred godly lessons, that a mother on her death-bed gave to her children* (London, [1670?]).

within compasse.[114] Andrew Jones's *Dying mans last sermon* was equally success-ful as a godly chapbook. Already in its twelfth edition by 1665, it was still in print in 1683.[115] By the late seventeenth century, the 'last legacy' had become a market-ing device to entice devout buyers, a catch-all title that encompassed a wide var-iety of pious writing, as well as a vehicle for partisan apology and political martyrology.[116] Encapsulated in several Whig broadsides, William Lord Russell's final admonitions to his wife (a 'fruitful vine') and children before being put to

[114] *Keepe within compasse: or, the worthy legacy of a wise father to his beloved sonne* (1620; STC 14899.3); M. R., *The mothers counsell, or live within compasse* ([1630]; STC 20583). Both titles were frequently reprinted. A similar text, 'fitted for all sorts, both yong and old' was John Norden, *The fathers legacie* (1625; STC 18607). See also Patrick Scot, *A fathers advice or last will to his sonne* (1620; STC 21859).

[115] Andrew Jones, *The dying mans last sermon. Or, the fathers last blessing left, and bequeathed as a legacy unto his children* (1661; Wing H945E).

[116] See Edward Burton, *The fathers legacy: or Burtons collections* (1649; Wing B6159); Henry Delaune, *Patrikon doron, or a legacie to his sons* (1651; Wing D887); F. S., *A dying fathers living legacy, to his loving son* (1660; Wing S22); *The advice of a father, or counsel to a childe directing him how to demean himself in the most important passages of his life* (1664; Wing A634); *The fathers legacy: or counsels to his children* (1678; Wing F555).

death for opposing the accession of the Catholic James II in 1683 were presented 'for the good of all Christian families'.[117]

Like funeral sermons and textual memorials, last legacies were understood as 'lively monuments' of the loving solicitude of those who composed them.[118] The group of books that appeared after their authors' deaths as 'mother's counsells' or 'blessings' provides a rich seam of evidence of how the intergenerational dynamics of the deathbed acquired new dimensions in the domain of print.[119] The widow Dorothy Leigh insisted that resorting to this medium was the only way she could ensure that her 'scrole' of 'godly counsailes' would be permanently preserved for the edification of her orphaned children. Although she excused her presumption in stepping into the shoes of her dead husband, her actions did not constitute a violation of coverture. Hoping that her book would inspire them to record instructions for their own offspring, she envisaged 'an apostolic succession of advice' down the generations and sought to create an unbroken line of faithful witness coinciding with the one carried by blood. She also claimed the right to select the names of her future grandchildren (Philip, Elizabeth, James, Anna, John, and Susanna). These, she explained, would serve as a constant prompt to remembrance for their bearers.[120] The 'Register of heavenly Meditations' which the Catholic Elizabeth Grymeston left to her son Bernye was similarly intended as 'a portable *veni mecum*' and 'Counsellor', 'in which thou mayest see the true portraiture of thy mothers minde'. She justified putting pen to paper 'the rather for that as I am now a dead woman amongst the living, so stand I doubtfull of thy fathers life'.[121] Appearing after her decease, the book attests to the capacity of the last testament to 'circumvent the cultural restriction on women's speech'.[122]

---

[117] *The last legacy, or affectionate and pious exhortation, and admonitions of the late William Lord Russel* (1683; Wing R2349).

[118] The quotation is from Francis Osborn's popular *Advice to a Son. Or directions for your better conduct, through the various and most important encounters of this life* (Oxford, 1658 edn; Wing O513), sig. A3v–4r. First published in 1655, this text was a more pragmatic and cynical guide to material success.

[119] Literary critics have paid considerable attention to this genre. See esp. Betty S. Travitsky, 'The New Mother of the English Renaissance: Her Writings on Motherhood', in Cathy N. Davidson and E. M. Broner (eds), *The Lost Tradition: Mothers and Daughters in Literature* (New York, 1980), pp. 33–43; Kristen Poole, ' "The Fittest Closet for all Goodness": Authorial Strategies of Jacobean Mothers' Manuals', *Studies in English Literature, 1500–1900*, 35 (1995), 69–88; Marsha Urban, *Seventeenth-Century Mother's Advice Books* (Basingstoke, 2006); Felicity Dunworth, *Mothers and Meaning on the Early Modern Stage* (Manchester, 2010), ch. 7; and Jennifer Heller, *The Mother's Legacy in Early Modern England* (Farnham, 2011). See also Susan C. Staub (ed.), *Mothers' Advice Books*, The Early Modern Englishwoman: Printed Writings 1500–1640, ser. 1, part 2, vol. 8 (Aldershot, 2002). The discussion here draws on Alexandra Walsham, 'The Mother's Legacy: Women, Religion and Generational Transmission in Post-Reformation England', in Susan Karant-Nunn and Ute Lotz-Heumann (eds), *The Cultural History of the Reformation*, Wolfenbütteler Forschungen (Göttingen, 2020), pp. 227–47.

[120] Dorothy Leigh, *The mothers blessing: or, the godly counsaile of a gentlewoman, not long since deceased, left behind for her children*, 7th edn (1621; STC 15404), sig. A5v, pp. 1–4, 14–16, 24–9. Quotation from Urban, *Mother's Advice Books*, p. 45.

[121] Elizabeth Grymeston, *Miscellanea. Prayers. Meditations. Memoratives* ([1608?]; STC 12410), sig. A2r.

[122] See Susan E. Hrach, ' "Heare Councill and Receive Instruction": Situating the Mother's Legacy in Manuscript', in Michael Denbo (ed.), *New Ways of Looking at Old Texts* IV, Papers of the Renaissance English Text Society 2002–2206 (Tempe, AZ, 2008), pp. 207–15, at p. 207.

Elizabeth Jocelin's *Mothers legacie* (1624) was another set of pearls of spiritual wisdom dispensed by a gentlewoman who correctly predicted her demise in childbirth. Edited by Thomas Goad after its author died, Jocelin's book presented itself as both a solace to its 'twinne-like sister' (the daughter who survived her) and a 'deputed mother' for her instruction. Goad consciously played the role of midwife in ushering the product of her literary labours into the world, seeing in them 'the lineaments of her own parentage': the devout Protestant piety of her father William Chaderton, Master of Queen's College, Cambridge, and later bishop of Chester and Lincoln. In his role as executor, he presented her bequest as beneficial not merely to 'her hoped issue', but also 'the common kindred of Christianity'.[123]

Such texts invited their readers to eavesdrop on the private pronouncements that parents made in anticipation of their own imminent expiry, which was the precondition for their publication. They allowed them vicariously to experience the moment of death and to hear the words uttered by people on the threshold of departure from this world. As the minister Richard Mayhew put it in his *Charisma patrikon, a paternal gift* (1676), a guide to growing in grace and faith, 'a book may speak when men are speechless; yea, when men are lifeless'.[124] The puritan poet Anne Bradstreet wrote to her children,

> This book by any yet unread,
> I leave for you when I am dead.[125]

Surrogates for speech, parental blessings and legacies projected the voice of living writers into a future from which they knew they would be missing. Exploiting media that were simultaneously promiscuous and intimate, the pose they adopted was both prospective and retrospective. Tools by which people who had passed from earthly life could communicate with succeeding ones, such texts reflect a vibrant tradition of communication between the generations that was strengthened by the reverence in which early modern people held their dead ancestors and their elders in faith.

In turn, many of these manuscripts and printed books became reservoirs of spiritual edification for fellow believers. A manuscript in the Friends' House Library incorporates a fine copy of William Penn's famous farewell letter to his wife and children, written 'if I should never see you more in this Worlde'. This has been transcribed alongside other texts, including the exhortations of an unknown Quaker preacher to the 'Dear Babes' and 'Lambs', 'for whom my soul travelleth in Birth'.[126] Copied out by Mary Franklin, the letters and last speeches that William Jenkyn, Henry Cornish, and other nonconformists left as legacies for their

---

[123] Elizabeth Jocelin, *The mothers legacie, to her unborne childe* (1624; STC 14624), sigs A3r–5v.

[124] Richard Mayhew, *Charisma patrikon, a paternal gift, or, the legacie of a (dying) father, to his (living) children* (1676; Wing M1438), sig. A7r.

[125] *The Works of Anne Bradstreet*, ed. Jeannine Hersley (Cambridge, MA, 1967), p. 240.

[126] FHL, MS VOL 62/5 (Compilation of letters and transcriptions once owned by the Braithwaite family), items 38 and 23.

children before they were executed for complicity in Monmouth's rebellion in 1685 supplied religious sustenance to this Presbyterian lady and her heirs.[127] The Blackmore family archive preserves Chewning Blackmore's last legacy of godly advice to his offspring, begging them 'to Remember the great End for which you ware sent in to the World for that you may Glorifi God' and ending with an admonition to be 'Chearful' and love and bear with one another (Fig. 6.6).[128] Subsequently deposited in Dr Williams' Library, these documents were envisaged as sources of inspiration for other dissenters.

Susanna Bell similarly left an account of the spiritual experiences that had converted her into a regenerate Christian to her mourning children. Taken from her mouth by one of them when 'she was in a very weakly condition', this described the inner struggles that accompanied her admission as 'a Babe of Christ' and her ongoing efforts to grow further in faith after she and her husband emigrated to New England. Enumerating the family's providential deliverances from plague, fire, and earthquakes, it traced the process by which she acquired 'experimental' knowledge of the grace of her election. Prepared for publication by the pastor of her congregation in London, Thomas Brooks, the published version of this inspiring autobiographical narrative written late in life became a paper monument to this godly matriarch.[129]

The language that contemporaries used to describe their literary bequests to living relatives was generational as well as testamentary. Women often compared the maternal labours they carried out in writing with their role in bringing forth children and nurturing their tiny bodies by breastfeeding, but men used this trope too. Ellis Crispe described the religious reflections written between 1622 and 1626 which he left to his kindred and friends as a 'poore decreped infant'. Among them was a record of his own covenant with the Lord and a translation of the Latin epitaph on the tombstone of his grandfather Thomas Crispe, a 'worthie & zealous servant of God', in the church of Marshfield, Gloucestershire:

> Lord graunt unto his children, and their child-
> rens children from one generation to
> another such graces of they sperrite
> that they may tread in his stepps
> and walke in thy waies.[130]

The personification of the book as a living child further reflects the effort to reconstitute the presence of the dead in a world from which purgatory had been removed.

[127] CL, MS I.h.37 (Mary Franklin, copies of letters and speeches). This archive has now been edited by Vera J. Camden: *Being Dead Yet Speaketh: The Franklin Family Papers* (Toronto, 2020).

[128] DWL, MS 12.40 ('Original Letters and Family Papers &c of the Blackmore Family'), item 140.

[129] *The legacy of a dying mother to her mourning children, being the experiences of Mrs Susanna Bell, who died March 13. 1672*, ed. Thomas Brooks (1673; Wing B1801), pp. 38, 52, 49.

[130] CL, MS I.f.2 (Spiritual diary of Ellis Crispe, 1622–6).

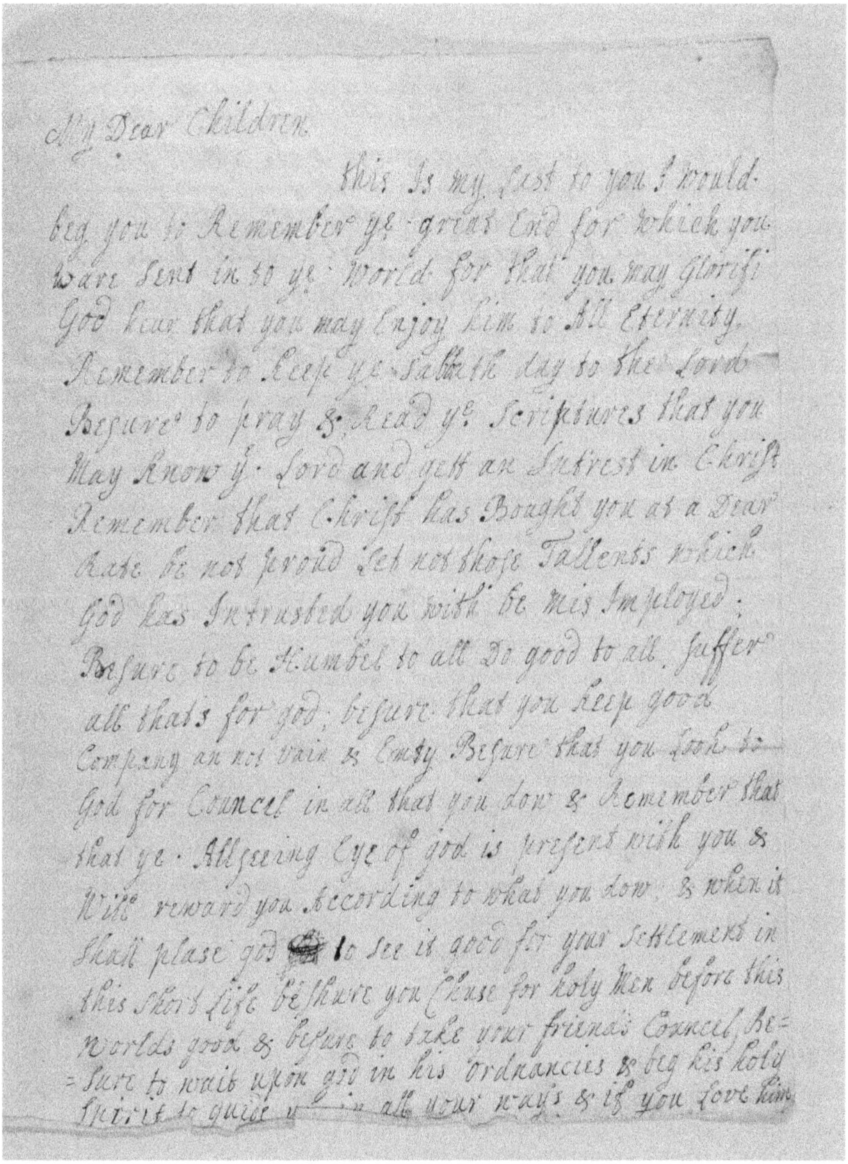

My Dear Children.

this Is my last to you I would beg you to Remember ye great End for which you ware sent in to ye world for that you may glorifi God hear that you may Enjoy him to All Eternity Remember to keep ye Sabbath day to the Lord Besure to pray & read ye Scriptures that you may know ye Lord and gett an Intrest in Christ Remember that Christ has Bought you at a Dear Rate be not proud Let not those Tallents which God has Intrusted you with be mis Imployed: Besure to be Humbel to all Do good to all suffer all thats for god; besure that you keep good Company an not vain & Emty Besure that you Look to God for Councel in all that you dow & Remember that that ye Allseeing Eye of god is present with you & will reward you According to what you dow & when it shall plase god to see it good for your settlement in this short life be there you Chuse for holy men before this worlds good & besure to take your friends Councel be=sure to wait upon god in his ordinances & beg his holy spirit to guide y in all your ways & if you love him

Fig. 6.6 Chewning Blackmore's legacy to 'My Dear Children'.

Source: Dr Williams's Library, London, MS 12.40 ('Original Letters and Family Papers &c. of the Blackmore Family'), item 140.

Moving seamlessly between the biological family and a wider Christian one, mothers' and fathers' legacies may be compared with those that devoted ministers bestowed upon the congregations they had served for decades. The work of a Gloucestershire minister and grandfather, *Maltbey's morsels for mourners* deployed the familiar idiom of experimental predestinarianism, describing itself as a 'new borne Babe, which might have beene obscured and buried with him, had it not with a Religious Care bin preserved' and printed for the little flock over which he had charge in 1633.[131] Rector of Ubley in Somerset for forty-four years, William Thomas composed his treatise of Christian and family duties— catechizing, praying, sermon repetition, and psalm-singing—before his decease, so that his parishioners might keep his teachings in perpetual remembrance.[132] Many of these publications were prepared for the press by clerical sons and heirs. John Dunton's *Remains* were edited by his son, who disappointed his father by not entering the Church like his grandfather and great-grandfather before him, pursuing a lucrative career as a Protestant bookseller instead. Among the eight treatises he printed was a friendly dialogue between 'a moderate conformist' and a parishioner about the heated debates that fractured the Restoration Church. Exhorting conforming Protestants and Presbyterians to unite against the popish enemy, it was an irenic call for cooperation between reformed 'bretheren'.[133]

Such texts helped foster the sympathetic assumption that all members of the inclusive institution that was the Church of England were members of the family of God. They alleviated the tensions between inclusion and separation that were inherent within Protestant ecclesiology. The Massachusetts pastor John Higginson's *Our dying saviour's legacy of peace to his disciples in a troublesome world* (1686) was addressed to the entire household of God that made up the visible church on earth. 'Being under the infirmities of Age, and not like to live long, being 70 Years old, which in Scripture-account is the ordinary period of mans life', he left it to his covenanted people of Salem, Guilford, and Saybrook as 'a thankful Remembrance' of God's gracious dealings with him in his 'Pilgrimage upon Earth' and particularly his early years in the 'wilderness'.[134]

Some took up the theme of 'Being dead, he yet speaketh' to address more diffuse communities. Richard Baxter's *Last legacy* was a series of 'select admonitions and directions to all sober dissenters'.[135] Published in Douai in 1654, Thomas Bayly's *Legacie left to Protestants* addressed eighteen issues in dispute between the

---

[131] John Maltbey, *A grand-fathers legacy; or Maltbey's morsels for mourners* (1633; STC 17216).

[132] See William Thomas, *Practical piety, or the pastor's last legacy to his beloved people* (1681; Wing T987B), sigs A2r, A3v.

[133] John Dunton, *Dunton's remains: or, the dying pastour's last legacy to his friends and parishioners* (1684; Wing D2619G). See treatise 6.

[134] John Higginson, *Our dying saviour's legacy of peace to his disciples in a troublesome world, from John 14.27* (1686; Wing H1956), sigs A2r–5r.

[135] *Mr Richard Baxter's last legacy in select admonitions and directions to all sober dissenters* (1697; Wing B1297). See also *The last will and testament of Sir John Presbyter... with divers admonitions and legacies left to his deare children* (1647; Wing L526).

Church of Rome and its heretical enemies. The bishop of Hereford, Herbert Croft, left a printed guide to anti-Catholic controversy to his diocese in 1679, the year of the Popish Plot, along with the substantial library that had enabled him to write it.[136] The 'widow's mite' bequeathed by Alice Hayes of Tottenham, who had been taunted with the derogatory nickname 'Quaker' in her youth, was designed to stir a new generation of Friends to bear faithful witness to the truth.[137] These were works that helped to bring the abstract entities that subsequently became known as denominations into being.

Other textual bequests addressed age and social cohorts. They spoke to young people and to old ones crippled by infirmity and crowned with 'gray hairs and wrinkles of Age'. Directed towards a 'rising generation' composed of 'all ranks, ages and sexes', they were engines for the creation of communities defined by the shared experiences of marginalization and empowerment that comprised the successive stages of England's prolonged and contentious Reformation. Further by-products of the radical transformation of traditional commemorative culture this wrought, they gave expression to the belief that these were people who had both seen and made history.[138] Addressed to both families of blood and families of faith, they invoked and crystallized multiple senses of generational identity.

Remembering the Reformations

Next I investigate the interrelated questions of how contemporaries remembered the ongoing cycle of religious change. Setting aside the distorting preoccupation with the rise of individual subjectivity that has dominated studies of early modern life-writing, more recent work has emphasized the communal environment out of which diaries and memoirs grew. It has situated introspection and interiority within the context of 'an overpowering concern with the Christian community', recognizing such texts as 'multi-layered sites of conversation' between the social and the self. It has taught us the value of adopting a broad definition of autobiography that is alive to its 'generic unfixity' and hybridity.[139] The ensuing

[136] [Thomas Bayly], *A legacie left to Protestants* ([Douai], 1654; Wing B1512); Herbert Croft, *The legacy of…Herbert, Lord Bishop of Hereford, to his diocess, or a short determination of all controversies we have with the papists* (1679; Wing C6966).
[137] *A legacy, or widow's mite; left by Alice Hayes, to her children and others* (1723).
[138] For legacies to age cohorts, see William Lydford, *Lydford's legacie: or, an helpe for young people* (1658; Wing L3548); Samuel Wakeman, *A young man's legacy to the rising generation* (Cambridge, MA, 1673; Wing W279), quotation at pp. 3–4; Christopher Ness, *A divine legacy, bequeathed unto all mankind, of all ranks, ages and sexes* (1700; Wing N454). For legacies to social cohorts, in this case the congregations of ministers ejected on 'Black Bartholomew's Day', see Richard Fairclough, *A pastors legacy to his beloved people: being the substance of fourteen farewell sermons* ([1663]; Wing F106); Edward Hancock, *The pastors last legacy and counsel. Delivered in a farewel sermon preached at St Philips in Bristol* (1663; Wing H640).
[139] For some key contributions within the literary scholarship, see Joan Webber, *The Eloquent 'I': Style and Self in Seventeenth-Century Prose.* (Madison, WI, 1968); Meredith A. Skura, *Tudor Autobiography: Listening for Inwardness* (Chicago, 2008); A. C. Spearing, *Medieval Autographies:*

discussion connects the narratives that people wrote about formative events with the powerful incentives they felt to instruct living relatives and as yet unborn descendants. It locates them within the 'communities of remembering' that are biological and social generations.[140] Inspired by the observation that 'autobiographical memory is not only a record, it is a resource', it shows how men, women, and children recurrently reinvented themselves.[141] To make sense of their lives they were obliged to fall back on inherited cultural schemes and to create 'fictive concords with origins and ends'.[142] 'Suspended between past and future', their reminiscences must be seen as 'a variation of a loop of the imagination'.[143] This was a process that evolved over the course of each individual's progress from infancy, childhood, and youth to middle and old age, and of the life cycles of the religious movements that marked this era. As it passed from people who had witnessed dramatic moments to their descendants and became second-hand testimony, memory underwent further mutations. Always coloured by hindsight, remembering the Reformations involved a mixture of spontaneous and strategic forgetting. The present was haunted by the past, which had multiple afterlives.[144]

For those caught up in its first bewildering phase in the 1530s, 1540s, and 1550s, persecution, sacrifice, and suffering served as a significant stimulus to record-keeping. Relating his tribulations as the first Protestant bishop of the Irish see of Ossory, John Bale's *Vocacyon* (1553) was written to console his afflicted co-religionists in England and his 'exyled bretherne' in Europe. The former Carmelite friar described his 'miraculouse deliveraunce' from 'the greedy mouthes of devourying lions' to the safety of asylum in Germany to encourage them to hope that they too would either be preserved from the 'tyrannouse molestacions' of the

---

The *'I' of the Text* (Notre Dame, IN, 2012); Kathleen Lynch, *Protestant Autobiography in the Seventeenth-Century Anglophone World* (Oxford, 2012). For historical treatments, see Michael Mascuch, *Origins of the Individualist Self: Autobiography and Self-Identity in England, 1591–1791* (Cambridge, 1997); James Amelang, *The Flight of Icarus: Artisan Autobiography in Early Modern Europe* (Stanford, CA, 1998); Rudolf Dekker, *Egodocuments and History: Autobiographical Writing in Its Social Context since the Middle Ages* (Hilversum, 2002); special issue on ego-documents edited by Mary Fulbrook and Ulinka Rublack, *German History* 28/3 (2010). The quotations are from Margo Todd, 'Puritan Self-Fashioning: The Diary of Samuel Ward', *JBS*, 31 (1992), 236–64, at 254; Andrew Cambers, 'Reading, the Godly, and Self-Writing in England, c.1580–1720', *JBS*, 46 (2007), 796–825, at 824; Smyth, *Autobiography in Early Modern England*, pp. 1, 14.

[140] The pioneering theorist is Tamara K. Hareven, 'The Search for Generational Memory: Tribal Rites in Industrial Society', *Daedalus*, 107 (1978), 137–49. For some other reflections on these themes, see Robyn Fivush, 'Remembering and Reminiscing: How Individual Lives are Constructed in Family Narratives', *Memory Studies*, 1 (2008), 49–58; Amy Corning and Howard Schuman, *Generations of Collective Memory* (Chicago, 2015).

[141] John A. Robinson, 'Autobiographical Memory: A Historical Prologue', in David C. Rubin (ed.), *Autobiographical Memory* (Cambridge, 1986), pp. 19–24, at p. 23.

[142] Mark Freeman, quoting Frank Kermode, in 'Telling Stories: Memory and Narrative', in Susannah Radstone and Bill Schwarz (eds), *Memory: Histories, Theories, Debates* (New York, 2010), pp. 263–77, at p. 266.

[143] Shore and Kauko, 'Landscape of Family Memory', p. 230.

[144] Marek Tamm (ed.), *Afterlife of Events: Perspectives on Mnemohistory* (2015), esp. Aleida Assmann, 'Theories of Cultural Memory and the Concept of "Afterlife"', ibid., pp. 79–94.

papists by God's gracious mercies or be selected to wear the greater crown of martyrdom for 'his truthes sake'. 'No chosen chylde receyveth he to enherytaunce, without much correction,' he wrote in a text that self-consciously evoked the rhetoric of the Pauline epistles to neophyte Christians. Composed in the immediate aftermath of these testing events, Bale's memoirs were an ebullient celebration of his calling as a member of the 'elect vynyarde' of the Church.[145] They imposed coherence on a moment of acute emotional and physical crisis and wove it into the fabric of his identity as an early convert.

Others looked back on episodes in their childhood and youth that marked them for life. Recalling how he had been whipped by his father for reading Tyndale's New Testament forty years earlier, William Maldon of Chelmsford said that he 'felte not the strypes' but 'as trewely as the Lord liveth I rejoiced that I was betten for Christ's sake'. Written 'not for any vayne glory', but 'the prayse and honour of our God', Maldon's narrative wiped the severe sting of his punishment out of his remembrance.[146] John Louth, later archdeacon of Nottingham, was just 3 years old when his father—who was carrying his son in his arms at the time— was mortally wounded in an affray with two of his neighbours in 1522, allegedly instigated by the monks of Sawtry Abbey. Mediated by his surviving parent, his own close escape from harm evidently fostered a lasting hatred of the Catholic priesthood and cemented his commitment to the Protestant faith. Here a memory trace from his childhood has 'been translated back into a plastic and visual form at a later date', aided by the stories his mother told him. Recollecting this violent event in 1579, he also dated it on a timeline that began with the birth of the Reformation: 'Ao 5 post Lutheri predicationem'.[147]

Individuals eager to carve out a niche for themselves in Foxe's Actes and monuments sent their own memoirs to the martyrologist. Edward Underhill supplied notes of his interrogation and imprisonment during Mary's reign, when he was arrested for composing a scurrilous ballad against the Catholic establishment and mocked by his peers as a 'hoote gospellar'. Fifteen years on, his liberation from 'thatt lothsume gayle off Newgate' and from 'the cumepany off the weked' seemed akin to the redemption of God's servants in Scripture. Insisting that he had never bowed his knee to Baal and been present at the 'blaphemus masse', he too constructed himself in the image of Christian heroes new and old.[148] In a text headed 'God is my deffense', Thomas Mountain, minister of the London parish of St Michael Tower-Ryall, told the tale of his incarceration in the Marshalsea and

---

[145] John Bale, The vocacyon of Johan Bale to the bishoprick of Ossorie in Irelande his persecutions in the same & final deliverance (Rome [Wesel?], 1553); STC 1307), fos 6v, 41v–42r, 8r, 47v. See Oliver Wort, John Bale and Religious Conversion in Reformation England (2013).

[146] John Gough Nichols (ed.), Narratives of the Days of the Reformation, Chiefly from the Manuscripts of John Foxe the Martyrologist, CS, OS 77 (1859), pp. 348–51. See Chapter 1 above, p. 34.

[147] Ibid., pp. 35–9. This is an example of what Sigmund Freud called 'screen memories': The Penguin Freud Reader, ed. Adam Phillips (2006), pp. 541–60, at p. 559.

[148] Nichols (ed.), Narratives, pp. 132–76, at pp. 149, 159–60, 172.

his 'paynful perygrynasyon[s]...for the testymonye of the truthe, and keapynge of a good consyence'.[149] Those who escaped the fires of Smithfield and survived to see Protestantism restored in 1558 instinctively viewed their own experiences through the lens of Foxe's famous history. They shoehorned the messy inconsistencies that mark human life into familiar biblical and hagiographical moulds, creating new 'social selves' in dialogue with the 'inner eye' of those who composed them, which were repeatedly recast in keeping with an ever-changing religious and cultural climate.[150]

Men and women who later became upright Protestants reconfigured their personal pasts to excuse or occlude the less than courageous behaviour in which they had engaged between 1553 and 1558, when many chose the more comfortable path of conformity. The small vellum roll on which Archbishop Matthew Parker listed the milestones in his academic and clerical career is one such exercise in repressing memory of the decision to 'tarry' within the realm rather than resist or take flight. Repressing the awkward fact that this architect of the Elizabethan Church was neither a martyr nor an exile but a Nicodemite, it reinterpreted his active compliance with the Catholic regime as a form of victimhood.[151] It effaced a more ambiguous and chequered version of the Marian past than the official one.[152] Others expressed regret at their past failings in the records they left for their posterity. The parenthetical phrase that the Kentish gentleman Richard Dering inserted in a memorandum regarding his marriage at a Mass in Queen Mary's time is a tiny, telling gesture of repentance: 'lord forgive me'.[153]

Written for her children in 1610 at the age of 85, Rose Hickman's carefully crafted account of the troubles she had endured for the reformed faith as a young married woman is another striking example of retrospective self-fashioning (Fig. 6.7). Half a century after the events in question, she remembered her family's relocation to the Low Countries in the mid-1550s as a period of fiery trial, highlighting the sacrifices she and her husband had made in leaving England, reproving the covetousness that had prevented her sister-in-law from following suit, and extenuating the casuistical compromises they made during these difficult times. Glossing over their pragmatic choice of Catholic Antwerp above Calvin's Geneva as their place of refuge, she declared: 'I accompted all nothing in comparison to libertie of conscience for the profession of Christ.' This is a narrative suffused with yearning for that heroic era and her determination to be counted among the

---

[149] Ibid., pp. 177–217, at pp. 216–17.

[150] Drawing on the insights of Mary Fulbrook, *Dissonant Lives: Generations and Violence through the German Dictatorships* (Oxford, 2011), esp. pp. 2–3.

[151] See Cambridge, Corpus Christi College, MS 583. This is discussed by Ceri Law in 'Compromise Refashioned: Memory and Life-Writing in Matthew Parker's Roll', in Walsham, Wallace, Law, and Cummings (eds), *Memory and the English Reformation*, pp. 257–70.

[152] For the persistence and manipulation of the Nicodemite legacy, see Robert Harkins, 'Elizabethan Puritanism and the Politics of Memory in Post-Marian England', *HJ*, 57 (2014), 899–919.

[153] FSL, MS V.b.96, fo. 201r.

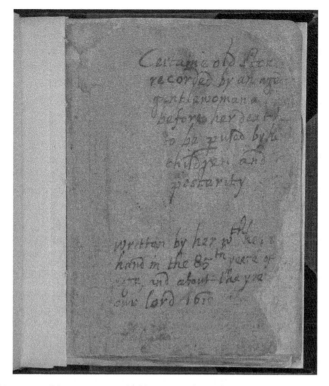

Fig. 6.7 'Certaine old stories recorded by an aged gentlewoman a time before her death, to be perused by her children and posterity. Written by her with her own hand in the 85ᵗʰ yeere of age, and about the yeer of our lord 1610'. The memoir of Rose Hickman.

Source: © British Library Board, Additional MS 43827A. All Rights Reserved/Bridgeman Images.

godly people whom the 'cruell papists' had oppressed. Integrating memories of her parents' illicit adherence to the Gospel in Henry VIII's reign and the providential deliverances of her son William during his childhood, it is at once a Protestant chronicle and a genealogy. Left as a mother's legacy, it was lovingly transcribed by her great-great-granddaughter Elizabeth as a writing exercise in 1667, together with an epitaph celebrating the 'happy blessings' bestowed upon this godly matron who had 'kept the sacred faith with constancy / Even in the midst of persecutions rage'. By the late seventeenth century, the 'certaine old stories' recorded by this aged gentlewoman had entered into family legend.[154]

---

[154] Maria Dowling and Joy Shakespeare (eds), 'Religion and Politics in Mid-Tudor England through the Eyes of an English Protestant Woman: The Recollections of Rose Hickman', *Bulletin of the Institute of Historical Research*, 55 (1982), 94–102. Rose died in 1613. Three manuscripts of her memoirs, which are seventeenth-century copies, were given to the BL by a descendant: Additional MS 43827 A and B; Additional MS 45027. The last is the writing exercise by Elizabeth Hickman. For the epitaph, see fo. 7v, which is followed by a list of her offspring dated 1637.

Subtly embellished as they were copied, such memoirs reflect the compound of pride, pain, discomfort, and guilt that accompanies the recollection of traumatic events.

The same patterns of partial forgetting and strategic remembering can be discerned among England's Catholics. Mediated by the scribes who recorded them, the life stories of adolescent boys who entered the English Colleges at Rome and Valladolid often highlight the spiritual shortcomings of mothers and fathers who were schismatics and heretics. The tales of reconciliation and conversion they told circumscribed patriarchal authority and emphasized role reversal: young people remembered their path to becoming true Catholics in accordance with the tropes of youthful enlightenment trumping degenerate age which were firmly entrenched within Christian culture.[155] As we saw in Chapter 1, the Benedictine monk Augustine Baker was similarly frank about the faults of his conservative parents, mere 'neutrals in religion' who had unwittingly lapsed into church papistry, schism, and apathy in the 1560s. Tempering shame with affection, he remembered his father's devout daily habit of vocal prayer aided by a primer and his mother's proclivity for quiet contemplation, which he had inherited from her. He clung to the conviction that it was only the former's 'conjugal estate' and care for his wife and children that had dissuaded him from his 'inclination and desire' to abandon his heretical homeland and go into voluntary banishment. His parents' steady drift away from the old faith formed a counterpoint to Baker's own journey towards it, culminating in his decision to devote his life to Christ. In turn, the memoirs of this 'venerable father' became treasured relics, edited and preserved by his fellow priests, disciples and friends in the order.[156]

Another text that traces the transference of allegiance from a blood family to a superior spiritual one is the conversion narrative of Catherine Holland, who defied her overbearing Protestant father to become an Augustinian sister. Written towards the end of her life at the behest of her confessor, it was inflected by the 'Miseries of decrepit old Age' she shortly expected to exchange for the 'heavenly Mansion'. Mentioned in her obituary, this precious history was subsequently deposited in the community's archive.[157] It must be analysed alongside the forms of 'subsumed' and 'anonymous autobiography' Victoria van Hyning has excavated from convent chronicles. As she shows, monastic self-writing was simultaneously superfluous and vital. Evincing 'the need to speak without being named', it reflected their authors' status as metaphorically dead to the world.[158]

---

[155] See Chapter 1 above, p. 77. Lucy Underwood, 'Youth, Religious Identity, and Autobiography at the English Colleges in Rome and Valladolid, 1592–1685', *HJ*, 55 (2012), 349–74, at 373–4.

[156] *Memorials of Father Augustine Baker and Other Documents Relating to the English Benedictines*, ed. J. McCann and H. Connolly, CRS 33 (1933), pp. 15–19, 53–4. See above, p. 47.

[157] Catherine Holland, 'How I Came to Change My Religion'. This is edited as the Appendix to Victoria Van Hyning, *Convent Autobiography: Early Modern English Nuns in Exile* (Oxford, 2019), quotations at pp. 340–1. See also ch. 2.

[158] Ibid., pp. 35, 266.

The transmission of such texts served to strengthen the bond between the generations and cement their attachment to a common religious past. The very process of remembering history was inextricably linked with remembering one's biological and spiritual ancestors.[159] Sometimes this served to collapse the distinction between personal experiences and inherited memory. The alderman and elder of the Dutch stranger church of London, John La Motte, whose mother and father had fled Ypres in the first decade of Elizabeth's reign to escape the duke of Alba, identified so closely with the 'great sufferings and bloody persecutions' of his family and fellow Protestants in the Low Countries that he recounted them to his household and guests 'in so punctual and feeling a manner, as if he had been an eye-witness, yea a sharer in them'. Although he died a full century later, he still thought of himself as part of the diaspora of Reformed refugees, describing his own memory as 'a living chronicle' of the tumultuous times that had prompted their exile. Indeed, he consciously reactivated a past that his own ancestors may have preferred to forget.[160] Like Moses or Abraham, La Motte's long life enabled him to breach the alleged divide between communicative and cultural remembering. It mimicked a tradition of familial memory which, as Rachel Greenblatt has demonstrated, was as vibrant in the Jewish communities of early modern Europe as it was among the ancient Hebrews.[161] It demonstrates the totemic resonance that painful experiences continued to carry for later generations.[162]

When second- and third-generation Protestants remembered events retailed to them by their parents and grandparents, they too engaged in forms of creative alteration and deliberate erasure. In an account of the divine blessings bestowed upon his family written in 1607, for instance, the Yorkshire gentleman Sir William Wentworth recast the story of his own conception in 1561 to remove incriminating traces of devotion to the discredited cult of saints. He quietly transformed the story of how a vision of St Anne and pilgrimage to her miraculous well at Buxton had helped his mother and father to overcome their failure to produce a male heir into a Protestant tale about the appearance of an angel and a journey to the Derbyshire shrine resurrected as a spa and celebrated for its natural healing

---

[159] See the perceptive comments of Joanne Bailey, 'The Afterlife of Parenting: Memory, Parenting and Personal Identity in Britain, c.1760–1830', *Journal of Family History*, 35 (2010), 249–70, and eadem, *Parenting in England, 1760–1830: Emotion, Identity and Generation* (Oxford, 2012), pp. 125, 128, 138, and ch. 5.

[160] Fulk Bellers, *Abrahams interment, or, The good old-mans buriall in a good old age* (1656; B1826), sig. F4r. See also Samuel Clarke, *The lives of sundry eminent persons in this later age* (1683; C4538), part 2, p. 102. See Johannes Müller, 'Permeable Memories, Family History and the Diaspora of Southern Netherlandish Exiles in the Seventeenth Century', in Erika Kuijpers, Judith Pollmann, Johannes Müller, and Jasper van der Steen (eds), *Memory before Modernity: Practices of Memory in Early Modern Europe* (Leiden, 2013), pp. 283–95; idem, *Exile Memories and the Dutch Revolt: The Narrated Diaspora, 1550–1750* (Leiden, 2016), esp. ch. 4.

[161] See Greenblatt, *To Tell Their Children*, ch.3 and p. 191.

[162] On this theme, see Paloma Aguilar and Clara Ramírez-Barat, 'Generational Dynamics in Spain: Memory Transmission of a Turbulent Past', *Memory Studies*, 12 (2019), 213–29.

properties in the mid-Elizabethan period. Taking the guise of 'a wellfavored gentlewoman of a mydle age', the heavenly visitor said that her name was 'God's pitty' and took a box of ointment out of her pocket with which she anointed the genitals of his father, who was then gravely ill with a burning fever. As well as commanding him to wash in the spring and give thanks for his deliverance, she also revealed many things to come, which Sir William surmised were predictions 'of some particuler prosperitees of his house and posterity'.[163]

Others glanced back at the popish past with greater ambivalence. In his critical account of the Henrician assault upon the religious houses written around 1590, Michael Sherbrooke recalled a conversation with his father thirty years after the suppression regarding his part in dismantling the fabric of a local monastery. In response to his son's demand, 'how came it to pass you was so ready to distroy and spoil the thing that you thought well of?', he replied: 'What should I do...might I not as well as others have some Profit of the Spoil of the Abbey? For I did see all would away; and therefore I did as others did.' Sherbrooke implicitly distanced himself from a generation that had been content to engage in the wholesale destruction of a worthy institution.[164] The manuscript memoirs of the Holles family of Lincolnshire are equally revealing of changing attitudes. Gervase Holles, a Royalist who compiled them while in exile in the 1650s, praised the liberality of his great-great-grandfather, a former lord mayor of London who had erected the market cross at Coventry in 1539 and was 'the restorer or rayser of our family'. While observing that 'his care for his soule' accorded with 'the superstition of those dayes', he nevertheless deplored the 'impious persons' responsible for damaging his tomb. His outrage at this egregious act of vandalism was sharpened by the renewed iconoclasm that coincided with the Civil Wars and Interregnum. Citing the memories of 'severall olde people who could very well remember him', he noted that his maternal grandfather had opposed the pulling down of St Mary's church in Grimsby, but 'was overballanced by the greater and more sacreligious number, some of whom they named to me with this observation that almost all their posterity came to beggary'.[165] Such texts reflected an emerging shift in sentiment, as regret about the 'fatal effects' of the Protestant revolution waned and a mellower view of monasticism gradually set in.

Family memoirs were often emended to conceal notorious ancestors. A book of 'diverse necessary remembrances' compiled by successive generations of the Dering family bent over backwards to deny that a monk of Canterbury convicted of treason in the wake of the Nun of Kent affair was a blood relative. By suggesting that the man in question had simply adopted the name of his former

[163] J. P. Cooper (ed.), *Wentworth Papers, 1597–1628*, CS, 4th ser., 12 (1973), pp. 28–9.

[164] BL, Additional MS 5813, fos 20v–21r. This manuscript tract is printed in A.G. Dickens (ed.), *Tudor Treatises*, Yorkshire Archaeological Society 125 (Leeds, 1959), p. 125. See also p. 33.

[165] Gervase Holles, *Memorials of the Holles Family 1493–1656*, ed. A. C. Wood, CS, 3rd ser., 55 (1937), pp. 20–4, 214.

patron, it redeemed the Dering line from political disloyalty.[166] A descendant of
the Tracys of Gloucestershire similarly dismissed the claim that a forebear was
implicated in the assassination of 'that turbulent and ambitious Prelate' Thomas
Becket, as a case of mistaken identity: 'tis evident that there were others of the
same Name living at that Time'. Although Becket's defence of papal power and
'violent Invasion of the Royal Prerogative of his Sovereign' made him the fore-
most target of Henry VIII's campaign to consign parts of Catholic history to
oblivion, acknowledging the presence of a murderer in one's pedigree was clearly
best avoided.[167]

Silence was an alternative device for effecting amnesia. The elimination of
inconvenient predecessors converged with efforts to play up the precocious
Protestant credentials of others. The Tracys proudly recalled their most illustrious
forebear: the Henrician evangelical of Toddington whose heretical will led to the
posthumous exhumation and incineration of his body by order of the chancellor
of the diocese of Worcester in 1531. Proclaiming his complete assurance of salvation through Christ's merits alone, this exemplary testament circulated scribally
in England, before being published in Antwerp in 1535. Leaving its imprint on
the preambles of many subsequent wills, it turned its author into a Protestant
hero: 'one of the first that embrac'd the Reform'd Religion in this Kingdom'.[168] The
Oldys family co-opted John Olde or Oldus into its ranks, 'an eminent Champion'
of the Gospel who had fled overseas in Mary's reign, explaining the different
spelling of his name by 'the unsettled Orthography of those Days'.[169] More legitimately, the Commelines of Gloucestershire celebrated an ancestor who had been
executed by the Spanish Council of Blood in Brussels in 1568 for attending
Calvinist hedge-preaching and founding a house church. This catastrophe led his
family to retreat to the northern Netherlands, where they stayed until 1621, when
his descendant sought asylum in England from 'the great dissensions and civil
commotions' within the Dutch Church catalysed by the controversial theology of
Jacobus Arminius.[170] Having a Protestant martyr in one's ancestry lent families a
cachet similar to the blue blood of royalty. William Whately's father-in-law was
the son of 'that tried and prepared Martyr John Hunt who was condemned to be

[166] FSL, MS V.b.96, fo. 205v.
[167] GA, D2153/N11 (Sudeley Archives), p. 11. A later family history glossed this differently, noting
the 'too Forward Officiousnes towards king Henry the Second' that had compelled William Tracy to
participate in the death of 'that pertinatius Prelate' and the chapel he had founded in Tewkesbury 'for
expacion of which so blouddy Offence': D2153/02 (photocopy of 'Series sive Prosapia
Antiquae…Familiae', 18th century).
[168] GA, D2153/N11, p. 16 and D2153/02. The latter confuses the chronology, suggesting that this
had occurred in 'ye tyme of Edward the Sixt'. See John Craig and Caroline Litzenberger, 'Wills as
Religious Propaganda: The Testament of William Tracy', JEH, 44 (1993), 415–31; Caroline
Litzenberger, 'Tracy, William (d. 1530)', in ODNB, and Chapter 3 above, p. 201.
[169] BL, Additional MS 4240 (Memoirs relating to the Oldys family), fo. 3r.
[170] GA, D1233/35 (Papers relating to the Commeline family), letter from Thomas Commeline,
11 July 1888.

burnt for Religion, but was saved from the execution thereof by the death of Queene Mary'. Fortuitously spared by a contingent event, he was almost, but not quite a Protestant saint.[171]

By contrast, England's Catholics keenly emphasized the uncompromising devotion of their predecessors to the Church of Rome. Georges Kenneb, a gentleman from Tournais and benefactor of the English convent of Nazareth in Bruges, boasted that his forebears were 'of the kindred of St Thomas of Canterbury, who were banished with his exile out of England'.[172] Others underlined their links with relatives who had made the ultimate sacrifice. The book of clothings of the Franciscan nuns at Brussels for 1620 noted the admission of Dorothy Whiting, niece of the last abbot of Glastonbury, who was executed for resisting the dissolution; the following year Jane Yates, granddaughter of Francis Tregian, 'whose bodie is kept in the Jesuites church at lisbon in Portugall with great veneration', took the habit at the age of 16.[173] Studiously cultivated by their kith and kin, the memory of distinguished forebears who had died in defence of their religion was critical to the formation of English Catholic histories of persecution. The oral traditions passed onto children were coloured by the collective history that was crystallizing in writing and print.[174]

Dissenters similarly sought to locate themselves in a noble line of stalwart non-conformists. The great-great-grandson of a couple who had left Rouen and settled in Southampton in the early 1560s, the Congregationalist minister Samuel Say assiduously preserved evidence of his Huguenot heritage, together with the memory of his father Gyles, vicar of St Michael's church in the same city until his ejection on Black Bartholomew's Day 1662.[175] Members of the mid-seventeenth-century sects also indulged in genealogical sleight of hand when it came to establishing their religious pedigrees. The Dymonds backdated their membership of the Society of the Friends by a generation, 'too hastily' assuming that the Axminster clothier Philip had become a Quaker in the 1650s, as the early twentieth-century descendant who compiled the chronicles of this 'clan' sheepishly confessed. He added that there was no foundation to the associated tradition that his remains were buried in the Friends' burial ground at Membury.[176] These pious fictions were commensurate with the tissue of legend that accumulated

---

[171] William Whately, *Prototypes, or the primarie precedent presidents out of the booke of Genesis* (1640; STC 25317.5), sig. a2r.

[172] Caroline Bowden (ed.), *The Chronicles of Nazareth (the English Convent) Bruges 1629–1793*, CRS 87 (Woodbridge, 2017), p. 21.

[173] Richard Trappes-Lomax (ed.), *The English Franciscan Nuns 1619–1821 and the Friars Minor of the Same Province 1618–1761*, CRS 24 (1922), pp. 7, 8.

[174] See also Lucy Underwood, 'Childhood, Family and the Construction of English Catholic Histories of Persecution', in Tali Berner and Lucy Underwood (eds), *Childhood, Youth and Religious Minorities in Early Modern Europe* (Basingstoke, 2019), pp. 223–53.

[175] DWL, MS 12.107 (the Say Papers), no. 25 (Gyles Say's memorandum concerning his mother).

[176] FHL, MS 278 (Chronicles of…the Dymond Clan…Part I, The First Five Generations 1595–1870, arr. Charles William Dymond), p. 8.

around George Fox himself, who remembered his own mother as coming from 'the stock of the martyrs' and spoke of his father as an 'honest man' who had the 'seed of God in him'.[177]

Spiritual journals and diaries were also exercises in selective recollection. 'Writing to redundancy' was another mode of 'scripting the self'. As Tom Webster has commented, the 'thoroughgoing destruction of conventional selfhood' required to create the 'new man' of Colossians 3.10 was paradoxically a recipe for reinvention. 'The material site' of the past 'became an object, like Scripture, of meditation and, unlike Scripture, of active re-making'.[178] Such texts afford insight into how people brought up as Protestants negotiated the psychological hurdle of being members of a generation which had not been called upon to suffer for its faith and which enjoyed the Gospel as a birthright. They bespeak a mixture of gratitude for the blessings of peace and prosperity and the tacit wish that their authors might be spiritually tried and tested like their evangelical predecessors. They trace the search for marks of election and the emotional experiences of regeneration that substituted for dramatic conversions from popery, as well as the inner battles with anxiety, sin, and atheism that replaced the crises of conscience that had afflicted their persecuted ancestors. Imitating the rhythms of Augustine's *Confessions*, they document the perennial struggles with diabolical temptation and the overpowering sense of providential intervention that marked the every-day life of ardent Protestants.

From the late Elizabethan diary of the Cambridge divine Samuel Ward to the 'Booke of Rememberance' that the Northamptonshire gentlewoman Elizabeth Isham completed in 1638, these texts construct a subjectivity that is sometimes oblivious to wider political and ecclesiastical events, centring instead on the inner religious life cycle of the writer. Isham's text evinces an admiration for the liturgy of the Church of England that Isaac Stephens has christened 'Prayer Book Puritanism'. For Isham, memory itself was 'an everlasting libraery' through which God revealed his mysterious intentions for the individual believer.[179] The separate, single-folio sheet on which she recorded brief details of her domestic routine, needlework, reading, and family births and deaths in discreet compartments was

---

[177] *A journal or historical account of the life, travels, sufferings, Christian experiences and labour of love in the work of the ministry of...George Fox*, ed. Thomas Ellwood (1694; F1845), p. 1. See William C. Braithwaite, *The Beginnings of Quakerism*, rev. and ed. Henry J. Cadbury (Cambridge, 1955), p. 29.

[178] Tom Webster, 'Writing to Redundancy: Approaches to Spiritual Journals and Early Modern Spirituality', *HJ*, 39 (1996), 33–56, quotations at 42, 48; Pollmann, *Memory in Early Modern Europe*, ch. 1.

[179] Ward's diary is Cambridge, Sidney Sussex College, MS 45, edited in *Two Elizabethan Puritan Diaries*, ed. M. M. Knappen (Chicago, 1933). Princeton University Library, RTCO1 (no. 62): Elizabeth Isham, 'My Booke of Rememberance'. For an online edition, see https://warwick.ac.uk/fac/arts/ren/researchcurrent/isham/, accessed 8 June 2022. For her meditations on memory, see fo. 32r. For a detailed study, see Isaac Stephens, *The Gentlewoman's Remembrance: Patriarchy, Piety, and Singlehood in Early Stuart England* (Manchester, 2016), esp. chs 1, 5.

a 'textual memento' that encapsulated the larger narrative using the techniques of artificial memory.[180] By contrast, Nehemiah Wallington's multiple notebooks obsessively chart God's 'marcys' to him and his 'groth' as a Christian in tandem with his consuming interest in topical events. Torn between his compulsion to pour out his heart onto the page and his concern that this was a dangerous distraction, his writings were both an attempt to construct a sanctified self and to chronicle the critical new chapter in human history he believed he was witnessing in the turbulent years of the 1640s and 1650s, when England's second Reformation seemed imminent, but never quite came to fruition. They gave expression to his sense that he was part of a special generation.[181]

The new challenges presented by the revolutionary events of the mid-seventeenth century were a further fillip to recording the recent past in writing. Survivors of the sectarian violence unleashed by the bitter Civil Wars engaged in forms of recuperative remembering. Legal depositions by Protestant victims of the Irish Rebellion of 1641 reflect attempts to digest and forget harrowing events such as the mass drowning at Portadown bridge. Rumour, hearsay, and printed news fused with private experience to create narratives that drew on established stereotypes of Protestant martyrdom, but edited out details of sexual assault, rape, and murder that were literally unspeakable.[182] In petitions for compensation and redress, the memories of maimed soldiers and war widows were likewise filtered through euphemistic formulae that repressed the horrific circumstances of their suffering, concealed shameful behaviour such as desertion, and eschewed provocative language in the interests of healing past divisions. Artisans, husbandmen, and labourers set aside the very nomenclature of the 'Rebellion' in favour of more neutral and rueful titles such as 'the late unhappy war' or 'the troubles'. As Mark Stoyle remarks, far from 'uncomplicated reproductions', such texts give us access to 'artful pastiches' in which genuine recollections of wartime experience are passed through the sieve of familiar narrative conventions.[183] They alert us to

---

[180] Northampton, Northamptonshire Record Office, MS IL3365, discussed in Margaret J. M. Ezell, 'Elizabeth Isham's Books of Remembrance and Forgetting', *Modern Philology*, 109 (2011), 71–84, at 84.

[181] David Booy (ed.), *The Notebooks of Nehemiah Wallington, 1618–1654* (Aldershot, 2007). The fullest study remains Paul S. Seaver, *Wallington's World: A Puritan Artisan in Seventeenth-Century London* (1985).

[182] For transcriptions of the depositions, now in Trinity College Dublin, see http://1641.tcd.ie, accessed 8 June 2022. See, e.g., Naomi McAreavey, 'Re(-)Membering Women: Protestant Women's Victim Testimonies during the Irish Rising of 1641', *Journal of the Northern Renaissance*, 2 (2010), 1–16; *eadem*, 'Portadown, 1641: Memory and the 1641 Depositions', *Irish University Review*, 47 (2017), 15–31. See also Mícheál Ó Siochrú and Jane Ohlmeyer (eds), *Ireland 1641* (Manchester, 2013) and Susan Broomhall, 'Disturbing Memories, Narrating Experiences and Emotions of Distressing Events in the French Wars of Religion', in Kuijpers, Pollmann, Müller, and van der Steen (eds), *Memory before Modernity*, pp. 253–67.

[183] Mark Stoyle, '"Memories of the Maimed": The Testimony of Charles I's Former Soldiers, 1660–1730', *History*, 88 (2003), 207–26, at 209–10; Imogen Peck, 'The Great Unknown: The Negotiation and Narration of Death by English War Widows, 1647–60', *Northern History*, 53 (2016), 220–35.

the ways in which people curated accounts of themselves designed to 'reconcile the events of the past with their present identity', a task that combined partial, partisan remembering with 'a healthy dose of forgetting'.[184]

Those who switched sides found it necessary to edit their private papers after the Restoration. Sir Thomas Mainwaring, whose father was a captain of the horse in the Parliamentary forces and who himself took the Solemn League and Covenant while a student at Gray's Inn, grew increasingly disillusioned with the Interregnum regime and was probably involved in Booth's uprising in 1659. His overt opposition to the Cromwellian order secured him a baronetcy in 1660. His diary entry for 30 January 1649 seems to reflect both a convenient form of amnesia about the regicide and a subsequent correction in keeping with the official Stuart narrative of the year. Initially he recorded that 'nothing remarkeable' had happened that day. Later this was crossed out and replaced with 'King Charles the first was murtherd'.[185]

The tribulations of the loyalist Anglican clergy and their families during the Civil Wars and Interregnum were also funnelled through the fallible organ of memory. The fractured testimonies John Walker collected from the children of these ministers in the early eighteenth century reveal the lasting psychological scars left by the humiliations they suffered over many decades, as well as the strategies of silence that made remembrance of them bearable. In the knowledge that their reminiscences might become public, their offspring practised reticence, burying scandalous elements and presenting their parents as victims of puritan persecution. They vindicated the behaviour of sequestered ministers by reproving other siblings who, like the clerical son of Robert Dixon, 'ran with the Multitude and saved his Bacon…in stead of suffering as our Father had done'.[186] 'Gravitationally attracted to one cataclysmic event', the king's execution, these narratives are created artefacts that repress memories that were too painful to articulate. Deponents confused events they had witnessed themselves with those subsequently related to them, and they drew convenient moral lessons when notorious oppressors suffered unfortunate sudden deaths. Some were astute enough to recognize that the second-hand stories they told about their relatives would be 'suspected to be partiall'.[187]

Later family histories recalled the religious and political turmoil of the English Revolution in ways that were likewise coloured by published histories.

---

[184] Imogen Peck, *Recollection in the Republics: Memories of the British Civil Wars in England, 1649–1659* (Oxford, 2021), ch. 5, esp. pp. 166, 175.

[185] CRO, DDX 384 (Diaries of Thomas Mainwaring, 1649–88), fo. 3r.

[186] See Fiona McCall, 'Children of Baal: Clergy Families and Their Memories of Sequestration during the English Civil War', *HLQ*, 76 (2013), 617–38, quotation at 629. On 'forgetting as humiliated silence' and the 'effacement of grievous memory traces', see Paul Connerton, 'Seven Types of Forgetting', *Memory Studies*, 1 (2008), 59–71, at 67–9.

[187] Fiona McCall, *Baal's Priests: The Loyalist Clergy and the English Revolution* (Farnham, 2016), ch. 2, quotations at pp. 23, 56.

Descendants of Edward Bridgeman, bishop of Chester, who went into hiding near Oswestry in Shropshire after his estate was confiscated, were invited to assimilate his experiences into the inspiring legend of Anglicanism under the cross that was steadily crystallizing in public and private discourse: the reader 'may easily form to himself the Distresses & Persecutions he underwent during the time of the Great Rebellion when Episcopacy was abolished in England'.[188] An account of the Newports of High Ercal in Staffordshire described the financial sufferings of a forebear devoted to Charles I who was ordered by Parliament to pay £170 to support 'fanatical preachers', after which he fled overseas. Reconciling his actions with the family's subsequent dissatisfaction with the conduct of James II, 'which pointed at the Destruction of the civil as well as religious Liberties of England', required some neat footwork, as did the staunch support of its eldest son Francis, a privy councillor to the same king, for the Glorious Revolution. He 'had the glory of appearing among that illustrious Band of Patriots at the Trial of the Seven Bishops when Religion and the Laws of England found Shelter in the Breasts of an English Jury on the 29th June 1688'. This was a history that vindicated his reputation as a Protestant patriot by ironing out evidence of vacillation, compromise, and inconsistency.[189]

Nonconformists such as Thomas Jolly remembered their responses to the moral predicaments posed by the Clarendon Code in similar ways. The doubts by which they were beset were partially eclipsed by the stout resistance and patient endurance they knew it was their responsibility to embrace. Their bravery in the face of persecution continued to loom large in the dissenting imagination after the Act of Toleration.[190] Such texts helped to construct an image of unflinching commitment to Presbyterianism that was enhanced by the additions made by their descendants. Begun after his removal from the parish of Coley in 1666, following the Five Mile Act, Oliver Heywood's autobiographical reflections were intermingled with reminiscences of his own godly ancestors, including his father Richard, whose appetite for fasting, conferences, and other Christian exercises attracted the hostile attention of officious apparitors.[191] John Rastrick, who spent fourteen years as vicar of Kirkton in Lincolnshire, wrote two accounts of the 'passages' of his life. One, defending the events that led up to his nonconformity, was published in 1705.[192] A second, composed around 1714, which remained in

---

[188] SRO, P1720 (Genealogical and historical account of the family of Bridgeman of Great Lever in Lancashire).

[189] SRO, P1725 (Genealogical and historical account of the family of Newport of High Ercal, afterwards Earls of Bedford, 18th century), pp. 6–8.

[190] DWL, MS 12.78 (Notebook of Thomas Jolly), no. 12: narrative 'of some passages of my sufferings these twenty years upon the account of non-conformity', c.1679.

[191] The Rev. Oliver Heywood B.A. 1630–1702: His Autobiography, Diaries, Anecdote and Event Books, 4 vols, ed. J. Horsfall Turner (Brighouse, 1882), vol. i, p. 77.

[192] An account of the nonconformity of John Rastrick (1705). This was also incorporated in Edmund Calamy's A defence of moderate non-conformity, 3 vols (1703–5).

manuscript, was dedicated to his son and heir William. He instructed the latter to rewrite it in the third person and make a copy for each of his siblings, but only after he had excised a chapter on his family troubles, prayers, and devotions, as well as 'whatsoever may be thought indecent, and of no use'. For his eyes only, these sections were to be removed before the book entered into the mainstream of inherited memory. Addressed to 'the children of my Old Age', the preface presented the text as the story of 'what the Lord hath done for my Soul... what I have done be worthy of nothing but forgetfulness; yet, what God hath done for me is worthy of a written and grateful Memoriall'.[193] Symbiotically linked with the public histories of puritan moderation and irenicism assembled by Edmund Calamy, such texts cemented the identity of ejected ministers as a distinct cohort of Dissenters. Personal accounts of Quaker suffering and convincement performed the same function, feeding into the two volumes compiled by Joseph Besse in the 1750s.[194] Across the ecclesiastical spectrum, religious culture was fundamentally shaped by autobiographical and social memory of the trials and tribulations of past generations.

The Memory of the People

The forms of first-person narrative and eyewitness testimony analysed above must be set alongside bodies of source material that blur the boundary between bureaucratic documentation and private life-writing. At first glance, the administrative records that were by-products of the growth of the Tudor state and the Church as an economic institution may seem unpromising sources for understanding how contemporaries experienced the Reformation as it unfolded and how it came to be remembered in subsequent decades. But financial accounts and parish registers are dynamic forms in which individual voices can be heard if we listen carefully.[195]

Instituted by Thomas Cromwell in 1538, parish registers sometimes served as a medium for articulating coded critiques of the religious policies of the Henrician and Edwardian regimes. For conservative incumbents like the former Benedictine monk Thomas Botelar of Much Wenlock in Shropshire who weathered these stormy decades, they provided a space in which to voice discontent about recent events. Extending from 1538 to 1562, the brief entries in Botelar's register betray his regret at the surrender of the local monastery in 1539 and the destruction of images and relics of the Anglo-Saxon virgin St Milburga by the ecclesiastical commissioners in 1547. They record how he read Henry's proclamation against

[193] HEHL, MS HM 6131, printed in Andrew Cambers (ed.), *The Life of John Rastrick, 1650–1727*, CS, 5th ser., 36 (Cambridge, 2009), pp. 27–9.
[194] See Chapter 4 above, pp. 321–2.   [195] Smyth, *Autobiography*, chs 2, 4.

the heretical books of Frith, Tyndale, and Wyclif and tell of the delight with which people in the local town of Bridgnorth greeted the renewal of traditional religion under Mary I, 'casting up their caps and hats, lauding, thanking and praising God Almighty with ringing of bells and making of Bonfires in every street'. The long passage that marks the accession of Elizabeth I on 17 November 1558 documents an act of subversion: Botelar followed orders in proclaiming this from the pulpit, but only after celebrating a High Mass to St Catherine and praying for the soul of the deceased queen in his best cope. By contrast, the only note he made on the day Henry VIII died in 1546 was a plea for God Almighty to pardon him. Punctuated with obits of the last priests and priors of various religious houses and of his fellow brethren at Shrewsbury Abbey, Botelar's register is a subdued but pointed lament for the passing of a generation. It turns a genre invented by the Tudor state into an instrument of private protest.[196]

Registers compiled by the married ministers of the Church of England, meanwhile, frequently merge into a form of genealogy, recording the life cycles of wives and children, and in turn of the incumbent himself.[197] Self-consciously memorial objects, some served to commemorate the parish community and its worthies. Recopied by successive clerks and by local antiquaries, they gave expression to a sense of communal identity rooted in an understanding of the Reformation as a moment of temporal disjuncture when superstition and idolatry had been vanquished.[198]

Transcending their status as inventories and balance sheets, churchwardens' accounts also served as books of shared memory. In the case of Christopher Trychay, the conservative vicar of Morebath between 1520 and 1574, they supply 'a uniquely expansive and garrulous commentary' on the affairs of this remote Exmoor village during a moment of revolutionary upheaval.[199] Such texts coexist in our archives with items that have too often been lazily categorized as 'commonplace books'. The well-known narrative of the Tudor Reformation written by Robert Parkyn, curate of Adwick-le-Street near Doncaster, resides within one such eclectic compilation. Alluding to Proverbs 28:12 (*'Regnantibus impiis: ruina*

---

[196] This only survives in later copies: Bodl., MS Gough Shropshire 15 (a transcription by James Bowen of Shrewsbury made in 1756) and C. H. Hartshorne, 'Extracts from the Register of Sir Thomas Butler, vicar of Much Wenlock in Shropshire', *Cambrian Journal*, 4 (1861), 81–98. Both transcriptions are printed in W. A. Leighton, 'The Register of Sir Thomas Botelar, Vicar of Much Wenlock', *Transactions of the Shropshire Archaeological and Natural History Society*, 6 (1883), 93–132, quotations at 104, 106, 108, 111–12. This is discussed briefly by Coster, 'Popular Religion and the Parish Register', pp. 106–8.

[197] The minister of All Saints, Little Bookham, in Surrey used the parish register to record genealogical information about himself and his predecessor: Surrey HC, BKL/1/1.

[198] Andrew Gordon, 'The Paper Parish: The Parish Register and the Reformation of Parish Memory in Early Modern London', *Memory Studies*, 11 (2018), 51–68. See also Simone Hanebaum, 'Sovereigns and Superstitions: Identity and Memory in Thomas Bentley's 'Monumentes of Antiquities', *Cultural and Social History*, 13 (2016), 287–305.

[199] Eamon Duffy, *The Voices of Morebath: Reformation and Rebellion in an English Village* (New Haven, CT, 2001).

hominum' : 'when the wicked rule, men are ruined') and apparently intended for wider consumption, this is an uncompromisingly critical account of the 'grevus matteres' brought to pass by Henry VIII, Edward VI, and the 'cruell tiranntes & enemisseis to God and holly churche' who were his advisers. Displaying his utter contempt for 'abhominable heresie', it too culminates in a celebration of the 'gratius' Queen Mary's accession and the revival of 'all olde ceremonies laudablie usyde before tyme'. Composed around 1555, it bespeaks Parkyn's relief at the snuffing out of Protestantism, before breaking off abruptly with a brief report of Mary's premature departure from 'this transitory lyffe' in 1558, which seems to have been added subsequently. This was an event that rendered him speechless. He evidently wanted to bury everything that followed in oblivion.[200]

Cumulative texts compiled by successive office holders, town chronicles afford further insight into how individuals and communities responded to the religious revolutions that swirled around them: from the destruction of images and chantries and the dismantling of Catholic worship to the campaigns that led to the cessation of mystery plays and popular pastimes in English provincial towns such as Worcester, Chester, and Shrewsbury. Their laconic entries served as a repository of information for posterity and, as Judith Pollmann has argued, an archive of the present for the future. Beneath the surface of the studied neutrality that characterized the genre, chroniclers ventriloquized their own views through the prodigious signs and natural disasters that denoted divine approbation and anger.[201]

Chronicles flourished in a context in which renewed urgency was being attached to preserving the documentary memory of towns and cities. London invented a new officer known as the Remembrancer in 1571.[202] In some chronicles, the annals of urban history and news are interspersed with undisguised affirmations of Catholic and Protestant piety. Adam Wyatt's 'journall' of 'things observeable' in Barnstaple from 1586 to 1611 commented wryly on the parallels between puritan sermon-gadding and Catholic 'trentals' of intercessory masses and pilgrimages and sarcastically recorded the story of the 'petie Skolemaster', 'one of the Anabaptistical & Precise Brethren', who wanted his child to be

---

[200] A. G. Dickens, 'Robert Parkyn's Narrative of the Reformation', *EHR*, 62 (1947), 58–83, at 64, 73, 75, 79, 82, 83.

[201] See Alexandra Walsham, 'Chronicles, Memory and Autobiography in Reformation England', *Memory Studies*, 11 (2018), 36–50, which discusses WAAS, 009:1/BA 2636 parcel 11 (no. 43701), fos 155–59, edited by Diarmaid MacCulloch and Pat Hughes in 'A Bailiff's List and Chronicle from Worcester', *Antiquaries Journal*, 75 (1995), 235–53; William Aldersey's 'Collection of the maiors who have governed this Cittie of Chester': CRO (ZCR 469/542); and Shrewsbury, Shrewsbury School, MS Mus X, a chronicle of Shrewsbury covering 1372–1603 known as 'Dr Taylor's Book'. Judith Pollmann, 'Archiving for the Present and Chronicling for the Future in Early Modern Europe', in Liesbeth Corens, Kate Peters, and Alexandra Walsham (eds), *The Social History of the Archive: Record-Keeping in Early Modern Europe*, P&P Supplement 11 (2016), 231–52.

[202] Gordon, *Writing Early Modern London*, pp. 123–4; Robert Tittler, *The Reformation of the Towns in England* (Oxford, 1998), pp. 211–20.

christened 'Doe well'. He saw the burning of Tiverton as an instance of the 'Digitus Dei' for the town's lack of compassion for the poor and was dismissive of recusants who preferred to 'go to Goal [gaol] then to Church': 'much good might it doe them'.[203] Defying reports of the 'death of the chronicle', the production and preservation of such texts is a measure of the reinvigoration of this scribal genre in the era of print and another index of the force exerted by family sentiment.[204] Mixing national and local chronology and institutional and personal memoranda, their polyvocal character reflects their status as multigenerational endeavours. Too often plundered for facts, they have been insufficiently exploited as evidence of how the Reformations were remembered, forgotten, contested, and reinvented.

Unearthing the reactions of the learned and literate is hard enough; taking the pulse of the populace at large is even more challenging. Pioneering work on popular perceptions of the past by Keith Thomas, Adam Fox, Daniel Woolf, and Andy Wood has drawn attention to a powerful strand of nostalgia for a world in which hospitality, charity, and social reciprocity were allegedly widespread.[205] Rose-tinted visions of bygone days breed in the gap between how the world seems and how people wish it could be. Counterintuitively, they are as much an emanation of hopes about the future as a form of longing for an idyllic earlier era. Rooted in the experience of temporal, spatial, and emotional dislocation, nostalgia is an amalgam of memory, affect, and fiction.[206] Fuelled by the 'rude transitions rendered by history', as Fred Davis has observed, it is itself an agent of 'the generation of generations'.[207]

In early modern England, the Reformations were a significant trigger for this ambivalent sentiment.[208] It became a commonplace to speak of the 'merry world' before the advent of bible-reading and preaching. The phrase 'It was never merry' served as a shorthand for a lost age when it was possible to buy 'twenty eggs for a penny' and when 'all things were cheap'. Linking the onset of Protestantism with economic decline and the old religion with material plenty, this proverbial saying

---

[203] *The Lost Chronicle of Barnstaple 1586-1611*, ed. Todd Gray (Exeter, 1998), pp. 62, 83, 82, 89.
[204] Cf. D. R. Woolf, 'Genre into Artefact: The Decline of the English Chronicle in the Sixteenth Century', *SCJ*, 19 (1988), 321–54; *idem, Reading History in Early Modern England* (Cambridge, 2000), ch. 1.
[205] Keith Thomas, *The Perception of the Past in Early Modern England: The Creighton Trust Lecture 1983* (1983), pp. 11–22; Adam Fox, *Oral and Literate Culture in England, 1500–1700* (Oxford, 2000), pp. 221–3 and ch. 4; Daniel Woolf, *The Social Circulation of the Past: English Historical Culture 1500–1750* (Oxford, 2003), ch. 9; Andy Wood, *The Memory of the People: Custom and Popular Senses of the Past in Early Modern England* (Cambridge, 2013), ch. 1, esp. pp. 67–78.
[206] For some stimulating discussions, see Svetlana Boym, *The Future of Nostalgia* (New York, 2001); the special issues of *Memory Studies*, 3 (3) (2010), edited by Nadia Atia and Jeremy Davies, and *Parergon*, 33 (2) (2016) edited by Kristine Johanson; Janelle Lynn Wilson, 'Here and Now, There and Then: Nostalgia as a Time and Space Phenomenon', *Symbolic Interaction*, 38 (2015), 478–92; and Achim Landwehr, 'Nostalgia and the Turbulence of Times', *History and Theory*, 57 (2018), 251–68.
[207] Fred Davis, *Yearning for Yesterday: A Sociology of Nostalgia* (1979), pp. 49, 111–15.
[208] The word 'nostalgia' was first coined by the Swiss physician Johannes Hofer in 1688, to describe a fatal form of homesickness. It was in use in English from the early 18th century. See *OED*, s.v. 'nostalgia'.

was apparently pervasive among the 'simple sort'. William Perkins recorded it among the 'common opinions' of the poor and ignorant which required correction by diligent catechizing.[209] Similar opinions emerged from the mouths of the characters that populate the lively puritan dialogues created by George Gifford. In Gifford's *Countrie divinitie*, Atheos firmly resists the admonitions of Zelotes, insisting 'I will follow our forefathers, nowe there is no love, then they lived in friendshippe, and made merrie together, nowe there is no good neighbourhood: nowe everie man for himselfe, and are readie to pull one another by the throate.' 'It was never merry since men unlearned have medled with the scriptures.' To his companion, this 'dunghill mirth... which men complaine of to be molested, and say it was happie in olde time' was both illusory and contemptible. The golden age remembered by the papists was a figment of their 'carnal' imaginations.[210]

Gifford's characters echoed a topos rooted in the early Reformation. Tellingly, evangelicals had frequently deployed it in dramatizations of the conflict between youth and age. Thomas Becon made it the complaint of an elderly priest against the precocious apprentice with whom he disputed and by whom he was outmanoeuvred: 'it was never mery with us, sythens such ionge boyes presumed to reade the scriptures'. In the Edwardian interlude *Lusty Juventus*, the figure of Hypocrisie laments that things have deteriorated 'since children where so boulde... every boy wil be a teacher / The father a foole, and the chyld a preacher'. The origins of decline are located in youthful presumption.[211]

As Harriet Philips comments, the association of the merry world with medieval Catholicism was ironically in large part an invention of the godly themselves.[212] The memories such texts enunciated were not authentic recollections but rather reflections of deep-seated anxieties about Protestantism's struggle to implant itself in the hearts and minds of ordinary people. They embody popular resentment of the reformers' obsession with the vernacular Bible and the pretentious piety of those who displayed one 'in every window'. The puritan polemicist John Field wielded this trope against the 'darke broode' of lapsed Catholics for whom Robert Persons wrote his famous manifesto for recusancy in 1581, condemning those who whispered in corners and on alebenches, linking the demise

---

[209] William Perkins, *The foundation of Christian religion gathered into six principles* (1618; STC 19717), sig. A3r.

[210] George Gifford, *A dialogue between a papist and a protestant* (1582; STC 11849), fo. 1r; idem, *A briefe discourse of certaine points of religion which is among the common sort of Christians, which may be termed the countrie divinitie* (1582; STC 11846), pp. 4–5, 17, 19.

[211] G. Menewe, *A plaine subversion or turning up syde down of all the arguments that the popecatholykes can make for the maintenance of auricular confession* ([Wesel?], 1555; STC 17822), sig. Ee5r; R. Wever, *An enterlude called lusty Juventus* (1550; STC 25148), sig. C3r. See Kristine Johanson, 'Never a Merry World: The Rhetoric of Nostalgia in Elizabethan England', in Alessandra Petrina and Laura Tosi (eds), *Representations of Elizabeth I in Early Modern Culture* (Basingstoke, 2011), pp. 210–27.

[212] Harriet Phillips, *Nostalgia in Print and Performance, 1510–1613: Merry Worlds* (Cambridge, 2019), pp. 40–3.

of the days of 'good chere' when one might have '24 egges for a peny' with the end of the Mass and the rise of 'these Gospellers'.[213]

The same strain of surmised nostalgia runs through Francis Trigge's *Apologie, or defence of our dayes* (1589), which sought to counteract the 'murmurings' that seemed to be in 'everyman's mouth', by 'plainly' proving that 'our dayes are more happy & blessed than the dayes of our forefathers'. Trigge refuted claims that the Reformation had destroyed prosperity and good fellowship and brought greater scarcity, dearth, oppression, and inflation. He did not deny that the earth now 'waxeth olde and barren' and was less fruitful than in its 'flourishing youth', but he repudiated the suggestion that Protestantism was responsible for precipitating the decline of the world. 'Thus is the nature of man', he said, 'ever lothing things present, and longing for things absent...bragging of things past, and slacke in things present.' Denigrating those who clung to the 'olde beaten waye of Papistrie', Trigge's *Apologie* endeavoured to extinguish false memory of the time before the putting out of the lights and pulling down of the abbeys. It sought to reinstate the sixteenth-century Reformation as the dawn of a bright new era of 'Sunneshine', albeit one built upon the foundation of another type of nostalgia: nostalgia for the pristine Christian past corrupted by the papacy over the course of the Dark Ages.[214]

Some of those who made unguarded statements of this kind rankled their contemporaries sufficiently to find themselves presented before the church courts. Grumblings that it 'was never merry since priests were married' or 'sithence the Scriptures were so commonly preached' could earn those who uttered them an official ticking off, but most such mutterings were just ignored.[215] The idea that the era before 'the alteration of the religion' was a golden time when goods were inexpensive and landlords benevolent also finds repeated expression in the thousands of depositions Andy Wood has painstakingly excavated from the Court of the Exchequer. In the statements the courts drew from old men with long memories to resolve disputes over customary rights, the suppression of parish gilds, chantries, and monasteries is repeatedly recalled as a critical fault line, a watershed that marked the decline of neighbourliness and the rise of avarice and greed. 'Apparently independent of any doctrinal justification', these were people who 'rejected Protestantism on the basis of novelty'. They saw Henry's Reformation as an aggressive exercise in asset-stripping. The absence of theological content in these legal documents is scarcely surprising: to articulate doctrinal dissent would have been to court trouble and risk prosecution. In 1621 a gentleman called Henry More was hauled up before the Star Chamber to answer the charge that he

[213] John Field, *A caveat for Parsons Howlet* (1581; STC 10844), sigs D8v–E1r.
[214] Francis Trigge, *An apologie, or defence of our dayes, against the vaine murmurings & complaints of manie* (1589; STC 24276), title page, sig. A3r, pp. 7–8, 1, 14.
[215] Christopher Haigh notes several examples in *The Plain Man's Pathways to Heaven: Kinds of Christianity in Post-Reformation England* (Oxford, 2007), pp. 203–4.

had called Henry VIII a tyrant, his daughter a bastard, and said that the Protestant religion 'did spring out of the saide kinges…Codpeece'.[216]

More gave voice to a strand of seditious Catholic memory that channelled Nicholas Sander's vituperative narrative of the origin and progress of the 'Anglican schism'. This was closely linked with polemical nostalgia for a time before 'first Luther and then Calvin had set their feete on English grounde' and turned the world upside down. In a retort to John Jewel written in 1564, Thomas Dorman contrasted the charity, simplicity, and sobriety of the pre-Reformation period with the envy, malice, vice, and 'busie bodie curiositie' that now reigned.[217] Edged with anger and resentment, the nostalgia of recusants and church papists could take on a belligerent cast.[218] Harking back to an idealized past which simultaneously supplies a blueprint for the future is the default position of those who find themselves on the losing side of history.

However, most of those who fondly recalled 'abbey time' and the 'merry world' were people who had complied with the Elizabethan settlement. They reminisced about an era of friendship and plenty that was largely a fantasy. The rhetoric of declension they employed was a counterpoint to the clerical chorus of lament about the descent into indifference and apathy that marked the Reformation's second generation. In seeking to shake their parishioners out of this lethargy, ministers often took up the story of Lot's wife looking back to iniquitous Sodom and being turned into a pillar of salt, which became a paradigm of backsliding and its divine punishment.[219] These two nostalgias were mutually reinforcing.

Intriguingly, as Harriet Lyon has shown, yearning for the monastic past gathered pace at precisely the moment that the dissolution was passing out of living memory. It was less a mental trait of the generation that had directly witnessed the seismic events of the Reformation than of its successors.[220] Together with a more general sense that times had been better in a distant past that few could now remember first-hand, its distinctive tones can be detected in mournful ballads like *Times alteration* (1630), in which nostalgia for an age of simplicity, modesty, and warm hospitality—wine, beer, and good cheer—is personified in the guise of an elderly man recalling the era when 'this old cap was new'. The 'brave dayes' he knew 'a great while agone' are not chronologically defined, but vaguely described as 'two hundred yeere' since. Characterized by an absence of luxury, pride, usury,

---

[216] Wood, *Memory of the People*, ch. 1, quotations at pp. 92, 78.

[217] On Sander, see Chapter 5 above, pp. 341–2. Thomas Dorman, *A proufe of certeyne articles in religion, denied by M. Juell* (Antwerp, 1564; STC 7062), fo. 138r–v.

[218] On nostalgia as subaltern memory, see Nadia Atia and Jeremy Davies, 'Nostalgia and the Shapes of History', *Memory Studies*, 3 (2010), 181–6.

[219] See above, pp. 311–12, and Alexandra Walsham, 'Remembering Lot's Wife: The Sin of Nostalgia in the English Atlantic World', in Harriet Lyon and Alexandra Walsham (eds), *Nostalgia in the Early Modern World: Memory, Temporality, and Emotion* (Woodbridge, forthcoming 2023).

[220] Harriet Lyon, *Memory and the Dissolution of the Monasteries in Early Modern England* (Cambridge, 2021), ch. 4.

and bribery, this 'time of yore' was also one free of pesky 'puritans'.[221] This is a song predicated on the perception of historical rupture and change for the worse. Recurrently reprinted as a broadside, it reflects nostalgia's chameleon-like flexibility. The Merry England it invoked was less a Catholic one than a time and place untroubled by the hotter sort of Protestants. A vehicle for anti-puritanism, it enshrined a sense of resentment that was intensified by the militant sabbatarianism provoked by the Caroline defence of Sunday sports and pastimes and festive wakes and ales.[222] By the mid-seventeenth century, Merry England had been relocated to Elizabeth's reign.[223] The English Revolution had the effect of shunting this forward into the early Stuart era, especially after Parliament's notorious decision to abolish Christmas in 1644.

The unprecedented turmoil of these decades reinforced other features of this evolving post-Reformation culture of nostalgia. It invested the perception that Protestantism had eradicated spirits, goblins, and ghosts from the land with an air of sadness. Where earlier writers had celebrated the demise of the magical world as a desirable side effect of the defeat of popery, for later authors this was a cause of regret. In 'Remaines of Gentilisme and Judaisme', John Aubrey complained that literacy had 'put all the old Fables out of dores' and that 'the divine art of Printing and Gunpowder have frighted away Robin-good-fellow and the Fayries'.[224] The rural folklore he sought to recover was not merely a carrier of nostalgia; perceived to be in danger of disappearing altogether, it had also become its object. Aubrey's efforts reflected the conflation of orality and 'superstition' that was a further consequence of the Reformations. Over time, the Catholic memories of an enchanted sacred past exiled from official discourse into the realm of speech ceased to be a source of embarrassment and became the quarry of antiquarians searching for an elusive primitive culture.[225]

The Civil Wars fostered renewed concern about the vulnerability of the medieval culture of remembrance that became the target of godly rites of violent oblivion. Transforming the bare ruined choirs of monasteries and defaced statues, images, and monuments into focal points for Royalist concerns about sacrilege, they fed the impulse to preserve them on paper. As Margaret Aston concluded in

---

[221] *Times alteration: or, the old mans rehearsall* (1629; STC 10271). For an insightful discussion, see Phillips, 'Old, Old, Very Old Men', 92–4.

[222] On which, see Ronald Hutton, *The Rise and Fall of Merry England: The Ritual Year 1400–1700* (Oxford, 1994).

[223] Thomas, 'Perception of the Past', pp. 20–3.

[224] John Aubrey, 'Remaines of Gentilisme and Judaisme', in *Three Prose Works of John Aubrey*, ed. John Buchanan-Brown (Fontwell, 1972), p. 290, 203. See Lauren Kassell, '"All was this Land Full Fill'd of Faerie" or Magic and the Past in Early Modern England', *Journal of the History of Ideas*, 67 (2006), 107–22.

[225] See Alison Shell, *Oral Culture and Catholicism in Early Modern England* (Cambridge, 2007), esp. ch. 2. See also Alexandra Walsham, 'Recording Superstition in Early Modern Britain: The Origins of Folklore', in S. A. Smith and Alan Knight (eds), *The Religion of Fools? Superstition Past and Present*, P&P Supplement 3 (Oxford, 2008), 178–206.

a seminal essay published in 1973, 'The very process of casting off the past gener-ated nostalgia for its loss. And with the nostalgia came invigorated historical activity.'[226] The motives that drove learned labours of love like Roger Dodsworth and William Dugdale's *Monasticon Anglicanum* coalesced with the sentiments encapsulated in grimly satisfying stories about the judgements visited upon pur-itan vandals. They nourished a corpus of local legend that conflated the exploits of Thomas and Oliver Cromwell in destroying striking religious and civic land-marks, blaming the former for the work of the latter and according many aes-thetic crimes to the Lord Protector for which he bore no responsibility. Their distant but common ancestry helped to compress the two men into one in popu-lar memory, as well as to present Thomas as the 'grandparent' of Oliver, the standard-bearer of the 'bless'd Reformation'.[227]

The telescoping of time evident in these anecdotes reflects a broader tendency to reassign traumatic developments to more recent periods. Philip Schwyzer has seen the language of 'lateness' as a mechanism for prolonging the moment of loss and postponing the impulse to forget. It reflects the warping and curving effects of memory: a capacity to distort temporality and confuse chronology that is a by-product of nostalgia's Janus-faced stance in relation to the past and the future. A sliding scale capable of moving in both directions, it can serve as a source of shelter as well as 'an impetus for a radical utopia'.[228] In Restoration England, long-ing for the 'good old cause' was accordingly a vessel for seditious republican memories of the Civil Wars and Interregnum. A temporary taste of victory swiftly followed by the experience of defeat was the recipe for a bittersweet remembrance of these momentous decades that was harnessed to support the ongoing struggle against 'popery' and 'arbitrary government' after 1660. If this fostered solidarity among disparate bodies of people for whom the reinstatement of monarchy was a source of regret, it also fuelled hope for a new revolution. While the debt that this discourse owed to scripts forged in the 1650s must not be overlooked, some of those who deployed it were people whose memory of the events in question was not personal but mediated by previous generations. It was cultivated within reli-gious and political communities and transmitted down families by oral and scribal tradition in a manner that challenged the 'mnemonic hegemony' pursued

---

[226] Margaret Aston, 'English Ruins and English History: The Dissolution and the Sense of the Past', *Journal of the Warburg and Courtauld Institutes*, 36 (1973), 231–55, at 255. See also Alexandra Walsham, *The Reformation of the Landscape: Religion, Identity and Memory in Early Modern Britain and Ireland* (Oxford, 2011), pp. 273–96.

[227] See Alan Smith, 'The Image of Cromwell in Folklore and Tradition', *Folklore*, 79 (1968), 17–39; Walsham, *Reformation of the Landscape*, pp. 530–1. For Thomas as the 'grandparent' of Oliver, see [Peter Hausted], *Ad populum: or, a lecture to the people* (1644; H1154), pp. 7–8.

[228] Philip Schwyzer, '"Late" Losses and the Temporality of Early Modern Nostalgia', *Parergon*, 33 (2016), 97–113; Kristine Johansen, 'On the Possibility of Early Modern Nostalgias', *Parergon*, 33 (2016), 1–15, at 14–15.

by the restored Stuart regime.[229] In Marianne Hirsch's terms these were 'post-memories': they were the memories of people whose birth post-dated the developments they claimed to remember.[230]

The durability of nostalgic tropes of medieval plenty provides a further example of this process. By the late seventeenth century, the notion that such statements were part of the proverbial speech of elderly people was antique, but it continued to be reiterated as if this was still true. The 'four Pillars of Popery' John Mayer described in 1653 included the hackneyed saying that 'this is the old religion wherein our fore-fathers lived, that were wiser and more pious than the people of these times', which was said to be current 'at this day'. When the Somerset rector William Thomas reproved 'old ignorant creatures [who] have us'd to proclaim the Times of Popery here in England better than the latter Times of the Gospel, because all things were cheap' in 1675, anyone born before the Henrician Reformation would have been more than 120 years old.[231] The demographic odds were firmly against this: most of the generation that had lived through the break with Rome must have been long gone.

Even so, this was a society that had its share of centenarians. In a context in which precise measurement of numerical age was still evolving, claims to longevity cannot always be taken at face value. Nevertheless, stories of prodigious long-livers offer oblique access to how humble people remembered England's long Reformation and how these memories changed over time. The clergyman Andrew Willet had met a 124-year-old man at Eversden in Bedfordshire who could recall the battle of Bosworth Field in 1485, 'being then as he affirmed…fifteen'.[232] Thomas Parr was reputed to be 152 when he died in London in November 1635, having travelled there from a small hamlet in Shropshire at the expense of a curious nobleman. Crowds flocked to see this ancient husbandman, but he soon expired in the impure air of the capital. Buried in Westminster Abbey, he posthumously became a celebrity. His body was the subject of an autopsy by the eminent physician William Harvey, and the water poet John Taylor published a biography about this 'old, old, very old man' in doggerel verse (Fig. 6.8). Heralding him as a 'living mortall Monument', Taylor situated him in a generational chain that stretched back to the Conquest, imagining that:

---

[229] Edward Legon, 'Remembering the Good Old Cause', in Edward Vallance (ed.), *Remembering the Early Modern Revolutions: England, North America, France and Haiti* (2019), pp. 11–25; idem, *Revolution Remembered: Seditious Memories after the British Civil Wars* (Manchester, 2019), esp. chs 5, 8. On the 'debt to existing scripts', see Peck, *Recollection in the Republics*, pp. 81, 90–4.

[230] Marianne Hirsch, *The Generation of Postmemory: Writing and Visual Culture after the Holocaust* (New York, 2012).

[231] John Mayer, *A commentary upon the whole Old Testament* (1653; M1424), p. 457; William Thomas, *Scriptures opened and sundry cases of conscience resolved* (1675; T990), p. 75.

[232] Andrew Willet, *Hexapla in Genesin, that is, A sixfold commentarie upon Genesis* (1632; STC 25687), p. 65.

The Olde, Old, very Olde Man or Thomas Par, the Soune of Iohn Parr of winnington in the Parish of Alberbury: In the County of Shropshire who was Borne in 1483 in The Raigne of King Edward the 4th and is now liuing in The Strand, being aged 152 yeares and odd Monethes 1635 He dyed Nouember the 15th And is now buryed in westminster 1635

Fig. 6.8 'The Olde, Old, very Olde Man'. Thomas Parr, aged 152. Line engraving by Cornelius van Dalen (c. 1700).

Source: Wellcome Library 925i. Wellcome Collection. Public Domain.

> They (by succession) might from Sire to Son
> Have been unwritten Chronicles, and by
> Tradition shew Times mutability.
> Then Parr might say he heard his Father well,
> Say that his Grand-sire heard his Father tell.

The postscript described 'the changes of Manners, the variation of Customes... the shiftings of Fashions, the alterations of Religions, the diversities of Sects, and the intermixture of Accidents' that had occurred since his alleged birth in 1483, fifty-five years before parish registers began. His lifetime had spanned every phase of the Tudor Reformations: brought up in Roman Catholicism, he had seen Henry VIII 'cast the Popes Authority out of this Kingdome' and restore the 'Primitive Religion' and observed its progress under Edward VI until the 'bloudy alteration' during the reign of Mary I, before witnessing the return to Protestantism and its consolidation under Elizabeth and her Stuart successors. Parr had apparently taken the dissolution of the monasteries, the onset of the

English liturgy, and other ecclesiastical upheavals firmly in his stride: 'hee held it safest to be of the Religion of the King or Queene that were in being, for he knew that hee came raw into the world, and accounted it no point of Wisedome to be broyled out it'. At least in Taylor's witty pen portrait, Parr was a conformist and temporizer by instinct. He had known times when 'men were so mad' as to worship stocks, blocks, saints, and idols as well as those when they were foolish enough to bow at the name of Jesus and regard surplices as the rags of the beast. Neither papist nor puritan, he was a bemused spectator upon, rather than an engaged actor in the religious upheavals of the early modern era.[233]

Outliving Parr by sixteen years, Henry Jenkins, an illiterate Yorkshire fisherman who died in 1670 at 169, was reputed to be the 'oldest Man born upon the Ruines of this Postdiluvian World'. The account of this Methuselah published in the *Philosophical Transactions of the Royal Society* said that he recollected the 'Dissolution of the Monasteries' well and remembered his master drinking many a glass with the last abbot of Fountains. In Jenkins's memory the suppression of the religious houses was twinned with a cosy vision of the tradition of pre-Reformation hospitality it had brought to an end. Mediated by a local gentlewoman called Ann Saville, the chronological framework for his reminiscences may thus be hers rather than his.[234]

For many, however, memory of the past revolved around the life cycle rather than historical watersheds. The legal proofs of the age of feudal heirs studied by John Bedell, Margaret McGlynn, and Joel Rosenthal reveal that only a minority used external occurrences to fix the dates of their birth; most referred to family rites of passage—baptism, marriage, death, and burial. By the later sixteenth century, as literacy increased, the evidence they presented was often written and textual rather than oral, including entries in the books of hours in which parents recorded the nativities and obits of their children. The gauge by which the majority marked the passing of time remained the passage of the generations.[235]

The long memories of the elderly were repeatedly compared to those of the Hebrew patriarchs, whose extended lifespans made them enduring repositories of wisdom: for 'the continuance of remembrance of matters, and deducing of them to posteritie the better'. Their days were lengthened, said William Whately, 'that

---

[233] John Taylor, *The old, old, very old man: or the age and long life of Thomas Par* (1635; STC 23782.5), sigs B4v, C3r, D2v–D3r. On Taylor as a cultural amphibian, see B. S. Capp, *The World of John Taylor the Water Poet, 1578–1653* (Oxford, 1994).

[234] Tancred Robinson, 'A Letter giving an Account of one Henry Jenkins a Yorkshire Man, who Attained the Age of 169 Years', *Philosophical Transactions of the Royal Society*, 19 (1695), 265–8. This is included in a volume of letters of the Savile and Finch families, 1626–1720: BL, Additional MS 28, 569, fos. 158r–159r.

[235] John Bedell, 'Memory and Proof of Age in England, 1272–1327', *P&P*, 162 (1999), 3–27; Margaret McGlynn, 'Memory, Orality and Life Records: Proofs of Age in Tudor England', *SCJ*, 40 (2009), 679–720; Joel Rosenthal, *Social Memory in Late Medieval England: Village Life and Proofs of Age* (Basingstoke, 2018).

by the life of one godly man, the truth which then was not put in writing, but by word of mouth delivered from man to man might be kept more pure and undefiled'.[236] In other words, they were key agents of what Assmann calls 'communicative memory'.

In turn, memory was frequently conceptualized as an aged person. In a comedy of 1607, it is the name of a character described as 'an old decrepit man' wearing a black velvet cassock and fur gown, with a watch, staff, and white beard.[237] Like chronicles and clocks, the old could be relied upon as timekeepers, by contrast with the young, whose moist brains meant that their memories were short and slippery.[238] Simultaneously, those very advanced in years were known to be prone to dementia and senile forgetfulness: a seventeenth-century commonplace book noted how 80-year-old Theodore Beza, Calvin's successor in Geneva, had completely lost his short-term memory, though he could still recite any verse from the Pauline Epistles 'perfectly by heart' in Greek and remember things he had learnt many decades earlier.[239] The vulnerability of human remembrance to a range of a physiological, climatic, and dietary contingencies was also widely recognized. One member of the Royal Society even tried to calculate mathematically how unreliable testimony became as it was transmitted over distance and time.[240]

The elderly were, nonetheless, an important cultural resource. They were regularly called upon to testify in court, and their authority as trustworthy custodians of inherited information was inflected by assumptions about gender. The commonplace that mothers and nursemaids were responsible for passing on idle stories predated Protestantism, but it was strongly reinforced by the reformers' disdain for the unwritten traditions that the papists elevated on a par with Scripture. 'Old wives' tales' became a convenient anti-Catholic shorthand for 'superstition'.[241] The wider epistemological shifts that were marginalizing the 'weaker sex' in the sphere of intellectual endeavour should not be allowed to eclipse the critical role that women continued to play in domestic education.[242] Mothers and wives remained critical figures in the transmission of religious advice, genealogical information, and family history to succeeding generations.[243]

---

[236] Gervase Babington, *Certaine plaine, briefe, and comfortable notes upon everie chapter of Genesis* (1592; STC 1086), fo. 26r; Whately, *Prototypes*, p. 51.

[237] Thomas Tomkis, *Lingua: or the combat of the tongue* (1607; STC 24104), sig. D3v.

[238] Henry Cuffe, *The differences of the ages of mans life: together with the original causes, progresse, and end thereof* (1607; STC 6103), p. 125.

[239] YML, MS 122, fo. 127v. For a reproduction, see https://exhibitions.lib.cam.ac.uk/reformation/artifacts/the-treasurehouse-of-the-mind-memory-in-commonplace-books/, accessed 8 June 2022.

[240] *The philosophical transactions and collections, to the end of the year 1700. Abridg'd and dispos'd under general heads*, 3 vols ([1716]), vol. iii, pp. 662–5.

[241] Foxe, *Oral and Literate Culture*, ch. 3. See, e.g., Henry Bullinger, *Fiftie godlie and learned sermons divided into five decades*, trans. H[enry] M[iddleton] (1577; STC 4056), p. 673.

[242] Daniel Woolf, 'A Feminine Past? Gender, Genre and Historical Knowledge in England, 1500–1800', *AHR*, 102 (1997), 645–79.

[243] See Katharine Hodgkin, 'Women, Memory and Family History in Seventeenth-Century England', in Kuijpers, Pollmann, Müller, and van der Steen (eds), *Memory before Modernity*, pp. 297–313.

Arguably, our sources conspire to privilege the recording of what Eamon Duffy calls the 'conservative voice'. The popular memories of the Reformation past they preserve are usually begrudging, if not openly critical ones.[244] Dismissed as 'fond', 'distracted', and 'frantic' by the privy councillors to whom they wrote impassioned letters, self-styled prophets who preached repentance, denounced Antichrist, and demanded far-reaching reform of the Church have not, by contrast, featured prominently in revisionist accounts. Miles Fry, who requested an audience with Lord Burghley to convey an 'embassage from God' in 1587, called himself Emmanuel Plantagenet and claimed to be the son of God and Queen Elizabeth, from whom he had been carried away at birth by the angel Gabriel. His mission was not 'to redeme the worlde but to shewe the end of generation and the love betwene christe and his church'. An Aldgate glover named Robert Dickons predicted famine, sword and pestilence, while the 'Christian Vintener' John Castle, who sent verses criticizing the religious settlement, was labelled a 'crazy Puritan'.[245] Such documents attest to a rival current of remembrance of the religious upheavals of the sixteenth century. Like the seditious recollections of the puritan revolution and godly republic which circulated after 1660, they provide insight into the alternative, if unrealized visions of radical religious reformation.[246]

Others seem to have firmly internalized the idea that Elizabeth's accession was the birthday of the Gospel and the moment at which popery had finally been routed. The petitions presented to the Long Parliament in defence of the Book of Common Prayer in the early 1640s give expression to the perception that the entrance of this monarch 'of blessed memory' was a critical turning point. A document emanating from Shropshire called for the Church to be reduced 'unto the purest and perfectest times of Queene Elizabeth'.[247] The bonfires and bell-ringing that marked the anniversaries of England's providential deliverances may have been initially orchestrated by the state, but over time they became forms of Protestant habitus, perpetuating memory through the performance of calendrical ceremonies that annually re-enacted the patriotic narratives examined in Chapter 5.[248] Anti-Catholic polemic likewise left a lasting local imprint. Salacious

[244] Eamon Duffy, 'The Conservative Voice in the English Reformation', in *idem*, *Saints, Sacrilege and Sedition: Religion and Conflict in the Tudor Reformations* (2012), pp. 213–32.

[245] See BL, MS Lansdowne 99 (Burghley Papers), fos 12v–13v, 18r–20v, 70r–73v. Philippa Carter explores some of these in 'Frenzy in Early Modern England' (PhD thesis, University of Cambridge, 2021), ch. 5. Jonathan Willis is also currently engaged in a study of this fascinating cache of letters.

[246] Legon, *Revolution Remembered*. See also Karl Gunther, *Reformation Unbound: Protestant Visions of Reform in England, 1525–1590* (Cambridge, 2014), ch. 7; and Susan Royal, *Lollards in the English Reformation: History, Radicalism and John Foxe* (Manchester, 2020), who emphasizes the radical ideas that Foxe's *Actes and monuments* mediated to later generations of Dissenters.

[247] Judith Maltby (ed.), 'Petitions for Episcopacy and the Book of Common Prayer on the Eve of the Civil War, 1641–2', in Stephen Taylor (ed.), *From Cranmer to Davidson: A Church of England Miscellany*, Church of England Record Society 7 (Woodbridge, 1999), pp. 103–68, at p. 160. See also pp. 119, 141, 159, 161, 165, 166.

[248] David Cressy, *Bonfires and Bells: National Memory and the Protestant Calendar in Elizabethan and Stuart England* (1989).

tales of lecherous monks and naughty nuns whose illicit liaisons were facilitated by underground passages attached themselves to ruined abbeys, together with stories of the infanticide of illegitimate offspring.[249] Memories of the moral misdemeanours of the medieval religious were shaped by the incriminating reports sent to Thomas Cromwell by the Henrician commissioners for the dissolution.[250]

It is ironic that recent understanding of early modern perception of the past has been so coloured by those who wished that Reformation had never happened and who yearned to turn back the clock. Yet we overlook the capacity of Protestant historiography to seep into cultural consciousness at our peril. Forgetting the perspective of those who considered the Middle Ages an era of benighted ignorance and for whom broken idols were symbols of triumph over error and darkness is another dimension of the myth of the English Reformation.[251]

Heirlooms

Thus far this chapter has focused on textual and oral traces of how contemporaries remembered the religious upheavals of the sixteenth and seventeenth centuries. But the material world too remained a touchstone for competing memories of this turbulent period. If material objects have social lives of their own, in turn they perform biographical and autobiographical functions. Their itineraries through space and time cement collective identities and demarcate the boundaries of natural and artificial kinship groups.[252] Via their transmission down the generations, they are transformed into heirlooms.

A Middle English term for a tool or implement bequeathed to one's legal heirs, the word 'heirloom' was in the process of floating free of its original legal definition as a chattel connected with a particular building and becoming a term for describing the treasured possessions that people left to their descendants.[253] Sedimented with successive layers of significance, heirlooms operate like

---

[249] See Walsham, *Reformation of the Landscape*, pp. 482–5.

[250] For the long life of this strand of polemic, see also Harriet Lyon, '"Superstition Remains at this Hour": *The Friers Chronicle* (1623) and England's Long Reformation', *Reformation*, 24 (2019), 107–21.

[251] Diarmaid MacCulloch, 'The Myth of the English Reformation', *JBS*, 30 (1991), 1–19.

[252] Arjun Appadurai (ed.), *The Social Life of Things: Commodities in Cultural Perspective* (Cambridge, 1986), esp. Igor Kopytoff, 'The Cultural Biography of Things: Commoditization as Process', ibid., pp. 64–91; Janet Hoskins, *Biographical Objects: How Things Tell the Stories of People's Lives* (New York, 1998). See also Hans Peter Hahn and Hadas Weiss (eds), *Mobility, Meaning and the Transformation of Things* (Oxford and Oakville, CT, 2013), and esp. *eidem*, ibid., 'Introduction: Biographies, Travels and Itineraries of Things', pp. 1–14.

[253] *OED*, s.v. 'heirloom'. See also Edward Phillips, *The new world of English words, or, a general dictionary* (1658; Wing P2068), s.v. 'heirloom'; John Cowell, *The interpreter, or, a book containing the signification of words* (1658; Wing C6644), s.v. 'heyre loom'.

palimpsests, 'sustaining both personhood and collective memory'.[254] Their dur-ability is emblematic of family continuity, but they can also trigger counterfactual thinking.[255] Giving expression to bonds of obligation and emotion, affinity and consanguinity, the remembrance evoked by material artefacts is as much a conse-quence of the dynamic bodily encounter between humans and things as of any cognitive process.[256]

Protestantism's vehement assault upon traditional assumptions about the local-ization of the holy provided a mandate for a comprehensive purge of sacred objects in the early stages of the Reformation. Vestments, plate, altar stones, and other forms of redundant liturgical furniture were swept from parish churches in Edward's and Elizabeth's reigns. Often these items invited the faithful to pray for the souls of their donors. Spurs to salvific remembering, they reflect the inter-weaving of liturgy and genealogy in traditional religion. Some were rescued by relatives, who voluntarily returned them when Queen Mary ascended the throne. Others were recycled as domestic tablecloths, cushion covers, vessels, and sinks. The transmutations they underwent never entirely effaced the resonances of the Catholic past which they carried forward into the future.[257] The migration of such objects from ecclesiastical settings into the home reversed the journey made by medieval heirlooms bequeathed for religious use, conjoining the life cycle of an individual with that of the faith community.[258] Concealed from public view, they became part of the apparatus of private worship within the recusant household. An exquisite fourteenth-century silver pyx decorated with scenes of the life of Christ, for instance, remained in the possession of a Northumbrian dynasty until it was sold to the Victoria and Albert Museum in 1950 by the widow of the last of the Swinburnes (Fig. 6.9).[259]

Medieval relics expelled from cathedrals and monasteries in 1530s likewise became part of the personal patrimony of Catholic families. Anne Vaux possessed a piece of Thomas Becket's hair shirt, while a silver reliquary containing a sec-tion of his skull was in the safekeeping of a wealthy Elizabethan gentleman who

---

[254] See Robert Gilchrist, *Medieval Life: Archaeology and the Life Course* (Woodbridge, 2012), pp. 237–51.

[255] Anna Green and Kayleigh Luscombe, 'Family Memory, "Things" and Counterfactual Thinking', *Memory Studies*, 12 (2019), 646–59.

[256] Andrew Jones, *Memory and Material Culture* (Cambridge, 2007), ch. 1.

[257] See Alexandra Walsham, 'Recycling the Sacred: Material Culture and Cultural Memory after the English Reformation', *Church History*, 86 (2017), 1121–54.

[258] See Roberta Gilchrist, 'The Materiality of Medieval Heirlooms: From Biographical to Sacred Objects', in Hahn and Weiss (eds), *Mobility*, pp. 171–82.

[259] V&A, M. 15&A-1950 (silver pyx, *c*.1310–25).

Fig. 6.9 The Swinburne pyx (silver and silver gilt, England, *c*.1310–25).
Source: © Victoria and Albert Museum, London, M. 15&A-1950.

had it repaired and ornamented at his own expense.[260] The dissolution also afforded opportunities for people lower down the social scale to acquire hallowed remnants. A Staffordshire yeoman kept a relic of the Anglo-Saxon Saint Chad, first bishop of Lichfield, in his bedhead, a location that suggests it was regarded as a protective amulet as well as a precious heirloom.[261] These sacred remnants forged links between biological and spiritual kin scattered by the proscription of the Catholic religion. The Jesuit John Poyntz gave the arm bone of St Thomas Cantilupe of Hereford to his sister in Paris, a companion of Mary Ward and later third superior of the Institute, in 1651. Such items wove webs between families, natal and spiritual, linking those still at home with those in exile and providing a material focus for the hope that their faith would, in due course, be restored to dominance.[262]

---

[260] For a list of relics in the possession of Anne Vaux and her sister, see TNA, SP 14/19, fo. 136; John Gerard, *The Autobiography of an Elizabethan*, ed. and trans. Philip Caraman (1951), p. 50.
[261] *Records of the English Province of the Society of Jesus*, 7 vols in 8, ed. Henry Foley (1877–84), vol. ii, p. 231.
[262] Virginia C. Raguin and Naomi Reed Kline, 'Relics and the Two Thomases: Thomas of Canterbury and Thomas of Hereford as Bishop Martyr and Bishop Confessor', in Virginia C. Raguin (ed.), *Catholic Collecting: Catholic Reflection 1538–1850: Objects as a Measure of Reflection on a*

The corporeal remains and personal belongings of sixteenth- and seventeenth-century martyrs served the same functions. Elizabeth More, the eighteenth-century prioress of the Bruges Augustinians, donated a vertebra of her celebrated ancestor Sir Thomas to the convent.[263] His hair shirt also circulated within the family before being absorbed into ecclesiastical ownership.[264] Fragments of the Elizabethan and Jacobean missionaries hanged, drawn, and quartered as traitors likewise formed a focal point for collective Catholic memory.[265] Like the convents abroad, the homes of the laity became shrines and reliquaries, enclosed spaces in which they came into close proximity with sacred materiality.[266] If some of these illicit objects were body parts, others were more ephemeral items. Remarkably, the fragile calyx of the flower that Thomas Maxfield carried with him to the scaffold at Tyburn in 1616 and clutched as he died survives among Maxfield's letters in the Archives of the Archdiocese of Westminster.[267]

For some of those who salvaged them, the remains of these martyrs were remnants of their own blood relatives. When he was arrested at Leicester in 1582, William Hanse was carrying 'a drop of his brother's blood that was hanged for the Catholic religion'. Upon entering a Franciscan nunnery in the Low Countries in 1624, the sisters Elizabeth, Grace, and Marie Ingleby brought with them one of the limbs of their executed uncle Francis as part of their dowry.[268] The miracle-working right hand of the celebrated Jesuit Edmund Arrowsmith was inherited

Catholic Past and the Construction of Recusant History in England and America (Worcester, MA, 2006), pp. 69–78, at p. 76.

[263] James Kelly, *English Convents in Catholic Europe, c.1600–1800* (Cambridge, 2020), pp. 155–6. See also Corens, *Confessional Mobility*, pp. 149–56; Claire Walker, 'The Embodiment of Exile: Relics and Suffering in Early Modern English Cloisters', in Giovanni Tarantino and Charles Zika (eds), *Feeling Exclusion: Religious Conflict, Exile and Emotions in Early Modern Europe* (Abingdon, 2019), pp. 81–99.

[264] Victoria van Hyning, 'Competing Lives and Contested Objects: Thomas More's Hairshirt and the Production of Memory', in Walsham, Wallace, Law and Cummings (eds), *Memory and the English Reformation*, pp. 303–17.

[265] See Alexandra Walsham, 'Skeletons in the Cupboard: Relics after the English Reformation', in *eadem* (ed.), *Relics and Remains*, P&P Supplement 5 (Oxford, 2020), 121–43, and *eadem*, 'Mobile Martyrs and Forgotten Shrines: The Translation and Domestication of Relics in Post-Reformation England', in Anton M. Pazos (ed.), *Relics, Shrines and Pilgrimages: Sanctity in Europe from Late Antiquity* (2020), pp. 181–202.

[266] Robyn Malo, 'Intimate Devotion: Recusant Martyrs and the Making of Relics in Post-Reformation England', *Journal of Medieval and Early Modern Studies* 44 (2014), 531–48. See also Abigail Brundin, Deborah Howard, and Mary Laven, *The Sacred Home in Renaissance Italy* (Oxford, 2018), ch. 4.

[267] AAW, St Edmund's College, Ware MS 16/9/7. The back of the letter is endorsed 'Flowers which Mr Maxfield caryed in his hand to Tiburn'. This letter was originally kept at St Edmund's College, Ware. See 'The Life and Martyrdome of Mr Maxfield, Priest, 1616', ed. J. H. Pollen, in *Miscellanea III*, CRS 3 (1906), 30–58. For a fuller analysis, see Alexandra Walsham, 'Relics, Writing, and Memory in the English Counter Reformation: Thomas Maxfield and His Afterlives', *BCH*, 34 (2018), 77–105.

[268] Claire Cross (ed.), *The Letters of Sir Francis Hastings 1574–1609*, Somerset Record Society (Yeovil, 1969), p. 25; Kelly, *English Convents*, pp. 155–6.

by members of his maternal family, the Gerards of Bryn Hall in Lancashire, who kept it as an heirloom, lending it out to local Catholics at times of medical emergency.[269] Memory and genealogy fused with thaumaturgy in the cults of these Counter-Reformation saints-in-waiting.

Items of devotional jewellery also became badges of dissident identity closely linked with ancestry. An early sixteenth-century enamelled gold rosary now in the Victoria and Albert Museum was once owned by Lord William Howard, son of Thomas, fourth duke of Norfolk, who beheaded as a traitor in 1572. Augmented around 1600 with two extra beads depicting his patron saints, until 1934 it was owned by an old Catholic family, the Langdales of Houghton Hall in Yorkshire.[270] Another artefact that clearly became a focus for remembering the religious and political resistance of past generations of recusants is a pendant brooch bearing the sacred monogram 'IHS' said to have belonged to a later William Howard, Viscount Stafford, who was executed for his alleged complicity in the Popish Plot in 1680.[271] Such objects played their own part in rewriting official narratives and in recasting predecessors on the receiving end of state violence as Christian confessors.

The biographies of these Catholic things find parallels in the corpus of Protestant material culture that Andrew Morrall, Tara Hamling, and other scholars are busy uncovering in all its rich variety. Tableware, furniture, and other types of domestic decoration became vehicles of personal and public memory, as well as instruments for teaching moral and cultural values. They were emblems and props in a mnemonic system that relied upon visualizing abstractions as concrete entities.[272] Some drew explicit attention to their identity as heirlooms. The oak dining table Peter Catterall commissioned for Crooke Hall in Lancashire in the 1630s included a panel inscribed 'AN ARELOME TO THIS HOUS FOR

---

[269] Bede Camm, *Forgotten Shrines: An Account of Some Old Catholic Halls and Families in England and of Relics and Memorials of the English Martyrs* (1910), pp. 188–9; *Records of the English Province*, ed. Foley, ii. 69.

[270] V&A, M.30–1934. See https://collections.vam.ac.uk/item/O17851/the-langdale-rosary-rosary-unknown/, accessed 8 June 2022.

[271] V&A, M.248–1923. See https://collections.vam.ac.uk/item/O33878/pendant-unknown, accessed 8 June 2022.

[272] David Gaimster, 'Pots, Prints and Propaganda: Changing Mentalities in the Domestic Sphere 1480–1580', in *idem* and Roberta Gilchrist (eds), *The Archaeology of Reformation 1480–1580* (Leeds, 2003), pp. 122–44; Andrew Morrall, 'Protestant Pots: Morality and Social Ritual in the Early Modern Home', *Journal of Design History*, 15 (2002), 263–73; Andrew Morrall, 'Inscriptional Wisdom and the Domestic Arts in Early Modern Northern Europe', in Natalia Filatkina, Birgit Ulrike Münch, and Ane Kleine (eds), *Konstruktion, Manifestation und Dynamik der Formalhaftigkeit in Text und Bild* (Trier, 2012), pp. 121–38; Tara Hamling, *Decorating the Godly Household: Religious Art in Post-Reformation Britain* (New Haven, CT, 2010); Alexandra Walsham, 'Domesticating the Reformation: Material Culture, Memory and Confessional Identity in Early Modern England', *RQ*, 69 (2016), 566–616; Victoria Yeoman, 'Reformation as Continuity: Objects of Dining and Devotion in Early Modern England', *West 86th: A Journal of Decorative Arts, Design History, and Material Culture*, 25 (2018), 176–98.

EVER', with his initials and a date. Evidently intended as a permanent fixture in the room, this monumental object symbolized the house as both a seat and a lineage.[273] So too did the standing silver cup with a gilt cover engraved with the word 'earlome' listed in the will of Sir Thomas Langton of Walton in the Dale, Lancashire, dated 4 April 1569, which was to be given to his cousin, heir, and namesake when he turned 21.[274] Over time, such artefacts often became detached from the buildings for which they were originally purchased and travelled to new locations with their erstwhile inhabitants or with the people who inherited them. Others openly announce their status as remembrancers: one seventeenth-century slipware jug admonishes its user 'WHEN THIS YOU SEE REMEMBER ME. OBEAY GODS WOURD'. The same formulation appears on a delftware mug marked 'MARY FAYERTHORNE WHEN THIS YOU SEE REMEMBER MEE ANNO 1647'. Here the text simultaneously commemorates the named individual and anthropomorphizes the object itself.[275] It both conveys her memory to her posterity and serves as a marker of the passing of time, quotidian and eternal.

Many such items originated as christening and marriage gifts. Presented by godparents on the occasion of an infant's baptism, silver apostle spoons continued to be passed down families after the Tudor Reformation, despite the suspect iconography of the saints and Virgin Mary with which they were decorated.[276] Others were newly commissioned. One dating from 1706 records the birth of the twins Mary and Elizabeth Harcum, who died, together with their mother, shortly thereafter. Given by their uncle, it was probably kept in memory of this triple tragedy.[277] Many Adam and Eve chargers bear the initials of couples and the year of their wedding, their biblical imagery serving as a stimulus to fertility as well as a warning of the dangers of lust and greed.[278] Used or displayed in the context of the midday meal, such objects enhanced the symbolic valence of eating within the

[273] Tara Hamling, ' "An Arelome to this Hous for Ever": Monumental Fixtures and Furnishings in the English Domestic Interior, c.1560–c.1660', in Andrew Gordon and Thomas Rist (eds), *The Arts of Remembrance in Early Modern England: Memorial Cultures of the Post-Reformation* (2013), pp. 59–83, at pp. 64–6.

[274] G. J. Piccope (ed.), *Lancashire and Cheshire Wills and Inventories: From the Ecclesiastical Court, Chester, the Second Portion*, Chetham Society (Manchester, 1857–61), p. 251.

[275] BM, 1887,0307,D.26 (17th-century slipware jug): https://www.britishmuseum.org/collection/object/H_1887-0307-D-26, accessed 8 June 2022. For the Mary Fayerthorne mug, see Louis L. Lipski, *Dated English Delftware: Tin-Glazed Earthenware 1600–1800*, ed. and aug. Michael Archer (1984), p. 162.

[276] For examples, see V&A, M.70–1921 (silver-gilt spoon, 1450–1500): http://collections.vam.ac.uk/item/O118113/spoon-unknown/, accessed 8 June 2022; M.85–1959 (parcel silver gilt spoon, 1635): http://collections.vam.ac.uk/item/O78643/spoon-wade-robert-ii/, accessed 8 June 2022. See Abigail Gomulkiewicz, 'Religious Materiality in Elizabethan Essex (1558–1603)', *Material Religion: The Journal of Objects, Art and Belief*, 16 (2020), 275–97.

[277] Edward Town and Angela McShane (eds), *Marking Time: Objects, People and their Lives, 1500–1800* (New Haven, CT, 2019), p. 116.

[278] See Chapter 3 above, pp. 223–35, and Alexandra Walsham, 'Eating the Forbidden Fruit: Pottery and Protestant Theology in Early Modern England', *Journal of Early Modern History*, 24 (2020), 63–83.

godly household, as well as memorializing key junctures in the human life cycle. Samplers and tapestries were other treasured family possessions that performed memory work. Incorporating the names and birthdays of the girls who stitched them to demonstrate their accomplishment in the art of embroidery, they too were often preserved as mothers' legacies.[279] Inlaid and engraved mourning rings were equally evocative of deceased relatives and friends. 'In memory of RR 1664' and 'When this you see remember me' are among the inscriptions on specimens in the British Museum (Fig. 6.10).[280] A delftware mug memorializing Mary Turner, who died aged 2 years and 14 days on 2 September 1752, is particularly poignant. Reflecting the imperative to remember a child who, like so many in these centuries, expired prematurely, this was an object specifically designed to stop the work of forgetting.[281]

Sometimes the only surviving traces of ancestral heirlooms are references to them in wills. Lena Cowan Orlin has cautioned against sentimentalizing the items

Fig. 6.10 Mourning ring inscribed 'In memory of RR. 1664' (gold, London, attr. to Thomas Cockram, 1646).
Source: © The Trustees of the British Museum, AF.1533.

---

[279] The Fitzwilliam Museum has an extensive collection of samplers. See Kate Chedgzoy, *Women's Writing in the British Atlantic World: Memory, Place and History 1550-1700* (Cambridge, 2007), pp. 20–1; Sophie Cope, 'Women in the Sea of Time: Domestic Dated Objects in Seventeenth-Century England', in Merry E. Wiesner-Hanks (ed.), *Gendered Temporalities in the Early Modern World* (Amsterdam, 2018), pp. 47–68.

[280] BM, AF. 1533 (mourning ring, 1646): https://www.britishmuseum.org/collection/object/H_AF-1533, accessed 8 June 2022; and AF. 1401(posy ring, *c.*1679): https://www.britishmuseum.org/collection/object/H_AF-1401, accessed 8 June 2022.

[281] Fitz., C.1583-1928 (tin-glazed earthenware mug 1752).

recorded in probate documents, arguing that they index legal ownership rather than feeling. Yet it is hard to see them as 'empty vessels', wholly bereft of affect.[282] By contrast, Susan James approaches them as 'archives of emotion' and as a 'seminal tool in fashioning an identity worthy of memorial recognition'.[283] Creating a bond between the giver and the receiver, they spin webs that bind siblings, offspring, godchildren, and heirs together across the generations. Clothing and jewellery were common bequests to favoured friends and relations at every level of society, while the simple tokens of maternal love left by unmarried mothers when they deposited their infants at London's Foundling Hospital—buttons, beads, coins, and fruit pips—were intended to serve as mementos of the women who left them.[284]

The wealthy could afford to give more. A testament left by the widow Millicent Jekyell of Burton Dassett and Stowe in Norfolk, dated 15 January 1582, incorporated precise instructions for the dispersal of her possessions to her children: the sapphire ring she bequeathed to her son, the two feather beds she left to her daughter, and the 'little pot of silver' that had once belonged to his father which she left to her grandson.[285] The bequests of Mary Salvin in 1683 included a pottinger to her niece and a posset cup to her godson. Transcribed and kept among the family's papers, a copy of her will sits alongside a 1741 memorandum about the three gold crucifixes given to the daughters of a later descendant, which were themselves legacies of their grandmother. In the absence of the actual objects, the text describing them has become an heirloom itself.[286] The subsequent trajectories of such items were sometimes depicted in diagrams that resemble family trees, including a curious 'genealogy' of the four Penelope watches Tom Blower from Leicestershire left to his four nieces in the nineteenth century.[287] In turn, the elaborate heraldic pedigrees commissioned by the gentry and nobility became part of the material culture of generational memory.[288] A Jacobean pedigree of

[282] Lena Cowen Orlin, 'Empty Vessels', in Tara Hamling and Catherine Richardson (eds), *Everyday Objects: Medieval and Early Modern Material Culture and Its Meanings* (Farnham, 2010), pp. 299–308.
[283] Susan E. James, *Women's Voices in Tudor Wills, 1485–1603: Authority, Influence, and Material Culture* (Farnham, 2015), pp. 282, 67, 60. See also Lisa Liddy, 'Affective Bequests: Creating Emotion in York Wills, 1400–1600', in Michael Champion and Andrew Lynch (eds), *Understanding Emotions in Early Europe* (Turnhout, 2015), pp. 273–89.
[284] Miles Lambert, 'Death and Memory: Clothing Bequests in English Wills, 1650–1830', *Costume*, 48 (2014), 46–59; Tanya Evans, *'Unfortunate Objects': Lone Mothers in Eighteenth-Century England* (New York, 2005); Jeanine Hurl-Eamon, 'Love Tokens: Objects as Memory for Plebeian Women in Early Modern England', *Early Modern Women: An Interdisciplinary Journal*, 6 (2011), 181–6.
[285] NRO, GUN 92/1–18 (Rolfe family records), pp. 10–11.
[286] DCRO, D/Sa/F43-6 (Notes of legacies and gifts of gold and jewellery of the Salvin family, 1733–1842).
[287] LLRRO, DG6/E/35 ('Genealogy of 4 Penelope Watches').
[288] See Richard Cust, 'The Material Culture of Lineage in Late Tudor and Early Stuart England', in Catherine Richardson, Tara Hamling and David Gaimster (eds), *The Routledge Handbook of Material Culture in Early Modern Europe* (2017), pp. 247–74.

the Heskeths of Rufford is even decorated with small stylized portraits (Fig. 6.11).[289] This biographical object literally visualizes prominent members of the Catholic dynasty which it commemorates.

Family portraiture flourished despite Protestant worries about the blurred boundary between idolatry and memory. The painting dated 1628 reproduced as Fig. 6.12 is a memento mori. Filled with allusions to the transience of time and the fragility of life, it probably depicts Elizabeth Holme, her husband Thomas Hill, and their two young children. Reminding its viewers of their own mortality, its external folding panels are painted with the figures of Youth and Age and the rebuses 'WEE MUST/DIE ALL' and 'YET BY/CHRIST LIVE ALL'. Its triptych format harks back to the Catholic past and a tradition associated with depictions of the Holy Family, even as it gives expression to a theological and visual culture in transition.[290] This group portrait depicts a Protestant nuclear family which it implies has been predestined to salvation in its entirety.[291] The oil of William Brooke, 10th Baron Cobham and his family dating from 1567 doubles as a memorial to his childless sister Elisabeth, who died of cancer two years earlier. Her posthumous place in the picture, hovering over her niece, namesake and god-daughter, signifies that she remained a living presence in their memory (Fig. 6.13).[292] By contrast, the large triptychs that Lady Anne Clifford commissioned for her two daughters reunite the vertical line of several generations in a horizontal picture that is surrounded by textual inscriptions that summarize family history. They also include imagined portraits of her tutor and governess.[293] These deploy the same strategy as several paintings of Thomas More and his family which bring the famous humanist together with descendants who could not, in fact, have sat together for the portrait in a pleasing fiction of family intimacy.[294]

[289] BL, Additional MS 44,026 (Pedigree of the Hesketh family of Rufford, Lancashire).

[290] V&A, W.5-1951 (painting of the Holme family, 1628). On the use of triptychs for post-Reformation dynastic portraits, see Jane Eade, 'The Triptych Portrait in England, 1585–1646', *The British Art Journal*, 6 (2005), 3–11.

[291] See Tarnya Cooper, 'Visual Memory, Portraiture and the Protestant Credentials of Tudor and Stuart Families', in Walsham, Wallace, Law and Cummings (eds), *Memory and the English Reformation*, pp. 318–33.

[292] Susan E. James and Katlijne Van Der Stighelen, 'New Discoveries Concerning the Portrait of the Family of William Brooke, 10th Lord Cobham, at Longleat House', *Dutch Crossing: Journal of Low Countries Studies*, 23 (1999), 660–101, at 73.

[293] Karen Hearn, 'Lady Anne Clifford's Great Triptych', in Karen Hearn and Lynn Hulse (eds), *Lady Anne Clifford: Culture, Patronage and Gender in Seventeenth-Century Britain*, Yorkshire Archaeological Society, Occasional Paper 7 (Leeds, 2009), pp. 1–24.

[294] V&A, P.15-1973 (portrait miniature of Sir Thomas More, his household and descendants, painted 1593–4). The item was bequeathed by Anne Louise Strickland in memory of the Rev. J. E. Strickland. Nostell Priory, West Yorkshire, National Trust 960059 (Rowland Lockey, after Hans Holbein the Younger, *Thomas More and His Family*, c.1594).

Fig. 6.11 Pedigree of the Hesketh family of Rufford, Lancashire, *c.*1615.

Fig. 6.12 The Holme family portrait (oil on panel, English school, 1628).
Source: © Victoria and Albert Museum, London, W.5-1951.

Fig. 6.13 William Brooke, 10th Baron Cobham, and his family (oil on panel, English, attr. to the Master of the Countess of Warwick, 1567). His dead sister stands on the right.
Source: Longleat House, Wiltshire. Wikimedia Commons.

These heirlooms must be set alongside the many bibliographical ones now within the collections of archives and libraries. As described in Chapter 5, recusants continued to insert births and deaths into medieval primers long after religious legislation had rendered these texts illegitimate.[295] These interpolations served to personalize texts that Virginia Reinburg has called 'archives of prayer', turning them into archives of Catholic memory.[296] The pages of missals and other liturgical books rescued from dissolved monasteries and convents also became convenient spaces in which people recorded nativities and obits.[297] Genealogical information has often been added to the calendars, tying remembrance of dead relatives to remembrance of the saints whose abolished feast days they still illicitly commemorate. Even with censored indulgences and pardons, they were tangible tokens of pious dissidence.[298]

If many such books demonstrated family fidelity to the old faith, others helped to paper over the gaping genealogical cracks created by the Tudor Reformation. Kept because they served as a tangible link to deceased ancestors, they index the gradual assimilation of dynasties into the official Protestant religion.[299] Ceasing to be aids to intercession, they became convenient devices for record-keeping. The Lyme Park Missal, for instance, contains entries for five generations of the male heirs of the Legh family from 1422, ending with the last recusant member in 1635. Wives and sons are included, as well as the name of a chantry priest, but daughters are excluded.[300] A fifteenth-century Latin psalter once owned by the Fortescue family probably survives because it bears this inscription on the first flyleaf: 'my grandfathers booke'.[301] Later inheritors of such texts turned an indulgent blind eye to their 'popish' elements, treasuring them as relics of their progenitors.

The sentiments they evoked were not, however, always affectionate. The extraordinary sentence that Henry Lord Stafford added to the 'noate' of his sister

[295] See Chapter 5, above, pp. 398–9. Kathleen Ashley traces the origins of this practice in 'Creating Familial Identity in Books of Hours', *Journal of Medieval and Early Modern Studies*, 32 (2002), 145–65. For a fuller exploration of this theme, see Alexandra Walsham, 'Heirloom Books and Archives of Memory in Early Modern England' (forthcoming).

[296] Virginia Reinburg, *French Books of Hours: Making an Archive of Prayer, c.1400–1600* (Cambridge, 2012).

[297] e.g. Bodl., MS Rawlinson liturg.e. 41 (15th-century manual according to Sarum use for a convent), the calendar of which contains entries relating to the families of More and Bramley. This has also been used a diary.

[298] e.g. CUL, Additional MS 10079 [G] (Sarum book of hours, [Bruges?, c.1460–70]). This was probably in the possession of the Martyns of Long Melford, but later passed into the possession of the Rookwoods of Hengrave Hall. See Francis Young, 'Early Modern Catholic Piety in a Fifteenth-Century Book of Hours: Cambridge University Library MS Additional 10079', *Transactions of the Cambridge Bibliographical Society*, 15 (2015), 541–59.

[299] Some examples include HEHL, MSSHM 58285 (Book of hours belonging to the Felbrygge family of Norfolk, 1375–1425); Bodl., MS Hatton 4 (Latin psalter and Sarum book of hours with genealogical information relating to the Edward Windsor, 3rd Lord Windsor of Stanwell, AD 1559–72) and the Roberts hours, discussed on p. 399 above.

[300] Owned by the National Trust, this is cited in Peter C. Jupp and Clare Gittings (eds), *Death in England: An Illustrated History* (New Brunswick, NJ, 1999), p. 133.

[301] HEHL, MSSHM 56911 (15th-century English psalter which belonged to the Fortescue family).

Dorothy's birth in October 1526 he transcribed from 'my mothers old praier boke' into the family cartulary hints at a bitter falling out between the two siblings: 'It had ben better [best?] she had never ben borne.' This may have been over the differences in religion: while Henry shared the conservative piety of his parents, Dorothy (later a lady-in-waiting to Elizabeth I) was a fervent Protestant who fled to Geneva with her husband in 1555, where one of her sons was baptized the following year, with John Calvin serving as his godfather.[302] Dorothy's elder brother Henry seems to have been eager to forget her.

After the sixteenth-century Reformation, books of common prayer and bibles took over as family registers (Fig. 6.14).[303] As we have seen, Broughton and Speed's popular genealogies of Christ sometimes sit immediately alongside

Fig. 6.14 Genealogical notes of the Graham family: *The holy bible* (London, 1676), flyleaf and title page.
Source: North Yorkshire County Record Office, Northallerton, ZKZ/4/9.

[302] SRO, D (W) 1721/1/1/1, p. 400. The word in question has been corrected. Simon Adams, 'Stafford, Dorothy, Lady Stafford (1526–1604)', in *ODNB*. See also Karen E. Spierling, *Infant Baptism in Reformation Geneva* (Aldershot, 2005), pp. 105, 115–16.
[303] See Femke Molekamp, '"Of the Incomparable Treasure of the Holy Scriptures": The Geneva Bible in the Early Modern Household', in Matthew Dimmock and Andrew Hadfield (eds), *Literature and Popular Culture in Early Modern England* (Farnham, 2009), pp. 121–35. See, e.g., the extensive notes of the Blennerhasset family in the flyleaves of an edition of the Bishops' Bible published in 1575: HEHL, RB 294479–80.

personal pedigrees. Some filled blank pages with prose narratives about family history or overtly advertised their provenance as parental gifts. The Marian martyr Rowland Taylor inscribed his last will and testament in a book presented to his son Thomas in which he looked forward to being reunited with the rest of his children—Susan, George, Ellen, Robert, and Zachary—in heaven.[304] Francis Newby noted inside his Geneva Bible that his father Samuel had given it to him in 1645 'with a charch to keep it as: long as I live'. This is also tooled in gilt on the book's leather binding (Figs. 6.15 and 6.16).[305] Others travelled down the maternal line. A 1675 Book of Common Prayer bequeathed to Margrett Pelham by her father was in turn passed down to her own daughter on her decease.[306] The noblewoman Susannah Beckwith dedicated her bible to her daughter and namesake:

> Susannah Beckwith my deare childe I leave this booke as the best jewell I have, Reade it with a zealous harte to understand truly and uppon all though readest either to confirm they faith or to Increase thy repentance...bee not wearie of well doing for in due season thou shalt reape if thou fainte not.

Much like the mother's legacies discussed above, this annotated book offered spiritual direction in anticipation of the testator's own death.[307]

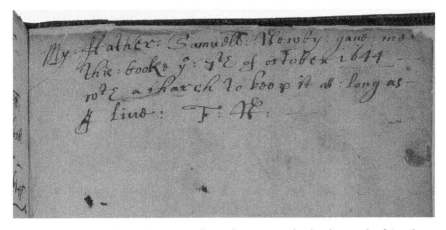

Figs. 6.15 and 6.16 'My Father Samuell Newby gave me this booke ye 7th of October 1644 with a charch to keep it as long as I live': *The bible translated according to the Ebrew and Greeke* (London, 1580), flyleaf and binding.
Source: Folger Shakespeare Library, Washington DC, STC 2129, copy 1. Folger Digital Image Collection.

---

[304] D. Andrew Penny, 'Family Matters and Foxe's *Actes and Monuments*', *HJ*, 39 (1996), 599–618, at 602.
[305] *The bible translated according to the Ebrew and Greeke* (1580; STC 2129): FSL STC 2129, copy 1.
[306] *The book of common prayer* (Oxford, 1675; Wing B3642): CUL, SPCK.4.1675.1.
[307] *The bible translated according to the Ebrew and Greeke* (1597; STC 2168): BL, 464.c 5 (1.). See Femke Molekamp, *Women and the Bible in Early Modern England: Religious Reading and Writing* (Oxford, 2013), pp. 36–7.

Figs. 6.15 and 6.16 Continued

An even more touching testimony to the power of the generations in preserving memory is a King James version encased in an embroidered binding worked by the mother of Mrs Mary Arbuthnot. In turn her daughter exhorted her own child to 'continue it down to posterity' within the family if she herself had no offspring. Later owners duly perpetuated the tradition of recording births, marriages, and deaths until the late 1780s, in fulfilment of 'the desire of my ancient

Fig. 6.17 'The Guift of my Dear and tender Mother': Embroidered binding worked by the mother of Mary Bradley, later Mrs Arbuthnot, 1654–1707. *The Holy bible containing the old testament and the new* (London, 1640). Cambridge University Library, BSS. 201.C.40. 5.

Source: Cambridge University Library, BSS. 201.C.40. 5. Reproduced by kind permission of the Syndics.

parent' (Fig. 6.17).[308] After her demise, Lady Frideswide Goulston's elaborately embroidered, red-ruled bible functioned as twin memorial to a mother and her son Morris, whose death in 1721, aged 17 years, 7 weeks and 3 days, is inscribed

---

[308] *The holy bible containing the old testament and the new* (1640): CUL BSS.201.C.40.5. For this object, see https://exhibitions.lib.cam.ac.uk/reformation/artifacts/the-guift-of-my-dear-and-tender-mother-an-embroidered-bible, accessed 9 June 2022.

on the second flyleaf.[309] The textile bindings that women stitched for the heirloom books they left to their children made them into material foci for remembering their creators.

Some subsequently passed to collateral branches of families. A quarto edition of the King James version bound with the Book of Common Prayer and Psalms dated 1663 records that it was bequeathed to Acton Chaplin Havelock, nephew of 'the last direct descendant' of the Chaplins of Aylesbury, Buckinghamshire, when she died unmarried, aged 81, in 1893.[310] Another, now in the Leicestershire Record Office, was a gift to George Clarke from his grandmother Elizabeth, who prayed to God 'he make good use of it', in 1678/9. It documents each stage of its meandering journey via siblings, cousins, wives, husbands, and in-laws to the year 1878, when Sophia Percy Herrick left it 'as an Heirloom to the Owner of Beau Manor for ever', the country house in which it had continuously resided for the preceding two hundred years.[311] Detached from the biological family and transferred to a physical location, this book illustrates the ongoing link between objects and the landed estates of particular lineages.

Transmitting devotional works to relatives was a favoured mechanism for ensuring that faith itself became a family inheritance. Lollards passed on copies of the illicit texts that marked them out as 'known men and women' to their relatives and friends, cementing connections within this clandestine heretical community. The copy of Wycliffe's 'Wicket' that Joan Austy brought to her second marriage had been entrusted to her by her first husband, John Redman, on his deathbed in the early years of the sixteenth century.[312] Bequeathing books that were badges of confessional identity was a way of performing the parental duty of building up household religion and cementing relationships within it. Anne Dalton's copy of Lewis Bayly's popular *Practice of piety* (1640) was a gift from her 'dear mother', while an English edition of the Italian Jesuit Orazio Torsellino's *The history of our blessed lady of Loreto* (1608) has this mark of ownership on its flyleaf: 'Martha Chambers her boock / given to mary mereing her Sister whoe departed this / life October the 8: 1699'.[313] The Graham family of Norton Conyers in Yorkshire

---

[309] *The holy bible* (1619), bound with *The book of common prayer* (1618), John Speed, *The Genealogies* and *idem*, *The whole book of psalms* (1618): HEHL 438000: 656. Ann Rosalind Jones and Peter Stallybrass argue that embroidery was a medium through which women inserted themselves into a memory culture of inheritance that was predominantly male in orientation: *Renaissance Clothing and the Materials of Memory* (Cambridge, 2000), esp. pp. 156–8.

[310] *A book of common prayer* bound with *The holy bible* (Cambridge, 1663): HEHL, 602964.

[311] *The holy bible containing the old testament and the new* (1648): LLRRO, DG9/2609.

[312] See Susan Brigden, *London and the Reformation* (Oxford, 1989), p. 89.

[313] Orazio Torsellino, *The history of our blessed lady of Loreto*, trans. Thomas Price (St Omer, 1608; STC 24141): CUL 6000.e.154. The book also contains five manuscript poems indicative of fervent Catholic devotion, including 'My vow of Pilgrimage to Loreto and Rome' and 'My Vowe to St Winifride's [well in Flintshire]'. These are in a different and earlier hand. I am grateful to Jason Scott-Warren for drawing this item to my attention.

handed down an octavo copy of Charles I's *Eikon basilike* (1649) that was emblematic of its Anglicanism, along with a King James bible filled with genealogical information.[314] A note on the flyleaf of a 1627 edition of John Cosin's controversial *Collection of private devotions* written by Charles E. Underwood in 1876 reveals that it had belonged to his great-great-great-great-grandmother Laetitia Gregory of Westhope, Herefordshire. By then it had been preserved within the family for seven generations.[315]

Annotations and other traces of ownership enhanced the status of books as tangible emblems of ancestral memory. Elizabeth Isham cherished the edition of Henry Bull's *Christian praiers and holy meditations* (1566) she inherited from her great-grandfather, which he had marked 'in many places that he liked'. Perusing it was a prompt to imitating his exemplary piety: 'it doth much rejoice mee…to tred in the self same stepes towards haven wherein my forefathers have walked'.[316] Adam Winthrop passed down to his heirs a distinctive set of hermeneutic habits along with the annotated books he carried across the Atlantic Ocean with him to New England. Reading itself was a family affair.[317] Others, like the devout Presbyterian Katherine Gell of Derbyshire, passed down the books in which they kept notes of the hundreds of sermons they had heard during their lifetimes: when her unmarried daughter Elizabeth died in 1704, the archive included more than one hundred stitched and unbound volumes.[318]

Such texts are compelling examples of what Ulinka Rublack has called 'grapho-relics'.[319] A mere fraction of those still in private hands, many early modern manuscripts that have ended up in institutional repositories must be assessed in the same light. From chronicles and commonplace books to memoirs, almanacs, funeral sermons, and diaries, these too reflect the crucial part that mothers, fathers, and children played in preserving traces of individual lives in an era of constant religious upheaval. Like the plethora of recipe books investigated by Elaine Leong, in which culinary, medical, and veterinary prescriptions are

[314] NYCRO, 4/10/2/27 and ZKZ/4/9.

[315] John Cosin, *A collection of private devotions* (1627; STC 5816): Bodl. copy, shelf mark Don.f.323. Charles Underwood was vicar of Westhope. Another hand in pencil on the same page notes his death in 1880(?) and is marked 'TR Underwood'.

[316] Princeton University Library, MS RTC01, no. 62 (Elizabeth Isham's 'Book of Rememberance'), fo. 16v, cited in Alec Ryrie, 'Protestants', in Anna French (ed.), *Early Modern Childhood: An Introduction* (Abingdon, 2020), p. 125.

[317] Richard Calis, Anthony Grafton, Madeline McMahon, Jennifer M. Rampling, Christian Flow, and Frederic Clark, 'Passing the Book: Cultures of Reading in the Winthrop Family, 1580–1730', *P&P*, 241 (2018), 69–141.

[318] See Ann Hughes, '"A Soul Preaching to itself": Sermon Note-Taking and Family Piety', in Elizabeth Clarke and Robert W. Daniel (eds), *People and Piety: Protestant Devotional Identities in Early Modern England* (Manchester, 2020), pp. 63–78, at pp. 70–1. For another example, which has also been used as a genealogical register, see FSL, V.a.437 (Sermon book of Dorothy Phillips). On the passing down of sermons within clerical dynasties, see Hannah Yip, 'The Familial Afterlives of Parochial Sermons in Early Modern England', *Reformation*, 27 (2022), 125–40.

[319] Ulinka Rublack, 'Grapho-Relics: Lutheranism and the Materialization of the Word', in Alexandra Walsham (ed.), *Relics and Remains*, P&P Supplement 5 (2010), 144–66.

juxtaposed with genealogical memoranda and spiritual meditations, these too are part of 'the paperwork of kinship'. Compendia of family wisdom co-created by multiple generations, they are another telling index of the transmission of emotion and remembrance along both matrilineal and patrilineal lines in early modern England.[320]

This was a process that involved both transcription and custodianship. Now in the Folger Library, Sir Francis Fane's commonplace book was given to his son at his coming of age. Incorporating several epistles that 'fell from my worthy progenitors penne upon the like occasion', this 'litle mannuall' is an heirloom enclosed within an heirloom. It opens with the advice that Francis's grandfather, the eminent puritan and founder of Emmanuel College, Cambridge, Sir Walter Mildmay left as a 'memoriall' to his heir Anthony, copied 'out of the originall', and includes the letters that Francis's mother and grandmother had sent him in imitation of the spiritual guidance that Lois and Eunice gave to Timothy in New Testament times.[321] Other texts followed the same path. Walter Boothby's 'Nosegay of Everlasting Orifficall Flowers, gathered out of Heavens paradice' is a voluminous mid-seventeenth-century compilation of sermon notes, edifying meditations, and transcriptions of letters written to his offspring and siblings in their middle years. It includes an extended 'counsell' addressed to his 'deere and loving Children Rebekah, Thomas Francis Mary & Hanna', which he entreats them to 'carefully peruse, and indevour contienably to follow...as my blessing I bequeath it fully to you all'. This is dated 1640, but the names of two further daughters, Sarah and Martha, have subsequently been inserted into the list. A marginal note summarizes this as 'The Bowells of a tender father to his pretious babes'. The preservation of the manuscript is itself a measure of filial affection.[322]

The same instincts explain the survival of the loose papers of Elizabeth, countess of Bridgewater. Collected and transcribed by family members after her decease in 1663, these are another archive of family remembrance, prefaced by genealogical notes and heart-rending prayers for the infants she lost to childhood illnesses—her 'girle Frank', her 'boy Henry' and her 'Deare Girle Keatty', who was

---

[320] Elaine Leong, *Recipes and Everyday Knowledge: Medicine, Science and the Household in Early Modern England* (Chicago, 2018), ch. 5. Examples include BL, Additional MS 45196 (Recipe book of Anne Glyd, 1656–1700); BL, MS Additional 34,174 (Twysden family papers); FSL, MS V.a.366 (Rebeckah Winche, *c*.1666); YML MS 228 ('A book of receiptes 1633', with genealogical notes of the Wentworth family). See also Margaret Ezell, 'Domestic Papers: Manuscript Culture and Early Modern Women's Life Writing', in Michelle M. Dowd and Julie A. Eckerle (eds), *Genre and Women's Life Writing in Early Modern England* (Aldershot, 2007), pp. 33–48.

[321] FSL, MS V.a.180 (Sir Francis Fane, commonplace book, compiled *c*.1655–6). See also Susan E. Hrach, 'Maternal Admonition as Devotional Practice: Letters of Mary Fane, Countess of Westmorland', *ANQ: A Quarterly Journal of Short Articles, Notes and Reviews*, 24 (2011), 63–74.

[322] Bodl., MS Eng. C. 2693 (Walter Boothby, 'A Nosegay of Everlasting Orifficall Flowers, gathered out of Heavens paradice'), p. 768. The death of a further son, George, in infancy in 1641 is recorded on the paste-down.

taken by smallpox aged just a year and 10 months.[323] Augmented by those who inherited them, such texts fused together the memory of several generations. A small red-ruled octavo booklet in which the stepdaughter of Lady Constance Lucy preserved her last dying words in 1675 also contains the story of the lingering illness this lady (whose own mother had died in childbirth) bore with Christian patience, added by a grieving relative. This manuscript is a double monument to the memory of two women bound by law, affection, and blood.[324] However, the emotions to which heirloom books attest were sometimes more mixed. Sir Henry Slingsby's daughter Barbara transcribed the catechism sent to her shortly after her father's execution for conspiring to restore the Stuart monarchy in 1658 'to presearve in memorie the last Legasie he left mee', despite the fact that it contained elements 'contrary to the faith and Doctrine of the church of Ingland which I profes', which she quietly redacted.[325] Here, loyalty to a parent overrode scruples about theological orthodoxy.

Godly biographies and autobiographies were similarly passed down as legacies and amplified by those who inherited them. Mary Honeywood combined a 'historicall narration' of her father, vindicating his honour against the 'envious calumnies of Injurious Det[r]actors', with instructions to her sons, daughters, and nephews to imitate their grandfather's 'religious care and pious industry'. Pinned to the first page is a list of the 'ages' (or birthdays) of the children of Sir Thomas and Sir John Honeywood, including a child that died in the womb. This text apparently travelled down the maternal line to Mary's eldest daughter Elizabeth and was later given to Elizabeth Lee 'affter my Sister died'.[326] Mary Franklin's account of her spiritual 'experence' was inserted in a book of sermon notes taken down by her husband, before being bequeathed to her children, who endorsed it with the words 'She being dead yet speaketh.' It passed to the last surviving grandchild, Mrs H. Burton, who, 'being now very Low in pocket and not able to purchase a memorand[um] Book att this time', reused it as a diary in 1782.[327] Such items

---

[323] BL, MS Egerton 607 (Prayers, meditations, and devotional pieces, by Elizabeth, countess of Bridgewater, collected after her death in 1663). Her meditations on the Old Testament, elaborately bound and clasped, are HEHL, Rare Books 297343.

[324] FSL, MS V.a.166 (Elizabeth Lucy, 'An account of the Lady Lacy written to a particular friend of hers...with Mar. Eyre's account of the last moments of the authoress, c.1675).

[325] HEHL, MSSHM 43213 (Catechism compiled by Sir Henry Slingsby, transcribed by Barbara Slingsby Talbot, 1687). See also *A father's legacy. Sir Henry Slingsbey's instructions to his sonnes* (1658; Wing S3995). Paula McQuade has identified the source of the catechism as *The key of paradise*, a Catholic devotional manual published by the Jesuit John Wilson: see *eadem*, *Catechisms and Women's Writing in Seventeenth-Century England* (Cambridge, 2017), ch. 4.

[326] Bodl., MS Rawlinson D. 102 ('M Honywoods Life her Father').

[327] CL, MS I.h.33 (Robert Franklin, notes of sermons with 'Mary Franklin her Experience' and Mrs H. Burton, devout meditations). See also MS I. i. 25 (Letters of Robert Franklin and his wife, 1670). See *Being Dead Yet Speaketh*, ed. Camden; Vera J. Camden, 'Dissenting Devotion and Identity in *The Experience* of Mary Franklin (d. 1711)', in Clarke and Daniel (eds), *People and Piety*, pp. 185–202.

allow us to witness the operations of an intricate web of intergenerational relations that endured across several centuries.

Sometimes texts of this kind escaped from the private into the public domain. Composed in 1627, Sir Anthony Hungerford's account of his conversion from the Romish religion—'the seedes whereof beinge sowen in childhood grewe up with me for many yeares till it pleased God in mercy to pluck it upp by the rootes'— found its way into print, alongside the tract he wrote to reclaim his 'deare mother' to the Church of England. Readers were allowed to eavesdrop on the 'memoriall' he left to his children Margaret, Edward, Anthony, and Frances, to whom they thereby became honorary siblings.[328]

Other heirlooms were also made into common property via this medium. Appended to Richard Baxter's *Breviate* of the life of his wife Margaret was the funeral sermon preached to mark her mother Mary's death, together with transcriptions of the letters she had sent to her daughter, who had kept them as a 'Treasure'. Baxter hoped that this 'Paper-Monument', published 'for the use of all, but especially of their Kindred', would prove more lasting than the marble tombstone to Mary that had perished in the Great Fire of London. Correspondingly, his book served as a memorial of his cherished companion of nineteen years.[329] The Essex minister Anthony Walker's biography of his spouse Elizabeth was likewise a receptacle for the religious directions she had left to her two surviving daughters in a large octavo book neatly bound, gilded, and ruled in red. Containing memoranda of God's providences to the family and records of their eleven children, 'besides some abortive or untimely births', this was a text her husband selectively transcribed as an act of commemoration. His aim, like hers, was 'That the generation to come might know them, even the Children which should be born, who should arise and declare them to their Children: That they might set their hope in God, and not forget the works of God; but keep his Commandements' (Psalm 78: 6–7).[330] Print transformed these intimate traces of personal lives into a spiritual resource for the whole household of faith.

A final example underscores the vital role that both sexes performed in the making of family memory. In a long passage in her autobiographical reflections, the Yorkshire gentlewoman Alice Thornton described the disappearance of her

[328] BL, Additional MS 42,504 (Sir Anthony Hungerford's autobiographical treatise, 1627), fo. 3r. On 12v there is a list of the births of this children, ending 'benedicat deus'. This is printed as an appendix to Hungerford's exhortation to his mother to abandon Catholicism: *The advise of a sonne professing the religion established in the present Church of England to his deare mother a Roman Catholike* (Oxford, 1639; STC 13972), p. 39–62. The 1616 edition does not include the 'memoriall'.

[329] Richard Baxter, *A breviate of the life of Margaret... wife of Richard Baxter* (1681; Wing B1194), pp. 81–2, 94.

[330] Anthony Walker, *The holy life of Mrs Elizabeth Walker* (1690; Wing W305), pp. 5–7. On this text and the broader phenomenon, see Marie-Louise Coolahan, 'Literary Memorialization and the Posthumous Construction of Female Authorship', in Andrew Gordon and Thomas Rist (eds), *The Arts of Remembrance in Early Modern England: Memorial Cultures of the Post-Reformation* (2013), pp. 161–76, at pp. 172–6. See also Chapter 4, above, p. 275.

father's book of advice to his son George during the chaos of the Civil Wars in 1643. Committed to the custody of an uncle by her mother with an exhortation 'to preserve it as the richest jewell she had', it was later seized by Parliamentary soldiers, along with other estate papers. Its loss was a tragedy over which she shed many tears. Alice thanked divine providence that although the original autograph manuscript had 'soe unhappily gone from the whole family', a copy made by a cousin, Timothy Dodsworth, had later come to light. Rejoicing in its recovery, she conscientiously preserved this facsimile for her own posterity. Her own extended account of God's mercy in preserving this parental legacy was intended to prompt acknowledgement of:

> the blessing we injoyed in his life...wherein he imitated the great father of the faithful, Abraham, to instruct and teach his house and children in the waies of God, and to command us by his holy writeings, a pledge of his lasting love and caire of our precious soules to all posterities, not only of us, but even of many more good people.

She implored her children and grandchildren to frame their lives accordingly, as an effective means 'to intaile an eternall blessing upon your seed's seed after you'. '[L]ett not, I beseech you, his honor be stained in you that are his branches.' In short, Alice Thornton urged her offspring to resurrect her dead father by becoming like him. In turn, she was determined to ensure that her own memoirs, written to vindicate her conduct in a series of family quarrels, would not perish. An eyewitness to the 'fury of the warres', she was all too conscious of the vulnerability of her own archive to the vicissitudes of time. Transcribed several times at her behest, the original was bequeathed to her eldest daughter Alice, wife of Thomas Comber, dean of Durham, and faithfully kept within the family for successive generations until the nineteenth century. The flyleaf bears an inscription by her great-great-grandson dated 1789.[331]

A perpetual incentive to storytelling, heirlooms derived their patina and resonance from their relationship with the key moments in the human life course of which they served as remembrancers. They stand 'for the passage of time and the successive nodes in the genealogical chain that link the family', provoking 'an emotional response which stimulates a temporal effect'. They transport their possessors back into history but also forward into the future.[332] To handle these

---

[331] *The Autobiography of Mrs Alice Thornton*, ed. Charles Jackson, Surtees Society 62 (1875), pp. 187–92. See BL, Additional MS 88897/1 and 2. Add MSS 88897/1 has been edited by Raymond A. Anselment as *My First Booke of my Life* (Lincoln, 2014). On the tangled history of these and another lost manuscript, see Anselment's introduction; *idem*, 'Seventeenth-Century Manuscript Sources of Alice Thornton's Life', *Studies in English Literature, 1500–1900*, 45 (2005), 135–55; *idem*, ' "My First Booke of my Life": The Apology of a Seventeenth-Century Gentry Woman', *Prose Studies*, 24 (2001), 1–14.

[332] Gilchrist, *Medieval Life*, pp. 243–4.

domestic texts and objects is to touch the elusive past we seek. They are products of a culture of memory-making and record-keeping that was decisively shaped by the generations.

Archives of Reformation

Lastly, we must examine the creation and curation of the very libraries, archives, and museums upon which we rely. The years of research that have culminated in this monograph have coincided with the so-called 'archival turn', a historiographical development that has sharpened my scrutiny of the caches of papers, annotated books, and heirloom objects that have formed the bedrock of my inquiry.[333] Turning the telescope around, this section makes the repositories I have used the subject rather than the object of study.[334] It argues that the generations, understood as both a biological unit and a social cohort, were vital agents in the formation of the early modern archive and, thereby, of our knowledge of England's religious past.

The Henrician Reformation had a devastating impact on medieval institutional libraries and archives. Monastic and ecclesiastical collections built up over centuries were dispersed and dismembered. Many ancient manuscripts were destroyed as vessels of 'superstition' and 'idolatry' in the heady days of the 1530s. Acquired as chattels along with the decommissioned sacred buildings in which they were kept, others were literally put to 'profane use' in privies or deployed to rub boots and scour candlesticks. Lay purchasers of dissolved religious houses indifferent to these redundant old books sold them off as scrap or wastepaper to bookbinders and shopkeepers, who recycled them. John Aubrey remembered that in his 'grandfathers days the Manuscripts flew about like Butterflies'.[335]

---

[333] See Eric Ketelaar, 'Archival Turns and Returns: Studies of the Archive', in Anne J. Gilliland, Sue McKemmish, and Andrew J. Lau (eds), *Research in the Archival Multiuniverse* (Clayton, Vic, 2017), pp. 228–68.

[334] For some recent developments in this field, see Ann Blair and Jennifer Milligan (eds), 'Towards a Cultural History of Archives', special issue of *Archival Science*, 7/4 (2007); Randolph C. Head (ed.), special issue of 'Archival Knowledge Cultures in Europe, 1400–1900', *Archival Science*, 10/3 (2010); Filippo de Vivo, Andrea Guldi, and Alessandro Silvestri (eds), 'Archival Transformations in Early Modern Europe', special issue of *European History Quarterly*, 46/3 (2016); Elizabeth Yale, 'The History of Archives: The State of the Discipline', *Book History*, 18 (2015), 332–59; Corens, Peters, and Walsham (eds), *Social History of the* Archive, esp. introduction, pp. 9–48 and *eaedem* (eds), *Archives and Information in the Early Modern World*, Proceedings of the British Academy 212 (Oxford, 2018), esp. introduction, pp. 1–25. Markus Friedrich provides a powerful overview in *Die Geburt des Archivs: Eine Wissensgeschichte* (Munich, 2013); *idem*, *The Birth of the Archive: A History of Knowledge*, trans. John Noël Dillon (Ann Arbor, MI, 2018).

[335] See Ronald Harold Fritze, '"Truth hath Lacked Witnesse, Tyme Wanted Light": The Dispersal of the English Monastic Libraries and Protestant Efforts at Preservation, c.1535–1625', *Journal of Library History*, 18 (1983), 274–91; Nigel Ramsay, '"The Manuscripts Flew about like Butterflies": The Break-Up of English Libraries in the Sixteenth Century', in James Raven (ed.), *Lost Libraries: The Destruction of Great Book Collections since Antiquity* (Basingstoke, 2004), pp. 125–44; James P. Carley,

The spoliation of abbeys and priories was succeeded by Edward VI's order of 1549 that cathedrals and parish churches be purged of liturgical service books—antiphoners, missals, processionals, and ordinals—which perpetuated 'ignorance' and sustained conservatives in the hope that Catholicism would soon be reintroduced. Torn between their desire to banish popery and their deep regret at the wanton destruction of the nation's intellectual patrimony, antiquaries such as Leland and Bale called for the preservation of some 'worthy monuments' for posterity. If 'great and speedy diligence be shewed', urged John Dee in a petition to Mary I in 1556, 'the remanents of such incredible store' could still be saved for future generations.[336]

As Jennifer Summit has shown, the process of salvaging the spoils of the monastic libraries entailed winnowing the chaff from the wheat. Matthew Parker, Stephen Batman, and other Protestant collectors carefully sifted the material that had escaped annihilation, rescuing texts that had polemical utility to a religion desperately seeking to defend its antiquity and establish its own pedigree, and discarding the rest. The private libraries they assembled reified the priorities and prejudices that underpinned the historical narratives analysed in Chapter 5. Annotated with appropriate health warnings, some traditional Catholic works were kept as a kind of prophylactic against backsliding to popish error. Reclassified as bibliographical antiquities, manuscripts and incunables were removed from the idolatrous institutions in which they had formerly been read to the sanitized setting of libraries such as Thomas Bodley's in Oxford. These served not as sacred gateways to salvation but laboratories for 'a particular form of scholarly alchemy, in which the straw of medieval belief could be spun into the gold of early modern knowledge'. The pre-Reformation books they absorbed ceased to be conduits of grace and became artefacts of history.[337]

Lollard treatises and Bible translations survive in disproportionate numbers precisely because they provided evidence that the reform of true religion had begun before Martin Luther. The very visibility of the rich textual tradition connected with the Wycliffite heresy was a by-product of the earnest evangelical quest for precocious precursors.[338] Families played their own part in preserving relics of the premature Reformation. The flyleaf of a Lollard bible now in Lambeth Palace Library lists the christening dates of the Essex couple John and Constance

---

'The Dispersal of the Monastic Libraries and the Salvaging of the Spoils', in Elisabeth Leedham-Green and Teresa Webber (eds), *The Cambridge History of Libraries in Britain and Ireland*, vol. i, *To 1640* (Cambridge, 2006), pp. 265–91.

[336] Hughes and Larkin (eds), *Tudor Royal Proclamations*, vol. i, pp. 485–6; Julian Roberts and Andrew G. Watson (eds), *John Dee's Library Catalogue* (1990), p. 194.

[337] Jennifer Summit, *Memory's Library: Medieval Books in Early Modern England* (Chicago, 2008), ch. 3 and p. 138.

[338] Richard Rex suggests that 'the seductive abundance of manuscripts' has led scholars to accord the sect greater importance than it is due: *The Lollards* (Basingstoke, 2002), p. 143. The definitive study of Lollards and their books is Anne Hudson, *The Premature Reformation: Wycliffite Texts and Lollard History* (Oxford, 1988).

Fig. 6.18 'This book I will (God willing) leave for an heirloome to my right heires of
Bramhall William Davenport 1620': Fifteenth-century Wycliffite translation of the Bible.
Source: Cambridge University Library, Additional MS 6680. Reproduced by kind permission of the
Syndics.

Tey's eight children between 1543 and 1557, together with the names of their
godparents, while a splendid early fifteenth-century folio bible in Cambridge
University Library is inscribed: 'This book I will (God willing) leave for an heirloome to my right heires of Bramhall William Davenport 1620' (Fig. 6.18).[339]
These texts are genealogical in a double sense: they document the lineage of the
Protestant faith as well as family history. Their presence attests to a project of partial remembering that skewed the contents of the scholarly libraries formed in
embryo in the sixteenth century, as well as the personal ones with which they
coexisted.

The magnificent medieval manuscripts that leading Elizabeth antiquaries were
responsible for reclaiming from oblivion obscure the fact that some contemporaries regarded printing as the best method of archiving. As Tony Grafton has
demonstrated, the ecclesiastical histories and quasi-facsimile editions of Anglo-
Saxon texts prepared and published by Parker and his team were envisaged as a

---

[339] LPL, MS 25, front flyleaf; CUL, Additional MS 6680, fo. 6v. This inscription was subsequently
tooled in gold on the red leather binding in which it was encased in the nineteenth century. I am
grateful to Mark Rankin for drawing my attention to the Lambeth bible. See his 'Reading the Wycliffite
Bible in Reformation England', in Elizabeth Solopova (ed.), *The Wycliffite Bible: Origin, History and
Interpretation* (Leiden, 2017), pp. 426–49, at pp. 439–40.

more durable record than the mouldering documents they had snatched from the wreckage of the dissolution. The concept of the archive Parker forged in conjunction with his colleagues was one that elided the distinction between scribal texts and printed reproductions.[340] Foxe's *Actes and monuments* and the collected works of Tyndale, Frith, and Barnes he edited in 1573 reflected a similar confidence that the invention of the mechanical press was a providential gift to assist in the vital task of dispelling darkness, spreading the light of the Gospel, and ensuring that the writings of these 'learned fathers of blessed memory' and 'chiefe ryngleaders in these latter tymes' remained 'as perpetual Lampes... to posteritie'.[341] It was a powerful preservative of the ephemeral and fragile, akin to formaldehyde.

The codex, in short, was conceived as a robust and portable archive. Foxe's multivolume tome of documents transcribed from official records and gathered from eyewitnesses was an arsenal of evidence designed to convince his papist enemies, as much as to sustain and embolden his co-religionists. On the one hand, a rather motley crew of medieval Dissenters with highly idiosyncratic opinions were remoulded as proto-Protestants and presented monochromatically, via 'touches of cosmetic surgery', as a 'secret multitude of true professors'.[342] On the other hand, radical factions like the Freewillers were quietly eliminated from his history. Damaging evidence of the theological conflicts over predestination that had splintered the Protestant cause in the 1550s was quietly omitted.[343] *Actes and monuments* was a collaborative enterprise which swelled in size over time as additional, unsolicited testimonies were sent in by relatives, friends, and disciples of the Marian martyrs, together with gory tales of the providential punishments suffered by their erstwhile persecutors. A compilation of oral histories *avant la lettre*, it captured the experiences of the men, women, and children whom it helped to construct as a special generation.

Belated recognition of the ways in which Foxe's book has indelibly coloured our understanding of the Reformation is beginning to be matched by awareness of the counter-archives England's Catholics created to correct the distorting impression left by Protestant ones. Presented as an unvarnished and impartial record, as Liesbeth Corens has argued, the very form taken by the collections of

---

[340] Anthony Grafton, 'Matthew Parker: The Book as Archive', *History of Humanities*, 2 (2017), 15–50. On the importance of the manuscript codex and the technology of the book as a key format for archiving, see Randolph C. Head, *Making Archives in Early Modern Europe: Proof, Information and Political Record-Keeping, 1400–1700* (Cambridge, 2019), esp. pp. 54–5, 60–9, 308–9.

[341] John Foxe, *Actes and monuments* (1563); *The whole workes of W. Tyndall, John Frith, and Doct. Barnes, three worthy martyrs, and principall teachers of this Churche of England*, ed. John Foxe (1573; STC 24436), sigs A2r–3v.

[342] Patrick Collinson, 'Truth and Legend: The Veracity of John Foxe's Book of Martyrs', in A. C. Duke and C. A. Tamse (eds), *Clio's Mirror: Historiography in Britain and the Netherlands* (Zutphen, 1985), pp. 31–54; repr. in *idem, Elizabethan Essays* (1994), pp. 151–77, at pp. 163 and 167.

[343] Thomas Freeman, 'Dissenters from a Dissenting Church: The Challenge of the Freewillers, 1550–1558', in Peter Marshall and Alec Ryrie (eds), *The Beginnings of English Protestantism* (Cambridge, 2002), pp. 129–56.

martyrological documents compiled by Christopher Greene and Ralph Weldon was a tactic in the confessional battles that continued to rage in the eighteenth century. 'Unbiased method and partisan purposes were not mutually exclusive.'[344] Editing out the unseemly rifts over missionary strategy and ecclesiastical governance that had divided the Catholic community, these archives served as 'secure sites of forgetting'. Like the royal Spanish repositories studied by Arndt Brendecke, they advanced 'hidden agendas of oblivion and concealment' even as they proclaimed their commitment to unveiling the truth.[345] The 'tacit narratives' they enshrined paradoxically paraded their own neutrality.[346]

Dissenting Protestants also displayed a strong archival impulse from the beginning. The 'registers' of 'sundrie memorable matters' assembled by puritan activists in Elizabeth's reign were devices for exposing the deficiencies of the Church of England and its inadequate discipline and ministry. Partly published in 1593, this voluminous body of correspondence and official documentation was one arm of a political project to remodel this flawed institution in the image of Calvin's Geneva. Within it was a withering analysis 'of the generation of Antichrist the Pope, the reveled childe of perdition and his successours' by Anthony Gilby, together with 'an hundred pointes of poperie remaining, which deforme the Englishe reformation.'[347] In this polemical archive, the genealogy of falsehood sat alongside accounts of the troubles of the godly 'brethren' at the hands of the bishops. It later passed into the possession of Roger Morrice, the ejected vicar of Duffield in Derbyshire, and thence into Dr Williams's Library, which was established in 1729 for the benefit of nonconforming clergy and students. Augmented by donations of books, manuscripts, and portraits, the legacy Daniel Williams left to his fellow Dissenters was both a treasury of history and memory and a register office for recording the birth of the children who represented their future.[348] The collections engrossed by the Presbyterians and Congregationalists and the scholarly editions subsequently published by their historical societies likewise created and

[344] Liesbeth Corens, 'Dislocation and Record-Keeping: The Counter Archives of the Catholic Diaspora', in Corens, Peters, and Walsham (eds), *Social History of the Archive*, pp. 268–87, at p. 285; Corens, *Confessional Mobility*, ch. 6.
[345] To echo observations made by Arndt Brendecke, '"Arca, Archivillo, Archivo": The Keeping, Use and Status of Historical Documents about the Spanish Conquista', *Archival Science*, 10 (2010), 267–83, at p. 271; *idem*, 'Knowledge, Oblivion, and Concealment in Early Modern Spain: The Ambiguous Agenda of the Archive of Simancas', in Corens, Peters, and Walsham (eds), *Archives and Information*, pp. 131–49, at p. 132. See also Friedrich, *Birth of the Archive*, p. 72.
[346] Eric Ketelaar, 'Tacit Narratives: The Meanings of Archives', *Archival Science*, 1 (2001), 131–41.
[347] [John Udall], *A parte of a register, contayninge sundrie memorable matters, written by divers godly and learned in our time, which stande for, and desire the reformation of our church, in discipline and ceremonies* ([Middelburg, 1593?]; STC 10400), fos 55–72; Albert Peel (ed.), *Seconde Parte of a Register: Being a Calendar of Manuscripts under that Title Intended for Publication by the Puritans about 1593, and now in Dr Williams's Library, London*, 2 vols (Cambridge, 2012; first publ. 1915).
[348] Alan Argent, *Dr Williams's Library 1729–1773: 'A Good Library, Under the Direction of the Dissenters'*, Friends of Dr Williams's Library Seventieth Lecture (2017). The registers are now in TNA, under class RG5.

perpetuated a pedigree for the English nonconformist tradition. Both have contributed to the construction of the 'vertical' denominational histories, dominated by a form of tunnel vision. As Patrick Collinson argued in a classic essay, they fostered an illusion of uninterrupted continuity and a sense of sectarian segregation and exclusion that obscures the horizontal and lateral ties that bound together members of this religiously pluralistic society.[349]

Record-keeping was also a natural reflex of the early Quaker movement. The sect was precocious in its efforts to create an archive of its ordeals via the media of script and print. It appointed its own paid recording clerks, starting with Ellis Hookes, establishing a tradition of secretarial diligence, information gathering, and transcription that supplied the ingredients for Joseph Besse's two-volume compendium of Quaker sufferings and laid firm foundations for the Friends House Library.[350] It prioritized the certification of births, marriages and deaths, in imitation of the books of generation in Scripture and 'after the manner of the Holy men of God', though the children of parents who fell short of the expected high standards could find themselves excluded. The local Meeting refused to record the offspring of Arthur Dekens of Southwark, for instance, 'hee having not walked as becomes a friend professing truth'. In turn, George Keith demanded that the date at which young Friends were 'convinced' should be listed alongside their natural nativity.[351] Quakers such as Thomas Ellwood collected and copied out the epistles and writings of 'ancient Friends' for their own and others' edification. One of the letters in a small folio has been scratched out so that every word is indecipherable.[352] The official archives of this sect were edited to reinforce its reputation for purity and to remove sources of scandal. They helped to craft its image as a tight-knit spiritual community unspotted by contact with the surrounding world. Begun by Lodowick Muggleton's friend and disciple Alexander Delamaine, the Muggletonian archive was similarly modelled on the 'Great Book' of life and combined a register of blessings with correspondence in a large folio.

[349] Patrick Collinson, 'Towards a Broader History of the Early Dissenting Tradition', in C. Robert Cole and Michael E. Moody (eds), *The Dissenting Tradition: Essays for Leland H. Carlson* (Athens, OH, 1975), pp. 3–38; repr. in *idem, Godly People: Essays on English Protestantism and Puritanism* (1983), pp. 527–62. See also *idem*, 'The Vertical and the Horizontal in Religious History: Internal and External Integration of the Subject', in Alan Ford, James McGuire, and Kenneth Milne (eds), *As by Law Established: The Church of Ireland since the Reformation* (Dublin, 1995), pp. 15–32. For a fuller development of the argument in this paragraph, see Alexandra Walsham, *Archives of Dissent: Family, Memory and the English Nonconformist Tradition*, Friends of Dr Williams's Library Seventy-Third Lecture (2020).

[350] See David J. Honneyman, 'Ellis Hookes (1635–1681): First Recording Clerk of the Society of Friends', *Quaker History*, 72 (1983), 43–54; Richard T. Vann, 'Friends Sufferings: Collected and Recollected', *Quaker History*, 61 (1972), 24–35; Brooke Sylvia Palmieri, 'Truth and Suffering in the Quaker Archives', in Corens, Peters and Walsham (eds), *Archives and Information*, pp. 239–62.

[351] Richard T. Vann and David Eversley, *Friends in Life and Death: The British and Irish Quakers in the Demographic Transition, 1650–1900* (Cambridge, 1992), pp. 15–17. See also J. S. Rowntree, 'History of the Friends' Registers', *The Friend*, NS, 43 (1903), 73. On Keith, see Chapter 4 above, p. 293.

[352] FHL, MS VOL 316 (Epistles and writings of early Quakers, collected and copied by Thomas Ellwood, 1639–1713), p. 68.

Rediscovered in a Kent farmhouse in 1974, it bears traces of its curation by the faithful followers who preserved it within their family before depositing it in the British Library.[353]

Historians are becoming increasingly aware of the extent to which ecclesiastical archives and libraries bear the imprint of the very confessional values whose formation they study. In the wake of the sixteenth-century Reformation, Europe's churches organized the records they engendered to buttress myths of origin that were central to their identities. Marginalized or magnified by those who categorized them, such narratives played their part in the making of historical facts about a contested religious past. They not only suppressed segments of it; as Jesse Spohnholz's recent study of the Calvinist Synod of Wesel has demonstrated, they even 'remembered' events that had never occurred.[354] 'Archives do not simply arrive or emerge fully formed; nor are they innocent of struggles for power in either their creation or interpretative applications,' writes Antoinette Burton. 'Though their own origins are occluded and the exclusions on which they are premised often dimly understood', they are themselves 'artefacts of history'.[355]

In England, where reform was sponsored by the state, this process ineluctably shaped the institutional repositories of the English monarchy and the ancient universities, which came to instantiate the versions of historical knowledge and cultural memory that Protestant politicians and collectors wished to bequeath to posterity.[356] The dissolution of the monasteries not only entailed a radical reordering of their documentation; it also necessitated new administrative processes to catalogue the assets which the Crown had confiscated.[357] The Henrician schism from Rome was an important precondition for archival expansion as an instrument of government and for the establishment of the forerunner of the State Paper Office. The mass of manuscript material engendered and gathered by Robert Beale as Clerk of the Privy Council buttressed the ecclesiastical policies of the Elizabethan regime.[358] His Jacobean successor, Thomas Wilson, secretary to Robert Cecil and keeper of the records at Whitehall, described in 1616 how he had been appointed 'to peruse, regester, abstract, & putt in order' the king's papers, which he found 'in extreame confusion' and 'reduced' into 'due order &

[353] The archive consists of eighty-nine volumes: BL, Additional MSS 60168–60256. See William Lamont, 'The Muggletonians 1652–1979: A "Vertical" Approach', P&P, 99 (1983), 22–40; idem, Last Witnesses: The Muggletonian History, 1652–1979 (Farnham, 2006).

[354] See Jesse Spohnholz, 'Archiving and Narration in Post-Reformation Germany and the Netherlands', in Corens, Peters and Walsham (eds), Social History of the Archive, pp. 330–48; idem, The Convent of Wesel: The Event that Never was and the Invention of Tradition (Cambridge, 2017).

[355] Antoinette Burton, 'Introduction: Archive Fever, Archive Stories', in eadem (ed.), Archive Stories: Facts, Fictions, and the Writing of History (Durham, NC, 2005), pp. 1–24, at p. 6.

[356] See Summit, Memory's Library.

[357] Vanessa Harding, 'Monastic Records and the Dissolution: A Tudor Revolution in the Archives?', European History Quarterly, 46 (2016), 480–97.

[358] Nicholas Popper, 'From Abbey to Archive: Managing Texts and Records in Early Modern England', Archival Science, 10 (2010), 249–66.

forme' over the course of 'teen painefull yeares'.[359] Public archives were presifted by these invisible technicians to facilitate selective remembering and deliberate forgetting.[360]

Scholarly work on archives as agents of early modern state-building has been predicated on a divide between public and private that is in the process of being refined. As Alan Stewart and Arnold Hunt have highlighted, the boundaries between the personal and bureaucratic were porous and fluid: if secretaries often retained official papers in their possession, their own letters sometimes ended up being jumbled with the records they kept as royal officials. To obviate this risk, Beale had urged that they be kept apart in a separate box or chest, but many remained promiscuously intermixed. He left his own archive of papers as a legacy to his only child, a daughter who married Sir Henry Yelverton. Sir Robert Cotton's will bequeathed his collection to his son Thomas, with the stipulation that they be handed on to his own heir, John. Ultimately both sets of papers ended up in the British Museum. Sir John Cotton arranged for their purchase by the nation in 1701, anxious to prevent them from falling into the hands of 'two illiterate grand-sons'. The varied afterlives of such records reflect the permeable membrane between the early modern household and the state.[361]

Ironically, some of the most intimate documents I have encountered were preserved by secretaries and clerks in official dossiers. Providing a first-hand account of how an evangelical merchant family responded to the Henrician and Edwardian Reformations in the 1540s, the illuminating letter books of the Johnsons of London came into the hands of the Lord Chancellor in 1553 following their bankruptcy and are now in The National Archives. Reports of clashes between the 'abhominable harlett of Babylon' and the Lutheran cause sit alongside consolatory letters sent to comfort grieving relatives which attest to their sincere solifidian convictions.[362] Robert Markham's moving epistle to his parents explaining the reasons for his conversion to Catholicism and his departure overseas in 1592—being 'distract of sences for feare of death' and unable to 'sleepe or take any rest so monstrous is the horror of my Conscience'—is among the Burghley papers because his father sent it to the Lord Treasurer in a bid to demonstrate his own religious orthodoxy and political fidelity.[363]

---

[359] TNA, SP 14/88, fo. 83 (Thomas Wilson to James I, 10 August 1616).

[360] Alluding to Steven Shapin, 'The Invisible Technician', *American Scientist*, 77 (1989), 554–63.

[361] Alan Stewart, 'Familiar Letters and State Papers: The Afterlives of Early Modern Correspondence', in James Daybell and Andrew Gordon (eds), *Cultures of Correspondence in Early Modern Britain* (Philadelphia, PA, 2016), pp. 237–52, quotations at pp. 240–1 and pp.250–1; Arnold Hunt, 'The Early Modern Secretary and the Early Modern Archive', in Corens, Peters and Walsham (eds), *Archives and Information*, pp. 105–30. See also Michael Riordan, '"The King's Library of Manuscripts": The State Paper Office as Archive and Library', *Information and Culture*, 48 (2013), 181–93.

[362] TNA, SP 46/5–7, analysed in Tankard, 'John Family and the Reformation', quotation at p. 475. The fate of the archive is discussed on p. 489.

[363] BL, Lansdowne MS 72, fos 121r, 122r. See Chapter 1 above, pp. 81–2.

Beale himself copied out the last letters that the Welsh separatist John Penry wrote to his spouse Elinor and his infant daughters Deliverance, Comfort, Safety, and Surehope from prison on the eve of his execution in April 1593. The first was a testimony of his love to 'so deare a sister and so lovinge a wife', urging her not to yield to 'the ordinaunces of the beast' and to bring up their 'seed' in the way of the Lord. The second was to be given to his children 'when they come to yeres of discretion and understandinge'. It urged them to take heed to avoid the 'poluted inventions' of 'Antichristes Kingdome', to grow in grace and godliness, and to willingly embrace persecution for Christ's sake. He was confident that if they continued in holy fear of God 'unto the ende...then shall you and I have a blessed meetinge in the great daye of his appearaunce'. '[T]he sole and only patrimonie' he bequeathed to each of them was a bible, which he charged them to read night and day.[364]

Many other domestic papers and personal memoranda have found their way into provincial archives. Deposited by later generations, they bear witness to the genealogical itch of their forebears. The late medieval and early modern periods saw the steady rise of the family book and archive. Italian *ricordanze* and English cartularies testify to an instinct to document honour and lineage that extended beyond the accumulation of physical proofs of landowning rights and titles to the preservation of written remains of revered predecessors. These encompassed both muniments and monuments. Families self-consciously became communities of records. The archival traces that they left behind were a manifestation of their future-mindedness—of their desire to build a bridge to their descendants. As Eric Ketelaar has argued, such archives were thereby transfigured into forms of cultural patrimony.[365] The steady displacement of 'life cycle' models of record-keeping, which present archives as places where documents go to die, by the idea of a more elastic 'continuum' that recognizes their repeated reuse has helped to lay the foundations for these new trends in interpretation. It highlights their capacity to function simultaneously as organizational and social memory from the time of their creation.[366]

As we have seen, the conceptualization of written, material, and printed remains as legacies to posterity was invested with fresh significance by the Reformations. Protestants derived from Scripture the conviction that they were duty-bound to keep enduring records for subsequent generations. In a sermon

[364] BL, Additional MS 48064 (Papers of Robert Beale relating to Religious Affairs, 1535–93), fos 19v–21v, 22v–24v.

[365] Eric Ketelaar, 'Muniments and Monuments: The Dawn of Archives as Cultural Patrimony', *Archival Science*, 7 (2007), 343–57, and *idem*, 'The Genealogical Gaze: Family Identities and Family Archives in the Fourteenth to Seventeenth Centuries', *Libraries and the Cultural Record*, 44 (2009), 9–28. See also Randolph Head, 'Family Archives: The Paradox of Public Records and Private Authority', in Maria de Lurdes Rosa and Randolph C. Head (eds), *Rethinking the Archive in Pre-Modern Europe: Family Archives and their Inventories from the 15th to the 19th Century* (Lisbon, 2015), pp. 31–6. Forthcoming work by Maura Kenny of the City University of New York and Imogen Peck of the University of Warwick will further illuminate family record-keeping practices in England between 1400 and 1800.

[366] See Elizabeth Shepherd and Geoffrey Yeo, *Managing Records: A Handbook of Principles and Practice* (2003), pp. 5–10. I am grateful to Kate Peters for discussion of this topic.

preached at Paul's Cross on 5 November 1614, William Goodwin underlined the duty of registering God's blessings 'with Characters that shall never be blotted out', so 'that they may never be forgotten but had in perpetual remembrance'. There were two reasons why the Lord required this: first, to ensure that the living would know and take notice of them, and second, in order 'that all ages and posterities succeeding them may have them in memory and remember them'. Goodwin's extended meditation on this theme described how, before the Flood, the patriarchs had such excellent memories that their hearts were their 'libraryes' and 'storehouses'; afterwards, when human lives were shortened and people grew corrupt and deceitful, they were obliged to resort to writing and to erect pillars, monuments, and tables to combat their forgetfulness. Speaking on the tenth anniversary of the Gunpowder Plot, he echoed Psalm 107 in beseeching his hearers to write down the deliverances vouchsafed to the English nation 'for the generations that are to come & that the people yet unborn may praise the Lord'. 'Tell this unto your children, and unto your childrens children, for if you forget it, the stones in the street will remember it, the timber in the wall will remember it, and record it, all will condemn you, of unthankfulness.'[367] The generations he invoked were both natural and spiritual kin. They were people bound by faith as well as by blood.

Goodwin's implied audience consisted of Protestants, but these precepts left a powerful impression across the confessional spectrum, from Catholics to Dissenters. Ranging in format from loose papers to bound volumes, the domestic archives families constructed in response to these biblical imperatives intertwined genealogical data with records of momentous events. Personal and public memories were seamlessly combined in texts and collections that made piety 'the subject as well as the object of remembrance', as well as 'the means of its transmission through time'.[368] Prefaced by the word 'Emmanuell' in godly Protestant style, the book of 'diverse necessary remembrances' compiled by three generations of the Dering family, Richard, Antony, and Edward, is a compact archive that survives in the Folger Shakespeare Library alongside other manuscripts, including notes of a theological dispute with the Catholic Thomas Doughty and a single leaf from a family history prepared as a 'fatherly love to my post[erity]'.[369] Written for his son Frescheville in 1658, Gervase Holles's 'Parentela et Parentalia Hollesiorum' was a set of biographies compiled as 'an act of piety to those that are dead and gone, whose memories every day (more and more) threatens to forgottennesse', so that those left behind 'may behold both the features and dispositions of their deceased

[367] DWL, MS 12.10 (Commonplace book of P. P. with notes of sermons), fos 7v, 9v, 10r–v, 12r.

[368] To quote Sundar Henny, 'Archiving the Archive: Scribal and Material Culture in 17th-Century Zurich', in Corens, Peters, and Walsham (eds), *Archives and Information*, pp. 209–35, at p. 225.

[369] FSL, MS V.b.96 (Dering family, 'A booke of diverse necessary remembrances'); MS X.d.531 (Papers of the Dering family, c.1450–1680), no. 16. See also MS Z.e.27 (Sir Edward Dering, history of the Dering family from the time of the Conquest, c.1635); MS V.b.307 (Notes for a history of the Dering family, c.1631); MS V.b.297 (Catalogue of Sir Edward Dering's books, c.1640–2); MS X.d.530 (Commonplace book, begun c.1605); MS X.d.488 (Notebook of Edward Dering illustrating a theological dispute with the Catholic Thomas Doughty, c.1639–40).

ancestors and retrieve (as it were) a conversation and entercourse with those whom death hath silenc'd'. Left to his daughter following his death, along with directions that it be transcribed into a book of vellum 'to be kept in perpetuity in the family', this was a text that self-consciously preferred 'candor' over 'fictions' and 'false eulogies'.[370] In the case of the Verney family of Buckinghamshire, the archive that passed down fourteen generations from 1495 to 1810 contained thousands of letters, as well as 'acres of parchment' and paper in the form of pedigrees, antiquarian transcriptions, maps, and estate documents. Sir Ralph (1613–96) was so loath to destroy anything that he cut holes to remove confidential items.[371] With an eye to sanitizing their posthumous memory, others, such as Edward Sackville, fourth earl of Dorset, burnt papers that were injurious to their family or friends.[372]

Archival impulses can also be observed among upwardly mobile people further down the social scale. The family papers of the Kays of Woodsome in Yorkshire chart their industry not only in building houses and acquiring farmland but also in instructing their young in devotion and husbandry. They include the 'fatherly farewell' that John Kay, 'bearinge a Ca[r]efull zeale unto my Successors', wrote in 1576 to provide them with 'holesome lessons' regarding their adoption and 'newe regeneracion' and their own spiritual duties as parents.[373] Though largely a record of the properties he owned and leased, the volume that the Devonshire farmer Robert Furse compiled for his son and 'all his Sequelle' in the early 1590s began with a prayer and an admonition to remember 'our awnseters or pryenytores' and let their 'honeste good and godly acts and lyves be a scolemaster to you and to yours for ever': allthoffe some of them wer but sympell rude unlernede and men off smalle possessyones substance habillyte or reputasion, yt I do wysshe and exhorte you all that you sholde not be asshamed of them nor mocke dysdayne or spyte them.[374]

Male custodianship of documentation may have a tendency to produce a historical memory that revolves around men, but, as we have seen, women were energetic genealogists, remembrancers, and transmitters of religious and household wisdom. Key agents of transgenerational memory, via the medium of the mother's legacy, they were the creators of 'matriarchives'.[375] Excluded from the

---

[370] *Memorials of the Holles Family*, ed. Wood, pp. 2, 8, xii, and 192, respectively.
[371] Susan Whyman, *Sociability and Power in Late Stuart England: The Cultural Worlds of the Verneys, 1660–1720* (Oxford, 2002), p. 5.
[372] A. P. Newton (ed.), *Calendar of the Manuscripts of Major-General Lord Sackville, K.B.E, C.B., C.M.G, Preserved at Knole, Sevenoaks, Kent*, vol. i, *Cranfield Papers, 1551–1612*, HMC, Octavo Series 80 (1940), pp. xiv–xv. On letter-burning, see Arnold Hunt, '"Burn this Letter": Preservation and Destruction in the Early Modern Archive', in Daybell and Gordon (eds), *Cultures of Correspondence*, pp. 189–209.
[373] FSL, MS X.d.445–449 and W.b.482–484 (Papers of the Kay family of Woodsome, Yorkshire, c.1561–1642). The 'fatherly farewell' is W. b. 484, quotations at pp. 1, 5.
[374] Anita Travers (ed.), *Robert Furse: A Devon Family Memoir of 1593*, Devon and Cornwall Record Society, NS 53 (Exeter, 2012), pp. 10–23, at p. 11.
[375] William H. Sherman, *Used Books: Marking Readers in Renaissance England* (Philadelphia, PA, 2009), ch. 3, developing a concept formulated by Jacques Derrida, *Archive Fever: A Freudian Impression*, trans. Erick Prenowitz (Chicago, 1996), pp. 35–6. See also James Daybell, 'Gender, Politics

main family archive by its patriarchs, the spiritual autobiography written by the unmarried gentlewoman Elizabeth Isham was a 'book of rememberance' designed to ensure that her own mother did not 'die in oblivion' and to continue the tradition of bequeathing maternal advice to her nieces.[376] Anne Clifford similarly curated the correspondence of her 'blessed' mother Margaret, countess of Cumberland, as a memorial, arranging and annotating it to highlight particular aspects of her life, especially her relationship with her daughter.[377]

Recusants felt an imperative to archive evidence of the faith of their ancestors and co-religionists as well as their lives. The voluminous 'flowers of fathers' that Thomas Jollet transcribed and intended to 'burye & intombe... till some ioyfull daye cause their happy Resurrection' were envisaged as a kind of time capsule, to be opened when the Church of Rome was restored to its rightful dominance, as well as a monument to the heroic company of Catholics who had suffered 'detriment in bodie lands or goodes' since the beginning of Elizabeth's reign. Uncompromisingly hostile to the 'Calvinian congregation', it is a text which seeks to nurture hatred of the 'viperous brood' of 'the very sonnes of Satan' in the next generation. The 1,800 pages which comprise it are a sacred treasury of Catholic memory whose survival is a simultaneously a testament to piety.[378] The papers of the Mauleverer family of Ingelby Arncliffe in North Yorkshire include indulgences, letters of confraternity, and charters relating to the former Carthusian house Mount Grace Priory, which remained a site of defiant Catholic pilgrimage in the seventeenth century, alongside household accounts and pedigrees.[379] Those associated with the Salvins of Croxdale, Co. Durham, contain leaves from a medieval monastic register, a grant of royal pardon relating to the Northern Rebellion, and a dispensation from eating flesh in Lent, while the Rookwoods of Stanningfield kept documentation relating to the executions of two successive ancestors named Ambrose for high treason in 1606 and 1696, together with pleas against recusancy fines and petitions for the revocation of orders of banishment. They preserved a record of resistance and resilience in the face of 'the turnynge vicissitude of this woorldes revolution' in a book that was passed down from heir to heir with the prescription that they 'continue to sett downe the family as it increaseth'.[380] The archival instincts of Catholics were

---

and Archives in Early Modern England', in *idem* and Svante Norrham (eds), *Gender and Political Culture in Early Modern Europe, 1400–1800* (2017), pp. 25–45.

[376] Stephens, *Gentlewoman's Remembrance*, pp. 7–9, 234–5, quotation at p. 31.

[377] James Daybell, 'Gendered Archival Practices and the Future Lives of Letters', in Daybell and Gordon (eds), *Cultures of Correspondence*, pp. 210–36, esp. pp. 223–33.

[378] Bodl., MS Eng. Th. b.1–2, quotations from vol. i, p. 3–4; and vol. ii, p. 403. This has been comprehensively studied by Katie McKeogh, 'Sir Thomas Tresham (1543–1605) and Early Modern Catholic Culture and Identity, 1580–1610' (DPhil thesis, University of Oxford, 2017). See also *eadem*, ' "Flowers of Fathers": Resistance and Consolation in a Catholic Manuscript Compilation, Bodleian MSS Eng. th. b. 1-2', *HLQ*, 84 (2021), 307–51.

[379] NYCRO, ZFL (Mauleverer family papers).

[380] DCRO, D/Sa/F 1–408 (Salvin family papers), items 7, 390; CUL MS Hengrave 76/1. For edited extracts from this archive, see Francis Young (ed.), *Rookwood Family Papers 1606–1761*, Suffolk Records Society 59 (Woodbridge, 2016).

intensified by awareness of the fragility of their family histories to the hostility and malice of Protestant heretics. The manuscript compiled by Thomas Meynell in 1614 summarized records that had been rescued by his uncle Robert from the three great chests of documents brought from Byland Abbey to the church of Northallerton following the dissolution. He prefaced this register of his fervent commitment to the Catholic religion with a passionate attack on the sacrilege sanctioned by the Henrician Reformation:

> when tyme inlarged vilanie to commit all profane and sinister actes, nothing was spared how holy soever it was. All was turned up side downe, and the bodyes of saintes and other heroicall persons being wrapped in lead were turned out thereof and the lead sould to plunderers, books and pictures were burned, Evidences not Regarded: all was subject to violence and Rapine.

Part chronicle, part prayer roll, this portable archive stores up the record of the past and present to preserve it for the future.[381]

Nonconformist families were no less assiduous in curating their religious inheritance. The apparently miscellaneous papers preserved by the descendants of dynasties of Presbyterian and Congregationalist ministers like William and Chewning Blackmore and Samuel Say were framed to recall their ennobling travails. Highlighting their exemplary domestic devotion and enhancing the image of moderation and propriety cultivated by martyrological memorials like Edmund Calamy's, the strategies of selection and editing deployed by successive relatives demonstrate how the memory of Dissent was subtly reinvented in subsequent decades.[382] So does the account of the imprisonment of Henry Singer for nonconformity in 1665 inscribed in a bible bequeathed to his son by his grandfather around 1681. This has been augmented by details of the Singers' involvement in the Monmouth rebellion and the emigration of other relatives to America with the Quaker William Penn. Copied out in rough facsimile in the nineteenth century, some of these stories were oral traditions that had probably been embellished as they were transferred onto paper.[383] Material remnants of individual lives coexist with memorials of the religious communities of which those people were members. The Braithwaite family papers, presented by a twentieth-century descendant named Janet to the Library of the Society of Friends in 1929, for instance, incorporate a set of transcriptions of the testimonies of eminent seventeenth-century

---

[381] NYCRO, ZIQ/MIC 2050 (Thomas Meynell's MS of 1614). See Sarah Bastow, 'The Piety of Thomas Meynell: No Thing was Spared How Holy Soever it was', *Reading Medieval Studies*, 43 (2017), 29–54.

[382] DWL, MS 12.40 ('Original letters and family papers &c of the Blackmore family'); MS 12.107 (Papers of the Say family). For a fuller discussion, see Walsham, *Archives of Dissent*. On the role of dissenting ministers as posthumous guardians of the reputation and memory of their friends, see Tessa Whitehouse, *The Textual Culture of English Protestant Dissent 1720–1800* (Oxford, 2015), ch. 6.

[383] Somerset HC, A/DNO/1 (History of the Singer family copied from the family bible, 1595–1851).

Friends.[384] The families who created the archives of nonconformity that have come down to us were thus the gatekeepers of its history.

The migration of the scribal traces of ordinary lives into public archives indexes the breaking of the generational chain. If this is a function of the genetic lottery that has extinguished some lineages, equally often it attests to a conscious effort to prevent them from dissolving into oblivion. Printed books and bodies of private documentation that have passed into the hands of provincial record offices and been acquired by national libraries reflect the longer-term process that has transformed them into cultural assets. Some, like a seventeenth-century copy of John Bunyan's *Signs from hell* with genealogical details of Peter and Elizabeth Street and their seven children, became part of parish libraries.[385] Others were gifts and bequests to repositories established by churches and sects: the Harris family's 1577 Geneva bible bears marks of its provenance, together with this twentieth-century notice: 'I give to the Society of Friends my black leather Elizabethan bible and I express the wish that this bible will be exhibited at the Central Library at Friends House Euston Road London.'[386] This piece of family history has become public property. John Milton's bible, with a genealogy written in his own hand and continued by his amanuensis after he went blind, is so valuable that the British Library keeps it under lock and key and produces it to readers only with special permission.[387]

The case of Dionys Fitzherbert, who had two copies of her spiritual autobiography made for the Bodleian and Sion College Library in 1633, reminds us that the instinct to leave legacies to 'posterity' (understood as a collective noun denoting the beneficiaries of a particular inheritance, culture, or tradition) long predated the nineteenth century. It underlines the point that ostensibly private documents were frequently intended to be a resource for the future. Fitzherbert's vivid account of the workings of her afflicted conscience was 'An Anatomie for the Poore in Spirit' designed to edify fellow members of 'the glorious and renouned Church of England' she embraced as 'our deare Mother'.[388] Generations, defined as both biological and social cohorts, were the crucible in which patrimony consciousness grew.[389] Archives, in other words, are by-products of the 'irrepressible...force and authority of transgenerational memory'.[390]

The presence of such texts in archives is often less a consequence of antiquarianism and connoisseurship than of affect and sentiment. The survival of

---

[384] FHL, MS 62/5.
[385] Surrey HC, PSH/RIP/16/1 (Parish records of St Mary's, Ripley).
[386] FHL, MS S 469 (Harris family bible).
[387] BL, MS Additional 32,310 (quarto edition of the *Holy bible*, 1612).
[388] The two copies are Bodl., MS Bodley 154 and LPL, MS Sion L40.2/E47. For her reverence for the Church of England, see Bodl., MS e. Mus. 160 (Original papers of Dionys Fitzherbert), fo. viii r. In the sixteenth and seventeenth centuries, the word 'posterity' referred both to blood descendants and to all future generations. See *OED*.
[389] See Ketelaar, 'Muniments and Monuments', who builds on Jean-Michel Leniaud, *Les Archipels du passé: Le Patrimoine et son histoire* (Paris, 2002).
[390] Derrida, *Archive Fever*, p. 35.

ephemeral items like the single sheet of paper on which Frances Matthew, wife of Tobie, archbishop of York, wrote the names of her children and their godparents further attests to the tremendous tenacity of family memory at a time when many children died in their infancy (Fig. 6.19).[391] Some explicitly signal their status as touchstones of emotion: a note in pencil on an envelope enclosing a disintegrating 'geonoligie' of the Coussmaker family of Westwood in Surrey, who ancestors fled Flanders to escape the Dutch Revolt, reads 'very tender'.[392] Many folders and boxes I have called up from the vaults contain an eclectic mix of items: fragmentary texts, scraps of cloth, deer bones, and ancient horoscopes. Inside heirloom prayer books and bibles that have been conserved as genealogical registers I have found pressed flowers, handwritten recipes, and sepia photographs.[393] Once objects that allowed people to reach across time, they have gradually shed their original significance like a dead skin. In other instances, a rival impulse has prevailed. Families have given photocopies and transcriptions while retaining the originals or reclaimed the heirlooms they had previously deposited, leaving only ghostly traces in indexes and catalogues.[394]

The paper shrines to generational memory I have been describing suggest that the older sense of *archivum* as a treasury of precious objects retained its vitality into and beyond the early modern period.[395] The wooden boxes, embroidered caskets, and carved chests in which early modern people kept such documents and artefacts in turn became memorials to past generations. Emptied and reused to archive more recent pasts, they reify the metaphorical conceptualization of memory as a receptacle for storage.[396] Emerging out of Renaissance cabinets of curiosities, modern museums themselves have accumulated collections in similar ways. They too are repositories that were shaped by the Reformations. The collections of John Tradescant, Elias Ashmole, and Ralph Thoresby that formed the

---

[391] YML, MS 322 (Frances Matthew's record of the births and baptisms of her children, 17th century).

[392] Surrey HC, 7052/7/1 (Pedigree papers of Macclesfield Forbes Coussmaker).

[393] e.g. WAAS, 705: 295 Parcel 5 (Hornyhold family papers: horoscope, deer bone); Dorset HC, D. 1962/3/2 (King James New Testament (Oxford, 1680) with register of the Richards family and pressed leaves and flowers); Surrey HC, 2953/1/8/1–7 (family bible inscribed 'Ann Iveson 1758', with genealogical notes and photographs); HEHL 438000:250 (*The book of common prayer* (Cambridge, 1673) with recipes); Devon HC, 5282M/F/13 and 13a (plant pressings found in Humphrey Prideaux, *The old and new testament connected in the history of the Jews and neighbouring nations* (1720)).

[394] e.g. SRO, 4714/1 (Photocopies of a bible owned by the Semple family of Northern Ireland, with genealogical notes and other memoranda, 1630–1787) and LLRRO, 26D53/2680/(Bible belonging to Robert Shirley said to have been bound and embroidered at Little Gidding, returned to the depositor in 1965).

[395] See Head, *Making Archives*, pp. 13–14.

[396] See Heather Wolfe and Peter Stallybrass, 'The Material Culture of Record-Keeping in Early Modern England', in Corens, Peters, and Walsham (eds), *Archives and Information*, pp. 179–208; Friedrich, *Birth of the Archive*, ch. 6. For an illuminating study of one such box, see Michèle Barrett and Peter Stallybrass, 'Printing, Writing and a Family Archive: Recording the First World War', *History Workshop Journal*, 75 (2013), pp. 1–32. On memory as a chest and container, see Frances A. Yates, *The Art of Memory* (1966), chs 6, 15; Mary Carruthers, *The Book of Memory: A Study of Memory in Medieval Culture* (Cambridge, 1992), ch. 4; *eadem, The Craft of Thought: Meditation, Rhetoric and the Making of Images, 400–1200* (Cambridge, 1998), pp. 14–21.

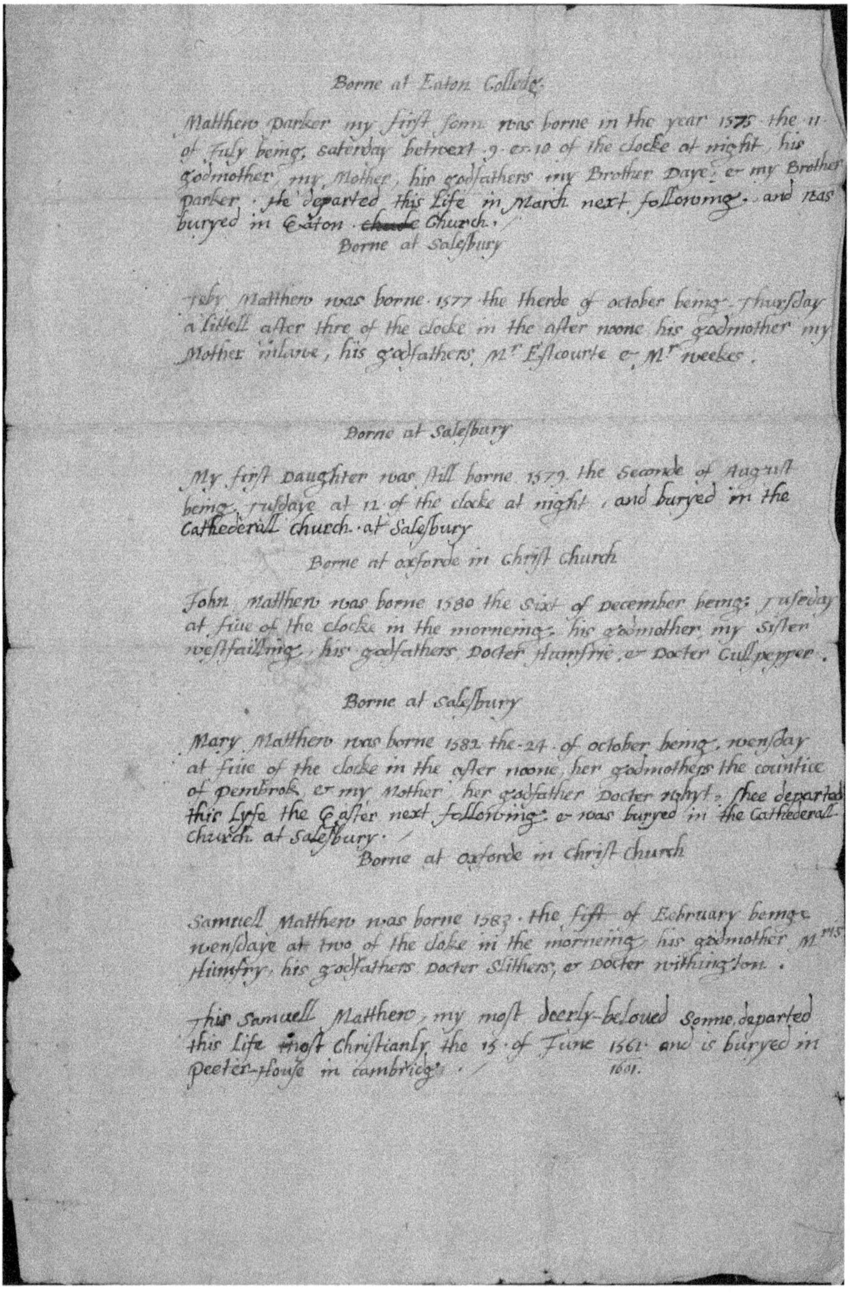

Borne at Eaton Colledg

Matthew Parker my first sonn was borne in the year 1575 the 11 of July being saterday betwext 9 & 10 of the clocke at night his godmother my Mother, his godfathers my Brother Daye & my Brother parker; He departed this Life in March next following. and was buryed in Eaton ~~churche~~ Church.

Borne at Salesbury

Toby Matthew was borne 1577 the therde of october being thursday a littell after thre of the clocke in the after noone his godmother my Mother inlawe, his godfathers Mr Estcourte & Mr weekes.

Borne at Salesbury

My first Daughter was still borne 1579 the Seconde of August being tusdaye at 12 of the clocke at night, and buryed in the Cathederall church at Salesbury

Borne at oxforde in Christ church

John Matthew was borne 1580 the Sixt of december being tusday at fiue of the clocke in the morneing his godmother my sister westfailing, his godfathers Docter Humfrie & Docter Cullpepper.

Borne at Salesbury

Mary Matthew was borne 1582 the 24 of october being wensday at fiue of the clocke in the after noone, her godmothers the countice of pembroke & my Mother her godfather Docter whyte, shee departed this Lyfe the Easter next following & was buryed in the Cathederall Church at Salesbury.

Borne at oxforde in Christ church

Samuell Matthew was borne 1583 the fift of Ebruary being wensdaye at two of the clocke in the morneing his godmother Mrs Humfry his godfathers Docter Slithers, & Docter withington.

This Samuell Matthew, my most deerly beloued Sonne departed this Life most Christianly the 15 of June 1561 and is buryed in Peeter-House in cambridge. 1601.

Fig. 6.19 Frances Matthew's record of the births and baptisms of her children (17th century).

Source: York Minster Library MS 322.

basis for our national museums absorbed some items that had previously been venerated as relics, together with other material remnants of 'superstition' and 'idolatry'.[397] They were places where, recategorized as 'antiquities' and 'rarities' and deactivated by their relocation from consecrated spaces, formerly sacred objects could be appreciated anew. No longer items that gave hope of salvation, now they were treasured as embodiments of a lost past. Their value lay not in their timelessness but in the fact that they were time-bound. James Simpson has suggested that the very existence of modern museums is predicated upon iconoclasm. These are institutions that replicate reformed fear of numinous images and neutralize them as objects of taste, allowing them to be viewed without taint of sin.[398]

Museums have also become places of asylum for religious and liturgical artefacts expelled from monasteries and churches in the sixteenth century, often via the Catholic homes in which they were initially preserved in anticipation of England's reversion to Rome. Absorbed into the ownership of families who were their temporary custodians, empty reliquaries and holy vessels eventually became heirlooms, before being bequeathed to missionaries, colleges, and convents overseas.[399] The recent return of many relic and manuscript collections to the safekeeping of Douai Abbey in Berkshire following the closure of religious houses due to lack of vocations replicates earlier patterns of movement.

The meandering itineraries and biographies of these Catholic objects parallel those taken by the many specimens of Protestant material culture discussed in this book: commemorative pottery, silverware, embroidery, needlework, portraits, and furniture. Broken up into lots and sold to collectors, items that once memorialized their former creators, donors, owners, or recipients have thereby lost their capacity to evoke those dead ancestors. The absence of stories of their provenance, however apocryphal, represents a second layer of forgetting. Yet if the movement of these cross-generational gifts and personal keepsakes into museums often marks the end of a family tradition of transmission, sometimes, by contrast, it testifies to a determination to ensure the preservation of this heritage for the nation. A gold ring set with a crystal enclosing a miniature of the martyred Charles I, for instance, was a Cameron family heirloom left to the Victoria and Albert Museum in 1909 by the spinster who inherited it, while the early eighteenth-century portrait of the four young daughters of the wealthy

---

[397] See John Tradescant, *Musaeum Tradescantianum: or, a Collection of Rarities Preserved at South-Lambeth neer London* (1656; Wing T2005), esp. pp. 42–9 and Michael Hunter, 'The Cabinet Institutionalised: The Royal Society's Repository and its Background', in Oliver Impey and Arthur MacGregor (eds), *The Origins of Museums: The Cabinet of Curiosities in Sixteenth- and Seventeenth-Century Europe* (Oxford, 1985), pp. 159–68.

[398] See Woolf, *Social Circulation of the Past*, pp. 191–7; James Simpson, *Under the Hammer: Iconoclasm in the Anglo-American Tradition* (Oxford, 2010), esp. pp. 121, 138–44, 157–8.

[399] See Raguin, *Catholic Collecting, Catholic Reflection*.

Dutch merchant Sir Matthew Decker passed down the family line until it reached the 7th Viscount Fitzwilliam, who bequeathed it with the rest of his art collection to the University of Cambridge in 1816.[400] Involving a transfer of guardianship, the trajectories of these two items embody the transition from communicative to cultural memory that the foregoing pages have traced but also qualified and complicated.

This chapter has investigated the generations as agents of remembering and forgetting, commemorating and inventing. It has explored the shifting ways in which people memorialised loved ones after the end of intercessory prayer via speech, text, and object, in juxtaposition with the imperative that drove so many to leave moral and spiritual legacies to their descendants. The picture that has emerged has further softened the sharp disjuncture between the living and the departed that the Tudor Reformation has been credited with effecting. It has underlined the diachronic links that continued to connect contemporaries with their deceased ancestors and their anticipated heirs, as well as the synchronic ones that they forged with their fellow Christians in this world. These influenced how people recollected the religious changes they had experienced and witnessed and the selective memories of these events, etched with embarrassment, pride, sadness, nostalgia, and anger, which they passed on to the next generation.

Kate Hodgkin has commented that 'the time of family memory looks to both past and future: it holds the dead in the minds of the living, and transmits the responsibility for remembrance forward to children and grandchildren.'[401] This is an insight that applies equally well to the overlapping families of blood and faith that this book has investigated. It also helps to illuminate the oral, textual, and material traces which they left behind. In turn, the life cycles of these traditions, documents, and monuments have much to tell us about the confessionalization of memory in the post-Reformation era. The product of efforts to dictate how posterity remembers the past, the archives, libraries, and museums in which they now lie are the refracting lenses through which we view this formative period. Alongside the chronicles, histories, and martyrologies composed by competing churches and sects, they have contributed decisively to constructing the historiographical paradigms and models of periodization we have inherited. These paradigms and models are themselves genealogical in the sense that they privilege linear stories of origin and descent. Emanations of the generations as communities of imagination, emotion, and memory, they too shape our knowledge of the English Reformations.

[400] V&A, M.1–1909 (gold ring set with crystal enclosing a miniature, 17th-18th century); Fitz., Founder's Bequest 1816 (437). On the latter, see Avery, Calaresu, and Laven, *Treasured Possessions*, p. 231.
[401] Hodgkin, 'Women, Memory and Family History', p. 312.

Conclusion

> Memorandum: that Mr Ric. Wilbraham my Grandfather died the 2^d
> day of February 1612 being the Purification of our blessed Lady,
> about 9 of the clock at night, being Tuesday. Anno. 10mo Jaco:

This neatly inscribed entry was the first of the 'Remembrances' Thomas
Wilbraham inserted in the quarto notebook which he appears to have inherited,
probably from his own father, in the same year. He took seriously his responsibility to keep up the tradition of record-keeping initiated by his ancestor Richard,
the second son of Ralph Wilbraham, a member of a junior branch of a prominent
Cheshire family with a particularly complex and tangled pedigree. Richard was
born on 13 August 1525, and his life spanned nearly the whole of the first century
of England's extended Reformation. It began not long after Martin Luther's provocative challenge to papal indulgences and in the same year as Germany erupted into
the popular rebellion that has become known as the Peasants' War. In 1534, when
Richard was 9, Henry VIII declared himself Supreme Head of the Church, precipitating an ecclesiastical schism from the Church of Rome that would have far-
reaching consequences for his kingdom. His childhood and rise to manhood
occurred against the backdrop of a bewildering phase of religious change. He
married Elizabeth Maisterton, who gave birth to his first son and namesake in
January 1552, five years after the precocious young Protestant prince Edward VI
came to the throne. Three other sons followed in quick succession, the fourth,
Ralph, being born on 'the sonday next before the feast of thannunciation of our
blessed lady', 20 March, 1558, sixth months before Mary I's premature death ter-
minated the passionate but controversial Counter-Reformation over which this
pious Catholic queen had presided. The end of 'her most gracious raigne' is noted
on the same page, followed by the accession of Elizabeth I, 'whome god longe
preserve'. At some point later the words 'most gracious' were crossed out, which
suggests that the writer no longer aligned himself with the faith of his forefathers
and looked back upon this period as an embarrassing aberration in the history of
the English nation. When Richard's 'deare loving wyffe' died in 1589, he recorded
her demise in a formulation that showed his firm belief that she, 'by Chrystes
mercy is in heaven [above]'. He evidently hoped and prayed that she was one of

God's elect, predestined to be saved. At some point in the preceding years, Richard had become a Protestant.[1]

It is unclear when Richard Wilbraham began writing the notebook which he bequeathed to his descendants and which opens an intimate window into the social universe I have explored in this monograph. It may have been later in life, as his own children grew up and had offspring of their own and he became conscious of his own advancing age and bodily frailty. By the early years of the seventeenth century, he was nearly 80, and his handwriting was becoming quite shaky. Part chronicle, part genealogy, part journal, Richard's book intermingled civic and public history with family memory. Starting with the conquest of the Scots at the Battle of Flodden Field in 1513, it served as a record of notable events, including the burning of the steeple of St Paul's cathedral in 1561, local floods, and consuming urban fires which broke out 'by godes sufferaunce', and the serious outbreak of plague in Nantwich in 1604 which killed 500 people before it ceased. Simultaneously, continued by his male heirs in the same vein, it was a register of the births, marriages, and deaths of members of their immediate households, as well as the extended web of their wider kith and kin—from 'cosens', step-siblings, in-laws, and godparents to 'best beloved' friends. These two chronologies and calendars occasionally converge: in a note added at the end of the book Thomas's mother Elizabeth deposed that he was born on St Peter's day in 'the yere nexte after the great Spanish fleete came to invade Englannd', 29 June 1589. This was a family that came to define its own seminal dates in relation to the providential landmarks that punctuated the timeline of the Reformation.[2]

In due course, Thomas himself passed away in October 1643. The early part of his section of the family book of remembrances tells of his admission to Lincoln's Inn and Brasenose College, Oxford, and his travels in Europe in the company of the French ambassador. These sit alongside memoranda about the fashionable alterations made to the family residence and the refurbishment of the pulpit and pews in the parish church of Acton in 1633. Less impersonal in tone than those of his predecessors, Thomas's entries include the story of his recovery from a dangerous sickness after Christmas 1631 ('God make me never to be unmindful of his great mercies') and the death of his eldest son aged 12, a terrible affliction which he prayed he might use for his own spiritual improvement. He commemorated this lamented lost child, 'one of my greatest temporall comforts...every way answerable to my owne harts desire', by calling his sixth son, who was born two months later, after him. In 1636 Thomas erected a double monument to the memory of his grandfather, who had died in 1612, and his firstborn child, who passed

---

[1] CRO, DDX/210/1 (Wilbraham Family Diary, 1513–1962), fos 13r, 1v, 8r. On the Wilbraham family, see James Hall, *A History of the Town and Parish of Nantwich, or Wich Malbank in the County Palatine of Chester* (Didsbury, 1972 facsimile edn; first publ. 1883), pp. 424–39.

[2] CRO, DDX/210/1 (Wilbraham Family Diary, 1513–1962), fos 3v, 52r.

away in 1633 before reaching his prime. The Latin inscription on the black marble tablet announces that although they never knew each other, the 88-year-old man and 12-year-boy lie 'sleeping together', united in death and 'veiled in Night' (*una obdormiscunt senex proavus, puerq' pronepus…hic velati nocte quiescunt*). The devotion, wisdom, and judgement of the elder found a mirror in the kind disposition and precocious mind of the godly youth, who consciously mimicked the Wilbraham ancestor whom he never knew.[3]

The years following the outbreak of fighting in 1642 were tumultuous for this Royalist gentleman, a member of Charles I's privy chamber who was imprisoned in his own house for refusing to support the Parliamentary war effort against the king and forced to seek refuge in Sussex. Perhaps preferring to bury them in oblivion, Thomas himself made no reference to these scarring experiences, leaving his son Roger to describe his father's troubles during the English Revolution, along with a brief but affectionate sketch of his character as an exemplary husband, parent, and master. Roger survived his two elder brothers, Richard, who perished in infancy, and Thomas, who died following a haemorrhage, aged 27, in December 1649.[4]

Roger proved to be the most prolific of the Wilbraham family record-keepers, as well as an assiduous antiquary and dedicated collector and chronicler of the history of Nantwich. Educated in Derbyshire and Cambridge, he passed his late adolescence and early adulthood under the cloud of the Civil Wars, during which the town served as a garrison for Roundhead troops. 'The Resentment I had of that Bloody Scene which was acted upon the Person of our Soveraign K. Ch. 1. 30 Jan. 1648[9]' precipitated a debilitating ailment that impaired his health for many years to come. His early married life coincided with the Interregnum, and he remembered the winter of 1659 as having 'afforded little else but Distractions… these Countries were full of discontented Soldiers'. The Restoration seemed like a miracle, 'Englands Jubile'. Roger compared Charles II's return after so long in exile and 'after the Martrydome of his Father by those Bloody Regicides' to the joyous re-entrance of King David to Jerusalem after his period of asylum in Mahanaim. The Great Fire of London in 1666, which 'did not spare our Mother church, with 86 of her Daughters, as Fagots about a Stake', also left a profound impression.[5] To a committed member of the Church of England, the conflagration seemed like a symbolic, architectural echo of the Marian burnings of Protestant heretics immortalized in John Foxe's *Actes and monuments*. Roger's fervent piety extended to preserving 'memorable instances of divine justice' against sinners in the vicinity of Nantwich, from notorious drunkards, swearers, and Sabbath-breakers to sexually promiscuous widows and the 'audacious slut' who was an incorrigible

---

[3] Hall, *History of the Town and Parish of Nantwich*, p. 320.
[4] CRO, DDX/210/1, fos 18r–v, 19r–v, 21r. [5] Ibid., fos 22v, 23v, 24r.

pilferer and thief. The untimely ends of these notorious evildoers provided patent evidence of the Almighty's active intervention in human affairs.[6]

Roger clearly regarded the fertility of his wife Alice, who was also his cousin, as a sign of approbation and as a cause for celebration. He was proud to have been the progenitor of eleven children, including twins, 'within the compasse of xii yeers & vi weeks' between 1657 and 1669. Even in an era of high infant and childhood mortality, he had more than his share of personal sadness. Seven of his offspring predeceased him, including his eldest daughter, who died within a few hours of her birth on 22 April 1658, before she could be baptized. The darkest year was 1675, which began with the death of the vicar of Acton, 'a burning & shining Light', to be followed by the demise of his 6-year-old son Richard in May 'of a stoppage in his Breast'. '[A] fresh Tyde of Griefe' broke upon his parents two months later when his 18-year-old brother Thomas, who had returned from Oxford to console them, took ill with a violent fever and later expired. Roger and Alice were both bereft and suffered both mentally and physically in the aftermath of this second tragedy. Alice spent the first anniversary of Tom's death in 1676 privately in her closet. After supper with her husband, she retired to bed. She awoke at midnight with a slight cold and cough, sighed four or five times, and died without warning. The sudden passing of his 'chiefest earthly Comfort' and 'best companion', 'an ornament to her Sex & a Crown to her Husband', left Roger numb. Afflicted by insomnia, he spent his sleepless nights musing on a suitable 'monument' by which to transmit her memory to posterity, eventually settling on the conversion of three buildings in Nantwich into an almshouse for half a dozen elderly and indigent widows.[7] The years that followed were lonely and melancholy ones, 'mostly made up of Griefs & disappointments', though he knew he must endure them because they were 'appointed of God'. An earthquake in 1690, which toppled the upper half of his hall chimney, prompted this reflection: 'God grant us to make use of these shakings, to sitt looser to the World.' He died, aged 85, in 1707 and was recalled by his son as 'exact in his Devotion...just in his dealings, & sober in conversation with men, charitable to the poor, carefull & cautious in worldly affairs'.[8] His own memorial in Nantwich church, erected by his son Randle, bears the family's arms and crest and records him as a man of 'sound morals, great wisdom, and upright life', who, 'though given to the study of religion and letters, yet failed not in his duty to his friends or his country' (*morum vero gravitate, scientiae copia, vitae integritate...qui religionis et literarum studiis penes totus incubuit, Nec amicis interim, nec patriae defuit*). It recalls his spouse as a woman, who 'though she was allied to him in kindred and in name, was still more so by her love and her virtue' (*cognatam sibi, et cognomine, amore et virtute multo intimius conjunctam*).[9]

---

[6] Ibid., fo. 49r–50v.   [7] Ibid., fos 21r, 25r, 26r–v.   [8] Ibid., fos 28r, 30r, 30v.
[9] Hall, *History of the Town and Parish of Nantwich*, p. 321.

The four generations of Wilbrahams who kept this remarkable family chronicle during the sixteenth and seventeenth centuries enjoined upon their successors the solemn duty of continuing it. Some were more diligent than others. The next Roger Wilbraham left a rather cursory account of his life, largely confined to the death of his wife in childbirth in 1737 and his removal to Nantwich as a widower the following year. Writing in 1816, a later descendant, George Wilbraham, noted that the 'last Remembrancer' had set down only two articles and vowed 'in some degree to supply the deficiency'. Lamenting the negligence of those who had 'so imperfectly fulfilled' the task set by their ancestors, his son in turn undertook to fill the lacunae.[10] After his death in 1852, George Fortescue Wilbraham took over the role. It then passed to his brother, who completed his seventy-ninth year on 29 July 1896, a milestone he marked with the words 'Praise to God for all his mercies'.[11] The twentieth-century portion of the diary records that the village of Upper Luddington in Warwickshire was damaged by German bombs on the night of 28 November 1940; the writer's brother became a prisoner of war the following June. The family's fortunes had been steadily eroding since before the turn of the century, and successive heirs were obliged to sell parts of the estate and its associated treasures to cover the cost of death duties. In 1953, crippled by the 'excessive taxes' imposed by the Labour government, George Hugh de Vernon Wilbraham and his wife moved from Delamere Manor to a smaller house called Sweet Briar Hall. Dying childless, George passed the duty of writing the diary to his brother Ralph, who described how his father had sold Titian's painting of his mistress in 1926, along with many other pictures, the library of books, and furniture and silver from several other residences. With the assistance of his mother, he was able to purchase a few small keepsakes of family interest, including the medicine cabinet that had once stood in her bedroom. A veteran of both world wars and the recipient of the Military Cross, in 1944 he accepted the post of County Director of the Cheshire Red Cross. The last entry in this extraordinary book records that he was awarded a voluntary service medal for fifteen years of continuous work for this body in 1962.[12]

It was 'by favour' of Captain Ralph Wilbraham that a Xerox copy was deposited in the Cheshire Record Office, where it now resides. The location of the original is unknown: it is pleasing to think that it may have been faithfully continued by his children and grandchildren. Even as a photographic facsimile, this notebook is a touching artefact. Its meandering journey through four and a half centuries bears testimony to the tenacity of family memory and its capacity to triumph over vicissitudes, ruptures, and disjunctures. Now part of the public archive of the county, it has become a piece of cultural heritage, together with the collection of printed pocket almanacs Roger Wilbraham used as remembrancers between c.1660 and

[10] CRO, DDX/210/1, fos 36v–37r.   [11] Ibid., fo. 45r.   [12] Ibid., fos 46r–47v.

1700. On the blank flyleaves of one of these, bound in brown leather and com-
puted for 1652, he reflected on the heart-rending events of 1675, when, in the
wake of his wife's death, he earnestly wished that he might follow her to
'Everlasting Rest...seeing that I cannot live with out her'. Her demise was also
recorded on the back cover of *The Oxford almanack for the year of our lord God
1673*, together with a note revealing that this tiny volume had been 'my Son
Toms...who to my great Griefe died 2 yeeres after. 8 September 1675'.[13] When I
opened this precious textual relic and read the poignant message that it has carried down the generations, I could not but feel deeply affected.

The Wilbraham papers are a moving meditation on the themes at the heart of
Generations: age, ancestry, and memory. As we have seen, in early modern
England the word 'generation' had multifarious meanings. If it was a term that
described lineal descent and the act of producing offspring, it was also an item of
vocabulary deployed to denote a chronological period or unit of time and to
characterize a group of coevals who had lived in or through it. Part of a language
rooted in Scripture that was simultaneously genealogical, medical, social, temporal, and historical, in its several, closely interwoven senses 'generation' was
integral to the protracted religious revolution that convulsed this country in the
sixteenth and seventeenth centuries.

Three principal threads of arguments have supplied the warp and weft of this
book. The first claim developed in foregoing pages is that the English Reformations
shaped the generations, as well as interrelationships between them, in compelling
ways. By abolishing purgatory, indulgences, and intercessory prayer, Protestantism
formally severed the links between the living and the dead. In theory it ruled out
the possibility that departed souls could return to the earth as ghostly spirits.
Meanwhile, the doctrine of predestination left little scope for future-proofing
mechanisms that could change the fate of people in the afterlife and smooth their
path to paradise. Fiercely contested and criticized by England's resilient Catholic
community, Reformed theology also provoked troubling questions about the
eschatological destination of distant ancestors born before the dawn of the
Gospel. Contemporaries regularly worried that beloved parents and grandparents
who had lived in the time of popery were now languishing in hell. In practice
affection, compassion, and pride often prevailed, papering over the cracks that
religious revolution opened up between the generations on either side of the
divide created by the Henrician schism. Family and friends who had passed from
this life remained ever-present in the imagination of those left behind. In short,
they remained an age group.

At the same time, the capacity of the Reformations to foster recurrent spasms
of intergenerational conflict cannot be denied. While the tensions they fostered

---

[13] CRO, DBW/P/J/9 (Diary of remembrances compiled by Roger Wilbraham, 1643–76); DBW/
P/J/10 (Diary of remembrances compiled by Roger Wilbraham, 1672–3).

between youth and age, parents and children, and kith and kin may have fulfilled predictions and reinforced well established stereotypes, the pain this caused was real and palpable. Many families were permanently fractured by faith, including the ruling royal houses of the Tudors and Stuarts. And yet, by sanctioning clerical marriage, the Protestant Reformation must also be credited with having generated new ones. Out of it emerged the novel phenomenon of the clerical family, and in due course dynasties of preachers and pastors who followed in the footsteps of their fathers and whose sisters and daughters tended to marry within the same circles. Fresh forms of spiritual kinship and fellowships evolved to compensate for those that were the casualties of radical religious change. The new families of love and societies of friends that were the distinctive by-product of its successive phases nuance suggestions that the translation of Christianity undermined the bonds of horizontal solidarity that bound people of all ages. On the contrary, together with the English Catholic convents and religious houses established in exile, they attest to their continuing strength in the wake of the Tudor Reformation and the striking and counterintuitive ways in which they were reconstituted by the process of confessionalization.

The second argument I have advanced is that the Reformations created generations. They did so, like more recent revolutionary movements, in and through the medium of memory. They forged imagined communities that reflected perceptions of the past as well as hope and speculation about the future, and gave rise to present-centred senses of identity that found most telling expression in the potent concept of 'generation work'. Impassioned calls for people to rise to this challenge, grasp the opportunity to make history, and herald the Second Coming may have peaked among the Fifth Monarchists in the 1650s, but generational consciousness was not simply a product of this millenarian moment and of the shocking rupture to the fabric of English society that was the regicide. It was also an outgrowth of the convulsions of the mid-sixteenth century, when revered institutions, structures, and practices had been dismantled and repudiated by order of the state and when many individuals who resisted official orders found themselves the victims of judicial violence. Among some, this fostered an apocalyptic outlook.

It was in the realms of retrospective and vicarious remembrance that awareness of being part of a particular generation developed. One index of this was nostalgia for the sufferings that had tested, tried, and ultimately purified their religious forebears, a yearning that served as a counterpoint to conservative longing for the lost Catholic world. Another was a preoccupation with tracing the vertical descent of the churches and congregations to which people belonged. This is a neglected dimension of the genealogical fever of the era.

The Reformations created generations in a further sense, by encouraging the building up of churches through the act of sexual reproduction. They placed a premium on the devout family as a seedbed of faith and proclaimed procreation within holy wedlock as a critical mechanism for the transmission of the true religion. Among some English puritans and Protestants emphasis on the benefits of nurture came to be accompanied by the tantalizing idea derived from the book of Genesis that grace could itself be hereditary and that election might, in some sense, run in their veins. Renewed emphasis on the original sin humanity derived from its first parents, Adam and Eve, came to be offset by the conviction that the godly could, in fact, help to secure the salvation of their own children. Although adoption was the most common metaphor for describing the mysterious process by which people became aware that they were members of Christ's special flock, wishful thinking crystallized into confidence that saving faith was an ancestral birthright: the inheritance promised to Abraham's seed, which set them apart as a 'race' or a breed. With this came the twin challenges of recapturing the fervour that had animated the first generation of converts and of combating the indifference and complacency that accompanied the institutionalization of charisma.

The pattern was repeated within the ranks of Roman Catholics and the sects, albeit shaped by different ideological imperatives. Forced to centre their spiritual and sacramental life within the domain of the home, the Catholic community likewise saw the education and upbringing of children as critical to its long-term survival as a minority faith which never quite abandoned hope that it might be restored to dominance again. For the later Quakers too, diligent instruction of the young was vital in shoring up the boundaries of a movement whose priority had become careful consolidation rather than exponential evangelical growth. Convincement thereby became a learnt experience. The logic of the long and plural Reformation I have traced was the steady convergence of families of blood with families of faith. Generations, I therefore contend, were both born and made. In the early modern environment, their genealogical, social, and historical dimensions cannot be separated.

Thirdly, this book has argued that the English Reformations were themselves invented by the generations in two respects. They were made by the actions and utterances of the young, middle-aged, and old, whose life cycles were also implicated in it in significant ways. These operated as both a spur and a brake on change. They drove some to engage actively in both advancing and resisting reform, by tearing down symbols of the old religion and taking drastic steps to prevent the spread of heresy. If they fostered heart-melting experiences of spiritual regeneration and rebirth, they also attenuated the disruptive impact of religious upheaval on everyday life. Sometimes, of necessity, family ties and friendships had to be prioritized. Tempering zeal, they promoted continuities and ambiguities that paradoxically enabled the sixteenth-century Reformation to take root in English society. They also helped people to weather the storm of the bitter Civil Wars that broke out a century later, as the unresolved tensions at its heart came to a head, and to navigate the challenges of the tumultuous era between the Restoration and the Glorious Revolution, when Dissenters and Catholics suffered renewed discrimination and persecution. They eased as well as complicated the tensions surrounding the rampant pluralism and de facto toleration that were the undesired children engendered by England's unruly Reformations.

These Reformations were also created by men, women, and children who preserved and passed down traditions about them orally, scribally, and via the new technology of print. They were fabricated by people determined to record and transmit stories of their own lives and those of their biological and spiritual relatives to posterity as legacies, together with digests of religious wisdom and parental advice. The accounts they composed with their descendants in mind were both clouded and sharpened by emotion and by the tricks played by their own selective and fallible memories. Silently edited and quietly embellished as they were transcribed, they helped turn ordinary people into heroes like those who populated the pages of histories and martyrologies. Simultaneously, they effaced pragmatic compromises and equivocations that subsequently became a source of shame and embarrassment. Such texts not only refashioned their authors and subjects. They also remoulded the messy, haphazard, and composite process that we know as the 'Reformation' itself. They helped to turn a jumble of somewhat inconsistent elements into a defining historical event, to fix it in time as a significant turning point, an imperfect experiment, or an appalling calamity. For others, it remained an aspiration for the future, an agenda that reflected their critical appraisal of its earlier phases as seriously defective. These documents were kept as memorials to departed relatives and bequeathed along with other material objects as heirlooms, and their very presence in our archives, libraries, and museums is an index of the generational processes that this book has analysed. Accordingly, they are the filters through which we view the social history of the English Reformations. Coloured by triumphalism, prejudice, anger, and affect, they have helped to perpetuate the denominational narratives and historiographical paradigms that shape our vision of the early modern past.

Finally, it is necessary to reflect upon the wider methodological insights that this book yields for historians of other contexts and periods. For all the emphasis they placed on the *longue durée*, the Annalistes discarded the concept of generations as schematic and reductive. Lucien Febvre famously declared: 'better forget it.'[14] Here, I have sought to rehabilitate it as an enriching framework for analysing a period distant from the revolutionary convulsions to which its emergence has generally been linked. Firmly rejecting the lingering assumption that generations as self-conscious social cohorts are by-products of the acceleration of history associated with the advent of modernity, I have underlined the creative agency that they exercised in the sixteenth and seventeenth centuries. Transcending

---

[14] Lucien Febvre, 'Générations', *Revue de synthèse historique* (June 1920), cited in Pierre Nora, 'Generation', in *Realms of Memory: Rethinking the French Past*, vol i, *Conflicts and Divisions*, trans. Arthur Goldhammer (New York, 1996), pp. 499–531, at 507.

the constraining dichotomy of the individual and the collective, generation has proved a flexible tool with which to explore the interplay between powerful discourses and the tissue of lived experience. It has enabled me to illuminate the intersections between the human and spiritual life cycles, to investigate the overlap of communicative and inherited memory, and to delineate the matrix within which horizontal and vertical senses of belonging coexisted. It is a device that offers the prospect of doing justice to change over time without falling into the trap of teleology.[15]

Instead of trying to define generation with any precision, I have actively embraced its ambiguities. This has proved especially valuable in analysing a religious movement that understood itself in generational terms. As we have seen, genealogical thinking lay at the core of Christianity, a faith that revolved around memory of the birth of the son of God whose death redeemed the world. Its history was the story of repeated attempts to return to its roots and recapture its original purity. In turn, its historiography over the last half-century has entailed a series of generational turns, in which the revisionism of younger scholars has supplanted the preferred interpretations of their elders in the field.[16] This has been both invigorating and limiting, not least by artificially separating the synchronic and diachronic dimensions of Reformation history and by obscuring the extent to which our own interpretations of it are products of the very processes we seek to study.[17] A generational approach is salutary in 'its affirmation of knowledge as perspective'.[18] Like the generation, as a discipline, history looks backward to the past, shaped by the present, and with an eye to the future. It too is a form of genealogy.

I conclude, however, as I began: by resurrecting the voices of the generations that witnessed and experienced the religious transformations of the sixteenth and seventeenth centuries, which speak to us across the fabric of time and permit the dead to communicate with the unborn. The medium through which I do so is Thomas Bentley's *Monument of matrons* (1582), a vast compendium of devotions which its author, the churchwarden of the parish of St Andrew's, Holborn, described as 'a domesticall librarie plentifully stored' for posterity. Its fifth 'lamp' assembled prayers for women of 'all sorts and degrees' and at every stage of the life cycle. This was a legacy for the wider Protestant family of faith as well as a memorial to his own wife Susan, who had died delivering his third child Nathaniel

---

[15] See Alexandra Walsham, 'Migrations of the Holy: Explaining Religious Change in Medieval and Early Modern Europe', *Journal of Medieval and Early Modern Studies*, 44 (2014), 241–80.

[16] See Nathan Perl-Rosenthal, 'Comment: Generational Turns', *AHR*, 117 (2012), 804–13.

[17] See James Simpson, 'Diachronic History and the Shortcomings of Medieval Studies', in Gordon McMullan and David Matthews (eds), *Reading the Medieval in Early Modern England* (Cambridge, 2007), pp. 17–30.

[18] Michel Foucault, 'Nietzsche, Genealogy, History', in *idem*, *Language, Counter-Memory, Practice: Selected Essays and Interviews*, ed. Donald F. Bouchard, trans. Donald F. Bouchard and Sherry Simon (Ithaca, NY, 1980 edn), pp. 139–64, at p. 156.

the previous year. It was a repository of meditations for virgins, wives, midwives, mothers, daughters, mistresses, maids, and widows, some of which his spouse may have composed and said herself. Collectively, these prayers reflect the poly-valency of the term 'generation' and illustrate the intimate links between religion, lineage, and the life cycle I have untangled in this book. A prayer for women in labour observes that the generation of offspring is the means 'whereby not onlie this world is replenished; but a Church which doth celebrate thy name for ever, is gathered unto thee'. A petition for the use of newly married couples implores that 'we...may most happily, prosprouslie, and joifullie, like fruitefull parents, seeing our childrens children, unto the third and fourth generation, live long togither unto our perfect age in thy holie love'. 'The old womans praier' is a contemplative reflection on her impending end:

> O God of our fathers, and Lord of all grace, throughout all nations, all ages, and generations, past, present and to come...grant I humblie beseech thee not onlie unto my selfe, which am now become aged, and full of daies; but also unto whomsoever thou hast given the blessing of long life and manie yeares, to live in this vale of miserie, to be mothers of manie children, to multiplie upon the earth, to increase heere thy kingdome, and to be as organs and instruments of thee...that thou wilt vouchsafe alwaies to indue me, and all sage and ancient matrones, with the spirit of truth, understanding and knowledge...so shall it come to passe, that now at all times, and in all ages, from tender youth, to verie old age, through generations, and all posterities, thy holie name shall be magni-fied in righteousness and true holines, with all joifulnes, lauds, thanks-giving, heere and for ever in the everlasting world to come, through thine onlie free grace in the merits most pretious of thine onlie Sonne our Lord Jesus Christ, Amen.[19]

[19] Thomas Bentley (ed.), *The monument of matrons: conteining seven severall lamps of virginitie, or distinct treatises* (1582; STC 1892), sig. B3r; *idem, The fift lampe*, pp. 130, 64, 184–5. See the introduc-tion to the facsimile edition, ed. Colin B. and Jo B. Atkinson, *The Early Modern Englishwoman: A Facsimile Library of Essential Works*, ser. III, vols iv–vi (Aldershot, 2005), pp. xiv–xv.

Manuscript Sources

Aberystwyth, National Library of Wales

Additional MS 1120E (annotated copy of *The Holy Bible, containing the Old Testament and the New with annotations and parallel Scriptures* (1690)).

Great Sessions (Flintshire Gaol Files), 4/970/5/19 (Certificate of recusants, April 1581).

MS 7192B (copy of John Reynolds, *The Scripture Genealogy beginning at Noah* (Chester, 1739) owned by the Lloyd family).

Brighton, East Sussex Record Office

ASH 3501 (Elizabeth Ashbornham, manuscript prayers given to her eldest daughter Elizabeth Cornwallis, 1635).

PAR 505/1/1/1 (Parish register of Westham, Sussex).

Cambridge, Cambridge University Library

Additional MS 6680 (Wycliffite translation of the Bible, 15th century).

Additional MS 8499 (Diary of Isaac Archer, 1641–1700).

Additional MS 10079 [G] (Sarum book of hours, [Bruges?, *c*.1460–70]).

MS Gg.4.13 (Collections, chiefly historical, concerning George, duke of Buckingham, and his times, early 17th century).

MS Hengrave 76/1 ('*Vetustissima Prosapia Rookewodorum de Stanningefilde, in Comitatu Suffolciae*', 17th–19th century).

MS Ii.vi.2 (The 'Roberts Hours', Flemish, late 14th/early 15th century).

Cambridge University Archives:
VCCt.III 11 (Vice Chancellor's Court records, 1577–1605).

Cambridge, Corpus Christi College

MS 29 (Peter of Poitiers, 'Genealogia historiarum' and Petrus Comestor, 'Historia Scholastica', *c*.1200–25).

MS 437 (Biblia, Latin, *c*.1200–99, with abbreviated copy of Peter of Poitiers, 'Genealogia historiarum').

Cambridge, Massachusetts, Harvard University Houghton Library

MS Eng. 1015 (Stephen Batman, 'A book of the coppies', before 1584).

Chester, Cheshire Record Office

D 6120 (Pedigree of the Bruen of Bruen Stapleford family, 11th–16th centuries).

DBW/P/J/9 (Diary of remembrances compiled by Roger Wilbraham, 1643–76, kept in a printed almanac).

DBW/P/J/10 (Diary of remembrances compiled by Roger Wilbraham, 1672–3, kept in a printed almanac).

DCB/1363/9 (Pedigree of Eaton Family of Blackden, 1570–1674).

DDC/15/25 (The line of the House of York, or the White Rose, to Hannah, wife of Roger Maddock of Chester, shoemaker, 18th century).

DDX 95 (Illuminated pedigree roll of the Brereton family of Malpas, Cheshire, c.1564).

DDX/210/1 (Wilbraham Family Diary, 1513–1962, photocopy of original).

DDX 384 (Diaries of Thomas Mainwaring, 1649–88).

DMD/O/1 (Letters and papers of the Henry Family, including extracts from the diary of Philip Henry, c.1670s, unfoliated booklet transcribed in 1878).

P20/13/1 (Churchwardens' accounts of St Mary's, Chester, 1536–1684), 9 May 1644.

ZCR 469/422 (Draft letter from Thomas Aldersey to his brother Robert, offering consolation on the death of a child, 1690).

ZCR 469/542 (William Aldersey's 'Collection of the maiors who have governed this Cittie of Chester', 17th century).

Dorchester, Dorset Record Office

D 53/1 ('A Private Chronology of Denis Bond ESQre of Lutton in the Isle of Purbeck Made A.D. 1636 & 1640', with notes by Thomas Bond of Tyneham. Copied from his transcription by Lilian Mary Garneys Bond, 1919, with entries added by her).

D 1962/3/2 (King James New Testament (Oxford, 1680) with genealogical register of the Richards family)

Durham, Durham County Record Office

D/Lo/F 325–332 (Londonderry Estate papers).

D/Sa/F 1–408 (Salvin family papers).

D/St/C1/1/3 (Pedigree of the Bowes family, 16th–18th centuries).

Edinburgh, National Library of Scotland

MS 6489 (Lady Anne Halkett, Meditations, 17th century).

MS 6491 (Lady Anne Halkett, Occasional Meditations, 1660–3).

MS 6492 (Lady Anne Halkett, Occasional Meditations and Select Contemplations, 1668–71).

MS Wodrow Folio XXV 1–2 (Wodrow manuscripts).

RB. s.2166 (4) (annotated copy of *The holy bible* (1627), bound with the *Book of Common Prayer*, belonging to the Stewart family, the earls of Moray).

Exeter, Devon Heritage Centre

528B/Z/1 (Pedigree of the Giffard family, *c.*1628).
1262M/O/FZ/2 (Fortescue family papers, volume of thoughts on religious matters, 1664–78).
3799M/3/O/8/2 (Report of speeches of Browne, a merchant, 1596).
5282M/F/13 and 13a (Humphrey Prideaux, *The old and new testament connected in the history of the Jews and neighbouring nations* (1720) and pressed leaves, ferns, and grasses).

Gloucester, Gloucestershire Archives

D1233/35 (Papers relating to the Commeline family).
D2153 (Sudeley Archives).

Kew, The National Archives

C 1/1322 (Court of Chancery Proceedings).
PROB 11/19/377 (Will of John Andrewe otherwise called Geilis of All Hallows Gracechurch, London, 15 March 1520).
SP 12, 14 (State Papers Domestic, Elizabeth I, James I).

Liverpool, Liverpool Record Office

920 MAT (*The Christian's Complete Family Bible* (1767), owned by the Mather family, dated 1770).

London, Archives of the Archdiocese of Westminster

St Edmund's College, Ware MS 16/9/1–8 (Correspondence by and about Thomas Maxfield, executed 1616).
Series A, vol. IV (Correspondence of the secular clergy and miscellanea, 1586–94).

London, British Library

Additional MS 4240 (Memoirs relating to the Oldys family).
Additional MS 4275 (Ralph Thoresby, collection of letters of conformist and nonconformist divines).
Additional MS 5813 (Michael Sherbrooke, 'Falle of religious howses, colleges, chantreys, hospitals &c', *c.*1590).
Additional MS 18002 (Genealogy from Noah, *c.*1422).
Additional MS 32310 (quarto edition of the *Holy bible,* 1612).

Additional MS 33747 (Robert Le Wright yearbook, 17th century).

Additional MS 34169–72 (Diaries of Isabella, wife of Sir Roger Twysden kept in a series of almanacs, 1645–61).

Additional MS 34174 (Miscellaneous papers relating to the Twysden family, 17th–19th centuries).

Additional MS 34660 (Commonplace book of the Brigden family).

Additional MS 37127 (*The compleat history of the old and new testament: or a family bible* (1735) owned by the Smith family).

Additional MS 42504 (Sir Anthony Hungerford's autobiographical treatise, 1627).

Additional MS 43827 A and B (Rose Hickman, 'Certaine old stories recorded by an aged gentlewoman a time before her death to be perused by her children and posterity', 1610).

Additional MS 44026 (Pedigree of the Hesketh family of Rufford, Lancashire).

Additional MS 44,062 (Notebook owned by Lancelot Ridley, 1568–1771).

Additional MS 45027 (Transcription of Rose Hickman, 'Certayne old Storyes Recorded by an Aged Gentlewoman', late 17th century).

Additional MS 45196 (Recipe book of Anne Glyd, 1656–1700).

Additional MS 47882 (Hopton family illuminated pedigree roll, late 17th century).

Additional MS 48064 (Papers of Robert Beale relating to Religious Affairs, 1535–93).

Additional MSS 60168–60,256 (Muggletonian archives, 17th–20th centuries).

Additional MS 74251A (Illuminated genealogy of the Weston family, c.1632–3).

Additional MS 88897/1 and 2 (Autobiographical writings of Alice Thornton, 1668–1707).

Arundel MS 381 (Tabulae Theologiae, 14th century).

Egerton MS 607 (Prayers, meditations, and devotional pieces, by Elizabeth, countess of Bridgewater, collected after her death in 1663).

Egerton MS 2255 (John Speed, 'Jesus of Nazareth', c.1616).

Egerton MS 2884, no. 10, fo. 21 (Anonymous advice of a father to his son, late 17th century).

Egerton MS 2877 (Commonplace book of Gilbert Freville, 1579–1622).

Harley MS 4928, (Sir Thomas Shirley, 'The Genealogicke Historie of the Howse of Shirleys... Inriched with divers Figures & discourses of Antiquitie', 17th century).

Lansdowne MS 72 (Burghley Papers, 1592).

Sloane MS 271 (Robert Smart, Papers relating to the puritans, with sermons and family memoranda, 1551–1617).

Sloane MS 761 (Timothy Sullivan, Genealogy and Pedigree to Adam, 1682).

Sloane MS 2498 (Genealogical tables from Creation to AD 902, owned by the Guide family).

Sloane MS 3945 (Mary Love, 'The Life of Christopher Love', 1651).

Stowe MS 72 and 73 (Genealogical chronicles of the kings of England to Edward IV, 15th century).

London, Congregational Library

MS I.f.2 (Spiritual Diary of Ellis Crispe, 1622–26).

MS I.h.33 (Robert Franklin, notes of sermons with 'Mary Franklin her Experience' and Mrs H. Burton, devout meditations, 17th century).

MS I.h.37 (Mary Franklin, copies of letters and speeches).

MS I.h.52 (Memorandum book with contemporary records of births, marriages, and deaths in the Mitchell, Crosby, Moody, Ingby, and Robinson families, 1646–1739).

MS I. i. 25 (Letters of Robert Franklin and his wife, 1670).

London, Dr Williams's Library

MS 12.10 (Commonplace book of P. P. with notes of sermons, 17th century).
MS 12.40 ('Original letters and family papers &c of the Blackmore Family', arranged by Charles Edward Blackmore Bowker, 1888).
MS 12.78 (Notebook of Thomas Jolly, 17th century).
MS 12.107 (Papers of the Say family).

London, Friends House Library

MS 278 ('Chronicles of…the Dymond Clan…Part I, The First Five Generations 1595–1870', arr. Charles William Dymond).
MS S 469 (Geneva bible (1577) owned by the Harris family).
MS VOL 62 (Compilation of letters and transcriptions once owned by the Braithwaite family, 1660–1794).
MS VOL 316 (Epistles and writings of early Quakers, collected and copied by Thomas Ellwood, 1639–1713).
TEMP MSS 752 (Commonplace book of Mary Penington, late 17th–early 18th century).

London, Lambeth Palace Library

MS 19 (Descent of the Kings of England from Adam, c.1533–4).
MS 25 (Bible in English, late 14th century).
MS 66 (A chronicle of the world from the Creation to 1525).
MS 310 (William Cecil, Pedigrees and Historical Notes, 16th century).
MS 766 (Genealogy of Jesus Christ, late 16th–early 17th century).
MS Sion L40.2/E47 (Dionys Fitzherbert, 'An Anatomie for the Poore in Spirit. Or the case of an afflicted conscience layed open by example', 1608–38).
MS Sion L40.2/E49 (Johann Carion, 'Chronicon', c.1600).

London, Parliamentary Archives

HL/PO/JO/10/1/60 (Records of the House of Lords, June 1641).

Matlock, Derbyshire Record Office

D1689/1 (*The summer of the whole scripture* (1607), Geneva bible belonging to the Taylor family).
D3850/F21-77 (Longsdon family papers).
D5430/76/9 (Commonplace book of Edward Bagshaw, vicar of Castleton).

Northallerton, North Yorkshire County Record Office

PR/KN 23/1/7 (Commonplace book, 18th century, part of the parish records of St John the Baptist, Knaresborough).

ZFL (Papers of the Mauleverer family of Ingelby Arncliffe).

ZIQ/MIC 2050 (microfilm of Thomas Meynell's manuscript, 1614).

ZKZ (Papers of the Graham family of North Conyers, 1404–2016).

Norwich, Norfolk Record Office

GUN 92/1–18 (Rolfe family records).

LEST/NE 2 and 2/1 (Sir Nichols Le Strange, 'Short notes for my sons profit', 1669).

LEST/NE 7 (Le Strange family papers, 'A treaty concerneing marriages of first cozens or cozen Germans', 1630).

LEST/OD 2 (Pedigree of the Le Strange family, 1655).

Oxford, Bodleian Library

MS 950 (Hugh Broughton, tables of chronology and genealogy, c.1600).

MS Additional A. 119 (Fairfax family letters, copied by Mary Arthington, c.1680–1700).

MS Ashmole 1789 (John Dee, 'A playne discourse, and humble advise, for our gratious Queene Elizabeth', late 16th century).

MS Bodleian Rolls 5 (Genealogical history of the kings of England, c.1485).

MS Bodley 154 (Dionys Fitzherbert, 'An Anatomie for the Poore in Spirrit Or The Case of an afflicted Conscience layed open by Example', 1633).

MS Carte 251 (Samuel Carte, 'Chronological relation of extraordinary events... from the earliest times to the beginning of 1700').

MS e. Mus. 160 (Original papers by or addressed to Dionys Fitzherbert, 17th century).

MS Eng. C. 2693 (Walter Boothby, 'A Nosegay of Everlasting Orifficall Flowers, gathered out of Heavens paradice', mid-17th century).

MS Eng. th. b.1–2 (Commonplace book associated with the Tresham family, early 17th century).

MS Gough Shropshire 15 (Transcription of the parish register of Much Wenlock, Shropshire, by James Bowen of Shrewsbury, dated 1756).

MS Hatton 4 (Latin psalter and Sarum book of hours with genealogical information relating to the Edward Windsor, 3rd Lord Windsor of Stanwell, AD 1559–72).

MS Jones 14, item 3 (George Hakewill, 'The Wedding Robe, or a treatise touching the unlawfulness of Protestants marriages with Papists divided into three parts', 17th century).

MS Rawlinson D. 102 (Mistress Mary Honeywood's Life of her Father, c.1635).

MS Rawlinson D. 1308 (Lady Mary Carey's Meditations and Poetry, transcribed by Charles Hutton, 17th century).

MS Rawlinson D. 1345 (Theological Tracts, 17th century).

MS Rawlinson liturg.e. 41 (15th-century manual for a convent, Sarum use).

MS Rawlinson Q.f.1 (copy of *This prymer of Salisbury use* (1552) owned by the Ramsay family).

MS Vet. B1 f.115 (annotated copy of Robert Persons' *A Conference about the Next Succession* (1594/5)).

MS Wood D 7 (2) (Assorted notes of Ralph Sheldon, 17th century).

Oxford, The Queen's College

MS 141–143 (Sir Thomas Shirley, 'The Catholike Armorist', 17th century).

San Marino, Henry E. Huntington Library

Ellesmere MSS (Ellesmere papers).
Hastings Personal Papers.
MSSHM 6131 (Life of John Rastrick, 1650–1720).
MSSHM 15369 (Commonplace book of Elizabeth Hastings, Countess of Huntingdon).
MSSHM 43213 (Catechism compiled by Sir Henry Slingsby, transcribed by Barbara Slingsby Talbot, 1687).
MSSHM 56911 (15th-century English psalter which belonged to the Fortescue family).
MSSHM 58285 (Book of hours belonging to the Felbrygge family of Norfolk, 1375–1425).
Rare Books 283000: Richard Bull, *Extra-illustrated Biographical History of England, from Egbert the Great to the Revolution* (1769–74).
Rare Books 297343 (Elizabeth Egerton, countess of Bridgewater, Manuscript meditations on the several chapters of the Old Testament, *c*.1620).
Stowe Temple Brydges Papers.
Stowe Temple Personal Papers.

Shrewsbury, Shrewsbury School

MS Mus X ('Dr Taylor's Book', chronicle of Shrewsbury 1372–1603).

Shrewsbury, Shropshire Archives

MI 1841/1 (King James Bible (Edinburgh, 1715) owned by the Calcott family).
P257/Q/1/1 (Will of Joseph Jones, 1729).

Stafford, Staffordshire Record Office

4714/1 (Photocopies of pages in a bible owned by the Semple family of Northern Ireland, with entries of births, marriages, deaths, and other memoranda, 1630–1787).
D (W) 1721/1/1/1 (Stafford MSS, The Great Cartulary, 16th–17th centuries)
D1057/O/1 A-B ('Memorandum & Manuscript of Congreves of Stretton, Staffordshire', 1580).
P1720 (Genealogical and historical account of the family of Bridgeman of Great Lever in Lancashire, 18th century).
P1725 (Genealogical and historical account of the family of Newport of High Ercal, afterwards earls of Bedford, 18th century).

Taunton, Somerset Heritage Centre

A/DNO/1 (History of the Singer family copied from the family bible, 1595–1851).
DD/BR/ba/1 (Pedigree of the Poulett family, compiled *c*.1627–35).
DD/EN/115 (Notebook begun by William Boules in the late 17th century, with notes on chronology and the Bible).
DD/PH/221 (Letters and drafts of letters of Sir Robert Phelips; Literary Extracts; Miscellanea, *c*.1583–1706).
DD/SK/4/4/14 (Genealogical notes on the Harcourt and Skrine families taken from the family bible 1680–1894).

DD/WO/63/3/1 (Pedigree of Elizabeth Downe, showing fictitious descent from Edmund, earl of Cornwall, c.1620).

DD/X/LY/1 (Pedigree of the Lyte family, 13th–16th centuries).

Washington DC, Folger Shakespeare Library

MS V.a.11 (Thomas Hunt, 'A Bosome Companion or The Fathers advice to his Children', 1690).

MS V.a.22 (Francis Western's copy of 'Englands Elizabeth her life and Trobles, during her minoritie, from the Cradle to the Crown', c.1700).

MS V.a.166 (Elizabeth Lucy, 'An account of the Lady Lacy written to a particular friend of hers…with Mar. Eyre's account of the last moments of the authoress, c.1675).

MS V.a.180 (Sir Francis Fane, commonplace book, compiled c.1655–6).

MS V.a.269 ('A true historicall Relation of the Conversion of Tobie Matthew to the holie Catholick Fayth', 1640).

MS V.a.228 (Book of hours, Sarum use, c.1500).

MS V.a.233 (Letter of Sir Henry Sidney to his son Philip, copy c.1600).

MS V.a.346 (Nathaniel Bladen, advice to a son, 1694).

MS V.a.366 (Recipe book of Rebeckah Winche, c.1666).

MS V.a.427 (Michael Dalton, 'A Breviary of the state of the Roman (or Westerne) Church and Empire, the decay of true Religion; and the rising of the Papacy; from the tyme of our Lord and Saviour Jesus Christ, till Martin Luther', 1634).

MS V.a.436 (Notebook of Nehemiah Wallington, 1654).

MS V.a.437 (Sermon book of Dorothy Phillips, 1616–17, with births, marriages, and deaths relating to the Hanmer family of Selattyn, Shropshire, 1588–1722).

MS V.a.474 (Diary for 1665, kept in interleaved copy of George Wharton, *Calendarium Carolinum* (1665)).

MS V.a.480 (Writing tables, 1580?).

MS V.a.511 (Elizabeth Ashbornham, Instructions for my children, or any other Christian, c.1606–c.1750).

MS V.a.531 (Writing tables owned by Alicia Gardiner and her son, 18th century).

MS V.a.666 (Mary Caryll of North, recusant devotional text, c.1680–1700?).

MS V.b.96 (Dering family, 'A booke of diverse necessary remembrances', c.1595–1644).

MS V.b.155 (Laurence Cromp, Genealogy of the Boun or Bohun family, 1690).

MS V.b.232 (Thomas Trevelyon Miscellany, 1608).

MS V.b.297 (Catalogue of Sir Edward Dering's books, c.1640–2).

MS V.b.307 (Sir Edward Dering, notes for a history of the Dering family, c.1631).

MS W.b.482–484 (Papers of the Kay family of Woodsome, Yorkshire, c.1561–1642, 18th-century copies).

MS X.d.212 ('The precepts of Sir W[illia]m Cecill Lord Treasurer of England 1596 To his Son Rob[er]t, 1604', later copy)

MS X.d.530 (Commonplace book, begun c.1605).

MS X.d.531 (Papers of the Dering family, c.1450–1680).

MS X.d.445–449 (Papers of the Kay family of Woodsome, Yorkshire, c.1561–1642).

MS X.d.488 (Notebook of Edward Dering illustrating a theological dispute with the Catholic Thomas Doughty, c.1639–40).

MS X.d.539 (Sir Charles Cornwallis, precepts to his grandchild, 7 November 1614).

MS Z.e.27 (Sir Edward Dering, history of the Dering family from the time of the Conquest, c.1635).

MS Z.e.41 (Pedigree of the Taylor family, Shadoxhurst, Kent, 1665).

Wigston Magna, Leicester, Leicestershire and Rutland Record Office

2D31/349 (Roos family pedigree, c.1684).

26D53/2556 (Dispensation granted by Thomas Cranmer, archbishop of Canterbury, for the marriage of Francis Shirley and Dorothy Congreve, 8 April 1535).

26D53/2681 (The Great Pedigree of the Shirley family, 1632).

DE3214/12424 (Pedigree roll of the Draycott family, 1604–62).

DE5833/2 (Manuscript elegy to Sir John Moore, written by Elkanah Settle, 1702).

DG6/E/35 ('Genealogy of 4 Penelope Watches', 19th century).

Woking, Surrey History Centre

2953/1/8/1–7 (*The Holy Bible* (Edinburgh, 1719) inscribed 'Ann Iveson 1758', with genealogical notes and photographs).

3996/1 (Photocopy of manuscript notes in the Revell family bible, 1708–1875).

7052/7/1 (Pedigree papers of Macclesfield Forbes Coussmaker).

BKL/1/1 (Parish register of All Saints, Little Bookham, Surrey, 1642–1758).

LM/1654 (Loseley manuscripts).

PSH/RIP/16/1 (Copy of John Bunyan, *Signs from hell,* now part of the parish records of St Mary's, Ripley).

Worcester, Worcester Archive and Archaeological Service

009:1/BA 2636 parcel 11 ('1641 Miscellanea').

705:134 BA 1531/79/20 (Lechmere family genealogical notes, mid-17th century).

705: 295 Parcel 5 (Hornyhold family papers).

York, York Minster Library

MS 122 (Commonplace book of the family of Marmaduke Rawdon, 17th century).

MS 228 ('A book of receiptes 1633', with genealogical notes of the Wentworth family).

MS 322 (Frances Matthews's record of the births and baptisms of her children, 17th century).

Index

For the benefit of digital users, indexed terms that span two pages (e.g., 52–53) may, on occasion, appear on only one of those pages.